Gareth Scott on *Cloncion* (7b - page 266)

# Fax13
# Costa Blanca
# Mallorca
# El Chorro

### Alan James
### Mark Glaister

based on original books by
Alan James
Alan Cameron-Duff
and Rab Anderson

Published by ROCKFAX in April 2001
Illustrations © ROCKFAX 1996, 1998, 2001

Text, topos and maps
by Alan James and Mark Glaister.

Additional text and topos
by Rowland Edwards, Rab Anderson, Alan
Cameron-Duff, Nick Verney, Stephen Kirby,
Dennis Morrod and Karen Yeow.

Computer artwork, design and layout
by Alan James and Mark Glaister.

Photography as credited.

Original ROCKFAX design by Ben Walker,
Mick Ryan and Alan James.

Printed by Clearpoint Colourprint, Nottingahm

Distributed by Cordee
(Tel: (+int) 44 (0) 116 254 3579)

# ROCKFAX
rockfax.com

Sheffield, UK and Bishop, CA, USA
Email UK: alan@rockfax.co.uk
Email USA: mick@rockfax.com
RRP £18.95 ($27, 30 Euros)

ISBN 1-873341-65-2

9 781873 341650

# NEEDLE SPORTS

Call in to our shop at:
56 Main Street, Keswick
(017687 72227)
or visit us at:
www.needlesports.com

# BMC Insurance

**Unbeatable value** for cover **you can trust ..**

### The BMC Travel & Activity Insurance Guide

- **Sun Trek** — low cost options for hill walking and trekking
- **Sun Rock** — popular climbing cover
- **Sun Ski & Climb** — comprehensive cover for mountaineering and winter sports
- **Sun Peak** — competitive premiums for ascents in the Greater Ranges

The choice is yours – 3 days to annual, UK, Europe or Worldwide

Request your copy by **Phone:** 0161 445 4747 **Fax:** 0161 445 4500 or **E-mail:** insure@thebmc.co.uk

Insure Online – www.thebmc.co.uk

# CONTENTS

Introduction .................................................. 5
Rock + Run Gear Page ..................................... 8
Grades ...................................................... 10
ROCKFAX ................................................... 12
Symbol and Topo Key ..................................... 17
Introducción (Español) ................................... 18
Introduction (Français) .................................. 20
Einführung (Deutsch) .................................... 22
Advertiser Directory ..................................... 24
Acknowledgments ........................................ 27

## COSTA BLANCA

Contents .................................................... 29
Introduction ............................................... 31
Logistics ................................................... 33
Crag Selection Table ..................................... 34
Area Map ................................................... 36
The Crags ........................................... 37 to 215

## MALLORCA

Contents ................................................... 216
Introduction .............................................. 218
Area Map .................................................. 219
History ..................................................... 220
Logistics .................................................. 223
Crag Selection Table .................................... 224
The Crags ......................................... 226 to 287

## EL CHORRO

Contents ................................................... 288
Introduction .............................................. 290
Area Map .................................................. 291
Logistics .................................................. 293
Crag Selection Table .................................... 294
The Crags ......................................... 296 to 359

Index ....................................................... 360

Chris Gore climbing *Lourdes* (8a - page 328) on Makinodromo, El Chorro. (Insets on the crux sequence) Photos: Mark Glaister

# INTRODUCTION

The delights of a winter-sun climbing holidays are now well known to most northern European climbers. Overheard conversations at the climbing walls regularly feature the words Sella, Sa Gubia and El Chorro as frequently nowadays as they used to feature the words Stanage, Tremadog and Bosigran twenty years ago. Even many die-hard "I'll never clip a bolt in my life" types have been tempted by a cheap air fare, an apartment overlooking the sea and 25 degree tempera-

tures on Christmas day, to stray from the path of righteousness and indulge themselves. However none of this would have caught on if it wasn't for the fantastic climbing found in the main locations. The rock formations, and routes, in the Costa Blanca, Mallorca and El Chorro are as spectacular and wonderful as you could wish for and the variety and extent of the climbing is enough to bring a smile to the face of even the grumpiest traditionalist. It isn't just about single pitch sport routes on bolted crags near the road, indeed probably my most memorable experiences have been on day-long routes, on major mountain crags, with loose rock, tricky route finding and a high degree of commitment. Amongst the pages of this book you will find many routes which drop into this category. Whether your preference is grade 4 slabs or 8c overhanging tufas, 12 pitch routes in the mountains or intense three move sequences by the road, there is everything to choose from in the three areas covering all abilities and styles of climbing. All you need to do is sit back, find an inspiring route and plan your next climbing holiday.

## THE GUIDEBOOK

The Costa Blanca, Mallorca and El Chorro have been brought together in this single book to give you all you need for many years worth of climbing holidays. Such is the quantity of climbing in the three areas that we have had to put in a lot of effort to squeeze it all into a manageable guide and this current edition should give you plenty to go at with nearly 3000 routes from grade 2 to 9a+! Those who own one of the previous editions will find many additional routes and crags and a lot of improvements to the existing information.

All the routes and crags are illustrated with approach maps, topos or photo-topos and text descriptions. If you do not like reading long-winded descriptions, or English is not your first language, then you should still be able to use the guide. Conversely, if you hate maps and your brain cannot cope with 2-dimensional representations of a 3-dimensional world, there are always the text approaches and route descriptions to fall back on. We have also added character symbols to this book which gives you another impression of a climb before you set off. Those of you who have never used a ROCKFAX guidebook before may want to familiarise yourself with some of the symbols and topos on page 17.

### GUIDEBOOK FOOTNOTE

The inclusion of a climbing area in this guidebook does not mean that you have a right of access or the right to climb upon it. The descriptions of bolts and other forms of fixed gear within this guide are recorded for historical reasons only and no reliance should be placed on the accuracy of the description of the nature and position of bolts and other fixed gear. The grades set in this guide are a fair assessment of the difficulty of the climbs. Climbers who attempt a route of a particular standard should use their own judgment as to whether they are proficient enough to tackle that route. This book is not a substitute for experience and proper judgment. The authors, publisher and distributors of this book do not recognise any liability for injury or damage caused to, or by, climbers, third parties, or property arising from such persons seeking reliance on this guidebook as an assurance for their own safety.

# Have you visited the "other" Mallorca?

- Quaint mountain casitas
- Beautiful hotels
- Delightful villas & apartments

**Specialists in
Deià, Sóller and Pollença**

Tel : 0113 2786862
www.alternativemallorca.com

## BEHAVIOUR

Please read any access information carefully and respect any restrictions due to nesting birds or other reasons. Please respect the local environment, don't drop litter or walk, or drive, unnecessarily off the described tracks. If you need to go to the toilet then please use proper facilities whenever possible. When it isn't possible, make sure you walk a long distance from the beaten tracks and bury it well. Do not start fires anywhere.

## HISTORY

One significant omission from earlier editions of this book was historical details on the climbers and equippers of the routes. In this edition we have made start to the ultimate task of fully documenting the historical details for the areas. In the Costa Blanca this has reached the extent where many first ascensionists, and/or equippers, are listed with the route, or the crag. In Mallorca there is a short historical piece which outlines the main events and protagonists of the development there. We have as yet not managed to assemble much data for El Chorro but hopefully this will come to light for future editions. In all areas we would like thank the local climbers for the effort they put in to equip and maintain the crags.

## LOGISTICS

All the information about flights, accommodation, transport is listed with the individual area introductions. **Costa Blanca** - see page 33, **Mallorca** - see page 223, **El Chorro** - see page 293.

**Child-Friendly Crags**
In previous ROCKFAX guidebooks we have outlined certain crags which may be regarded as 'child-friendly' and I often get asked this question by parents before they make a trip. The criteria for this is that they should be reachable with a child-carrier backpack, and have a reasonably safe and well protected area underneath for children to play safely. In this edition of this book I haven't added the information to specific crags since it has become clear that there are few locations in all three main areas which easily pass the child-friendly test. As a general rule those parents wishing to go climbing with their small children would be best advised to head for the Costa Blanca or Mallorca since El Chorro is very poor in this respect. Check the ROCKFAX web site for more details of child-friendly crags - rockfax.com

**Trips Without Hiring a Car**
Although for all three destinations a hire car is advisable, it is possible, for those on a tight budget, to have a winter-sun holiday without hiring a car. The best location for this type of holiday is El Chorro where you can reach most of the climbing on foot and getting from the airport to the main area is relatively straightforward (see page 293). In the Costa Blanca it is possible to camp at Sella, which will give enough climbing for most, and it should be possible to pick up lifts with other climbers to reach other destinations. Getting to Sella from the airport can be hard work though (see page 33). Mallorca is the worst venue for those without a car although it is still possible to get around (see page 223).

## FEEDBACK - rockfax.com

The ROCKFAX web site is an important source of extra information for all climbers, especially in the areas covered by our guidebooks. Each book has a lot of backup information which is constantly updated and many now have pdf downloadable updates (Portable Document Format - *a universal format which can be viewed and printed out on all modern computers using the free application Adobe Acrobat Reader*). Before you make a trip to any of the three destinations in this book you are well advised to take a look at rockfax.com to check for any new information or topos for the area you are visiting.

If you do find anything that you think would be of interest to us regarding the three areas then please get in touch. It is through the help of climbers that we have been able to put together this updated edition.

Alan James
March 2001

# ROCK+RUN GEAR PAGE

With any climbing trip, having the right gear is an important part of the experience. If travelling by air you will be limited to the amount of gear you can take so it is important to make the right decisions before you set off.

## ROPE

Probably the most important bit of kit is the thing that will stop you hitting the ground. For most of the routes in this guidebook you will only need a single 10mm or 11mm rope. A longer rope (55m or 60m) is recommended though since some of the pitches are more than 25m long, so you need an extra bit to lower off. Routes where this is known to be the case tend to be indicated in the text, but always take care when lowering by putting a knot in the end of the rope. Some routes need twin 50m x 9mm ropes for abseil descents. Once again this is indicated in the text. A good solution to keep your luggage down is to take one 9mm rope and climb any twin rope routes with a 9mm and a 10mm.

Bolt clipping at El Chorro. Photo: Alan James

## CLIMBING KIT

There are many 'trad' routes in this book which are well worth considering, however, because of the extra gear, it is worth planning the routes before your trip. For these you will need a full rack of wires, hexes and cams. Even if you don't intend to do any full trad routes it is a good idea to carry a small set of wires for sport routes with missing, or badly placed, bolts. Check each of the three main section introductions for more gear information.

All three areas have multi-pitch climbs on which it is strongly advised that you wear a helmet. You will also need to carry an abseiling device to descend and it is well worth carrying prussik loops in case of difficulty (it is a good idea to work out how to use them before you end up dangling hopelessly from the end of a rope). Again it is worth deciding whether you are going to attempt a multi-pitch before your trip.

For most of the more conventional sport routes 15 quick-draws will be enough. A couple of extra ones may be required for belays on multi-pitch routes. Also take a screw-gate or two for secure belays.

## OTHER GEAR

Beyond the usual holiday gear there are certain other things which you may like to think about. Spain is hot and you will get dehydrated, a situation which will probably be made worse by a few beers in the evening. If you do a long route carrying a sturdy water bottle is essential. For those with sensitive skin a light coloured long-sleeve shirt, a neck scarf and a hat is also a good idea to stop you turning pink. However it isn't always hot and in Winter the temperature can drop dramatically once the sun disappears. In this instance a light wind proof, or the ubiquitous belayer's duvets, are very welcome.

# UKClimbing.com

## *The best place for climbing on the web*

- **Searchable Crag and Wall Databases**
- **Regular Features and News**
- **Weather Forecasts for Crags**
- **ROCKTALK Discussion Forum**
- **Six Other Forums**

Dave Pickford making the second ascent of *The Monk's Satanic Verses* (E8 6c) at Lower Sharpnose, Cornwall, England.
Photo: Mark Glaister

# GRADES

The grades for the three areas have now been brought into line with common consensus opinions. Mallorca used to be a bit of an oddball with extremely hard grades and El Chorro was always known for having soft-touches. Hopefully these discrepancies have now been ironed out.

## ROUTE GRADES

| Sport Grade | British Trad Grade (well protected routes only) | UIAA | USA | Australian |
|---|---|---|---|---|
| 1 | Mod (Moderate) | I | 5.1 | 4 |
| 2 | | II | 5.2 | 6 |
| 2+ | Diff (Difficult) | III | 5.3 | |
| 3- | | III+ | 5.4 | 8 |
| 3 | VDiff (Very Difficult) | IV- | 5.5 | 10 |
| 3+ | | IV+ | 5.6 | 12 |
| 4 | Sev (Severe) | V- | | |
| 4+ | HVD (Hard Very Difficult) | V | 5.7 | 14 |
| 5 | HS (Hard Severe) 4a | V+ | 5.8 | 16 |
| 5+ | VS (Very Severe) 4c | VI- | 5.9 | |
| 6a | HVS (Hard Very Severe) 5b | VI | 5.10a | 18 |
| 6a+ | E1 5a / 5c | VI+ | 5.10b | 19 |
| 6b | E2 5b / 6a | VII- | 5.10c | 20 |
| 6b+ | E3 5c / 6a | VII | 5.10d | 21 |
| 6c | E4 6a / 6b | VII+ | 5.11a | 22 |
| 6c+ | | VIII- | 5.11b | 23 |
| 7a | E5 6a / 6c | VIII | 5.11c | 24 |
| 7a+ | | VIII+ | 5.11d | |
| 7b | E6 6b / 6c | IX- | 5.12a | 25 |
| 7b+ | | | 5.12b | 26 |
| 7c | | IX | 5.12c | 27 |
| 7c+ | E7 6c / 7a | IX+ | 5.12d | 28 |
| 8a | | X- | 5.13a | 29 |
| 8a+ | E8 6c / 7a | X | 5.13b | 30 |
| 8b | | | 5.13c | 31 |
| 8b+ | E9 7a / 7a | X+ | 5.13d | 32 |
| 8c | | XI- | 5.14a | 33 |
| 8c+ | E10 7a / 7b | XI | 5.14b | 34 |
| 9a | | XI+ | 5.14c | 35 |
| 9a+ | | | 5.14d / 5.15a | 36 |

Above is a very complicated looking Grade Conversion Table. The reason it is so complicated is that grades are complicated and very difficult to compare. By using this table, you should get a rough idea of what the equivalent Spanish/French grade is compared to your domestic leading grade. It is worth remembering that because sport routes are relatively safe sometimes the moves can seem disproportionately hard for their equivalent grades. If you find yourself struggling on a route which you think has been undergraded then let us know. Conversely if you find yourself cruising to the top of a route, which was three grades harder than anything you had ever done elsewhere, enjoy your moment of glory and then, when you sober up, drop us an email and let us know that it might have been a bit overgraded.

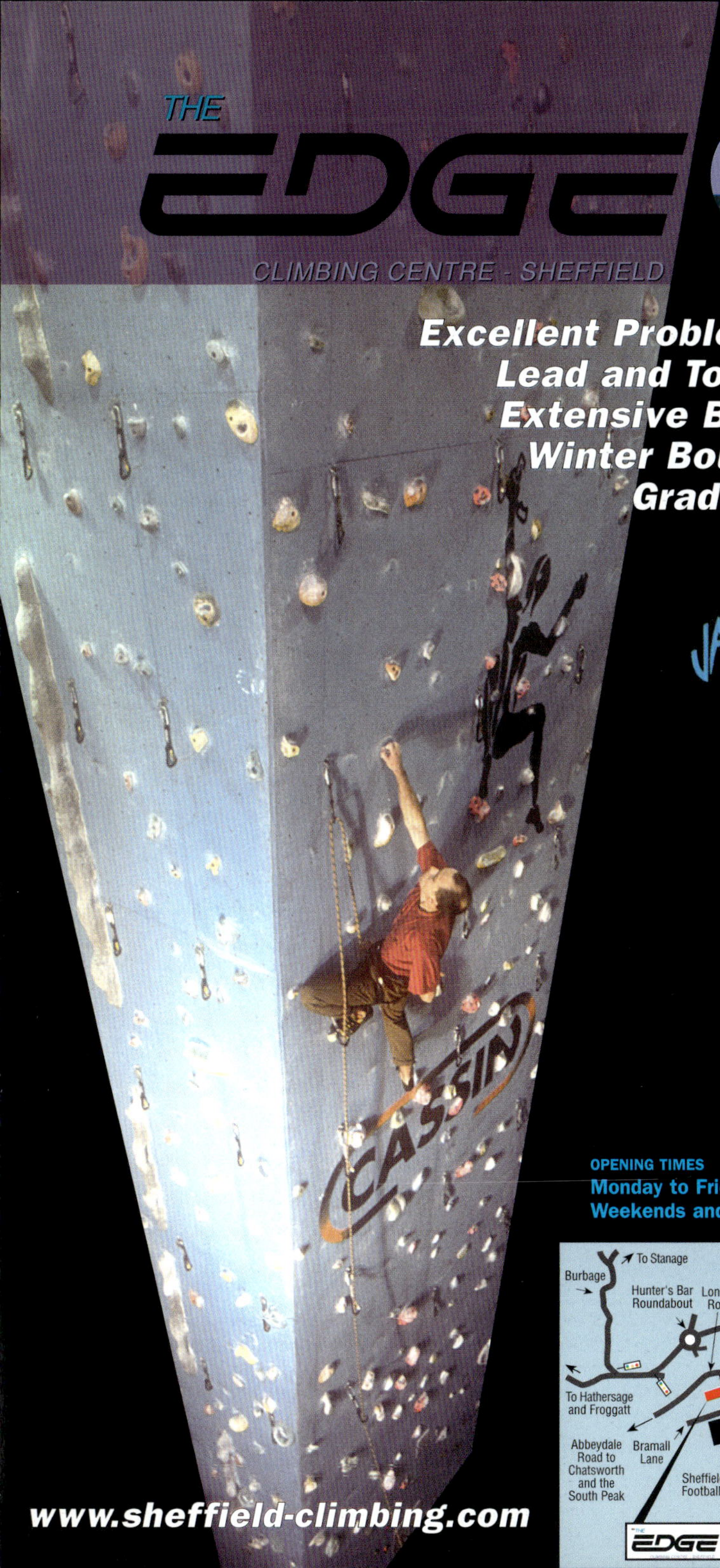

# THE EDGE
## CLIMBING CENTRE - SHEFFIELD

**Excellent Problems and Routes**
**Lead and Top-rope Climbing**
**Extensive Bouldering Walls**
**Winter Bouldering League**
**Grades for Everyone**

Guidebooks
Harnesses
Hardware
Clothing
Ropes
Boots
Pads

The **EDGE** CLIMBING CENTRE
John Street / Bramall Lane
Sheffield S2 4QU
Tel: 0114 275 8899
Fax: 0114 273 8899

**OPENING TIMES**
Monday to Friday: 10am to 10:30pm
Weekends and Bank Holidays: 10am to 8pm

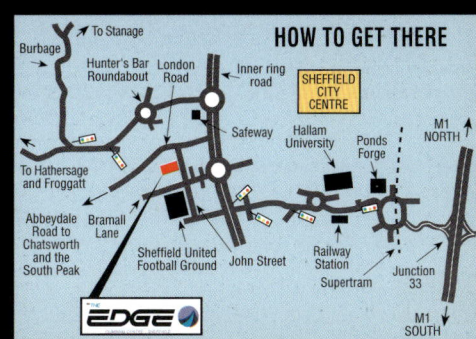

www.sheffield-climbing.com

# ROCKFAX

### YORKSHIRE GRITSTONE BOULDERING (2000)
rockfax.com/yorkshire_bouldering
All the bouldering on the brilliant gritstone outcrops of Yorkshire, England.
320 pages, nearly 3500 problems over 17+ locations.
*"..one day all guidebooks will look like this"* - Simon Panton, Climber, February 2001

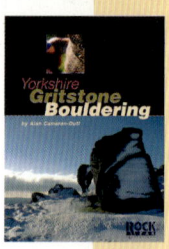

### DORSET (2000)
rockfax.com/dorset
Sport climbing, trad climbing, deep water soloing and bouldering on the south coast of England. 1500 routes on 272 pages including 32 pages of colour.
*"Mighty fine; a job well done"* - Mike Robertson, OTE, May 2000

### COSTA DAURADA (1998)
rockfax.com/costa_daurada
Winter sun destination near Barcelona in northern Spain. Single pitch sport climbing on perfect limestone. 172 pages, 1000+ routes and all major areas.
*"It is the most comprehensive and up-to-date guide available for this area, superseding the Spanish guide."* - - John Adams, Climber, March 1999.

### PEAK BOULDERING (1998 and 2000)
rockfax.com/peak_bouldering
Gritstone bouldering in the Peak District, near Sheffield, England. The only guidebook available. 2nd Edition - 224 pages, 38 locations and 1600+ separate problems.
*"Having had a chance to use the guide for myself, plus liaising with others, it has become apparent that it is pretty damn good."* - Neil Bentley, High, August 1998

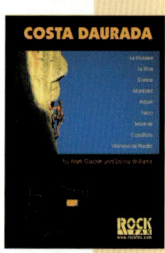

### NORTH WALES LIMESTONE and NORTH WALES BOULDERING (1997)
rockfax.com/north_wales_limestone
Sport and traditional climbing found on the spectacular Ormes of Llandudno. Also includes a bouldering guide to North Wales. 224 pages, 800+ routes, 34 separate crags.

### RIFLE - BITE THE BULLET (1997)
Sport climbing on the limestone of Rifle Mountain Park in Colorado. 72 pages, 200+ routes.

### PEMBROKE (1995)
Traditional climbing on the Pembrokeshire Coast of South Wales. All the important routes are included. 112 pages, 450+ routes.

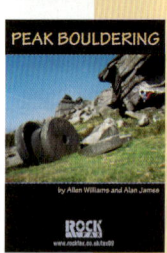

### BISHOP BOULDERING SURVIVAL KIT (1999)
All the information you need for bouldering around Bishop in California.

### THE LAKES (1994)
Limestone section to be included in YORKSHIRE and SOUTH LAKES LIMESTONE.

## NEW BOOKS

### PEAK LIMESTONE (2001)
rockfax.com/peak_limestone
All the best trad and sport routes on Peak limestone in one book.

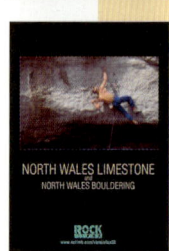

### YORKSHIRE and SOUTH LAKES LIMESTONE (2001)
rockfax.com/yorkshire_limestone
All the best trad and sport routes on Yorkshire and South Lakes limestone in one book.

### VEGAS ROCKS (2001)
rockfax.com/vegas
The limestone and sandstone cliffs around Las Vegas. Check web site for more details.

All books are available from your local retailer or Cordee (3a DeMontfort Street, Leicester, LE1 7HD. UK. Tel: (+int) 44 (0) 116 254 3579) or by credit card using the safe online ordering at:
rockfax.com/shop.html
email: alan@rockfax.co.uk

A climber on *Septiembre* (8b+ - page 165), Sector Wild Side, Sella on the Costa Blanca
Photo: Keith Sharples

# Finca la Campana

.Com

Parties

Hot bike trails

Your base-camp close to the crags offers bunkhouse, doubleroom, or cottage accommodation. All selfcatered and with pool. Mountainbike and caving tours.

Cottage with views

Exploring caves

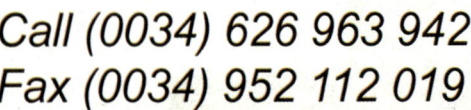
Call (0034) 626 963 942
Fax (0034) 952 112 019

Chuck Pettigrew on
*Pilier Dorada* (6c - page 325)
on El Polvorin, in the Central Gorge
of El Chorro.
Photo: Kim Hawker

# 'LITTLE ANGELS TO ROCK GODS'

## Awesome Walls Climbing Centre

**OPEN**
**MON - FRI**
**12 - 10**
**SAT - SUN**
**10 - 6**

16.5m LEAD WALL OVERHANGING BY 8m

12m FREE-STANDING FEATURED PINNACLE

44 BOLT LINES, 3 ROUTES ON EACH

SEPARATE TOP-ROPING AREA

AWESOME NEW BOULDERING WALL

*Voted 'best new Wall' by OTE*

NO MEMBERSHIP/JOINING FEES

COURSES, TRIPS & PARTIES

GEAR SHOP & CAFE

4 BOULDERING AREAS WITH MARKED PROBLEMS

AWCC, St.ALBANS CHURCH, ATHOL ST.,
OFF GREAT HOWARD ST., LIVERPOOL L5 9XT

**TEL/FAX - 0151 2982422**

Email - ddouglas@netcomuk.co.uk

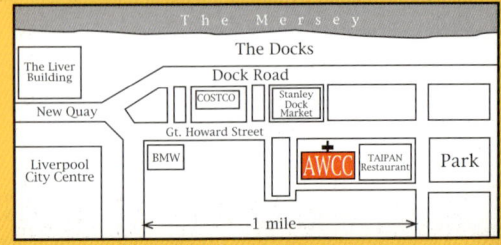

# TOPO and SYMBOL KEY

## Route Symbols

 A good route

 A very good route

 A brilliant route

 An unknown route

 A poor route. A bag of ......!

 Technical climbing involving complex or trick moves.

 Powerful moves requiring big arms

 Sustained climbing, either long and pumpy or with lots of hard moves

 Fingery climbing - sharp holds!

 Fluttery climbing with big fall potential

 A long reach is helpful/essential

 A route which needs wires and friends

 A route which has ENPs - see page 113

## Area Symbols

 **Approach** Approach walk time and angle

 **Sunshine** Approximate time when the sun is on the crag

**Restrictions** Climbing is not allowed at some times

 Slabby climbing

 Vertical wall climbing

Steep climbing

 Lower-offs on most routes

 Some multi-pitch routes

 Crags where you belay on the top

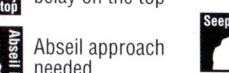 Abseil approach needed

 A crag with dry climbing in the rain

 A windy and/or cold buttress

 A crag which stays wet after rain

## Topos

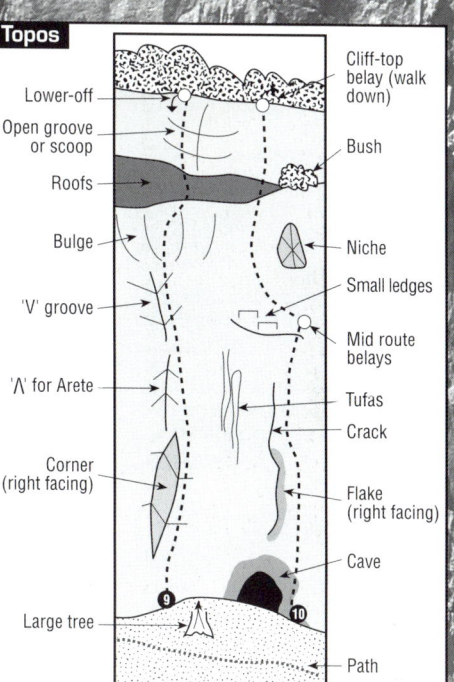

Lower-off, Open groove or scoop, Roofs, Bulge, 'V' groove, '∧' for Arete, Corner (right facing), Large tree, Cliff-top belay (walk down), Bush, Niche, Small ledges, Mid route belays, Tufas, Crack, Flake (right facing), Cave, Path

## Maps

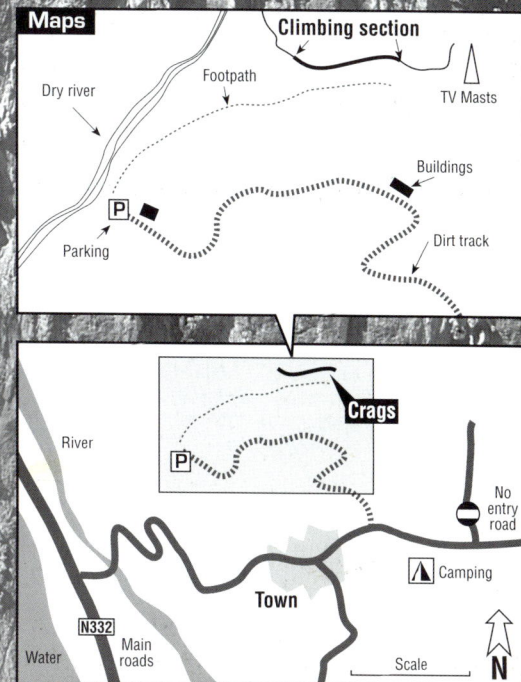

Climbing section, Dry river, Footpath, TV Masts, Buildings, Parking, Dirt track, River, Crags, No entry road, Camping, Town, N332, Water, Main roads, Scale, N

# INTRODUCCIÓN (Español)

Bienvenido a la tercera guía de escalada ROCKFAX que cubre las zonas de la Costa Blanca, Mallorca y El Chorro en España. Las primeras dos ediciones de este libro han sido consideradas por escaladores del mundo entero como la mejor y más fiable fuente de información sobre estas tres zonas, y nos complace presentar esta nueva versión expandida del libro.

La escalada en estas tres zonas es de lo mejor que se puede encontrar en España. Hay de todo para satisfacer a los escaladores sea cual sea su nivel o preferencia. En la Costa Blanca encontrarás la selección más amplia con muchas paredes de vías de un sólo largo como Sella, Gandía y el Vinalopo y también varias zonas montañosas importantes como el Puig Campana, el Peñón d'Ifach o el Divino. Mallorca acoge algunas de las mejores vías deportivas duras de España sobre formaciones rocosas maravillosas, en Fraguel y Alaró por ejemplo, pero existe igualmente una amplia oferta de vías más fáciles desde Sá Gubia a los acantilados de Cala Magraner y Santanyí. La sección final abarca la roca dramática alrededor del Chorro, la atracción principal siendo el desfiladero mismo. También se incluyen en esta sección varias zonas cercanas al Chorro como Loja, El Turón o la increíble cueva de Archidona.

### LA GUÍA

Este libro contiene toda la información necesaria para todas las vías y paredes principales en las tres zonas y, en muchos casos, es la única guía actualizada que existe. Toda la información viene bien ilustrada con mapas de aproximación, croquis y símbolos, así que para los que no hablen mucho inglés no les será difícil tanto llegar a los diferentes sectores como evaluarlos.

### MATERIAL

La mayoría de las vías en este libro pertenece a escuelas de escalada deportiva totalmente equipadas. Existen algunas vías en las tres zonas que se pueden clasificar como vías 'tradicionales', y que requieren un juego completo de fisureros y friends.

- Este símbolo se usa para vías que requieren protección natural (fisureros y friends).

- También hay varias vías en la Costa Blanca que usan el sistema ENP, y que se indican con este símbolo. El sistema ENP se explica en la página 113.

### INFORMACIÓN ADICIONAL

Desde 1996 la guía de la Costa Blanca, Mallorca y El Chorro ha sido continuamente actualizada y mejorada a través del website de ROCKFAX, y todos estos comentarios han sido incorporados a este libro. Sin embargo queremos seguir mejorando la calidad informativa y nos interesan todos vuestros comentarios y opiniones sobre la guía. Estos se recopilan regularmente en hojas actualizadas gratuitas que se pueden imprimir, en formato PDF, desde el website de ROCKFAX – rockfax.com. Estas hojas actualizadas contienen modificaciones y evoluciones, vuestras opiniones acerca de grados y vías y, de vez en cuando, croquis completos para nuevos sectores.

### ROCKFAX

ROCKFAX consiste de Alan James en el Reino Unido y Mick Ryan en los Estados Unidos. Llevamos nueve años produciendo guías de escalada sobre zonas situadas en todo el mundo. Podrás encontrar información detallada sobre todas nuestras publicaciones en nuestro website – rockfax.com - y en la página 12.
Email (Reino Unido): alan@rockfax.co.uk. Email (Estados Unidos): mick@rockfax.com.

## Símbolos de las vías

 Vía buena

 Vía muy buena

 Vía fantástica

 Vía desconocida

 Vía mala

 Escalada técnica que requiere movimientos complejos o ingeniosos

 Movimientos de fuerza que requieren brazos sólidos

 Escalada de continuidad, larga y con botellas garantizadas o con muchos movimientos duros

 Escalada de dedos – ¡Agarres cortantes!

 Escalada alarmante con posibilidad de caídas grandes

 Gran envergadura útil / esencial

 Vía que requiere algunos fisureros

 Vía que tiene ENP – ver página 113

## Símbolos de las paredes

 **Aproximación** Tiempo de aproximación y pendiente

 **Sol** Horas aproximadas en que la pared está al sol

 **Restricciones** Escalada prohibida durante ciertos períodos

 Placa

 Vertical

 Desplomado

 Descuelgues en la mayoría de las vías

 Algunas vías de varios largos

 Reunión en la cima

 Rápel necesario

 Protegido de la lluvia

 Frío / expuesto al viento

 Chorreo Permanece mojado después de llover

## Croquis

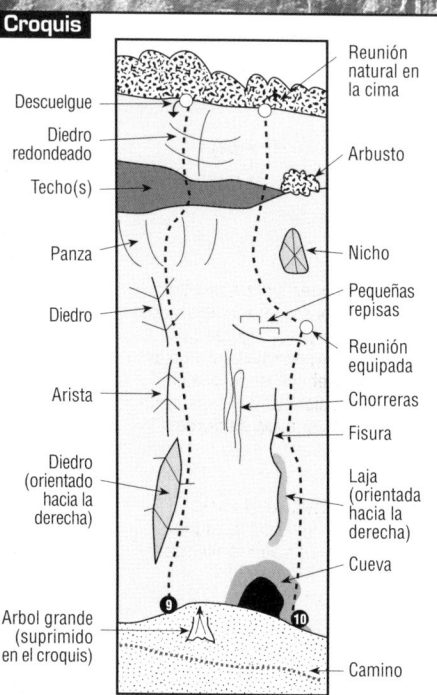

## Mapas

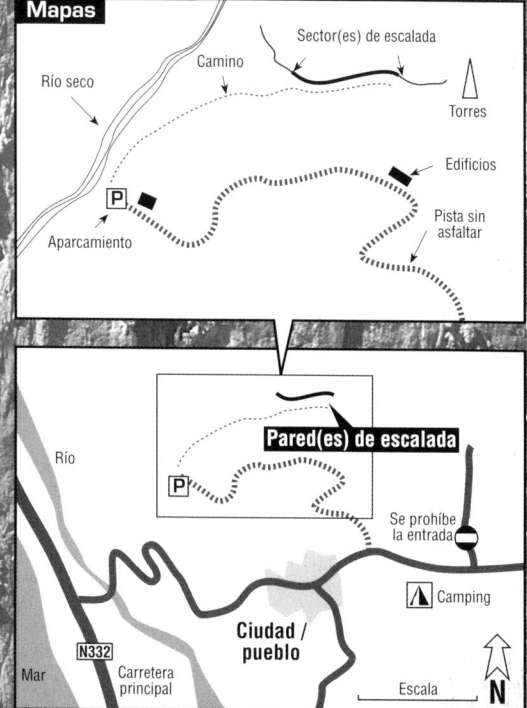

# INTRODUCTION (Français)

Bienvenue au troisième guide d'escalade ROCKFAX qui comprend la Costa Blanca, Majorque et El Chorro en Espagne. Les grimpeurs du monde entier ont considéré les deux premières éditions de ce livre comme la meilleure source d'information sur ces trois endroits, et nous sommes heureux de présenter cette nouvelle version élargie du livre.

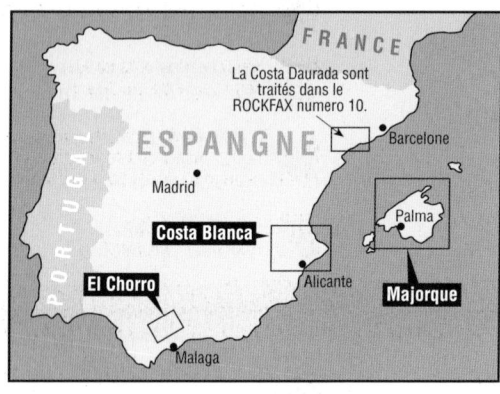

On peut dire que l'escalade comprise par ces trois endroits est du mieux qui puisse se trouver en Espagne. Il y a tout pour satisfaire aux grimpeurs quel que soit leur niveau ou préférence. A la Costa Blanca on trouvera la sélection la plus diverse avec des parois comprenant des voies d'une longeur comme Sella, Gandía ou le Vinalopo et aussi plusieurs secteurs montagneux comme le Puig Campana, le Peñon d'Ifach ou le Divino. Majorque abrite quelques-unes des meilleurs voies sportives dures d'Espagne sur des formations rocheuses merveilleuses, à Fraguel et Alaró par exemple, mais il existe également une large gamme de voies plus faciles à Sá Gubia et aux falaises longeant la mer à Cala Magraner et à Santanyí. La section finale comprend les rochers dramatiques autour de El Chorro, l'attraction principale étant la gorge même. On trouvera également dans cette section plusieurs secteurs près de El Chorro comme Loja, El Turón ou l'incroyable grotte de Archidona.

## LE GUIDE

Ce livre contient tous les renseignements nécessaires pour toutes les voies et tous les secteurs principaux dans les trois endroits et, dans beaucoup de cas, est le seul guide actualisé qui existe. Tous les renseignements se trouvent bien illustrés par des plans de situation, des topos et des symboles; c'est à dire, ceux qui ne parlent pas beaucoup d'anglais n'auront pas de difficultés pour trouver et évaluer les différents secteurs.

## MATERIEL

La plupart des voies dans ce livre font partie d'écoles d'escalade sportive tout à fait équipées. Il existe quelques voies dans les trois endroits qu'on pourrait classifier comme des voies 'traditionnelles', et qui nécessitent un jeu complet de coinceurs et de friends.

- Ce symbole s'utilise pour des voies qui nécessitent une protection naturelle.

- Il existe aussi plusieurs voies à la Costa Blanca qui utilisent le système ENP, et qui sont indiquées par ce symbole. On explique le système ENP à la page 113.

## RENSEIGNEMENTS ADDITIONAUX

Depuis 1996 le guide de la Costa Blanca, Majorque et El Chorro est continuellement actualisé et amelioré à travers le website de ROCKFAX, et tous ces commentaires ont été incorporés à ce livre. Nous voudrions pourtant continuer à ameliorer la qualité de l'information et nous accueillerons tous vos commentaires et toutes vos opinions sur le guide. Ceux-ci sont dressés dans des feuilles actualisées gratuites que l'on peut imprimer, en format PDF, d'après le website de ROCKFAX – rockfax.com. Ces feuilles actualisées contiennent des modifications et de nouveaux développements, vos opinions sur les cotations et les voies et, de temps en temps, des topos complets pour de nouveaux secteurs.

## ROCKFAX

ROCKFAX consiste d'Alan James au Royaume-Uni et de Mick Ryan aux Etats-Unis. Ça fait neuf ans qu'on crée des guides d'escalade sur des endroits situées dans le monde entier. On pourra trouver des renseignements sur toutes nos publications sur notre website – rockfax.com - et à la page 12. Email (Royaume-Uni): alan@rockfax.co.uk. Email (Etats-Unis): mick@rockfax.com.

## Symboles des voies

 Bonne voie

 Très bonne voie

 Voie majeure

 Voie inconnue

 Mauvaise voie

 Escalade technique nécessitant des mouvements complexes ou astucieux

 Requiert des bras solides pour des mouvements de force

 Escalade de continuité, longue et avec bouteilles garanties ou bien avec beaucoup de mouvements durs

 Escalade à doigts – prises coupantes!

 Escalade angoissante avec possibilité de grandes chutes

 Les grands seront avantagés.

 Voie nécessitant quelques coinceurs.

 Voie ayant des ENP – voir page 113

## Symboles des parois

 **Approche** Temps de marche d'approche et pente

 Dalle

 Moulinettes sur la plupart des voies

 Protégé de la pluie

 **Soleil** Heures approximatives auxquelles la paroi est exposée au soleil.

 Vertical

 Quelque voies de plusieurs longueurs

 Relais au sommet

 Venté et exposé

 **Restrictions** Escalade interdite pendant certaines périodes

 Surplomb

 Rappel nécessaire

 Suintement Reste mouillé après la pluie

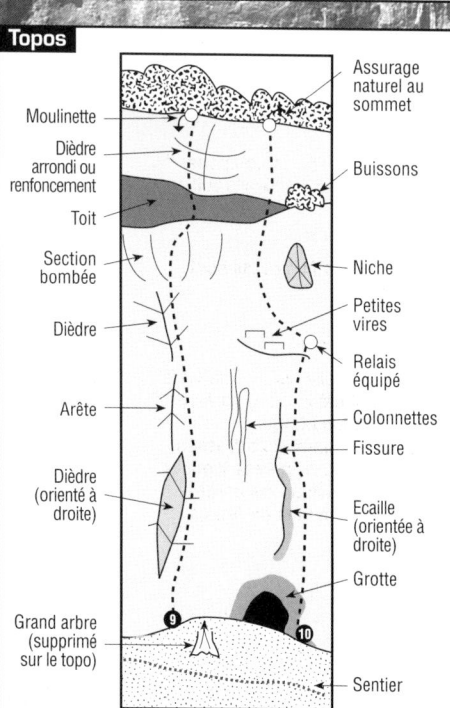

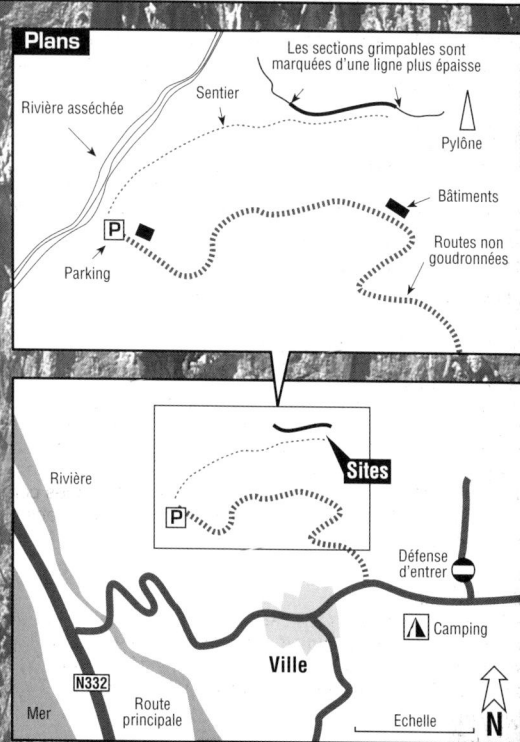

# EINFÜHRUNG

Willkommen zur 3. Auflage des ROCKFAX Kletterführers, der die Gebiete Costa Blanca, Mallorca und El Chorro in Spanien beinhaltet. Die ersten beiden Auflagen dieses Buches wurden von Kletterern der ganzen Welt als die besten und umfangreichsten Kletterführer für diese drei Gegenden anerkannt. Daher freuen wir uns jetzt, diese erweiterte, neue Version des Buches herauszubringen.

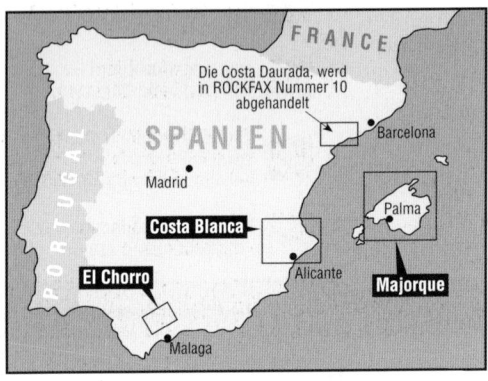

Die Klettermöglichkeiten in diesen drei Gebieten gehören zu den besten, die Spanien zu bieten hat. Es gibt für jeden Kletterer etwas, unabhängig von seinen Fähigkeiten und Vorlieben. An der Costa Blanca findet man die grösste Auswahl. Es gibt sowohl viele Sportrouten mit einer Seillänge wie z.B. Sella, Gandía und der Vinalopo Felsen, als auch einige höhere Felsen mit alpinem Charakter wie Puig Campana, Peñon d'Ifach und Divino. Mallorca bietet einige der besten, schweren Sportrouten Spaniens, die an wunderschönen Felsen wie Fraguel und Alaró liegen. Weiterhin gibt es dort ein grosses Angebot an Routen im leichteren Schwierigkeitsgrad, ausgehend von Sa Gubia weiter zu den Klippen am Meer von Cala Magraner und Santanyi. Der letzte Abschnitt beschreibt den imposanten Felsen rund um El Chorro, wobei die Schlucht selber den Mittelpunkt bildet. In diesem Kapitel sind auch einige weitere Gebiete in der Nähe von El Chorro beschrieben, wie Loja, Turon und das beeindruckende Archidona.

## DER KLETTERFÜHRER

Dieses Buch beinhaltet alle Informationen, die für alle Hauptrouten und Felsen in den drei Gebieten benötigt werden. In den meisten Fällen ist es der einzige aktuelle Führer, der erhältlich ist. Alle Informationen sind durch Karten, Topos und Symbole illustriert, die es ermöglichen auch ohne umfassende Englischkenntnisse die verschiedenen Gebiete zu erreichen und Routen auszuwählen.

## AUSRÜSTUNG

Die meisten Kletterrouten in diesem Buch beschreiben Touren auf voll ausgerüsteten Sportkletterfelsen. In allen drei Gebieten existieren auch ‚traditionelle' Routen, die eine volle Ausrüstung bestehend aus Klemmkeilen und Friends voraussetzen.

- Dieses Symbol kennzeichnet Routen, die die Verwendung von Klemmkeilen und Friends erfordern.

- Im Gebiet Costa Blanca gibt es einige Routen, die das ENP System verwenden und durch dieses Symbol gekennzeichnet werden. Dieses wird auf Seite 113 beschrieben.

## WEITERE INFORMATIONEN

Über die ROCKFAX Web-Seite wurde der Führer Costa Blanca, Mallorca und El Chorro seit 1996 regelmäßig aktualisiert und verbessert. Alle dort vorhandenen Kommentare wurden in das neue Buch eingearbeitet. Auch weiterhin möchten wir die Qualität des Buches verbessern und sind daher an Kritik und Anregungen zu diesem Buch sehr interessiert. Aktualisierungen werden regelmäßig auf unserer ROCKFAX Web-Seite im PDF-Format zum Herunterladen zur Verfügung gestellt. Diese beinhalten sowohl Veränderungen und Neuerungen sowie gelegentlich Topos von neuen Gebieten, als auch Ihre Meinung zu Schwierigkeitsgraden und Routen.

## ROCKFAX

ROCKFAX sind Alan James in England und Mick Ryan in Amerika. Seit 9 Jahren veröffentlichen wir Führer von Klettergebieten in der ganzen Welt. Details zu unseren Veröffentlichungen befinden sich auf unserer Web-Seite – rockfax.com und auf Seite 12.
Email (UK): alan@rockfax.co.uk  Email (USA): mick@rockfax.com

## Symbole

 Lohnende Kletterei

 Sehr lohnende Kletterei

 Brilliante Kletterei

 Eine unbekannte Route

 Unschöne Kletterei. Besser etwas anderes unternehmen ...

 Technisch anspruchsvolle Tour mit trickreichen Zügen.

 Anstrengende Züge. Erfordert dicke Oberarme.

 Durchgehend anstrengende Tour; entweder anhaltend schwer oder mit einer Reihe harter Züge.

 Kleingriffige, rauhe Kletterei - nichts für zarte Hände.

 Heikle Kletterei mit hohem Sturzpotential, aber nicht allzu gefährlich.

 Lange Arme sind hilfreich.

 Kletterei, die Sicherung durch Klemmkeile u.ä. erfordert.

 Eine Route, die das ENP System verwendet – siehe Seite 113

## Felsymbole

 Zugang Zeit und Steilheit des Zugangsweges.

 Sonnenschein Zeit, zu der der Felsen in der Sonne liegt.

Beschränkungen Klettern ist zu bestimmten Zeiten verboten

 Plattige Reibungsprobleme

Hauptsächlich senkrechte Probleme

 Hauptsächlich steile Probleme

 Umlenkungen existieren in den meisten Routen

 Mehrere Seillängen

Felsen, mit Standplätzen auf der Spitze

 Falls Abseilen notwendig

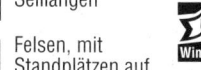 Trockener Fels bei Regen

 Dem Wind ausgesetzt

 Rinnwasser

## Topos

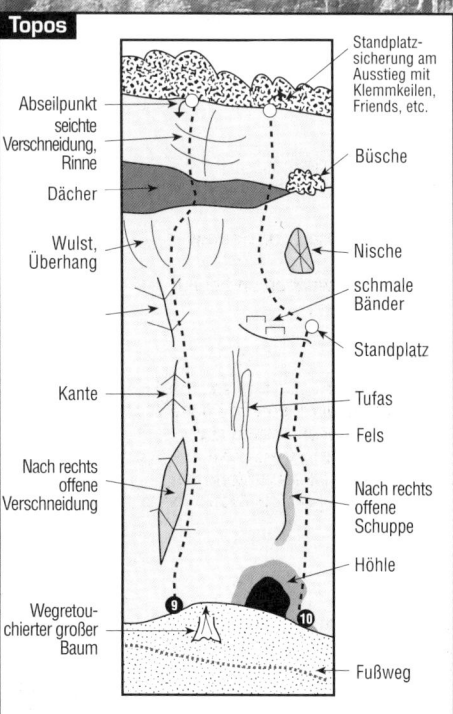

## Karten

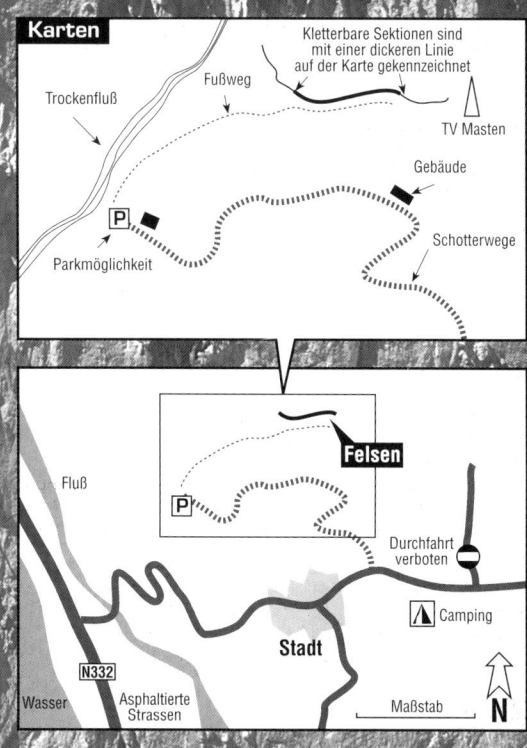

# ADVERTISER DIRECTORY

**UKClimbing.com**

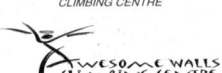

ROCKFAX is very grateful to the individuals, companies, shops and climbing walls, who have supported this guidebook.

**ALTERNATIVE MALLORCA (Page 6)** - Mallorca accommodation
Alternative Mallorca, 60 Stainbeck Road, Meanwood, Leeds, LS7 2PW
Tel: 0113 278 6862  Fax: 0113 274 2204
Web site: www.alternativemallorca.com

**AWESOME WALLS (page 16)** - Climbing wall
AWCC, St. Alban's Church, Athol Street, Liverpool, L5 9XT. Tel: 0191 2303793
Email: ddouglas@netcomuk.co.uk

**BENDCRETE (Inside Back Cover)** - Climbing walls, MORPHIX holds, bouldering mats
Bendcrete, Aqueduct Mill, Tame Street, Stalybridge, Cheshire, SK15 1ST.
Tel: 0161 3383046 Fax: 0161 3387956
Web site: www.bendcrete.com   Email: info@bendcrete.com

**BMC INSURANCE (Page 2)** - Insurance
Tel: 0161 445 4747 Fax: 0161 445 4500
Web site: www.thebmc.com   Email: insure@thebmc.co.uk

**ESMERO PROPERTY SERVICES (Page 30)** - Costa Blanca accommodation
Esmero Property, 38 Ortembach 16A, Buzón 8, 03710 Calpe, Alicante, SPAIN
Tel & Fax: 00 34 96 583 0260 or UK: 0208 8526079
Email: ianm@arrakis.es

**FINCA LA CAMPANA (Page 14)** - El Chorro accommodation
Finca La Campana, El Chorro, Alora, Malaga, SPAIN.
Tel: 00 34 626 963 942 Fax: 00 34 952 112 019
Web site: www.el-chorro.com

**LA ASMOLADORA (Page 30)** - Costa Blanca accommodation
Pam and Derek Cornthwaite, La Asmoladora, Parcent, Costa Blanca
Tewl & Fax: 00 34 96 640 5429. Tel (UK): 01433 639536
Web: www.holiday-rentals.com/asmoladora Email: dcornth@attglobal.net

**NEEDLESPORTS (Page 2)** - Shop and online shop
Needlesports, 56 Main Street, Keswick, Cumbria, CA12 5JS.
Tel: 017687 72227 Fax: 017687 75593
Web site: www.needlesports.com   Email: info@needlesports.com

**ROCK + RUN (Page 8)** - Shops and online shop
The Lakes - 3-4 Cheapside, Ambleside, Cumbria, LA22 0AB. Tel: 01539 433690
Sheffield - 98 Devonshire Street, Sheffield, S1 4GY. Tel: 0114 275 6429
Mail Order - Tel: 015394 32855
Web site: www.rockrun.com   Email: info@rockrun.com

**SCARPA (Back cover)** - Climbing footware
The Mountain Boot Company Ltd., 8 Nelson Street, Newcastle-u-Tyne, NE1 5AW
Tel: 0191 232 3565   Fax: 0191 222 1764
Web site: www.scarpa.co.uk   Email: info@scarpa.co.uk

**SNOW & ROCK (Inside front cover)** - Shops
M25 Superstore - 99 Fordwater Road, Chertsey,  KT16 8HH. Tel:01932 566 886
Bristol Superstore - Shield Retail Centre, Bristol, BS32. Tel: 0117 914 3000
Kensington - 188 Kensington High Street, London, W8 7RG. Tel:0207 937 0872
Hemel Ski Centre - St. Albans Hill, Hemel, HP3 9NH. Tel:01442 253 305
Holborn - 150 Holborn, Corner Gray's Inn Road, EC1N 2LC. Tel: 0207 831 6900
Sheffield Ski Village - Vale Road, Sheffield, S3 9SL. Tel: 0114 275 1700
Birmingham - 14 Priory Queensway, Birmingham, B4 6BS. Tel: 0121 236 8280
Web site: www.snowandrock.com

**TERRACOTTAGES.CO.UK (Page 32, 222, 292)** - Accommodation
Tel: 01695 624143
Web site: www.terracottages.co.uk

**THE EDGE CLIMBING CENTRE (Page 11)** - Climbing wall
The Edge Climbing Centre, John Street, Sheffield, S2 4QU.
Tel: 0114 275 8899 Fax: 0114 273 8899
Web site: www.sheffield-climbing.co.uk   Email: info@sheffield-climbing.co.uk

**UKCLIMBING.COM (Page 9)** - Climbing web site
Web site: www.ukclimbing.com

**ZERO 95 (Page 6)** - Costa Blanca Shop
Avda. Gabriel Miro, 14, 03710 CALPE (Alicante). Tel: (00 34) 96 583 0589
Web site: web.jet.es/zero95

**CLASSIFIEDS**
**THE MOUSE HOUSE (Page 32)** - Costa Blanca accommodation
**HOTEL LA COSTERA (Page 32)** - Costa Blanca accommodation and restaurant
**LA ALIMONA CHICA (Page 292)** - El Chorro accommodation

Lewis Grundy on an un-named 6b (*Route 2* - page 265) on Sector Del Medio, at Alaró on Mallorca. Photo: Jane Grundy

Jon Dunne climbing the superb, but un-named, 6c+ (*Route 24* - page 73) at Lliber, on the Costa Blanca.
Photo: Dave Simmonite

# ACKNOWLEDGMENTS

The most important people who need thanking are the climbers who have equipped and climbed the routes in this book, without them we would have nothing to climb.

Alan James. Photo: David Ranby

There are over 200 other people who have had a hand in producing this book by giving feedback for the updates which have been available on the ROCKFAX web site for the last 4 years. Thanks are due to all who contributed in this way. The feedback has ranged from an email with a single grade change to five page documents of topos and text. Everything has been welcome and please keep it coming. The following people have all sent feedback in some form: Adam Hocking, Adrian Berry, Adrian Martin, Al Austin, Al Evans, Al Scott, Alan Little, Alan Randall, Alec Burns, Alessandro Bellini, Alex Masters, Allen Price, Andi Dick, Andreas Polster, Andrew Earl, Andrew Roberts, Andy Birtwistle, Andy Hyslop, Andy Jones, Andy Kirk, Andy Mackintosh, Andy Say, Angela Soper, Anne-Marie Nuttall, Anthony Prendergast, Arran Deakin, Ben Heason, Bev Hull, Bill Pattison, Bob Bennett, Bob Smith, Bridget and Jeremy, Carl Dawson, Chris Doyle, Chris Gore, Chris Heald, Chris Howell, Chris Sims, Christian Strunz, Chuck Cuthbert, Clare Dyson, Colin Goodey, D. McAulay, Dave Booth, David Bowler, Dave Douglas, Dave Garner, Dave Law, Dave Lyon, Dave Wilcock, David Chadwick, David Toon, Don Roscoe, Doug Reid, Eddie Church, Franck Vilpini, Frank Thompson, Gary Baum, Gary Gibson, Georg Hoffman, George Ridge, George Wright, Gerard O'Sullivan, Giles Stone, Goi Ashmore, Guy Maddox, Hans-Thomas Thiel, Harry Engwirda, Heinz Wurzer, Henry Wurzer, Howard Jones, Huw Jenkins, Iain Mann, Ian Dunn, Ian Henderson, Ian Gray, Ian Krauklis, Ingo Ronner, Jane Meeks, Janet Horrocks, Jill Whittaker, Jim Arnold, Jo George, John Bull, John Cardy, John Codling, John Earl, John Fletcher, John Harwood, John Mountain, John Scott, John Smith, John Tombs, John Walton, John Watson, John Wilson, John Zangwill, Jon Ashdown, Jon Barton, Jon deMontjoye, Jon Pearson, Jon Read, Karen Beattie, Kate Arnold, Keith Wadsworth, Kepa Laitsaari, Kevin Davey, Lee Bartrop, Lisa Curry, Lynn Leadbeater, Mandy Payne, Marina Bloj, Mark Bull, Mark Garthwaite, Mark Haigh, Mark Lawrence, Mark Medley, Mark Savage, Martin Basil, Martin Christmas, Martin Cooper, Martin Crocker, Martin Komstadius, Martin Wilkinson, Matt Ward, Matthew Farwell, Mel Griffiths, Michael Doyle, Michael Muendel, Mick Nally, Mike Arnold, Mike Brier, Mike Gutteridge, Mike Kerby, Mike Raine, Mike Searson, Neil Stabbs, Nicola Bowden, Nick Easton, Nick Longland, Nick Malden, Nick West, Nigel Slater, Nigel Tuckley, Oliver McCreath, Paddy Gibson, Paul Brooks, Paul Green, Paul Jennings, Paul McClorey, Paul Stallard, Percy Bishton, Perry Hawkins, Pete Oxley, Peter Owens, Phillippa Poland, Richard Barnes, Richard Fox, Richard Sewards, Rick Kruze, Rick Sewards, Rob Stone, Rob Taylor, Roger Everett, Roger Laycock, Ron Fawcett, Ron James, Sami Salonen, Sam Moore (and ICOC), Sebastian Schwertner, Seth Barber, Silvia Pearsons, Simon Brown, Simon Caldwell, Simon Jinks, Simon Marsh, Simon Mooney, Spike Pycroft, Stefan Ringmann, Steve Anthony, Steve Blake, Steve Crowe, Steve Fletcher, Steve Green, Steve Mayers, Steve Plackett, Steve Quinn, Steve Swygart, Steve Taylor, Stuart Greenall, Taina Jaaskelainen, Terry Taylor, Thomas Jekel, Tim Bancroft, Tim Bevis, Tommy Smith, Tre Wilson and Uwe Lindenau. There may be other who have been swallowed by my various email packages over the years. If your name has been missed off then please accept my apologies.

Mark Glaister. Photo: Emma Williams

Thanks also to Mark Glaister for the work he has put in to update the El Chorro section; to Rowland Edwards for providing great topos and information for various areas in the Costa Blanca; to Nick Verney for his efforts in Mallorca; to Stephen Kirby, Dennis Morrod, Miquel Riera and Karen Yeow for topos to crags in the Costa Blanca and Mallorca; to Alan Cameron-Duff and Rab Anderson, the co-authors of the previous editions; to Juan Varela-Nex for the translations and feedback; to Michael Pangels and Nicole Hoyer for a translation at the last minute and also extensive feedback; to David Mora García for helping find the historical details in the Costa Blanca; to Chris Craggs for his books to the areas; to Kev Howett and Mike Owen for help with earlier books and to the following for giving feedback above and beyond the call of duty - Andreas Bachner, Keith Sharples, Johnny and Stella Adams, Neil Foster, Richard Davies, Dave Musgrove, Dave Cobley, Andy Hartley and Tomas Ratajczak. For their photographic contributions thanks are due to Biel Santandreu, Lewis Grundy, Keith Sharples, Dave Cobley, Kim Hawker, Jane Grundy, Dave Simmonite, Rowland Edwards, Mark Edwards, John Wilson and Micki Palmer.

Mark would like to thank Emma Williams, Chris Gore, Jon Hofor, Drew Haigh, James 'Caff' McHaffie, Rob Knight and Sheridan Bridal for their help with the El Chorro section.

Over the years I have made many trips to the three areas in this book. My climbing partners have all helped to produce this guide by agreeing to go to all the obscure places and by putting up with my questions and frantic drawing sessions. These people are Sophie Milner, Mr and Mrs Ranby, Jon Young, Mr and Mrs Park, Tim Seaborne, Mr and Mrs Grundy, Andy Burnett, Mr and Mrs Cross, Andy Bowman, Mr and Mrs Scott, Dave Idenden, Steve Anson, Chrissy Dorn, Lousie Crawford, Simon Baker, Caroline Fanshawe, Craig Smith, Molly Heitz and Carolyn Falder.

Thanks also to Mike James and Johan Louwerse for their proof reading, Liz James for her general help and support and Mick Ryan for doing his stuff in the States.

Finally I would like to thank the three most special people, who will soon become four - Henriette, Hannah and Sam.

What's next?

Alan James
March 2001

## COSTA BLANCA

| | |
|---|---|
| Climbing Information | 31 |
| Logistics | 33 |
| Crag Selection Table | 34 |
| Area Map | 36 |
| | |
| Gandía | 37 |
| Salem | 47 |
| Montesa | 56 |
| Aventador | 59 |
| Bellús | 64 |
| Jalón Valley | 70 |
| Olta | 78 |
| Peñon d'Ifach | 80 |
| Sierra de Toix | 88 |
| Mascarat Gorge | 104 |
| Bernia Area | 110 |
| Echo Valley | 113 |
| Ponoch | 136 |
| Puig Campana | 138 |
| Sella | 146 |
| Alcoy | 177 |
| Agujas Rojas | 180 |
| Reconco | 183 |
| Peña Rubia | 186 |
| Cabreras | 191 |
| Salinas | 199 |
| Forada | 207 |

Craig Smith climbing *The Naked Edge* (6c - page 175) on El Elefante at Sella on the Costa Blanca. Photo: Alan James

# Costa Blanca

by Alan James

Additional text and topos
by Rowland Edwards

# Costa Blanca: Calpe - La Fustera - Moraira - Sierra Altea
# VILLA AND APARTMENT RENTALS

The Calpe area has, over the past 15 years, developed into one of the main rock climbing areas in southern Europe. The mild winter climate is ideal for climbing and the easy accessibility to Sella, Gandia, Mascarat and Toix makes Calpe the ideal base. We have been providing accommodation for climbers for many years and appreciate your needs and requirements. For those non-climbers visiting our area you may wish to explore some of the white-washed Spanish villages set amongst pines or vines or simply 'flop out' on an unspoilt white sandy beach. A colourful and bustling street market can be found each day of the week so practice your haggling and grab a bargain. Feeling energetic? Then take a walk to the top of the Peñon (see photo) - 300 metres high and experience a view never to be forgotten.

For our comprehensive brochure please contact:

**Mrs Wendy Brown**
Tel: 0208 8526079

or

**Mrs Rosemary McKernan**
38 Ortembach 16A, Buzón 8
03710 CALPE (Alicante)
Spain
Tel: (00 34) 96 5830260
Fax: (00 34) 96 5830260
Mobile: (00 34) 689 336020
Email: ianm@arrakis.es

- Wide range of private villas with or without pools
- Quality apartments
- Car hire and cot hire
- Experienced English management

# La Asmoladora
*"Paradise between mountains" - Gabriel Miro*

## Parcent, Costa Blanca

Situated near the small pueblo of Parcent in the peaceful Jalon Valley, finca La Asmoladora is located in the centre of the climbing areas of the Costa Blanca. It is surrounded on three sides by spectacular mountains. The nearest crags are five minutes away and all the main Costa Blanca areas are within easy reach.

The finca is an excellent rural base for all mountain activities and for climbers preferring to avoid the overcrowded tourist areas of the coast.

It has superb self-contained, self-catering accommodation sized and equipped for groups of two, four and eight people. It can accommodate a total of fourteen. The photograph shows our three Casitas each for two people.

For relaxing before or after climbing, La Asmoladora has twelve acres of almond, olive and vine terraces to wander in, a tennis court, mountain bikes and a large barbecue area and swimming pool.

**MORE INFORMATION**
Contact owners Pam and Derek Cornthwaite
Email: dcornth@attglobal.net
Phone/fax (Spain): 00 34 96 640 5429 (Oct - May)
Phone (UK): 01433 639536 (Jun - Sep)
Web: www.holiday-rentals.com/asmoladora

# COSTA BLANCA

The Costa Blanca has become the largest and most popular area in Spain for visiting climbers. The wealth and variety of climbing in the area is truly staggering, and for every partially developed crag there are at least two other slightly less accessible ones which haven't been touched yet. But it is the variety in the climbing which keeps people coming back here. It is not just roadside clip-ups since there are huge trad routes on the Puig Campana, and in the Echo Valley, and majestic, fully-bolted, multi-pitch extravaganzas on places like the Peñon and the Ponoch. You can switch from doing one long route in the mountains on one day to ticking a dozen routes on a crag three minutes from the car on the next.

In the Costa Blanca the weather and general holiday atmosphere which are also part of the attraction. There is something uniquely appealing about climbing a route on Christmas Day, on a superb cliff in the blazing sunshine, while staying in an apartment in a nearly-deserted Benidorm or Calpe and relaxing afterwards with a few beers on the beach. The routes cover all grades and styles with probably the widest choice of lower-grade Winter-Sun-Rock available in Spain. But there is also lots of hard stuff, adventurous stuff and esoteric stuff. If you explore the area a bit, you will be rewarded.

Since the first two editions of this book most climbers have got to know the wider delights of the area beyond the very popular venues of Toix, Gandía and Sella. Although some of the crags require long car journeys, places like Reconco, Forada, Salinas and Cabreras are well worth the effort. In this book we have added the major trad climbing crags of the Echo Valley as well as three other new venues - Bellus, Montesa, Ponoch and Agujas Rojas. All the other areas have also been significantly enhanced. We have also added information about the first ascensionist, or route equipper, to as many routes as possible and thanks are due to David Mora García and Rowland Edwards for their help in this task, plus the writers of the local guidebooks to Vinalopó and Sella. Where details of individual routes are not known we have tried to credit the major developers at the crags.

## CLIMBING INFORMATION

### Access
A few of the crags have access restrictions because of nesting birds (Cabreras, Salinas and one face of the Peñon). Details are with the route pages. Most of the other areas can be reached all year round.

### Grades
The grades in the Costa Blanca tend to be consistent with other areas. Certain crags like Gandía have reputations for harder grades but most of these anomalies have been removed by now.

### Gear
If you wish to get the most out of the area then you are well advised to bring a rack of wires and cams with you. There is some brilliant trad climbing to be found including the ENP routes in the Echo Valley (see page 113). Most of the bolted routes require up to 15 quickdraws and many are more than 25m long making a 60m rope essential if you want to lower off. If you are doing a lot of multi-pitch routes then you will need two 50m x 9mm ropes. For more information on gear see page 8.

### Other Books
*Guía de Escalada del Ponoch* by Carlos Tudela (1998)
*Guía de Escalada Puig Campana* by Carlos Tudela (1995)
*Escalada Sella* by Ignacio Sánchez and José Miguel García (1999)
*Escaladas en el medio y alto Vinalopo* - various authors (1995)
*Costa Blanca Rock* by Chris Craggs (1997)
There is an old guide to *Peñon d'Ifach* (including the Toix Ridge and Mascarat) by Roy de Valera (1989) which probably isn't available any more.

### Other Areas
The Costa Blanca is so vast that we haven't space here to cover the many other crags in the area. You can be assured that there are many other crags however we have covered most of the ones within comfortable driving distance. As new crags come to light full topos will appear on the ROCKFAX web site - rockfax.com/costa_blanca

On the Costa Blanca near town of Benissa and A7 motorway junction 63 (see map page 70) *the Mouse House* offers:

- double bedroom
- single bedroom
- living room
- kitchen
- full bathroom
- use of swimming pool
- private entrance & parking

Call/fax. 00 34 96597 3042
for tariff & availability.

Check for more details at
www.villarama.com

*If it will all fit?*

## ZERO 95
### Climbing Shop

Avda. Gabriel Miró, 14
03710 CALPE (Alicante)
Tfno. 965830589
http://web.jet.es/zero95
(see main advert on page 6)

## Costa Blanca: Calpe - La Fustera - Moraira - Sierra Altea
## VILLA AND APARTMENT RENTALS

UK Contact: **Mrs Wendy Brown**, Tel: 0208 8526079
Spain Contact: **Mrs Rosemary McKernan**, 38 Ortembach 16A, Buzón 8, 03710 CALPE
Tel & Fax: (00 34) 96 5830260, Mobile: (00 34) 689 336020, Email: ianm@arrakis.es
(See main advert on page 30)

## HOTEL LA COSTERA
*La Costera, Calle San Jose, N/1, Finestrat 03509, Alicante*

Tel and Fax: 00 34 965878629
Email - oasiswingfield@ctv.es

Accommodation in double or twin rooms
*(From 3000psts per twin room per night)*
Restaurant open to non-residents

### terracottages.co.uk

Holidays in Spain and Mallorca
Visit www.terracottages.co.uk
For a great selection of holiday accommodation
Villas, Country Houses, Cottages, Apartments

Phone Stu 01695 624143
SPANISH COSTAS, MALLORCA
EL CHORRO, COSTA DAURADA

**Car Hire**

- WALKING
- MOUNTAINEERING
- SKY MOUNTAINEERING
- ICE CLIMBING
- COSTA BLANCA CLIMBS
- ADVENTURE CLIMBS
(P. Ifach, P. Campana, Ponoch,..)
- SPAIN CLIMBING

## DAVID MORA GARCÍA

Climbing & Mountaineering Instructor
Spanish Mountaineering School EEAM

escola valenciana
d'alta muntanya

CONTACT: Santa Ana, 5-2ºC, 03201 – Elche, Alicante (Spain)
Tlf: (+34) 96 544 94 82 E-mail: davidmora@mixmail.com

# COSTA BLANCA LOGISTICS

More on the ROCKFAX web site at - rockfax.com/costa_blanca

## WHEN TO GO
Of the three areas in this book the Costa Blanca has the best climate for the cold months like December and January where the coastal strip is often be warm and dry when inland areas are dull and wet, and you can celebrate Christmas Day with an ascent of a classic route. The late Autumn can bring storms but is likely to be very pleasant temperature-wise. Probably the best time is Spring when you can be fairly sure of plenty of good climbing and a sun tan. The Summer months will only bring the sun tan with the added bonus of expensive air fares, and impossibly hot crags.

## FLIGHTS
There are loads of flights to Alicante leaving from most major European airports at every conceivable time of day, throughout the year. Prices vary from ultra-cheap £50 specials to £200+ in the most popular times. Luckily the popular times are in mid-summer when Spain is far too hot for climbing but you can still expect to pay near $200 for trips at Christmas and Easter. The best place to buy is from one of the many low cost flight shops now in existence. Local ones (hence local phone calls) advertise in the yellow pages under 'Travel Agents and Tour Operators'. National ones advertise in the travel pages of the broadsheet newspapers. It is always worth at least two calls since prices, and availability, can vary dramatically. There are also plenty of bargains to be had on the Internet these days.

## ACCOMMODATION
### Villas and Apartments
The most popular option for accommodation on the Costa Blanca is to take advantage of the vast number of cheap holiday apartments available on the coast in Benidorm and Calpe. The Benidorm options are usually available in 'flight plus accommodation' packages and can prove to be good value, especially for couples or small groups. A lot of these are available without pre-booking simply by turning up and looking for the 'places to rent' signs. Booking a villa or an apartment separately tends to prove more pleasant and luxurious. In the case of villas you will often have a complete overkill of things like swimming pools, barbecues, balconies, televisions and dishwashers. None of these things are unwelcome but it can seem a bit strange when compared to camping in Llanberis Pass. If you are in a large group (6 to 10) and are travelling at a preferred time (Spring, Autumn and Winter) then hiring a villa will also be the cheapest option; from as low as £20/person/week. There are also some delightful inland casitas and villas which should prove very attractive for those who wish to get away from the hustle and bustle of the coast. For villas and apartments or inland accommodation check some of the adverts to the left and on page 30 and 118. Also there is an updated list on the ROCKFAX web site at rockfax.com/costa_blanca/cbaccom.html

### The Refuges and Camping
There is only one refuge in the Costa Blanca and that is at Sella (see page 147). It is well equipped, with a small shop but you will need to take some basic camping gear (sleeping bag, etc.) if you are wanting to stay inside. The whole refuge is sometimes closed during quiet periods. It can get very busy during Spanish holidays, which are not at the same time as British holidays. You can also camp outside the refuge which is probably the only place in the Costa Blanca worth considering for camping although there are other sites available.

## SHOPS
There are plenty of large supermarkets in Benidorm and Calpe and down the whole coastal strip. It is worth remembering that opening times are slightly less favourable on Sundays and holidays than in Britain, but better than in Germany. Also remember that most shops will shut down from 1pm to 4pm every day.

### Climbing Shops
Zero '95 in Calpe is the only climbing shop in the area (see advert on page 6).

| COSTA BLANCA | PAGE | No. of ROUTES | ↓VS ↓4 | VS 4 | HVS 5 | E1 6a | E2 6b | E3 6c | E4 7a | E5 7b | E6 7c | E7 8a↑ | Sport Routes | Some Trad Routes | Some ENP Routes | Some Multi-Pitch Routes |
|---|---|---|---|---|---|---|---|---|---|---|---|---|---|---|---|---|
| GANDÍA | 37 | 136 | 1 | 5 | 19 | 23 | 23 | 24 | 24 | 18 | 9 | 9 | Sport | | | |
| SALEM | 47 | 125 | 4 | 5 | 14 | 22 | 22 | 15 | 14 | 10 | 6 | 2 | Sport | | | |
| MONTESA | 56 | 46 | | 1 | 7 | 15 | 11 | 8 | 2 | 2 | | | Sport | | | |
| AVENTADOR | 59 | 74 | | 1 | 11 | 26 | 21 | 5 | 3 | 2 | | | Sport | | | Multi-pitch |
| BELLÚS | 64 | 111 | | 2 | 10 | 29 | 32 | 23 | 12 | 4 | 1 | | Sport | | | |
| JALÓN VALLEY | 70 | 79 | 1 | 3 | 12 | 20 | 11 | 12 | 8 | 10 | 2 | | Sport | | | |
| OLTA | 78 | 20 | | 2 | 6 | 1 | 3 | 4 | 2 | 1 | 1 | | Sport | | | |
| PEÑON D'IFACH | 80 | 22 | | | 4 | 3 | 7 | 4 | 4 | | | | Sport | Trad | | Multi-pitch |
| SIERRA DE TOIX | 88 | 146 | 2 | 23 | 32 | 30 | 23 | 11 | 11 | 9 | 2 | 3 | Sport | Trad | ENP | Multi-pitch |
| MASCARAT | 104 | 31 | | 2 | 12 | 3 | 2 | 4 | 5 | 2 | | | Sport | Trad | | Multi-pitch |
| BERNIA AREA | 110 | 23 | | 1 | 6 | 3 | 7 | 4 | 2 | 2 | | | Sport | Trad | | Multi-pitch |
| ECHO VALLEY | 113 | 96 | 7 | 6 | 11 | 22 | 22 | 6 | 8 | 1 | 4 | 9 | Sport | Trad | ENP | Multi-pitch |
| PONOCH | 136 | 2 | | | | | | 2 | | | | | Sport | | | Multi-pitch |
| PUIG CAMPANA | 138 | 25 | | 1 | 4 | 7 | 6 | 4 | 2 | 1 | | | | Trad | ENP | Multi-pitch |
| SELLA | 146 | 215 | 5 | 5 | 20 | 30 | 26 | 42 | 33 | 21 | 16 | 17 | Sport | Trad | | Multi-pitch |
| DIVINO | 167 | 47 | | 2 | 4 | 6 | 5 | 7 | 7 | 4 | 7 | 5 | Sport | Trad | | Multi-pitch |
| ALCOY | 177 | 35 | | | 5 | 8 | 4 | 4 | 5 | 3 | 2 | 1 | Sport | | | |
| AGUJAS ROJAS | 180 | 38 | | 2 | 1 | 5 | 3 | 3 | 5 | 7 | 5 | 2 | Sport | | | |
| RECONCO | 183 | 30 | | | 5 | 7 | 9 | 3 | 5 | 1 | | | Sport | | | |
| PEÑA RUBIA | 186 | 67 | | 1 | 10 | 10 | 10 | 7 | 8 | 5 | 2 | 3 | Sport | | | |
| CABRERAS | 191 | 71 | | 3 | 10 | 29 | 15 | 6 | 5 | 3 | | | Sport | | | Multi-pitch |
| SALINAS | 199 | 77 | | 1 | 11 | 10 | 18 | 8 | 7 | 9 | 6 | 4 | Sport | | | |
| FORADA | 207 | 91 | 1 | 2 | 17 | 16 | 6 | 17 | 18 | 9 | 1 | 4 | Sport | | | |

| Approach walk | Sunshine or shade | Access restrictions | Dry in the rain | Windy and exposed | SUMMARY |
|---|---|---|---|---|---|
| 10 min | Lots of sun | | Dry in the rain | | A very popular crag with lots of steep walls and tufas. Reasonable grade spread but the easy routes are not very good. One of the best venues for grade 7 climbers. Now rocketed into the super-hard grades with Sector Bovedón. |
| Roadside to 15 min | Sun and Shade | | | | Sheltered crag in a small valley. Easy access and good mid-grade routes. Over-bolted in places and the hard routes aren't very interesting. |
| 3 min | Lots of sun | | | | Small well-positioned crag above an attractive town with a castle. A good grade spread and plenty in the 5 and 6 grade range. Most of the routes are only short. |
| 10 min | Lots of sun | | | Windy | An old crag which has been well re-geared. Nicely situated above a river. Plenty of slab climbs but can get a bit repetitive and some of the lines are hard to follow because of over-bolting. Very sunny with no shelter. A few good hard routes. |
| 5 min | Lots of sun | | | | Short and very well-sheltered crag in a ravine. A good venue for an easy or short, day or worth combining with Montesa or Aventador. Still being developed so there may be new routes. |
| 2 min to 10 min | Sun and Shade | | | | Several small crags dotted about a wide valley. Plenty to go at across the grade range and it is possible to tick two crags in a day. Well placed for people staying in Calpe. Lliber is the pick of the bunch. Good in bad weather. |
| 20 min | To mid Afternoon | | | Windy | Beautifully situated buttress on long ridge overlooking Calpe with magnificent views. Quality rock and routes from 4 to 6c including 2 of the area's classics. Some hold chipping on the harder routes and quite a long approach walk. |
| 20 min | Afternoon | Restrictions | | Windy | One of the main landmarks of the Costa Blanca next to Calpe. Superb long trad climbs and several stunning fully-bolted, multi-pitch routes. Easier routes have a justifiably reputation for looseness, but they are still good. |
| Roadside to 25 min | Sun and Shade | | | Windy | A favourite old area which probably still has the widest selection of easier climbs. Some of the Sea Cliffs are getting a bit worn out and there are many better places to climb. Sea Cliffs offer a complete contrast with superb, isolated trad routes. |
| 10 min to 20 min | Sun and Shade | | | Windy | Atmospheric an very varied area. One classic easy multi-pitch route and several hard wall climbs. Experience can be tempered by traffic noise but the positions are memorable. |
| 10 min to 20 min | Lots of sun | | | Windy | Two small venues on the beautiful long ridge of rock above Benidorm. Altea Col is worth a look for those operating above 6a, Bernia has harder routes although there are a few easy trad lines. |
| 1 min to 1 hour | Mostly sunny | | | Windy | A massive area including the largest selection of trad climbing in the guide. Several big walls with a lot of multi-pitch routes on them including many which require the ENP protection system (see page 113). |
| 25 min | Lots of sun | | | Windy | One of the most awesome pieces of rock in the area. Home to many long trad routes and a few fully-bolted sport routes, two of which are described here. |
| 1 hour | Lots of sun | | | Windy | Magnificent mountain crag with huge long routes. A wonderful place to spend a day providing you climb fast enough. Well worth the effort of the walk-in. Good routes across the grades. |
| 1 min to 20 min | Sun and Shade | | Dry in the rain | | The largest crag in the book. It has everything from short easy routes to long traditional multi-pitch jobs. Plenty of routes for everyone and enough appeal to spend your whole holiday here. |
| 10 min to 1 hour | Lots of sun | | | Windy | Majestic towering face dominating the Sella valley. A complete contrast to the short bolted routes below with many long multi-pitch climbs requiring an adventurous big-mountain approach. |
| 5 min | Lots of sun | | | | Unattractive crag in an urban setting. Mostly powerful steep climbing on pockets and the quality routes are all in the 7th grade. Good for those who need an outdoor climbing wall but don't go here for the easy stuff. |
| 1 min | Sun and Shade | | | | Beautifully situated towers in a woodland setting. Small set of mainly-harder routes on good rock. |
| 20 min | Lots of sun | | | Windy | Delightful slabby crag in a pleasant setting. Easy access and a good selection of mid-grade routes. Another alternative for people who are sick of Toix. Not much hard stuff but not much easy stuff either. |
| 10 min | Evening | | | | Small crag with small routes. May be of interest if you are passing but don't make a special trip. Easy routes are okay but hard routes are chipped. |
| 15 min | Morning | Restrictions | | Windy | Superb well-situated pinnacles. A great alternative to Toix Oeste with lots of excellent two pitch slab routes. The only drawback is the drive from the coast. Not much hard stuff. One restricted buttress - Feb to Jul. |
| 5 min | Morning | Restrictions | | Windy | Delightful new crag in a beautiful position. Reasonable grade spread but, although the hard routes are the main attraction, some of them are a touch 'created'. Gnarly approach drive. No climbing from Feb to Jul. |
| 10 min | Sun and Shade | | Dry in the rain | Windy | One of the best crags around consisting of an impressive fin with contrasting sides. One cold and steep with some of the best hard routes in the area; and the other slabby and sunny with a great position. |

## COSTA BLANCA LOGISTICS Continued....

### GETTING AROUND

Unless you are staying at Sella and plan to climb there all week, you advised to hire a car. These can be booked before your trip and picked up at the airport. The local agents often offer better value than the larger companies and give a better service once you are there, especially in the event of something going wrong. The usual practice is to pick up the car full of fuel, when all companies will sting you for an extra 7000 psts for the petrol, and return it empty. This can make a memorable return journey to the airport, with the engine running on fumes, and your flight departure time only half an hour away.

**Without a Car -** As mentioned above, your option for a car-less holiday in the Costa Blanca is probably restricted to Sella which has easily enough climbing to keep you busy. Getting to Sella can be tricky - first get a bus to Villajoyosa and then hitch, or get a taxi, up the valley to Sella.

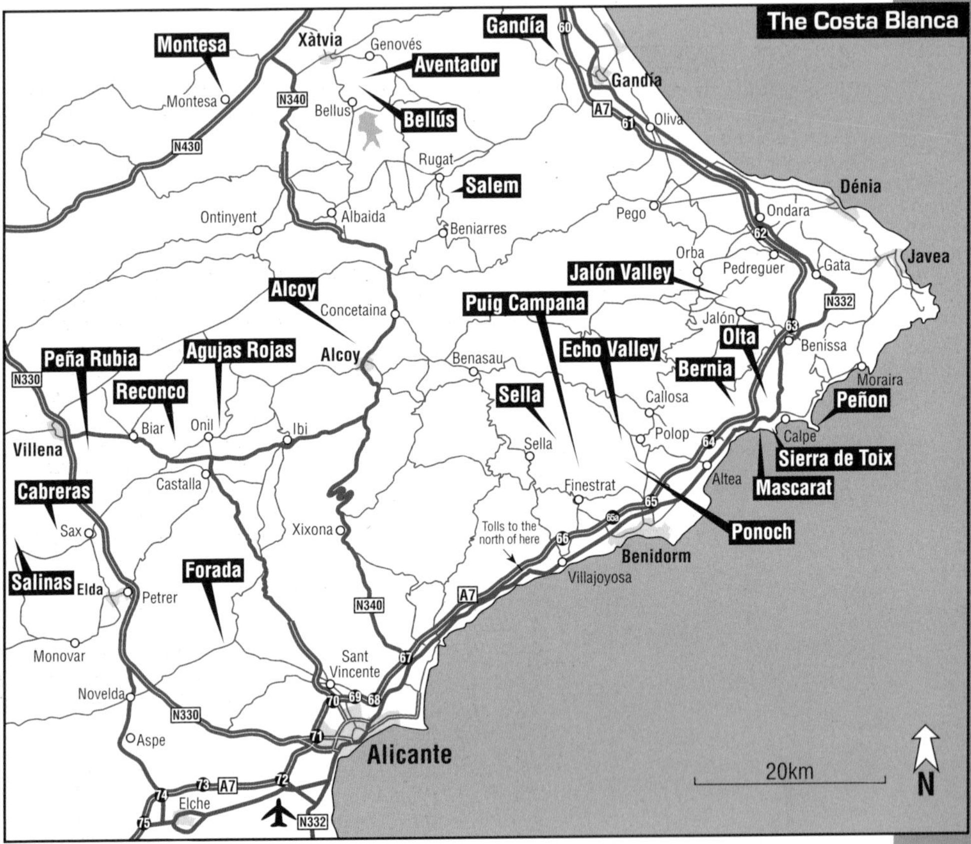

Getting to many of the crags will necessitate spending a lot of time on the expensive A7 toll road (the tolls are only applied on the tourist sections from Villajoyosa to Gandía). You can avoid the A7 by using the N332 coast road but, be warned, this road is horribly slow and congested, with frequent bottle-necks at the many small towns it goes through. Most of the inland roads are also a slow and narrow although there are many road improvements taking place at the moment which is dramatically improving road access across the whole area. The problem with all the improvements is that it is putting the crag approach information out of date faster than we can print new editions. If you find the road layouts have changed then please let us know (email - alan@rockfax.co.uk). Any new information will be put onto the ROCKFAX web site - rockfax.com/costa_blanca

# GANDÍA

The first impression of this crag as you approach is that it is significantly less impressive than most of the bits of rock you have just driven past. However first impressions can be deceptive and when you get involved with the routes you will find some immaculate climbs on near-perfect rock formations. There is a good grade range and, although it isn't one of the better areas for people leading below 6a, there are still plenty of easier routes dotted around the crag. Most of the best climbing is on steep bulging tufas in the harder grades and the crag is an absolutely essential destination for those operating at 7a/7b. Some of the harder routes are a bit chipped but the best bits tend to be swinging around on the tufas and pockets at the bottom on natural holds. The easier climbs are mostly on grey slabs and walls with fingery and technical climbing. In the past there has been a restriction on certain routes owing to nesting birds and these routes were even debolted to stop people climbing them. Most of the routes have now been rebolted and it appears now that you can climb here all year round, on all the routes.

## ASPECT AND CLIMATE

The crag faces south, catches all the sun going and isn't too exposed to the wind. It suffers from some seepage and many of the hard tufa climbs become impossible after rain. However if it is raining, and the water hasn't had a chance to seep through, then you will may find a dry route here, albeit a hard one. El Bovedón is certain to stay dry in the rain but the routes are all very hard.

## APPROACH

Drive north on the toll A7 to junction 61. Exit at junction 61 and turn left towards Gandía at the next junction. Drive through Bellreguart to the new roundabout and take the second exit signed to 'Valencia'. Once on the bypass, ignore the exit sign-posted for the 'Albaida' (unless you are headed for Salem or El Aventador) and take the next exit, signed to 'Barx'. Turn left under the N332 and then under the motorway. Take the first right, signed 'Raco de Tomba' and park down this road, below the crag.
See page 46 for approach to El Bovedón.

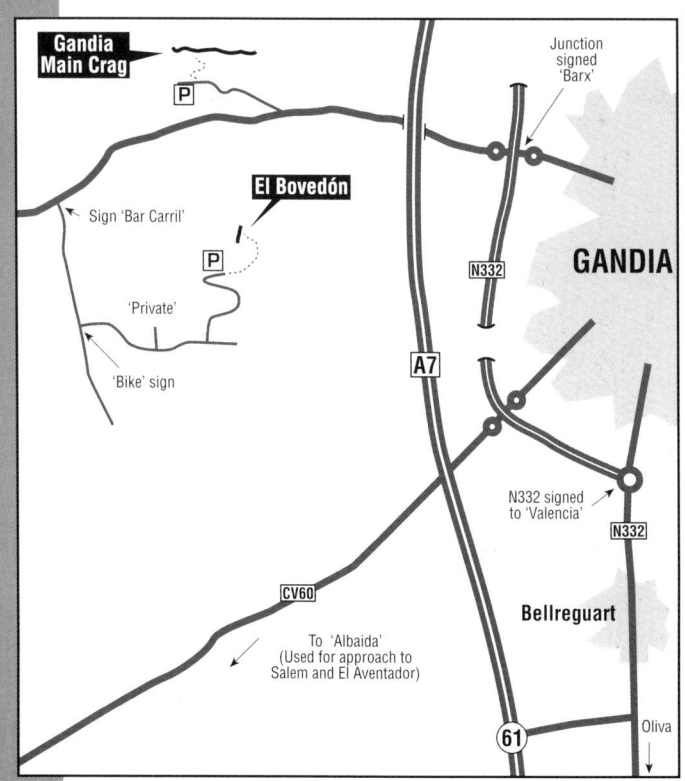

## THE ROUTES

The routes here are the work of Club Alpi de Gandía, principally Juan Carmelo Merino, Pep Ginestar, Miguel Cebrián, Xavi Calabuig and Albert Monzó. They have been developing the crag since the mid 1980s and have done an excellent job in maintaining the bolts, lower-offs and approach paths. Some rebolting was done in 2000. The grades in this book are mostly the same as those given by the locals and they tend to be at the upper end of their respective ranges.

# COSTA BLANCA - Gandía

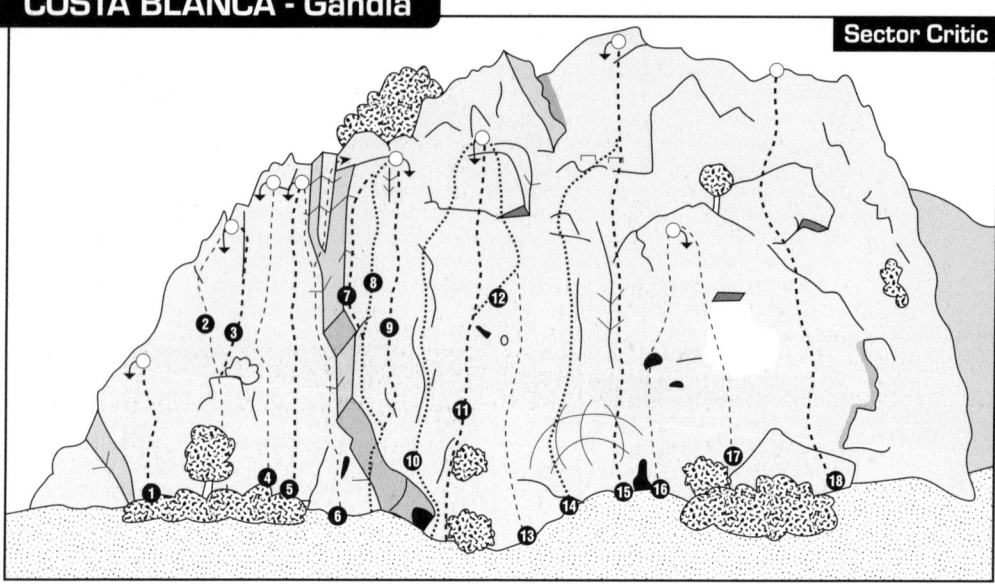

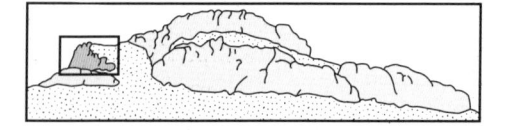

**Sector Critic**

## SECTOR CRITIC
At the extreme left-hand side of the crag is a buttress which is separated from the main areas by a narrow gully. This wall receives the sun later than the main crag - cool in the mornings, warm in the evenings.
**ACCESS** - This is the one buttress on which there are still a few debolted routes which are indicated with the 'no entry' symbol.
**APPROACH** - To get there, walk left from where the approach path hits the crag, underneath the cave in Sector Hydraulics. The most prominent feature of the buttress is the long narrow corner of *Gran Diedre*. The first routes are on the wall left of this corner.

**1. Margarila** .................... 6a+
2 bolts and not much excitement.

**2. Espero groc** ................. 6b

**3. Diagnosis superficial** .......... 6b

**4. Pasando de poli** ............. 7b

**5. Ja estic mort** ............... 7a+
Just to the left of a line of rusty old bolts.

**6. Gran diedre** ................. 5+
Although this route has been debolted you can climb it on wires.

The next three routes all start in the same place and are eliminates based on the arete and wall right of the corner.

**7. Selectiva** ................. 6c

**8. Espolón why** .............. 6c

**9. Megaloceras** .............. 7a
The crux is polished, but it is avoidable on the right.

**10. Aguiles** ................. 5
Good climbing. Needs wires for the crack.

**11. Piccolissima** ............ 6a
The first bolt is at 8m, so take few wires. Even when you get there it is a long reach!

**12. Terra lliure** ............. 5+
The easiest way up the wall but a wire or two is needed for the bottom section.

**13. PSAN** .................... 6b

**14. Beniarrés** ............... 5

**15. Tallà** .................... 5
The long, open corner, and headwall.

**16. Garbancito** .............. 6a

**17. Stick fluish** .............. 5+

**18. Bloc calgut** .............. 4+
A long route which wanders to the top of the buttress. Needs wires.

West facing wall
5m to 15m routes
Best grades - 5+ to 7a

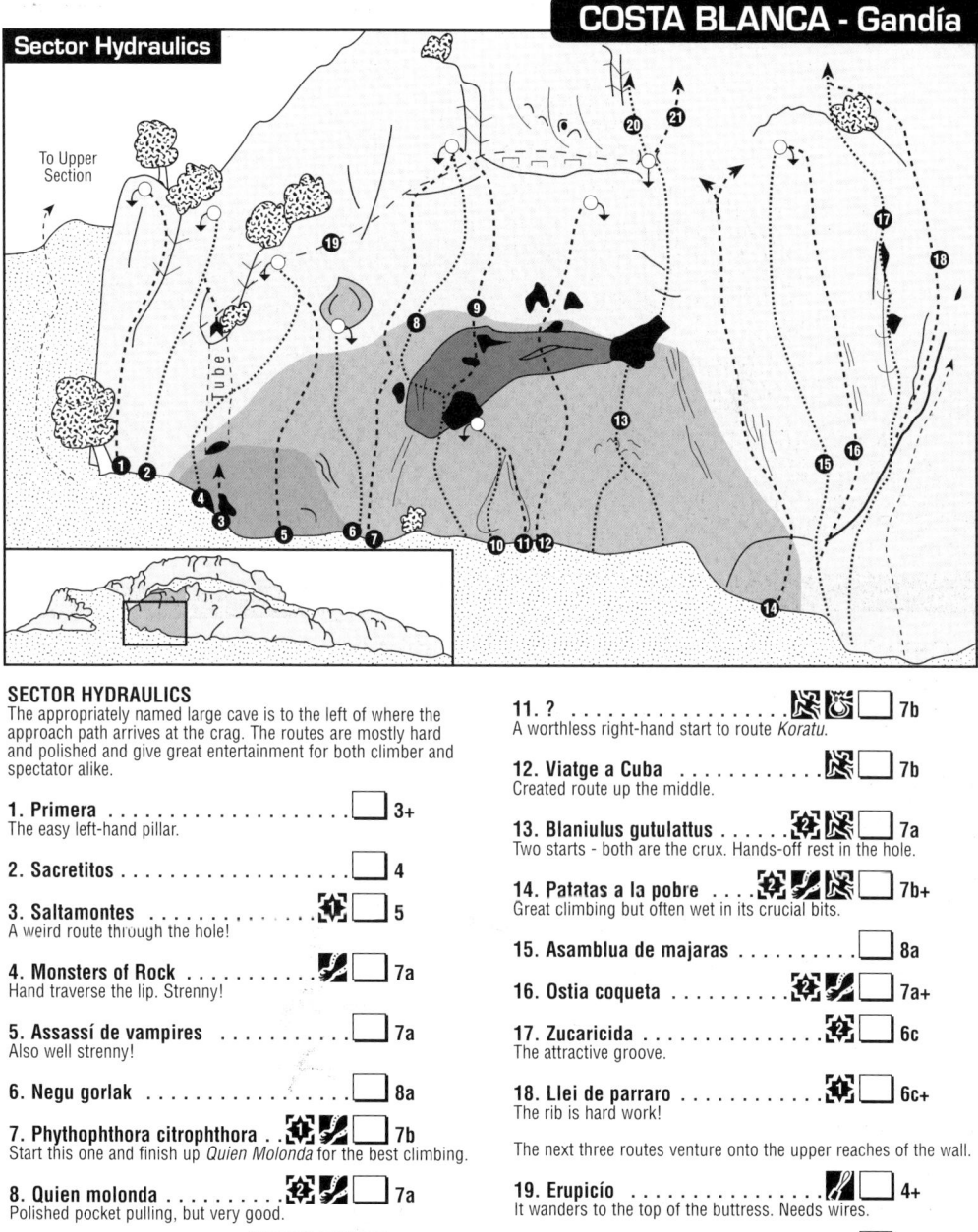

# COSTA BLANCA - Gandía

## Sector Hydraulics

The appropriately named large cave is to the left of where the approach path arrives at the crag. The routes are mostly hard and polished and give great entertainment for both climber and spectator alike.

**1. Primera** ................... 3+
The easy left-hand pillar.

**2. Sacretitos** ................. 4

**3. Saltamontes** ............... 5
A weird route through the hole!

**4. Monsters of Rock** .......... 7a
Hand traverse the lip. Strenny!

**5. Assassí de vampires** ....... 7a
Also well strenny!

**6. Negu gorlak** ............... 8a

**7. Phythophthora citrophthora** .. 7b
Start this one and finish up *Quien Molonda* for the best climbing.

**8. Quien molonda** ............. 7a
Polished pocket pulling, but very good.

**9. Spherique Voice** ........... 7a+
A great trip in upside-down-land. Buckets all the way (except for one bit).

**10. Koratu** ................... 7b
Short and fierce.

**11. ?** ........................ 7b
A worthless right-hand start to route *Koratu*.

**12. Viatge a Cuba** ............ 7b
Created route up the middle.

**13. Blaniulus gutulattus** ..... 7a
Two starts - both are the crux. Hands-off rest in the hole.

**14. Patatas a la pobre** ....... 7b+
Great climbing but often wet in its crucial bits.

**15. Asamblua de majaras** ...... 8a

**16. Ostia coqueta** ............ 7a+

**17. Zucaricida** ............... 6c
The attractive groove.

**18. Llei de parraro** .......... 6c+
The rib is hard work!

The next three routes venture onto the upper reaches of the wall.

**19. Erupicío** ................. 4+
It wanders to the top of the buttress. Needs wires.

**20. Pagaràs amlo costo** ....... 6a
Up a short groove. Wires needed if you climb *Erupicío* to reach the start.

**21. Séstrema en la brena** ..... 5+
Wires needed if you climb *Erupicío* to reach the start.

South facing cave
5m to 20m routes
Best grades - 6c to 7b+

# COSTA BLANCA - Gandía

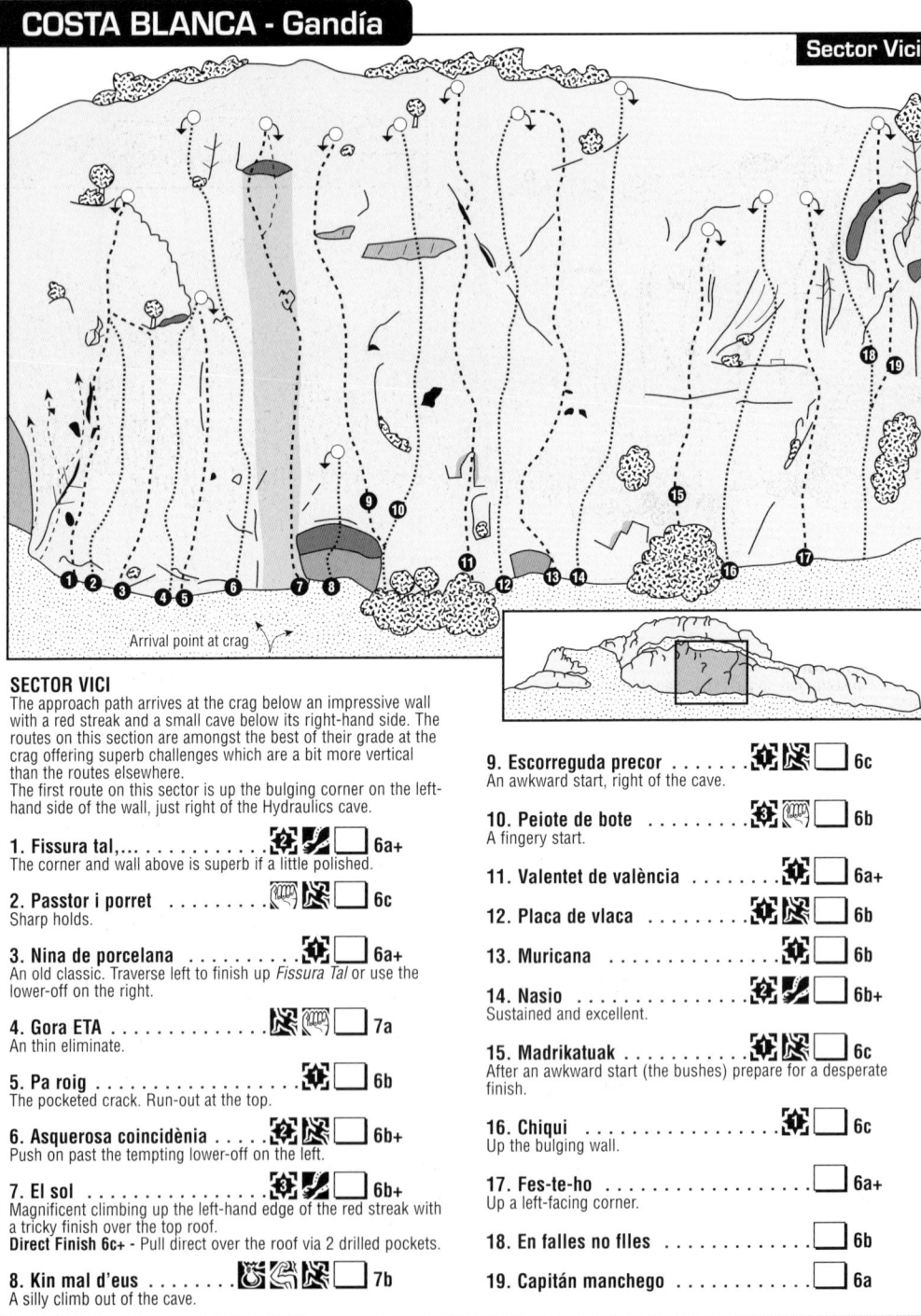

**Sector Vici**

*Arrival point at crag*

## SECTOR VICI
The approach path arrives at the crag below an impressive wall with a red streak and a small cave below its right-hand side. The routes on this section are amongst the best of their grade at the crag offering superb challenges which are a bit more vertical than the routes elsewhere.
The first route on this sector is up the bulging corner on the left-hand side of the wall, just right of the Hydraulics cave.

**1. Fissura tal,** .............. 6a+
The corner and wall above is superb if a little polished.

**2. Passtor i porret** .............. 6c
Sharp holds.

**3. Nina de porcelana** .............. 6a+
An old classic. Traverse left to finish up *Fissura Tal* or use the lower-off on the right.

**4. Gora ETA** .............. 7a
An thin eliminate.

**5. Pa roig** .............. 6b
The pocketed crack. Run-out at the top.

**6. Asquerosa coincidènia** .............. 6b+
Push on past the tempting lower-off on the left.

**7. El sol** .............. 6b+
Magnificent climbing up the left-hand edge of the red streak with a tricky finish over the top roof.
**Direct Finish 6c+** - Pull direct over the roof via 2 drilled pockets.

**8. Kin mal d'eus** .............. 7b
A silly climb out of the cave.

**9. Escorreguda precor** .............. 6c
An awkward start, right of the cave.

**10. Peiote de bote** .............. 6b
A fingery start.

**11. Valentet de valència** .............. 6a+

**12. Placa de vlaca** .............. 6b

**13. Muricana** .............. 6b

**14. Nasio** .............. 6b+
Sustained and excellent.

**15. Madrikatuak** .............. 6c
After an awkward start (the bushes) prepare for a desperate finish.

**16. Chiqui** .............. 6c
Up the bulging wall.

**17. Fes-te-ho** .............. 6a+
Up a left-facing corner.

**18. En falles no flles** .............. 6b

**19. Capitán manchego** .............. 6a

South facing wall
15m to 25m routes
Best grades - 6a+ to 6c

Lots of sun · 10 min · Vertical · Lower-offs

40

# COSTA BLANCA - Gandía

## Sector Fundicio

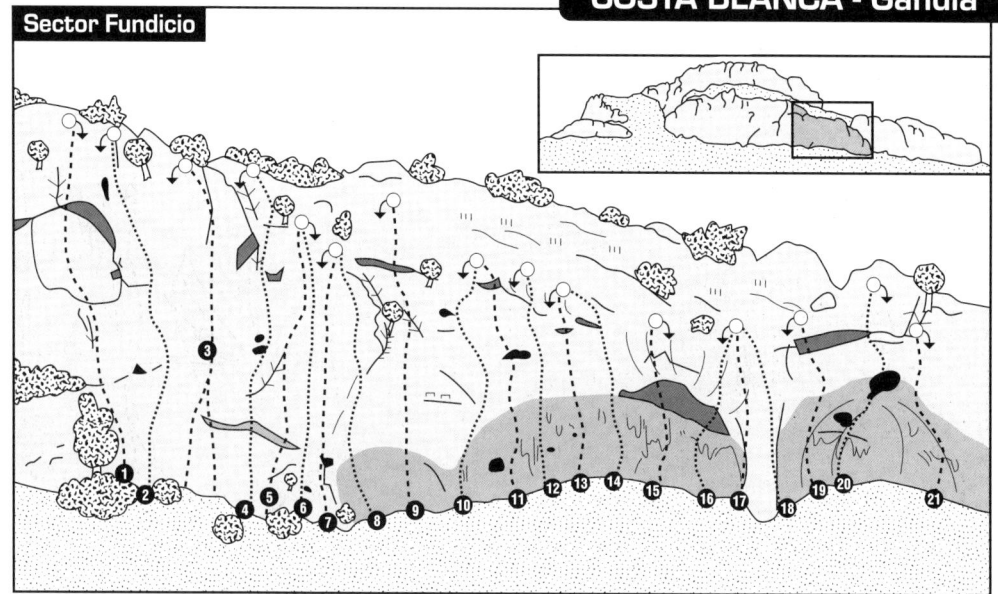

### SECTOR FUNDICIO
This steep sector has some long easier routes on its left-hand side, and an impressive bulging wall on its right. It is situated to the right from where the approach path arrives at the crag.

**1. Kaya** .................. 6a+
Up an orange wall.

**2. Nupices** ................ 6b+

**3. Milan kundera** ............ 6a+
There are two starts, both about the same grade.

**4. Chitiri, chitiri** ............. 4+

**5. La insoportable** ........... 6a

**6. ?** ..................... 5+
An eliminate.

**7. La levedad** .............. 5

**8. El ser** .................. 6a

**9. Tamborinaes** ............. 6a
Steep climbing, but good holds.

**10. Puntín d'ernestín** ............ 7a
Debolted.

The next wall gives the best climbing in this sector.

**11. El rigio** ................ 6b+
The last bolt is badly placed. A hard finish.

**12. Pepes troika** ............ 6b

**13. Ultima albertencia** ....... 6b+

**14. Amorrada al piló** ........ 6b

**15. Pere** .................. 6c+
Tufas and jugs all the way.

**16. ?** ..................... (7b/c)
Steep climbing left of the pillar.

**17. A mi no mafecta** ........ 6c
The left-hand side of the pillar.

**18. Espanya no mapanya** ..... 7b
A very short and intense crux move.

**19. En medium** ............. 7c

**20. Dia de borratxera** ....... 7c
Heave between the holes and prepare yourself for the disappointingly technical finish.

**21. Joc de mans** ............ 6c+
An unlikely looking route up the steep right-hand side of the small cave.

South facing wall
10m to 20m routes
Best grades - 6a to 6c

# COSTA BLANCA - Gandía

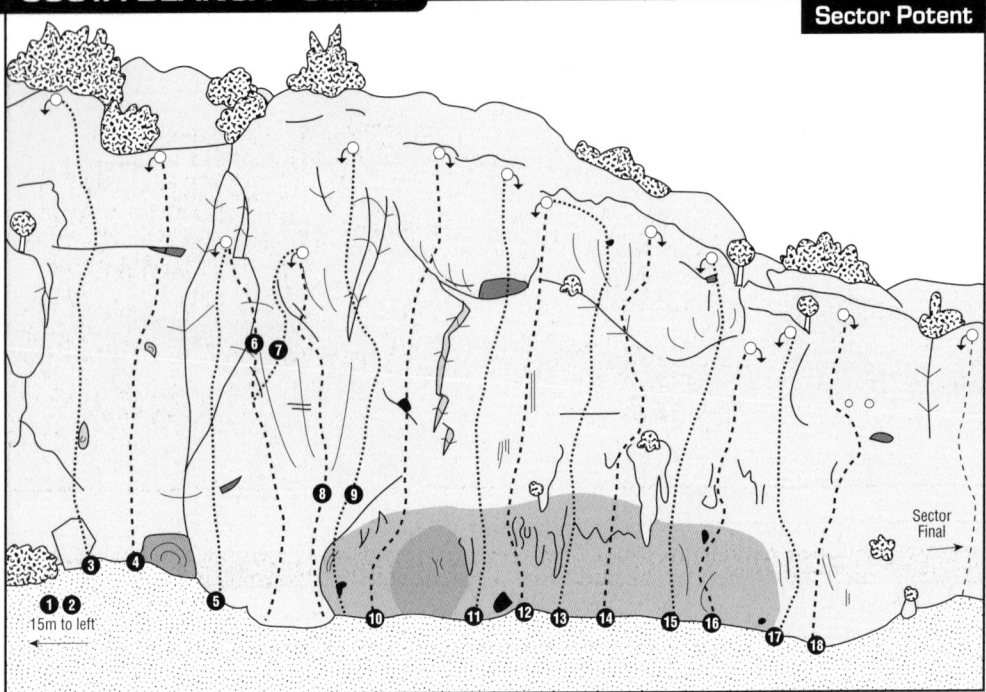

## Sector Potent

### SECTOR POTENT
For those leading 7a to 7b you will struggle to find a better wall than this in the whole of the Costa Blanca. The climbing and the rock formations are superb. Tick more than 3 routes here in a day and you will have earned your evening beer.

**1. ?** ........................ 4+
15m left off the topo. The left-hand line

**2. Novatillos** ............... 5+
The right-hand line up the centre of the slabby grey wall.

**3. Maqui popeye y la sirla** ........ 6b
Start by a block.

**4. Donde hostias ...** ......... 6b
Good moves but escapable.

**5. Juputa** ................ 6b+
A steep start but the crux pulls are on the thin grey wall right of the upper corner.

**6. Tercer left** ............. 7b
The orange wall past a hard move then take the left-hand branch.

**7. Tercer right** ............ 7b
The right-hand branch.

**8. Muluk el tarqui** ......... 7a+
Superb, intricate climbing with a big finish.

**9. Sugar glass** ............ 7b
Given 7c+ before. Shares start with *Muluk el Tarqui*.

**10. Botoia sakatu** ........ (7c/7c+)
Start left of the recess.

**11. Enya** ................ 7c
Steep fingery wall right of the big flake.

**12. ?** .................. 7b
Excellent. Hard to on-sight if you don't find the hidden hold.

**13. Baila al alba** ......... 7b
Some of the bolts are twin pairs.

The main feature of this wall is the magnificent elephant's trunk tufa. The next route is just to the left of this.

**14. Dos super carrozas** ...... 7a
Brilliant moves past a heart-shaped hole and onto the trunk. Eases above.

**15. Don diego** ............ 7a
Another great route with a steep start which is okay if you don't think about it too much.

**16. Jaque mate** ........... 7a+
A powerful start and a bit of a tricky finish, if you are pumped, which you probably will be.

**17. Solta el mos** .......... 7a+
Less steep but has a (chipped) fingery finish.

**18. ?** .................. (8a)
Hard and fingery with a blank section.

South facing wall
15m to 25m routes
Best grades - 6c to 7c

# COSTA BLANCA - Gandía

**Sector Final**

## SECTOR FINAL
The last section is relatively disappointing. The wall tapers and has less of the interesting formations Gandía is famed for, however there are a few interesting wall and slab climbs.

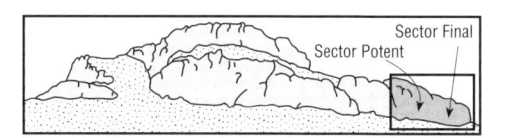

**1. Groceries** .............. 7a
An excellent quick and pumpy pitch.

**2. A Mano** ............... 7a
Much pumpier than it looks.

**3. ?** ..................... (7a/b)
The left-hand line out of the cave.

**4. ?** ..................... 7a+
The steep central line has one hard move to leave the glued flake.

The next route is right of a small cave.

**5. ?** ..................... 6c+
Very poor. An awkward move above the cave.

**6. ?** ..................... 7a

**7. ?** ..................... 6c
Up the steep leaning wall.

**8. Bum bum ipanime** .......... 5
The open corner, moving right at the top.

**9. Beato andres hibernon** .... 6a
The wall right of the corner with a tricky rock-over to start. Hard if finished direct.

**10. Leones** ............... 5
A steep and technical start. Much easier above.

**11. Fetiche** .............. 6c
An indifferent start leads to a spectacular finish over the roof.

**12. Abu abdallah** .......... 6b+
A short route with a tricky roof.

**13. Sense goma no hi ha concil** ... 6a
Finish over a small roof.

Around the corner, just off the topo, are two more routes.

**14. 3/4 d'hora** ............ 6a+
The left-hand line.

**15. Vergonya** ............. 5
The right-hand line.

South facing wall
10m to 15m routes
Best grades - 6a+ to 6c

# COSTA BLANCA - Gandía

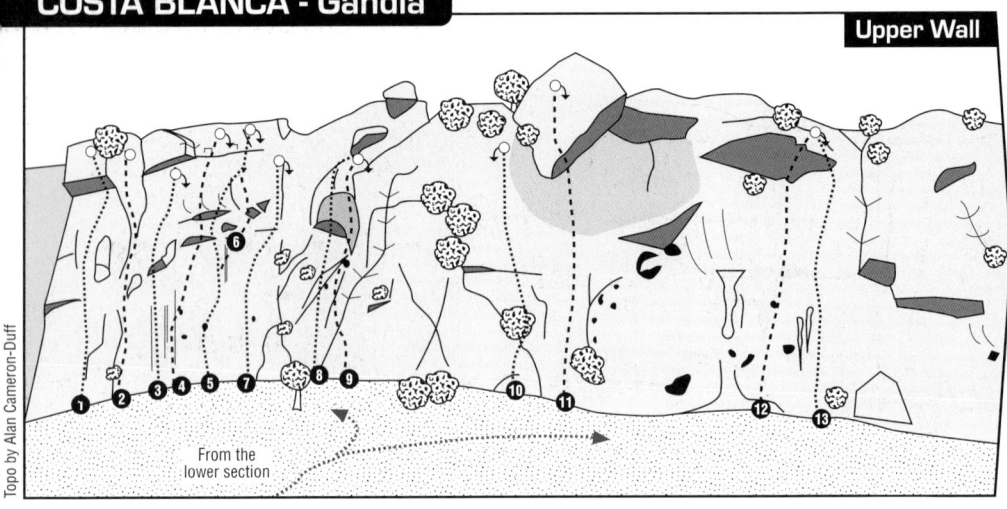

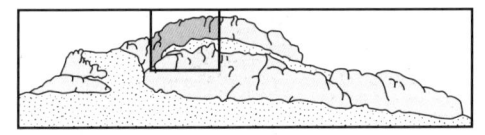

## Upper Wall

**UPPER WALL**
The final section gets far less traffic than the other bits but has been described as the best sector at Gandía. It is situated above the lower walls and can be a bit cooler than the lower sectors if there is a breeze blowing.
**APPROACH** - It is best reached by the steep gully left of Sector Hydraulics. This gully is quite steep and requires some scrambling so take care. At the top of the gully head across rightwards to reach the routes. It can also be reached by the gully between Sectors Fundició and Potent and also from the far right-hand end.

There are two traditionally protected routes up the pillar on the left, below a roof. The first bolted route is below the left-hand side of a wall with a line of bulges at half-height.

**1. Pep camarena** . . . . . . . . . . . . . . 5
The grey slab leading to a steep finish. No bolts or lower off.

**2. Derribos arrias** . . . . . . . . . . . . 5
Another bolt-less wonder to the right.

**3. Eva luna** . . . . . . . . . . . . . . . . . . . 6c
Start by a block.

**4. Derribos arrias** . . . . . . . . . . . . . . . 6b
Finish at a lower-off above a ledge.

**5. Sandbag** . . . . . . . . . . . . . . . . . 7a
Direct past a hole and up the steep wall above. With a name like this, believe the grade at your peril!

**6. Boca de grimper** . . . . . . . . . . 6b+
The cop-out version of *Sandbag* avoids the bulge on its right-hand side.

**7. Gualeta** . . . . . . . . . . . . . . . . . . 6c
Up the smooth grey wall. The thread is the first runner.

**8. Gnatleta** . . . . . . . . . . . . . . . . . 6c
Right of a good-looking corner.

**9. Rosarito** . . . . . . . . . . . . . . . . . 6b

There is then a gap of about 15m. The most obvious feature of the next section is a spectacular flying fin.

**10. Esfínter disfalet** . . . . . . . . . . 5+
The wall left of the fin has one hard move.

**11. Sarcófago** . . . . . . . . . . . . . . . 7b+
Direct to the fin then pull over with difficulty.

**12. Anatema maranata** . . . . . . 7b
The roof right of the fin crossed on its right-hand side.

**13. Cellas cortos** . . . . . . . . . . . . 6a+
Superb climbing up and right of the roof.

# COSTA BLANCA - Gandía

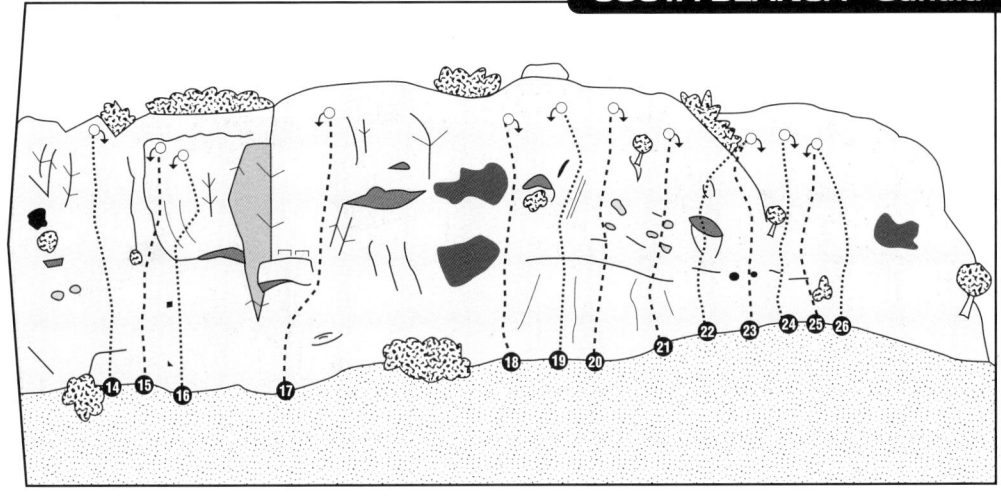

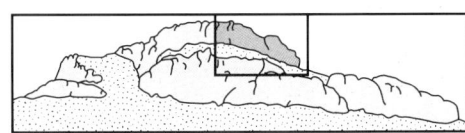

There is then a gap of about 15m of very climbable looking rock. Considering that everything else at this crag has been bolted, this section may soon sprout some routes.
The next wall is just left of a gently bulging section.

**14. Guirigay** .................. 6a

**15. ?** ........................ (6c)

**16. Tranquilized** ............. 7a
Climb the wall via some holes, then pull rightwards through the bulge.

Right of the bulge is a large hanging corner.

**17. Des carà** ................. 6b+
The wall right of the corner.

**18. ?** ........................ 7a
Climb through the right-hand side of the red caves then make ahrd move onto the wall above.

**19. Boltxerique** .............. 6c
Unlikely looking for the grade.

**20. Vulcano** .................. 6c+
Fun bucket pulling to a technical finish.

**21. ?** ........................ 6c
Excellent.

**22. Lo qui siqui** ............. 6a+
Buckets lead through a roof into a scoop in the wall above.

**23. Mol de turd** .............. 5
Finish up a slanting crack.

**24. ?** ........................ 6a

**25. Kamari** ................... 6a
Good holds.

**26. Cató-en-pels** ............. 5
Left of a cave.

South facing wall
15m to 25m routes
Best grades - 5 to 7a

45

# COSTA BLANCA - Gandía

### El Bovedón

## EL BOVEDÓN
This cave gives some superb hard routes which should make the Costa Blanca more attractive to climbers operating in the upper grades. It faces east and is well sheltered.

**APPROACH (See map on page 37)** - Drive to Gandía. Continue past the turning for the main crag for 900m then turn left (signed 'Bar Carril'). Drive on for another 900m and turn left again. Drive down here for about 450m to the second turning on the left (which is a surfaced road just past a large green gate). Take this and drive to the end of the road. Park leaving room for cars to turn. Follow the path across a slope and back left to reach the crag (5 mins).

1. ? .............................. (4)
Scrappy route up the left-hand edge of the crag.

2. ? .............................. (6a)

3. ? .............................. (7a/b)

4. ? .............................. 6b
Reasonable little rib at far left-hand side of crag.

5. ? .............................. 7a+
Broccoli wall leading to steep bulge. A touch friable.

6. ? .............................. (7b)
Wall leading to friable bulge.

7. ? .............................. 7a+
Hard start up bulging wall then easier rib above.

8. ? .............................. 6b+
Wall behind trees. Good climbing with nice finish.

9. ? .............................. 6c
Another good grey wall.

10. ? .............................. 8a
Past a project. A steep start and long wall above.

11. ? .............................. 7c+
Start up the block to the right and traverse left, crossing the next route. Another topo has this at 7a+.

12. ? .............................. 8b
Direct through the lower bulge.

13. ? .............................. 7c
Straight up from the start of route 12.

14. ? .............................. 8a+
The long wall starting up the block.

The main cave routes are so steep that they get hardly any sun. The routes are very complex follwoing pocket lines which cross each other. There are bolts all over the place but the actual intended route lines are is unclear. Ask a local!

15. La Negra .............................. 8c+

16. Mestizaje .............................. 8c+/9a
Links *La Negra* to *Malsoñando*.
FA. Pedro Pons 2.2001

17. Malsoñando .............................. 8c

18. ? .............................. 7c

19. ? .............................. 7c+

20. ? .............................. 8a+
A long diagonal pitch.

21. ? .............................. 8c

22. ? .............................. 8b

23. ? .............................. 7a+
Good long route with a tricky lower section. Loose in middle.

24. .............................. 7b+

25. .............................. 6a+
Right of the cave.

26. .............................. 6a+

East facing wall and cave
20m to 40m routes
Best grades - 7c to 8c+

# SALEM

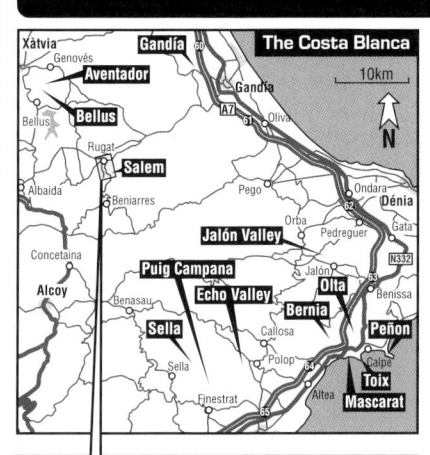

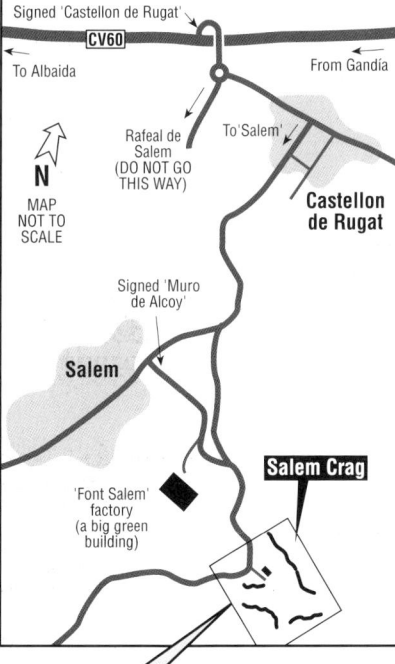

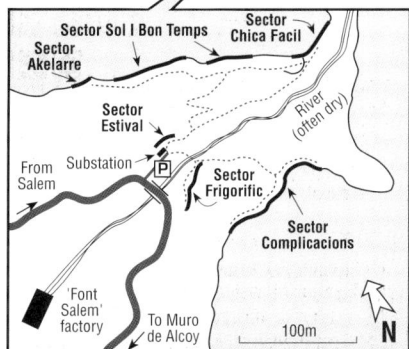

Despite the slightly sinister association Salem is a friendly crag with loads of accessible and well-bolted climbing. The various walls offer both sun and shaded routes as you require them. The rock is generally good with smooth flowing limestone, covered in small solution pockets, on the right-hand side, and more broken and cracked walls on the left-hand side. As with most recently bolted crags, the gear and lower-offs are all solid and well-positioned .... lots of them ... all over the place ... in fact far too many, and this actually detracts from one or two sectors.

Many visitors here make the mistake of just climbing on the two sectors near the parking - Frigorific and Estival. Both these offer some good routes, especially in the easier grades, however you will get much more from the crag if you venture up onto the higher side walls and explore the place a bit.

Bolts have a habit of disappearing on the easier routes by on Sectors Frigorific and Estival. Some people may find a small rack of wires useful just in case.

## APPROACH

Salem lies 25km west of Gandía, just off the road between Castellon de Rugat and Muro de Alcoy. Most people based in the Calpe area will want to approach the crag from Gandía. Follow the approach to Gandía described on page 37, until the first turn off on the ring road. This road is the CV60 signed to 'Albaida'. After 20km turn off towards 'Castellon de Rugat'. At a roundabout turn left (direction 'Castellon de Rugat/Salem') and drive into the village of Castellon de Rugat, then turn right following the 'Salem' sign. After 2.3km, just before you enter Salem, turn left (signed 'Muro de Alcoy'). Follow a winding road until you see a large green factory (Font Salem) on the right. The road swings around over a small bridge and you will see Sector Frigorific just above the road. Park on the dirt track in front of a small substation. This all takes about 1 hour from Calpe.

## ASPECT AND CLIMATE

The crags form a 'V' shape running into a short valley, sheltered from the wind. Extremes of temperature may be encountered as the crags on the right-hand side of the valley face northwest and only get late afternoon sun, whilst the crags opposite face south and bask in the sun until late afternoon.

## THE ROUTES

Salem has been developed principally by Domingo Rus and also Salvador Guerola, Emilio Perales and Lluis Ortiz.

47

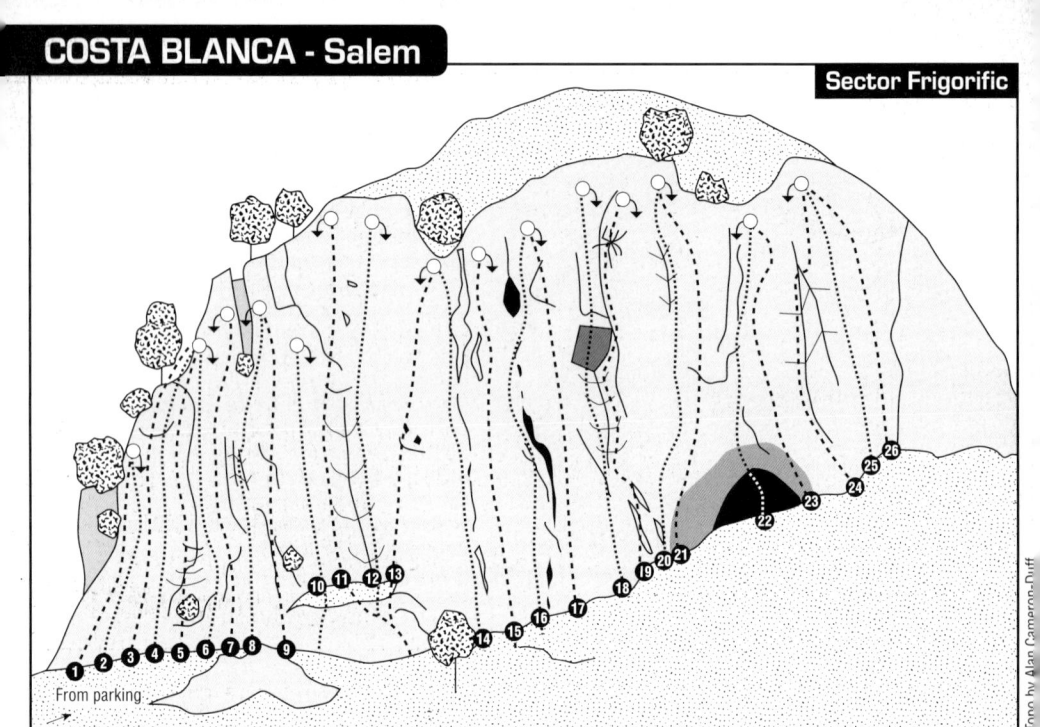

# COSTA BLANCA - Salem

**Sector Frigorific**

## SECTOR FRIGORIFIC
Opposite the substation is a steep smooth wall of compact blue limestone, with lots of curvy features and a small cave in its right-hand end. The routes are mostly single pitch and are so tightly packed that, in some places, it is difficult to distinguish individual lines beneath the patchwork of bolts. If every alternate route on this buttress was de-bolted then it would leave some really good lines in the 6b to 7a range, with some interesting 5s on the left-hand side. Most of the harder routes are pointless eliminates. All the bolts are new and the rock is solid.

The first line starts up the short compact grey slab just over the stream bed.

**1. El kiki** .................... 6c
Tricky moves past 3 bolts. Harder than it looks!

**2. El gro** .................... 6b
A slightly easier version of *El Kiki*.

Routes 3 to 6 all share the same lower-off.

**3. Alaxuplala** .................... 6a
Slink right past the 3rd bolt.

**4. Suc d'avespa** .................... 5

**5. Xupla polen** .................... 5
Up the scoopy corner.

**6. Mikel i altres broxes** .................... 5

**7. Mikel caga flors** .................... 5

**8. Guerola que vola a la casola** .................... 5
Nice climbing up the slab and the rounded fin above.

**9. Camalot** .................... 5

The next routes start from a grass ledge.

**10. El graduado** .................... 5+

**11. No hay billetes** .................... 6a+
Climb the left side of the steepening groove.

**12. Bájame una estrella** .................... 7a+
Superb climbing up the groove with a naughty rest possible on the left, before the final flourish.

**13. Fort battle** .................... 7b+
Climb a streak past pockets and up the steep wall above. The only worthy filler-in route.

**14. La pelusa de la parrusa** .................... 6b+
A good route up the line of pockets.

**15. Ahora corre La sangre** .................... 7b+
Non-line to the right.

**16. Cuidao, cuidao** .................... 6b
The orange groove has a sharp crux move.

**Sector Frigorific**
NW facing wall, 5m to 20m routes
Best grades - 5 to 7b+

48

# COSTA BLANCA - Salem

## Sector Estival

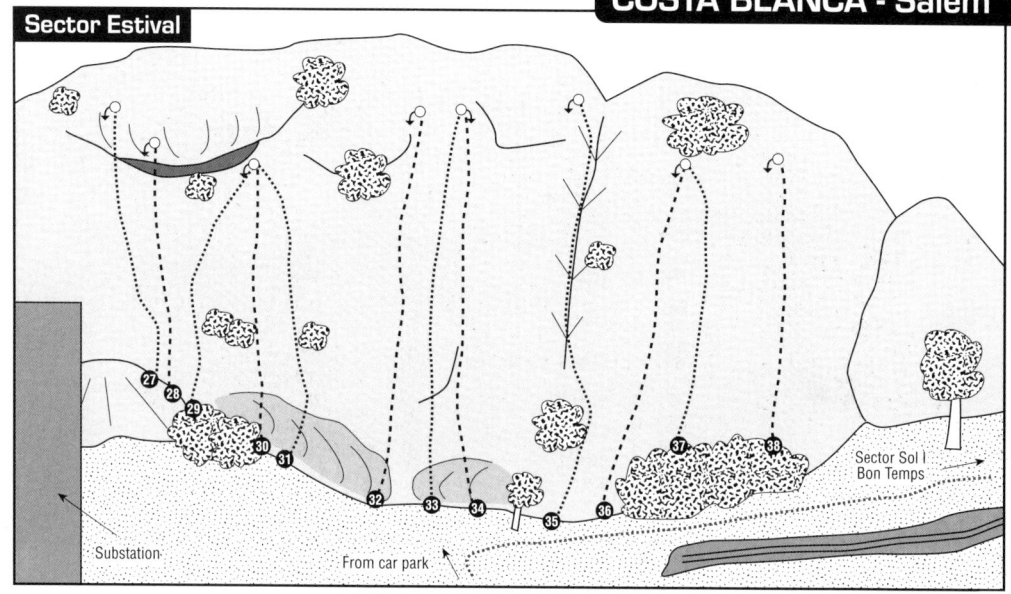

### SECTOR ESTIVAL
The opposite side of the car park has a vegetated little wall which is useful for those after the lower grades. None of the climbs is spectacular but the could be useful for people who wish to attempt their first leads. The rock is sharp but the routes are well bolted providing the first bolts haven't been nicked.
The first route starts on a platform behind some bushes.

**17. No es lolo todo lo que lo que** — 8a
A blank-looking affair up the blue wall.

**18. S'asbara** — 6c+
An artificial line up the left-hand side of the groove and over a small bulge.

**19. Eau dansissam** — 6c
The right-hand side of the groove has a hard start. It's a path above though.

**20. Temps al temps** — 7a+
Sharp pockets up the wall out of the left side of the cave. Another hard start.

**21. Quo vadis troni** — 8b/7a+
A terrible route which is so close to route 20 that it is route 20!

**22. I de major sere un octau** — 7b
The line of sharp pockets out of the cave, and up a tiring crack in the arete.

**23. Caña dulce** — 7b
A dreadful climb up the right-hand side of the cave and wall above.

**24. Somnis de tardor** — 5+
The corner gives the best easier route on the buttress.

**25. Mai ribe a temps** — 6a+
The slabby wall around the arete has one hard move.

**26. Sfinter-man el hombre karaña** — 5

**27. Acces denegat** — 6a
Up the wall and over the small roof.

**28. ?** — (5+)

**29. R2 dedos** — 3+

**30. C3 pedos** — 4+
A crack and slab.

**31. Boulder Rock** — 6c
Nasty little number out of the scoop.

**32. Xeroki** — 4
Nice start and easy finish.

**33. U2** — 4+
Easy after the first move.

**34. Moscataca** — 4
Boltes removed.

**35. Passeig dominical** — 3+

**36. La bruixa de salem** — 4+

**37. Negra neusl els set gigantes** — 4

**38. Naxcuda en lliure** — 3
Bolts removed.

### Sector Estival
South facing wall, 5m to 10m routes
Best grades - 3+ to 5+

# COSTA BLANCA - Salem

## Sector Sol I Bon Temps - Left

### SECTOR AKELARRE
This small sector consists of a couple of small caves up the hillside leftwards from the main Sector Sol I Bon Temps. Routes 1 to 3 are in the left-hand cave and are listed from left to right although no real details are known about them.

1. ? .................... (7b/c)
2. ? .................... (7b/c)
3. ? .................... (7b/c)

The right-hand cave has two more routes. There may be another route here now.

4. **Akelarre** ............... 6a+
Tricky moves, up over a bulging roof, on the left-hand side of the cave.

5. **El hombre de humo** ...... 7c
Powerful moves over the stacked roof in the centre of the cave.

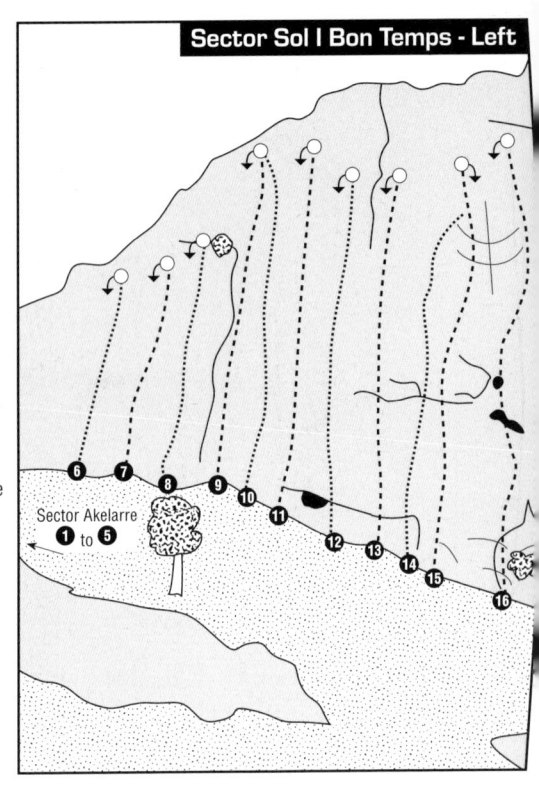

### SECTOR SOL I BON TEMPS - LEFT
This area consists of a couple of open sunny walls high on the hillside above Sector Estival. With good rock and lots of well-bolted routes packed closely together, only the steep walk-in is preventing it from being the ultimate convenience crag.
**APPROACH** - Walk up past Sector Estival and continue more steeply, zig-zaging up the hillside, over some scree to reach the base of the Sector Sol I Bon Temps Right. Continue over some broken rock to an exposed slab below the left wall.

6. **El lobo veloz** ................ 6a+
A short slight line up the grey slab left of the groove.

7. **Samurai** .................... 6b

8. ? .......................... 6b+

9. **A tot ostia** ................. 6a+
Up the right-hand side of the shallow groove. A long pitch.

10. **Oferta explosiva** ........... 6b
A hard start.

11. **Super nova** ............. 6b
Technical climbing up a clean grey wall on stuck on holds.

12. **Chinahauk** .............. 7a
Intricate technical moves.

13. **Paraboles lejanos** ..... 7a
Another technical route on little edges.

14. **Siniestro total** .......... 6c
Good climbing up past the small ledge and into the clean grey scoop above. Badly bolted low down.

15. **Tirant de roc** ........... 6b+
More of the same, with a steeper start some sharp slots.

16. **Seguix l'animal** ....... 6b+
Past a diagonal cave.

---

**Sector Akelarre**
South facing caves, 10m to 15m routes
Best grades - 6a+ and 7b/c

50

# COSTA BLANCA - Salem

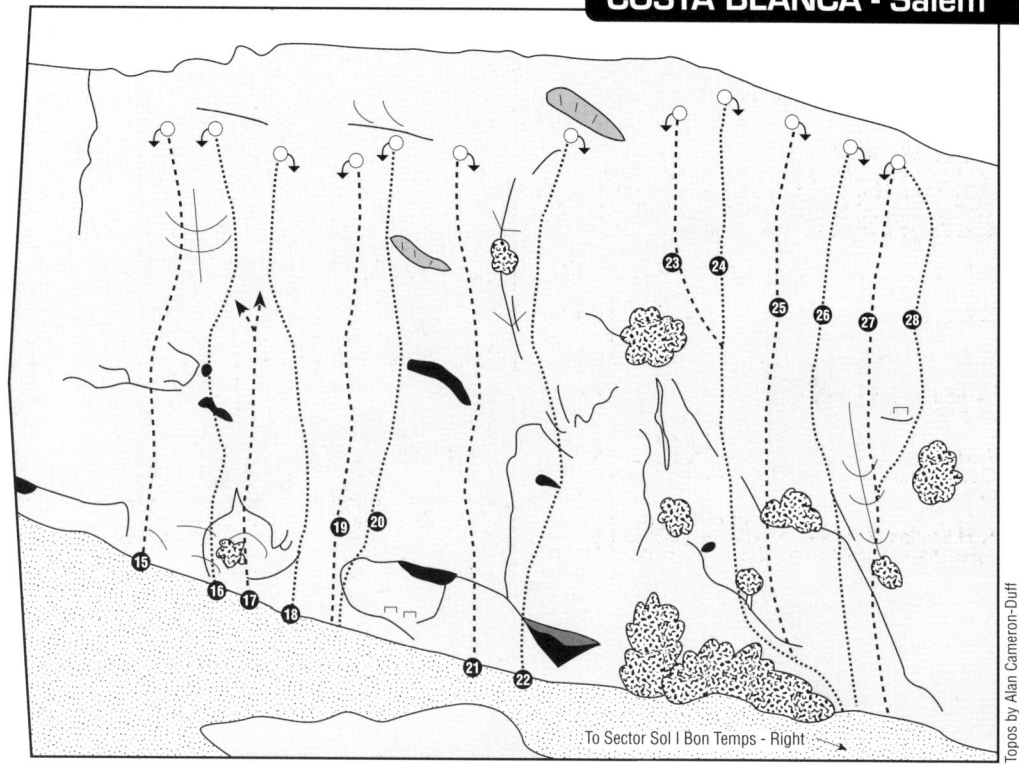

**17. Azul marcia ilusion** ... 7a
Climb strenuously out of the right-hand side of the hollow to finish up either of the adjacent routes.

**18. ?** ... 6c
The line of silver bolts.

**19. Repos celestial** ... 6c
Same start as route 18 but clip the bolts on the right.

**20. La bola del nas** ... 7b
Past a diagonal slot. The third clip is desperate.

**21. Reuníon tumultuosa** ... 6b
Follow a crack in the wall.

**22. Las mollas de riglo** ... 6a
Up the pillar and chossy corner above.

The next routes are 10m further right, past a large bush.

**23. Plan de choque** ... 6b
Start in the bushes. Take the left-hand line of bolts in the headwall.

**24. Paquete e medidas** ... 6c+
The right-hand line of bolts in the headwall.

**25. Que se mueran los feos** ... 6c

**26. Tarugo** ... 6b+
Climb the gully to the open scoop.

**27. Mabel's** ... 6a
Past a tufa on the right-hand side of the scoop.

**28. El cedro torre** ... 5+
The right-hand edge of the scoop.

**Sector Sol I Bon Temps - Left**
South facing wall, 10m to 30m routes
Best grades - 6a+ to 7a

# COSTA BLANCA - Salem

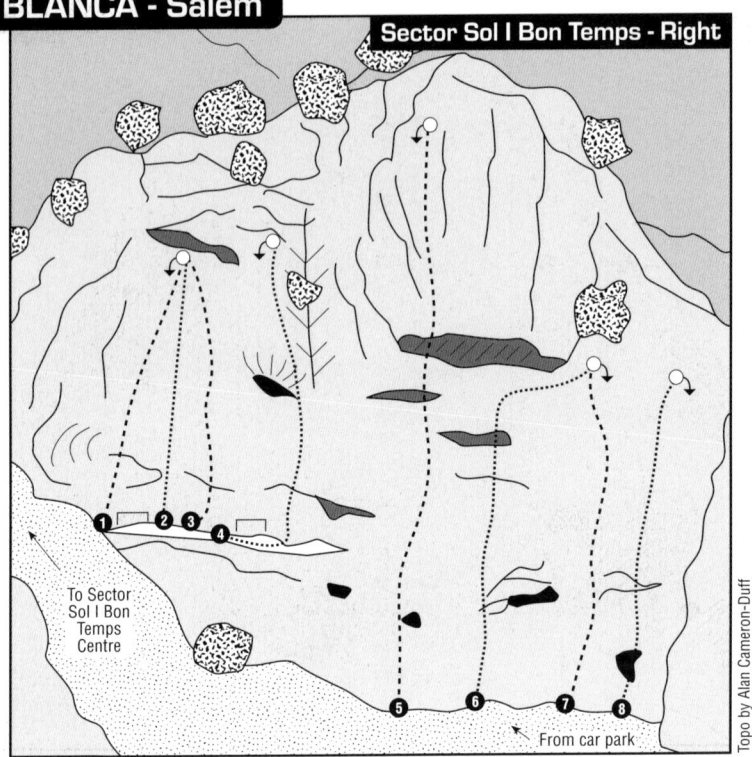

## Sector Sol I Bon Temps - Right

### SECTOR SOL I BON TEMPS LOWER
Further down the hill from the fine Sol I Bon Temps wall is a smaller, and slightly scrappier section.
**APPROACH** - Walk up past Sector Estival and continue more steeply, zig-zaging up the hillside, over some scree to reach the base of the crag.

The first routes start from a ledge on the left-hand side of the crag.

1. Tovarich .................... 6c+
2. Tulukremlin ................ 6c
3. Con iberia ya habrias volado ...... 5
4. Pelut I pelat ................. 6b
Climb the wall to the right of the ledge, then take the left side of the shallow groove past a deep hole.

5. Síndrome de soletat ...... 7a+
The best route on this sector. Climb the yellow wall to the left-hand side of the roof and continue up interesting rock to a lower-off just beneath the ledge.

6. Un montón de ostias ........ 7a+
Climb the centre of the wall to below the roof then scuttle rightwards to a lower-off.

7. Sarvachof ................. 6c
Direct to the lower-off to the left of the roof.

8. Culo flojo .................. 6a+
A poor line on the right-hand edge of the wall.

South facing wall
10m to 15m routes
Best grades - 6c to 7a

**Sector Chica Fácil**

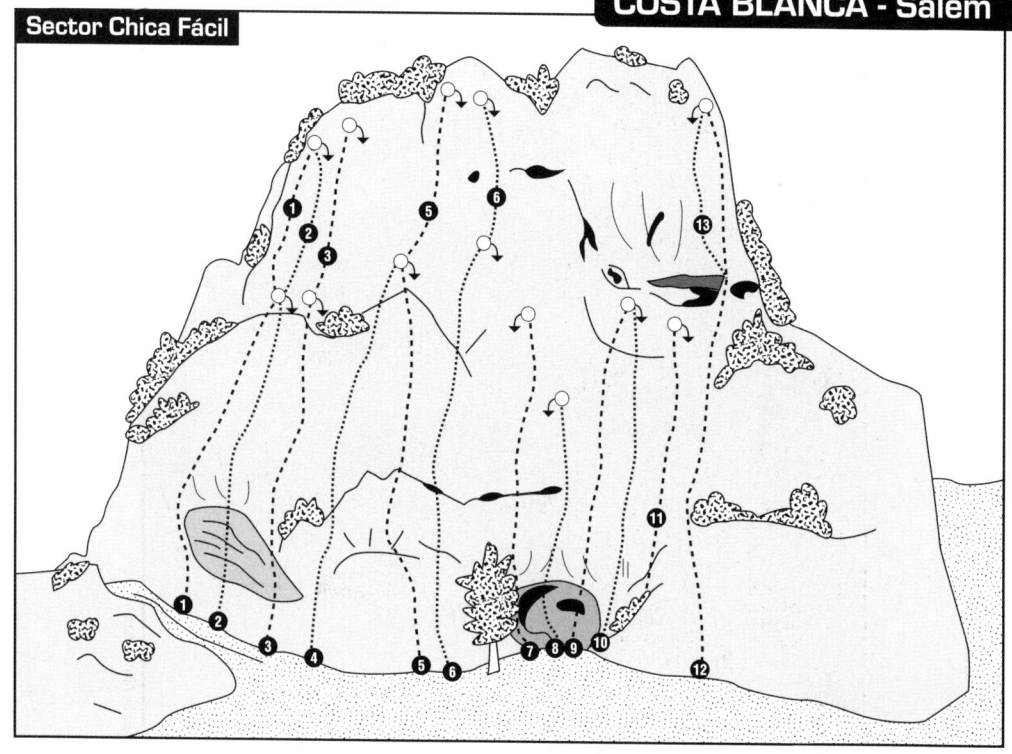

# COSTA BLANCA - Salem

## SECTOR CHICA FÁCIL
The final section of cliff, on the sunny side of the valley, is a big wall undercut at its base by a couple of caves. It is not as vegetated as it first appears and offers some fine two pitch routes, on good rock. If you climb these routes with a single 50m rope it will take two abseils to descend.

**APPROACH -** This sector can be reached directly from the parking spot, without slogging all the way up the hill. From Sector Estival locate an indistinct path which contours across the hillside. It is also easy to drop down the hillside from Sector Sol I Bon Temps - Lower.

The first route starts just left of a bulge.

**1. Astisores perilloses** .......... 6a,5+
The sharp, pocketed wall has a hard start. Finishing up pitch 2 of the next route gives a good 2-star combination.

**2. Atmosfera** .......... 7b,6a+
Straight through the cave.

**3. Honeymoon** .......... 6b+,6b+
Up the flake on the right-hand side of the bulge.

**4. La fuerza del viento** .......... 6a+
A single pitch on the left-hand side of the central section.

**5. Despedida de soltero** .......... 6a,6b

**6. Chica fácil** .......... 6a,6b
A good route starting just left of the tree.

**7. Caza de brujas** .......... 6b+
The left-hand side of the cave and groove above.

**8. El gordo de mi mesota** .......... 6c+
Straight out of the centre of the cave.

**9. Solo para aboyados** .......... 6c
The blanker right-hand side of the cave.

**10. Estreno duro** .......... 6b
The wall right of the cave.

**11. No me toques que me rompo** .......... 6a

**12. El principo del fin** .......... 5+
The rambling right edge of the buttress.

**13. El demoño dojo** .......... 6b+
A better route which seeks the good rock left of the arete.

SE facing wall
10m to 40m routes
Best grades - 6a to 6b+

# COSTA BLANCA - Salem

## Sector Complicacions

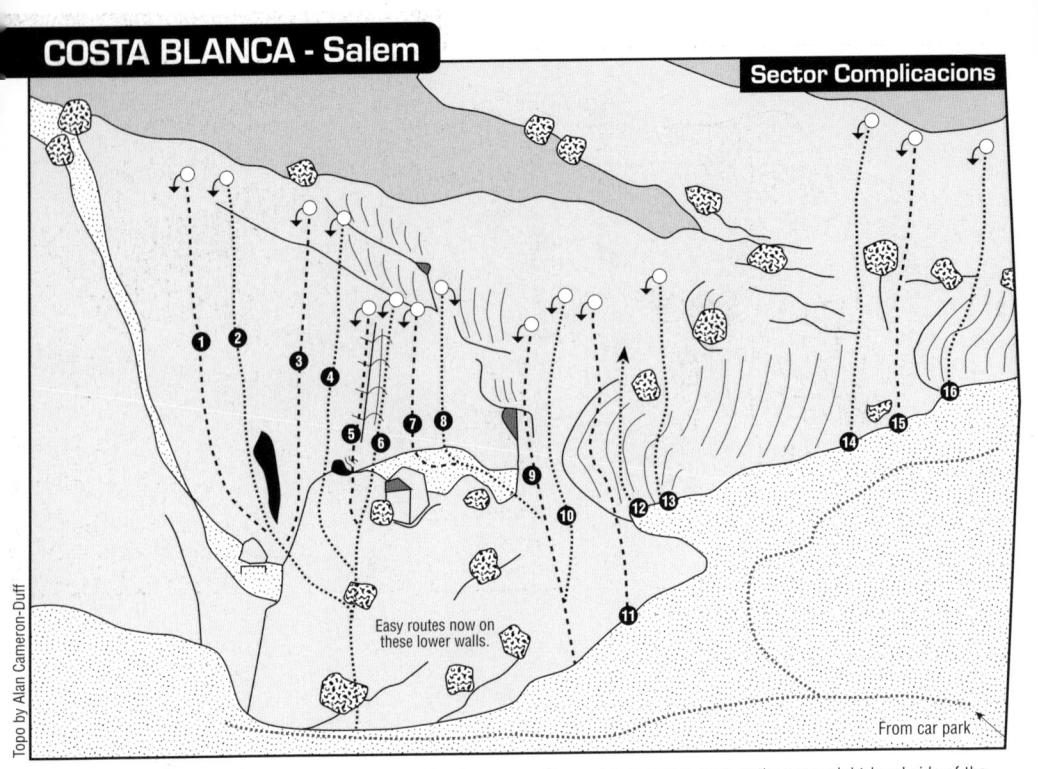

### SECTOR COMPLICACIONS
This is the long and complex crag running up the north facing hillside. It consists of smooth compact limestone covered in small pockets with rounded hollows and caves but the quality rock is a bit spread around. The base below the crag slopes making gearing up awkward and the lack of sun means the place can be freezing (or a welcome shady spot in hot weather).
**APPROACH** - Walk past the left-hand side of Sector Frigorific and follow the path up the hillside.

The first routes described are on the buttress above a vegetated slab. This used to just have a single line of bolts up it but recently it has been bolted with several easier routes. No grades are known but most will be in the 4 to 6a range.

**1. Jesuita bim bam** .......... 6a+

**2. Estoy frito tres delicias** ....... 6b+
Just left of a tall cave.

**3. Tbo negro** ........... 7b
Blank climbing right of the cave.

**4. No mola portar els collons a la gola** ......... 6b+

**5. Chimpangali** .......... 6b+
The crack left of a rounded pillar. Can be started from the higher ledge on the right.

**6. Viuda negra** .......... 6a
The rounded pillar direct. Can be started from the higher ledge on the right.

The next four routes start on the upper right-hand side of the vegetated apron-slab.

**7. Expolon** ................... 6a

**8. Semilla negra** .......... 7a+
A steep bulge.

**9. Calvorotas** ............... 6a
A long route up the pillar.

**10. Monomakina** .......... 6c
Entertaining.

**11. Chube pachi** ....... 7a+
An excellent little problem.

**12. Baja chocho** ............. 7b?
The local topo has this route at 7b! It looks impossible to me.

**13. Droga dura** ....... 7c
It has more holds than the 7b!

**14. A miches** ............. 6a+
A long reach over the initial bulge gains the more amiable headwall.

**15. Lluvida acida** ............. 7a

**16. Marka pasos** ............. 7b
Starts in the curved recess, a massive reach from an undercut to gain vertical rock above.

# COSTA BLANCA - Salem

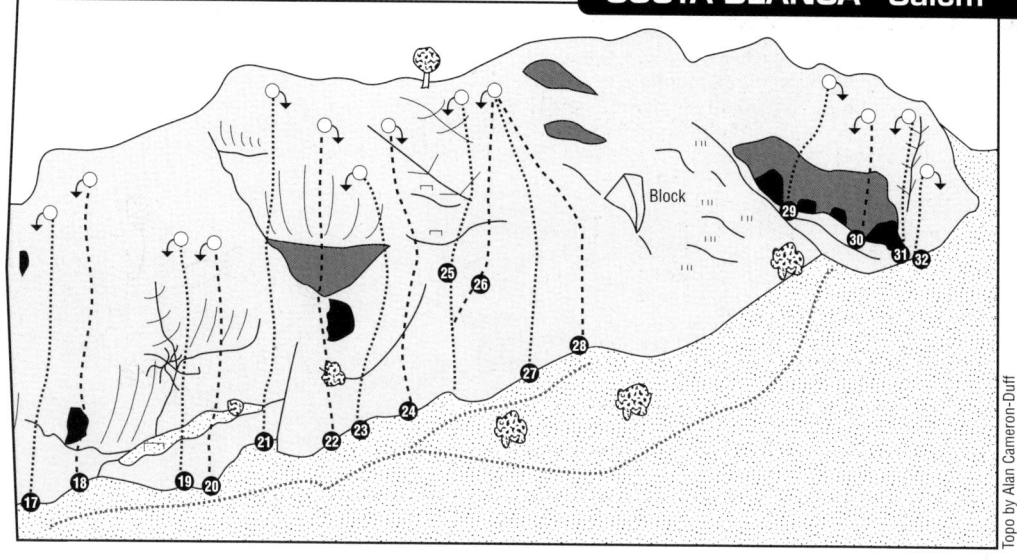

The routes on this sector begin just to the right of a large curiously shaped hole in the rock, just uphill from route 16.

**17. Tu et punxes tio** ....... 6c+
The clean, pocketed wall just left of the hole.

**18. Pelas pa las pilas** .... 7c+
A rather fearsome blank-looking wall above the hole.

**19. Melodía de seducción** .......... Project

**20. Temblores** ................ Project

**21. Tómate un respiro** ........ (7b+)
The route up steep rock just left of the bulging roof was given 7a in the local topo, but it is much harder than this. It may have lost holds.

**22. Pedromina la piruleta** .. 7b
Spectacular moves on massive pockets over the roof.

**23. El silencio de los borregos** ........ 7c
A harder version of the last route. Powerful!

**24. Con agua me clorofoma** ...... 6b
Good climbing just right of the bulging roof.

**25. Celtas cortos** ............ 6c

**26. Tírate al ruedo** ........... 6b+

**27. Les granotes minja** .......... 6b+

**28. Sed de libertad** .............. 6a
The slab left of a flying arete.

Up around the corner is a small cave.

**29. Altamira** ............ 7b
The left-hand end of the cave. A bit short.

**30. Mierda en los dedos** ....... 7a
The right-hand end of the cave, up a short pillar.

**31. Diedrosuro** ................ 5+
Up the groove past three bolts.

**32. Nicho para un bicho** .......... 7a
Up the bulging arete to a lower-off in the middle of nowhere.

North facing wall
10m to 30m routes
Best grades - 6a to 7c+

# MONTESA

Montesa is a fine little crag consisting of walls of good compact rock, in a splendid position. At first sight the routes look a bit disappointing since many are quite short, however the climbing is continually interesting with absorbing moves from start to finish. The rock is a sandy limestone with a very rough pockets which will make mincemeat of your tender finger tips so take care. The crag has a good range of features including some cracks, chimneys and small overhangs but mainly it is about pocketed walls and slabs.

Included here are two of the main buttresses. There are more routes on the pinnacle in front of the main walls (Tormo Gros) and there is also another sector to the left of Paret de la Mola (El Raco del Boticari). A full topo is available from Camil's Rock Bar in the town for the bargain price of 500pts. Funds from the sale of this topo are used to help pay for maintenance of the crag so, if you enjoy climbing here, please buy the topo.

### APPROACH

Montesa is next to the N-430 between Albacete and Valencia. From the coast either head north to Gandía, and then drive inland towards Xàtiva, or drive to Alcoy and pick up the N340 heading north towards Xàtiva.
Once in, or near, Xàtiva, pick up signs for Albaceta and the N430. Once on the N430 dual carriageway, continue for a few junctions until you can turn off to Montesa. Follow the signs for the Castillo, turning right and go out of the town, up around the back of the castle. Go over the top of the hill and take a very sharp right at the first bend coming back down into the town. Park by a fountain and some picnic tables. The crag is three minutes up a hill from here.

### ASPECT AND CLIMATE

Most of the crag faces south and catches the sun. It isn't very exposed to the wind but will give no shelter in the rain.
The block of Tormo Gros has a north facing side which gives shade. The routes on this wall are relatively friendly grades from 4 to 6a+ and a couple at 6b+.

### THE ROUTES

The routes have been equipped by the local climber Ricard Jimenez. He tends to hang around the Camil's Rock Bar.

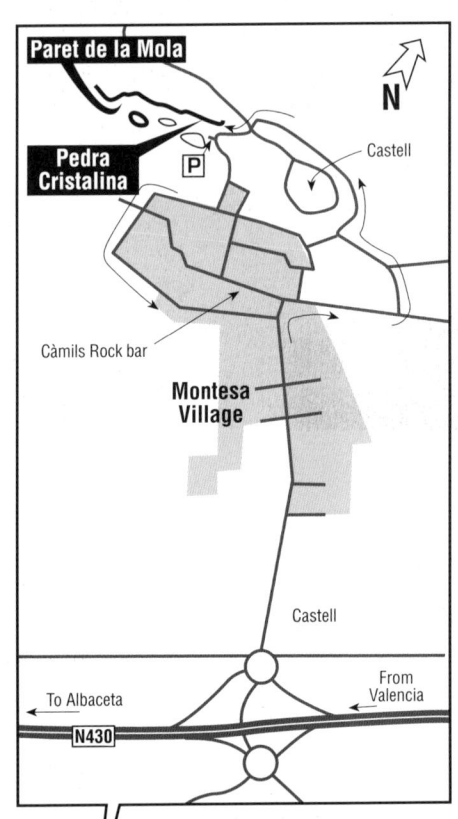

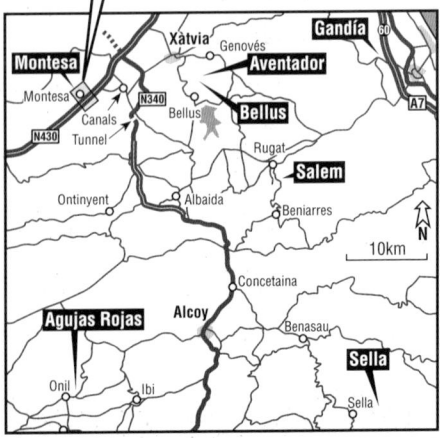

# COSTA BLANCA - Montesa

## Paret de la Mola

### PARET DE LA MOLA
The main area described is the two buttresses behind the free-standing tower of Tormo Gros.

**1. Wiski a go-go** .............. 7a+
Off the topo to the left is a thin wall.

**2. Per si plou** ............... 5 (A3)
Curious route in the corner. There is a report of a 6a+ in this area as well.

**3. Dagón** .................. 6b+

**4. Ningún Drama** ............ 6c

**5. Sense titól** ............... 6c+

**6. La fura Deus** ............. 6b

**7. Tuli-lola** ................. 6a

**8. Fornicadors** .............. 6b+

**9. La bola del drac** .......... 4

**10. L'oratge** ................ 6b

**11. Diedre ecologic** .......... 5+

**12. Per aci Mixel no passa** ..... 6b+

**13. Diedre güay** ............. 5

**14. Elo Deu del vent** ......... 5+
Big pockets.

**15. Epiliano dels collons** ....... 5+

**16. Pic-pic** ................. 5+
Flake crack with big pockets.

**17. La Panxa** ............... 6b

**18. Pepemite** ............... 6a+

**19. La lluita dels caps** ........ 6b+

**20. Xila/Virgo** .............. 5+
Start in the grove then cross the next route.

**21. Virgo/Xila** .............. 6a+
Hard crack at the start, step back left before the finish.

**22. Insubmisió** .............. 6a+

The rest of the routes are off the photo-topo.

**23. Qué morro** .............. 6a+
Hard slab rightwards, then join *Insubmisió*

**24. Te la mango** ............. 6c
Arete just left of a crack. The crack start is also 6c.

**25. L'espectacul** ............. 6c
Thin start up right-hand side of the wall.

**26. L'home dur** .............. 6b
Start left of a crack then cross it and finish up the pillar.

**27. El nas de Roseta** ......... 6a+
Right-hand side of the pillar.

South facing buttresses
15m to 20m routes
Best grades - 4 to 6c+

# COSTA BLANCA - Montesa

**Pedra Cristalina - Left**

## PEDRA CRISTALINO
The short walls to the right of the central area of Paret de la Mola have a set of technical climbs on compact rock. The climber on route 11 should give you the scale of the crag.

**1. Estornuts** .................... 6b+
Only 3 bolts to lower-off.

**2. Llagrimes en la perda** ..... 7b
Short and fierce.

**3. Baltario, el frare escalador** .. 6b

**4. Caxi-baxe** ......... 7a+

**5. ?** ..................... (7b)
Direct line left of the corner.

**6. Ferrán JB** ............. 6c
The arete.

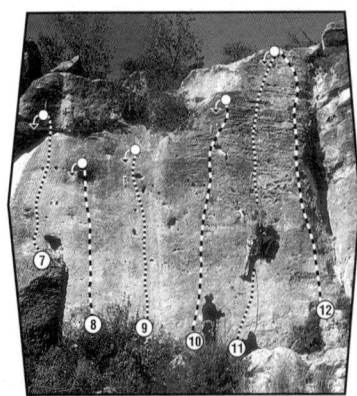

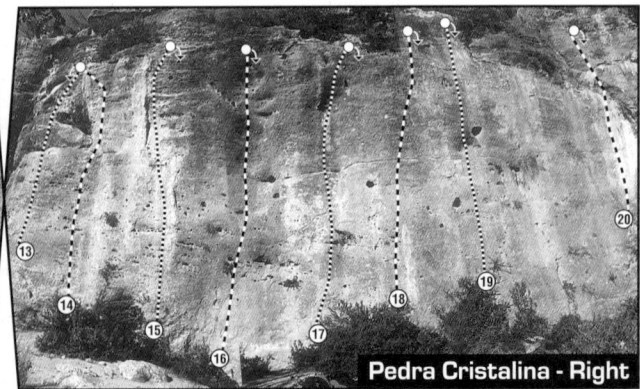

**7. Agárramela por el cuello** ... 6b+
Left of a big pocket.

**8. Menir** ................. 6a+
2 bolts to lower-off. Hard to start.

**9. ¡A la mili quillo!** .......... 6a+
A reachy start. Good pockets above.

**10. Cristalina** ........... 6a+
Another hard start.

**11. Colorines** ............... 6a+
Green and blue bolts.

**12. Diedre besuco** ............. 5
The corner.

**13. La teoría de la palanca** ...... 6a
A one-move-wonder.

**14. El paso del embolo** ......... 6a

**15. El forat negre** ....... 6a+
Up the tufas.

**16. Pepe Blai** ............. 6a+
The open scoop.

**17. Patiras tendinitis** ......... 6c
There might be a warning in the name.

**18. Patiras d'estrenyiment** .... 6c

**19. La petjada de tico** ......... 6a+
In between 2 holes.

**20. Snake-men** ............. 6c
Further right is a short white wall.

**Pedra Cristalina - Right**

Short south facing wall
6m to 15m routes
Best grades - 6a to 6c

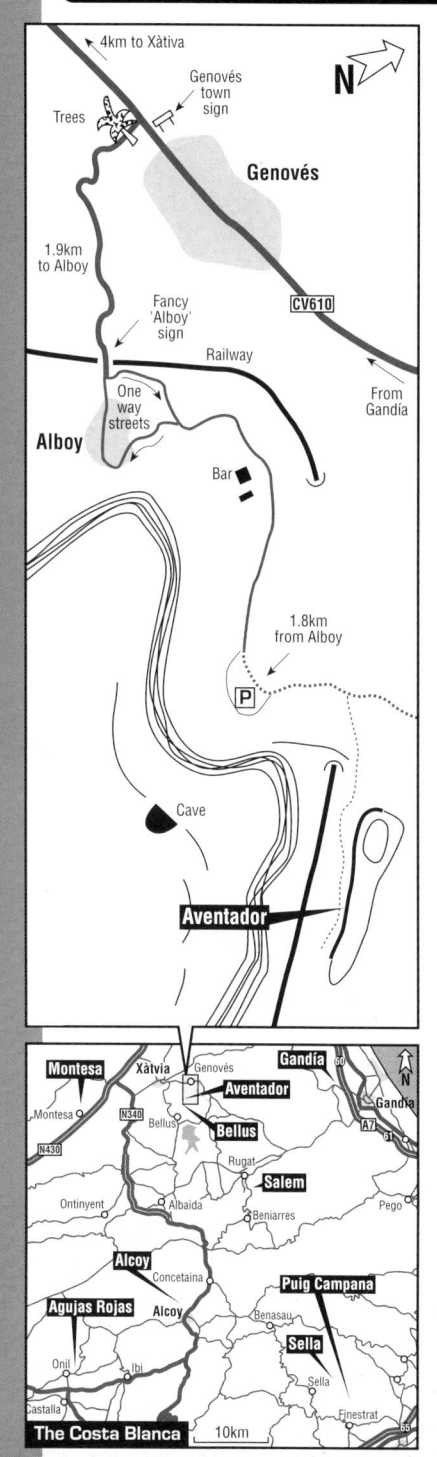

# AVENTADOR

Aventador consists of a long wall of well-pocketed compact rock, with some good slabby face climbing and the odd steeper route. The crag is situated in a splendid, sunny position and the river below provides a delightful swimming spot. The lines are all pretty parallel, hence you can get the *done one done 'em all* feeling with some of the routes, however if you dot about the crag a bit there is plenty to keep you interested for a few visits. On certain sections the various routes tend to get a bit mixed up with each other since there aren't many features and there are lots of bolts. It isn't uncommon to find yourself straying onto another route while climbing upwards in a straight line. It is worth noting that the rock is very sharp and can take its toll on your finger tips especially if you try and cram a lot of routes into the day.

## ASPECT AND CLIMATE

The crag faces southwest, which means it receives the sun from mid-morning onwards. In summer it can be too hot but it is fine for the rest of the year. It is exposed to wind and there is relatively little shelter under the crag.

## APPROACH

Most people based in the Calpe/Benidorm area will want to approach the crag from Gandía. Follow the approach to Gandía described on page 37, until the first turn off on the ring road. This road is the CV60 signed to 'Albaida'. After 12km, turn off this road towards Xàtiva on the CV610. After 18km always following Xàtiva signs, you will arrive at the town of Genovés. 50m after passing the 'leaving Genovés' sign, turn left by some trees (signed 'Estudio del Pintor Vicente'). Follow this road for 1.9km and turn left (signed 'A Chopada') immediately you have crossed a railway bridge, after passing the fancy 'Alboy' sign. After 400m you come to a T-junction. Turn left and follow the road for a further 1.4km and park at a flat terrace on the right, just before the track winds uphill. From here walk up the track and break out rightwards to the crag which is now obvious on the hillside above you.

El Aventador can also be reached by following the N340 from Alcoy to Xàtiva. In Xàtiva pick up signs for the CV610 towards 'Genoves and Gandía'. This brings you into Genoves from the other end so turn right on entering the village.

## THE ROUTES

This historic crag was one of the first places in Spain to be developed for sport climbing in the early 1980s. This was principally the work of Salvador Guerola and Emilio Perales and their friends.

# COSTA BLANCA - Aventador

## Sector Alto Bronx

### SECTOR ALTO BRONX
At the left-hand end of the crag is a prominent steep cave. The first routes are located some distance up the slope, past a section of loose yellow rock, to the left of the cave. These two routes have the added attraction of staying in the shade a lot longer than the rest.

**1. La suplente del presidente** ..... 6c

**2. Porri** .............. 6b
This short route may have a second pitch at 6a which will need some wires.

To the right is a loose yellow wall with two old trad routes. Further right again is a bush.

**3. Placa cósmica** ............ 6b+
Start left of a bush. 'Placa Cosmica' is painted on the rock.

**4. Spectrum** ............... 6b
The same start as above then break right. 1) 6b, 2) 6a+

To the right of the bush are more lines of bolts.

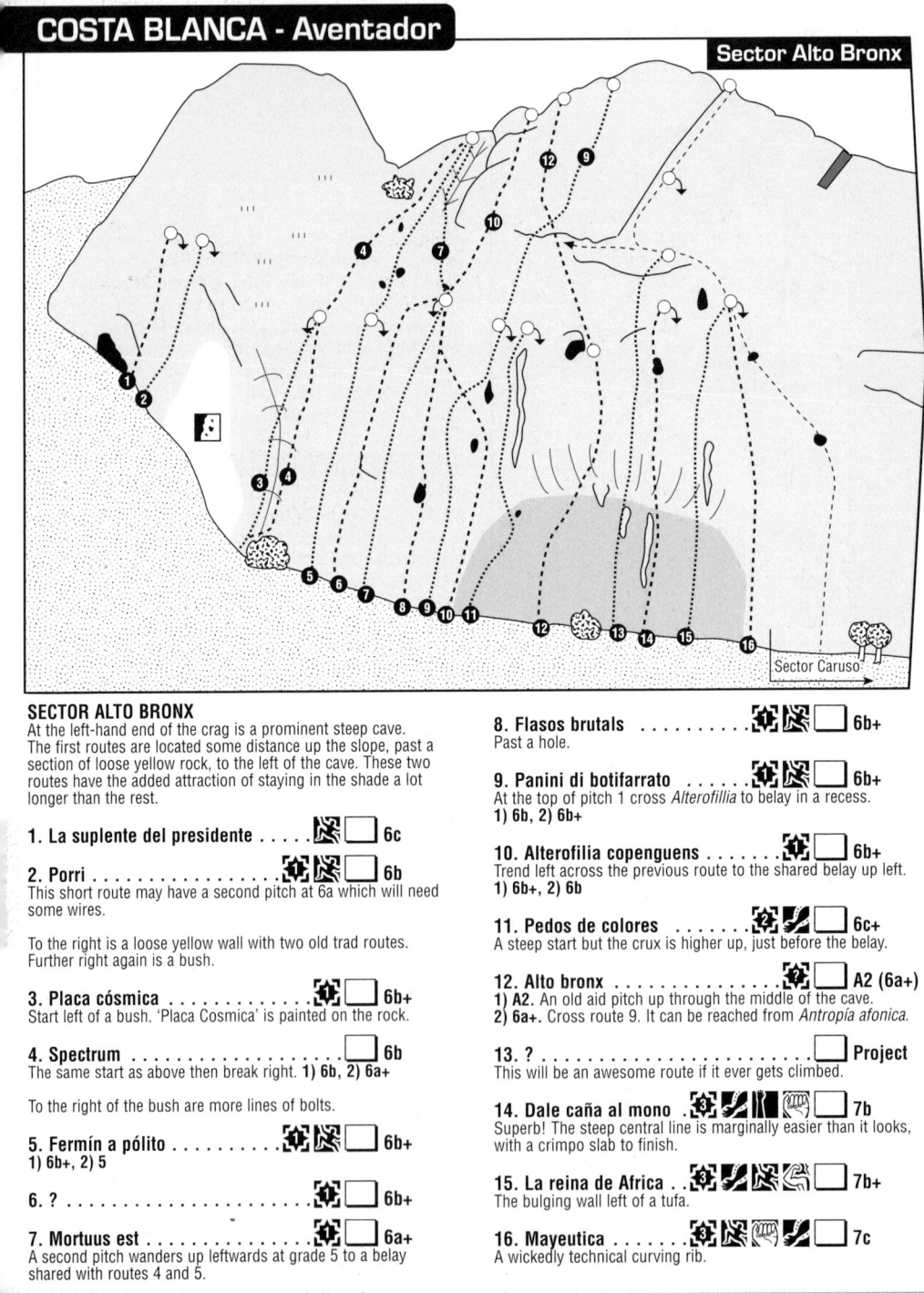

**5. Fermín a pólito** ......... 6b+
1) 6b+, 2) 5

**6. ?** ..................... 6b+

**7. Mortuus est** ............. 6a+
A second pitch wanders up leftwards at grade 5 to a belay shared with routes 4 and 5.

**8. Flasos brutals** ......... 6b+
Past a hole.

**9. Panini di botifarrato** ..... 6b+
At the top of pitch 1 cross *Alterofillia* to belay in a recess.
1) 6b, 2) 6b+

**10. Alterofilia copenguens** ....... 6b+
Trend left across the previous route to the shared belay up left.
1) 6b+, 2) 6b

**11. Pedos de colores** ....... 6c+
A steep start but the crux is higher up, just before the belay.

**12. Alto bronx** .............. A2 (6a+)
1) A2. An old aid pitch up through the middle of the cave.
2) 6a+. Cross route 9. It can be reached from *Antropía afonica*.

**13. ?** ....................... Project
This will be an awesome route if it ever gets climbed.

**14. Dale caña al mono** ....... 7b
Superb! The steep central line is marginally easier than it looks, with a crimpo slab to finish.

**15. La reina de Africa** ..... 7b+
The bulging wall left of a tufa.

**16. Mayeutica** ............. 7c
A wickedly technical curving rib.

South facing wall
10m to 45m routes
Best grades - 6a+ to 7c

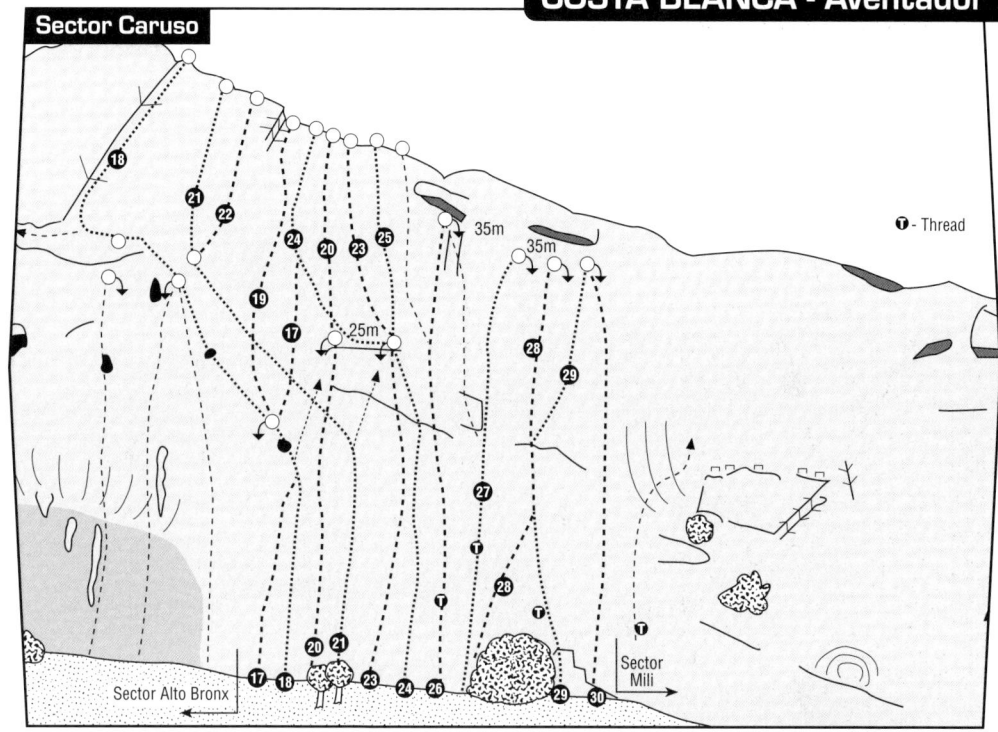

## SECTOR CARUSO

To the right of the cave is tall smooth wall with some long 2 pitch routes. The routes here follow very complex lines and there are a number of direct variations which confuse matters. Also, some of the easier pitches are only sparsely bolted which makes picking the line out hard. The names painted at the base, the prominent cable-belay shared by several routes and the finishing corner of *Carbono 14* are fairly reliable features. Two abseils, or twin 50m ropes for one abseil, are needed to descend.

**17. Mesclaillos guerola** . . . . . . . . 6b
40m. A long direct line best split at a belay on *Antropía Afonica*.

**18. Antropía afonica** . . . . . . . . 6a+
1) **6a+.** Climb up around the edge of the cave ignoring the first belay in favour of a higher one below the corner. Alternatively use the belay on *Tremolando* for a good single pitch.
2) **6a.** Finish up the corner.

**19. Variation C** . . . . . . . . . . . . . . . . 6b
An upper pitch left of the corner of *Carbono 14*.

**20. Trembolando estoy** . . . . . . . . 6b
1) 6b, 2) 6b. Finish to the right of the corner of *Carbono 14*.

**21. Astolfo hinkel** . . . . . . . . . . . . 6a+
1) **6a+.** The line travels across left above *Antropia* to a belay on the upper wall. A good alternative is to climb direct to the lower-off on *Carbono 14*.
2) **6c.** A hard finish or attempt the easier.....

**22. Aisenkouen** . . . . . . . . . . . . . . . . 6b
A right-hand finish to *Astolfo*.

**23. Karuso** . . . . . . . . . . . . . . 6a
1) **6a.** An excellent pitch with a fluttery crux.
2) **5+.** Given a higher grade in another topo.

**24. Carbono 14** . . . . . . . . . 6a
1) **5+.** A sparsely bolted pitch but the easiest way up the wall.
2) **6a.** Traverse left across several other routes eventually reaching a short corner high on the wall.

**25. Extrema unción** . . . . . . 7a
An upper pitch. Start up either of the previous two routes.

The next routes are very long single pitches from which you can't lower off.

**26. Vomitera óptica** . . . . . . . . 6c+
Name scratched on the rock. The left-hand finish is *Vampiro*, 7a.

**27. Astrokangrena bucólica** . . . . . . 6b
The left-hand finish is *Asgarramenta Lumbar*, **6c+** finishing at the *Vomitera* belay.

**28. Aci em pegaras** . . . . . . . . . . 6b
Start left of the bush.

**29. Cristal pardo** . . . . . . . . . . . . . . . . 6b+
Start right of the bush. Shares its middle section with the previous route.

**30. Calla pixorro** . . . . . . . . . . . . . . . . 6b
Thinly bolted at the bottom but easy climbing.

South facing wall
20m pitches to 45m routes
Best grades - 6a to 7a

# COSTA BLANCA - Aventador

## Sector Mili

Long pitches - 60 rope to lower-off

⊙ - Thread

← Sector Caruso

Sector Navarro →

### SECTOR MILI
The crag now turns slabby and the routes become less impressive, although there are some good easier challenges.

**31. Mili** .................... 4+
*Mili* and *Trimomia* probably take the same line up the lower wall. The easier finish is on the right at the top.

**32. Trimomia** ............... 6a+
Wires may be needed for the start shared with *Mili*.

**33. Gueles marxoses** .......... 6a+
High first bolt but easy climbing following a long diagonal to finish at a corner. Confused with *Mili* in previous guides. Many will want split the route at a stance on the ledge.

**34. Pepsiman** ................ 6a
Start just left of a tree and continue just right of a bush.

**35. Albomina** ................ 5+
A right-hand variation on *Pepsiman*.

**36. Cefalograma** ............. 5+
Start between two trees and climb the left-hand line. A long pitch which can be spilt at the mid-height stance.

**37. Coconuts** ................ 6a
The right-hand line, from between trees.

**38. Jorge negrete** ............ 6a
Finish just left of the final corner of *Gueles marxoses*.

**39. OV** ...................... 6a+
Good climbing leading to a hard finish.

**40. Coneiximent de mosquit** ..... 6b
Start as for *Ov* but move right to a large block, then tackle the bulging wall above.

**41. Luis mariano** ............. 6a+
Aim for the right-hand side of a large block.

**42. Collo que guai** ........... 6a+

**43. Mesinfoteles** ............. 6a
Pass a large hole on its left-hand side. The finish over the overlap is tricky.

**44. Amadeus** ................. 6a
Past some red graffiti and the hole on its right-hand side. Another hard finish.

**45. Pegamé en to el medio** ..... 6a+
The zig-zag corner.

**46. Ala anem** ................ 6b
A fingery wall finishing on a block.

**47. Has Cobrat?** .............. 6b
Past some red graffiti of the name. The top roof is hard and the final bolt awkward to clip.

**48. Tot es manec** ............. 6a
Start by 'PX' on the rock. Left of a hole.

**49. Pepe Carvalho** ............ 6a
The line is right of the hole. Desperate roof to finish.

**50. Jerónimo** ................. 6a

South facing wall
15m to 30m routes
Best grades - 5 to 6b

# COSTA BLANCA - Aventador

🔵 - Thread

Sector Mili

Sector Navarro

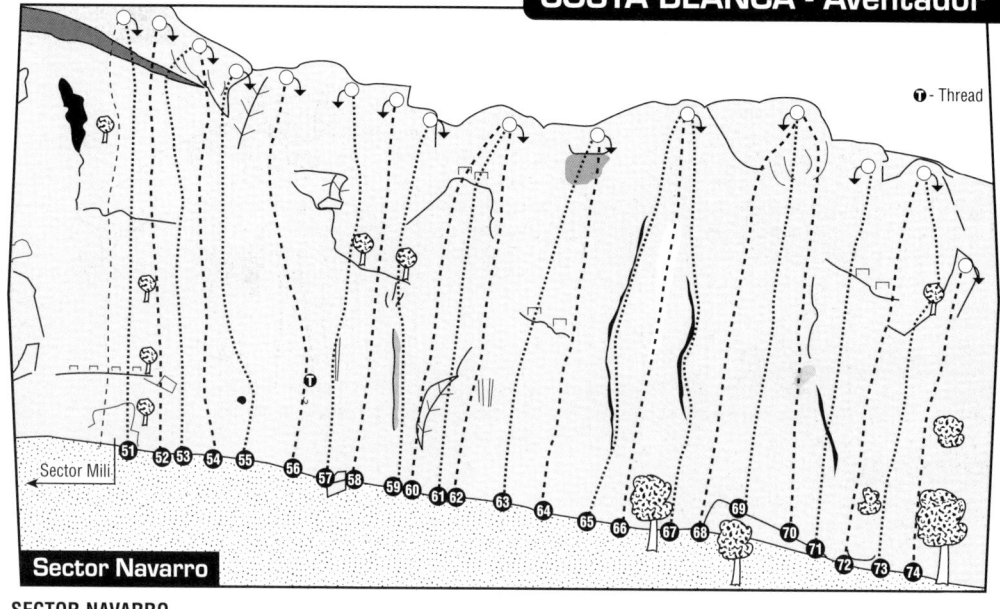

## SECTOR NAVARRO
The right-hand end of the crag has some great steep slab climbs in the easier grades..

**51. Que asco que tusca** ............ 6b

**52. Patetas de cargol** .......... 6b
Start by a scratched arrow. Finish either left or right.

**53. Cacau i tramus** ............ 6b

**54. Pase milions** ............ 6b+
Hard crux move.

**55. Blackmaster** ............ 6c+
Finish up a hanging arete.

**56. Afrodita** ............ 5+
The big corner high on the buttress, reached direct.

**57. Hermafordita** ............ 6b
Past a blunt tufa.

**58. Zapalastro** ............ 6c
With a steep finishing wall.

**59. BA** ............ 5
Up a flake, past a ledge to a hard finish.

**60. Mortadelo** ............ 5+

**61. Rompetechos** ............ 5+
Start up a little corner.

**62. Filemón** ............ 5+
Just left of twin blunt tufas.

**63. Carpanta** ............ 5+

**64. Arcadia** ............ 5
There is a white rock scar at the bottom.

**65. Vent** ............ 5
Follow the crack line.

**66. Pepet** ............ 6b+
Start just left of the tree and follow the white streak.

**67. Navarro** ............ 6a
The right-hand pocket line, right of the tree.

**68. Asterix** ............ 5+
Good climbing. Start from a block.

**69. Obelix** ............ 6a
Poor and contrived. Start from the block.

**70. Idefix** ............ 5+

**71. Rafa** ............ 5

**72. Pepe** ............ 5
The line is just left of where the name is on the rock.

**73. Dit** ............ 5

**74. La pelirroja ilustada** ............ 6a+
The last line on the wall.

South facing wall
15m to 25m routes
Best grades - 5 to 6b+

**63**

# BELLÚS

Bellús offers varied climbing in a secluded dry valley called The Barranco Fondo. This is a very pleasant spot, once the rubbish dump parking area is left behind, and should provide a good day's entertainment for climbers who are over-familiar with other crags in the Costa Blanca. It is probably not worth a visit on your first trip to the Costa Blanca but there are lots of shortish routes, across a reasonable grade spread, that are worth seeking out once you've sampled the grander delights of Sella, Gandía, and the other more major areas.
The topos and route information here have been cobbled together from a number of sources. There are some confusions in the route lines and many of the routes have no comments or character symbols. Please feel free to email these to ROCKFAX (alan@rockfax.co.uk) for inclusion in future guides, and make sure you check the rockfax web site (rockfax.com/costa_blanca) before your trip for any updates.

## ASPECT AND CLIMATE

The crag is a well sheltered sun-trap. There are no big overhangs here so there is little to do in the rain. Similarly there is not much respite from the sun either so this is not a summer time crag.

## APPROACH

Bellús village is situated about 8km south of Xàtiva on the N340. It can be reached along the slow roads from Sella, via Alcoy and Albaida. However from Benidorm or Calpe it is best to approach from the Gandía ring road via the CV60 and CV610 until a left turn in the small town of Quatretonda on the CV612 leads via the village of Benigàmin and across a dam to join the N340 immediately south of Bellús. Turn right on a dirt road immediately north of the village and at the junction of tracks turn left towards the obvious quarried walls. Keep left and park just before the tracks run out at the side of the quarry which is unfortunately now used as a tip. Walk carefully through the rubbish and soon pick up a delightful track running up the right side of the gorge. About 1 hour from Calpe.

### Cueva Pechina
There is another buttress situated above the river (almost opposite Aventador). This has 14 routes and is shady. Grades from the left - **5, 7b, 6c+, 7c+, 6c, Project, 7b+, 7a, 6a+, 6a+, 6b+, 6c+, 7a+, 7c.**
**APPROACH** - Go straight on at the crossroads and pass some farms. Leave the car and walk for 5 minutes, the cave is not visible until you reach the river.

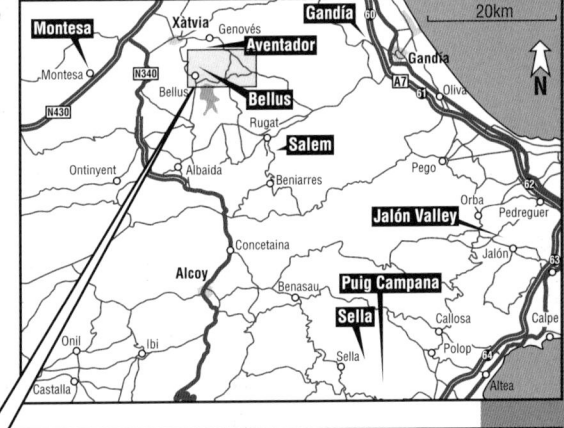

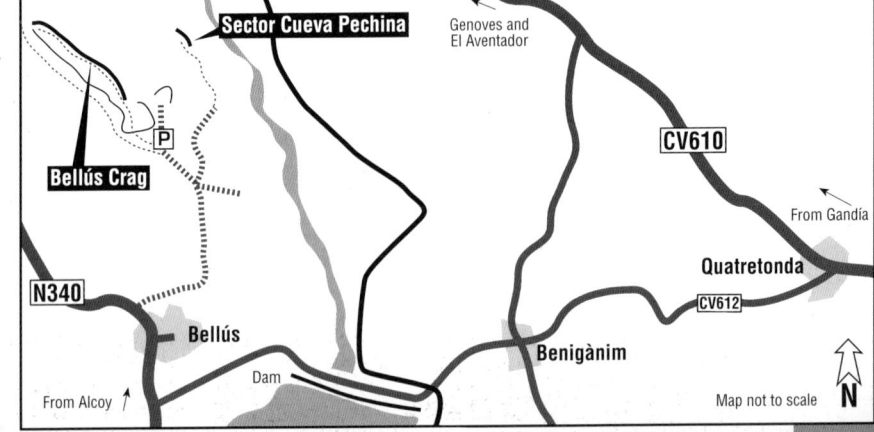

# COSTA BLANCA - Bellús

## Sector Balcón

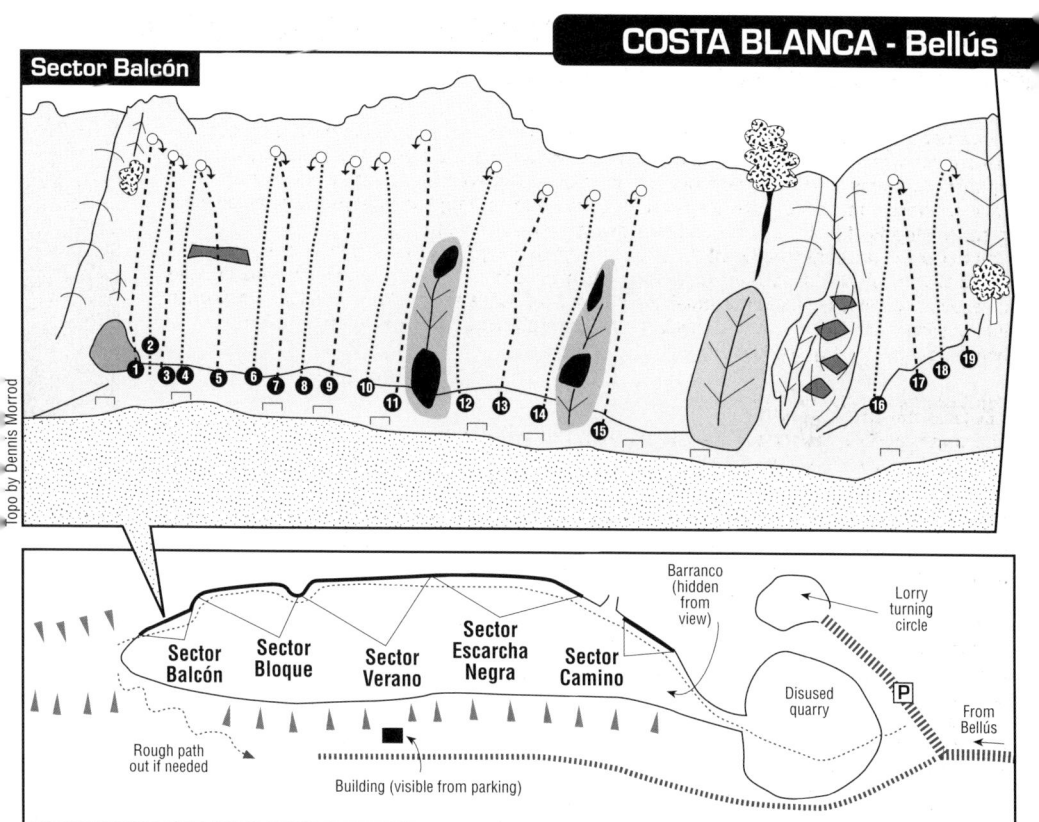

### SECTOR BALCÓN
The far left-hand end of the crag with short routes on steep, undercut, grey walls of good rock. Some of the routes have had their first bolt removed.

1. Ganimedes . . . . . . . . . . . . . . . 5
2. Europa . . . . . . . . . . . . . . . . . 5
3. Titán . . . . . . . . . . . . . . . . . . 5+
4. Júpiter . . . . . . . . . . . . . . . . . 6a+
5. Orión . . . . . . . . . . . . . . . . . 6c
6. Reina de saba . . . . . . . . . . . . 6c
Good climbing on positive holds.
7. Rinoceronte . . . . . . . . . . . . . 6c
8. Akenaton . . . . . . . . . . . . . . . 7a+
9. Salomón . . . . . . . . . . . . . . . 7a

10. Dulce castigo . . . . . . . . . . 7a+
Short, fingery crux.
11. Campurriano . . . . . . . . . . . 7b+
Steep and fingery.
12. Capitán América . . . . . . . . . 7b
Steep and fingery.
13. Acécarme el agujero . . . . . . 7b+
A steep climb with a dyno at the start.
14. Tutankamon . . . . . . . . . . . . 6b+
15. Cleopatra . . . . . . . . . . . . . 6b
16. Celtas Cortos . . . . . . . . . . . 6b
17. Columbia . . . . . . . . . . . . . 6a+
18. Airbag . . . . . . . . . . . . . . . 5
19. JB . . . . . . . . . . . . . . . . . . 5+

South facing wall
5m to 10m routes
Best grades - 5 to 7b+

Lots of sun — 5 min — Vertical — Lower-offs

Topo by Dennis Morrod

# COSTA BLANCA - Bellús

## Sector Bloque

**SECTOR BLOQUE**
Many of the routes on this sector are very short, sometimes only 2 or 3 bolts long and quite often the first bolt is missing! However the moves pack a lot in.

1. Yertu primituvu . . . . . . . . . . . . 6a+
2. Guapito bananas . . . . . . . . . . 6a+
3. Tócate los huesos . . . . . . . . . 6b
4. Peña el porru . . . . . . . . . . . . . 6b
5. Carne Val . . . . . . . . . . . . . . . . 6a+
6. Transilvania . . . . . . . . . . . . . . 6c
7. Dràcula . . . . . . . . . . . . . . . . . 6c+
8. Tarambanas . . . . . . . . . . . . . 6b
9. As de ases . . . . . . . . . . . . . . 7a
10. Masacre . . . . . . . . . . . . . . . . 6a+
11. Halloween . . . . . . . . . . . . . . . 6a
12. Xíus . . . . . . . . . . . . . . . . . . . . 6a+
13. Comanche . . . . . . . . . . . . . . 6b+
Sharp pockets.
14. Pierdo verticalidad . . . . . . . . 6a+
15. Colores de guerra . . . . . . . . . 6a
16. Asmático . . . . . . . . . . . . . . . . 6b+
17. Pedro Picapiedra . . . . . . . . . . 6b+
18. Pablo Mármol . . . . . . . . . . . . 5
19. Hells Bells . . . . . . . . . . . . . . . 5+
20. Consejo de guerra . . . . . . . . . 6a
21. Consejo de paz . . . . . . . . . . . 6b
22. Yeti . . . . . . . . . . . . . . . . . . . . 6a
Good juggy climbing.
23. A escobazos con Guerola . . . . . 6a
24. El atrofiat . . . . . . . . . . . . . . . 6a
Hard at the start.
25. El attolladero . . . . . . . . . . . . 6b+
26. Amordasat . . . . . . . . . . . . . . 6a

South facing wall
5m to 10m routes
Best grades - 5 to 6b+

## COSTA BLANCA - Bellús

**Sector Verano - Left**

### SECTOR VERANO - LEFT
This sector has the longest routes at the crag on steep shallow grooves, cracks and walls.

1. Invertidos de la ostia ........ 6c+
2. Les grapes ............... 6b+
3. Los mediocres ........... 6b
4. Micro .................. 6c
5. Pistacho ............... 6b
6. El pastiset ............. 6a
7. Momo .................. 6b+
8. Parasit ................ 6a
9. Bossím ................ 6a
10. Mister coki ............ 6b
    Looks very good.
11. Amors ................ 5+
12. Pobre Olivera .......... 6b
13. Karkamal ............. 6a+
14. El amagatall .......... 6a+
15. Capello .............. 6c+
16. No me siento las piedras ... 6a+
17. Yohan ................ 7a
18. Champions league ...... 7a
19. Harley Davidson ........ 6c+
20. Brea ................. 7a+
    Just left of a chimney.
21. Ostia a la cabeza ....... 7c
    Doesn't look like a 7c.
22. La pancheta de gueroleta ... 6b
    Looks harder than 6b.
23. Tridente .............. 6b
    Looks harder than 6b.
24. Moco de pavo .......... 7a
    Chipped pillar.

There is a big gap of climbable rock which has two routes Terminator (7b+) and Guerotex (6c+) listed but no bolts.

Gap of climbable rock to the next routes Sector Verano - Right →

South facing wall
5m to 18m routes
Best grades - 5+ to 7a

# COSTA BLANCA - Bellús

## SECTOR VERANO - RIGHT

**25. Duracel** .................. 7a
Good climbing up tufas.

**26. Atlanta** .................. 6b
Diagonal line of pockets.

**27. Popeye** .................. 6c
Line of tufas. One of the best routes at Bellús.

## SECTOR ESCARCHA NEGRA

The next section of rock has four routes around 2 niches. The local topo has 2 routes listed at 7a+ - *Cacaolat del Marroc* and *Alto Brons*. It is not know which of these next routes is which however none of them look as hard as 7a+.

**28. ?** .................. (6b/6c)
Red streak into a shallow groove. looks good.

**29. ?** .................. (6b/6c)
Past a small niche.

**30. ?** .................. (6b/6c)

**31. ?** .................. (6b/6c)

Further right, past a blank section, are 2 more unknowns.

**32. ?** .................. (6c)

**33. ?** .................. (6c)

**34. Código rojo** .................. 6c

**35. Sed de dromedario** .................. 6b
Orange groove.

**36. Sega** .................. 6a+
Left-hand side of a grey slab.

**37. Mega** .................. 6a+
Start below a small tufa boss at 2m.

**38. Esquirol** .................. 6a+
A fine grey slab.

**39. Psicosis** .................. 6b+

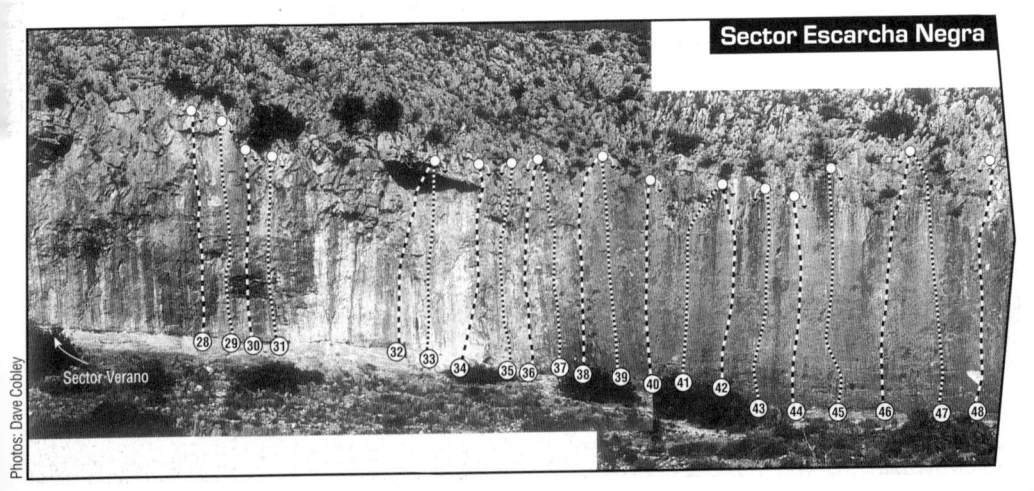

# COSTA BLANCA - Bellús

40. Alparrus . . . . . . . . . . . . . . . . 6a+
41. Sopletiste . . . . . . . . . . . . . . 6c+
42. Trance . . . . . . . . . . . . . . . . . 6c
43. Moreno . . . . . . . . . . . . . . . . 6b
44. Rompe gafas . . . . . . . . . . . . 6c+
45. Rompe cojones . . . . . . . . . . 7a
46. Maldita sea mi suerte . . . . . . 6b
Excellent, steep slab climbing.
47. Tiempo perdido . . . . . . . . . . 6c
Left of a white scar.
48. Cuerdas gastadas . . . . . . . . 6a+
Through the white scar.

The next 4 routes start behind a large bush. This bush provides the only shade at the crag and tends to be the gearing up spot.

49. A todo tren . . . . . . . . . . . . . 6b
50. La chicharra . . . . . . . . . . . . 6b
51. La porreta . . . . . . . . . . . . . . 6a+
52. La chufeta . . . . . . . . . . . . . . 6c
53. Sobaos . . . . . . . . . . . . . . . . 6b
Fingery crux on razor pockets.
54. Bujakes . . . . . . . . . . . . . . . . 6b
Red wall above cave.
55. Rayos uva . . . . . . . . . . . . . . 6c
Tricky tufa start to gain delicate hanging corner.

56. Aquí macabatde fotre . . . . . . 7a+
57. Carnestoltes . . . . . . . . . . . . 7a+
58. Los suaves . . . . . . . . . . . . . 6c
Left of short crack, low on the wall.
59. Kakaolate . . . . . . . . . . . . . . 6b
Just right of short crack.
60. Terrorista en la autopista . . 7b
Past a small hole at 3m. Painful holds.
61. Peligrosa María . . . . . . . . . . 6c
62. Alcatraz . . . . . . . . . . . . . . . . 6c
Long reaches between sharp pockets.
63. Siempre igual . . . . . . . . . . . 6b
Slab above ramp and broken wall.
64. Anfiteatro . . . . . . . . . . . . . . . 6a+
65. Sudores . . . . . . . . . . . . . . . . 6a+
66. Calores . . . . . . . . . . . . . . . . 5+
67. Temores . . . . . . . . . . . . . . . 5

**SECTOR CAMINO** - This short wall is situated 100m before the main crag. There is no topo included for these two but they are the first you you encounter on approaching the crag.

68. Flautus cercanas . . . . . . . . . 4+
The left-hand line.
69. Tambores lejanos . . . . . . . . 4+
The right-hand line.

**Sector Escarcha Negra**
South facing, 5m to 10m routes
Best grades - 5+ to 7a+

# JALÓN VALLEY

Just to the north of Calpe is a large open valley where there are a number of excellent small crags which are well situated for people staying in Calpe or Benidorm. Although none of the crags could be described as major venues, the climbing is good and the approaches easy. Virtually all of them make good rest-day or half-day venues.

The best of the crags is Lliber which is well worth a visit especially if you lead in the 6s and 7s. Alcalalí is very small but all seven routes are good, however they are all harder than 6b. L'ocaive has some good routes in the lower grades and is north facing making it useful in hot weather but very chilly at other times. Font d'Axia is a secluded little spot with a pleasant, west facing wall with friendly routes making it a good place to try leading if you are a beginner.

Two other crags mentioned are given brief coverage. Coves Rojes is very accessible, and has a few decent routes, but it is like climbing in a rubbish dump. Covatelles is very disjointed and close to the motorway but again there are a few worthwhile climbs.

While you are in the area it is worth checking out are the free wine tasting sessions on Sunday, at the 'Cooperativa La Virgen Probre' just outside Jalón. Also there is occasionally a street market in Jalón which is worth a look.

### APPROACH

Most crags are approached from the central village of Jalón. Detailed approach descriptions are included with the route pages. The recently opened Jalón by-pass has made negotiating the village much simpler. It used to be a bit of a bottleneck especially on market days.

### ASPECT AND CLIMATE

As mentioned above there is plenty to go at in the valley in most weather conditions. It usually receives the same weather as Calpe making it an option on wet days. Most of the crags apart from L'ocaive are well sheltered from the wind.

### THE ROUTES

The route have been developed by the Salem climbers and also climbers from the Centre Excursionista de Pedreguer and Grup Espeleo Gata.

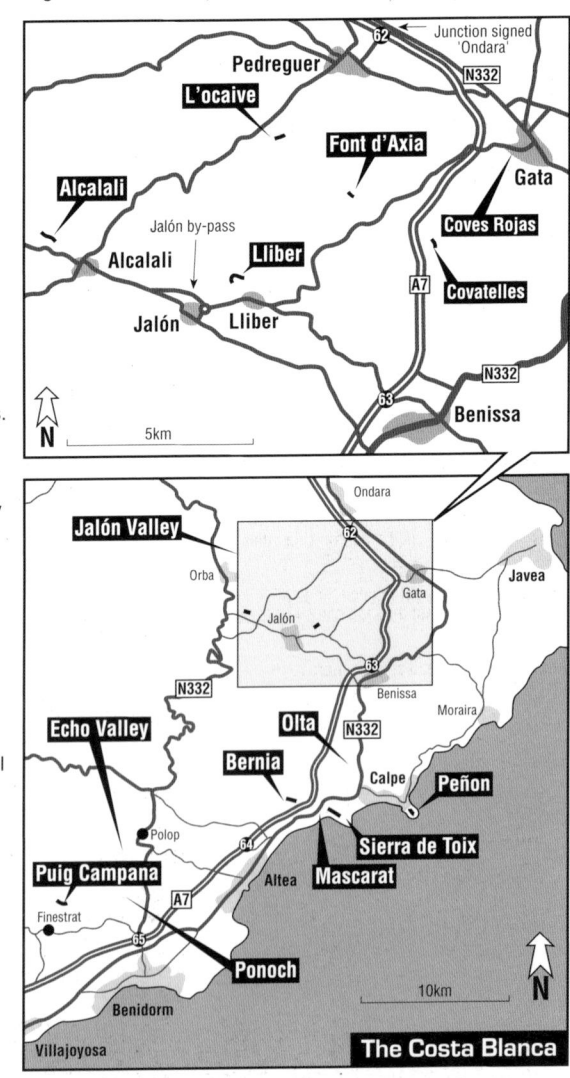

# COSTA BLANCA - The Jalón Valley

## Alcalalí

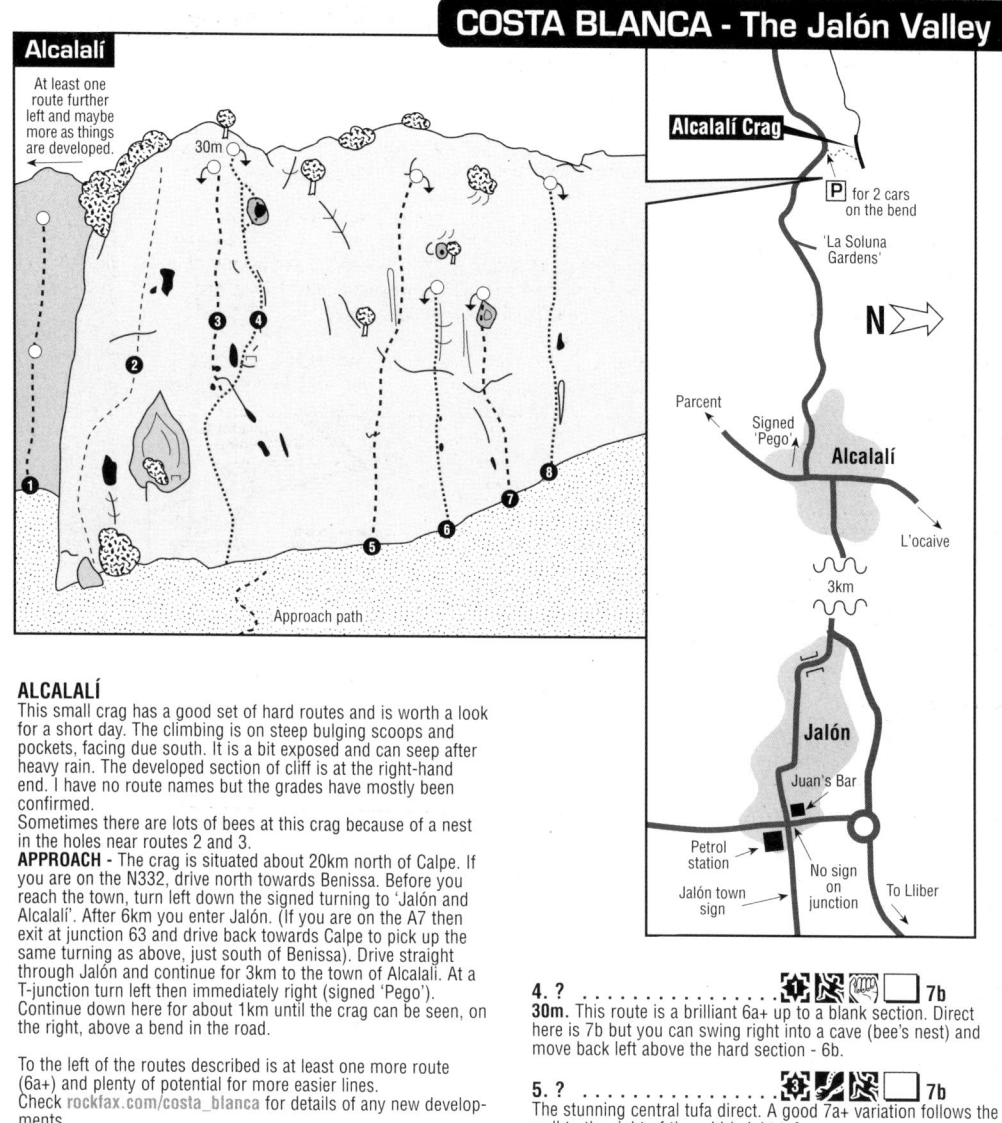

At least one route further left and maybe more as things are developed.

## ALCALALÍ

This small crag has a good set of hard routes and is worth a look for a short day. The climbing is on steep bulging scoops and pockets, facing due south. It is a bit exposed and can seep after heavy rain. The developed section of cliff is at the right-hand end. I have no route names but the grades have mostly been confirmed.
Sometimes there are lots of bees at this crag because of a nest in the holes near routes 2 and 3.

**APPROACH** - The crag is situated about 20km north of Calpe. If you are on the N332, drive north towards Benissa. Before you reach the town, turn left down the signed turning to 'Jalón and Alcalalí'. After 6km you enter Jalón. (If you are on the A7 then exit at junction 63 and drive back towards Calpe to pick up the same turning as above, just south of Benissa). Drive straight through Jalón and continue for 3km to the town of Alcalalí. At a T-junction turn left then immediately right (signed 'Pego'). Continue down here for about 1km until the crag can be seen, on the right, above a bend in the road.

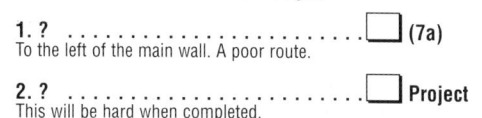

To the left of the routes described is at least one more route (6a+) and plenty of potential for more easier lines. Check rockfax.com/costa_blanca for details of any new developments.

The routes are described from left to right.

**1. ?** .................................... (7a)
To the left of the main wall. A poor route.

**2. ?** .................................... Project
This will be hard when completed.

**3. ?** .................................... 7b+
30m. A sustained start leads to a technical and fingery upper wall.

**4. ?** .................................... 7b
30m. This route is a brilliant 6a+ up to a blank section. Direct here is 7b but you can swing right into a cave (bee's nest) and move back left above the hard section - 6b.

**5. ?** .................................... 7b
The stunning central tufa direct. A good 7a+ variation follows the wall to the right of the mid-height tufa.

**6. ?** .................................... 6b+
Brilliant pulls between big pockets.

**7. ?** .................................... 6c
Finish above a little cave. Low in the grade.

**8. ?** .................................... 7a
A hard start up the elephants trunk which is very hard if you climb direct (there is a right-hand variant). Fine climbing up the wall above with another tricky move by the 5th bolt. This upper move can be by-passed bringing the whole route down to 6c+.

South facing wall
15m to 30m routes
Best grades - 6c to 7b+

# COSTA BLANCA - The Jalón Valley

Lliber - Left

## LLIBER

Lliber (pronounced 'zjee - bear') is the best of the crags in the Jalón Valley. The climbing is generally vertical, or gently overhanging, on broccoli-covered rock which is hard wearing on the fingers. It faces east, receiving the morning sun. The right-hand side is steep enough to give dry climbing in light rain and it is very sheltered from the wind.

**APPROACH** - The crag is situated about 20km north of Calpe. If you are on the N332, drive north towards Benissa. Before you reach the town, turn left down the signed turning to 'Jalón and Alcalalí'. (If you are on the A7 then exit at junction 63 and drive back towards Calpe to pick up the same turning as above, just south of Benissa). As you enter Jalón there is a petrol station on the left and 'Juan's Bar' opposite. Turn right here and right again at the next roundabout. As soon as you pass the Lliber town sign, cross a bridge and turn sharp left down a ramp which leads to a water channel. Drive down here and cross the ford. Continue towards the crag, which is obvious ahead of you on the left, and park by the almond groove. Don't be fooled by the huge red cliff that you can see from the road, this is rotten, loose and full of birds and bird shit.

The main climbing is on the left-hand wall which is terminated by a short grey slab left of a diagonal corner.

**1. Como un loco** .............. 6a
The left-hand side of the slab.

**2. Sansón sin pilila** ......... 5+
Direct up the slab.

**3. Sansón y dalila** .......... 6a
The slab just left of the corner.

**4. La desuirgada** ............ 6b+
Fingery wall and bulge. It can be started from the next route using the desperate 'blob' start but that is pointless.

**5. Agárrate como puedas** .. 7a
Use the glued-on blob at the start to gain better holds above. Usually requires a dyno. Impossible for the short?

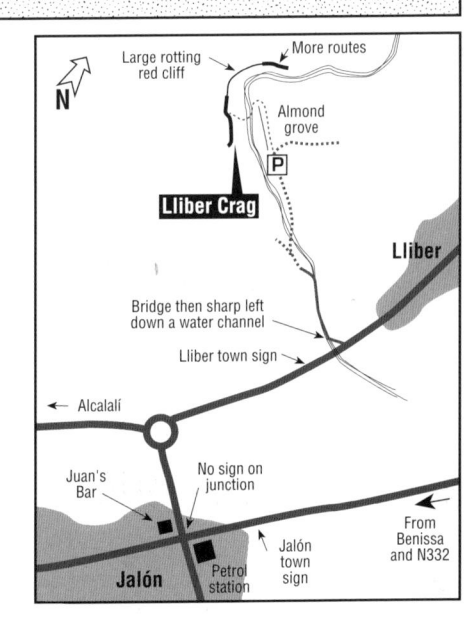

**6. Puta hili** ................... 6c+

**7. Toro salvaje** .............. 7a
Start behind a big tree.

**8. Hall 9000** ................. 6c+
Direct through a niche on painful small holds.

**9. El pas de la dent** ........ 6a

**Lliber - Right**

**COSTA BLANCA - The Jalón Valley**

The best climbing is on the very steep wall right of an open corner. The slope under the crag is terraced.

**10. Through the Magic Door** . . . . . . 6a
Climb the wall right of a corner onto a hanging grey slab. There is a loose flake near the top.

**11. Soc una aguileta** . . . . . . . . 6b
Finish at the same lower-off as above which also involves negotiaiting the loose flake.

**12. Techno manía** . . . . . . . . . . 7a+
The wall behind the tree has a hard finish over the roof. It is easier to go left at the roof.

**13. Tarzan de las monodedos** . . 7b
Very technical.

**14. La bella** . . . . . . . . . . . 7b
Superb climbing but probably impossible for the short. 1st bolt removed.

**15. La bestia** . . . . . . . . . . 7b+
Good climbing but too close to the corner.

**16. Sulacco** . . . . . . . . . . . 7a+
The wall right of the corner is fingery. 1st bolt removed.

**17. Caballo loco** . . . . . . . . 7a+
Make a hard start up a left facing groove. The wall above is much easier.

**18. Muévete como un huracán** 6c
The fine arete left of a corner. A tricky start with a hard third clip.

**19. Siempre en alguna parte** . . . . 6c
The wall right of the corner. Name at the bottom.

**20. Lliberpool** . . . . . . . . . . . 6b
Brilliant name, brilliant route! Long and sustained but never desperate but it is becoming polished.

**21. ?** . . . . . . . . . . . . . . . . 7b
A hard move at half-height, either dyno for a blob or climb to the left of it.

**22. ?** . . . . . . . . . . . . . . . 7b+
The bulging arete.

**23. ?** . . . . . . . . . . . . . . . 7c
Awkward, technical and sustained.

**24. ?** . . . . . . . . . . . . . . . 6c+
Superb climbing with a tricky finish to a strange hold. The lower section is also hard. See photo on page 26.

**25. ?** . . . . . . . . . . . . . . . 7c
Another hard route over the narrow roof.

**26. ?** . . . . . . . . . . . . . . . 7c+
The wall and roof on small holds then the blunt arete above.

**27. ?** . . . . . . . . . . . . . . . 6c
A hard move near the bottom and sustained in its upper section.

There are five more routes to the right of the rotten red cliff which are of questionable quality This section faces west and receives the sun until much later in the day.

The first route is *El Ultimo Hurcan* - **6c**, to the right is *Sir Lawcelot* - **7a+**. Above these two is a short pitch starting from a ledge, *La Corrida* - **6a+**. Some distance further right and below are two more routes, *Arthur Conan Doyler* - **6a+** and *Gangrejos a Gogo* - **6c**.

East facing wall
5m to 15m routes
Best grades - 5+ to 7a

# COSTA BLANCA - The Jalón Valley

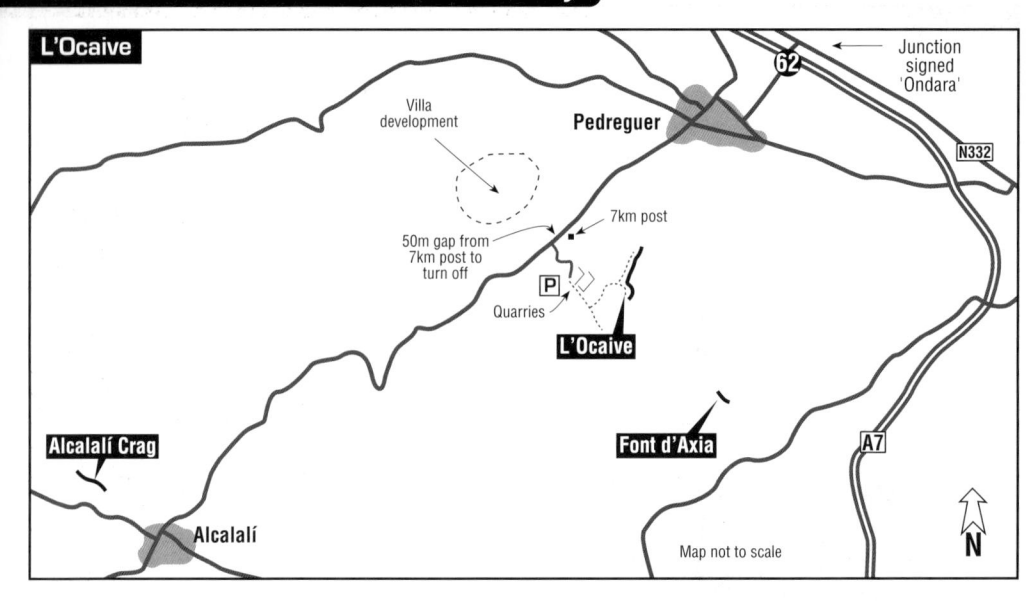

## L'OCAIVE

L'ocaive is a large and slightly vegetated crag with some scope for further development. Most of the existing routes are in the lower grades and give pleasant climbing on pocketed slabs. The most impressive feature of the crag, a large overhanging bay on its right-hand side, only yields a couple of routes at present. Most of the crag faces northwest so it is a good spot for hot weather but can be bitterly cold if there is a wind blowing.

**APPROACH (from North) -** L'ocaive is southwest of the small towns of Ondara and Pedreguer, which is just off the A7 to the north of Benissa and Calpe. Turn off the A7 at junction 62, signed 'Ondara', which takes you onto the N332. Turn right towards Gata, then right again towards Pedreguer. On the edge of Pedreguer turn left (inland) at a small roundabout towards 'Llosa de Camancho' and Alcalali. As you head down this road keep and eye on the kilometre posts and 50m after you pass the 7km post turn left drive up a short road to park on a grotty flat area (sometimes used as a firing range). The crag should be clearly visible on the hillside above you. From here follow a vague path up the hill taking one left turn, to the foot of the cliff.

**APPROACH (from South) -** An alternative to trying to negotiate Pedreguer is to approach from Alcalalí. This is also logical if you are combining L'ocaive with one of the other Jalón Valley crags. Just keep an eye on the km posts and turn right 50m before the 7km post.

### SECTOR HIDDEN ROCK
The first routes are on a scrappy little leaning block above an animal enclosure down and left of the main cliff.
There is a bolt line on the back of the leaning block which looks hard. The three routes described are on the less-impressive front.

**1. Lagarto cachas** .......... 7b+
A powerful but worthless boulder problem on tiny edges.

**2. Sins of Life** ............ 6c
Short and difficult.

**3. The Fly** ................. 6a
Short and easier.

### SECTOR PLACAS TOCHAS
The first routes are on the left-hand toe of the wall.

**4. Cuerpo de mujer** .......... 6a
1) 4+. Can be done on its own.
2) 6a. A good continuation.

**5. La esquina asesina** ....... 6a+
1) 4+. As for the previous route.
2) 6a+. A good slab leading to a hard finish.

**6. ?** ...................... 4+
The chimney/groove.

**7. Aluncina con la esquina** ... 5+
A good long pitch. This can be connected to the lower-off of route 5 for a good extension. There is a thread for protection.

# COSTA BLANCA - The Jalón Valley

L'Ocaive

**8. Si ta cais ta codes** ............ 6a

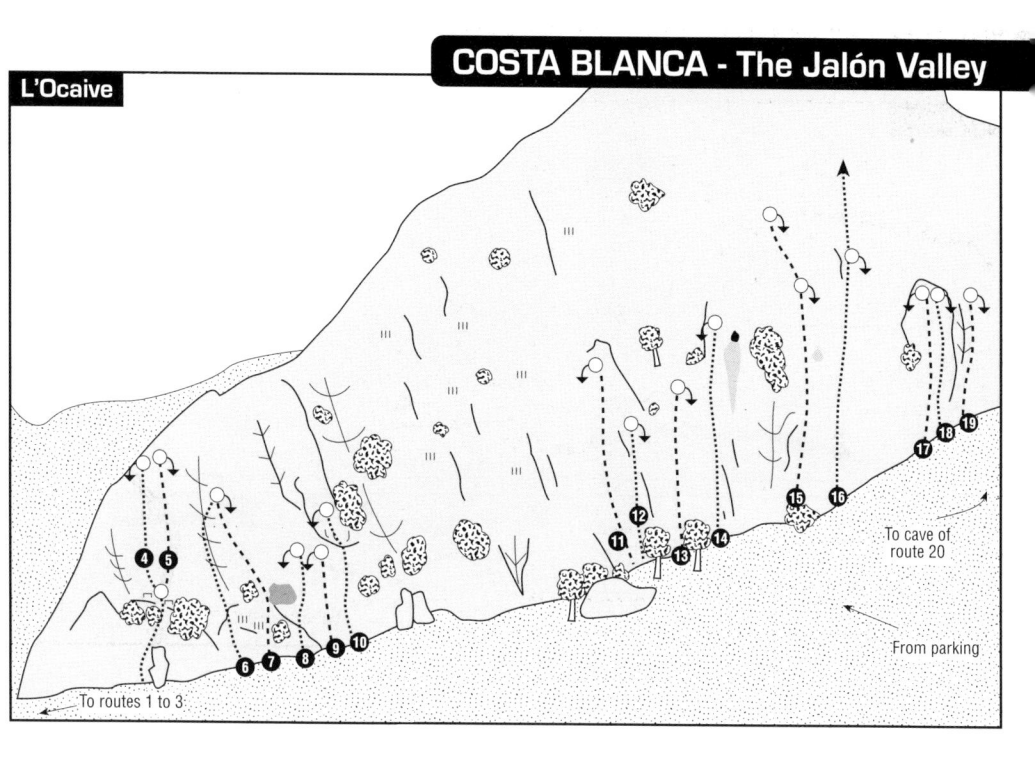

**9. No maclaro** ............... 6a

**10. El grajo del carajo** ....... 6b
A good slab on small pockets and edges, with a tricky bulge to finish.

## SECTOR MANIATICOS
The next routes are 20m up the slope, just right of a big rock below the face.

**11. Placa manía** ............ 6a
A long pitch which can be tricky if you follow it directly although there is a groove left of the upper bulge which is hard to avoid. There may be a 2nd pitch at 6a.

**12. No t'as vares** ............ 5+
Slab past two cracks.

**13. Amparito no me to el pito** .... 6a

**14. Hombres de papel** ........ 6a+
A tricky finish left of the orange streak.

**15. El medio de icaro** .... 7a,6b+
Start up the rib right of a scoop. A long rambling first pitch leads to a thin wall high up.

**16. 96 octanes** ........... 6a+
1) 6a+. Better climbing than it looks
2) 6a. ....especially if you continue up the second pitch.

## SECTOR LA ARANA
Further up the slope are three poor routes around a scrappy corner at the right edge of the butress.

**17. El Incrédulo** ............... 6a

**18. Chorazón salado** ........... 6a+

**19. Ella la araña** ............... 5+
Climb the chossy corner.

The next route starts at the back of the huge bay up and right.

**20. Los primos** ........... 6c+,6c+
Climb just left of the overhanging crack system on crumbly orange rock. Spectacular! There are bees in one of the holes.

**21. ?** .................... (7c/8a)
Up thin tufas starting from a cave entrance down and right of *Los primos*.

NW facing wall
5m to 30m routes
Best grades - 5+ to 6c

# COSTA BLANCA - The Jalón Valley

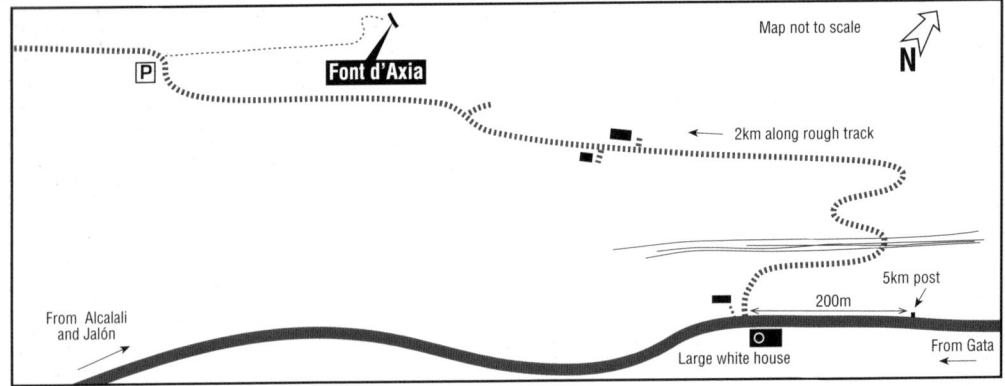

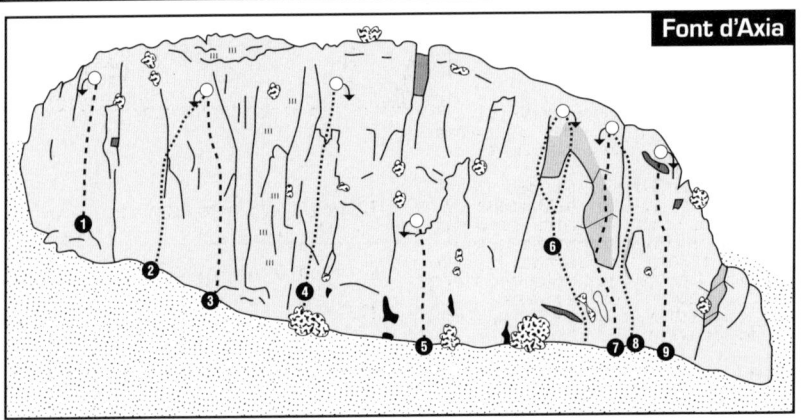

## FONT d'AXIA

Font d'Axia is not a great venue but it is in a useful location and has some routes which may be of interest to beginners or people who are just starting to lead. It faces southwest and is relatively sheltered from the wind.

**APPROACH** - Approach from Lliber. Locate a small turn off 200m west of the 5km post on the Gata to Lliber road on the map on page 70. This track is opposite a house with a turret. Follow the track for about 2km, across a river and keeping left at the only junction. Continue to a bend by a track and park opposite this then walk up it to the crag which you may have had a glimpse of on the drive in.

**1. Izquierda ruta** . . . . . . . . . . . . . . . . 3+
The best of the three easier routes.

**2. Savina** . . . . . . . . . . . . . . . . . . . . 4

**3. El paval** . . . . . . . . . . . . . . . . . . . 4

**4. Perell el cacaolat** . . . . . . . . . . . . 5+
Tricky moves on the pillar.

**5. ?** . . . . . . . . . . . . . . . . . . . . . . . 6b
Poor short route.

**6. La Ley del canteo** . . . . . . . . . . 6c
The left-hand finish is an easier 6b+.

**7. El drak** . . . . . . . . . . . . . . . . . . 5
The best route here. There is a half-height lower-off to give a short but unsatisfying 4. There is a loose block near the top.

**8. Les zapatelles del pastor** . . . . . . 5+
Corner past a big flake. Loose block finish.

**9. Frizer se transforma** . . . . . . . . . 6b
Bulging rib to recess.

West facing wall
10m to 15m routes
Best grades - 3+ to 6c

# COSTA BLANCA - The Jalón Valley

## COVATELLES
A small and rather insignificant crag is close to the motorway south of Gata. Worth a visit for the enthusiast.
**APPROACH** - The crag is approached from the road from Gata to Lliber and Jalón. To get on this road, drive north on the N332 to Gata (about 30 minutes from Calpe) or exit the A7 at junction 63 to pick up the N332. Once in Gata, turn left at a sign to 'Lliber' (just after the 'Javea' turning). The road doubles back down a straight section. Turn right at the bottom and head out of the town. Pass under the motorway, then after 2km, turn left (signed 'Cami de Gorges') after crossing a river. Go down a track and take a right fork under the motorway. Park just beyond. From here a path leads to the crag above.
**THE ROUTES** - There is a group of routes at the left-hand end of the crag. From the left they are - **6a+, 7a+, 5+, 6c**; then up and right - **5, 6b+**. Further right is a **5+** then a **5**. At the right-hand end of the crag is a horizontal cave; to the left of this are some more routes - **6a, 6a, 6a+** and **6b+**.

## COVES ROJES
This is a small, steep and sheltered crag above a riverbed just outside Gata. The central section of the crag, around a small cave, is quite good although the right-hand end isn't very impressive and it is all very 'urban'.
**APPROACH** - As for Covatelles. Take the road to Lliber out of Gata. As you head out of town you will see the 'Restaurante El Corral del Pato' on the right. Turn left here and go up a short hill. Follow the road leftwards then turn right and park in the lay-by overlooking the riverbed. The crag is underneath you. Follow the path at the left-hand end of the lay-by, past the inevitable barking dogs, then steeply down to the river bed. The routes are described from left to right starting on the far left below a large buttress split by a diagonal line of....

1. Beyond the City . . . . . . . . . . . . ?
2. La abeja maya . . . . . . . . . . . . . ?
Left-hand side of the main central buttress.
3. Vigen Asesina . . . . . . . . 7b+
The orange streak up the steep wall.
4. L'obila . . . . . . . . . . . . . . . . . . 5+
Right of a project. The steep left wall of a cave.
5. Sin mas ni menos . . . . . . . . 6b+
The best route at the crag. Climb spectacularly out of the cave.
6. Pajaro de hierro . . . . . . . . . 6b+
Tackle the short steep wall on enormous buckets.

The next four bolt lines are very poor. The section of rock is covered with glued-on stuff. Further right are some more routes.

7. S.C.E . . . . . . . . . . . . . . . . . . 5+
8. ? . . . . . . . . . . . . . . . . . . . . . . 6c
The steep wall after a tricky start.
9. Kao . . . . . . . . . . . . . . . . . . . 6a
The white streak.
10. De chuguita poco costa . . . . . . . . 6a
Wall to the right.
11. Eso es todo . . . . . . . . . . . . . . . . 6b+
12. ? . . . . . . . . . . . . . . . . . . . . . . . . 6a
Up the flakes to the right.

There are then four poor routes up the short wall to the right. Names and grades are unknown.

The next routes described are on the first bit of rock you see when approaching the crag.

13. Greticas . . . . . . . . . . . . . . . . . 6a
Climbs up near the arete behind the tree.
14. Bokimoll . . . . . . . . . . . . . . . . . 5b
15. Riendas sueltas . . . . . . . . . . . . 5+
16. La cachonda . . . . . . . . . . . . . . 6b
17. La fisura loca . . . . . . . . . . . . . 5+
Up the obvious flake crack.
18. Comas flotas . . . . . . . . . . . . . . 6c+
19. El gran paso . . . . . . . . . . . . . . 6a
20. Para herniaos . . . . . . . . . . . . . 5
21. Todo riesgo . . . . . . . . . . . . . . ?
Very sad indeed!

**Coves Rojes**
East facing wall, 5m to 15m routes
Best grades - 5+ to 6b+

# OLTA

The impressive ridge of rock which overlooks Calpe has a few routes on one small section just left of centre of the southern face. The rock is excellent and the views over Calpe are stunning with the Penon making a magnificent backdrop which is much-photographed on the superb arete route of *Tai Chi*. The other top drawer route is the stunning *Super Tufa Groove* which is one of the best 6b+ routes in the area.

The rock is quite sharp and a day here tends to take its toll on your finger tips. Some of the harder routes tend to have improved or fully-created holds which spoilt the experience a bit, but mostly the moves and climbing are excellent.

Hopefully one day more routes will be climbed up on this ridge since the potential of the much larger right-hand end hasn't been touched yet.

## ASPECT AND CLIMATE

The crag faces southeast and catches plenty of sun although in Winter the sun goes off the crag in the early afternoon. It is high and exposed to any wind.

## APPROACH

First you need to get onto the road to the 'Estacion F.C.' which leaves the N332 from the main Calpe junction. Getting onto this road is not that easy if you are approaching from the south. First you need to either turn off into Calpe and go around the first roundabout to come back under the N332, or over-shoot the junction and turn around so that you are coming south on the N332. Drive to the Station and cross the tracks. From the station follow the brown signs to 'Monte Olta' and 'Zona de acampada' and park by the (free) camping site. From here head up the hill to a track, turn left and walk along to a derelict water tank. A rough track leads from here up the hillside to the crag, which is visible above.

The old approach reached the water tank before parking. The track has deteriorated and the locals have decide not to allow access along here anymore. However there are reports that this approach is now open again.

## THE ROUTES

All the routes have been developed by Calpe resident Jens Muenchberg.

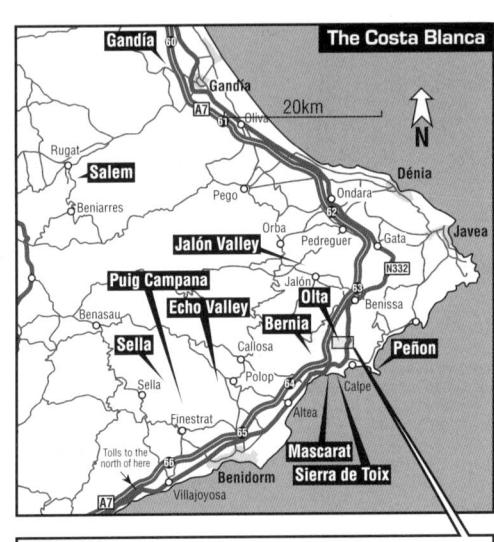

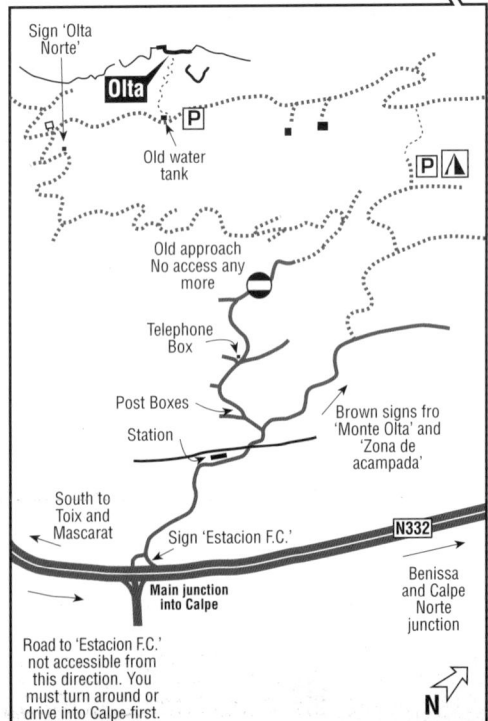

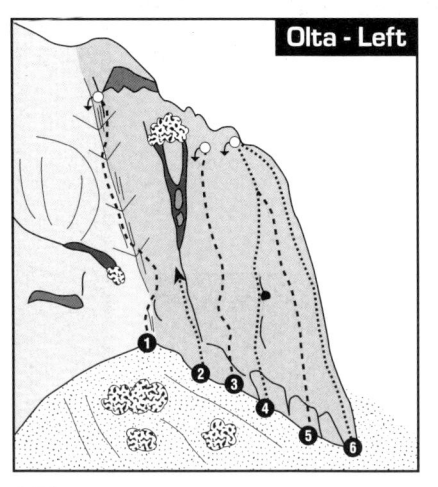

# COSTA BLANCA - Olta

**Olta - Left**

**7. Spanish Eyes** .......... 6b
The small bulge is the crux.

**8. Fantasía encanto** ........ 7b+
A thin slab and chipped wall.

**9. Ninja** ................ 7c
The tufa and (chipped?) wall above.

**10. Hillside Avenue** .......... 6c
An artificial line up bulges with a chipped finish.

**11. Halt Mich** .............. 6c+
Another line-less chipped route.

**12. Hola Olta** ............. 6c
Better climbing up the steepening slab.

**13. Vamos** ................ 5+
A hard start up the slab then move right above.

**14. Best of '95** ............. 5
A good slab pitch.

**15. Du Darfst** .............. 5
The best of the easier stuff up the clean slab.

**16. Turrón** ................ 5
Shared finish with *Du Darfst*.

**17. Das Buch der 5 Ringe** ........ 5
Hard if you go too far left - 6a.

**18. Touch Me Softly** .......... 4+
The corner.

**19. Christmas Dreams** .......... 5+
Very short wall with one hard move.

**20. Breakthrough** ............ 4
Just off the topo.

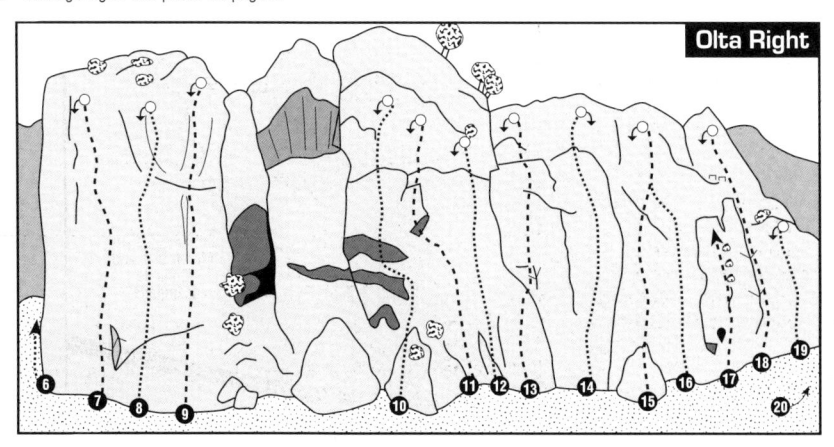

## OLTA
The largest feature of the crag is the huge white groove on its left-hand side. The wall further left looks to be made of excellent, climbable rock.

**1. Tufa-Groove** .......... 6b+
30m. Stunning climbing with less helpful holds than you expect but not that desperate. Steep for the grade - look where you end up on the lower-off!

**2. Tao** ................ 6a
30m. The crack leading to a wide chimney.

**3. Wings of Freedom** ..... 7a+

**4. Ki** ................ 6c

**5. Mulan** .............. 7a+
A thin eliminate with a reachy crux.

**6. Tai chi** ............. 6b
The superb arete. Probably 6c+ if you climb direct past the second bolt - most go right. See photo on page 3.

**Olta Right**

SE facing wall
10m to 30m routes
Best grades - 4+ to 6c

79

# PEÑON d'IFACH

One of the most striking landmarks in the whole of the Costa Blanca is the stunning 300m tower of the Peñon d'Ifach which towers over Calpe. The subject of the majority of the area's postcards must surely attract every climber's eye and those who have attempted routes here will know that the climbing does not disappoint.

The South Face of the Peñon is the more extensive of the two climbing areas. This huge wall rises up above an approach slope with a vertical, orange wall leading upwards to a top half riddled with caves, overhangs and groove systems. Many long routes find their way up the complex face to finish satisfyingly on the summit of the Peñon. There are a number of low to mid grade challenges which are popular classics requiring an early start and a decent rack of gear - *Valencianos* and *Vía UBSA* are examples. However the really big ticks are the superb, fully-bolted epics like *Costa Blanca, El Navigante* and *New Dimensions*. There are few sport routes to compare with these in the whole of the Costa Blanca.

The other climbing area is the North Face which faces inland and overlooks an environmental centre. The focus of interest created by the centre has led to a partial climbing ban on the North Face and an attempt to ban climbing on the entire mountain. Only the intervention of local climbers has prevented this happening.

All the routes are long multi-pitch climbs and will require 5 to 7 hours or more for a leisurely ascent although there are reports of people taking as long as 11 hours on *Gómez-Cano*. The fully bolted routes are well-equipped with double bolt belays making an abseil descent possible from most should things turn against you. The older classics are more sparsely equipped with fixed gear of variable quality. On these routes a decent rack is mandatory. A suitable rack would be a single set of wires and the odd large hex, with at least 15 quickdraws. The pitches tend to be long so it is advisable to take two 9mm ropes to help with rope drag. This is also useful if you have to abseil off at any stage. The rock is of variable quality. The smoother orange rock can polish to a high sheen and there is some loose material especially on the lower pitches. It is worth wearing a helmet, especially on the easier and more popular routes, since there is a lot of loose rock around. A top-tip to avoid rock fall is make sure you are on the mountain early so that there are fewer people above you! However you must also be very dainty with your feet on the ledges.

## ASPECT AND CLIMATE

The main climbing faces southwest and is warmed by the sun from mid-morning onwards, although its exposed position on a peninsula means it can get very breezy . It can also get cripplingly hot so carry water and sun cream. The North Face is a different proposition since it is mostly in the shade.

## APPROACH

If you are based in Calpe, you will know where the Peñon is. If you are driving up from further south, then take the Altea turn off the A7 (junction 64) and drive through the Mascarat gorge on the N332. Soon after turn off towards Calpe. Drive down this road which skirts the left edge of the town, past a supermarket on the left. Continue past all the half-built tower blocks towards the Peñon ahead. When the road veers around to the left, turn right (signed 'Peñon'). Keep going to where the road forks and take the right-hand branch. Drive down here to the harbour side and park. See route pages for approaches from here.

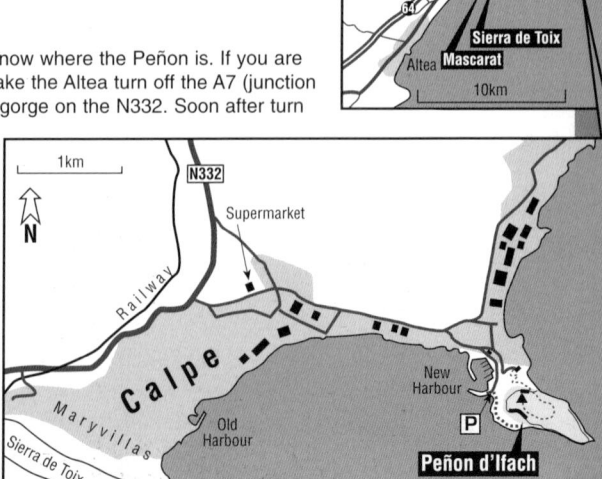

**North Face**

**COSTA BLANCA - Peñon d'Ifach**

Area of large rockfall. New line possible to the right.

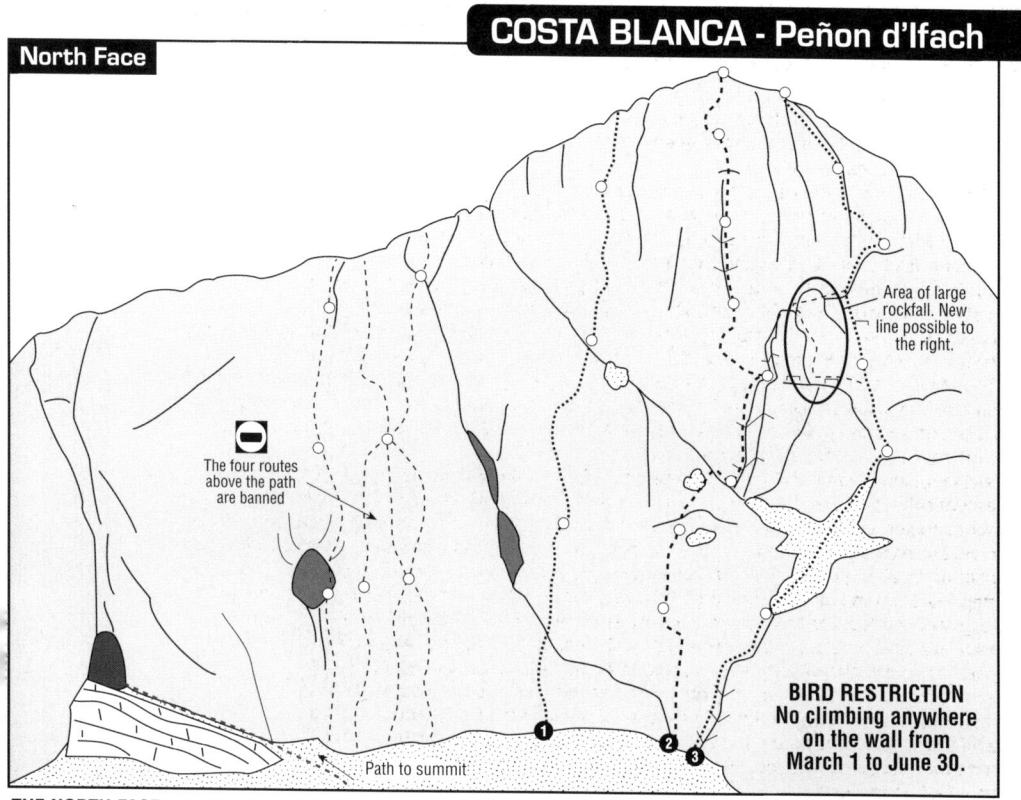

The four routes above the path are banned

Path to summit

**BIRD RESTRICTION**
No climbing anywhere on the wall from March 1 to June 30.

## THE NORTH FACE
This is the large white face which overlooks the town. Unfortunately the best climbing is banned. There are three long routes on the big wall to the right. The whole face is covered by a bird ban from April 1 to June 30.
**APPROACH** - Follow the main summit path from the visitor centre. This path zig-zags up the hill eventually swinging back left below the banned area. Just before this a little track leads up rightwards into a large bay where the routes are.
**DESCENT** - Walk down the main path which leads back through the tunnel below the North Face.

◼ **ACCESS** - NO CLIMBING FROM 1 MARCH TO 30 JUNE BECAUSE OF NESTING BIRDS.

The banned routes on the magnificent white wall above the path are all high quality routes with some fixed gear. From left to right they are: *Verde esmerelda* - 6a, *Taberna del puerto* - 6c+, *Asignatura pendiente* - 6b, *Vampiro* - 6c+.

The first described route is a bit of an unknown quantity up the wall towards the left-hand side of the bay.

### 1. Sinfonía de las Gaviotas . 6b+
I have not found anyone who has done this route but it is well recommended in the local topos. It is the only line on this side of the bay. Take a full rack since the fixed gear is probably a bit sparse.
*FA. Jorge Garcia, F.Tejeda*

The next two routes start by a chimney near the right-hand side of the bay, left of a large buttress dropping from the summit.

### 2. Roxy . . . . . . . . . . . . . . . . 6b
A scrappy first few pitches lead to an excellent finish high on the wall. Take a full rack with some large stuff.
1) **5, 30m.** Climb leftwards from the chimney to a crack. Follow this past to a ledge on the left.
2) **5, 20m.** Climb the corner above.
3) **5, 30m.** Climb the wall to the ramp which crosses the face. Descend rightwards to belay in a corner.
4) **5+, 30m.** Wander up the wall above then move right into a corner and follow this to a ledge.
5) **6b, 25m.** Traverse left in a good position then move up and back right to a crack. Hard moves lead up this to a stance.
6) & 7) **6a, 50m.** Follow the groove and crack upwards to an easing in angle. Easy climbing remains to the summit.
*FA. A.Ballard, J.M.Gonzalez 1981*

### 3. Pany . . . . . . . . . . . . . . . . 5
The most popular route on this face has suffered a rock fall recently. A new line has been found but it is a good but harder and the climbing is still a bit dirty low on the route. Take a full rack. The stances are mostly geared. Start at the chimney mentioned above.
1) **4, 25m.** Climb the chimney to a good ledge on the right.
2) **50m.** Bush-bash up to the top of the buttress on the right.
3) **3, 20m.** Climb a rib above.
4) **4+/5, 35m.** Climb straight up the wall to a ledge and continue to a stance on the top of the second buttress.
5) **4+, 30m.** Climb the slab on the left to reach a fine crack.
6) **4+, 30m.** Follow the crack to easy ground.
*FA. Panyella, Salas 1955*

North facing wall
200m multi-pitch routes
Grades - 5 to 6b+

# COSTA BLANCA - Peñon d'Ifach

**Valencianos Area**

Two more easy pitches to the top.

Start of routes ❷ to ❾

Photo: Alan James

82

# COSTA BLANCA - Peñon d'Ifach

## THE SOUTH FACE
The main area of interest for climbers is the magnificent South Face with its many superb, long and intricate climbs. The more popular routes are all frequently climbed and reasonably well geared, though there is still much loose rock. A helmet, and plenty of caution, is advised for the routes which start up *Valencianos* and the corner of *Diedro UBSA* since both these routes form large natural funnels channelling rock onto the lower pitches. **PLEASE TAKE GREAT CARE WHEN CLIMBING THESE ROUTES NOT TO DISLODGE ANY ROCK.** Another good idea is to be on the route by 8:30 am then you will be above most parties and may be able to finish the route in the shade.
**APPROACH** - From the harbour walk around the flat road along the waterfront just before the end of the track. Scramble steeply back leftwards along the base of the cliff.
**DESCENT** - From the summit follow the well-built footpath which zig-zags downhill and through a short tunnel, to emerge below the North Face, just above the visitor centre. This takes around 20 minutes.

## VALENCIANOS AREA
The first route follows the diagonal ramp, below the huge dome, leading to the prominent ridge at the top of the *Valencianos* slab.

### 1. Same ............ 6b
Although the climbing is good, and the chimney is an 'experience', the route is spoilt slightly by lack of grade consistency. Start by a cave below a crack system which leads to a rightwards trending ramp. The first two pitches can be by-passed on the right at 5. There are some bolts but take a small rack.
1) 6a+, 15m. Gain and climb the crack to the ramp.
2) 6b, 25m. The crux pitch up the corner above.
3) 4, 20m. Wander easily up and right to below a large chimney.
4) 6a, 25m. Climb the crack into the chimney and continue up this to an enclosed stance.
5) 5, 25m. Keep thrashing up the chimney until it opens out. Belay above on easier angled rock.
6) 4, 30m. Follow the slab to the ridge. Join and finish up the last three pitches of *Valencianos*, or make 4 careful abseils back to base.
FA. J.L.Moreno, Jordi Palas, Santi Llop

The shared start of routes 2 to 9 is in the centre of the bay, at the highest point of the approach slope. The name *Via Valencianos* is painted on the rock to the left.

### 2. Valencianos ............ 5+
The classic, and popular, easy route up the face. Although it is a big expedition, it is possible to retreat by rappel if things turn against you. There are some bolts and pegs but take a full rack.
1) 3, 35m. Climb first rightwards, then back left and to the base of the big white slab. Belay bolts on the left.
2) 3, 40m. Traverse/walk leftwards past bushes to gain a ledge running back right above the slab and belay directly above your second.
3) 5+, 30m. Climb the blocky corner at the right-hand end of the ledge past 2 bolts (crux). Move left to belay at the base of the upper slab.
4) 4, 20m. Climb left onto the slab to a bush belay.
5) 4, 45m. One long pitch leads to a superb belay on the ridge.
6) 4, 30m. Walk along the ridge then traverse to the left and climb a flake/crack to a bulge. Belay above on a spike.
7) 20m. Climb rightwards, taking the easiest line. Belay in a notch.
8) 30m. Easy climbing leads to the summit.
FA. A.Martí, M.Gómez, A.Botella, A.Tebar 1958

### 3. Polvos mágicos ....... 6a+
A direct version of *Valencianos*. It is possible to escape onto *Valencianos* at several points on the route, should the going get too tough. Take a full rack.
1) 2+, 35m. Pitch 1 of *Valencianos*.
2) 6a+, 25m. Climb the sustained, and slippery corner direct.
3) 5+, 30m. Pitch 3 of *Valencianos*.
4) 4, 20m. Meander up easy ground to gain the right edge of the upper slab, beneath the steeper headwall. Belay in a small recess.
5) 5, 30m. Follow the corner above to the ridge.
6) 4, 20m. Climb a groove to the ridge and then move left to easy ground.
7) & 8) 50m. The last two pitches of *Valencianos*.
FA. Pablo Ros, Miguel Devesa, Roy Valera

### 4. Virginia Díez ........ 6b
A short, bolted direct finish to *Polvos Magicos*. Well-positioned but a lot of effort to get there.
1) to 4) 6a+, 110m. As for *Polvos Magicos*.
5) 5, 25m. Follow the bolt line up the steep wall above the belay.
6) 6b, 25m. Continue steeply to finish up the prominent groove and watch out for the snake!
DESCENT - Either abseil off, or continue up the ridge to the top.
FA. Jaime Arviza, Miguel Díez 1991

### 5. Sensacion de vivir ..... 6b+
A superb fully-bolted line finishing up the left-hand side of the *Valencianos* slab. Take just 1 krab of wires for the first two pitches.
1) & 2) 6a, 60m. As for *Polvos Magicos*.
3) 6b+, 40m. Move right and tackle the left-hand of two bolted cracks.
4) 6a+, 50m. Climb up and onto the slab, and follow it to the ridge.
DESCENT - Either abseil off, or continue up *Valencianos*.
FA. Jaime Arviza, José Juan Quesada 1991

### 6. Pilar López de Sancho ...... 6c
A spectacular line up the great tower which hangs over the *Valencianos* slab. It shares the same slow start as the last route but the finish makes it worthwhile. Take just 1 krab of wires for the first two pitches.
1) & 2) 6a, 60m. As for *Polvos Magicos*.
3) 6b, 40m. Move right and tackle the right-hand of two bolted cracks.
4) 6c, 50m. Move easily back right and upwards and climb superb hanging groove onto the slab above.
5) & 6) 6b+, 80m. Continue in 2 pitches to the top.
There is another line of bolts breaking left to the arete from the top of pitch 5 at about 6c/7a.
DESCENT - Either abseil off, or follow the easy ridge to reach the summit path.
FA. Jaime Arviza 199?

### 7. Piratas ............... 5+
One of the original lines on this bit of wall. It has easy climbing but is seldom climbed and has much loose rock. Take a full rack.
1) to 3) 5+, 105m. As for *Valencianos*.
4) 4+, 25m. Climb up a corner then follow a ramp rightwards to a belay around an arete.
5) 4+, 20m. Follow the corner to a cave belay.
6) 5, 20m. Leave the cave on its right. Then climb up a crack to a pedestal belay.
7) 4, 25m. Climb the corner past some bushes to another belay.
8) 4+, 20m. Surmount the final bulge and continue to the ridge. Escape more easily to the summit path.
FA. Armand Ballard, J.M.Gonzalez 1979

South facing wall
Multi-pitch routes up to 300m
Best grades - 5+ to 6c

83

# COSTA BLANCA - Peñon d'Ifach

Costa Blanca Area

## COSTA BLANCA AREA
One of the most prominent features of the South Face is the huge pinnacle which forms a long corner on its right-hand side - *Diedre UBSA*. The front of this pinnacle has been developed with two superb, fully-bolted mega-routes which give a great day out for those who demand a bit more from their 'clip-ups'.

### 8. Los miserables ...... 6c+ (6b)
An excellent route with only 1 drawback; that is all the rambling it takes to get to the last two pitches. A two-star alternative is to substitute pitches pitches 3 and 4 of *Pilar López de Sancho*, moving right below the hanging groove to the base of pitch 5 below. Take a krab of wires for the first 2 pitches, and for the belay at the very top.
1) to 3) **6a+, 90m**. As for *Polvos Magicos*.
4) **6b, 20m**. An aimless pitch. Climb up and left, then back right to a ledge below the corner of *Piratas*. Now things improve.
5) **6c+ (6b) 40m**. Climb the wall just right of the corner past one short hard section (easily by-passable by climbing the corner on the left at 6b). Trend up and right to a ledge belay.
6) & 7) **6b, 50m**. Two superb pitches lead straight to the top through some steep bulging caves. A stunning finish.
FA. Jaime Arviza , Emilio Perales 1991

### 9. Costa Blanca .......... 6c+
A brilliant route which is one of the great routes of the area. The climbing is superb and independent and the finish is breathtaking. The route is fully equipped. Start as for *Valencianos*.
1) **15m**. Move up then right along a ledge to belay below a slab.
2) **6b+ 40m**. Climb onto a slab and make some thin moves up leftwards. Easier climbing leads up and right to a belay.
3) **6b, 35m**. Climb directly up the wall and grooves above.
4) **6a, 20m**. Continue to a stance on the edge of the pinnacle.
5) **6b+, 25m**. Step down and across the gully onto the wall behind. Surmount a small overhang and continue up the wall above with some sustained moves and long reaches.
6) **6b, 20m**. Straight up the wall above to the upper large cave.
7) **6c+, 30m**. Swing wildly out of the cave and grind to a halt at at thin move. After a rest above another hard move, involving a blind reach, reaches easier ground.
6a) & 7a) **6b, 50m**. A good way of avoiding the hard last pitch is to traverse the ledge of *Diedro UBSA* to join and finish up *Los miserables* - a three star alternative at 6b+ for the whole route.
FA. Jaime Arviza, Salvador Guerola 1993

### 10. Puto paseo ecológico .. 7a+
This fully-bolted 7-pitch monster has atmospheric and occasionally intimidating climbing. Start midway between *Costa Blanca* and *El Navigante*, below a line of new bolts inn the centre of the huge pillar.
1) **7a+, 30m**. Climb into a crumbly cave. Pull out right and up a leaning, compact wall (crux!). Easier climbing to a belay.
2) **6c, 20m**. Climb up past a rock scar, make a scary move leftwards onto a flake. Climb overlapped walls above to a belay.
3) **6b, 30m**. Climb a scary bulge, then easy ground to a big steep jamming/layback crack which leads to a belay.
4) **6c+, 20m**. A technical and exposed hanging arete leads to a belay on big ledge on top of the pinnacle.
5) **5, 25m**. Step down across the void to gain lovely, easy, smooth jamming cracks. A very pleasant respite.
6) **6c+, 30m**. A brilliant, big overhanging pitch up a band of perfect rock. Make ever-steeper moves up the big corner to a tricky capping roof. Completely out-there!
7) **7a?, 40m**. Bolts lead left towards a thread in a pocket, but there are no holds. Stretch left to clip the bolt out on the wall, and reverse back to base. Then drop down and traverse underneath a perfect top-rope left to pockets in the leaning wall. Lever up these to the aforementioned thread, and follow the thin corner above, past the odd chipped slot, to easy ground and the top. There may be a higher method of doing this traverse.
FA. Unknown but probably Jamie Arviza 1996/7

Belay ledge behind pinnacle

Approach via Polvos magicos

Diedro UBSA

Easy approach

SW facing wall
Multi-pitch routes up to 300m
Best grades - 6b to 7a+

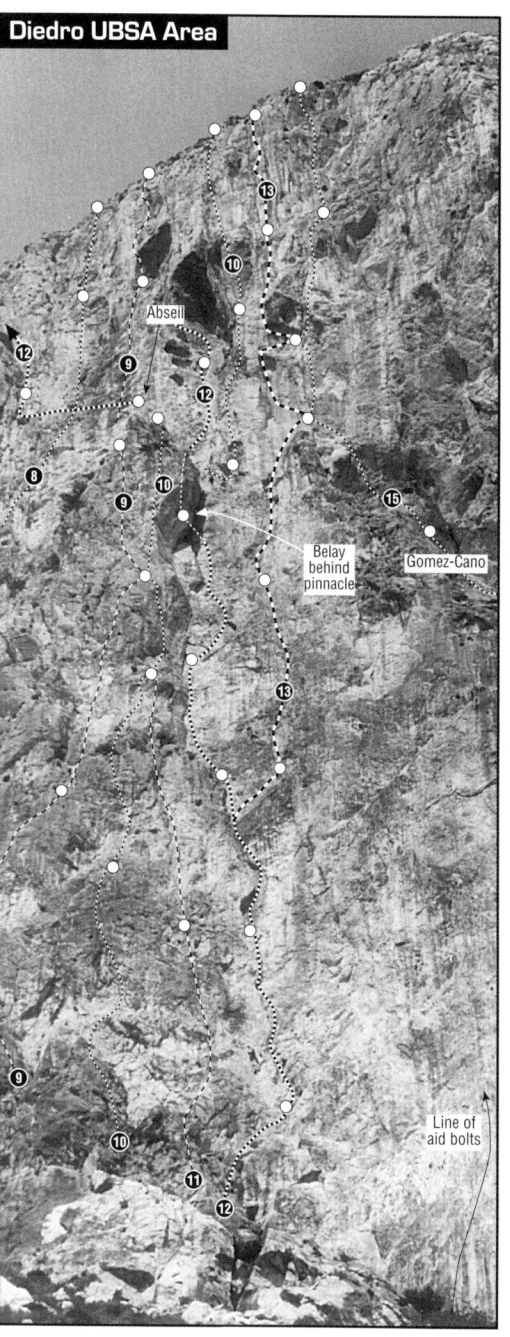

# COSTA BLANCA - Peñon d'Ifach

## Diedro UBSA Area

**11. Me estoy quedandо sin yemas** .......... (7a)
There is another line of bolts on the right-hand side of the pillar which is a free version of an old aid route. No further details are known beyond the rough pitch grades - **1) 7a, 2) 6b**.
It is included here mainly so that you don't mistake it for the last route.

### DIEDRO UBSA AREA
The long groove to the right of the large pinnacle provides the substance of one great old trad route and the start of a great new clip-up.

**12. Diedro UBSA** ........ 5+
A classic expedition which takes the groove to a belay behind the pinnacle and then continues to reach the large cave high up. From here the route escapes by spectacular abseil to gain a ledge and corner on the left which leads to the top. The route is slightly spoilt by the looseness of the first few pitches. Take a small rack although you may only place a couple of runners since there is a variety of fixed gear on the whole length of the route. Start left of the base of the groove by a large cactus bush.
**1) 15m.** Scramble up any line to a belay left of the base of the groove.
**2) 4+, 30m.** Climb awkwardly right to the groove then up to a stance in a chimney.
**3) 5+, 30m.** Continue bridging up the groove (possible stance before a hard section).
**4) 5, 25m.** Another pitch up the corner.
**5) 4, 30m.** Move right onto a slab and then back left and climb up to a shady stance behind a pinnacle.
**6) 5+, 25m.** Climb up to a jammed block and make a long move around this onto the wall above. Climb up and right-wards into a chimney to belay.
**7) & 8) 25m up, 8m down.** Scramble to the top corner of the cave and abseil off the large clump of tat onto a ledge below, swinging slightly left to the twin bolts.
**9) 3+, 30m.** Traverse across into the corner and move up to belay.
**10) 4, 35m.** Climb the corner to gain the ridge. Easy rock leads from here to the summit.
FA. Luis Riguez, Jose Guerrero, Pedro Oliva

**13. El navigante** ..... 7a
A magnificent route which is of the same calibre as *Costa Blanca*, if not even better. It follows a very steep and direct line up the centre of the face to reach a fine position high on the wall. A wire or two may be needed for the section shared with *Diedro UBSA* which also contains some loose rock.
**1) & 2) 4+, 45m.** As for *Diedro UBSA*.
**3) 5+, 15m.** Continue up the corner but step right and climb onto a small black glacis.
**4) 6b 30m.** Climb straight on some weird and wonderful holds and then smoother rocki above.
**5) 6b, 30m.** Another long pitch leads to a belay shared with *Gómez-Cano*.
**6) 6c, 15m.** Tackle a short steep arete (scary) or groove to the left (technical).
**7) 6a, 20m.** Climb the crack and groove above.
**8) 7a, 20m.** Climb the overhanging face above with one hard move (or aid - 6c). Continue on steep, pumpy rock then make an awkward traverse to the left. Scramble up easy rock to the summit.
FA. Salvador Guerola, Emilio Perales, Juan Terradez, Jaime Arviza 1991

SW facing wall
Multi-pitch routes up to 300m
Best grades - 5+ to 7a

# COSTA BLANCA - Peñon d'Ifach

**Gómez-Cano Area**

Line of aid bolts

Photo: Alan James

86 | Afternoon | 20 min | Vertical | Multi-pitch |

# COSTA BLANCA - Peñon d'Ifach

## GOMEZ-CANO AREA
Right of the pillar of *Diedro UBSA* a vast orange wall opens out with some huge caves high up. The lines on this section are all mountaineering-type routes are bigger undertakings than their neighbours to the left. Most have some loose rock and all require a full day with an early start to complete. It is also essential to carry water on the route plus twin 50m ropes in the event that you have to abseil off.

### 14. Manuel ............ 6b
A long route with a fine first pitch, but overshadowed by its neighbours above that. The upper sections have little quality fixed gear and there is much loose rock. Tack a full rack and prepare yourself for an adventure! Start below an attractive flow-stone wall.
1) **6b, 30m.** Follow the tatty gear up the steep wall. Move right to a groove and climb this to a stance.
2) **6a, 20m.** Climb a crack above then swing right to a stance.
3) **6a, 45m.** Climb a rib or groove above to a dodgy flake. This leads to a ledge. Continue up rightwards to the base of the first cave on *Gómez-Cano*.
4) **4, 45m.** Pitch 4 of *Gómez-Cano* but continue to the ledges above and move right through an arch to a poor belay.
5) **5+, 40m.** Follow either of two ribs above to a slab which leads up leftwards to a stance.
6) **5+, 35m.** Climb the chimney above then make hard moves out right. Climb the crack above and belay in a corner.
7) **6a, 30m.** Follow the crack and arete on the right to easier ground.
8) **3, 30m.** Easy ground leads to the top.
*FA. Manfred*

### 14a. Manuel Pitch 1 ........ 6b
The superb first pitch is often done in its own right and has just enough fixed gear. It is 45m long so you will need twin ropes to abseil off.

### 15. Vía Gómez-Cano .. 6b (7b+)
A massive mountaineering classic which takes in some incredible rock at a reasonable grade. It follows a long sweeping diagonal line through the series of huge honeycomb caves high on the wall. Take a full rack of gear including some foot slings for the aid pitch. Also take lots of water. Start below the diagonal crack where the name is painted on the rock.
1) **6a, 30m.** Climb the crack up rightwards, then move onto a flake which comes back left. Make a tricky move out right, past a bolt, to a sloping stance.
2) **5, 15m.** The groove above is awkward.
3) **7b+ or A0/5+, 40m.** Climb up a groove then move rightwards onto the wall. Head up here towards a steep-looking crack. Either climb smoothly up the crack, or swing around like a baboon on the pegs. 1 wire is needed on the peg ladder. Belay at the base of a huge cave.
4) **4, 35m.** Climb to the top left-hand corner of the cave and pull around into a large bay. Scramble across left and make some exposed moves on a short rib around into another cave system and two threads for a belay.
5) **3+, 40m.** Walk leftwards to peg and bolt belay on left edge of cave.
6) **20m.** Scramble up some spikes and flakes to the foot of a corner.
7) **6a, 30m.** Follow the corner then make tricky moves into the crack above. This leads to a stance in a chimney.
8) **6a, 40m.** Squirm up the chimney and the grooves above until you are forced right onto a ramp and an exposed belay.
9) **6b, 40m.** Climb up into a corner and follow this to a bulge. Move around this on undercuts and follow a corner above to easier ground. Scramble to the top from here.
*FA. Miguel Cano, A.Gómez-Bohorquez*

### 16. Línea Mágica ..... 6c+ (7b+)
Another long modern route which gives superb climbing and positions. A small rack is need for the section shared with *Gómez-Cano*. Start just left of *Gómez-Cano*.
1) **6b, 30m.** Climb the bolt line to join *Gómez-Cano*.
2) **& 3) 7b+ or A0/5+, 55m.** As for *Gómez-Cano*.
4) **6b, 20m.** Climb straight up a corner then through the roof of the cave in a position of some excitement! belay on the ledge.
5) **10m.** Traverse easily around the rib to belay beneath a bolt ladder in the next bay.
6) **6a, 40m.** Move up left through a bulge, then rightwards to a groove. Climb this then escaping right at a thread on the arete.
7) **6c+, 35m.** Climb up a wall to reach a steep section then pul through this (hard) to easier ground.
8) **5, 40m.** Scrambling remains.
*FA. Jaime Arviza, Esteban Clemente 1991*

### 17. Anglada Gallego ..... 6a
This long route follows the centre of the main face, between the two huge cave systems. It is a bit of an unknown quantity but judging by the other routes in the area will contain some superb climbing on suspect rock and old fixed gear. The climbing is a bit unbalanced, with all the hard stuff at the bottom. Start down the slope from the crack of *Gómez-Cano*. The name is on the rock.
1) **5+, 35m.** Climb up a wall and crack to a hanging stance.
2) **6a, 40m.** Climb rightwards, then up a wall. At its top move right to a stance in a corner.
3) **20m.** The corner leads easily to a great cave.
4) **5+, 40m.** Some strenuous corners on the left lead to a recess.
5) **5, 25m.** Follow the groove above to a junction with the well bolted line of *Línea Mágica*.
6) **5+, 40m.** Traverse right into a corner and climb it with difficulty at its top. Step left to another *Línea Mágica* belay.
7) **8) & 9) 120m.** Scramble easily up the gully to the col between the two summits of the Peñon.
*FA. J.M.Anglada, M.Angel, G.Gallego*

### 18. New Dimensions .. 7b
This amazing route up the awe-inspiring right-hand side of the vast South Face of the Penon. After a very hard first pitch (7a with aid) it relents and builds to a superb climax on the headwall. Take a small rack for the three easier pitches and prussik loops in case you fall off pitches 8 or 9.
1) **7b (7a min. to frig, E5 6b) 35m.** The line of black bolts is harder than it looks. The crux in the middle leads to a hands-off rest. Take a good breather here since the upper section is harder than it looks. A final hard move gains the belay - phew!
2) **7a, 35m.** Climb straight up the wide crack behind the stance and follow the line over two awkward bulges above. The line of bolts out to the left of the stance is an enjoyable alternative 6c pitch which gets a bit lost higher up by a thin slab.
3) **6b+, 50m.** A huge long pitch - take lots of clippers.
4) **6c+, 40m.** The hard short wall then easy ground above. Belay on a big ledge below the hanging seat - a good spot for lunch.
5) **5, 20m.** Step right around the corner past a peg. Follow the loose groove and step right onto a belay above a pillar.
6) **5+, 30m.** Teeter left (peg and bolt). Continue into a bay then left to a thread. Squirm back up (bolt) right to a ledge.
7) **5+, 35m.** Meander up to a rib towards a solitary bolt and belly-flop onto the next ledge. Walk right and pick your jaw off the ground after you have seen where the next pitch goes.
8) **6c, 25m.** Enjoy the position as you tip-toe up the groove, then launch up the big holds to grab the blobs. Pray they don't break off and clip all four bolts at the belay. Take a deep breath and stare downwards for 10 seconds.
9) **6c, 40m.** Follow the hanging groove to a thin pull (smallest holds on the route?) onto the wall above. Continue past a couple of ledges to a good stance.
10) **40m.** Scramble off rightwards past two grooves then double back left to reach the top.
*FA. Roy de Valera, Juan Carmelo Merino 1991*

---

SW facing wall
Multi-pitch routes up to 300m
Best grades - 6b to 7b

# SIERRA DE TOIX

The Sierra de Toix forms an impressive ridge overlooking Calpe to the north, and Benidorm to the south. The rock outcrops on the ridge are virtually continuous but only certain sections have been found worthy of development. In the past Toix has been over-sold and some people have left, disappointed after their week's stay, believing it to be the best climbing in the area. Well it certainly isn't the best but it does still have an important role in climbing in the Costa Blanca area. The crags are extremely accessible, with many good routes especially in the easier grades, and it will probably be visited at least once by most teams who come out here.

There is a wide variety in the climbing on the ridge from 5m five bolt slab climbs to wild virtual trad routes on the super-exposed sea cliffs. The best climbing is in the 5 to 6b range, but there are also some excellent harder routes on Toix TV and Toix Norte.

Many of the routes have become established classics over the years and they are beginning to get a bit polished. Since this was one of the first areas to be developed on the Costa Blanca, much of the gear is now looking a bit old and in need of replacement and it is often a good idea to carry some wires with you. If you are after a trad climbing experience then head for the Candelabra del Sol. This is now home to some amazingly-positioned, trad routes which will give a memorable day's outing.

## ASPECT AND CLIMATE

One of the main attractions of the Toix ridge is the climbing it offers in adverse weather conditions. If it is raining inland, a situation which is not totally unheard of in Winter, then there it is often dry here. Conversely, when the sun is beating down, it is possible to find somewhere here that you can escape from it. Obviously Toix Norte is in the shade, but for easier routes Toix Oeste in the morning and Toix Este in the afternoon are both worth considering. The exposed position on the headland does mean that it can be windy here, especially on Toix Oeste and Toix TV.

## APPROACH

The Toix ridge is situated high above the town of Calpe. All the various areas are reached from Maryvillas, a sprawling collection of holiday villas south of Calpe town and on the northern slopes of the ridge. The Maryvillas turn off is well signed on the N332 to the south of Calpe, just north of the Mascarat Gorge however you need to be travelling towards Calpe to turn into it. Once you are in Maryvillas it is very easy to get completely lost in the maze of roads which zig-zag up the hillside but stick to the approach descriptions listed with each crag, you should be okay. If you are driving up from further south, then take the Altea turn off (junction 64) and drive through the Mascarat Gorge on the N332.

## THE ROUTES

The older routes on Toix Oeste and Este were bolted in the mid 1980s by Erika and Pel, 2 swiss climbers. Toix TV was developed by Mark and Rowland Edwards in the mid to late 80s. The same pair also developed the Candelabra del Sol with some recent additions being made in te year 2000 and 2001. In the late 1990s Jens Muenchberg rebolted and added many routes to Toix Placa.

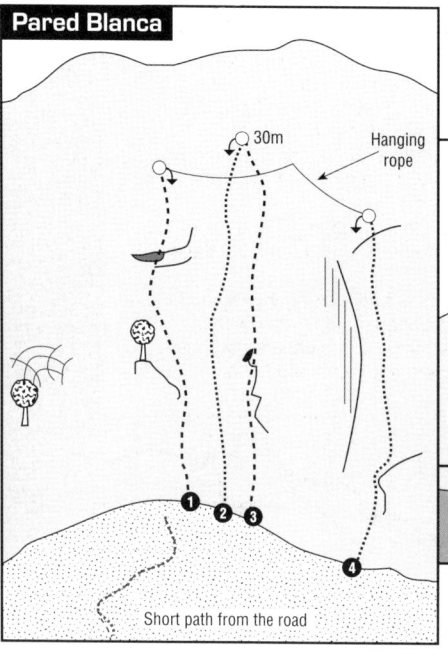

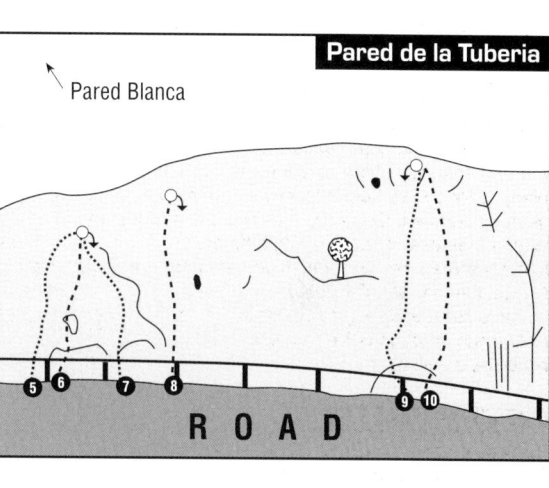

# COSTA BLANCA - Sierra de Toix

## TOIX NORTE
The northern side of the Toix Ridge is clearly visible from Calpe and is continuous for most of the length of the ridge, however only two small sections have so far been developed. The largest, and most impressive, section is Pared Blanca, the large white wall towards the right-hand end. Pared de la Tuberia is a shorter wall above the approach road.

**APPROACH** - Turn off the main road from Calpe, into Maryvillas, then take the following sequence of turns; right by the telephone, branch right at next junction, take next road on the left, continue straight past two other junctions (up to this point it is the same approach as for Toix TV) then turn sharp right at the next. The road then leads up the hill and doubles back under Pared de la Tuberia. Park further up the road.

## PARED BLANCA
... is the huge wall above you!
The routes are fully bolted, but the bolts are far apart.

**1. Por quien doblan las esquines** .......... 7b
The left-hand line passing a tree at half-height, and continuing over a roof.

**2. ?** ............... 7b+
A blank line which contains the odd chipped hold but is still very impressive.

**3. ?** ............... 7a+
The best route on this wall is sustained and pumpy with three cruxes. The last crux is at the top and the other two are well above the bolts which protect them. E5 6a gives the right impression.

**4. ?** ............... 7b
Another superb route to the right of the brown streaked groove. Heavy on your right arm.

## PARED DE LA TUBERIA
This is the wall above the road. On first acquaintance it seems a bit short and insignificant but the routes pack a lot in.

The first three routes share a lower-off.

**5. La Niña** ................ 6b+

**6. La Novia** ................ 6b

**7. La Viuda** ................ 6c

**8. Piñón** ................ 7a

The last two routes look a bit better than the others but are extremely painful and fingery at the top. The bolts are a bit 'tinny' as well.

**9. ?** ................ 7b
A desperate finishing move.

**10. ?** ................ 7a+

North facing wall
5m to 30m routes
Best grades - 6b+ to 7a+

# COSTA BLANCA - Sierra de Toix

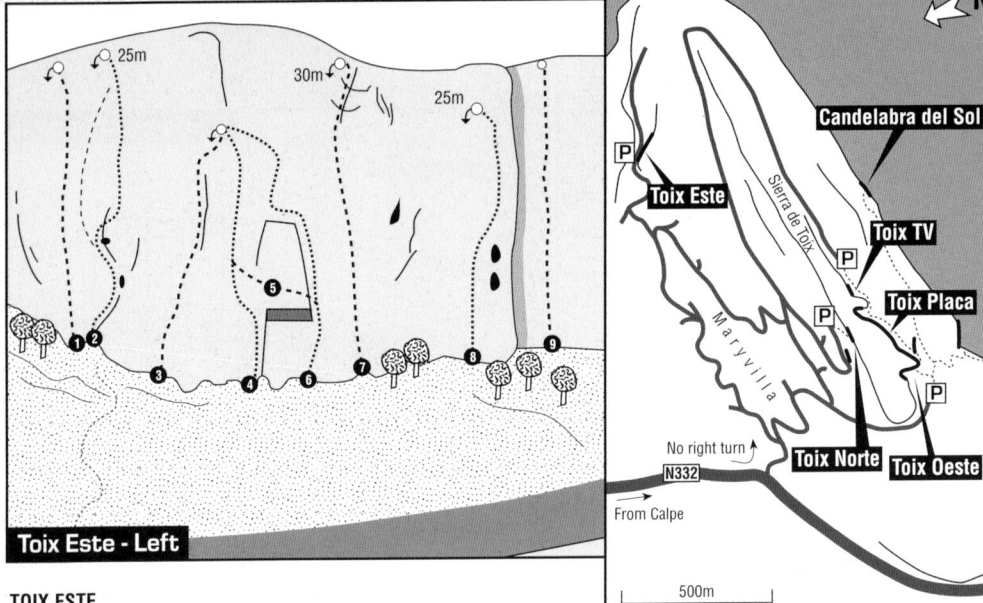

## TOIX ESTE

Toix Este is a popular roadside crag with glorious views over Calpe and the Peñon. The climbing varies from good long routes with fingery cruxes, to short little polished things on slightly dodgy rock. In general the better routes are towards the left-hand end of the crag. The gear is much the same as elsewhere on Toix, with the odd manky bolt and lower-off, but you will struggle to need a wire placement. This is a good airport day crag since it is easy to keep an eye on your gear.

**APPROACH** - Turn off the main road from Calpe, into Maryvillas then ignore everything except the following sequence of turns: branch left, branch right, middle of three, branch left, road joins from left, keep going and hey presto, there's a crag! Park behind the other white, blue or red hire cars.

**DESCENT** - Most of the routes on the left-hand side of the crag are more than 25m long. TAKE CARE IF YOU DESCEND BY LOWERING-OFF.

The far left-hand section of the crag is reached via a small path which leads up to the face from the road directly below.

**1. Hetti** .................... 4
The line is marked by arrows. 1) 4, 25m. 2) 4, 15m.

To the right is the name *Solar Energy* painted on the rock. There are some threads but no grade is known.

**2. Fluid Connection** .......... 6b+
An interesting initial section up the steep wall. Move right to gain a groove on the upper slab. The gear and belay are old.
**Fluid Connection Left (6b+)** - From the recess below the slab climb up left. Slightly inferior to its neigbour.

**3. Boro el toro** .......... 7a+
A very fingery slab with one chipped hold.

**4. Edward's Slab** .......... 6c
Teeter up the right-hand edge of the slab. Bolts may be missing.

**5. La tonta del bote** .......... 6b+
A slightly pointless variation. Start up *Vía de los fakiros* and traverse across to *Edward's Slab*.

**6. Vía de los fakiros** .......... 6b+
Climb up the right-hand side of the small roof, then step left and make a hard move up above (tricky clip for shorties).

**7. Hannah** .......... 6a+
A long route which follows the grey rib.

Routes 8 to 11 can be reached by a prickly scramble along the base of the main wall, or from below by the parking spot.

**8. Purple** .......... 4+
The slab just left of a cave.

**9. Sonja** .......... (4+)
There are some old threads visible on the wall just right of a vegetated gully.

**10. Spolli** .......... 4+
The crux bulge is at 20m. There is a lower-off at 25m otherwise it is a 40m pitch.

**11. Winter** .......... 6a
30m. A good route, with a hard start, up the slab continuing up steep rock above. Take care when lowering.

**12. Green** .......... 5+
Thin start, jugs above. The line is marked by paired bolts.

**13. "P"** .......... 5
A line of red marks up a thin crack. Joins *Green* near the top.

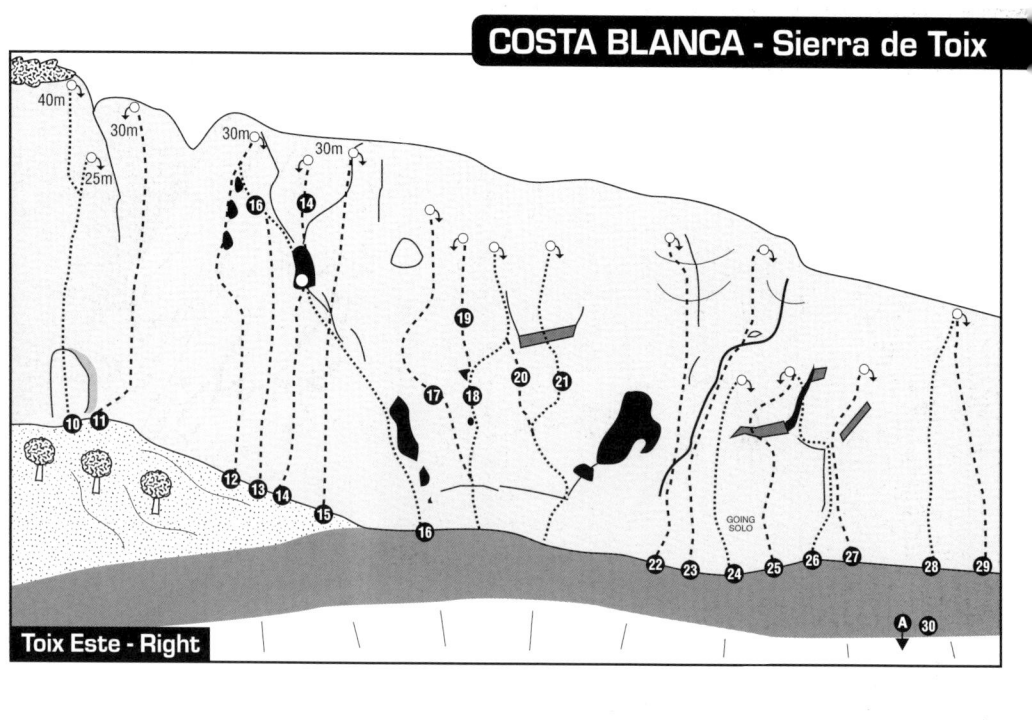

… **COSTA BLANCA - Sierra de Toix**

**Toix Este - Right**

**14. Vía la fina** ............ 5
A popular climb which is split at a stance in the cave. Leaving this is tricky! **1)** 4+, **2)** 5

**15. Silver** ................ 6a
Another technical slab climb which crosses *Vía pyramid*.

**16. Vía pyramid** ............ 5
A long diagonal line which is split at a stance in the cave of *Vía la fina*. **1)** 4+, **2)** 5

**17. Sol y bon temps** ........ 6b+
A fingery section at mid-height gives the difficulties.

**18. Vía yoyoba** ............ 6a+
The excellent central line has a hard move rightwards to reach the groove left of the roof.

**19. Vía yoyoba Direct** ...... 6c
Direct from where the parent route moves right.

**20. King Cucudrulu** ........ 7a
Only one teeny weeny little hard move!

**21. El oso y el mandrono** .... 6a+
Another popular route which has fine lower wall and a tricky roof to finish. Escape leftwards is possible.

**22. Green** ................ 5+
Start below the crack but break leftwards up the wall.

**23. La ramuna arenosa** ...... 5+
The big curving corner.

**24. Going Solo** ............ 6c
A polished technical nasty that has had far too many ascents.

**25. Graphic Whore** .......... 6c+
Friable low down but a good finish over the bulge.

**26. ?** .................... 6a
Poor and loose.

**27. ?** .................... 6a
Uses the same loose flake as route 25.

**28. Vía Nuts** .............. 6b
A traditional route to the left of the yellow bolts. Given a British grade of E3 5b!

**29. Yellow** ................ 5+
The line of yellow bolts is slippery, technical and balancy. The lower-off is old and unuseable. Either use the last bolt or a tree on the top (awkward).

There are a few more lines to the right but they are very poor. However on the far side of the road is a pair of bolts which are the abseil station to:

**30. Adois Daly** ............ 7c+/8a
A sustained and technical slab route which is similar to slate climbing.

NE facing wall
10m to 30m routes
Best grades - 5 to 7a

# COSTA BLANCA - Sierra de Toix

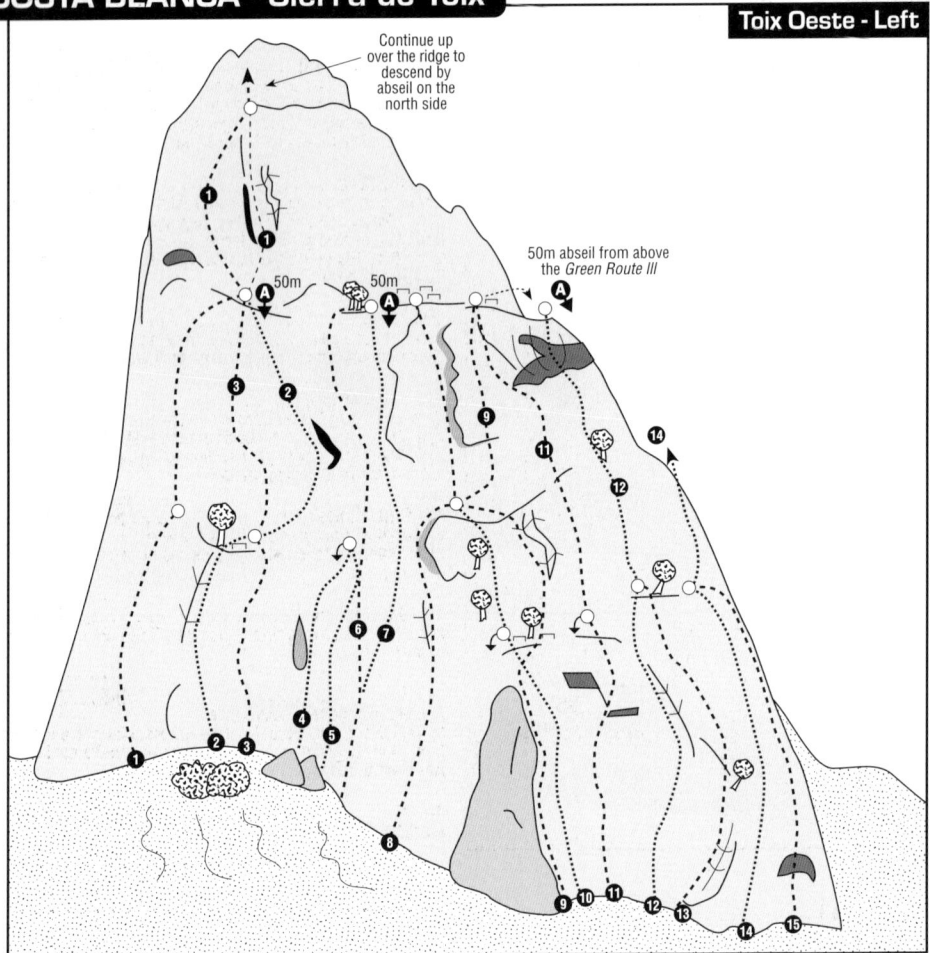

## Toix Oeste - Left

**TOIX OESTE**
The most popular climbing on the Sierra de Toix is found at Toix Oeste. For many people the climbing here is one of the reasons for coming to the Costa Blanca since there are all the benefits of bolted winter-sun climbing but at an easier grade than most other areas.
**GEAR** - Some of the gear on this crag is now getting very old. It is often a good idea to carry a small rack.
**APPROACH** - Turn off the main Calpe road (N332) at the junction signed to Maryvilla, on the northern side of the Sierra de Toix. Then turn right, right, right, left until you swing around under the cliff at the end of the road. Park here and walk down a wall which continues from the end of the road, until it is possible to break out leftwards up the hillside to the crag.
**DESCENTS** - It is possible to lower from some of the routes. The longer ones require an abseil. There are three good abseil belays marked on the topo above. These abseils require double 50m ropes. If you are climbing on a single rope then you will have to make two abseils. It is possible to scramble down from above the right-hand side but this isn't advisable since it is awkward and takes a long time.

The first routes are in the bay to the left-hand side of the crag.

**1. Amarilla** .......... 5
A long trip up the left-hand side of the wall with little fixed gear.
1) 4, 25m. Take the easiest line on the left-hand arete of the bay.
2) 5, 25m. Follow the steep wall (run-out) to a belay. It is possible to abseil off from here in one (45m).
3) 4, 20m. Follow the left-hand rib to another stance. There is a direct variation on this pitch at grade 5.
4) 30m. Follow easy ground up the ridge.
**DESCENT** - Abseil down the north side of the ridge (40m).

**2. Plata** .......... 6a
1) 6a, 20m. A steep pitch up the left-hand side of the bay.
2) 5+, 25m. Move right to gain a crack/groove follow this back left to a stance.
**DESCENT** - Abseil (45m).

92

# COSTA BLANCA - Sierra de Toix

## Toix Oeste - Right

Toix Placa
Toix TV

**8. Green Route II** ......... 5
50m. A good climb which finishes up the prominent flake high up. The gear is of a bit mixed quality but there is plenty of it. The pitch can be split at a mid-height stance just after the slab and before a tricky move on the upper wall.

**9. Ruta Díez** .............. 4
A trad route to the right of the pillar at the toe of the buttress.
1) **3, 20m**. Climb the pillar then step right into a groove which leads to a mid-height belay ledge.
2) **4, 25m**. Step right and take the easiest line up the wall. Descend by abseil.

**10. ?** ..................... 4+
Just right of a pillar. It is possible to continue up the *Green Route II* in one pitch, to finish at grade 5 (45m).

**11. Red Route II** ........... 5
Up the centre of the buttress in two pitches.
1) **5, 20m**. Follow the red paint to a ledge stance.
2) **5, 30m**. The easier upper section follows a couple of corners to finish left of a bulging section.

**12. Blue Route** ............. 5+
1) **5+, 20m**. The blue bolts show the way.
2) **5+, 30m**. Pull through the bulge slightly leftwards in a good position.

**13. Dire Straits** ............ 5+
20m. The name is starting to wear off. Finish up the *Blue Route* or lower off.

**14. ?** ..................... 4+
A good, fully-bolted, easier route.
1) **4+, 30m**. Climb direct from the lowest point of the buttress.
2) **4, 30m**. Continue up a corner all the way to the double bolts. Abseil off to the right.

**15. ?** ..................... 6a+
A couple of bolts which mark the line.

**16. ?** ..................... 4
The blocky corner and grooves has no fixed gear. Not very good.

**17. Red Route III** .......... 6a
20m. Another one! Unlike the other two *Red Routes*, this one is very short and you can lower off. Easier started from the left.

**18. Renov 5-** ............... 4+
1) **4, 25m**. Up a broken groove.
2) **4+, 20m**. The slab above.

**19. Green Route III** ........ 6a
This route follows the wall left of a curving groove.
1) **6a, 25m**. Start up a flake, belay in a niche.
2) **5+, 20m**. A few wires are required for the left-hand finish. The direct finish is a bit easier but not as good.

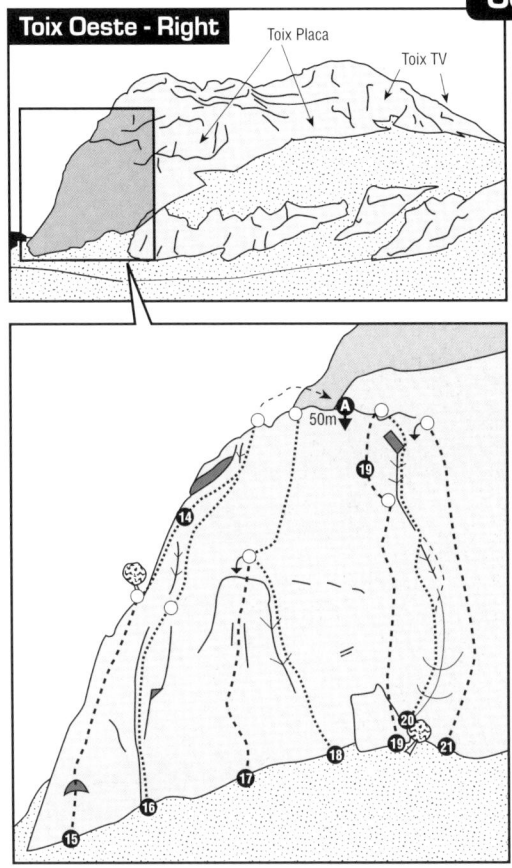

**20. El Menú de Día** ........ 6b+/5+
45m. The curving groove has two variations. The left-hand is harder. Both variations join and finish up the direct finish of the previous route.

**21. Black Route II** ......... 5
35m. The rib to the right of the curving groove is pleasant.

**3. Green Route I** ........... 6a+
A popular route which can be done in one pitch.
1) **6a+, 20m**. Climb direct to the prominent stance. Strenuous.
2) **6a+, 25m**. Direct up the steep wall.

**4. ?** ..................... 7a
A short, technical and worthless route.

**5. Red Route Direct** ........ 6c
lower off the belay of the previous route or continue up the next route.

**6. Red Route I** ............ 6a+
45m. This long, single pitch is one of the most popular routes on the crag (hence it is a bit polished). Take a lot of quickdraws. The start is the crux but the thin slab above provides an interesting finish. descend by abseil (45m).

**7. Black Route** ............ 6b+
45m. Start in the same place as the last route but climb the slab on the right. It is possible to miss out the hard bit by climbing the groove to the right at 6a.

West facing wall
Long single pitch and two pitch routes
20m to 50m. Best grades - 4 to 6a+

# COSTA BLANCA - Sierra de Toix

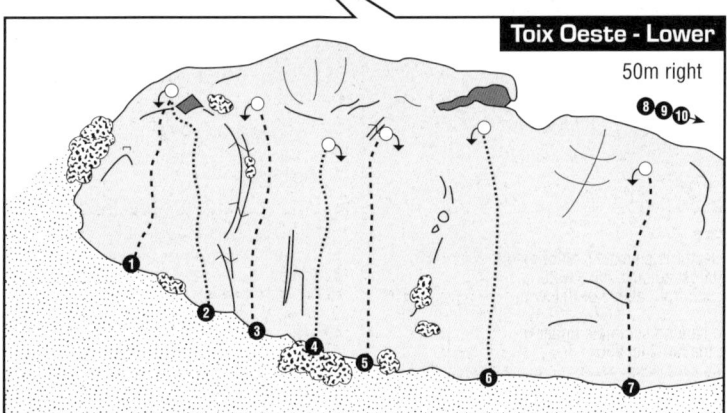

## TOIX OESTE - LOWER

To the right of the main Toix Oeste cliff is a gully and below this is a short wall with a number of easy bolted routes. None of these is mega-classic but they are all useful for beginners. The numbers along the base of the cliff don't correspond to the route lines. I have taken the liberty of copying Chris Craggs' made-up names for these routes.

**APPROACH** - Walk down rightwards from below the main Toix Oeste buttress.

**1. La roja una** .................. ☐ 3
Start by the number 1.

**2. Asombroso** .................. ☐ 3+
The same lower-off as *La roja una*.

**3. Costilla** .................. ☐ 4
Just right of the corner.

**4. La roja dos** .................. ☐ 4
Start by the number 2.

**5. Bella ruta** .................. ☐ 4

**6. Ocho fixe** .................. ☐ 4+

**7. La roja tres** .................. ☐ 5
Above the number 3. The line is marked by a bolt and a peg.

There may well be naturally protected routes on the walls to the right, with the numbers 4 and 5 at the bottom.

The next bolted routes are in a small recess, with an attractive tufa side-wall, 50m right of route 6.

**8. The Whole of Creation** .................. ☐ 6b+
Up a tufa on the left wall. No lower-off.

**9. ?** .................. ☐ (6c)
In the back of the bay.

**10. La roja seis** .................. ☐ 5+
The slab to the left of the '6'. No belay but you can scramble to the top and walk down the gully.

Short west facing wall
5m to 10m routes
Best grades - 3 to 5

# COSTA BLANCA - Sierra de Toix

## Toix Placa - Left

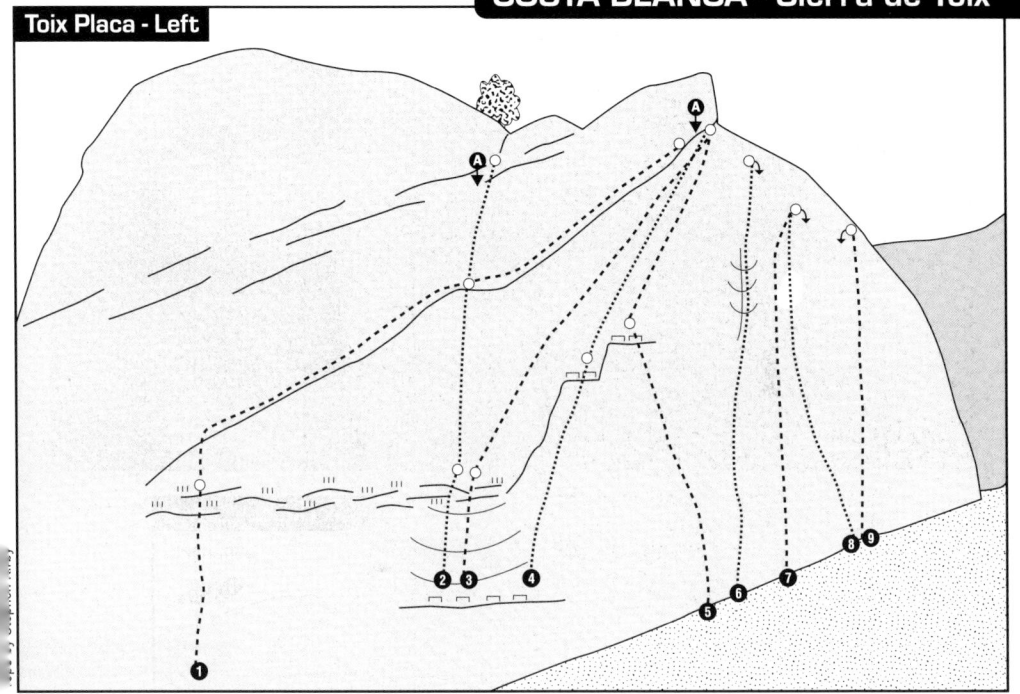

### TOIX PLACA - LEFT
This relatively new sector is an extension of the old Toix TV Lower which now almost adjoins Toix Oeste.

**APPROACH** - Approach from above or below both about as quick as each other.
From the Toix Oeste parking scramble under the main buttress and up the gully on the far side, above Toix Oeste - Lower.
From Toix TV parking drop easily down the hillside below the amphitheatre of Toix TV.

**GEAR** - Some of the first routes have strange assortments of pegs, bolts and threads but it is all adequate for a sport route. The majority of the climbs are well-bolted.

The first route starts in the gully.

**1. Omasus** . . . . . . . . . . . . . . . . . 5
An unclear route with a good top pitch but two very scrappy pitches leading up to a ledge level with the starts of the other routes.
1) **4, 20m.** Line of threads for first pitch.
2) **3, 20m.** Continue up vegetated rock to the mid-height ledge.
3) **4, 30m.** Unclear pitch - climb up rightwards?
4) **5, 20m.** Follows line of rightward tufa-ramp with well-spaced pegs for gear (and some aid if needed off a knotted rope).

The next routes start at the top of the gully. Scramble across onto a ledge to start.

**2. Lofi** . . . . . . . . . . . . . . . . . 4+
A direct line up towards a tree.
1) **3, 25m.** Easy climbing to a ledge.
2) **4+, 30m.** Threads, pegs and an ICE SCREW protect.
3) **4, ?m.** The top pitch is loose. Would make a better route doing the first two pitches of this and the last pitch of *Omasus*.
**DESCENT** - Abseil from the tree.

**3. Lara** . . . . . . . . . . . . . . . . . 4+
1) **3+, 25m.** Easy climbing to another ledge.
2) **4+, 40m.** Up and then right across a delectable slab. Bolts, threads and pegs.
**DESCENT** - Abseil off the shared belay.

**4. Anto** . . . . . . . . . . . . . . . . . 5
Starting from the same ledge as *Lara*.
1) **3, 30m.** A direct line up the slab.
2) **5, 40m.** Diagonally up right. A bit loose.
**DESCENT** - Abseil off the shared belay.

**5. Ana** . . . . . . . . . . . . . . . . . 4+
10m to the right of *Anto*.
1) **4+, 30m.** Very good and well bolted.
2) **4+, 40m.**
**DESCENT** - Abseil off the shared belay.

**6. Hewa** . . . . . . . . . . . . . . . . . 5
**50m.** Excellent long pitch up a slab to a small corner and then right behind a pinnacle. Good abseil bolt. Protected by threads, bolts and a jammed knot!
**DESCENT** - Abseil off the shared belay.

**7. ?** . . . . . . . . . . . . . . . . . 6a+
A little further up the slope. This route might not have fixed gear.

**8. Mushu** . . . . . . . . . . . . . . . . . 6a

**9. Ghost in the Shell** . . . . . . . . . . . . 6b+

West facing wall
30m to 100m multi-pitch
Best grades - 4+ to 6b+

# COSTA BLANCA - Sierra de Toix

**Toix Placa - Right**

## TOIX PLACA - RIGHT
Further up the slope is the wall previously called Toix TV - Lower. This wall is probably best approached from Toix TV parking.

**1. Kalk Stall Videnhul** .......... 6b
The line passes a white circle on the rock.

**2. Coming back to Life** .... 6b+
Very thin slab moves. High in the grade.

**3. Thalia** ................. 6b+

**4. No Name** ............... 6a+

**5. Pegasus** ................ 6a+
2 bolts at the start. An alternative finish can be made up the left-hand finish of *Cicky Bugger* which gives better climbing.

**6. Cicky Bugger** ........... 5+
30m. There are two finishes. The right-hand one goes up a scoop and is about the same grade.

**7. Heaven Is...** ............ 5+
Niuce balancy climbing.

**8. Johanna** ................ 5
Lots of pockets.

**9. Heti** .................... 4
35m. The lower half has bolts but at the top it is just threads however the climbing is good. Take care when lowering.

**10. 4 You** .................. 6a
30m. Hard at the start with a tricky clip for shorties.

**11. Semi Dulce** ............. 5+
30m. Some bolts shared with *4 You*.

**12. Steinbeisser** ............ 6a
30m.

**13. Fantasia** ............... 6a

**14. For my son Jens** ........ 6b
30m. An easy wall, then a big ledge, then a deceptive scoop.

**15. Aladdin** ................ 6c
30m. Easy to a very hard finish.

**16. Hafa** ................... 4+
1) 4+, 40m.
2) 4, 40m.
DESCENT - Abseil off.

**17. Hova** ................... 3
1) 3, 30m. The clean, slabby rib.
2) 3, 25m. Threads and bolts mark the line but break out left to a higher stance. *Noldis* goes right off this pitch.
DESCENT - Abseil off.

**18. Noldis** ................. 5+
1) 3, 27m. Threads up the clean rib below the amphitheatre.
2) 4+, 23m. Threads and bolts.
3) 5+, 25m. There are 2 alternatives. Left on old bolts, or right onj new bolts and threads. Both offer good climbing.
DESCENT - Abseil with care, the route is diagonal.

Up walls below and left of amphitheatre

West facing wall
Long 20m to 40m routes
Best grades - 4 to 6c

# COSTA BLANCA - Sierra de Toix

**Toix TV - Right**

To the Amphitheatre

## TOIX TV - FIRST WALL
A short wall in an impressive position. The climbing isn't brilliant but should provide some entertainment. Most of the route names are painted on the rock.

**APPROACH -** Turn off the main road from Calpe, into Maryvillas, then take the following sequence of turns, right by the telephone, branch right at next junction, take next road on the left, then continue straight on past three more junctions, all the time following signs for 'Mirador'. This should leave you on the road which rises up the hillside towards the seaward end of the Toix ridge. Follow this to the bend at the very edge of the world, and continue to a small parking spot below the TV transmitter, at the road end (popular with paragliders).
From the parking follow the right-hand line of red dots across the hillside to the crag. The left-hand (lower) line leads to the Amphitheatre.

The first routes are on the far left of the wall. You need to scramble up from the central gully to reach the starts.

1. Daddycool ............... 6a
2. Terminator ............... 6c+
3. Follow Me ............... 6c
4. Salida ............... 7a
   A good little route.
5. Gaudi Max ............... 6b

The next two routes start from the gully.

6. Cloud No.9 ............... 6a+
7. El baile ............... 5+

8. UB40 ............... 5+
   Two old bolts then join *Tropical Dreams*.
9. Tropical Dreams ............... 6a
10. Dear Renate ............... 5+
    The move around the small tree is tricky.
11. Verlassen + betrogen ............... 4+
    The old name has been crossed out.
12. Banana Joe ............... 5+
13. Universal ............... 6a
14. Gufelwufel ............... 5
    Through a small cave. Loose rock, threads and bolts.
15. Seduction ............... 6a+
16. ? ............... 4+
    Line of threads. Grade scratched on rock.

South facing wall
8m to 12m routes
Best grades - 5+ to 7a+

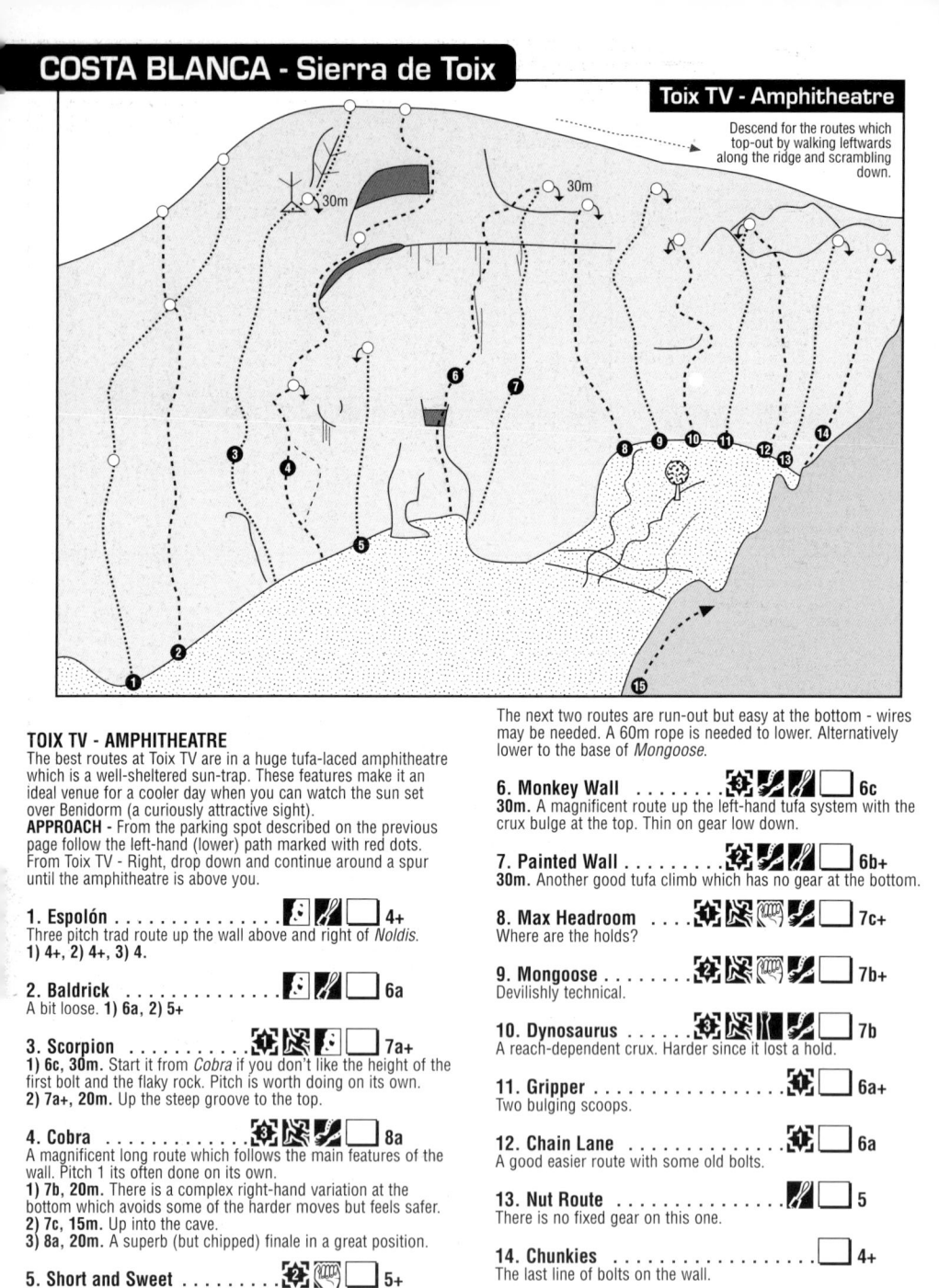

# COSTA BLANCA - Sierra de Toix

## Toix TV - Amphitheatre

Descend for the routes which top-out by walking leftwards along the ridge and scrambling down.

### TOIX TV - AMPHITHEATRE
The best routes at Toix TV are in a huge tufa-laced amphitheatre which is a well-sheltered sun-trap. These features make it an ideal venue for a cooler day when you can watch the sun set over Benidorm (a curiously attractive sight).
**APPROACH -** From the parking spot described on the previous page follow the left-hand (lower) path marked with red dots. From Toix TV - Right, drop down and continue around a spur until the amphitheatre is above you.

**1. Espolón** .................... 4+
Three pitch trad route up the wall above and right of *Noldis*.
1) 4+, 2) 4+, 3) 4.

**2. Baldrick** ................... 6a
A bit loose. 1) 6a, 2) 5+

**3. Scorpion** .................. 7a+
1) 6c, 30m. Start it from *Cobra* if you don't like the height of the first bolt and the flaky rock. Pitch is worth doing on its own.
2) 7a+, 20m. Up the steep groove to the top.

**4. Cobra** ..................... 8a
A magnificent long route which follows the main features of the wall. Pitch 1 its often done on its own.
1) 7b, 20m. There is a complex right-hand variation at the bottom which avoids some of the harder moves but feels safer.
2) 7c, 15m. Up into the cave.
3) 8a, 20m. A superb (but chipped) finale in a great position.

**5. Short and Sweet** ........... 5+
A short route up the middle. Wrongly called *Ombra* before.

The next two routes are run-out but easy at the bottom - wires may be needed. A 60m rope is needed to lower. Alternatively lower to the base of *Mongoose*.

**6. Monkey Wall** ............... 6c
30m. A magnificent route up the left-hand tufa system with the crux bulge at the top. Thin on gear low down.

**7. Painted Wall** .............. 6b+
30m. Another good tufa climb which has no gear at the bottom.

**8. Max Headroom** .............. 7c+
Where are the holds?

**9. Mongoose** .................. 7b+
Devilishly technical.

**10. Dynosaurus** ............... 7b
A reach-dependent crux. Harder since it lost a hold.

**11. Gripper** .................. 6a+
Two bulging scoops.

**12. Chain Lane** ............... 6a
A good easier route with some old bolts.

**13. Nut Route** ................ 5
There is no fixed gear on this one.

**14. Chunkies** ................. 4+
The last line of bolts on the wall.

**15. Black Adder** .............. 4+
The right arete of the amphitheatre. Sparse gear and 2 bolts.

SW facing amphitheatre
10m to 30m routes
Best grades - 5+ to 8a

# COSTA BLANCA - Sierra de Toix - Sea Cliffs

## Raco del Corv

**RACO DEL CORV**
Directly below Toix Oeste, a magnificent wall of exotic rock rises out of the sea. This is home to several sport and trad routes most of which are classics.
The beach below this wall is a very beautiful spot to swim or sunbathe and rarely has anyone on it.
**APPROACH** - The best approach is from the parking for the Mascarat Gorge (see page 104). From the parking spot, walk down to the beach. It is also possible to walk down here from below Toix Oeste, but this is steep and nasty.
**DESCENT** - The most common descent from these routes is to traverse the prominent grassy break at two thirds height, to a bunch of threads at its left-hand end. Make one abseil from here to another ledge below and left, then make one more 50m abseil to the beach. It is also possible to climb to the top of the crag and walk down, but there is no fixed gear on the upper section of the cliff.

**1. ?** ............ 7a+
A full 50m pitch up the line of abseil building to a steep finish at the top.

The next 6 routes share a common first pitch. Take the easiest line across the wall to a prominent sloping ledge.

**2. Sombre** .. 7b
A sustained and technical route. It is a bit chipped at the top, on the section shared with *Müne*. Take some small wires to supplement the spaced bolts.

**3. Müne** ........ 7b
A created route to the right which joins *Sombre* near the top.

**4. El Dorado 1** ............ 6a+
A brilliant climb on magnificent rock.
1) 6a+, 35m. From the sloping ledge make a hard rising traverse until you are below a wide crack. Swarm up this to a hanging stance above.
2) 6a+, 30m. Finish up the slab above, past a few bits of fixed gear, to the diagonal grassy break. Belay a long way up lleft along the sloping ledge.

**5. El Dorado 2** ............ 6b
Another superb route.
1) 6a+, 25m. From the ledge, traverse right until next to the hanging rope. Climb up some scoops then go diagonally rightwards to a small stance below a bulge.
2) 6b, 40m. Climb up slightly leftwards past some well-featured rock to the grassy break. Belay miles back.
There is a poorer alternative right-hand pitch 2 at bold 6b.

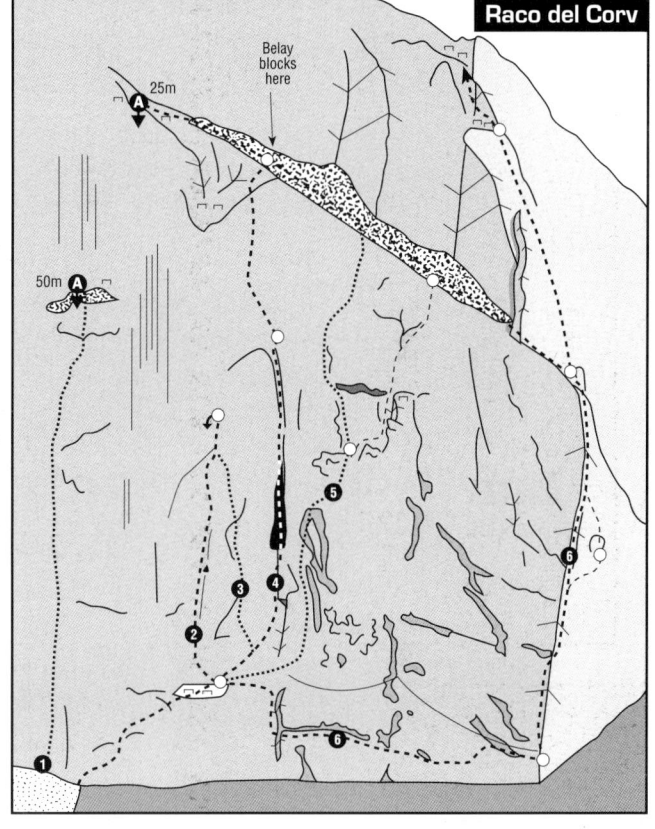

**6. Vía Missing Link** ... 6b+
This much-photographed route follows the magnificent arete. A full rack of gear is needed. Pitch 1 is difficult to protect, serious to second and shouldn't be underestimated, however you are only about 1m above the sea.
1) 6a+, 35m. From the sloping ledge move right then carefully down-climb, placing wires in a crack, to gain a low traverse line. Follow this awkwardly, staying just above the water, until it is possible to climb diagonally upwards (don't climb up too soon) to a scoop which leads to the hanging stance on the arete.
2) 6b+, 45m. Power up the arete above, first on the left, then on the right. From the diagonal break, either traverse left to gain the grassy ramp, or climb easily up the wall above to the top (50m).
**Variation - Lucas Nocturnes 6b**
2a) 6b, 25m. Just after the route swings around the arete, traverse right to a cave to belay.
3a) 6a+, 25m. Pull up above the cave and climb back to the arete above. Only a teeny bit easier than the original and less good.

SW facing cliff
50m to 80m multi-pitch routes
Best grades - 6a+ to 7b

# COSTA BLANCA - Sierra de Toix - Sea Cliffs

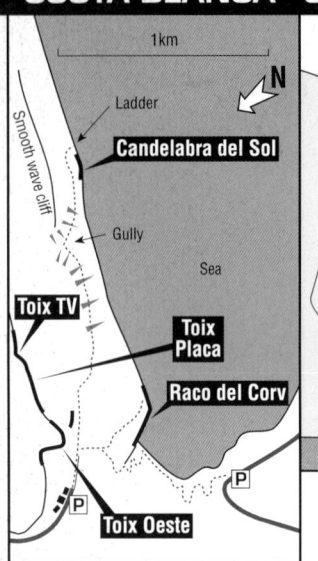

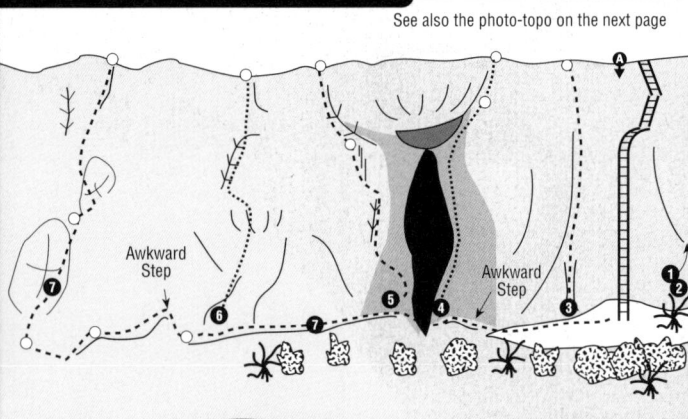

See also the photo-topo on the next page

## CANDELABRA DEL SOL
The southern side of the Toix headland forms a continuous sea cliff which is up 80m high in places. The potential for climbing here looks vast but much of the rock is loose and crumbly, however several routes have been developed in one section which give some extremely atmospheric climbing. Most of the routes on this section are part bolted, part ENP-equipped but also requiring a full rack of gear.

**APPROACH** - Approach from below Toix Oeste (see page 92). Follow the wall descending beneath Toix Oeste and continue on a rough path until a cairn appears on the right. From here a brilliantly well-cairned path leads for about 1km across the hillside, dipping into a wide gully at one point. Shortly after this, a smooth wave of rock appears on the left and the path drops down to the cliff top. Here some rickety ladders can be found which drop all the way down to a ledge above the sea. Descent (or ascent) of the ladders, without a rope, is definitive E8 2a, so it is best to abseil. Follow the ledge leftwards past one tricky step (grade 3) to a large cave.

### 1. Malice Aforethought — 6b
A big route in an impressive position. Start below a steep crack to the right (looking in) of the ladders.
1) **6b, 27m (E3 5c).** Mostly fixed gear although large cams may be needed. Climb the crack to a good ledge in the roof (belay possible to avoid rope drag). Climb the roof (2bolts) to the lip and swing out onto the steep wall on the right. Bridge out and climb the steep wall (bolts and a thread) trending right at the top and then left into the wide bay and good ledge.
2) **6a, 28m.** Climb the right wall to a good ledge and thread. Move up right to gain the arete and climb out onto the steep arete. Climb this direct to the top. Belay (Friends) well back on the right-hand side of the boulder.
FA. R.Edwards, D.Golding 28.12.00

### 2. Lady in Space — 6b
An excellent alternative upper pitch to *Malice*.
1) **6b, 27m.** As for *Malice*.
2) **6b, 30m (E3 5c).** Climb the wall on the right of the cave until it is possible to traverse left onto the opposite wall. Traverse this and make some hard moves up into the roof (threads). Continue out to the tip of the cave and then climb the short wall to the top.
FA. R.Edwards, M.Edwards, R.Mayfield 13.1.01

### 3. Goliath — 8a
**45m (E7 6b).** A hard route direct up the large tufas left (looking in) of the descent ladders. Start below a large overhanging pinnacle/rib, with a hole through its base. Climb the left-hand side of the pinnacle then move onto the arete. Follow the edge to below an overhanging groove (2 threads). Climb the groove direct to a crack (thread) and enter the chimney between the large tufas. Climb direct (2 threads) onto the overhanging headwall which leads strenuously (run-out) to a good thread. Continue to a slabby ledge (thread) and climb the steep groove to finish.
FA. M.Edwards, R.Edwards 24.11.00

The next three routes have old bolts and are unsafe at present.

### 4. Candelabra del Sol — 8a
**50m.** An amazing an impressive route but unclimbable in its present condition. It follows the steep back and side wall of the cave in one huge pitch. There is a second bolted line which follows the back of the cave, via a belay. This alternative is 7b+. Photo of the main pitch opposite.
FA. M.Edwards 1980s

### 5. The Flame — 7b
A superb pitch up a wonderful tufa. Take some wires to protect reaching the first bolt, and for the short second pitch (6a). The crux heave onto the tufa requires some commitment.
FA. R.Edwards 1980s

### 6. Raptured Dreams — 7a
The next line of bolts is a touch loose at the bottom. DON'T arrive at the top crack without some large wires otherwise you will find yourself on a gnarly E5!
FA. R.Edwards 1980s

SW facing cliff
50m to 200m multi-pitch routes
Best grades - 5 to 8a

Mark Edwards on
*Candelabra del Sol* (8a - opposite)
Toix Sea Cliffs.
Photo: Rowland Edwards

Jane Fisher on the traverse of
*Magical Mystery Tour* (5 - page 102)
Toix Sea Cliffs.
Photo: Rowland Edwards

# COSTA BLANCA - Sierra de Toix - Sea Cliffs

## CANDELABRA DEL SOL
The immaculate walls to the left of the ever-popular *Magical Mystery Tour* have been developed with some spectacular climbs. Most of these rely on trad gear and the occasional ENP (see page 113). There are some old bolts but please don't trust these. They may be replaced sometime in the future.
**APPROACH** - See previous page.

### 7. Rowland's Magical Mystery Tour  ★★★ ENP  5
This great expedition gives a memorable outing. There is some fixed gear, including ENPs (see page 113) to mark the line but take a full rack with you. Approach by walking leftwards (looking in) from the ladders. Competent climbers, especially those attempting the routes further left, will find the first 2 pitches possible without ropes however if you are unsure rope up.
**1) 3, 25m.** Traverse left to the arete and then left again, descending into the Candelabra del Sol cave.
**40m.** Walk/scramble left along ledges to the edge of the left wall and step around left onto a good ledge.
**2) 3, 10m.** Climb the wide crack on the left to a ledge then drop down left into a hollow.
**3) 4-, 20m.** Traverse left (old peg) to the arete and climb around this into a large scoop (poor bolt). Pull up over the overlap into an even larger scoop. Belay on old bolts and/or ENPs.
**4) 4, 25m.** Make an ascending traverse right across the wall of the scoop to the right arete (poor bolt). Climb this, trending right at the top, to reach a good ledge with 2 ENPs. Alternatively continue to traverse right into the next cave with 1 poor bolt and gear to belay.
**5) 5, 40m (VS 5a).** Climb right and up into the next cave. Climb left onto the arete (poor bolt) and go direct to a good ledge. Move right and climb the obvious groove, moving right at its top, to reach the top of the cliff.
*FA. R.Edwards 1986. Climbed solo, bolts placed later.*

### 8. Dimage ★★ ENP  6b+
Good climbing in an excellent position which starts as for *Magical Mystery Tour*.
**1) to 3) 55m.** As for *MMT*.
**4) 6a+, 25m.** Climb left onto a shattered pillar then move up and around left onto the steep wall. Climb this past an SENP (run-out at the top) to reach a small ledge and belay bolts.
**5) 6b+, 25m (E3/4 6a).** Climb right to a steep wall. this leads strenuously (3 SENPs) onto a good ledge (belay possible). Climb the short wall above and then the shallow groove on the left.
*FA. R.Edwards, M.Edwards, M.Jones 23.4.00*

### 9. Kubla khan ★★★ ENP  7b
A superb route which tackles the overhanging crack-line right of *Journey to Xanadu*. The route overhangs for its full length but, although the climbing is sustained, it is not technically difficult until the headwall of the cave. The moves here can be easily aided bringing the grade down to about A0/6b+. The route requires 3 or 4 SENPs (see page 113).
**1) to 3) 55m.** As for *MMT*.
**4) to 6) 75m.** As for *Journey to Xanadu*.
**7) 6a, 35m.** Climb the crack to the first cave (belay on *Journey to Xanadu*). Then continue up the crack into the next large cave.
**8) 7b, 40m (E5 6b).** Climb the wall on the left and bridge up the wide crack. Continue up the crack, past a number of threads, until you reach a steep wall. Climb out onto the overhanging wall (SENP) and climb this (2 SENPs) to a small ledge and belay (thread up on right and 1 SENP).
**9) 6b, 20m.** Climb the steep overhanging corner on the right and then the slab above to the top.
*FA. R.Edwards, M.Hesslinger 28.12.99*

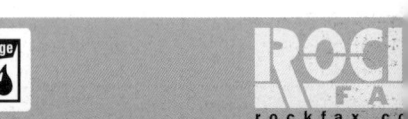

# COSTA BLANCA - Sierra de Toix - Sea Cliffs

Photo: Rowland Edwards

## 10. Rowland's Journey to Xanadu ... 6c
A fine, but hard, extension to *MMT* with some dramatically positioned pitches. The climbing is very committing and the route should only be undertaken by competent teams. Pitch 7 requires 6 SENPs (see page 113). Start as for *MMT*.
**1) to 3) 55m.** As for *MMT*.
**4) 4, 20m.** From the belay, traverse left around a pillar and cross over onto the slab. Climb this to the next bay.
**5) Abseil 25m.** Enter the narrow cave and abseil from the thread until you are in the bay just above the sea.
**6) 5, 30m.** Climb around the left edge onto the seaward face and traverse left to a narrow cleft. If the sea is calm, make a delicate, low traverse, or if the sea is rough, take a slightly higher one. Either way you end up on the far side of the cleft below a steep crack-line.
**7) 5, 20m.** Climb the crack to the first cave. A good stance.
**8) 6a+, 25m.** Traverse out onto the left wall (ENP). Climb direct (ENP) to a small slab and follow the crack above and left to a ledge. Climb the steep wall above (ENP) to reach a good ledge. 3 ENP belay. This point can also be reached by following the crack and wall to the left of pitches 6 and 7.
**9) 6c, 20m (E3 6a).** Climb up and right into the bay and then right again until you can step onto the top of a stalactite. Climb up (ENP) to a thin crack and follow this into a cave. Thread belay.
**10) 6a, 30m.** Climb up into the roof of the cave and move up and left onto the wall above. Climb this to a thread and then over the roofs on the left to the top. Thread belay.
FA. R.Edwards, M.Edwards, Michael Esslinger 11.12.99

## 11. Rowland's Promised Land ...... 6b
A magnificent long expedition passing through some of the most impressive rock scenery in the area. Allow 5-6 hours for the whole trip. Start as for *MMT*.

### Rowland's Promised Land continued....
**1 to 6) 105m.** As for *Journey to Xanadu*.
**7) 2, 18m.** Cross the gully onto ledges and follow these to a buttress (thread high up). Belay.
**8) 4, 25m.** Descend leftwards onto the ledges which cross the slab. Follow these to a corner and belay on wires or make a move lower to a good thread (hanging) belay.
**9) 4+, 25m.** Continue to traverse left along a thin flake above small foot holds until you reach a good stance below a steep pillar. This stance can also be reached by abseils from above.
**Higher (easy) alternative -**
**8a) 3, 50m.** Step down and around the corner then move up onto the sloping ledge running leftwards.
**9a) 3+, 10m.** Step down left onto the ledge below.
**10) 3+, 20m.** Move left into the next groove and climb the left-hand side of the pillar to a good ledge and thread belay.
**11) 6b, 30m (E2/3 5c).** Climb direct to the top of the pillar and then immediately move right for a few moves. Ascend rightwards (2 ENPs) then direct (ENP). From here ascend leftwards, crossing to a thread, and then to the hanging belay. Bolts.
**12) 6a, 25m.** Traverse left for a few moves and then ascent leftwards to a pocket. Continue direct to a good ledge at the base of the head wall. Nut belay.
**13) 6a+, 45m.** Climb the wall on the right, past 2 small pockets, direct to the small overhanging buttress on the right. Move right and climb the front of the buttress to a ledge. Climb the slabs and the short wall to the top.
FA. R.Edwards, M.Edwards, R.Mayfield, T.Phillips 17.10.00

**APPROACH FOR LAST 3 PITCHES ONLY -** On the approach walk to the ladder abseil, look out for the beginning of the broken crag above on the left and a large cactus on your right. Follow the lower track and find a cairn on the cliff edge. Abseil from a pair of staples below this cairn directly down the wall, passing one ledge and onto a lower one with two bolts. Abseil again (free in places) until you reach a ledge below a pillar, just above the sea. Belay. This is the end of pitch 9 of the traverse.

South facing cliff
50m to 75m multi-pitch routes
Best grades - 5 to 8a

# MASCARAT GORGE

The walls of the Mascarat provide some superb long routes in a weird and exciting setting. These routes are often gazed at in awe from the car as you whip through on your way to, or from, somewhere else but, if you are eventually tempted to give one of them a go, then there should be something at your grade. The road and traffic noise dominate the atmosphere a bit, although this is of little significance on the South West Face, and in the Gorge itself. Several of the long routes have become established classics on the Costa Blanca hit list with *Vía UBSA* being one of the more popular long, and relatively easy, routes around. Others are seldom climbed by visiting climbers, but are none-the-less worthwhile. The hard routes on the Hambre de Mujer Wall, and *Cleoplaca*, are all superb and popular.

## ASPECT AND CLIMATE

The tall walls give shady climbing on many of the routes and a cold wind can whistle down the Gorge in winter. This makes it a good place to head for in very hot weather but conversely a dreadful place if it is chilly. The longer routes on the South West Face are much more exposed to the sunshine and should all be considered as major full-day undertakings. Make sure you are well equipped with an appropriate rack of gear and take plenty of water and sun screen.

## APPROACH

The Mascarat is the bit with all the bridges, tunnels and huge towering walls of orange and grey limestone on the N332, just to the south of Calpe. Some of the routes start from the road level, and some start from the base of the gorge. The problem is what do you do with your car? If you can persuade someone to drop you off then this is by far the best option for the routes which start at road level. If you wish to climb in the gorge, or the route *Aurora*, then, turn off the N332 about 250m south (downhill) from the lowest tunnel signed towards 'Pueblo Mascarat'. Follow this road down past a bridge on a bend (the track up the gorge leads off from this bridge) and continue to a T-junction turn left and drive around to a parking area overlooking the Toix Sea Cliffs. Don't leave anything in your car. **NOTE** - this area is being built all over so it is possible that this parking spot may become inaccessible in the future. - check rockfax.com for update details.

To get to the routes walk up the gorge along the path from the bridge. The routes at road level can be reached by slogging up the steep bank on the left (looking up the gorge) to appear by the small tower.

## THE ROUTES

The first ascensionists of most of the long routes are shown with the routes. The shorter routes were done by various climbers including the Edwards and Nacho Sánchez.

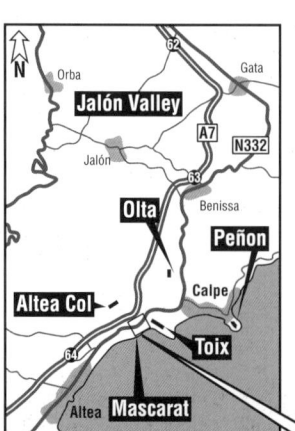

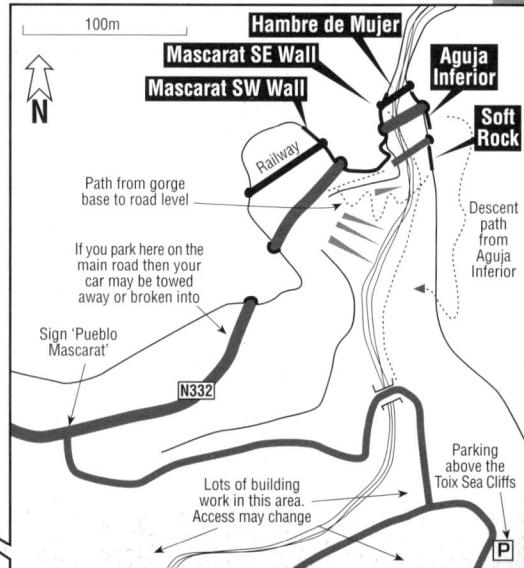

# COSTA BLANCA - Mascarat Gorge

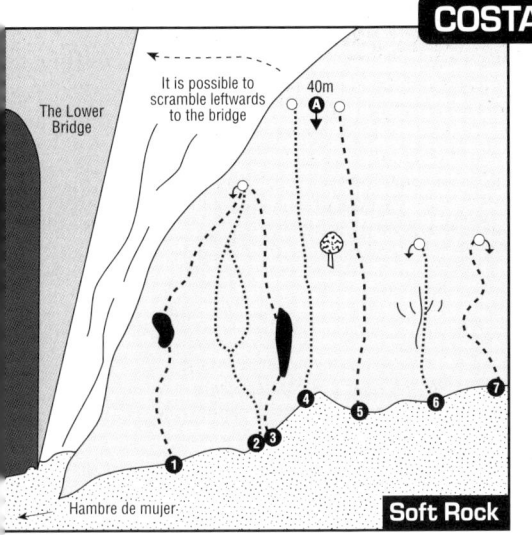

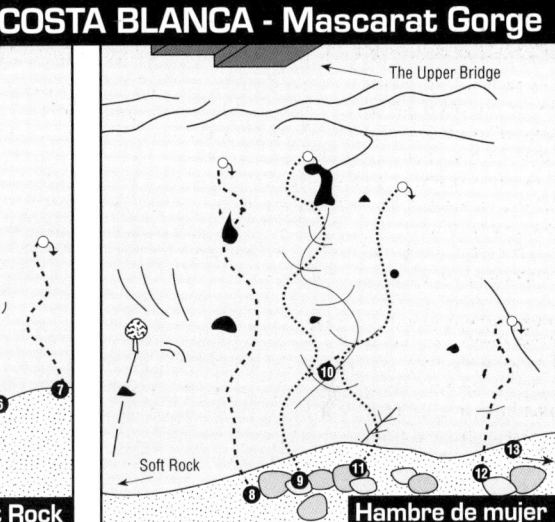

## MASCARAT GORGE
Deep in the gorge, which cuts through the towering walls of the Mascarat, are a couple of compact walls which have been developed with several single pitch routes. The atmosphere is somewhat enclosed and the area is liberally strewn with debris which has either been washed down the river (usually dry) or chucked off the bridges. However the climbing is good especially on the *Hambre de mujer* wall.

**APPROACH** - From the parking above the sea cliffs walk back down the road to the little bridge. From here an indistinct path leads off up the gorge.

## THE SOFT ROCK WALL
Just before the first bridge is a smooth wall on the right. This is the most popular wall in the whole Mascarat, but it isn't the best.

**1. Mujer contra mujer** . . . . . . . . . . 6a+
The left-most route on the wall, which goes through a small hollow.

**2. Marcia el último** . . . . . . . . . . 6a+
The wall between the two holes has two variations (both about the same grade). The first bolt is quite high.

**3. Auntie Bolt** . . . . . . . . . . . 6a
Climb up through the right-hand cave. The first bolt is above the cave, so take some gear.

**4. Soft Rock** . . . . . . . . . . . . 6a
40m. The wall right of the cave needs a bit of gear. Abseil off or walk left to the bridge and abseil down from below *Cleoplaca*.

**5. ?** . . . . . . . . . . . . . . . . . 4+
40m. A poor line up the wall to the right. Descend as for the previous route.

**6. Brother Wolf** . . . . . . . . . . . . . 5+
Pulling through a small bulge is the crux. Abseil off since the lower-off is poor.

**7. Sister Moon** . . . . . . . . . . . . . 6a
The last bolt is missing making it a bit bold. Wires won't help.

## HAMBRE DE MUJER WALL
As you walk deeper into the depths, the gorge towers above you and the walls close in ominously. This is not a place to get caught if there is ever water in this dry river, and the start to route 4 is proof that there sometimes is (but very rarely). On the left, directly underneath the new road bridge, is a wall very reminiscent of Huntsman's Leap in Pembroke, with routes of similar quality.

**8. El sherifico** . . . . . . . . . 7b
A superb route with a hard, reachy move near the bottom and a sustained and pumpy finish.

**9. Hambre de mujer** . . . . . . . 7a
A great route which gives a full body pump! It follows the superb snaking groove with just enough holds and some well-spaced bolts. It doesn't really have a crux but there are many easy moves either.

**10. Hambre Variation** . . . . . . . 6c+
By starting up *Hambre* ... it is possible to miss out the really hard bit of *Que Dios reparta suerte* and finish up the good top section.

**11. Que Dios reparta suerte** . . . 7c
The start is often wet, and always desperate. This is actually the first pitch of the original start of *Silphara* on the southeast Wall. This start was altered after a particularly savage storm removed the bottom five meters of boulders leaving some very blank rock.

**12. Lubricante vaginal en uno** . . . . 7a
A short little route with one hard move.

15 further up the gorge, where it narrows is one last wierd route.

**13. Abdul** . . . . . . . . . . . . . 7b
Start up a slabby pillar and then swing around the corner where it starts to get steep. One more hard move leads to a rest before the final bulge. The lower-off has a nowhere feeling about it.

# COSTA BLANCA - Mascarat Gorge

## Mascarat South West Face

**MASCARAT SOUTH WEST FACE**
The south side of the Mascarat Gorge has two huge faces separated by a ridge which runs down to the road by the disused road bridge. This ridge is the start of one of the more popular long routes in the area - *Vía UBSA*. The other routes are on the walls to either side and have complex approaches and descents, but they are all in an extremely atmospheric setting and provide some memorable full day adventures.

**GEAR -** The routes tend to have pegs or bolts by the hard bits, and on the stances, but a full rack of wires and a few friends is advisable.

**APPROACH (Routes 1 and 2) -** Cross the main road just below the middle tunnel. Fight through the bush on the other side to get yourself onto the scree slope leading to the railway. Slog up this, over the railway, until you can scramble easily up a band of rock on the right. The start of route 1 is marked by a cross and a pair of metal 'things'.

**TERRACE DESCENT (Routes 1 and 2) -** The routes top-out on the summit ridge. This can be followed to the top but there is an easy escape off leftwards along a terrace. Follow this across the hillside, and up a rock step, until it is possible to descend a gully on the left, onto the slope above the railway. This leads down to the road. Take care not to descend leftwards too early from the terrace. At the top of the gully it is possible to join the *Vía UBSA* descent described opposite.

### 1. Las Tetas de mi Novia  6b+
A good route up the left-hand side of a huge pillar, high up on the southwest face of the buttress. Full rack needed.
1) **6b+, 35m.** Climb the wall below the prominent groove past a variety of fixed gear. Make a hard move left into the groove to belay.
2) **6b, 45m.** Climb a groove above until forced left into another groove. Climb this until a move back right gains a well-pegged crack which leads to a stance.
3) **6b, 20m.** Traverse easily rightwards until you can climb up past a peg to gain a belay.
4) **6a+, 45m.** Climb directly above the stance trending rightwards to the ridge.
*FA. Roberto Lli, Quique Barber 28.1.84*

### 2. Espermació  6a
A seldom-climbed line up the right-hand side of the pillar.
1) **5+, 40m.** Climb the wall just right of *Las Tetas* ....
2) **5+, 45m.** Move up to gain a leftwards trending crack. Follow this to the left edge of the pillar, then climb another crack to a stance on top of the pillar.
3) **6a, 40m.** Move right then climb the wall to a grassy ledge. Escape rightwards from here to the ridge.
*FA. Salvador Guerola, Emilio Perales 22.2.86*

### 3. Vía UBSA  5+
A classic trip which has been wrongly called *Vía UPSA* for years. The route was once fully bolted but the gear has been removed to return the route to its big-mountain, trad character. Although there is only one hard pitch it should be considered as a serious undertaking for experienced teams only. In general it is easy to follow, as long as you look out for the bolts without hangers. A full rack is definitely needed to back up some of the belays. Start by the curious square tower on the lower road bridge.
1) **3, 40m.** Follow the easiest line up the pillar to belays under steeper rock.
2) **4, 35m.** Follow the cracked rib above the belay to where the ridge levels out.

**Vía UBSA continued....**
3) **2, 35m.** Scramble easily up the ridge to a grassy terrace. Walk along terrace to peg belay at foot of upper wall, below and left of a groove.
4) **4+, 40m.** Climb up and right to the foot of the groove, and climb it for 2-3m before pulling round onto the right edge (bolt). Follow a line of cracks up the wall to threads (possible belay) and traverse right to peg and thread belay.
5) **5+, 35m.** Climb the polished groove (old pegs, one new bolt) and continue in the same line to belay (threads, old bolt).
6) **4+, 30m.** Climb the wall above and left of the belay, then trend rightwards (pegs - optional bolt belay down and right) to the arete. Traverse right, around the arete, to exposed stance.
7) **4, 35m.** Continue traversing right to a groove - climb this and slabs above to the top.

**Vía UBSA DESCENT -** If you continue to the top there are two more excellent easy pitches, a scramble and a lovely ridge walk across the top. To descend you have to traverse the whole ridge until you reach a villa building site, descend through this then traverse back across the mountain to the descent gully described opposite. Instead of going down the normal descent gully, keep to the south of it and follow the bounding ridge and scramble down the hillside to join the road by the first tunnel entrance on the approach from Altea.
*FA. Unknown probably around 1974.*

**SW Face**
150m to 250m multi-pitch
Best grades - 5+ to 6b+

# COSTA BLANCA - Mascarat Gorge

**Mascarat South East Face**

## MASCARAT SOUTH EAST FACE
The rest of the routes start on the southeastern wall, but they top-out at the same place as *Vía UBSA*. Despite the enclosed atmosphere, the situations are superb. One slight draw back is the incessant traffic noise.
**APPROACH** - Climb over the railings on the middle road bridge then move up right to a ledge. Follow a groove to another ledge below the wall proper.
**DESCENT** - As for *Vía UBSA* or along the Terrace (opposite).

### 4. El Pajarón  6a+
The old classic of this wall, which for years has been known as *Vía Sulfada*. The approach is a bit scrappy, but after that it is solid and excellent. Full rack needed.
1) **4, 30m.** Scramble leftwards up vegetated rock to below a groove in the clean upper wall.
2) **6a, 35m.** Climb the groove then step right and move up into another groove. At the top of this step down left to a small ledge.
3) **6a, 30m.** Step right and climb up then move right again into a groove which leads to a stance.
4) **6a, 25m.** Move up behind the stance into a slabby groove and follow the crack above to a stance.
5) **5+, 30m.** Follow the red corner (no fixed gear) and a flake on the left to a ledge.
6) **5, 20m.** Continue to join *Vía UBSA* before its last pitch. Continue up *Vía UBSA* in one, or climb the groove and bulge on the left to the ridge (5).
FA. Salvador Guerola, Emilio Perales 1986

### 5. Finis Africae  7b+
**50m.** A desperate long route from the large grassy terrace, to the big cave at the end of pitch 3 on *Sylphara*. Abseil off.

### 6. Sylphara  7a
It originally started from the base of the gorge (see Hambre de Mujer Wall - route 4) but a storm altered the start, so nowadays it is best begin at bridge level. Full rack needed.
1) **5+, 35m.** From the right-hand end of the ledge, climb up a slab then traverse across rightwards to the cave.
2) **6a, 40m.** Leave the cave on its left edge and climb up to another cave.
3) **6a+, 35m.** Step left from the bottom of this cave and climb a leftwards trending groove to its top.
4) **7a, 35m.** The big one and it's not really aid-able! Follow the curving groove above to a good ledge at the top.
5) **5+, 20m.** Climb a corner then move right to belay.
6) **5, 40m.** Climb a short groove to a pillar. Belay at the top.
7) **4, 45m.** Move up then left to join *Vía UBSA* to finish.
FA. Ernesto López, Koke Pérez, Enrique Barberá 1979

### 7. Vuelo del aguila  6a+
A long and exposed climb taking the right arete of the steep face overlooking the gorge. Start as for *Sylphara*.
1) **3, 45m.** Traverse right on ledges to a long cave.
2) **6a, 30m.** Climb slabs right of the cave to 2 bolts. The crack on the right leads to shallow grooves and a cave. Bolt belay.
3) **6a, 50m.** Slabs on the left lead to a crack (bolt, ignore pegs going left). Climb the chimney on the right past overhangs to a groove. Move left below a roof then up a groove to a ledge on the left.
4) **5, 35m.** Climb the rightwards slanting groove then just right of the arete to a ledge.
5) **4, 40m.** Continue just right of the arete until you can step on to it. Climb the slab to a good ledge.
4a) **6a+, 35m.** Alternative pitch. Climb the groove above and pass a small cave on your left. Go direct to a cave.
5a) **5, 45m.** Climb into another cave on the left (nest) then up a groove to follow slabs and a chimney which lead to the arete. Follow this to a good ledge.
6) **4. 25m.** Follow the arete to a belay (peg).
7) **4+, 30m.** Follow the arete to a good ledge.
8) **4, 25m.** Climb the arete to and walk off.
FA. Unknown. P4 and P5 - R.Edwards, M.Edwards 1.95

**SE Face**
200m to 250m multi-pitch
Best grades - 6a+ to 7a

**107**

# COSTA BLANCA - Mascarat Gorge

## AGUJA INFERIOR
The 'Smaller Pinnacle' is the tower on the opposite side of the gorge to the main Mascarat walls. It has a striking clean triangular wall, which is obvious when driving north on the N332 - this is the home of *Cleoplaca*. There are also a number of other short hard climbs on this wall, plus several long routes.

**GEAR** - The single pitch routes are fully bolted with lower-offs. The long routes have some gear but a full rack is advisable.

**APPROACH** - All the routes bar one start at road level so you will either need to slog up the hill from the Sea Cliffs parking or be dropped off at road level.

**DESCENT** - For the routes which top-out there are 3 options.

**Option 1** - The safest an easiest option, but not the quickest, is to scramble along the summit ridge then break down the steep, but broken, slope on the right-hand side of the ridge. This slope leads down, over a couple of rock steps, to the road at the base of the gorge.

**Option 2** - On the upper slope of the previous descent, locate a cable and follow this back right, by means of a tricky scramble, to reach the terrace below routes 10 and 11. The path leads you to the bridge level.

**Option 3** - You can also walk along the ridge to the villas below Toix Oeste. This presents a problem with the car since it is then a long walk around to get back to the gorge. However it can be very useful if the team that dropped you off is then climbing at Toix Oeste.

The first route takes a long and exciting line, up the left-hand side of the pinnacle.

### 1. Boulder Mascarat y Terminar .......... 6a
This impressive route takes you to some exciting positions above the road. The first three pitches are fully bolted and descent is possible from above pitch 3. however the upper section does have some good climbing, including the crux pitch. Start by abseiling from the left-hand side (looking uphill) of the new road bridge, to a small ledge above the base of the gorge.
1) 5+, 45m. Climb across to a detached pillar, then move up a wall and make a delicate traverse left until you can reach a cave.
2) 4+, 35m. Pull steeply into the groove and follow it to a ledge.
3) 3, 20m. Scramble easily up a corner behind and onto a big ledge. You can escape leftwards here, back to the road.
4) 5+, 35m. Cross the ledge to below a big red corner. Climb the corner until you are forced left across a slab to a stance.
5) 4, 30m. Move left then climb up another corner, past a hole. Some big flakes lead more easily to a stance with a tree, below a steep crack.
6) 6a, 20m. The crack is hard to start but then leads more easily to the top.
FA. Javier Motes, Moises García, Enrique Barberá, Ernesto López

Above and right of the road tunnel are two more long diagonal grooves. The next route follows these.

### 2. Gede .......... 6a
The line is easy at the bottom then intricate at the top. The route is fully bolted except for the last easy pitch so take a small rack for this. The best approach is to walk around underneath the *Cleoplaca* wall, and follow the little tunnels through the cave to emerge just above the road. You can scramble directly to this point from the road but it's not as much fun.
1) 4+, 30m. Climb the groove above then traverse left to the other groove.
2) 5, 35m. Follow this groove then traverse left onto a big ledge.
3) 5+, 20m. Above the ledge is a big corner. Climb the wall to the right of the corner to a small stance.
4) 6a, 15m. Climb a steep flake behind the stance, then traverse around the pinnacle and move up to a well-positioned ledge.
5) 3, 30m. Scramble easily to the top.

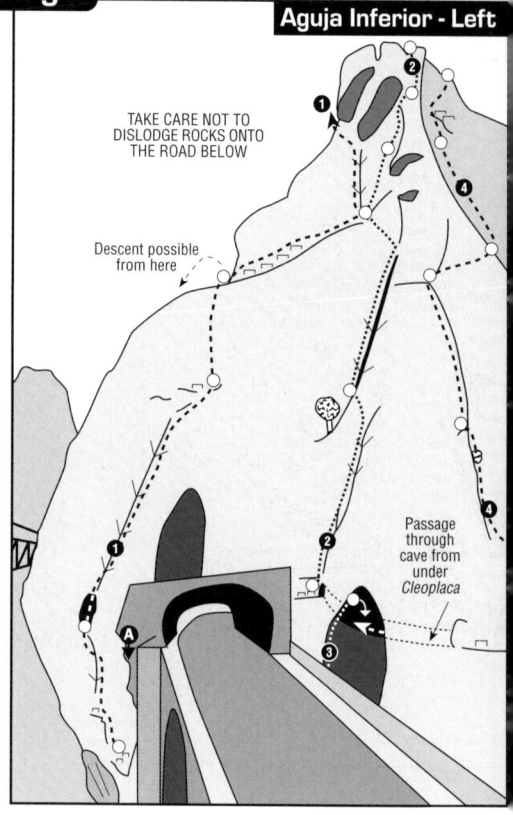

## Aguja Inferior - Left

TAKE CARE NOT TO DISLODGE ROCKS ONTO THE ROAD BELOW

Descent possible from here

Passage through cave from under *Cleoplaca*

### 3. ? .......... 6b+
A curious little route on the road side of the cave down and left of the *Cleoplaca* wall. It is just inside the cave and has a lower-off in space. Take care getting to the start.

### 4. Montesinos .......... 6a+
Another long route with two good lower pitches but it deteriorates higher up. Start from the old road bridge and walk across underneath the *Cleoplaca* wall. Scramble up a flake to the ledge directly below the wall and belay on the bolts.
1) 6a+, 30m. Move left to gain the groove-line, which bounds the face on its left. Climb this, past a deep hole, and belay on a small ledge on the left.
2) 5, 20m. Pull back right into the crack and follow it to a stance on the right.
3) 4, 15m. Traverse directly across the slab on the right, to the *Cleoplaca* belay. The sensible option is to abseil from here but:
4) 4+, 50m. Climb up the loose grooves above.
5) 4+, 50m. Follow the flakes to the left of the grooves then step back right before the top. Be very careful not to knock rocks onto the road from these upper two pitches.
FA. Juan Montesinos, Rafael Botella 1970s

**Left** - West facing wall
150m to 200m routes
Best grade - 6a

# COSTA BLANCA - Mascarat Gorge

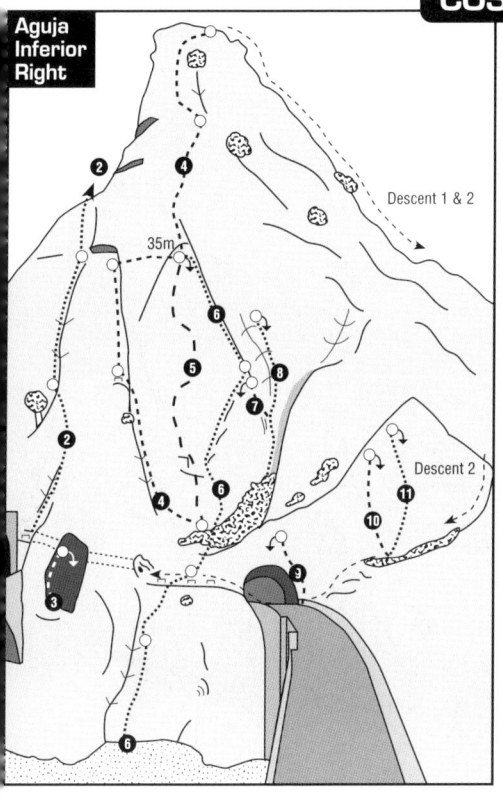

**Aguja Inferior Right**

**5. Cleoplaca** ............ 7b
One of the best technical challenges in the area, which is very testing on the fingers. The rope drag at the top can make the route impossible. Either climb it on twin 9mm ropes, or take a hanging stance on the flake after a tricky initial section. It is 35m from the grassy ledge to the belay.

**6. Aurora** .................... 6a
This one starts at the base of the gorge, between the two road bridges, and continues up the right-hand edge of the *Cleoplaca* wall.
1) **5+, 35m.** Climb the lower wall as direct as possible, to a stance and pegs on the right.
2) **5+, 10m.** Move left and make a hard move to reach the terrace below *Cleoplaca*. Belay on the bolts below the wall.
3) **6a, 30m.** Climb up to gain a ramp line which is followed with difficulty to a crack on the right.
4) **6a, 25m.** The crack above leads to the bolt belay at the top of *Cleoplaca*. Do yourself a favour and abseil off. However if you do need that summit sensation then continue up *Montesinos*.

The next routes are fully bolted with lower-offs.

**7. La Caravela** ............ 6c+
Start up the gully on the right and climb steeply to the belay on *Aurora*.

**8. Bridge of Spies** .... 7c
A magnificent, if slightly manufactured, route up the large curving arete to the right of the main wall.

**9. ?** .................. 7b
A stupid route above the tunnel entrance.

To the right is a short wall above a grassy terrace.

**10. To Be in England** ....... 7a
A wire is needed at the start (E5 6b).

**11. Crazy Inglese** .......... 6b+
The unappealing grade of E3 5b gives a better impression of this route. One peg and one thread.

**Right** - West facing wall
5m to 200m routes
Best grades - 6a to 7c

# BERNIA RIDGE AREA

There are two crags on the impressive ridge which drops down to the coast between Altea and Calpe. They offer very contrasting climbing, in an impressive situations on good quality rock. The Bernia Area consists of several sport and trad routes which pick lines out from the good bits of rock along the ridge. The sport routes tend to be in the higher grades and include the classic Magic Flute. The trad routes tend to be easier, following cracks and all of them end at lower-offs. Altea Col is a more exposed and isolated crag on the other side of the ridge above the old crag called Dalle d'Olla. It has a number of well-bolted sport routes.
The building development in the Altea Hills estate has now reached the Dalle d'Olla and climbing is no longer allowed on this crag.

## ASPECT AND CLIMATE

The Bernia Area face southwest and get lots of sun but is exposed to any wind. Altea Col is a morning-sun venue and may give some shelter but can't really be recommended in cold or very windy weather.

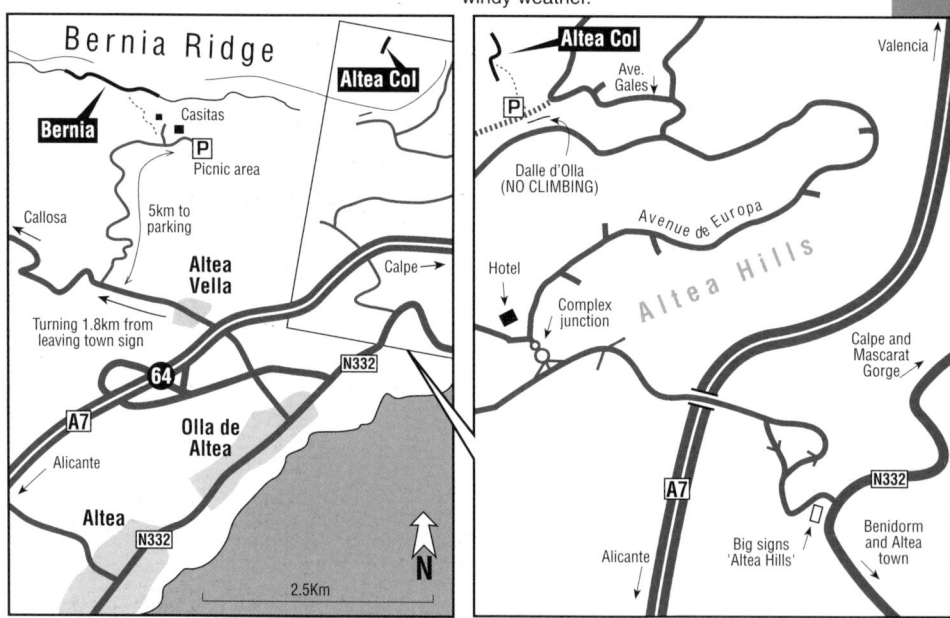

## APPROACH

**Altea Col -** Turn off the N332 at the big 'Altea Hills' entrance. Follow the road uphill, across the motorway to a complex junction by a large hotel. Drive around the fountains and head off rightwards up 'Avenue de Europa'. Follow this around until the 4th right turning 'Ave. Gran Bretagne'. Turn right then take the next left 'Ave. Gales'. Drive along here to a sharp bend where a dirt track (tarmac to this point) leads off leftwards (NOTE - this may change since there is a lot of development in this area). Park here and pick up a well-cairned path which leads off rightwards to the crag which can be clearly seen.

**Bernia -** From the N332 coast road at Olla de Altea, take the road inland towards Callosa d'En Sarrià. Go through Altea Vella and 1.8km from the leaving town sign turn off to the right, before a sharp right bend marked with chevrons. Drive uphill passing through the centre of a farm and past some gates on the right with 'Costera Blanca' on them. Continue climbing up the winding road until after 5kms you arrive at some 'Casitas' (small cottages) high above the coast. Park here, or at the small picnic area a little further on. From here you can see the jutting ships prow of the 'Sphinx' on the cliff above and too the left. To reach it contour leftwards along then up the terraces, over some flat slabs, up to some large boulders. Walk directly uphill from here to the base of the routes.

## THE ROUTES

Altea Col was developed by Calpe resident - Jens Muenchberg. The Bernia Area was developed by Mark Edwards and Rowland Edwards between 1986 and 1997.

# COSTA BLANCA - Bernia and Altea

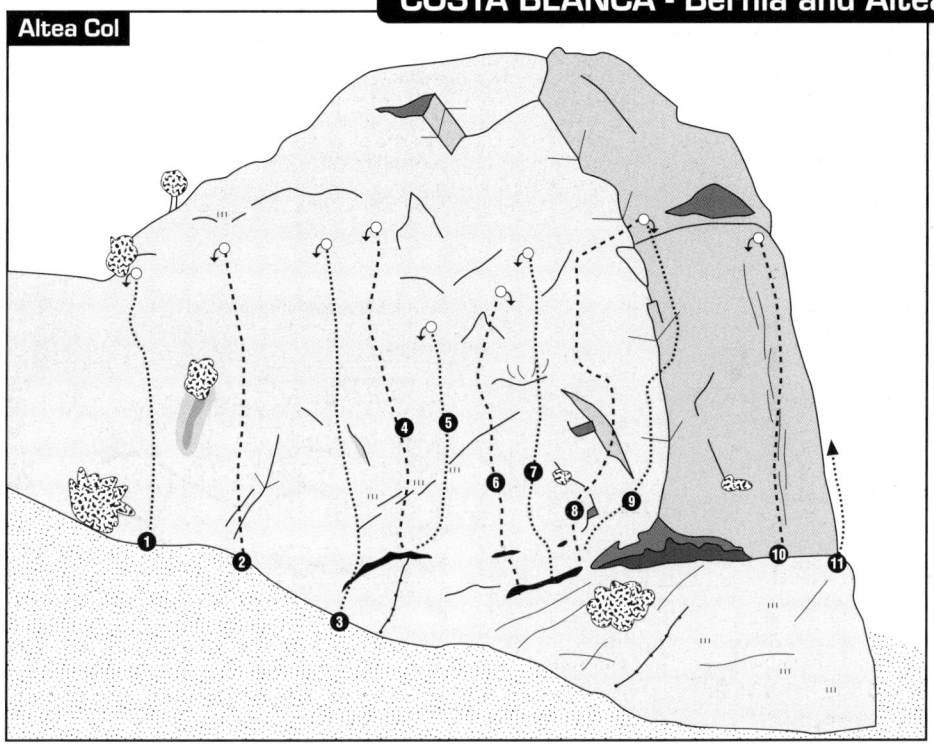

**Altea Col**

## ALTEA COL
The routes are described from left to right. The first two are in a small bay just right of the main wall.

**1. ?** .................... 6c+
A thin vertical wall on small edges with sparse bolts. Technically not too bad but a bit scary.

**2. ?** .................... 6c+
The right-hand wall of the bay past tufas and holes. 'Broccoli' rock at present but will improve with traffic.

**3. ?** .................... 6b
35m. The left-hand edge of the main wall.

There may now be another new route in the area of route 3.

**4. Tschook du ????** ...... 6b+
30m. A tricky start and sustained wall above. Good climbing all the way.

**5. Leo** .................... 6a+
28m. The easiest route on the wall with a more gentle start than its neighbours. It gets a bit technical above but is never desperate.

**6. Entre dos tierras** ......... 7a+
28m. A poor, unbalanced route which has a desperate start and then much easier climbing above.

**7. Walking on the Milkyway** ... 6c
28m. Another hard start with easier wall above (6a+).

**8. Soft and Huggy** ......... 6a+
Some sharp holds and well-spaced bolts. Move right to the shared lower-off.

**9. Kuscheltiger** ........... 6c+
Start as for *Soft and Huggy* but traverse right. The slab higher up provides the fingery crux.

**10. Salva mea** ................. Project
The tufa streaks will be very hard if it is ever climbed - 8a/b?

**11. Suse 4711** ............ 6b+
Around the corner from the start of *Salvea mea*.

East facing wall
20m to 30m routes
Best grades - 6a+ to 6c+

# COSTA BLANCA - Bernia and Altea

## Bernia

Right again is another project then past a gully are two cracks.

**5. Left Crack** .............. 6a+
A full rack needed. There is a lower-off.

**6. Right Crack** ............. 6a+
A full rack needed.

The next routes are on the magnificent prow.

**7. The Magic Flute** ....... 7b
Brilliant climbing but sadly the bolts are old and one is missing. Gain the tufa using pockets and then climb it to a belay, or continue up.....

**8. The Sphinx** .......... 8a
The exposed and spectacular prow gives a long and demanding pitch. From the belay a 6a+ pitch leads to the top.

**9. The Grand Diedre** ........ 6c
The big corner to the right of the prow.
1) 6c, 2) 6b+

About 100m to the right is a slab with a diagonal crack on its right-hand side.

**10. Secrets** ............ 7a+
The slab direct. Take a small rack.

**11. The Diagonal** .......... 6c
The crack itself in one long pitch. Some fixed gear but take a full rack.

**12. Mark in Time** ..... 8b
A big route up the steep, double curving wall 50m to the right. Lots of pockets.

**13. Dada Crack Left-hand** ....... 6a
The left-hand crack is followed to a lower-off.

**14. Dada Crack Right-hand** ...... 6a+
The right-hand crack to the same lower-off.

**15. El groove** ............. 5+
The crack and groove to a lower-off.

**16. The Slap** .......... 7a+
A bold wall to a lower-off.

## BERNIA

The most striking feature of the buttress is the huge ship's prow of *The Sphinx*. This is home to one of the best routes in the area - *The Magic Flute*.

The first route is a bit further left on a tall pillar.

**1. The Immaculate Arete** .. 7b+
A superb route up the huge arete starting up a grey slab.

To the right is a steep wall with a good set of routes and projects.

**2. Jayne's Project** ......... 6c
A slab leading to an overhanging wall with pockets.

**3. Paradise Lost** .......... 7a
Another slabby start but steep above.

Inbetween routes 3 and 4 are two projects.

**4. The First and Last** .. 8b
Start up a slab to reach a steep crack.

South facing walls
15m to 60m mostly single pitch
Best grades - 6a to 8a

# ECHO VALLEY

The Echo Valley is one of the most impressive mountainous limestone regions in the Costa Blanca. Just walking up the valley takes your breath away so you can imagine what it is like when you are actually on the routes. Compared to many of the other crags in the Costa Blanca it is relatively unspoilt and quiet which makes it a great venue for those who are after a bit of solitude far from the madding crowds. The appearance of the route information in this book, coupled with the improved access roads, is likely to make it a much more popular destination in future. Please try and keep it as unspoilt as possible, keep to the paths, take your litter home and respect the local flora and fauna.

The climbing is mostly traditional requiring hand-placed gear for virtually all of the routes. Many of the routes have been climbed using the Environmental Nut Placement system, or ENP. These devices are fixed into drilled holes in the rock and are designed to accept certain wire nuts which are placed in much the same way as you place a nut in a crack. This means that the routes retain their traditional character whilst allowing blank areas of rock to be relatively well-protected for the lead climber.

There is more information on the routes in the Echo Valley on the Compass West web site - www.compasswest.co.uk

## ENP USAGE

The ENP is a steel tube containing a hard plastic washer with a small stainless steel spring behind it. When you place the nut into the tube the nut pushes against the plastic washer and depresses the spring backwards. You can then turn the nut sideways through 90 degrees and release it so that the spring traps the nut in the pre-formed sides of the tube. The wires can be removed simply by pushing backwards against the washer, turning back through 90 degrees and letting the spring push the wire back out again. It should be remembered that ENPs are not bolts and should not be treated as such. They are solid but they need to be properly placed and you should obviously use wires which are in good condition.

There are currently two types of ENP which require a different wire nut to be used in each.

**The standard ENP -** This requires a Wild Country Rock 3, or Cassin 5 brass nuts.

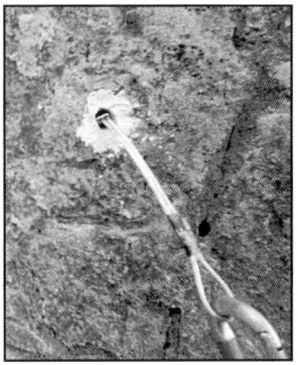

An ENP. Photo: Alex Masters

**The Super ENP (SENP) -** This requires an RP5.

There is no visual difference in outward appearance between the two devices, and you can't place wires for the ENP in the SENP, so you should make sure that you check the route notes in this guidebook carefully. All the descriptions tell you which kind of nut is needed and how many are placed on each pitch.

Tips on usage -

1) It is a good idea to round off the corners of the nuts with sandpaper. This makes them turn more freely in the ENPs. Most of the crags have a placement at their base which enables you to practice placing the wires.

2) Rock 3s have a tendency to slide up the wire when trying to remove them. This can be avoided by fixing the nut onto the head of the wire with tape or glue.

## ASPECT AND CLIMATE

**Echo One and Castillo -** These two areas face south and get all the sun that is going. They will also offer some protection from the cold north winds.

**Echo Two -** Receives the sun until mid afternoon, then it can become chilly in the winter. It makes a good venue for late afternoons and evenings in the hot season.

**Echo Placa, Col Llama and Haunted Walls -** These are all high crags which catch a lot of sun but are exposed to any wind that is blowing.

**Senyera -** Receives the sun until early afternoon but then it can get very cold. A good warm weather venue.

Although none of the above crags could be considered a reliable wet weather venue. If the wind is blowing from the west then the central section of Echo Two stays remarkably dry.

## APPROACH

**From the North -** Leave the A7 at junction 65 (Benidorm) and immediately turn south on the N332. Keep going to a right turn inland towards Callosa d'en Sarrià.

**From the South -** Leave at the the new Terra Mitica junction (Number 65a) and turn north onto the N332 towards Valencia. Keep going to a left turn inland towards Callosa d'en Sarrià.

You should be able to see the large hulk of the Ponoch and the taller Puig Campana on your left, you are aiming for the valley on the north (far) side of the Ponoch. Drive on for about 5km past many roundabouts. When you reach one signed La Nucia/Polop and Callosa straight on, and Guadalest to the left, turn left towards Guadalest, still on the CV70, going left through an industrial estate. After about 4km you will come to a roundabout with trees in its centre and a road/track leading off to the left (at the time of writing this track is unsurfaced but it may well be surfaced in the future). The roads, and road numbers, in the area of La Nucia and Polop are undergoing considerable modifications and you should expect some alterations to these directions. Please inform ROCKFAX of any changes.

**For The Castillo, Echo One and Echo Two -** Drive up the left turning off the roundabout and you will start to see the rock faces in the valley right of the Ponoch. The pyramid shape of Echo Two is very obvious. Echo One and Castillo are below that. Follow the track to a junction and park there, or just before. A path leads off up the hillside towards Echo One and the Castillo. The parking for Echo Two is further along the track. See crag pages for approaches from here.

**For Echo Placa and Col de Llama -** Continue from the parking spots below the Echos, along an increasingly rough track, to a chain-off track on the left by a casa. See crag pages for more details.

**For the Haunted Walls, Senyera and the Capella -** Starting from the roundabout with trees on the CV70 continue straight on towards Guadalest. After approximately 7km there is a surfaced road on the left, up a steepish hill (the first surfaced road on the left, by a large house surrounded by trees). Go up this road and take the first track on the left. Follow this for about 2km, taking no turning off to the right, until a small parking spot of the left (cairn). This is the parking for Senyera and La Capella. For Haunted Walls walk up the hill to the col which descends down into Sella. This same point can be reached from Sella but is slightly rougher. See crag pages for approaches from here. It is also possible to approach Senyera and La capella from below - see crag pages.

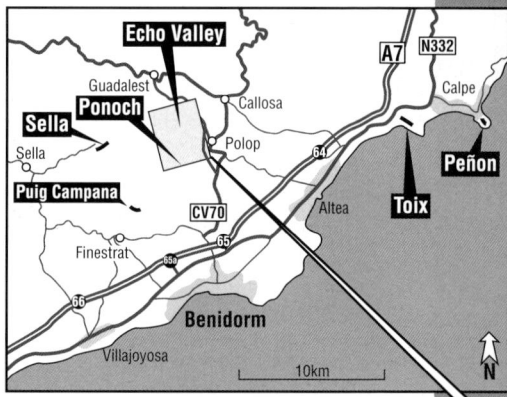

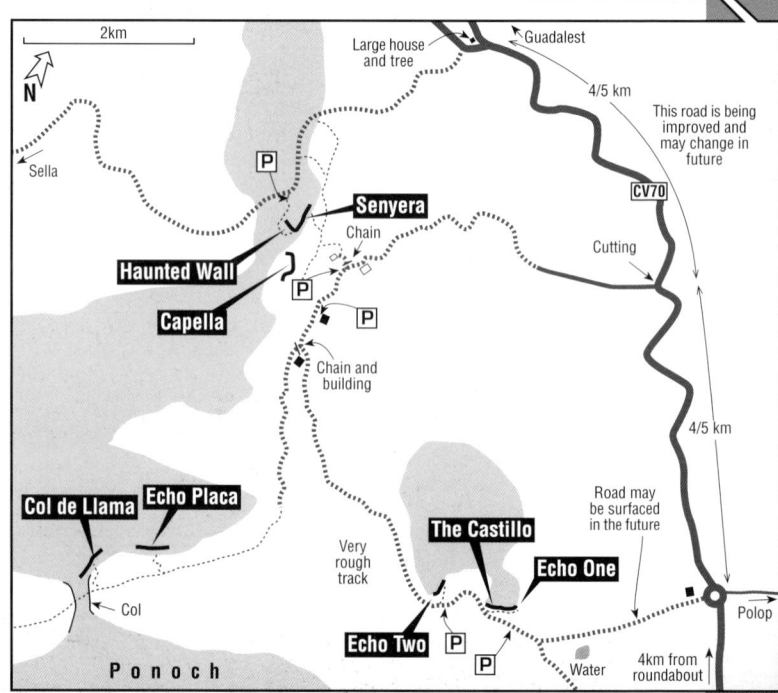

114

Castillo Lower - Left

# COSTA BLANCA - Echo Valley

## CASTILLO LOWER - LEFT
The Castillo stretches down virtually to the track. The lower left section has been developed with the only sport routes in the whole valley. These routes were equipped by unknown climbers.
**APPROACH** - From the parking follow the track uphill. Echo One and the orange wall of Castillo can be seen up on your right. Continue past a large boulder on the right to just before the rock faces meet the track (cairn on the left). Scramble up the banking at the side of the track (cairn) and follow a cairned-path up and right. Castillo Lower is the first crag you pass on the left.

The first five routes are on the short wall just above the track.

1. ? . . . . . . . . . . . . . . . . . . . . . . . . . ?

2. ? . . . . . . . . . . . . . . . . . . . . . . . . . ?

3. ? . . . . . . . . . . . . . . . . . . . . . . . 6c+
Slopers up the wall left of the groove.

4. ? . . . . . . . . . . . . . . . . . . . . . . . 6b+
Powerful climbing up the steep groove and over the bulge.

5. ? . . . . . . . . . . . . . . . . . . . . . . . 6b+
A rather strange climb forcing its way through and past a tree. The climbing is harder if the use of the tree is avoided.

Further up right are some longer routes.

6. ? . . . . . . . . . . . . . . . . . . . . . . . . 6a
A crack climb.

7. ? . . . . . . . . . . . . . . . . . . . . . . . . 6b

8. ? . . . . . . . . . . . . . . . . . . . . . . . . 7a
Long reaches over the final bulge.

9. ? . . . . . . . . . . . . . . . . . . . . . . . 7a+
The best line on the wall. The finish can be made harder if the use of the right-hand crack is avoided.

10. ? . . . . . . . . . . . . . . . . . . . . . . . 6c
30m. A long pitch crossing a ramp at mid-height.

11. ? . . . . . . . . . . . . . . . . . . . . . . . 6a

12. ? . . . . . . . . . . . . . . . . . . . . . . . 4+

13. ? . . . . . . . . . . . . . . . . . . . . . . . 6a
30m. Right of a tree-filled gully.

14. ? . . . . . . . . . . . . . . . . . . . . . . . 6b
The crux is the roof.

Further right are two long multi-pitch routes.

15. ? . . . . . . . . . . . . . . . . . . . . . . . 5
1) 5. A diagonal crack line. Can be done on its own.
2) 5. Scramble across right then follow the cleaner wall above.
**DESCENT** - By abseil down the next route.

16. ? . . . . . . . . . . . . . . . . . . . . . . . 6a
1) 6a. Can be done on its own.
2) Scramble across easy ground to the base of the upper wall.
3) 5. A vertical wall leads to another ledge.
4) 5. One more pitch to the top.
**DESCENT** - By abseil.

South facing wall
10m to 30m routes and multi-pitch
Best grades - 4+ to 7a+

# COSTA BLANCA - Echo Valley

**The Castillo**

Castillo Upper

Route 14 from Castillo Lower - Left

Approach from The Bay

Castillo Lower - Right

## CASTILLO LOWER - RIGHT
This wall is a very pleasant place to visit. Most of the routes are slab and crack climbing with plentiful trad protection.
**APPROACH (See page 112)** - From the parking follow the track uphill. Continue past a large boulder on the right to just before the rock faces meet the track (cairn on the left). Scramble up the banking at the side of the track (cairn) and follow a cairned-path up and right. The first crag on the left is the bolted section on Castillo Lower - Left. The next routes start just to the right of this.

**1. Little Bootie** . . . . . . . . . . . . . . . . 2
Climb the short wall and then the lower crack to the lower-off.
FA. R.Edwards 12.98

**2. Big Bootie** . . . . . . . . . . . . . . . . . 2
The other crack to the lower-off.
FA. R.Edwards 12.98

Lots of sun · 5 min · Slabby · Vertical · Lower-offs · Multi-pitch · Windy

# COSTA BLANCA - Echo Valley

**3. Whisky** .............. 2
Climb the next crack right of the previous 2 routes. Lower off.
FA. R.Edwards 12.98

**4. Arbole Directo** .......... 3+
Start directly below a small tree.
1) 3+, 20m. Climb the slab then move right to a crack just above the tree. Follow this to a lower-off or:
2) 3, 20m. Continue up the slabs and corner to join *The Wasp*.
FA. R.Edwards 12.98

**5. Domingo nerga** ....... 6a+
A fine climb with a good crack finish. Start as for *Abole Directo*. Climb the slab to just below the tree and move delicately out right onto the steep wall (ENP). Climb direct, then a long reach right. Continue up right and follow a crack to the lower-off.
FA. R.Edwards 12.98

**6. Vino tinto** ........... 6b
A bold route. Start below an overhanging corner. Climb the corner and then follow the steepening-slab leftwards. Make some hard moves past a jammed wire and continue up the slab. Lower off.
FA. M.Edwards 5.98

**7. Salir por encima** ...... 6a
A strenuous and well-protected roof pitch. Climb a corner to an overhanging crack. Climb this and the crack above to a lower-off.
FA. R.Edwards 11.98

**8. Strongbody** .......... 6a
Start just right of *Silar por encima*, below a slanting crack. Climb the crack onto a ledge. Continue direct then move right to the arete. Continue up the wall to reach the lower-off on the left.
FA. R.Edwards 12.98

**9. The Wasp** .......... 4
Good climbing with a spectacular finish. Start below a steep slab on the edge of the wall.
1) 4, 45m. Climb to and up a steep groove. Step into the groove on the right, which ends at a large block (belay possible). Climb the wall and trend right then direct to a ledge with a chain belay.
2) 3, 15m. Traverse easily leftwards along ledges to reach a large bay at the foot of an arete.
3) 4, 45m. Climb the arete into a slanting groove. Go up this and move right at its top onto a ledge (belay possible). Move left and climb the slab rightwards stepping left at the top onto a good ledge and trees.
4) 4+, 20m. (The sting) From the left end of the ledge climb direct to the steep wall above. Follow the leftwards-slanting fault line which leads to the top.
**DESCENT** - Climb rightwards to the belays of *Scorpion* and Abseil off from there.
FA. R.Edwards 11.98

**10. Mosca** ............ 3
Start right of *The Wasp* below a crack. Climb the short wall and enter the wide crack on the left. Follow this to a large block. Climb the wall behind and trend right over slabs and blocks to reach the belay.
FA. R.Edwards 11.98

**11. Mosca izquirda** .......... 3
Start by the right side of a large bush. Climb the slab until you can traverse left to a crack. Follow this to a ledge and then continue direct to the belay.
FA. R.Edwards 11.98

**12. Mosca directo** ......... 4
Start to the right of the large bush. Climb the slab until level with the large tree. Move slightly left and then direct to a ledge. Climb the corner on the right and then more broken rock to the belay.
FA. R.Edwards 11.98

**13. Scorpion** ......... 4+
A spectacular finish. Start below a large tree at half-height.
1) 4, 45m. Climb the leftwards-slanting slab to a recess and tree. The steep crack on the right leads to a tree. Pass this on the left then climb up until it is possible to move left across the wall to a thin crack. Follow this, and the broken rocks, to the belay.
2) 2, 20m. Climb the short wall onto the vegetated slab and ascend left to the base of the slabs on the left.
3) 4, 30m. Climb the slab and then the slanting corner to a recess. Go rightwards up the slanting arete then the short wall above. Move left and then back right, to avoid a bush, to a good ledge and belay.
4) 4+, 30m. Climb the crack to the head-wall and traverse left to the base of the steeper section. Climb the fault-line in the head wall and move right of a good flake. Pull over the roof and climb the slab to the belay.
FA. R.Edwards 11.98

## CASTILLO UPPER
The higher walls contain some striking cracklines.
**APPROACH-** Scramble up left from below The Bay (see next page) to the ledge below the wide crack in the middle of the wall. Alternatively climb one of the routes on Castillo Lower.

**14. The Cut** ......... 6b
Three contrasting pitches. Start below a thin crack, 4m left of a deep chimney.
1) 6b, 40m. Climb the slab direct to the thin crack. Follow this until it is then climb up the wall (bold) to a thread and continue up easier rock to a belay ledge.
2) 6a, 40m. Climb left (thread) to reach a rising traverse to a ramp. Climb this to its end and continue to a short groove. Climb direct over a block and traverse to a belay ledge on the left.
3) 5, 10m. Break out left and then surmount the bulge on the right then continue steeply to the top.
FA. M.Edwards, H.Lee 10.00

**15. Cosmic Messenger** .... 6a
A good climb through the overhangs at the top of The Castillo. Start left of the wide chimney.
1) 5+, 25m. Climb a crack on the left of the wide chimney to a sloping ledge. Go left to a thread belay.
2) 5+, 20m. Climb right to a sloping fault. Climb this then direct to below the tree. Pull over the overhanging block to gain a good belay just above the tree.
3) 6a, 25m. Climb up then left into the slanting crack-line and follow it in a spectacular position across the headwall to the top.
FA. R.Edwards, M.Edwards 6.1.01

**16. Force of Nature** ..... 7c
A powerful line which tackles the large overhangs at the top of the face after an easy start. Start below the large chimney.
1) 5, 35m. From the large ledge, climb the chimney and follow it to a ledge on the left.
2) 5, 25m. Follow the crack slanting left and then direct up a crack to belay above a tree.
3) 7c, 20m. Climb boldly up the right wall, moving right below a roof, to enter an off-width crack (large cams essential). Climb the crack to the roof and make some hard moves left to a spike (loose). Follow the crack above with increasing difficulty to finish up the overhanging head wall.
FA. M.Edwards 1999

South facing wall
20m to 120m single and multi-pitch
Best grades - 2 to 7c

**117**

# SPAIN

## Finestrat - Costa Blanca

### ACCOMMODATION on the Costa Blanca

Enjoy your stay on the Costa Blanca
Centrally placed for sport and multi-pitch climbing
Stay in Finestrat, a small traditional Spanish village with all amenitie
Area and route information supplied by an expert on the area

**Weekly courses**
**Private guiding**
**Rowland Edwards**
**UIAGM AMBG MIAC**
**Compass West**
**Tel/Fax 00 34 965878585**
**Web site - www.compasswest.co.uk**
**E-mail - compass-west@cliffhanger.com**

# COSTA BLANCA - Echo Valley

## ECHO ONE - THE BAY
The bottom left side of the bulk of Echo One is a wide depression known as The Bay.
**APPROACH (See page 112)** - From the parking follow the track uphill. Continue past a large boulder on the right to just before the rock faces meet the track (cairn on the left). Scramble up the banking at the side of the track (cairn) and follow a cairned-path up and right below the Castillo. To the right of this is the wide depression of The Bay. To reach it scramble up into the depression and make for the foot of the wall.
**DESCENTS** - Use the abseil from the top of Route 1. Routes 5 and 6 abseil from a fixed chain. It is possible to scramble back down but this isn't advised.

### 1. Mistaken Identity  4+
This route lies on the extreme left-hand side of the buttress. Start below a thin rib of rock below the seemingly vegetated wall - this is indeed a misleading impression. This route was first climbed with removable bolts. Staples were placed later - hence the name.
1) **3, 20m.** Fully bolted. Climb the rib and follow the steep walls and slabs to a palm-tree-covered ledge.
2) **3 (HS 4b) 30m.** Some gear is needed. Climb the steep wall on the right and follow the well-spaced line of bolts, trending right to a sloping ledge. Climb the steep slab to the roof above and trend right and up to reach the top. Abseil from the lower-off (50m).
FA. R. Edwards, Esther Edwards 4.97

### 2. Vía Carob  6b+
A good route with some interesting moves. Start lower down, and in a small bay to the right of *Mistaken Identity*, by a rib of rock which leads to a groove with a carob tree at its top. You can run the two pitches into one.
1) **6a, 25m.** Climb the groove to the chain lower-off / belay.
2) **6b+ (E3 6a) 25m.** Climb up rightwards and then directly up the steep wall and slab to the top (3 ENPs).
FA. R. Edwards 12.10.98

### 3. Cracks for Angels  6b
Start as for *Vía Carob* at the base of a narrow rib.
1) **6a, 30m.** Climb the rib and then ascend right along the top or bottom crack. Move up to the small roof on the left of the pillar and climb the crack to a belay on top of a flake. Bolts
2) **6b (E3 5c) 25m.** Climb the crack on the left to an ENP. Trend leftwards up the steep slab to the top. Belays and abseil point.
FA. R.Edwards, M.Edwards 21.4.98

### 4. The Pod  6b+
A superb route with two contrasting pitches. Start in the Bay below an orange-coloured overhanging pod. The first pitch is worth doing on its own but the second is also superb if you are up to it.
1) **6a (E3 5b) 25m.** Climb the crack directly to the pod. Climb this until it closes up and make a bold swing left on the short slab. Go right to the foot of a steep crack (2 ENPs). Climb the crack to a bolt belay (possible lower-off).
2) **6b+ (E3 6a) 25m.** Climb onto the right wall and go directly up this (3 ENPs) to the steep slab above. Follow this to the top of the crag.
FA. R.Edwards, M.Edwards 6.4.98

### 5. Rock Factory  6a+
**(E4 5c) 30m.** A bold route. Start in the wide bay below the clean sweep of rock which forms a large scoop. Follow the crack past the old tree then right passing two ENPs. From the last ENP climb right then straight up, following a steep slab, to a small overhang on the left. Climb over this and follow the groove to the belay and lower-off.
FA. R.Edwards, M.Edwards 5.98

### 6. Pictures of Perfection  5
**(VS 4c) 30m.** A short variation finish to the last route but it is at a consistent grade. Follow *Rock Factory* to its last ENP. From here, move right then up and across into a sloping groove. Follow this until it steepens then move right again into a flake good crack. Follow this to a good ledge and bolt and chain lower-off.
FA. R.Edwards, Esther Edwards 25.12.97

South facing wall
30m to 50m routes
Best grades - 4+ to 6b+

# COSTA BLANCA - Echo Valley

## ECHO ONE
This impressive cliff dominates this end of the valley.

**APPROACH (See page 112)** - From the parking follow the track uphill. Echo One and the orange wall of Castillo can be seen up on your right. Continue past a large boulder on the right to just before the rock faces meet the track (cairn on the left). Scramble up the banking at the side of the track (cairn) and follow a cairned-path up and right, below the Castillo. Continue along the narrow path until below the main face.

**DESCENTS** - For the routes which reach the top of the crag, abseil directly down the face via the fixed belays of the other routes.

Echo One

# COSTA BLANCA - Echo Valley

### 1. Diamond Solitaire ....... 🔲 5+
Start at the foot of a slabby ramp at the left side of the buttress below the first of two leftward-facing grooves.
1) 5, 22m. Climb the slab and then move left into a cave. Leave this onto a good ledge and belay (peg and nuts).
2) 5 (HVS 5b) 20m. Climb the steep groove on the right. Continue climbing the crack which leads to a ledge. Move left into a recess and belay (nuts).
3) 5, 25m. Climb the crack in the wall above the roof. Pull over this and trend rightwards into a bay with thread belay.
4) 4, 28m. Climb onto the block on the right move back left and continue straight up the steep slab to the top.
FA. R.Edwards, Mark Bonesteel 1.97

### 2. Diedro Edwards ....... 🔲 6a+
A long corner and face route with a slightly bold third pitch. Start in the centre of the face below a leftward-facing corner which starts 15m above the ground.
1) 6a, 25m. Climb the steep wall and make some difficult moves into the corner and follow this to a large recess.
2) 6a, 20m. Climb the corner to a large ledge above.
3) 6a+ (E3 5c) 25m. Follow the faint line of the depression in the centre of the orange wall above. Trend right to reach a wide crack and follow this to a tree-covered ledge.
4) 4, 40m. Climb the wall behind the belay to the top.
FA. R.Edwards, Mark Bonesteel 1.97

### 3. Movimento magic ....... 🔲 6a
A good long route. Start below a rightwards-slanting orange wall just to the right of the tower of Diedro Edwards.
1) 6a, 25m. Climb the slab to the base of the steep section (ENP) and climb this to the overlap. Ascend right and then up to a good ledge. Bolts.
2) 6a (E2 5b) 25m. Climb across the wall on the right to the arete (ENP). Go right again and then follow cracks left to a sloping ledge and belay bolts.
3) 6a (E2 5b) 30m. Climb up to the steep wall above. Go up and right passing two ENPs. Follow cracks and then trend right to a good ledge, tree on the right. Climb the vertical crack to a ledge.
4) 3, 20m. Climb the arete easily to the top.
FA. R.Edwards, D.Golding, W.Kersten 27.12.98

### 4. El murcielago ........... 🔲 6a
25m. A single pitch to a lower-off.
FA. R.Edwards, D.Golding, W.Kerston 27.12.98

### 5. St Valentines ....... 🔲 6b+
Quality climbing with short difficulties. Start just right of the scoop at the base of the wall, below a small cave high up.
1) 6b+ (E2 6a) 45m. Climb directly to the recess then straight up to the foot of a steep wall (just right of a white scar). Climb the pocketed wall (ENP at half-height) to gain a ledge. Go left into a groove and climb direct to a bolt belay.
2) 6b (E2 5c) 50m. Climb the slabby arete to the base of the wall above. Step right onto the steep overhanging wall. Go right (2 ENPs) and make a long move up and right to reach some broken cracks. Follow these right and climb the bulging slab on the right by a good pocket. Follow the arete to the base of a good crack going up on the right side of a tree. Follow the crack, passing the tree on the left, and up into a good recess.
3) 3, 20m. Either abseil back down the route from here or continue up the arete of Vía Esther to the top of the crag.
FA. P1 - R.Edwards, Dave Goldy 1.98, P2 - R.Edwards, M.Edwards, F.Beith 13.2.98

### 6. Initiation .............. 🔲 5+
(HVS 4c) 30m. A good route with a bold start. It finishes up a perfect crack, high up the wall of the prow, high up. Start just left of the pinnacle of Deception, below a series of slanting slots in the steep wall. Follow the slots until then continue up and across to a steep crack in the face of the prow. Climb this to a corner and up this to a slab which leads to the belays. Abseil off.
FA. R.Edwards and students 12.97

### 7. Second Blood .......... 🔲 5+
(HVS 5a) 30m. After a bold start this route follows the steep corner, on the right of the prow, high up. Start 3m to the right of a thin flake at the base of the wall below some deep broken cracks. Climb direct to the cracks and straight up to below the prow. Climb up to the left of the prow and continue up the steep crack to the roof. Go over this in a wild movement into a corner. Climb the wall on the left and continue to the belay.
FA. R.Edwards 12.98

### 8. Rough-Rider ...... 🔲 6c
(E4 6a) 30m. The hard moves are indeed rough on the skin. Start as for Second Blood, about 5m left of the pillar of Deception, below a series of rightward slanting slots. Follow the slots to the base of the steep rough wall on the right with a sling in a thread. Ascend rightwards (ENP) and make a long and bold move to reach the thread. Move up right into a shallow groove and follow this to a belay. Abseil off.
FA. R.Edwards, Geoff Cater, Sarah Nuttal 28.5.98

### 9. Deception ............. 🔲 6a
(E1 5b) 30m. A much better climb than it looks. Start below a pinnacle about 15m left of the right edge of the buttress. Climb the left-hand side of the pinnacle then move right into a small cave. Over this and follow the crack to its end. Move left and up to a flake then up to a good ledge and chain and thread belay. Abseil off or continue up one of the routes above.
FA. R.Edwards, Mark Bone Steel 1.97

### 10. Vía Diagonal ............. 🔲 5+
(VS 4c) 30m. An alternative start to Ricon De Placa.
FA. R.Edwards, Esther Edwards 12.12.96

### 11. Design and Form ........... 🔲 6a
(E2 5b) 25m. A counter line to Vía Diagonal.
FA. M.Edwards, Sarah Nuttal 11.98

### 12. Un Rincon de Placa ...... 🔲 4+
A wandering route but with good climbing and positions. Start at the extreme right side of the crag below an obvious corner.
1) 4+, 30m. Climb the corner then a steep wall to the wide gully. Cross over left to reach the belay ledge of Deception.
2) 4, 35m. Climb the slab behind the belay and then the left arete. Traverse down and left to reach a good ledge.
3) 4+ (VS 4c) 25m. Climb the groove to a large ledge.
4) 4, 28m. As for Diamond Solitaire.
FA. R.Edwards 12.96

### 13. Vía Esther ............ 🔲 5
A good route at the grade. It follows the right arete of the crag. Start at the extreme right end of the buttress below the arete. Reach this by a short scramble up ledges into a wide gully.
1) 4+, 25m. Climb across the steep short wall with a leftwards slanting crack then move up and across right onto the slab. Up this and then climb short grooves on the left to a small stance and thread belays.
2) 5, 30m. Climb the wall and move right into grooves which lead to a good ledge below the imposing head wall. Swing round right and climb the short wall onto a good ledge and thread belays.
3) 5 (VS 4c) 40m. Climb the wall left of the belay then ascend up and right to a crack. Go up this a short way until it is possible to move right onto the right arete. Climb direct until you can move left onto a good ledge and thread belays. Possible abseil descent from here.
4) 3, 20m. Climb the wall behind the belays and go direct to the top. A short scramble leads to the summit and a lower-off.
FA. R.Edwards, Esther Edwards 10.2.95

Large, south facing wall
30m single pitch, to 110m multi-pitch, routes
Best grades - 4+ to 6c

# COSTA BLANCA - Echo Valley

## Echo Two - Left

### ECHO TWO - LEFT
Once below this cliff it soon becomes apparent that it is a lot larger and steeper than you first imagined. All of the long routes find their way along natural lines mainly on leader-placed gear. Many of the first pitches of the climbs can be done on their own and make a useful short day.

**APPROACH (See page 112)** - Continue underneath Echo One until Echo Two. Park and follow the path up to the crag.

**DESCENT (Walking down from the summit)** - Once on the summit walk south (left -looking in) and scramble down the ridge, overlooking the climbs, until on a broad ledge. Walk down a sloping scree ledge (right - looking out) to an abseil point. A 25m abseil reaches the hillside. Walk down this making for the end of the crag on the left. Walk around the base of the wall. An escape on the north side can be made but with far more difficult down climbing.

### 1. Espolón de Echo ......... 3
(VDiff) 120m. The left-hand arete of the wall which has many variations. Start in the gully behind the left-hand side of the crag. Climb the steep wall rightwards to get onto the ridge and follow this easily to a large step. Climb the ridge on the left to the summit. 2 or 3 pitches.
*FA. R.Edwards 1998*

### 2. Vía de Polop ......... 5+
Start at the top of the slope which descends below the main face, below a long overhang at 10m up.
**1) 5 (VS 4c) 25m.** Climb up to the short crack on the left and up this onto the slab above. Trend right and then up to the blocks below the roof. Traverse left to the end of the blocks and then move up onto a small ledge and belays.
**2) 3, 10m.** Follow the shallow groove to a large ledge.
**3) 4, 28m.** Climb the pillar on the right and then move around the face into a cave.
**4) 5+ (VS 4c) 25m.** Climb the wall on the right. Move right and then up into a small cave. Climb left and up the narrow gully to a good ledge below the top headwall.
**5) 5+ (VS 4c) 40m.** Climb the short wall and then up to the overhanging groove above. Traverse right onto the slab and then up to a crack. Climb this and the short walls above to the top.
**DESCENT** - As left or abseil described on next page.
*FA. R.Edwards, Michael Esslinger 26.12.99*

### 3. Through the Looking Glass 🔒 6a
A good introduction to the style of climbing on this wall. The start is still slightly loose but not worryingly so. Start at the top of the slope below a leftwards slanting fault.
**1) 5+, 25m.** Climb the wall to gain the fault and follow this to a difficult move right to reach the arete. Go around this to a corner crack which is followed to a small roof. Pull over to a bolt belay.
**2) 5, 25m.** Traverse right along the break to the next bay (bolts on a project). Follow the line below the overlap (peg) and pull over this onto a wall and groove which is followed to the top. Move right to a good ledge and bolt belay.
**3) 6a (E1 5b) 30m.** Climb the steep wall on the right (2 threads) to follow the fault line right to a steep corner. Move up, then left, and climb direct to a small ledge (thread/nut belays).
**4) 5, 45m.** Climb the steepening slab direct to a short steep crack. Climb this to a ledge with a tree on the left (care with loose rock). Ascend left to the ledge below the top wall.
**5) 4+, 45m.** Climb onto the slab and head for the rightwards-slanting overhang. Follow this then move out right onto the slab . Cross to cracks on the right and follow these to a ledge. Climb the short walls to the top. Alternatively, you can finish up *Capricorn Encounter* or the right-hand finish of *El asesino*....
**DESCENT** - As left or abseil described on next page.
FA. R.Edwards, C.Morton, B,Rynne 2.1.01

### 4. Capricorn Encounter 🔒 6a+
Start just as the steep overhangs finish, below a scoop with a glued and bolted flake at its base.
**1) 6a+ (E2 5c) 25m.** Climb awkwardly into a scoop (SENP) then move left along a series of hand holds (SENP and threads) until you can make a wild move up and right. Continue direct to a good ledge. Move right and climb the steep arete above a small pillar abutting the ledge. Make some difficult moves up the arete and follow a crack to a good ledge and belays.
**1a) 6a.** Instead of climbing the pillar move down on right into a steep groove and climb this to the ledge.
**2) 5+, 25m.** As for *Looking Glass*.
**3) 6a+, (E2 5c) 30m.** Go up right (2 threads) then back left to a faint crack. Follow this and continue up left onto the slab. Ascend leftwards to a belay in a short corner.
**4) 5, 50m.** Climb the small pillar left of the tree and continue directly up the slab until below the overhanging block at its top. Climb up to this and pull over by a thin crack onto a ledge. Climb over ledges to a larger ledge at the foot of the headwall.
**5) 6a+ (E2 5b) 35m.** From the ledge. Climb the wall directly below the bush high up (2 SENPs). At the last SENP traverse right and ascend rightwards below a small overlap. At its end climb direct to a good ledge and finish up short wall to the top.
**DESCENT** - As left or abseil described on next page.
FA. R.Edwards, M.Edwards 23.12.00
FA. (pitch 5) R.Edwards, D.Whitley 25.2.01

### 5. Secundo Veces 🔒 6c+
Mainly bolted.
FA. M.Edwards, R.Edwards, J.Hoskins 3.01

### 6. ? (6b+)
Another possible project sport route.

### 7. Chilling Out 🔒 8a
First pitch of a hard new route which will be extended upwards.
FA. M.Edwards 2001

### 8. El asesino y redención 🔒 7a
A superb long route with interesting climbing and exciting positions. Start near the top of the slope below a well-defined groove/crack system with a small, ruined wall at its base.
**1) 7a (E4 6a) 20m. The Assassin.** This fine pitch can be done on its own. Climb into the overhanging crack with difficulty and follow this to the roof. Climb out over the roof and onto the left wall. Follow a thin crack and pockets to a niche and bolt belay. Lower off or continue up...

## COSTA BLANCA - Echo Valley

**El asesino y redención continued....**
**2) 6a, 18m. The Redemption.** Follow the groove (some loose rock) and then climb leftwards to the middle of the wall and bolts in a small cave.
**3) 6b (E3 5c) 28m.** A great pitch. Traverse left to a ledge below an overhanging wall with a large hole (thread). Climb this direct to a small ledge. Climb the overhanging wall, trending slightly right, to reach a good ledge with trees.
**4) 5+, 50m.** Climb slightly left and then straight up to a short steep wall. Climb this to another steep wall which leads to a good ledge. Traverse left to another ledge and belay below the head wall.
**5) 5+, 45m.** Climb the shallow groove and, at its top, traverse left onto a ledge. Continue to the top of the crag.
**Alternative finish -**
**5a) 6b (E3 5c) 45m.** Climb the wall direct passing a SENP. Continue in the same line to reach a good ledge. Climb direct to the top of the crag.
**DESCENT** - As left or abseil described on next page.
FA. (The Assassin) M.Edwards. 23.10.99. The rest - R.Edwards, M.Esslinger 11.99

### 9. Spanish Gold 🔒 Project
A multi-pitch project. Pitch 1 has been climbed already at 7a.
FA. (pitch 1) M.Edwards, R.Edwards 3.3.01

### 10. The Long Stretch 🔒 6b
Start right of the cracks of *The Assassin* below a steep, overhanging crack, with a thread runner high up.
**1) 6b (E3 5c) 20m.** Climb the wall on the left to reach the thread runner and make a long reach right into the groove. (This can also be reach by climbing the steep crack in the right wall). Once in the groove, climb past two holes and make a long reach right to a good hold. Trend right again to a ledge and chain belay.
**2) 6b (E3 5c) 18m.** Climb the groove direct to a ledge and chain belay.
**DESCENT** - Abseil off.
FA. M.Edwards, R.Edwards 1.00

### 11. The Dawning 🔒 6b
**(E3 5c) 20m.** An easier start to *The Long Stretch*. Start to the left of the next large chimney below a steep wall with a good horizontal break. Climb to the break and make a long reach left. Continue direct, and then slightly right, and up, to a good pocket. Trend slightly right to a lower-off.
FA. M.Edwards, R.Edwards, M.Hesslinger 12.12.99

### 12. Indigo 🔒 8a+
**(E8 7a) 15m.** A short but powerful climb. Start from the left end of the terraced wall, just right of a chimney, below a pocketed crack. Enter the crack and follow this with increasing difficulty to its end. Climb the overhanging wall above (2 SENPs) and then make powerful moves onto the hanging slab (1 SENP) and then to the lower-off.
FA. M.Edwards 10.00

### 13. Death Pulse 🔒 8a+
**(E8 7a) 20m.** A strenuous and overhanging route which is poorly protected. Start below the steep overhanging wall left of *Andromeda*, and below a slabby loose section of rock. Climb the loose rock below the wall up to the first large pocket in the overhanging wall above. Enter this and make a very dynamic move rightwards to a shallow scoop. Match on this then continue strenuously up large pockets to the final headwall. Climb a thin crack to its end and make difficult moves to gain the belay of *Andromeda*.
FA. M.Edwards 1.00

# COSTA BLANCA - Echo Valley

## Echo Two - Centre

### ECHO TWO - CENTRE
The right-hand side of the wall is even more impressive than the left. It contains several brilliant long routes.
**APPROACH** - See previous page.
**DESCENT (Abseil)** - At the top of *Diedro Edwards* is a large boulder on the edge of the wall. There is a rope sling and chain positioned on the wall to the right (looking out) of this boulder. Abseil to the top of the pitch 4, then to the top of the tower. Next to the top of pitch 1 and then to the ground.

### 14. Asteroid Storm ..... 7c+
**(E7 6b) 20m.** Less technical and with larger holds than *Death Pulse*. Large cams are useful. Start as for *Death Pulse*. Climb the loose rock to the steeper section and pull up powerfully into the large pocketed overhanging wall. Climb to the crack and continue to a large undercling. Pull up powerfully to join *Andromeda* which leads to the belay.
*FA. M.Edwards 1.00*

### 15. Andromeda ...... 7c
A very direct route up the centre of this very impressive wall. Retreat would be very difficult after pitch 3. The route has several SENPs. Start in the middle of the face, just left of a ruined wall and below a very steep overhanging crack.
**1) 6a (E2 5b) 20m.** A fine crack-pitch which is worth doing on its own. Enter into the base of the crack from the right where large broken rocks meet the base of the wall. Climb left along the ledges to the foot of the crack. Climb up into the crack and follow this to a hanging belay, or lower off.
**2) 7a, 25m.** Climb right onto the overhanging wall and go up this trending rightwards (2 SENPs) to a hidden pocket on the right. Climb direct to a large hole above and move left (SENP) to reach a very steep and wide groove. Climb this, passing some threads, to reach a belay on the right.
**3) 6a, 25m.** Climb the groove on the left and follow the line leftwards to the bottom of a steep slab. Climb onto this (SENP) and continue straight up to a traverse line going left. Follow this to some small caves and climb through these (SENP) to another larger cave.
**4) 7c (E6 6c) 38m.** Climb over the roof on the left (SENP) and then straight up to a 'bolted' flake. Climb straight up (SENP) to the roof above passing a number of thread runners. Climb over the roof and onto the ramp which is followed for a short way. Climb the wall direct (SENP) which ends on a small ledge and hanging belay.
**5) 6a, 35m.** Climb left (SENP) and then straight up the steep slab to a good ledge and belays.
**6) 6a, 40m.** Climb rightwards into a depression then left into a steep short groove. Go right again into another groove and follow this finishing up a slab at the top. Block belays.
*FA. R.Edwards, M.Edwards 2.5.99*

# COSTA BLANCA - Echo Valley

**16. Super 'G'** ..... 🎚️🔩🧗‍♂️ 8a
(E7/8 6c) 25m. A powerful line taking the cracks and flakes in the overhanging wall right of *Andromeda*. Surmount the lower bulge onto the slab (thread) and climb the overhanging wall. Pull over the first bulge to a sloping ledge (thread) then onto the overhanging wall and a thin crack. Follow this (1 SENP and peg). Climb strenuously up the flake /crack to its top and exit on right to large pocket (peg). Pull strenuously up to a small ledge and belays.
FA. M.Edwards 12.99

**17. Path of Excess Power** .. 🎚️🔩🧗‍♂️ 7c/8a
(E8 6c) 25m. A hard and unrelenting line of tufas up the steepest part of the overhang which uses the SENPs. Start left of *Mad Dog*. Climb the steep wall onto the slab and climb to a thread runner. Climb the first bulge to a small sloping ledge. Pull up to the larger pocket (stuck wire) and power up the overhanging wall by dynamic moves (3 SENPs) to a large hole. Climb out over the final bulge (SENP) and then continue (SENP) on easier rock to a ledge.
FA. M.Edwards 1.99

**18. Mad Dog** ....... 🎚️🔩🧗‍♂️ 8a
(E8 6c) 25m. One of the most strenuous crack climbs on this wall. Start below a overhanging crack, to the left of *La gloria escondida*, below a wide boulder stuck up against the base of the cliff. Climb the boulders either on the right or left and climb the slab which leads to the base of the overhanging crack. Follow the crack until it is possible to move left to a large flake. Climb right up the overhanging wall to a chain lower-off.
FA. M.Edwards, R.Edwards 15.5.99

**19. La gloria escondida
(The Hidden Glory)** ... 🎚️🔩🧗‍♂️ 7a+
A great route tackling the full length of the wall. Start in the centre of the wall below a rightwards slanting roof, about 20m up. The route uses the original ENPs.
1) 6a+ (E1 5c) 20m. Climb up the friable rock to the thread. Pull over the overlap and follow the line of 3 ENPS to a ramp going left. Follow this to the bay below the roof.
Lower off or continue up:
2) 7a (E4 6b) 25m. Climb the overhanging groove going left and swing out onto the overhanging wall on the left (2 ENPs). Climb across and up the overhanging wall on well-spaced pockets (2 ENPs). Continue left and up onto a leftwards traversing ledge which leads to a belay. Bolt.
3) 6a+ (E2 5c) 48m. Move right and climb the groove passing a tree. Climb directly up the shallow groove until the first ENP is reached. Traverse left along a sloping ramp (2 ENPs) to a shallow groove. Climb this (ENP) then move left to reach a large cave. Bolts.
4) 7a+ (E5 6b) 30m. Climb right along the ledge to the far end and swing round into a corner. Go up to the thread and climb onto the leftward sloping ramp. Follow this (3 ENPs) to the foot of the steeper rock going up to the roof. Climb up to the roof and go right to an ENP at the end of the roof. Pull over the roof, difficult, and move left to bolt belays. The extra bolts just above the roof are for the abseil descent.
5) 6a (E2 5c) 25m. Climb directly up the wall above the belay (2 ENPs) then traverse left to a long wide crack. Go up this then traverse left into the cave on the left. Bolts
6) 6a (E2 5c) 28m. Climb right out of the cave (ENP) to a thread. Go up then follow a line going left onto a small ledge. Climb the steep wall above (ENP) and then up the groove to a ledge on the left by a bush.
7) 5 (HVS 5a) 35m. Move along the ledge to the left and climb the slabs, walls and ledges to the top of the crag.
FA. R.Edwards, M.Edwards 20.2.98

**20. Dreammaker** ......... 🎚️🔩 6b
Exciting climbing with good protection. Start to the right of the overhanging wall of *La gloria escondida* and just to the left of *Voyage to Orion*, below a very shallow open groove.
1) 6a+ (E2 5c) 15m. Climb the steep wall to a block protruding from the wall (SENP). Go over this and enter the shallow groove on the right. Climb this (SENP high up) to reach a small ledge and belay. Lower off or:
2) 6b (E2 6a) 35m. Climb the groove (SENP) then move right (SENP) to gain a good hold below the roof. Climb this, and the crack above, to the base of a steep slab. Climb this to a large niche. Go over this to a small ledge and bolt belays.
FA. R.Edwards, M.Edwards, M.Jones

**21. Voyage to Orion** ...... 🎚️🔩🧗‍♂️ 6c+
A magnificent route with great positions, on perfect rock. Start as for *Diedro Edwards* below the steep crack and slight bulge. This route uses the original ENPs.
1) 6a, 30m. Climb the crack and traverse left towards a groove. At its base, move left again across a steep section into another shallow groove. Climb this to the roof (thread). Pull over the roof and swing wildly up and right onto a ledge. Climb the thin crack to a good ledge and a junction with *Diedro Edwards*.
2) 6c+ (E4 6a) 45m. Climb the shallow depression above to a sling. Continue up the slab (2 ENPs) but trend slightly right to a small cave. Move left and climb the overlap (2 ENPs). Move right again and climb the rough wall (3 ENPs) to a shallow bay. Climb directly over the bulge to a good ledge.
3) 6b, 30m. Move left into a cave. Pull over the roof and into a groove on the right (2 ENPs) and onto a ledge. Climb the steep rock, with large holes in it, passing a sling. Move right (1 ENP) and into a large groove. Follow this to its top. Bolt belay.
4) 6b, 30m. Climb the short, steep wall left of the ledge, past an ENP. Make a spectacular traverse left until you can climb direct (thread) to a recess. Move right then back left to follow cracks and grooves to the top of the route. Thread belay.
FA. R.Edwards, J.Toms, V.Leuchsner 15.1.98

**22. Diedro Edwards** ...... 🎚️🔩 6b
One of the classic routes of the valley with good protection. Start 5m left of the extreme right-hand side of the wall, just before the it heads upwards to the steep wall and groove of *Diedro Naranja*, and below a short overhanging crack. This route requires 2 original ENPs only.
1) 4, 25m. Climb the overhanging crack and then move left across a steep wall to the base of the first groove. Up this to the overlap and pull right into the groove above. Follow this to a good ledge on the left. Bolt belay.
2) 5+,25m. Climb the groove into the first cave. Pull over this and continue up the groove to belay in a second cave.
3) 4, 25m. Continue to follow the groove until the top of the tower - Bolt belay. These two pitches can be done as one but rope drag might be a problem.
4) 6a, 20m. Climb the steep groove above to the top of the pillar. Bolt belay.
5) 6b (E3 5c) 45m. Climb to the roof and move up and left (ENP). Continue to the small overhang (ENP). Exit right then left up cracks to slabs which are followed to the top of the climb. Belay on pinnacle on the right.
FA. R.Edwards, S.O'Rouke and Patty 1.97

**23. The Silent Sleeper** ...... 🎚️🧗‍♂️ 5
(VS 4c) 40m. A good easier route. Start on the right of the crag, at the lowest point, just to the left of a large boulder. Climb the slab past an old iron spike and ascend leftwards to a steep slab. Up this and move right into a corner. Go up this for a short way, to a old bolt, and climb directly up the wall to a ledge. Climb the steep wall into a shallow depression which leads to a wide bay with a thread belay. Abseil off from belay high up.
FA. R.Edwards, Esther Edwards 2.3.97

SE facing wall
15m, 20m single pitch to 190m multi-pitch routes
Best grades - 5 to 8a

# COSTA BLANCA - Echo Valley

## Echo Two - Placa Immaculada

# ECHO TWO - PLACA IMMACULADA

To the right of the main bulk of Echo Two is a big corner capped with a roof. Right of this is an immaculate wall of rock.
**DESCENTS** - It is possible to abseil off most of the routes on twin 50m ropes.

### 24. Sea of Dreams  6a+
(E3 5c) 48m. (See topo on previous page) Excellent climbing with a steep, tough groove to finish. Start in a recess, slightly above the toe of the buttress, and below a thin flake in the centre of the steep slab on the right. Climb up to the flake. From its top climb direct to gain a slab above. Climb this (ENP) to the foot of a groove and up this to a large recess and bolt belay. Abseil off.
FA. R.Edwards 12.4.98

### 25. The Sickle  6a+
(E2 5b) 50m. A long pitch. Start just left of the obvious groove of Complanos 61st. by a narrow rib of rock. Climb the rib and the wall above (2 ENPs) to a steep black wall on the left thread runner. Climb the slab above this to the base of an steep groove. Climb the groove to the large recess and belay. Abseil off.
FA. R.Edwards 10.97

### 26. Complanos 61st.  6b
A fine route with some very dramatic positions. Start below a groove just left of *Diedro de Naranja*.
1) 6a+, 45m. Climb the groove and follow the curving crack until you can pull over the overhang on the right (thread). Continue the crack to a slab. Follow this (ENP) to a groove on the right. Climb this to a small ledge and large recess. Lower off or:
2) 6a+ (E3 5c) 35m. Climb the slab on the left to the large slot on the left of the wall above (2 ENPs). Move left onto the steep wall (ENP) and follow a line of holes and cracks to reach a good ledge and bolt belay on the wall above.
3) 6b (E3 5c) 45m. Climb the steep wall on the left (ENP) to a thread. Ascend right into a shallow groove and follow this past some threads. Climb a steep wall (ENP) and move right onto a ramp and follow this to a steep crack which leads to the top.
**DESCENT** - Make 3 abseils to the ground. It is easiest to swing left onto the *Diedro Edwards* abseils as soon as possible.
FA. R.Edwards, Peter Milton 17.4.98

### 27. Diedro de Naranja  6b
A sustained route. Photo page 129. Start at the extreme right-hand end of the buttress below the very obvious orange groove.
1) 6a+, 25m. Climb the slabby rock on the left of the shallow groove then enter the groove proper where it steepens. Follow the groove by climbing direct on its left-hand side, and then direct again (thread). Belay in a recess (thread).
2) 6b (E3 5c) 25m. Climb the orange slab on the right and follow the sloping ramps rightwards (3 ENPs) to some good thread runners. Move right again and then straight up into a cave. Traverse right into the centre of the slab and follow this to the good ledge and belay. Abseil off.
FA. R.Edwards, M.Bonesteel, E.Revs Vilapiana 2.97

### 28. Naranja Directo  7a
A direct finish to *Diedro de Naranja* which climbs the upper wall above the undercling section.
1) 6a+, 25m. As for *Diedro de Naranja*.
2) 7a (E4 6a) 25m. From the cave move out left onto the overhanging wall and (ENP). Climb direct to a ledge on the right and then follow a series of pockets to the top.
FA. M.Edwards, R.Edwards 5.6.99

### 29. Solstice  8a
A hard direct finish to the next route, ...*Raven and Crow*.
1) & 2) 45m. As for *Raven and Crow* or *Diedro de Naranja*.
3) 8a, 15m. Swing boldly up left into two large holes (2 threads and 1 SENP) Climb up and follow pockets to enter a groove which is followed to a ledge. Bolt belay. Abseil off.
FA. M.Edwards, R.Edwards 15.5.99

# COSTA BLANCA - Echo Valley

### 30. Prayer to the Raven and the Crow  8a
A fantastic climb up the left-hand side of Placa Immaculada. Protection is mostly from SENPs. Start below the obvious scoop just right of *Diedro de Naranja* groove.
1) 7c, 18m. Enter the scoop and follow it direct, passing a large pocket/hole, to a good ledge (4 SENPs). Bolt and thread belay.
2) 8a, 28m. 7 SENPs and 2 ENPs. Step right below the bulge to the steep crack of *Going Nuts*. Climb this past two ENPs. From this point all the remainder of the gear is SENPs. Move left to a flake. Climb to a small overlap and trend diagonally right and climb the wall direct to a horizontal break. Climb direct again to easier rock and join *Diedro de Naranja* pitch 2. Continue up to the Solstice belay or continue to follow the line of *Diedro de Naranja* to the top belay on the right.
FA. M.Edwards, R.Edwards 15.5.99

### 31. Going Nuts  8a
(E7 6b) 50m. A superb and sustained route on perfect rock. Start 5m to the left of the flat-topped boulder right of *Diedro de Naranja*, and below a bulge in the wall above. Climb the easy, slabby depression to the steeper bulge. Climb up this (2 ENPs) and gain the sloping ledge (possible belay on left). Climb the overhanging flake crack and move direct to a scoop (2 ENPs) Making increasingly difficult moves to an easing of the angle of rock (2 ENPs). Move rightwards to below a shallow scoop (2 ENPs). Climb the scoop with difficulty (2 ENPs) to an easier ground and continue in a direct line up the wall (wires) passing a thread to reach belays on the large ledge. Abseil off.
FA. M.Edwards 2.98

### 32. Corredora de la medianoche (Midnight Runner)  7a+
(E4 6b) 45m. An excellent route which is very sustained and technical. Start just to the right of *Going Nuts* and to the left of a flat-topped boulder at the base of the wall. Head for a bulge in the rock on the right (ENP). Climb direct to a good ledge. Move up and then move right to a good thread. Climb direct and follow pockets to reach a blank section. Continue direct (three ENPs) to reach a good ledge on the right. Climb the narrow slab above (ENP) and then trend right to a belay. Abseil off.
FA. R.Edwards, M.Edwards 16.5.98

### 33. Children of Laughter  7a+
(E5 6a) 50m. A superb long pitch with good protection. Start from a small flat boulder at the base of the wall. Climb rightwards into the slight depression on the right and follow this until a move left to a lower-off (this section is grade 5 and can be done on its own). From the chain go left and then back right to a thread runner. Continue direct passing another thread to a slab (belay possible). Climb the steep slab trending right and then direct to a belay. Abseil off.
FA. R.Edwards, E.Edwards 20.6.98

### 34. Espolón Encantada  5
A good easier route. Start at the lowest point of the wall, on the right-hand side, just before it slopes back upwards. A series of small cracks heads up leftwards.
1) 4+ (VS 4c) 25m. Climb the cracks until it is possible to go right to a small arete. Climb this and then back right to a good ledge and thread belay by a small palm tree.
2) 5 (VS 4c) 40m. Climb the crack on the left and at its top move right onto a small ledge. Step right and past a thread runner. Continue directly up and then trend right up a slab, keeping just left of the vegetation, to reach a small stance and belay. A 50m abseil reaches the bottom.
FA. R.Edwards, E.Edwards 19.6.98

SE facing wall
50m single pitch to 120m multi-pitch routes
Best grades - 5 to 8a

# COSTA BLANCA - Echo Valley

**Echo Two - Placa Immaculada - Right**

## ECHO TWO - PLACA IMMACULADA - RIGHT
The final section is the dome-shaped buttress right of the immaculate wall.
**DESCENTS** - It is possible to abseil off all the routes on twin 50m ropes.

### 35. Vía los palmeres . . . . . . . . 5+
Start 3m to the right of *Espolón Encantada*, directly below the palm tree.
1) **5+ (VS 4c) 20m.** Climb slightly left across the slab and then move back right to climb direct to the palm tree. Move left below this and gain the ledge above. Belay.
2) **5+ (VS 4c) 35m.** From the ledge, climb right and then up the steep rock,. Follow the left-hand side of the slab (thread on right) to reach a narrow pillar. Go up this and then through broken blocks to a belay and abseil point.
FA. R.Edwards, E.Edwards 6.98

### 36. The Visionary . . 8a
**(E7 6c) 25m.** A superb, bold climb taking the black wall left of *Rock Dancer 2*. Start below the black streak and below prominent tufa bulge at 10m. Take a full rack including a full range of cams. Climb the slab towards the start of the black streak (threads). Climb boldly up the slab and make a delicate move out right to a pocket. Continue directly up the wall to twin pockets. Make a series of technical moves leftwards to stand on a sloping ledge. Move up leftwards and enter a shallow groove by some strenuous moves (thread). Climb up the wall above (run-out) trending towards a right-facing flake. Continue direct by less-steep rock, and the easy wall, to the roof. Climb this to the belay. Abseil off.
FA. M.Edwards, R.Edwards 25.11.00

### 37. Rock Dancer 2 . . . . . . . . 6a
A superb climb on good rock with good protection. Start 10m right of *Espolón Encantada*, below a steep slabby wall and two threads high up. Climb the short corner to the slanting crack and follow this for a short way. Traverse right then climb directly up the slab until it steepens. Climb up to the left of a threaded sling, then move right. Continue up then slightly right following a small crack. At its top, move left and then continue to climb the slabs to a ledge. Abseil off.
FA. R.Edwards, E.Edwards 20.12.99

### 38. Taurus . . . . . . . . . . . . 6a
**(E2 5b) 50m.** A good slab route with solid but well-spaced protection. Start 5m higher up the slope from *Rock Dancer 2*, in a small recess with a narrow corner on the left. Climb the narrow corner, then straight up to the steeper rock above. Climb left, then back right, then continue straight up the slab using hidden, but good holds. Make for a groove in the centre of the overhanging headwall. Climb the groove, and then the wall on the right, to reach an excellent ledge. Abseil off.
FA. R.Edwards, E.Edwards 4.99

### 39. Kfour . . . . . . . . . . . . 6c
**(E4 5c) 45m.** Excellent climbing but awkward to protect on the crux. Start as for *Taurus* in the small bay. Climb up the vegetated slab on the right and make for the right-hand side of a white stain on the wall above. Climb left onto the stained rock and an excellent small hand hold at head-height (small wire or friend above). Make some hard moves onto the good hold and climb leftwards (slots high up on the left) to a good ledge. Climb directly up to a shallow groove on the left and surmount the overlap on its left-hand side. Climb up to the base of the steep rock and climb the groove to the top. Abseil off.
FA. R.Edwards, M.Edwards 14.6.99

### 40. Yes to Dance . . . . . . . . . 6b+
**(E4 5c) 45m.** Another quality slab climb. Start at the right-hand side of the wall, below a rib of rock, where to rock ends and the vegetation starts. Climb the rib to a slab. Climb this to a steep black wall leftwards to a series of pockets on the steep wall leading left. Climb direct up into a shallow crack and groove, then up the wall to the overhanging rib above. Move right and climb the rib on the right to the top. Abseil off.
FA. R.Edwards 5.99

SE facing wall
50m single and two pitch routes
Best grades - 5+ to 8a

Rowland Edwards climbing *Diedro de Naranja* (6c - page 127) on Placa Immaculada, Echo Two.
Photo: Mark Edwards.

# COSTA BLANCA - Echo Valley

**Echo Placa**

## ECHO PLACA
The most obvious feature of the wall is the huge dihedral on the left-hand side. To the right of this the three cracklines of the other routes can be easily picked out.
**APPROACH (See page 112)** - From the parking at Echo Two continue up the track which zig-zags its way up the hill (can be rough at the top) until a casa on the left with a chain across a track (this is the path up to the climbs). Continue to drive along the track to until you can drop down another track on the right to a large building with a flat section in front. Park here and walk back to the path with the chain. (The casa can also be reach from the other direction (see map on next page)). This is the path leads up the valley to Echo Placa. Beneath the wall are some awkward (grade 2/3) broken ledges.

### 1. The Great Dihedral — 7a
The left-hand corner gives this impressive route. Scrambling up leftwards to the base of the corner (50m grade 3).
1) **6a (E1 5b) 50m.** Climb the corners and slab to a thread belay.
2) **7a (E5 6a) 50m.** Climb a wide crack past a bolt. Follow the steep corner above (bolts) to a roof. Pull over this to a belay.
3) **6b (E2 5c) 40m.** Continue up the corner over a small roof and caves to a final roof. Pass this on the right and belay at a pillar.
4) **40m.** Climb the pillar and easier rock to the top.
FA. R.Edwards, M.Edwards 1.90

### 2. The Forth Addition — 6b+
The easiest of the routes on the wall has one short hard section which is very friggable.
1) **3 (HS) 50m.** Scramble up easy ground to the base of the wall.
2) **4 (VS) 30m.** Climb up onto a ledge and follow this leftwards to the bottom of a corner.
3) **6a (E1 5b) 25m.** Follow the corner to a bolt belay.
4) **6b+ or 6a+ with aid (E3 6a) 40m.** Climb up then move right into a groove. Climb up (peg & bolt) then traverse right to a tree. Climb past the tree (or aid it using the bolts - NOT the tree). Continue up cracks to a belay.
5) **6a (E1 5b) 45m.** Climb the fault-line above, then move right-wards.
6) **4 (VS) 30m.** Climb right to a tree then up a shattered pillar.
FA. R.Edwards, S.Perez 27.3.93

### 3. Luna Sombre — 7a (6b)
A good route taking a long diagonal line across the wall. Start by scrambling up to the base of the wall (50m grade 3).
1) **4, 15m.** Climb a corner top a ledge.
2) **5+, 20m.** Cross leftwards to a rib and traverse left into a hollow. Climb the slab to a ledge.
3) **6b, 30m.** Climb left and up some grooves (pegs) then traverse delicately left to a slab. Climb this to a groove then move left to a corner which leads to a stance.
4) **7a, 30m.** Climb the groove then continue up a steep crack to a ledge.
4a) **6a, 35m. The easier variant.** Climb the groove then move right into another groove. Follow this, past a bolt, to a ledge.
5) **6a+, 50m.** Follow the steep crack on the right and the wall above, to a ledge.
6) **3, 40m.** Broken rock leads to the top.
FA. R.Edwards, E.Edwards, M.Edwards 26.3.90

### 4. Cracks in the Sky — 7b
A good climb on perfect rock. Start by scrambling up to the base of the right-hand side of the wall (50m grade 3).
1) **6a (E1 5b) 45m.** Climb a corner to a pillar on the left. Continue up a crack to a ledge, then traverse left to bolt belays.
2) **7b or 6b+ with aid (E5 6b) 25m.** Climb the steep wall on the left, past 6 bolts, to a good ledge and bolt belay.
3) **6c (E4 6a) 25m.** Follow the steep crack above to another ledge and bolt belay.
4) **6b (E2 5c) 50m.** Climb cracks on the right, then trend right to the arete (possible belay). Continue up thin cracks to a ledge.
5) **5 (HVS 5a) 35m.** Ascend rightwards then follow grooves and ledges to the top of the wall. Take care with loose rock.
FA. R.Edwards, M.Edwards 2.90

**DESCENTS** - From the top go rightwards and drop down the back of the wall. This will take you down a wide gully and around the base of another wall to the right. Continue down rightwards to your starting point.

South facing wall
200m multi-pitch routes
Best grades - 6a+ to 7b

# COSTA BLANCA - Echo Valley

**Col Llama**

## COL LLAMA
This remote part of Costa Blanca is far-removed from the hustle of the coast and many of the sea side crags. The climbing is mostly on solid rock, particularly after pitch one where it enters the groove system. A full set of nuts and cams is needed.
**APPROACH (From Polop)** - As for Echo Placa then continue up the footpath to the col. The wall on your right is split by a large corner at mid-height - this is the line of *Fields of Gold*.
**APPROACH (From Sella)** - Drive up the track from the main areas at Sella, past Sector Wildside. From here, continue for 1.5km, until a casa on your left, with a sign on the road pointing to Polop. Go up this track for 2km until you are on the col overlooking the Echo Walls area. The wall on your left is the Col Llama.

### 1. Name Unknown . . . . . . . 6a
The original route of this wall is a superb route which takes the lower corner then escapes left to another corner. The first pitch is vegetated and loose and the upper part of the route is solid but thin on gear for its grade. The main groove is superb. Start 8m right of the steep wall below a broken slab.
1) **5 (VS 4c) 35m.** Climb over broken ledges to a peg at 20m. Traverse left to reach the base of the groove.
2) **6a (E1 5b) 45m.** Climb the groove direct (two pegs and one bolt) to the good ledge below a steep wall.
3) **5 (HVS 5a) 35m.** Climb the steep wall and broken groove to reach a steeper 'V' groove . On the left is a steep wall with slanting faults in it,climb this and the broken ground above to reach a good ledge and peg belays .
4) **5 (VS 4c) 25m.** Climb the slab on the left and continue direct to a belay .
5) **4+ (VS 4b) 30m.** Climb the broken slab to reach the arete.
6) **4 (VS 4b) 45m.** Follow the ridge to the top.
FA. May have been climbed by Joe Brown in the late 80s. It has also been claimed by Spanish climbers in the early 90s

### 2. Fields of Gold . . . . . . . 6b
A great route which is well worth the approach walk. Start at the base of the wall, directly below the big groove, and below a small slanting corner in the middle of the lower wall.
1) **6b (E2 5c) 35m.** Climb direct to the small groove (2 bolts) Enter the groove (bolt) and go up this to the roof. Climb over this (bolt) and direct to a small ledge and bolt belay.
2) **6a (E1 5b) 45m.** Climb the groove (2 pegs) to a large ledge and bolt belays.
3) **5 (HVS 5a) 20m.** Climb the steep wall and the broken grooves on the right (bolt) to a steep crack on the right and small ledge.
4) **6b (E2 5c) 45m.** Climb to the top of the crack and traverse right (bolt) to a steep ramp. Climb this (2 bolts) to a good thread. Continue direct (peg) then ascend rightwards across the slab to a thread. Continue to traverse for a short while and then climb direct to a small ledge and bolt belays.
5) **6b (E2 5c) 25m.** On the left is a pillar with a thin crack. Climb the slab on its right and then enter the crack. Follow this and then the crack in the bulge above which leads to a small ledge and bolt belay. The last bolt belay - abseil off from here or go for the summit experience:
6) **4 (VS 4b) 25m.** Climb the slab on the left to the overhanging blocks and then onto the ridge proper.
7) **4 (VS 4b) 40m.** Continue to follow the ridge to the top.
FA. R.Edwards, S.Perez 9.5.95

**DESCENT** - Either, abseil back down after pitch five, from the last of the bolts belays, or continue to the top (well worth the climb) and descend south along the rim of the crags and down a scree slope and back north to the foot of the crag.

South facing wall
200m multi-pitch routes
Best grades - 6a to 6b

# COSTA BLANCA - Echo Valley

**Haunted Walls**

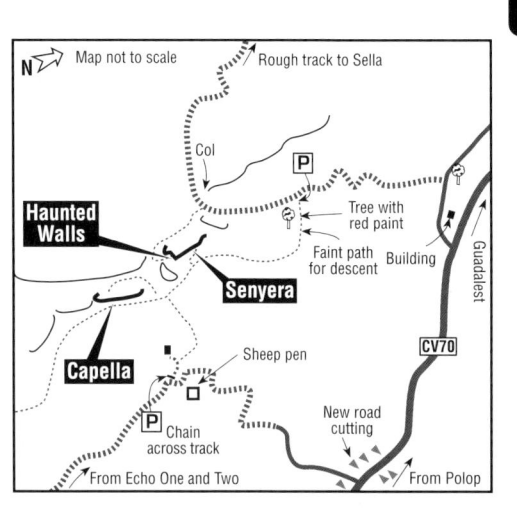

# COSTA BLANCA - Echo Valley

**Cracks of Tranquillity continued....**
4) 6b (E3/4 5c) 45m. A great pitch. Climb onto the opposite wall and follow the faint crack which gradually gets wider to full-hand width. Pull directly over the roof to a good ledge and belay.
5) 3 (Diff) 15m. Scramble over the pinnacle to the next arete.
6) 6a (E2 4c) 40m. Climb the centre of the arete to the top of the crag. Poor protection.
FA. R.Edwards, Mark Bonesteel, Esabel Carcera 15.3.97

## 3. The Exorcist  6c+
A very strong natural line on good rock which follows the second crack line from the right. There is a distinctive overhang about one third height.
1) 6a (E2 5b) 25m. Climb across ledges below and right of the crack to reach an ENP. Move up right into a groove (slightly suspect rock) at the top of this groove move right again (ENP) and into the main groove. Follow this to belay bolts below the overhang.
2) 6a+ (E3 5c) 35m. Large cams or hexes are useful. Climb to the roof then traverse the roof on the left to the vertical crack. Follow this to a ledge and bolt belays.
3) 6c+ (or 6a/A0) (E4 6a) 25m. 2 ENPs. Climb the crack on the right of the belay to the roof above. Climb the bulging roof above on its right-hand side and a thin crack free 6c+ (or 6a+ and A0). Continue up after the difficult mantelshelf to reach a bolt belay below some trees.
Scramble through the trees and then over a small pinnacle on the right and into a small forest. Cross this and a wide gully to the foot of a superb arete. Bolt belays.
4) 5 (VS 4c) 20 m. Climb the arete to the first staple and then traverse left (staple) to a belay ledge. Bolts.
5) 6a+ (E3 5c) 25m. Climb the shallow corner to the small roof and move left over this. Continue up the steep crack to a good ledge and bolt belays.
6) 5+ (HVS 5a) 30 m. 1 ENP. Climb the wall above and continue straight up to the trees at the top of the crag.
FA. R.Edwards, M.Edwards 1.96

## 4) The Phantom  6b
Superb climbing on the extreme right-hand vertical crack on perfect rock. Start at the very base of the crack by a small cave.
1) 6a+ (E3 5c) 28m. This is the original start but it is quite loose and strenuous. Climb the crack until a step left brings you to the base of the vertical crack. Climb this, passing a number of threads, to a good bolt belay. Or...
Start just left of the natural line of the crack at a short vertical white wall.
1a) 6a+ (E2 5c) 28 m. Climb loose but easy rocks to the foot of the white wall (ENP). Climb the wall by a faint crack (ENP) to good holds which end on a steep slab. Go up this, then traverse right into the big crack. Climb the crack, passing a number of good thread placements, to a good ledge and bolt belays.
2) 6b (E3 6a) 30m. Continue climbing the crack and move onto the left wall at the roof. Climb direct (ENP) and up to a thread. Continue to follow the crack to a good ledge and bolt belays.
3) 6a (E1 5b) 38m. Climb the steep wall left of the belay and traverse back right into the crack. Follow this to the second of two tree covered ledges.
4) 25m. Scramble through the trees to reach a bay on the far right.
5) Phantom Arete. 6a+ (E3 5c) 50m. Climb the blunt arete above the belay and follow the line of the arete (a few wires needed) to the first staple. Continue up the arete (one other staple and 7 ENPs). Head for the shallow groove on the left-hand side of the arete. The final section of the route is again protected by natural gear. Belay on two bolts on a good ledge on the left.
6) 5 (VS 4c) 35m. Climb the wall just right of the belay and then up ledges to the summit of the mountain.
FA. R.Edwards, M.Edwards 5.6.96

## HAUNTED WALLS
This dramatic area has several powerful lines on perfect rock. It does have a haunted and magical feel about the place since it's always so silent and peaceful - very much like the Pinnacle Wall of Cloggy.
**APPROACH** - From the parking described on page 114 walk (or drive) up the hill to the col. Take a horizontal traverse SSE across the hillside, heading for the end of the rocky ridge you can see in the distance. As you traverse the peaks on the left are the summits of The Cathedral and Haunted Walls. When you have finished the routes you descend these summits back down to your car. When you reach the end of the ridge climb upwards to a col and descend the other side to another col. Look left and you will see Haunted Walls with its vertical cracks and aretes. Descend easily to the base of the wall. This walk takes about fifteen minutes from your car.
**DESCENT** - All routes can be abseiled but, once on the top wall, it can be more problematic to abseil than to walk off. Descend down the NW side of the mountain, back towards the Sella track, and then down a gully and ridge to reach a scree slope. From here a short walk leads back to the car.

## 1. The Spectre  6a
Not a very good route in its present state but should become cleaner as ascents remove more of the loose rock. Start on the left side of the wall opposite the large off width crack. The routes starts up the wall on the left below a wide V-groove.
1) 5+ (VS 4c) 20m. Climb the steep wall and then move right and up to belay on threads below the steep groove.
2) 6a (E1 5b) 45m. Climb the steep dihedral (some loose rock) to the top of a pinnacle. Bolt belay.
FA. R Edwards, M Edwards 3.97

## 2. Cracks of Tranquillity  6b
One of the best crack climbs in the area and well worth the trouble of getting to this fantastic crag. This route climbs the third crack from the right.
1) 6a+ (5b) 27m. Climb the steep crack to a belay on the right.
2) 6a+ (5b) 27m. Climb the overhanging crack on the left and then traverse right to pass a tree. Move back left to climb the crack and then finish up a short wall on the left to belay bolts.
3) 5 (4c) 20m. Traverse left to a large block and then up to a thread on a slab. Move left onto the small pillar and up this to a good ledge and bolt belay.

South facing wall
150m multi-pitch routes
Best grades - 6a to 6c

**133**

# COSTA BLANCA - Echo Valley

## SENYERA

A beautiful wall with two splendid routes on it. It is actually just around the corner from the Haunted Walls but the routes start from a much lower level and are major full-day undertakings.

**APPROACH (From above)** - Starting from the parking spot described on page 112. 50m further on is another small parking space (small cairn). Descend a faint track from this first parking space to an old tree then traverse the path rightwards below the rock walls. You will see the Dru-shaped peak of Senyera. When directly below the peak look for a large boulder above the track with a small cairn. Follow the scree (less thorny) towards the gully on the left-hand side of the wall. *Nemisis* starts from the base of the wall. For *La Catedral* scramble up the rocks on the right to the base of the pillar with a groove on the left.

**APPROACH (From below)** - From the roundabout with trees on the CV70, mentioned on page 112, continue along the main road from about 3km towards Guadalest. At a new road cutting (may change) turn left onto a hard-topped track heading uphill. Follow this, which turns into a rough track, past a sheep pen on the left, to a wider area with a track leading off uphill to the right. Park here and walk up the track until a path leads off right (red paint). Follow this to a T-junction. Turn right for Senyera and walk 50m until level with a boulder (cairn) on the left and above the track. Keep to the scree (less thorny) and make for the gully on the left of the wall.

**DESCENT** - Climb over the top of the mountain and down the other side, heading rightwards. Cross a gully to a steep gully going down to the base of the mountain. The parking area in on the right (15 mins).

### 1. La catedral . . . 6b+

A tremendous route taking the full length of this beautiful rock face. Start on the right of the arete, just left of as narrow gully.
**1) 6a (E1 5b) 35m.** Climb the broken rocks of the wide arete until a move left in made into a shallow groove. Climb this for a short while (peg runner) then move right and up to a crack. Follow this until a move right can be made to reach a small ledge and thread belay.
**2) 5+ (E1 5b) 25m.** Climb the slab and make for a small overlap. Over this (2 bolts) and trend left to a small ledge right of a groove. Thread and peg belay.
**3) 4+ (VS 4b) 20m.** Climb across the groove and traverse left and slightly downwards to a ledge and bolt belay.
**4) 6a (E2 5b+) 40m.** Climb directly up the wall by a small groove (2 bolts) and into the upper section of the wall which is split by a series of thin cracks. Climb the centre of the wall (bolt) and the left to reach a bolt belay.
**5) 5+ (VS 4c) 25m.** Climb the slab on the left into a gully, follow this and then move back left onto the arete proper. Bolt belay.
**6) 4 (VS 4a) 20m.** Climb across broken loose rock to a cave on the left. Bolt belay.
**7) 6a (E1 5b) 40m.** Enter the groove on the left (bolt) and follow this over ledges and another groove to a good ledge on top of a tower (escape can be made from here on the right).
*La catedral continued....*
**8) 6b+ or 6a with aid (E3 or E1) 20m.** Climb onto the wall opposite the tower. Follow the crack right and then move back left to the centre of the wall. Continue straight up, then left and make some long moves to reach a good ledge and belay.
**9) 4 (VS 4b) 20m.** Climb the groove to a ledge.
**10) 4 (HS 4a) 30m.** Follow the arete to the top of the mountain.
*FA. R Edwards and students 5.95*

### 1a. Mediterranean Wall . . . . . . 6c+

A good direct start to *La catedral*. Start down to the left of the start of *La catedral* below the second of two ribs.
**1) 6c+, 38m.** Climb the rib heading for the sling high up. Pass this and make for the clean sweep of rock. Climb the faint crack and pockets to reach a hanging belay (bolts).
**2) 6b, 20m.** Go left to a crack and follow it moving right at the top to a ledge and bolt belay (end of pitch 3 of *La catedral*).
*FA. R.Edwards 1993*

### 2. Nemesis . . . . . . . . . 6a

A long and interesting route but with a little loose rock. Pitches 6 and 7 are particularly fine. Start at the very base of the wall as you enter the gully and on the right of the buttress.
**1) 6a (E1 5b) 30m.** Climb the cracks in the steep slab, moving right and then left to a good ledge and belay.
**2) 5+ (HVS 5a) 25m.** Continue up the edge of the wall passing some small overhangs to a bolts belay on the left.
**3) 4 (VS 4b) 15m.** Climb direct to below the orange overhang and a small ledge with a peg high up.

Big east facing wall
300m multi-pitch routes
Grades - 6a and 6b+

# COSTA BLANCA - Echo Valley

**Nemesis continued....**
**4) 6a (E1 5b) 30m.** Climb up a few meters and enter a steep crack. Climb this and then move right when possible to enter a steep crack which leads into a shallow groove. Follow this to a good ledge and bolt belays.
**5) 5+ (VS 4c) 20m.** Climb the crack on the left and the easier rock to a tree belay.
**6) Easy, 30m.** Scramble up and then left to the base of an arete to the left of the gully.
**7) 4+ (VS 4b) 50m.** Climb the steep cracks in the arete and then easier rock into a gully. At its top climb the chimney on the right to the top of a pillar. Climb the crack and chimney direct to a good ledge and bolt belays.
**8) 6a (E1 5b) 50m.** Climb across to the base of the left arete and climb this to the top of the tower.
**9) 4+ (VS 4b) 30m.** Climb the wall direct to the top of the route. A better, but much harder, finish is:
**8a) 6a+ (E3 5c) 50m - Phantom Arete.** Climb the blunt arete above the belay side and follow the natural line of the arete using natural gear to the first staple. Continue to climb the arete , Bolts. You are making for the shallow groove on the left side of the arete. The final section of the route is again protected by natural gear. Belay on two bolts on a good ledge on the left..
**9a) 5 (VS 4c) 35m.** Climb the wall just right of the belay and then up ledges to the summit of the mountain.
FA. (Pitches 1 to 5) R.Edwards, Betty Edwards 2.96
(Whole route) R.Edwards, Michael Esslinger 18.11.99

## LA CAPELLA
This stunning peak is known by Spanish climbers as Cima Notario/Perea but the locals call it La Capella. Described here is one majestic long route however there are other bolted routes on this wall which we hope to have information on in the future. Check rockfax.com.
**APPROACH** - Follow either approach to Senyera to the junction of the paths. Continue to follow the path (or turn left if approaching from below) until below the very impressive overhanging dihedral which splits one side of the wall. Go to the very base of the wall where a bolt can be seen just above the track.
**DESCENT** - Down the wide gully behind the mountain. At the bottom traverse right back to the path. (20 mins).

### 3. Diedro Edwards en la Capella .... 8a
This superb, hard route takes the only weakness on this very impressive wall. The rock is solid, the positions and atmosphere are both exciting and spectacular. Start at the base of the wall, just above the path, directly below an overhanging groove with a bolt. A full rack with wires and cams is needed.
**1) 6a+ (E1 5b) 25m.** Follow the line of pockets (2 bolts) to a ledge. Traverse left to a thread belay.
**2) 6b+ (E3 6a) 35m.** Climb just right of the belay to a bolt. Above this move right then straight the wall (bolt) and continue to a shallow scoop.
**3) 5+ (VS 4c) 40m.** Climb the pocketed slab above (well-spaced bolts) to a steep tower. Climb this (bolt) to a good ledge.
**4) 6c, 15m.** Climb onto the wall behind the belay then traverse right to a ledge below the large corner. Fully bolted.
**5) 6c+ (E4 6b) 30m.** Climb the overhanging corner direct to where it narrows (awkward past a small bush). Move right at the top and up the slanting groove to a hanging bolt belay. Well-spaced bolts but gear also needed.
**6) 8a or 7b with aid (E8 or E5) 40m.** Continue to follow the overhanging groove (well-spaced bolts). Climb the steep corner (gear needed) and pass the final overhang to reach a good ledge.
**7) 6b (E3 5c) 20m.** Climb the groove to another good ledge on the arete.
Escape can be made from here by traversing left over easy, but loose, rock **(5, 100m)**. Or continue up the arete above **(2 pitches of 5, 75m)**.
FA. R.Edwards, M.Edwards 2.89

La Capella

Big east facing wall
300m route
Grade - 8a

135

# PONOCH

The Ponoch is a very impressive face of rock, on an Alpine scale, that overlooks the town of Polop. However few Alpine tactics will be needed to conquer the two fine climbs described here since they are both fully bolted. The face is a good place for those who have enjoyed the style of climbing provided by routes like *Costa Blanca* and *Navigante* on the Peñon d'Ifach and would like to sample a bit more. The main south face is criss-crossed by many routes which involve trad gear but the two included here are predominantly long sport climbs albeit with some seriousness. Both are at times a little run-out, very exposed and, most importantly, exposed to significant rockfall from the huge face above. Rockfall should be expected at all times due to animal movements but if other teams are operating above it may be wise to climb elsewhere as the often easy upper pitches of the meandering trad routes follow loose ledge systems. A helmet is essential when climbing here.

We hope to add a few more routes to the list because this huge face demands attention from those keen to explore the more spectacular walls of the Costa Blanca. If you enjoy these two then you could try getting hold of a copy of the local guide to the mountain - *Guía de Escalada del Ponoch* by Carlos Tudela (1998).

## ASPECT AND CLIMATE

The enormous south face of the Ponoch is exposed to any sun that is going - great in the cooler Winter months but desperate in the heat since there is little shelter. If the wind is blowing then it is best to keep away. On the routes described retreat is easy should the weather close in.

## APPROACH

**From the North -** Leave the A7 at junction 65 (Benidorm) and immediately turn south on the N332. Keep going to a right turn inland towards Callosa d'en Sarrià.

**From the South -** Leave at the the new Terra Mitica junction (Number 65a) and turn north onto the N332 towards Valencia. Keep going to a left turn inland towards Callosa d'en Sarrià.

You should be able to see the large hulk of the Ponoch on your left. About 9km from the A7, by a roundabout with an industrial estate on the left, turn left (signed 'Guadalest'). At the second roundabout on this road (about 1.5km) turn left by a large house. Ignore the left branch and follow this road to park at a left turn with a chain and 2 cartwheels. Resist the temptation to drive past these since it is a private driveway leading to a villa not far above. Walk up the drive and continue via the dry stream bed. At a small cairn, scramble out of the gorge on the right and follow a path which zig-zags up the terraced hillside beneath the crag, aiming for an open bay. This is to the left of an obvious pinnacle, whose profile comes into view as you near the base of the crag. Don't linger at the base if there are parties above, since there is some loose rock.

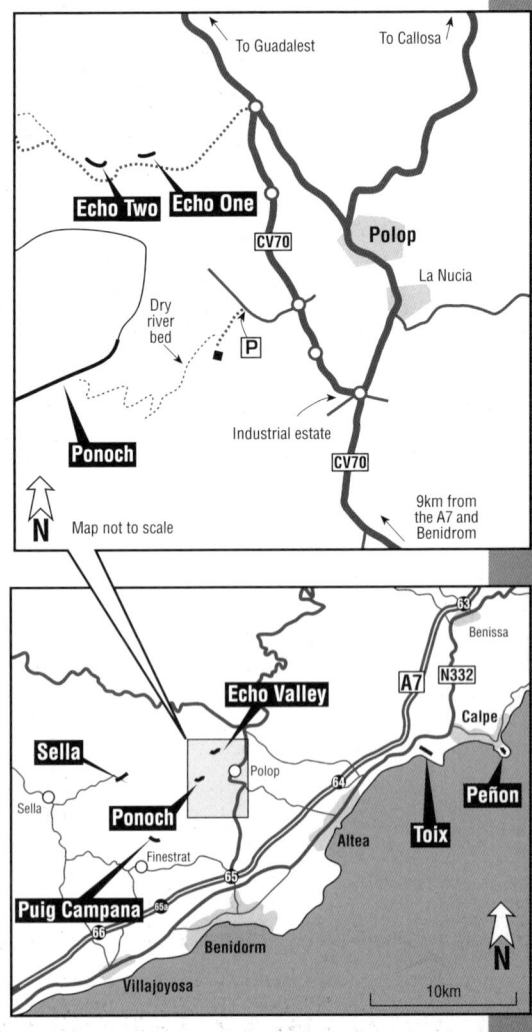

# COSTA BLANCA - Ponoch

## 1. Heroes del silenco  6c+
Another excellent, fully bolted route, giving sustained, fingery climbing on perfect rock. Start beneath the line of new bolts up a non-descript wall in the next bay around to the left of *Gorillas*.
1) **6a, 45m.** Follow the bolts up the wall to a good ledge.
2) **6a+, 25m.** Climb the concave wall and make an explosive move around the bulge. A tricky pitch.
3) **6b+, 45m.** The wall above has a fingery start and a desperate second clip. Things then ease considerably and enjoyable climbing leads to a stance in a break.
4) **6b+, 45m.** Traverse left, then steeply past some holes to pull out at the base of a smooth slab. Thin climbing weaves around the bolts before easier ground and a shallow groove reach a calcited stance with an assortment of belays.
5) **6c+, 30m.** Traverse left to a steep crackline. Follow this and make a desperate and blind pull onto the wall above. Move out right to easier ground, before another fingery shield, fortunately easier than it looks, gains easy ground and a belay.
**DESCENT -** Abseil down a new set of abseil stations off line to the right of the route (facing out).
FA. Chiri Ros, Isabel Pagan, Manuel Amat Castill 1991/92

## 2. Gorilas en la Roca  6c+
A fantastic route with contrasting climbing. There is some loose rock, so care is needed. The climb is fully bolted, though there is no belay at the top of the first pitch so take a couple of slings. Start at the back of the obvious bay, at the first easy ground to the left of the pinnacle/tower.

Gorilas en la Roca continued....
1) **6a, 45m.** Once you spot the new bolts, follow these negotiating a tricky bulge before the rock disappears and loose scrambling gains a big ledge. Belay by the scratched 'X' which shows the way and the start of the good climbing. Slings on a small bush and two good footholds should suffice.
2) **6b+, 45m.** Follow the rib, grooves and wall above by sustained, sharp gout d'eaux pulling.
3) **6c+, 40m.** Climb boldly to a bolt, then on to a shelf beneath a leaning wall. After a tricky start this gives superb climbing up the shallow groove systems running up its right-hand side. Pull out onto easier ground and continue to another good ledge.
4) **6a+, 30m.** No bolts are visible, but follow the step-ledges right for a couple of moves, before launching confidently upwards, whereupon the bolts do appear. Sustained but excruciating moves lead up the wall and rib to a belay.
5) **6b, 25m.** Cautiously gain a loose alcove and try not to imagine what built the nest! Exit rightwards before enjoying the perfectly formed leaning wall above.
6) **6b+, 35m.** Follow the wall leftwards, then back right before tackling the hanging groove. Trend back left with one tricky wall to reach a good belay.
**DESCENT -** Abseil carefully back down the route. When you reach the X ledge, scramble around the bay to the right (facing out) and descend a couple of steps to escape via an abseil station. This is above the batch of trivial single pitch routes on the wall to the left of pitch 1.
FA. Manuel Amat Castill, Antonio "Chiri" Ros 1989/90

West facing wall
15m to 20m routes
Best grades - 6a to 7b

# PUIG CAMPANA

As you drive up and down the coastline, there is one impressive bit of rock which stands high above all the other impressive bits of rock which you 'ooh and aah' at from your car. This is the 1400m high Puig Campana above the village of Finestrat. Along with the Peñon d'Ifach, this mountain has been a focus of climbing in the Costa Blanca since the 1960s. However owing to the long approach walks, and the existence of other significantly more accessible crags, Puig Campana hasn't been developed nearly as much as it deserves. Despite this it is still home to some superb and important routes, which will provide many memorable days of climbing for those into long traditionally protected climbs.

The actual climbing is seldom hard, except on the newer routes. The three main classics on the south face, *Espolón Central*, *Diedro Gallego* and *Diedro Magicos*, and *Espolón Finestrat* on the Aguja Encantada, are the only routes on which you are likely to have company.

### APPROACH

Puig Campana is approached from the village of Finestrat.

**From the North or South -** Leave the A7 at junction 65a (Terra Mitica) and turn southwards towards Alicante on the N332. Look out for a huge supermarket - the turning for this is also the turning for Finestrat.

Once in Finestrat, drive towards the mountain on the road to 'Font de Moli'. Continue along the metalled road, up the hill, around a series of bends and over a bridge. This is the popular point to start your walk up to the summit but, for climbing, it is quicker to continue for about 1km to a short track on the right-hand side of the road. Park here and follow a path up the hill for 200m. Just after some pine trees on the right, and by a cairn, is a small track leading off to the right.

**For Sector Central -** Follow the small path until it is possible to scramble up onto a big plateau. A well-marked path leads from here under the face.

**For Sector Aguja Encantada -** Continue along the lower path until the first track on the right at a junction marked by a cairn. Continue to another cairn which marks a track that zig-zags up the screes directly below the face. This sector stays in the shade longer than the main south face.

### GEAR

Many of the routes date from the 1960s hence most of the classics have little in the way of fixed gear. For these routes you will need a standard rack of wires, a few cams and a selection of big clunky stuff. Virtually every route requires double ropes since the pitches are long and descent is usually by abseil. A few of the routes here use the ENP system (see page 113).

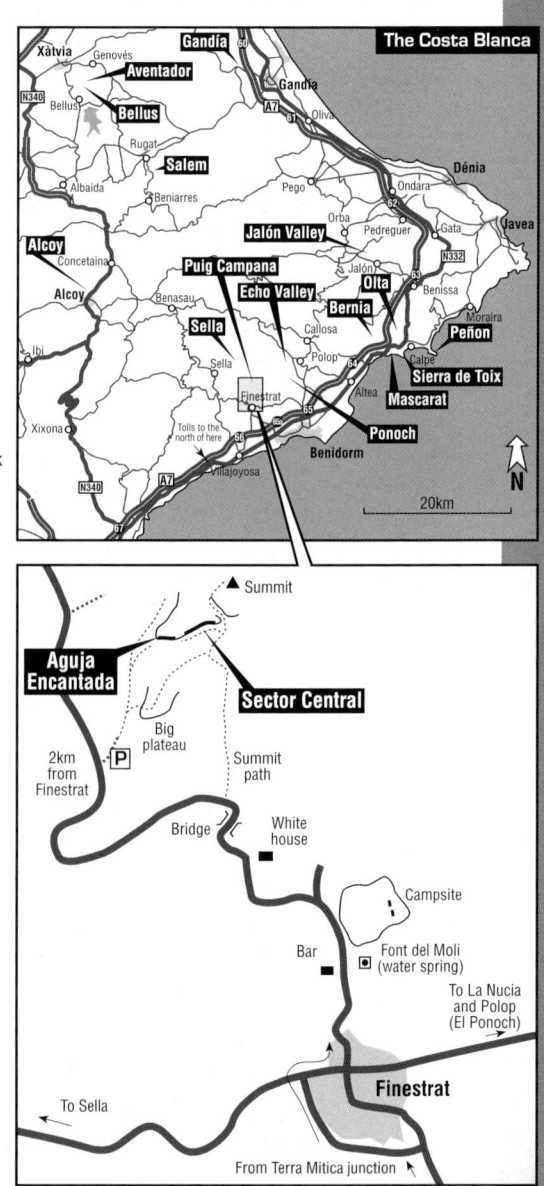

## ASPECT AND CLIMATE

This is a big mountain with a climate more familiar to alpine peaks than Spanish crags. The length of the routes means that it will take you most of the day to get up and down your chosen climb and, as there are no professional rescue teams in the region, it is best to chose the right climb according to your skills, gear and the available hours of daylight. It is obviously essential to carry water but also take some spare clothing for the upper sections, which are frequently colder than you might expect. Indeed the top is often shrouded in mist which makes descents difficult and potentially hazardous. Having said this, you are probably more likely to suffer from sunburn than anything else, so light long-sleeve tops and neck scarves are also a sensible addition to your gear along with the 'factor 15' sun cream.

**Puig Campana - Descents**

## DESCENTS

There are frequently problems when people try and descend the mountain, especially if darkness is falling. As a precaution you should always carry one head torch per person in case you get caught out and please try and familiarise yourself with the descent paths as you approach the mountain.

**DESCENT FROM THE TOP** - Follow the summit ridge over the top, then drop down to the col between the two main summits. A path leads down rightwards to the main summit path. Red dots point the way.

**DESCENT FROM THE TOP OF ESPOLÓN CENTRAL** - Scramble carefully rightwards, descending slightly into a easier angled area (marked by red dots and with fixed cables on most of the steep sections). Continue traversing around the bottom of a spur then over a ridge to start dropping down a steep gully. The main summit path lies below. Don't try and drop down the slope too early since this is where a lot of the accidents and problems have been caused in the past. The photo above shows the correct line. Note that the whole mountain is covered with goat tracks and goats don't always know where they are going.

**DESCENT BY ABSEIL DOWN THE ESPOLON CENTRAL LINE** - The abseil descent, down the left-hand side of the pillar, can be joined at various points from the routes to the right. From the large tree on the ledge at the top of pitch 8a) of *Espolón Central*, abseil from the bolt and thread belay to a ledge (50m). Walk left (facing in) to a cable thread and abseil to another ledge (50m). Walk left and down to another cable. Abseil 25m to a wide bay. Walk down around the base of a rib on the left (facing out) and descend easy rocks to the bottom.

# COSTA BLANCA - Puig Campana

## SECTOR CENTRAL - LEFT
The huge south face is a massive and complex bit of rock. There are routes all over it but only the main ones are outlined here.
**APPROACH** - See page 139.
**DESCENTS** - On previous page and described with the routes.

### 1. Espolón Central . . . . . . . 3 🔲 4+
The longest route in this book is a great mountaineering experience. It goes up the huge pillar on the left-hand side of the face at a relatively easy grade (British 'Severe' at most) but it can get more difficult if you stray off route. Some of the variations are listed below. It should not be underestimated and you must allow a lot of time to climb the route and descend. A fast ascent is 6 hours but allow yourself at least 10 hours of daylight.
**APPROACH** - Walk up the long band to reach the scree slope going up to the centre of the lower wall of the South face. You arrive on a wide ledge below the face itself. This is the area of the *Direct Start*. Continue to walk leftwards below this until you reach a small cairn below a short steep wall. This wall is not difficult and can be scrambled but some people may need to rope up. Continue to scramble up rightwards to reach the rib on the right, forming the edge of the buttress.
**1) 2) and 3) grade 3,120m.** Follow the right edge of the ridge selecting belays at convenient places. You finally reach the large ledge which splits this section of the mountain.
**1a) 3, 55m.** An alternative start is to continue up the broken ground, which now forms a gully, until you reach a groove with a large pine at its top. Climb right to the same ledge as above. Walk along the ledge until it disappears, above is a slab with many trees. The shorter option on the *Direct Start* joins the main route on this ledge.
**4) 3, 45m.** Climb the slab to the tree. Pass this on the left and continue up broken grooves and aretes, trending right, to reach another large ledge.
**5) 25m.** Walk and scramble horizontally right to the steep rocks on the arete proper and find some threads. Don't climb the broken grooves on the left or the slabs above the large ledge.
**6) 4, 25m.** Climb direct up the arete and belay on the next good ledge.
**7) 4, 50m.** Continue up the arete moving to the left at the top to reach a good ledge and peg belay. Retreat is possible from this point using an abseil bolt on the left.
**8) 4-, 35m.** Climb the groove on the left of the pillar and continue up easily to a large tree.
**9) 25m.** Continue right over ledges to the base of the wall.
**Alternative to pitches 8 and 9 -**
**8a) 4, 35m.** Climb the right side of the pillar then hand traverse left onto the arete, up this and the short wall above to a ledge.
**9a) 4, 25m.** Follow the arete to the base of the wall.
**10) 4, 50m.** Make a curving ark to the left and follow the groove to the top of the wall, or climb the centre of the wall to the top (slightly harder).
**11) 4, 50m.** Climb the arete above by the groove on the left. Continue up ledges to a good thread belay.
**12) 4, 50m.** Climb the ridge by cracks and grooves to the large ledge. Climb the zig-zag crack to a good belay but poor pegs.
**13) 4, 50m.** Climb the groove on the right and continue up easy ground.
A further 20m of scrambling reaches a boulder with a large red paint mark on it. From here a long traverse can be made to reach the far gully.
**DESCENT -** Descents in darkness are not uncommon, but are very undesirable. If you are unsure then you can abseil off from several points. See notes on previous page.
FA. J.Roig, C.Torregrosa, M.Gascon 1960s

### 2. Espolón Central Direct . . 3 🔲 5
A more satisfying way of climbing the route and only a touch harder than the original way. Start at the flat area, below a groove containing a small bush.

**Espolón Central Direct continued...**
**1) 3+, 30m.** Climb the short wall to a short groove. Up this to a ledge. Pass a bush on the right and continue up the broken groove to reach a good ledge below a steep wall.
**2) 5, 30m.** Climb left across the groove and up the arete (peg) to a ledge. Take care with loose rock on this pitch.
**3) 4-, 25m.** Traverse right to a series of broken grooves. Climb these (peg on the left) until on the second of two ledges.
**Shorter Version - 3a) 4-, 50m.** Climb directly up the grooves above to reach the large ledge mention in the normal start.
**4) 4-, 45m.** Ascend rightwards across a sloping slab. Then follow ledges right to reach a wide gully just left of the arete proper. Peg belay.
**5) 4-, 35m.** Cross the gully and climb onto the arete proper. Follow this to the next big ledge. Thread belay. The normal route joins from the right at this point - escape by abseil possible.

### 3. The Edward's Finish . . . . 2 🔲 5
A good continuation which takes you to the top of the mountain. Start at the top of pitch 13 of the main route.
**1) 175m.** Scramble up the broken ridge until you are below the jagged pinnacles. Don't stray off right on this scramble.
**2) 3, 35m.** Scramble over the first pinnacle and then descend leftwards into the gully on the left. Ledges now lead across the face of the last pinnacle. Belay possible half way along.
**3) 3, 20m.** Cross the gully and then climb up onto the col between the last tower and the main face.
**3a) 5, 50m.** The col can also be reached by climbing along the top of the pinnacles (3) and abseiling from the last tower to reach the col.
**3b) 4, 50m.** Keep right of the pinnacles until you reach a steep slab which is climbed to the col.
**4) 5, 30m.** From the col climb the steep slab direct to a small roof. Climb right onto a large ledge.
**5) 5, 45m.** Climb the depression on the right and then the wall above to reach a ledge and a tree. Climb the rib on the right to the top to reach a board ridge with small trees. A final 175 m of ridge scrambling reaches the notch at the top of the mountain.
**DESCENT -** See previous page.
FA. R.Edwards 12.84

### 4. Directisima . . . . . . . . 3 🔲 6a
An good three pitch route which can lead on to bigger things. Start below a leftwards sloping ramp, just left of the start of *Edge of Time*, below a large overhang high up.
**1) 4, 20m.** Climb the ramp to a good ledge.
**2) 6a, 40m.** Climb the steep wall to a shallow groove (pegs). Enter the steep groove on the right and climb and excellent crack to its top. Climb rightwards across slabs making for a cave high up. Thread and peg belay.
**3) 6a, 45m.** Climb the red groove. Near its top move right and climb the steep wall (threads) to reach less steep rock. Follow the cracks on the right to reach the belays of *Vía Julia*.
**DESCENT -** Abseil off or continue up one of the next two routes.
FA. Juan Marti, Pep Camarena 6.11.76

### 5. Nueva Edicion . . . . . 🔲 ENP 🔲 7a
Good, exposed climbing with several ENPs (see page 113) which has a UK grade of E4 6a. Start to the left of a ramp and directly below a faint crack coming down from the right side of an overhang high up. Small cairn against wall.
**1) 6b, 50m.** Follow the thin cracks (2 pegs) which lead to a shallow groove right of the roof. Climb this to belay on blocks.
**2) 6b, 25m.** Climb up to a pocket (thread) and continue to a large depression on the right. Follow the thin crack above to belay in another large depression.
**3) 6c, 35m.** Climb the steep wall above and left of the cave (2 ENPs). Join *Vía Julia* at the end of the layback.
**4) 6a, 45m.** Climb the groove on the left (peg) then move right and up to a tree. Make a rising traverse right across the wall to belay in a small niche on *Edge Of Time*.

# COSTA BLANCA - Puig Campana

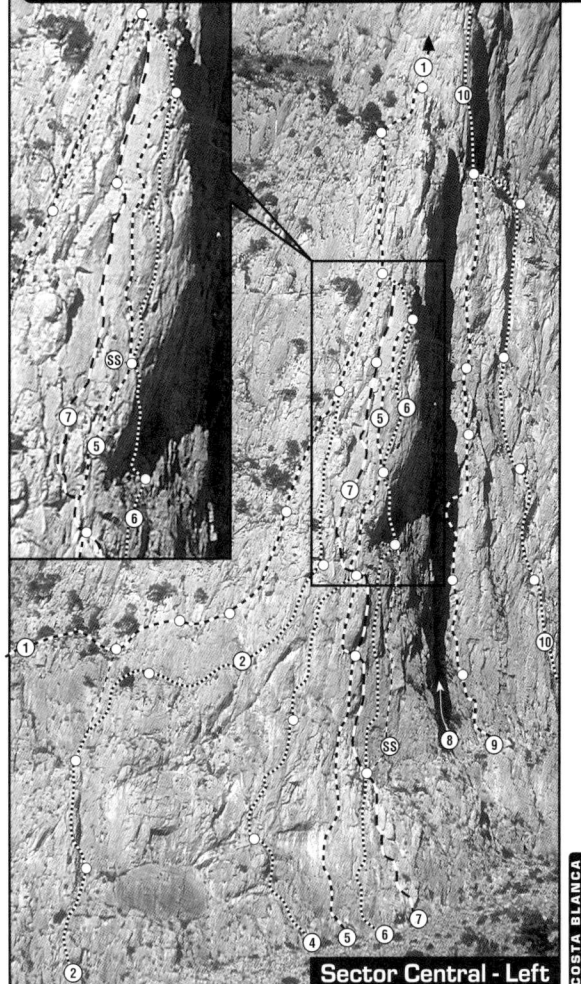

Nueva Edicion continued...

5) 6a, 25m. Climb to a thread and continue up a shallow depression (1 ENP). Move up and right, then direct to a large flake and crack. Belay here or in the groove of *Vía Julia* on the left.
6) 7a, 35m (E4 6a). Climb past the thread in the middle of the wall then straight up (3 ENPs). Follow the crack on the right to reach a ledge and belay on *Edge Of Time*.
7) 4, 25m. Climb the steep slabs to the ledges on the left and a belay shared with *Vía Julia*.
DESCENT - Either continue to join the descent for *Julia*, or, abseil back down *Edge of Time* via the bolt belays.
FA. R Edwards, C.Edwards 19.2.95

### 5. Edge of Time .......  6c
A good hard climb. Take a full rack. Start at the top of a ramp, just right of the cairn of *Nueva Edicions*.
1) 5+, 45m. Climb up to a faint groove. Follow the grooves rightwards to another wider one which leads to the belay ledge of *Vía Julia*.
2) 6c (E5 6a) 50m. Climb the thin flake above the belay to a thread. Ascend to a small ledge and then to a small groove. When it becomes steep move right (thread) and climb slabs and a small roof. Traverse right to belay.
2a) Sin Salida - 5+, 45m. Ascend right to the first shallow groove. Climb this then pull left into another groove. Follow cracks to a ledge. Climb the wall above (peg) then shallow grooves to a good stance.
3) 6a, 20m. Climb to a wall then move right to a ledge. Follow the groove on the left until a crucial hold leads onto the left wall. Move up past a peg to belay in a niche.
4) 6b, 40m. Follow the rightwards slanting cracks to a groove. This leads past a flake to a ramp and groove above (peg). Climb the steep crack to a ledge. Bolt belay.
4a) Sin Salida - 4, 25m. Climb left across the wall to a crack. Climb this to join and finish up *Vía Julia*.
DESCENT - Either continue to join the descent for *Julia*, or, abseil back down the route via the bolt belays.
FA. R.Edwards, C.Edwards

### 7. Vía Julia .......... 6a
A classic with some loose rock but great climbing. Take a full rack with a large Friend for pitch 4. Start at the foot of the pillar where the name is painted on the rock.
1) 4, 30m. Climb shallow grooves and cracks to a ledge can be reached by walking around to the right).
2) 6a, 45m. Climb the steep wall and cracks above to a ledge. Continue up more cracks to the top of a pillar. Can be split at the half-way flake.
3) 5, 25m. Move left, climb a groove and slab to an overhang (peg). Pull over into a groove (possible belay) then move left to a steep, wide crack. Climb this to a belay.
4) 4, 25m. Can easily run together with pitch 3. Climb cracks in the slab then a corner above.
5) 5, 30m. Follow the corner to join *Espolón Central*.
DESCENT - See previous page.
FA. Chema Rameirez, Manolo Pomares 10.82

### 8. Diedro Gallego ....... 6a
An old classic which follows the huge groove/corner in the centre of the South Face. Start in the bay up and right from where you arrive at the face, below the long crack.
1) 3, 20m. A wall leads past a tree to a chimney/crack.
2) 6a, 35m. Follow the crack to a cave.
3) 5+, 25m. Climb up to the roof then onto the face on the left and up into a small corner. Climb this and move right into a corner and spike belay.
4) 5, 20m. The corner above leads to the final chimneys.
5) 4+, 40m. Follow the chimney past 3 caves to a large cave.
6) 4, 30m. Bridge the final chimney then climb the right wall to the ridge of *Espolón Central*.
DESCENT - See previous page.
FA. M.Angel, J.Luis, J.Carlos García Gallego 4.77

### Sector Central - Left

The last two routes described are marked on the topo only. There isn't room here for full descriptions. If you go to rockfax.com/costa_blanca then you can download a free PDF document which contains the text descriptions of all of the long routes on the Costa Blanca including the two below.

### 9. Espolon Edwards ........ 6c+
A fine route up the narrow pillar of rock immediately to the right of *Diedro Gallago*. It relies on mostly fixed gear.
1) 5, 2) 6c+, 30 6c, 4) 6c+, 5) 6a+.
FA. R.Edwards, M.Edwards 7.1.01

### 10. Víaje en el tiempo . 6b
A long and traditional classic with a memorable pitch high up.
1) 5, 2) 6a, 3) 4+, 4) 6b (5+/A1), 5) 5.
FA. Chema Rameirez, Manolo Pomares 19.3.82

Huge south facing wall
150m to 400m multi-pitch routes
Best grades - 4+ to 7a

# COSTA BLANCA - Puig Campana

## Sector Central - Right

### SECTOR CENTRAL - RIGHT
The right-hand side of the huge south face contains the classic long 'Magic Corner'.
**APPROACH** - See page 138.
**DESCENT (For the long routes)** - There is an abseil line in between *Diedro Magicos* and *Rompededos*. From the belay at the top of *Diedro Magicos* make a 45m abseil to the ledge below. (This is where *Angalada - Cerdé - Gallego* joins). Make three 45m abseils from here down the line of *Rompededos*.

### 1. Diedro magicos — 6a+
One of the best mountain routes of its standard in the Costa Blanca. Start below the long groove which goes the full length of the right-hand side of the upper south face.
1) **5, 25m.** Climb the corner to a cave. Bolt belay.
2) **5, 25m.** Continue up the corner to another bolt belay.
3) **5+, 30m.** Follow the corner to a peg. Move right across the wall to a good ledge and bolt belay.
4) **4, 25m.** Move up then follow grooves and cracks leftwards to belay in a groove.
5) **6a+, 50m.** The crux. Climb up to another ledge and a possible belay. Move up to the roof above then a hard move right leads into a corner. Up this, then left to another corner which leads to the top. The pillar above leads to the top in four grade 4 pitches.
**DESCENT** - Above.
*FA. H. García Gallego 11.80*

### 2. Asesina a tu vecina — 6b+
A sparsely equipped sport route to the right of the corner of *Diedro Magicos*. Old bolts and run-out.
*FA. Chema Ramírez, Quique Barberá*

### 3. Rompededos — 6c
Another great route up the wall to the right of the long corner of *Diedro Magicos*. The first pitch is a fully-equipped sport route. Take a full rack for the last two pitches.
1) **6c, 45m.** Follow the bolts to a chain belay.
2) **6b+, 30m.** More bolts lead off above to a ledge.
3) **5+, 30m.** Climb steep grooves and flakes to the top wall. Harder moves around the bulge lead to a good ledge.
4) **6a, 30m.** Climb the slabs on the left to reach a good ledge.
**DESCENT** - Above.
*FA. A & F.Bayonas, B.Durán, J.Rodríguez, M.López 8.5.83*

### 4. Anglada - Cerdá - Gallego — 5+
A worthwhile route, which takes the right arete of the wall. Start well right of *Diedro Magicos*, below a pillar of broken rock.
1) **3, 15m.** Climb the pillar to a good ledge just right of a groove.
2) **5+, 45m.** Climb the slab until level with a crack. Move right to the crack then step left into another flake/crack. Follow this past a large ledge to another ledge.
3) **4, 45m.** The groove on the right leads back left to the top of a pillar. Follow the groove on the left to a large ledge and tree.
4) **4+, 45m.** Climb the grooves above to a corner (peg). Move right to another corner and climb this to a groove on the left. Continue to the large ledge above.
**DESCENT** - Walk left along the ledge to the abseil described above.
*FA. M.Anglada, Cerdá, M.A.Gallego 1.4.79*

Further right is a triangular wall with two shorter routes on it.

### 5. Tricolomanía — 6b+
The left-hand side of the wall has poor rock. Take a small rack.
1) **6b+, 45m.** Climb a groove then move left to a bolt. Move back right to a bolt line and struggle up this to the belay.
2) **6b+, 45m.** Continue up past a peg then move back right past some more bolts to a steep finish.
**DESCENT** - Abseil down the route.
*FA. Quique Barberá, Robert Llí 4.2.84*

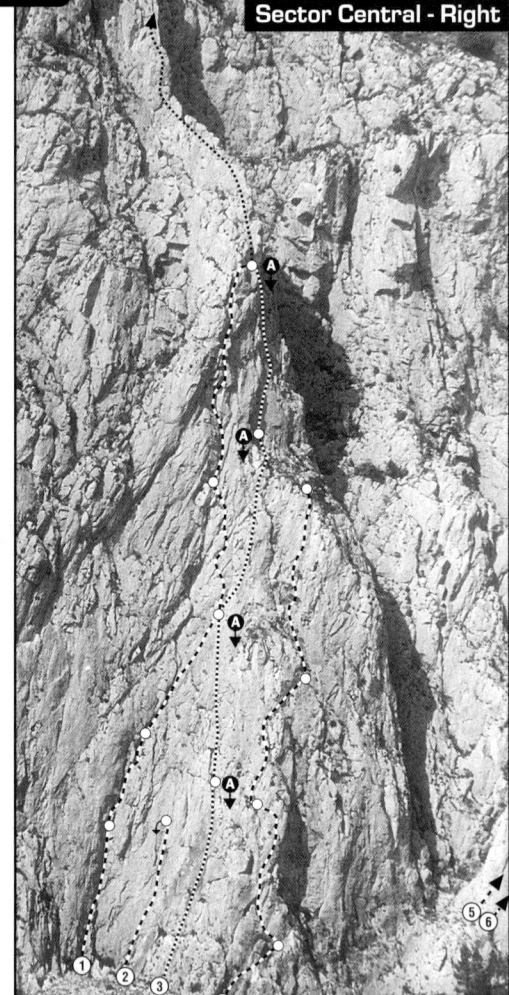

### 6. Cleptomanía — 6b+
The right-hand line also needs a small rack.
1) **6a+, 40m.** Climb the wall past 2 bolts, then move back left to a peg belay above a pillar.
2) **6b, 25m.** Move right and climb the wall (4 bolts).
3) **6b+, 25m.** Move across right to below a roof. Pull over the roof to finish.
**DESCENT** - Abseil down *Tricolomanía*.
*FA. Chema Ramírez, Manolo Pomares 6.11.82*

Huge south facing wall
50m to 175m multi-pitch routes
Best grades - 5+ to 6c

# COSTA BLANCA - Puig Campana

## AGUJA ENCANTADA - Left

The West Face of Puig Campana is an extremely complex bit of rock with many pinnacles and walls. By far the most impressive section is the Aguja Encantada - 'The Enchanted Pinnacle' - which has a number of fine trad climbs.
**GEAR** - Most of the routes require a full rack although there is some fixed gear. Two of the routes are equipped with the ENP protection device (see the notes on page 113).
**APPROACH** - See page 138.

### 1. La Flecher . . . . . . . . . . . . 6a
A fine route. Start below the pinnacle high up the slab. Take a full rack, including some large Friends.
1) 5, 25m. Climb cracks to the base of the pinnacle.
2) 5+, 20m. Climb the pinnacle, then step left and climb cracks to a big ledge.
3) 5+, 25m. The steep crack on the left leads to a ledge.
4) 6a, 30m. Climb up right then up the shallow groove above (bolt). At its top traverse left to the arete. Up this to a ledge.
5) 5, 20m. Follow cracks to ledges and a tree.
**DESCENT** - Abseil down the route.
FA. R.Edwards and students 23.3.94

The next two routes go to the top of the pinnacle and their upper sections are on the topo on the next page.
**DESCENTS (Routes 2 and 3)** - From the top abseil back down the routes to the mid-height ledge. From here abseil down *La Flecher*. Alternatively you can make two abseils down the back of the pinnacle into the gully behind, then scramble down the gully.

### 2. Aorangi . . . . . . . . . . . 6c+
An excellent route. The name is Maori for 'cloud piercer'. Take a full rack with some slings although the hard pitch is bolted.
1) 5+, 25m. Climb the slab to the pinnacle.
2) 5+, 25m. Climb the pinnacle then step onto the opposite wall. Climb the groove to a crack which leads to a ledge.
3) 6c+, 45m. The groove above is bolted until the top wall. Continue past a flake to the ledge above. Walk across the slabs to the wall behind.
4) 5, 20m. Climb the wall past a sloping ledge. Up left to belay.
5) 6a, 30m. Climb left over a small roof, then follow cracks and corners to the large ledge.
6) 3, 25m. Scramble across broken rock to the base of a long crack in the upper wall.
7) 5, 20m. A broken wall leads to a ledge.
*See topo on next page for next two pitches.*
8) 6b, 45m. Follow the crack then the wall on the left. Move back to the crack and up to a cave.
9) 6a+, 45m. Exit the cave up a chimney, cracks lead to the top.
FA. R.Edwards, S.Pérez 4.94

### 3. Dancing on Crystals . . . . 6c
A superb pitch with contrasting climbing. It has 6 ENPs (see page 113). Start below, and just right, of the large pinnacle.
1) 6a, 45m. Climb the slab rightwards, past a ledge, to belay below the red wall.
2) 6c, 30m. The groove above leads up the steep red wall to a ledge. 6 ENPs.
3) 6b, 20m. Climb the groove on the right to a ledge. Continue up to another ledge with bolt belays. 2 ENPs.
4) 5, 45m. Scramble across to a broken corner, then up the corner to a cave.
5) 6a, 30m. Climb the steep wall then move leftwards to a slab. Up this to a ledge. 3 ENPs.
6) and 7) As for *Aorangi*.
*See topo on next page for next two pitches.*
8) 6b+, 40m. Climb the crack of *Aorangi* but when just above 2 bolts pull right. Follow the crack to a cave belay.
9) 6b+, 50m. Climb the roof on the right then trend left to join and finish up *Aorangi*.
FA. R.Edwards, C.Edwards 19.3.96

West facing wall
150m to 250m multi-pitch routes
Best grades - 6a to 6c+

**143**

# COSTA BLANCA - Puig Campana

## AGUJA ENCANTADA - Right
The right-hand side of the Aguja Encantada is dominated by the long *Pillar de Finestrat*.
**APPROACH** - See page 138.
**DESCENTS** - The best equipped abseil is down *El Diamante*. Other descents are described with the routes.

### 4. Diedro Edwards-Pérez  7a
A quality climb which follows the right-hand side of the red wall. Take a full rack. Start below the right-hand side of the red wall.
1) **5, 25m.** Climb the wall to a good ledge.
2) **5+, 20m.** The black slab leads to the base of a steep wide crack.
3) **6a, 25m.** Follow the crack to a ledge and bolt belays.
4) **7a, 35m.** Climb the ramp to the corner, then up to a bolt. Climb a tufa past 2 bolts then make a hard traverse leftwards to a good ledge.
5) **6b+, 30m.** Follow the long corner above.
6) **6b+, 35m.** Climb the wall left of the belay to a ledge then up past pockets to a bolt. Move left then left again to a ramp. Climb over a roof (threads) and up a groove to a ledge.
7) **5, 35m.** Climb rightwards to an abseil station.
**DESCENT** - Abseil down *El Diamante*.
*FA. R.Edwards, S.Perez 18.4.94*

### 5. Pillar de Finestrat  6b+
A magnificent climb up the 'Enchanted Pillar'. Take a full rack. Start below the right-hand side of the red wall, by a cairn.
1) **5, 25m.** Climb the wall rightwards then move left to a cave.
2) **6b, 30m.** Climb up a groove and slab above, past 3 bolts, to a roof. Pull over this to a crack on the left then up to a ledge. Bolt belay.
3) **6b+, 30m.** Move rightwards past 2 bolts, then move upwards to a crack above a spike. Climb this then move right to belay.
4) **6a, 45m.** Climb rightwards then up, past blocks, to a small roof. Over this to the arete on the left. Then up to a cave.
5) **5+, 40m.** The groove above leads to the abseil station.
**DESCENT** - Abseil down *El Diamante*.
*FA. R.Edwards, A.Lloret 24.1.94*

### 6. El Diamante  6a+
A superb and popular route up the right-hand side of the pillar. There are bolts on the belays and blank section but take a full rack. Start below the right-hand side of the red wall, by a cairn.
1) **5+, 30m.** Climb rightwards up a ramp and grooves to the top of a pinnacle. Move right to belay.
1a) **7a+, 30m.** This pitch can be started more directly and is fully bolted although the bolts are well-spaced.
2) **6a, 25m.** Climb out right, over a bulge, then up a slab to a groove. Follow the groove to a ledge and bolt belay.
3) **6a+, 45m.** The groove above leads (2 bolts) to a slab (2 pegs). Continue up an arete (2 bolts) and at the last bolt traverse right to a ledge (possible belay). Climb the slab (thread and bolt) and wall above to a large cave.
4) **5+, 25m.** The pocketed wall leads up a slab to a ledge left of a tree.
5) **5+, 25m.** A groove in the arete leads to the abseil station.
**DESCENT** - Abseil back down the route.
*FA. R.Edwards, S.Perez 3.94. Direct - R.Edwards 4.94*

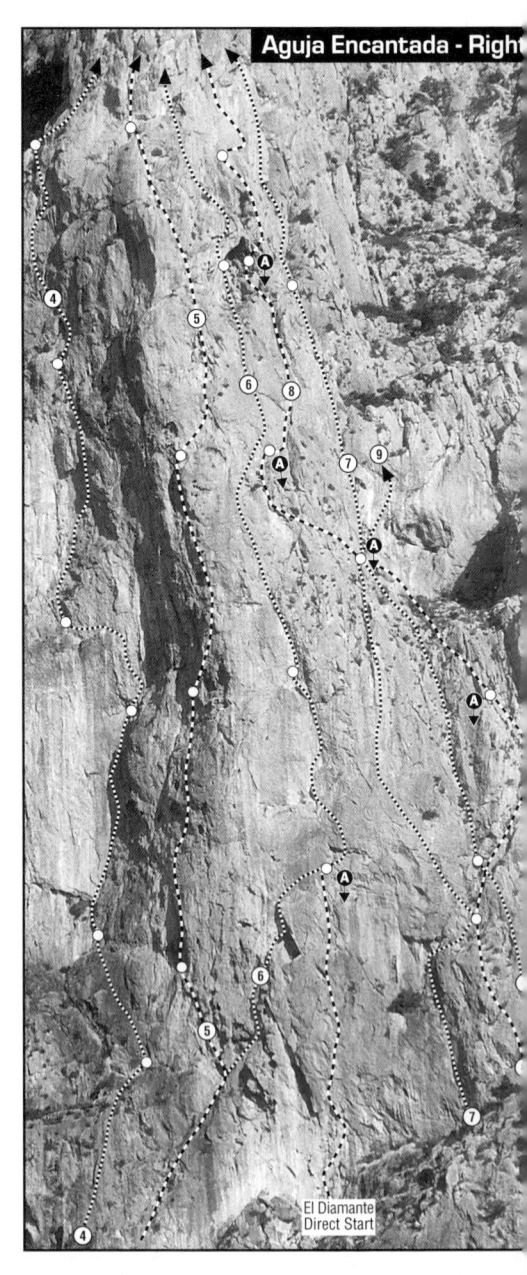

Aguja Encantada - Right

El Diamante Direct Start

# COSTA BLANCA - Puig Campana

## 7. New Generations 🔾 // ☐ 6b+
An excellent ENP route up the wall between the two older classics. Start below a slab, down and left of *Espolón Finestrat*.
1) **6b, 35m.** Climb the slab to a roof. Move right to a ledge and bolt belay. 4 ENPs.
2) **6b+, 50m.** Climb the slab above leftwards, then move up to a crack. Follow this to a ledge. 6 ENPs.
3) **6a, 40m.** The broken groove and wall above leads to another ledge.
4) **6a+, 45m.** Climb the slab on the right then up a steep groove. Swing right and move up and over an overhang on amazing holds. Continue to the abseil station.
**DESCENT** - Abseil down *El Diamante*.
FA. R.Edwards, C.Edwards 3.95

## 8. Espolón de Finestrat ...... 🔾 // ☐ 5
Another great classic at an easier grade than most of the routes on this sector. Some of the pitches can be combined if you are confident. Start by scrambling up the ramp below and right of the main pillar. Belay at a tree.
1) **5, 25m.** Climb the slab leftwards, past 2 bolts, to a ledge and bolt belay.
2) **4, 20m.** Follow easy ledges out right then back up onto a pillar with 2 ring bolts.
3) **3, 25m.** Follow the ramp leftwards to a grassy bay. Belay bolt on the left edge.
4) **4, 20m.** Climb leftwards into a groove. Up this to a pinnacle on the left. Ring bolt belay.
5) **5, 20m.** Climb the groove on the left. At its top either climb up left or go direct (harder) to a cave.
6) **5, 20m.** Follow the arete on the right and move left to belay.
7) **5, 40m.** Climb up right then move leftwards across a ledge. Climb a crack to an arete and follow this to the abseil station.
**DESCENT** - Either abseil down the line of *El Diamante* or; make 2 abseils to the ring bolts at the top of pitch 4, then 1 rightwards (facing in) to the left edge of the grassy bay. A short abseil from here gains the ring bolts at pitch 2 belay. 1 more to the ground.
FA. M.Pamares, F.Garcia 3.2.84

## 9. Talisman ...... 🔾 // ☐ 6a+
A fine route which can be used as a variation start to reach the fine upper pitches of *New Generations*. Start on top of a boulder 4m up from the start of *Espolón Finestrat*.
1) **6a, 20m.** Step on to the wall on the left and make an ascending traverse into the middle. Climb direct, then right, and direct again to reach a block. Move left to a good ledge to belay.
2) **5, 35m.** Move left to the base of a slanting groove with a small overhang. Climb over the roof onto the slab on the left. Follow this over another small roof and continue up the slab to reach easy ground. Belay below a blank slab on the right.
3) **6a, 25m.** Climb the right side of the steep pillar to a good hold. Move left to a flake hold (thread) and climb direct until a long move right enables some pockets to be used to gain a shallow scoop. Continue and finish up a block-chimney.
3a) **6a+, 25m.** A more strenuous pitch. Climb into the cave and then out right on to the face. Pull up into the next cave and move left into the shallow groove. Climb this to the large ledge above.
4) **6a+, 50m.** From the ledge move left and climb the pocked wall to the first overhang. Climb this and the one above to reach a blank slab. Climb this to the next roof and pull over this on to the slabs above. Continue in the same line, keeping slightly right, and make for a crack on the headwall. Pull into this and follow it to the top of the pinnacle.
**DESCENT** - As for *Espolón de Finestrat*.
FA. R.Edwards, R.Birch, B.Birch 26.11.00

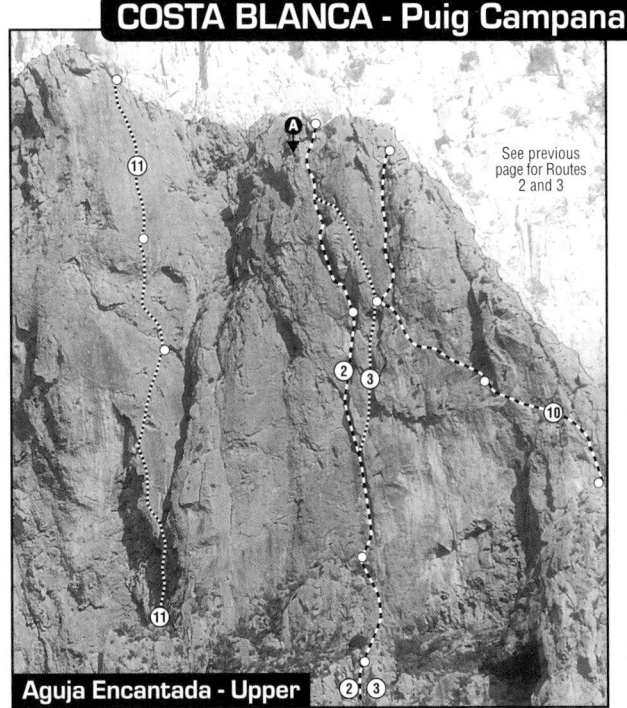

There are two more pitches listed here on the upper section, off the topo.

## 10. Flamingo Dancer ...... 🔾 // ☐ 6a+
A good finish to route 5,6,7 or 8. You will already have a full rack.
1) **5, 25m.** Climb over the top of the pillar and down into the gap. Move up to a good ledge below the right arete.
2) **5+, 25m.** Climb the broken groove on the left, then move left to belay below a corner. (The corner is a 6a pitch to the top.)
3) **6a, 40m.** Move left across the wall, past bolts, to a cave.
4) **6a+, 30m.** Climb back right to a groove and follow this to the top.
**DESCENT** - As opposite.

## 11. Corazón en la Roca . 🔾 // ☒ // ☐ 7b+
A sport route in an amazing position on the smooth wall behind the first pinnacle of Aguja Encantada. It can only be reached by climbing one of the lower routes first for which you will need a rack, but you can leave it on the ledge below the route. Start by crossing the ledge to a pillar.
1) **6b, 40m.** Follow the bolts up the pillar then out right onto the wall. This pitch can be split at a stance at 25m.
2) **7b+, 15m.** A hard pitch but it can be easily aided at 6c/A0.
3) **6a+, 30m.** One more pitch leads to the top.
**DESCENT** - Abseil down the route, then down *La Fletcher*.
FA. R.Edwards, S.Pérez 4.4.94

**Aguja Encantada - Upper**

See previous page for Routes 2 and 3

West facing wall
150m to 250m multi-pitch routes
Best grades - 5 to 7b+

# SELLA

Sella is the most important and extensive area in the whole Costa Blanca. There is so much climbing that you could easily spend a whole week's holiday here and only leave the valley to top up on your supplies at the supermarket. The most popular section is the long ridge in the centre of the valley which has a superb south face. However if you stray from the crowds then you will be rewarded with some peace and solitude. In hot weather the north facing Pared de Rosalía is worth considering with its great long routes in the mid and harder grades. Further along the road from the main area is the mecca for hard climbers called the Hidden Valley and you can't really miss the final jewel in the crown - The Divino sits majestically above everything and is worthy attention from all those who demand a little bit more from their climbing.

The climbing on the main area tends to be fingery and technical on single pitch slabs and walls. It is all well bolted with lower-offs. On the Pared de Rosalía it is worth getting your rack out, especially if you intend to tackle one of the longer routes. In the Hidden Valley you will find yourself grappling with tufas and pockets on wildly steep walls but it is only really worth considering if you lead 7a or above. The Divino has mainly long traditional routes but the lower section does contain sport routes albeit mostly in the harder grades.

One of the Bindhammer brothers on *Dosis* (8b+ - page 165) one of the best hard routes at Sella, on the Wild Side.
Photo: Keith Sharples

## ASPECT AND CLIMATE

The variety of the cliffs in the area makes it possible to find sun or shade when required throughout the year, although it is less of a winter-sun venue than you might think since the tall surrounding walls tend to keep the low sun off except in the middle of the day. Most of the crags are reasonably well sheltered by the walls of the valley except for the Pared de Rosalía and the Divino which are the walls of the valley. These two should be treated as mountain crags. The main area will dry quickly after rain. If it is raining then most of the Hidden Valley crags will stay dry, however they will seep after prolonged spells of bad weather.

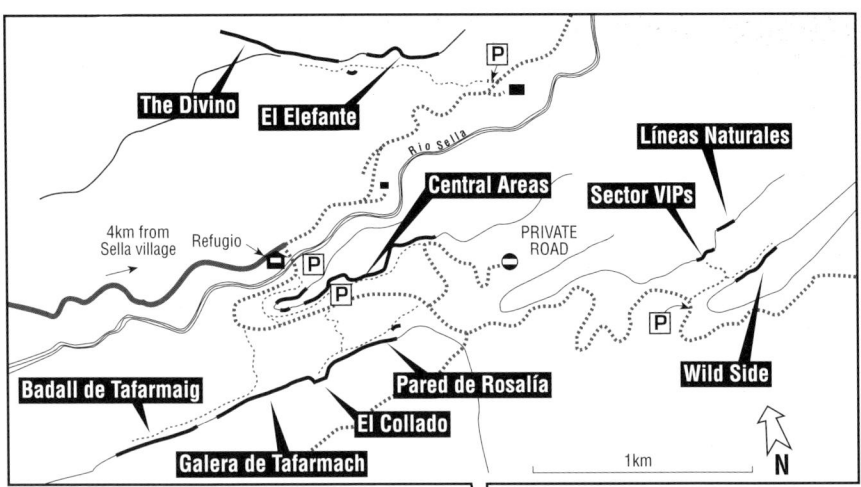

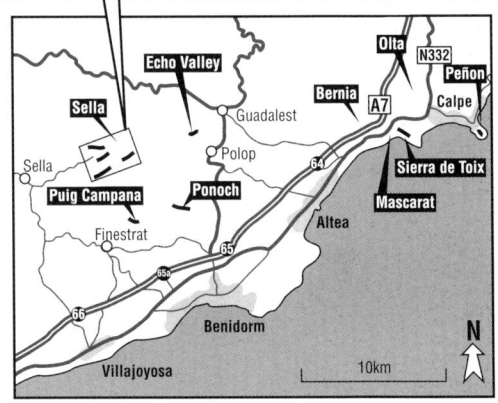

## APPROACH

Sella is situated about 20km inland from Villajoyosa on the A7 motorway.
**To reach it from the north -** Leave the A7 at junction 65a (Terra Mitica) and immediately turn south on the N332. Keep going to the mega supermarket and turn inland towards Finestrat. Drive around Finestrat, always following signs to Sella, and continue to a T-junction Turn right and eventually you arrive at Sella village. Just before entering the village, turn right down a short straight road and turn right again at the end of this. Follow this track for 4km to the refuge and crags.
**From the south -** Turn off the A7 at junction 66 and head inland following signs Sella to join the above description at Sella village.
Park near the large tower beneath the Cabeza de Rino or up the track underneath Techo del Rino.

## THE ROUTES

Many of the route equippers and first ascensionists are credited. The ones in the central area are mostly the work of Jose García and Nacho Sánchez who run the refuge.

## THE REFUGE

Only 50m from the climbing area, and underneath the inspiring wall of the Divino, is the climber's refuge. It is the only refuge in the Costa Blanca and there is space for 25 people inside and places to camp outside. The refuge sells drinks, 'bocadillos' (sandwiches), hot meals, beer, chalk and gas.
**For more information contact José or Nacho at: Casa-Refugio, Font de l'Arc, 03579 SELLA, ALICANTE, SPAIN
Tel: (00 34) 96 594 1019
or: (00 34) 96 597 2106**

Photo: Alan Cameron-Duff

# COSTA BLANCA - Sella

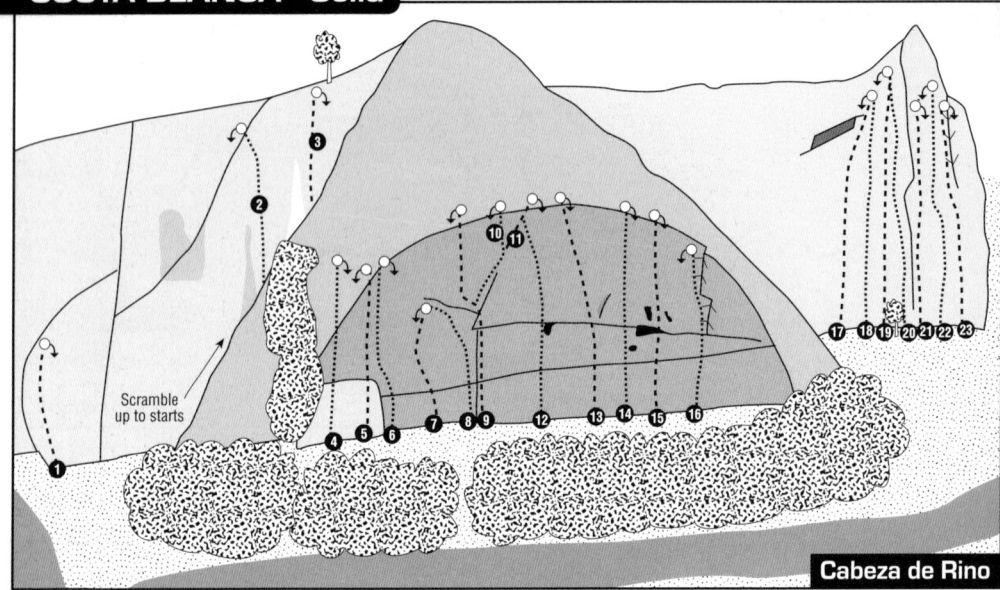

## Cabeza de Rino

### CABEZA DE RINO
The 'Rhino's head' is the crag directly opposite the refuge. It is shorter than most of the other sectors at Sella but the main section overhangs viciously giving some powerful routes. The right-hand side is a very popular easy area with some technical slab climbs which are unfortunately becoming a bit polished.

To the left of the overhanging wall are three routes.

1. **Bajo las ruedas** . . . . . . . . . . . . . . . 6a

To start the next routes scramble up the gully.

2. **La sombra de Caín** . . . . . . . 6c
30m. A long route which is worth seeking out.

3. **Compuesta y sin novio** . . . . . . . . . 6b+

4. **L'eura** . . . . . . . . . . . . . . . . . . . 6b

5. **Chapo el secundo y me bajo** . . . 6a

6. **?** . . . . . . . . . . . . . . . . . . . . . . ?

7. **Menestral Pescanova** . . . 7b+
A nasty move which uses a chipped one finger pocket.

8. **Síndrome del Betún** . . . . 7a+
Follow the diagonal line of pockets leftwards.

9. **Próximo Bautizo** . . . . . . . . 7a+
Climb up into the overhanging corner. Short but sustained.

10. **Comtitapel** . . . . . . . . . . . . 7a
The right-hand path is easier but no less strenuous.

11. **Diagonal** . . . . . . . . . . . . . . 7a+
Finish *Comtitapel* diagonally rightwards.

12. **Hombres de poca fe** . . . 8a
Extremely fingery and very steep.

13. **Multigrado** . . . . . . . . . 7c
A hideously rounded layback.

14. **Región Pagana** . . . . . . 7c
Some chipped holds.

15. **Julio César** . . . . . . . . . . . 6c+
Two hard sections but no real line.

16. **Chulerías** . . . . . . . . . . . . 6c
The last line is choss.

The slabby right-hand sector is up and right, next to the path which leads around onto the south side.

17. **Pequeñecos** . . . . . . . . . . . . . 3+

18. **Le Tina de Turner** . . . . . . . . 6a
Very polished.

19. **Tais tos tolais** . . . . . . . . . . 6b

20. **Frustración agrícola** . . . . . . . . . . . 5
The first bolt is high.

21. **Quisiera ser un octavo** . . . . . . 5
Well-spaced bolts but you can supplement them with wires.

22. **Verglas que sí** . . . . . . . . . . . . . . 5+
The lower-off is missing, use other routes.

23. **Registro sanitario** . . . . 6b+
The hard section can be by-passed on the left at 6a.

NW facing roof and slab
5m to 30m routes
Best grades - 3+ to 7c

# COSTA BLANCA - Sella

**Culo de Rino - Left**

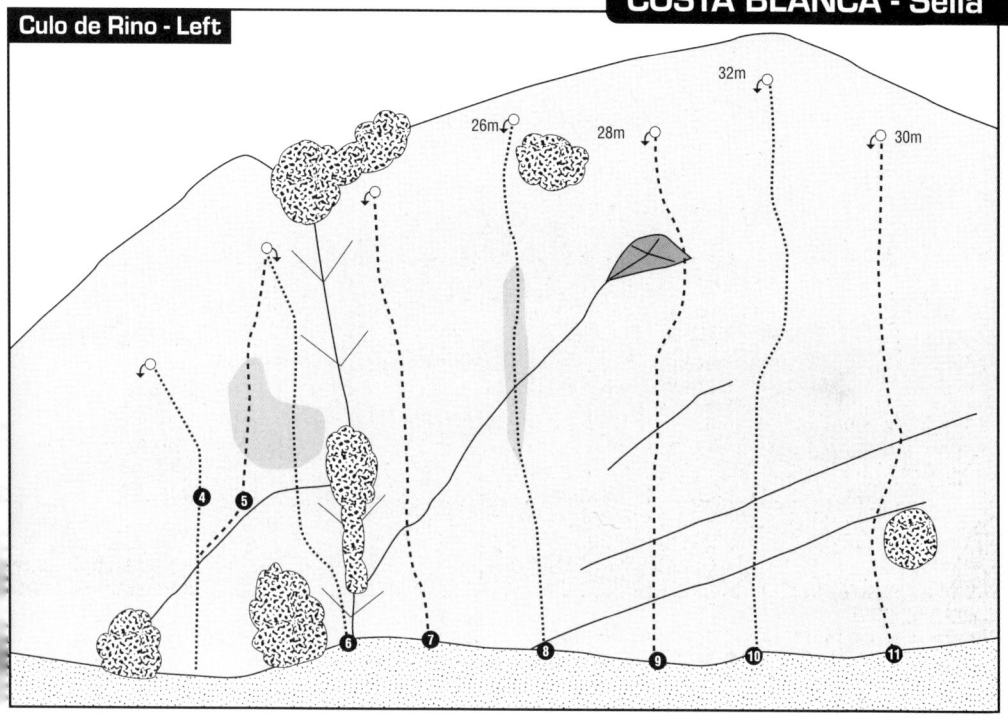

## CULO DE RINO - LEFT
The most popular climbing is on the sunny south side of the ridge. The first section is around the corner and up the hill from the Cabeza de Rino. The climbing is excellent and popular with a good selection of mainly slabby or vertical routes, on good rock, within 5 minutes of the car, but keep away from *Otigofrenicia*!

**APPROACH** - There are two ways of reaching the Culo de Rino. The first is to park opposite the refuge, walk up the road until you are almost level with the end of the Cabeza de Rino, then take a path up through the bushes and around leftwards to the base of the wall. Alternatively, drive up the dirt road past the refuge under the Cabeza de Rino until you are level with the Techo del Rino (which has a large square-cut overhang in it upper section) then turn left off the road into flat parking areas below the cliffs. The Culo de Rino is leftwards through the trees.

Before you get to the quality climbing there are three hidden routes on the other side of the Rhino's head. The bushes have grown around these routes and they are hard to find but they aren't really worth the effort anyway.

**1. Todo por la punta patria** .... 7c
Very short and very blank.

**2. Aqui no pinta nadie nada** ....... 5+

**3. Más fácil todavia** ............. 4+

Further up the slope the climbing improves.

**4. Timatiriticón** ................ 6a
Polished and a bit insignificant and the bolts are old.

**5. Pies de minino** ............... 5+

**6. Chusmaniática** ............. 6a
A fingery bulge provides the crux.

Take care when lowering off the next set of routes, they are all long and there have been accidents.

**7. Otigofrénicia** ........... 7c
20m. A fingery boulder problem up the blank wall just right of the corner.

**8. Denominacíon de origen** ..... 6a+
26m. A good wall climb.

**9. Camilo el rey de los kumbayas** .. 6b
28m. A good route up the big slab on nice rock.

**10. Valor y Coraje** ............. 6a+
32m. A very long pitch with some great climbing.

**11. Martillazos de maricona** ........ 6b+
30m. The next line has a poor start but improves higher up. Another very long pitch.

South facing slab
20m to **32m** routes
Best grades - 6a+ to 6b

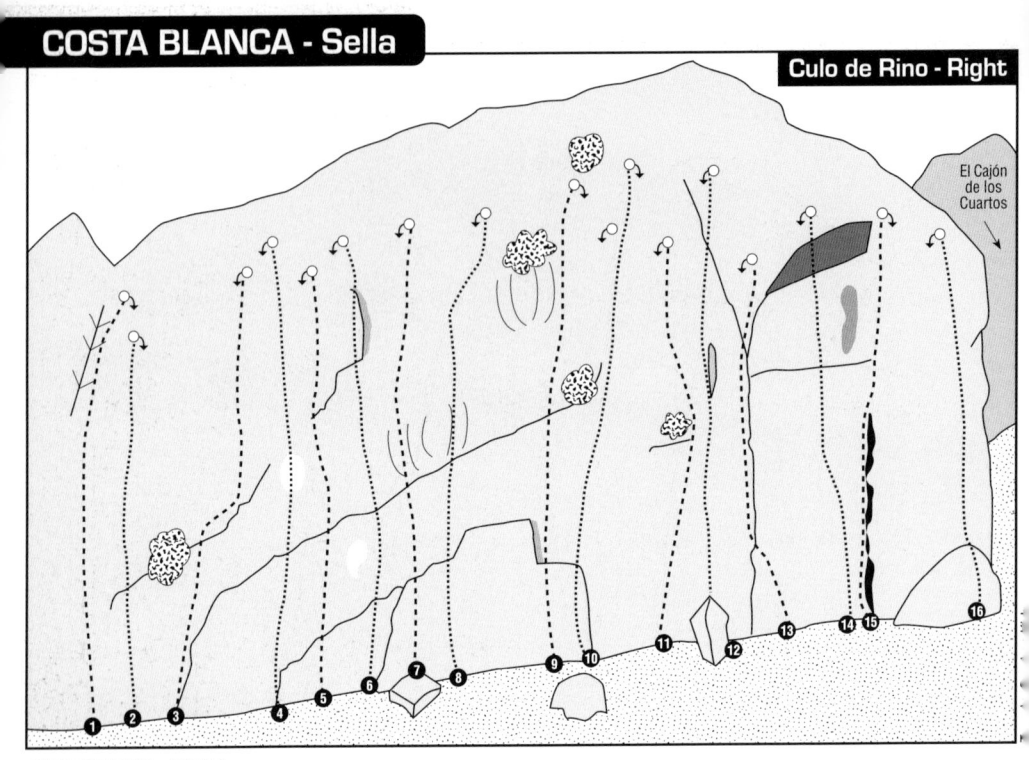

# COSTA BLANCA - Sella

## Culo de Rino - Right

El Cajón de los Cuartos

### CULO DE RINO - RIGHT
One of the most popular crags at Sella with plenty of good long routes. The left-hand side has some easy slab climbs. Further right the wall steepens up and gives some more technical numbers.

**APPROACH** - The wall is just to the left of the main car park below the overhang of Techo del Rino.

**1. Sense Novetat** . . . . . . . . . . . . . . . 6a+
2 bolts lead up into a corner, from here you need runners, shock horror!

**2. Los refugiados** . . . . . . . . . . . . 6a
A good little route with a stepp and sustained upper wall.

**3. A diestro y siniestro** . . . . . . . . . 5+
A fine steady route with the crux at the top.

**4. A golpe y porrazo** . . . . . . . . . . 5+

**5. Vía del Indio** . . . . . . . . . . . . . . 5+
Becoming very polished.

**6. Divinas Chapuzas** . . . . . . . . . . 6a
Start behind the pine tree, left of a cream rock scar. A reachy two-move-wonder with spaced bolts up the lay-back crack.

**7. Tú dirás** . . . . . . . . . . . . . . . . 6a+
Up the grey wall and over a small bulge. Steeper than it looks. The hard start can be avoided by using *Divinas Chapuzas*.

**8. Vino d'Oporto** . . . . . . . . . . . . 6c
A fingery route with the crux at the top.

In the past there has been a project up the wall in between routes 8 and 9 but currently it doesn't have any bolts.

**9. Guija loca** . . . . . . . . . . . . . 6c+
The grade is if you climb it direct at the start. You can by-pass this on the right which gives a 6c.

**10. Kina borregada** . . . . . . . . . 7b+
Bolted for a national climbing competition. Unlike most competition routes, it is vertical and fingery.

**11. Edward's Wall** . . . . . . . . . . 7a
A controversial route which was led with gear at E7 6b. Subsequently a bolted route was put up a similar line. Also called *No frenes mis instintos*. There is a lower-off to the left at the top.

**12. Suspiros de dolor** . . . . . . . . . 7a
Up the blank-looking wall past two chipped holds.

**13. La cosa** . . . . . . . . . . . . . . . 7a
The corner proves to be technical and painful.

**14. A golpe de pecho** . . . . . . . . 7a+
Sharp fingery holds up a wall and over a bulge.

**15. Con las manos en la cosa** . . . . . . . . . . . . . . . . 6c
A technical route up a tufa groove with some sharp holds.

**16. Días de lluvia** . . . . . . . . . . . 6a+
Steep and technical climbing on side-pulls and sprags. The first bolt is missing but it isn't a problem.

---

150 | Lots of sun | 2 min | Slabby | Lower-offs | South facing slab
15m to 25m routes
Best grades - 6a to 7b+

rockfax.co

# COSTA BLANCA - Sella

**El cajón de los cuartos**

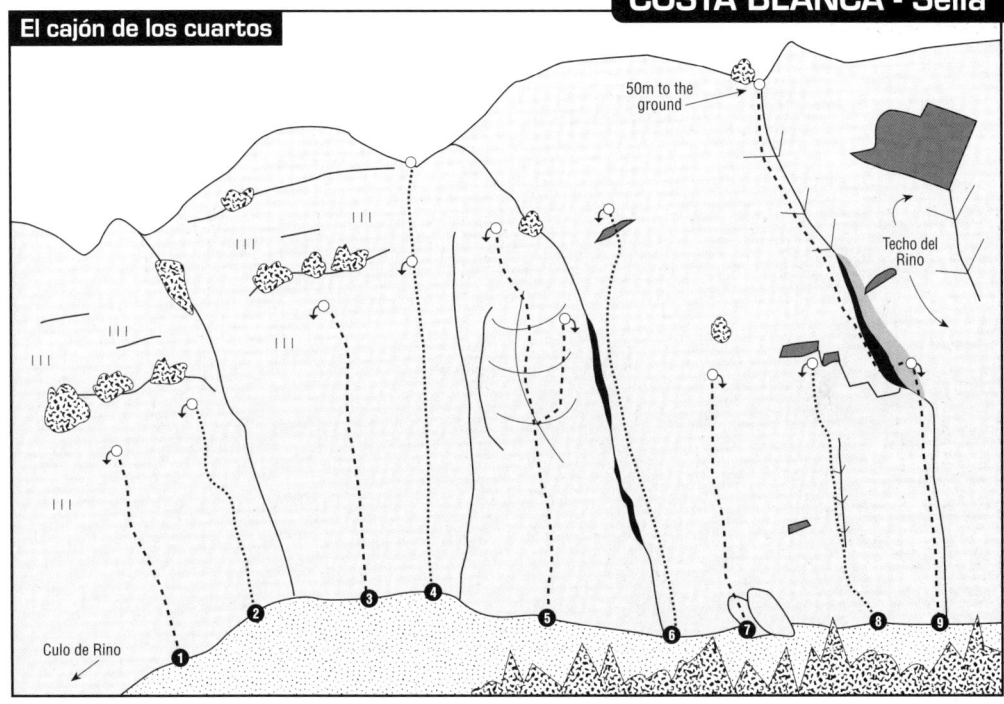

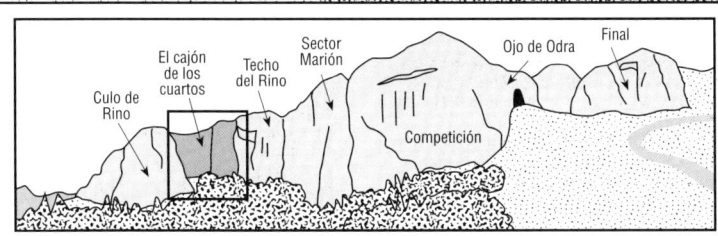

## EL CAJÓN DE LOS CUARTOS
A short section of bolted slabs with some popular easier routes. It is a good area for beginners. This is the bay above and left of the parking area.

**1. Dime dime** ............... 3+
Pronounced 'dee-may dee-may'. Popular and polished.

**2. Con mallas y a lo loco** .......... 3+

**3. Pequñecos II** ............. 4
The left-hand line in the centre of the bay.

**4. Pequñecos III** ........... 4+
1) **4+.** An entertaining, but polished, slab route.
2) **4+.** Less good then the 1st pitch but the view from the top is good.

**5. Porko niente lire** ......... 6c+/7a+
A technical little number up the smooth scoop with two finishes. The left-hand is longer and harder. The right-hand has its own lower-off. There is a devious middle line as well.

**6. Ciudado con mi sombrero** ..... 6a+
An excellent steep groove. The top crack can be by-passed on the left.

**7. Fulanita y sus menganos** ... 6b
Short but quite absorbing.

**8. Zig-zag atómico** ............... 6a
Up the wall behind the trees.

**9. Two Nights of Love** ......... 5+
1) **5+, 25m.** Climb right into the corner then follow this to a belay. Either lower off here or:
2) **4+, 25m.** Cross the gully and thrash up the slab and corner above to the top. One 50m abseil reaches the ground.

South facing slab
10m to 25m routes
Best grades - 3+ to 6b

# COSTA BLANCA - Sella

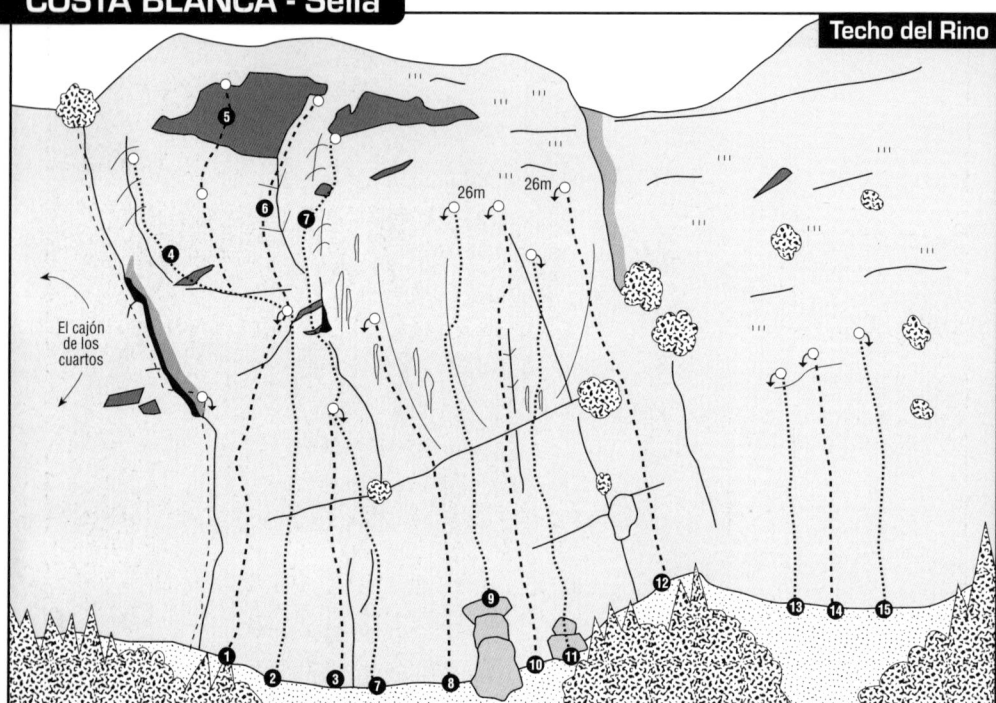

## Techo del Rino

### TECHO DEL RINO
This is the steepest sector on the main area at Sella, which is dominated by a huge square roof on its upper left, with the magnificent bulging wall of *Kashba* below and right.

**1. Blanco nato** .................. 6b
Polished start moves.

**2. Martín Galas** ........ 6b+
Technical wall climbing but a bit eliminate.

**3. Vaya tipo el de Oti** ....... 6c+
A clean slab, with some painful holds, leading to a steep finish.

The next three routes start from the belay at the top *Blanco nato*.

**4. Pesos pluma** ........ 6b+
From the belay, climb out left then up to the edge of the big roof. Exposed, technical and improbable.

**5. La Explanada** ...... 8b+
A tricky little 'created' roof climb.

**6. Vía Pecuaria** ......... 6b
A grip-trip out under the right-hand side of the roof!
DESCENT - Abseil off.

**7. Cardo Borriquero** .............. 6c+
1) 6a, 20m. Can be done in its own right.
2) 6c+, 20m. A fine exposed pitch.
DESCENT - Abseil off.

**8. Acróbata porcino** ........ 7a
The significant climbing is only short but it saves its best for the last move. See photo on page 176.

**9. Ssorbe verge** ........ 7b+
26m. A very bouldery middle section provides the difficulties.

**10. Kashba** ............. 6c+
26m. Classic climbing and one of the best routes at Sella.

**11. No me bajes tan...** ......... 7a
A one-move-wonder. Grab the side-pull and jump!

**12. El torronet** .............. 5+
26m. A great easier pitch on excellent rock. The first bolt is gone.

To the right of the main wall is another short wall with some frequently-climbed technical routes.

**13. Colp de Cot** .............. 6b+
A short and desperate section. Locally graded 6a+.

**14. Hola Patricio** ........ 6a
Good pocket pulling past well-spaced bolts.

**15. Puntea que no tienes ni idea** .. 6a+

152

South facing wall
15m to 30m routes
Best grades - 6a to 7b+

Lots of sun / Steep / 2 min / Lower-offs

# COSTA BLANCA - Sella

## Sector Marión

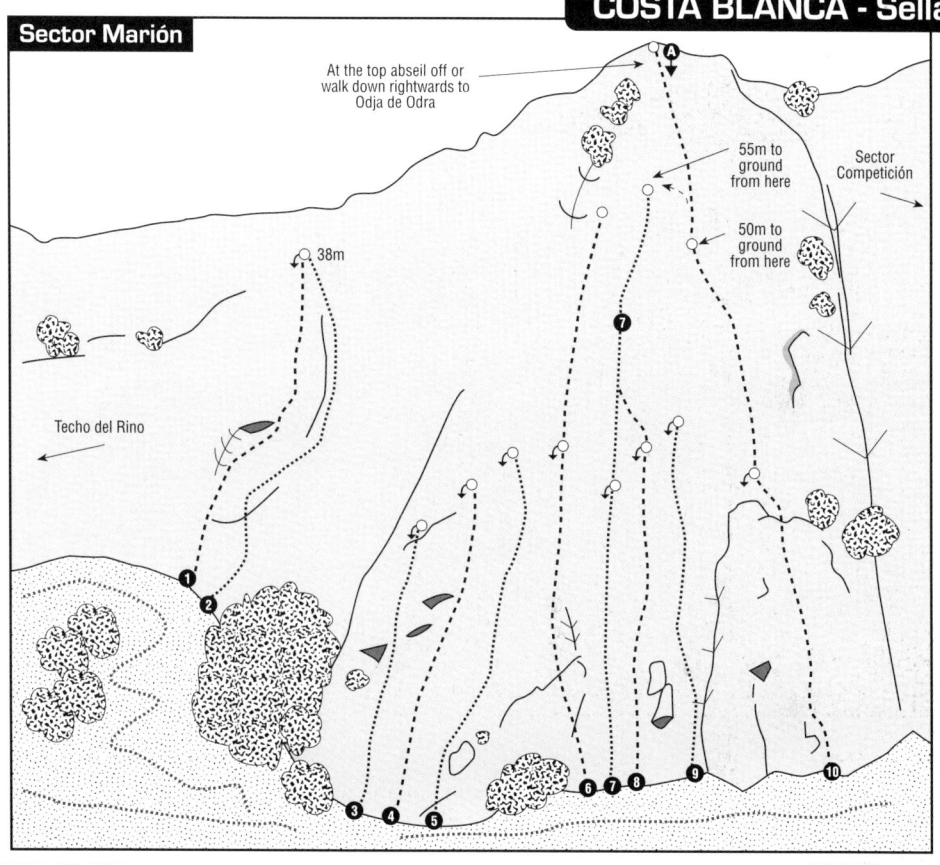

At the top abseil off or walk down rightwards to Odja de Odra

55m to ground from here
50m to ground from here

Sector Competición

Techo del Rino

**SECTOR MARION**
One of the classic features of Sella is the elegant long arete of *Marión*.

The first two routes are 38m and have very high first bolts which means you can lower off with a second rope and get to the ground before the knot reaches the first bolt. Take care whatever you do here.

**1. Culo Ipanema** .......... 6b+
38m. Good technical wall with a poor finish.

**2. Rosalind Sutton** .......... 6a+
38m. A poor lower wall leading to a nice crack at the top. Combine the lower bit of *Culo Ipanema* with upper bit of *Rosalind Sutton* for the best route - 6b+.

Down the hill, past the trees are some more routes.

**3. Bolt Tax** .......... 6a
Good technical climbing.

**4. Deja vu** .......... 5

**5. Cartujal** .......... 5+
Quality rock.

**6. Cul de sac** .......... 5
1) 5, 20m. The first line of bolts to the right of a bush.
2) 5, 20m. Continue in the same line. Abseil off.

**7. Prusik** .......... 5+
1) 5+, 20m. A popular pitch.
2) 5+, 30m. Be careful of the loose flake.

**8. Anglopithecus Britaniensis** .... 6a+
It is possible to continue up pitch 2 of *Prusik*.

**9. Mister Pi** .......... 5+
Start by bridging up the groove. Hard 6a if you stick to the most direct line but you can escape right to the crack.

**10. Marión** .......... 5+
The classic prominent arete offers one of Sella's most celebrated climbs. The grades suggested for the various pitches seem to vary wildly from person to person.
1) 5+, 20m. Hard moves over a bulge then trend left to ledges.
2) 4, 25m. Continue to another stance (50m to ground).
3) 4+, 20m. Follow a small groove to a tricky bulge (2 bolts). Pull over this then use the lower-off on the left (55m) or continue to the top on wires.

**DESCENT** - Make two abseils down the line. Alternatively, walk right along the ridge to reach the Oja de Odra cave from behind.

South facing slab
15m to 35m single and multi-pitch
Best grades - 5 to 6b

Lots of sun · 2 min · Slabby · Lower-offs · Multi-pitch

A climber
*Desbloquea que No* (5 - oppos
on Sector Competicíon, S
Photo: Keith Shar

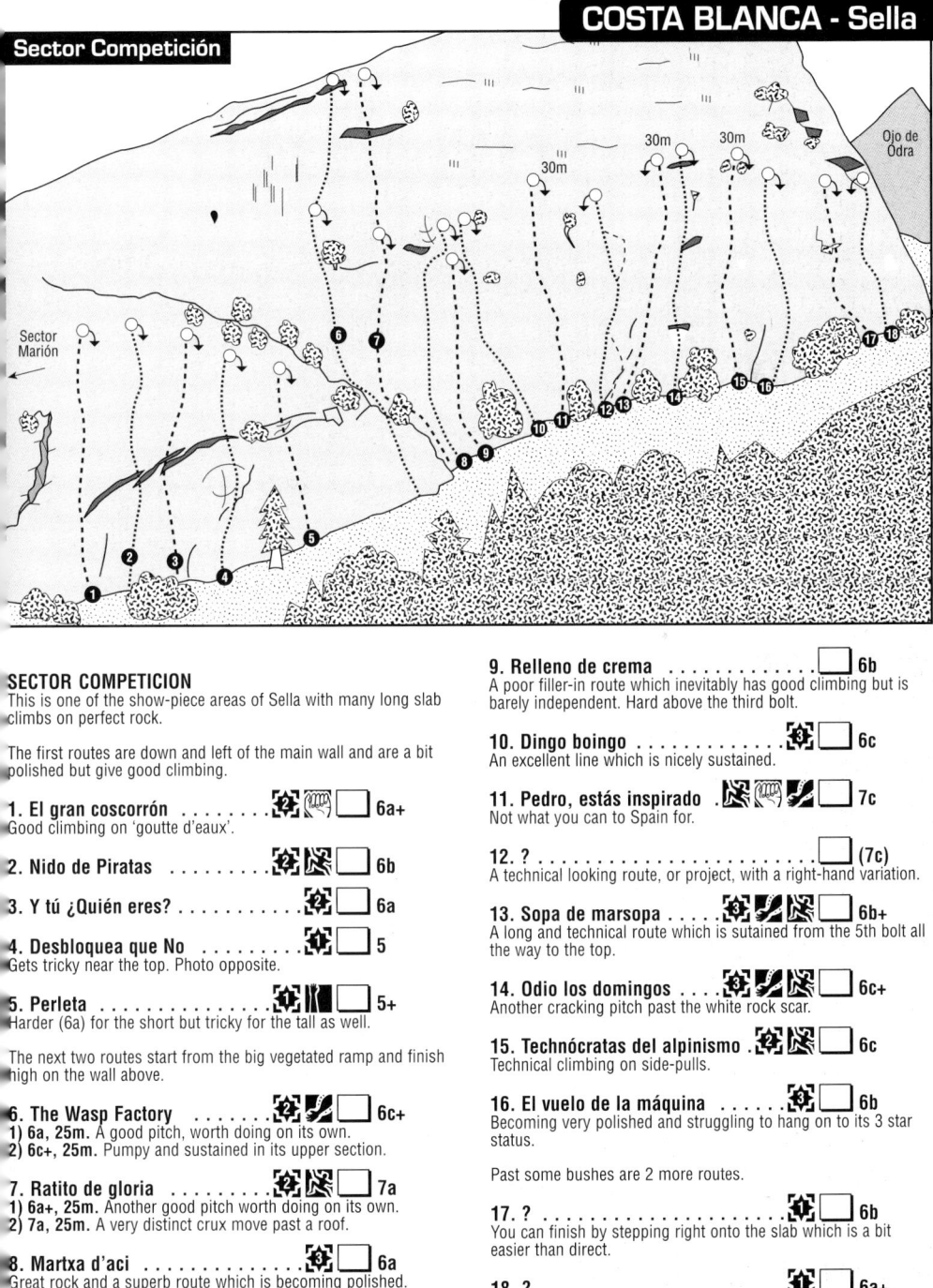

# COSTA BLANCA - Sella

**Sector Competición**

## SECTOR COMPETICION
This is one of the show-piece areas of Sella with many long slab climbs on perfect rock.

The first routes are down and left of the main wall and are a bit polished but give good climbing.

**1. El gran coscorrón** . . . . . . . . 6a+
Good climbing on 'goutte d'eaux'.

**2. Nido de Piratas** . . . . . . . . . 6b

**3. Y tú ¿Quién eres?** . . . . . . . . . 6a

**4. Desbloquea que No** . . . . . . . 5
Gets tricky near the top. Photo opposite.

**5. Perleta** . . . . . . . . . . . . . . . 5+
Harder (6a) for the short but tricky for the tall as well.

The next two routes start from the big vegetated ramp and finish high on the wall above.

**6. The Wasp Factory** . . . . . . . 6c+
1) 6a, 25m. A good pitch, worth doing on its own.
2) 6c+, 25m. Pumpy and sustained in its upper section.

**7. Ratito de gloria** . . . . . . . . . 7a
1) 6a+, 25m. Another good pitch worth doing on its own.
2) 7a, 25m. A very distinct crux move past a roof.

**8. Martxa d'aci** . . . . . . . . . . . 6a
Great rock and a superb route which is becoming polished.

**9. Relleno de crema** . . . . . . . . . . . 6b
A poor filler-in route which inevitably has good climbing but is barely independent. Hard above the third bolt.

**10. Dingo boingo** . . . . . . . . . . . . 6c
An excellent line which is nicely sustained.

**11. Pedro, estás inspirado** . . . 7c
Not what you can to Spain for.

**12. ?** . . . . . . . . . . . . . . . . . . . (7c)
A technical looking route, or project, with a right-hand variation.

**13. Sopa de marsopa** . . . . . . 6b+
A long and technical route which is sutained from the 5th bolt all the way to the top.

**14. Odio los domingos** . . . . . 6c+
Another cracking pitch past the white rock scar.

**15. Technócratas del alpinismo** . . 6c
Technical climbing on side-pulls.

**16. El vuelo de la máquina** . . . . . 6b
Becoming very polished and struggling to hang on to its 3 star status.

Past some bushes are 2 more routes.

**17. ?** . . . . . . . . . . . . . . . . . . . . 6b
You can finish by stepping right onto the slab which is a bit easier than direct.

**18. ?** . . . . . . . . . . . . . . . . . . . . 6a+

South facing slab
15m to 30m single and multi-pitch
Best grades - 5 to 6c

# COSTA BLANCA - Sella

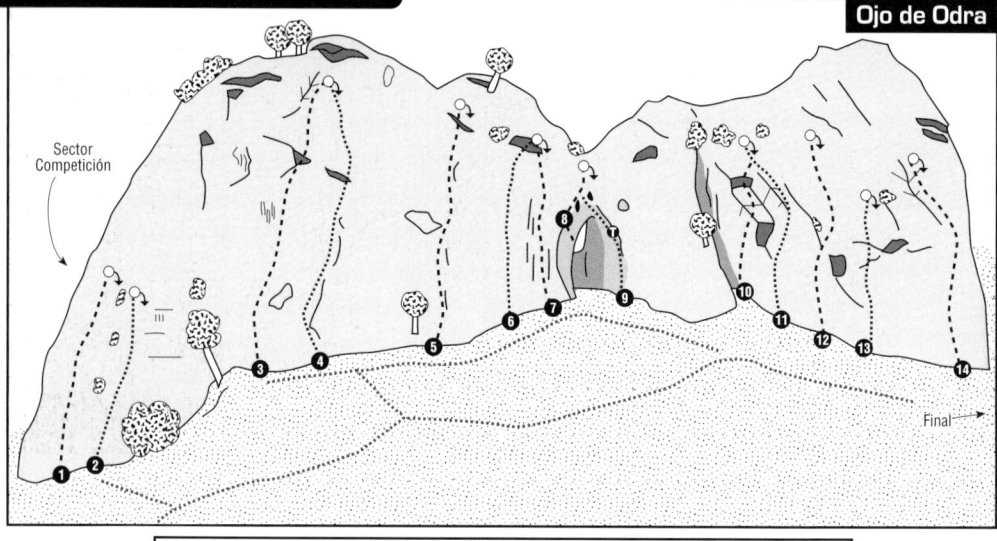

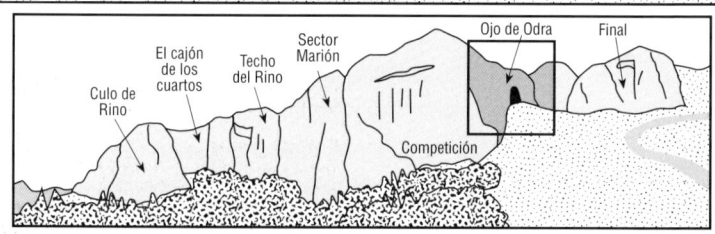

## Ojo de Odra

### OJO DE ODRA
Around the corner and up the hill from Sector Competición is a steep end wall leading to a shorter section with an amazing hole through it. Further right is another short wall which has seen some recent development.

The first two routes are just around the corner from Sector Competicion.

**1. Almorranas Salvajes** .......... 4+

**2. Alí Babá y los 40K** .......... 3+

The upper section of the wall has some steep, orange rock.

**3. Kamikaze** .......... 7a+
30m. A superb route with great climbing.

**4. Seventh Samurai** .......... 6c
30m. Even more run-out than its neighbour.

**5. Fisura con finura** .......... 6a
A fine line up the crack.

**6. Roberto Alcázar y Merlin** .......... 6a+
A technical start followed by a long reach then some juggy moves to the top.

**7. Espíritu de Satur** .......... 6c
There are no bolts visible for this route. The line on the local topo is just left of the cave.

Further up the hill is the famous hole known as Oja de Odra. If you scramble up the back of this hole you can get an amazing view of the Divino.

**8. Ojo de Odra** .......... 6c
Start in the hole and swing out of the left-hand side (looking in) on sharp, polished holes.

**9. Los coreanos** .......... 6c+
The line of pockets right of the hole past a sling.

**10. Els nuciers** .......... 7a
A bit of a non-line across the groove.

**11. Mel de roma** .......... 6b
Nasty fall possible from the last move.

**12. Skid Row** .......... 6b
Steep and strenuous on good holds.

**13. Los remeros** .......... 6c

**14. Balados para un sorde** .......... 6a+

South facing slab
15m to 30m routes
Best grades - 5 to 6b

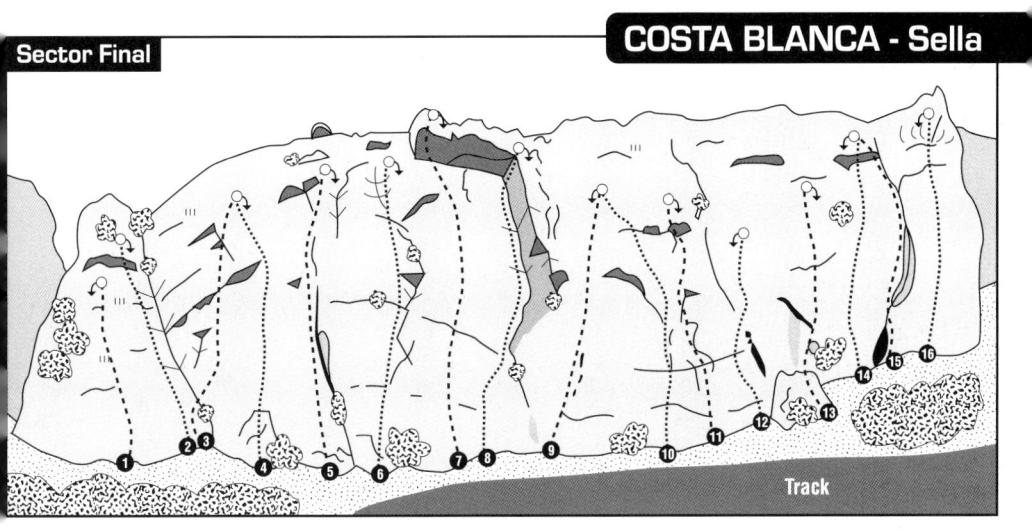

**Sector Final**

# COSTA BLANCA - Sella

**SECTOR FINAL**
This is the last area on the central popular section, the rock above here is on private land and should be avoided. This compact buttress of corners and intermittent cracklines has some great routes in the 6a+ to 6c range.
**APPROACH** - From the car park under the Techo del Rino, walk uphill beneath the crags, past Sector Ojo de Orda.
**Do not drive up the road and park under the cliff** - This is a private road and parking here upsets the local residents.

The first routes are on a slightly scrappier section of rock, to the left of the bend in the road.

**1. La vergüenza** . . . . . . . . . . . . . . . 3
Bolts removed.

**2. La vergüenza II** . . . . . . . . . . . 3+
Good for beginners.

**3. Speedy González** . . . . . . . . . . . 5+
Start at the groove then trend right across the wall.

**4. El Pixoncet** . . . . . . . . . . . . . 6a+
Polished on the crux moves but delightful climbing.

**5. Con mallas y a lo loco** . . . . . . . 5+
The groove/crack-line has a tricky start but is okay above.

**6. Aquí no nos dejan aparcar** . . 6a
A tricky little number with some thin moves at the bottom.

**7. Aquí tampoco** . . . . . . . . . . 6b+
Great climbing up the technical wall and over the roof.

**8. Wagageegee** . . . . . . . . . . . . 6a+
The big corner. Original climbed without bolts at E3 5c and with a more direct finish over the roof.

**9. Desperate Dan** . . . . . . . . . 6c
The awkward, pocketed crack.

**10. Kilroy was 'ere** . . . . . . 6c+
Technical and sustained.

**11. El Agüí** . . . . . . . . . . . . . . . . 6c+
The rightwards trending crackline.

**12. Grillos Navajeros** . . . . . . . 6c
Excellent technical climbing up a vague crack.

**13. Mandolin Wind** . . . . . . . . 7a+
A very hard start.

**14. Anno Dracula** . . . . . . . . . . 6c
Another hard start.

**15. ?** . . . . . . . . . . . . . . . . . . . . . 6a+
The crackline might be bolted. If not then use wires.

**16. I.Q. 18/30** . . . . . . . . . . . . . . 6b
Up the pillar behind the tree. Worth doing.

South facing wall
15m to 20m routes
Best grades - 3 to 6c+

157

# COSTA BLANCA - Sella

**Pared de Rosalia**

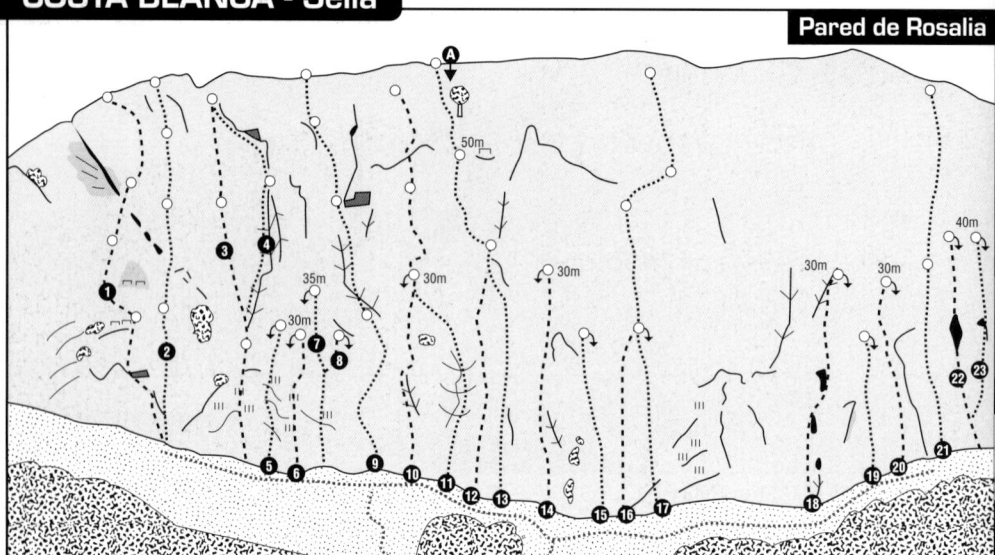

### PARED DE ROSALIA
This vast face is frequently stared at by climbers basking in the sun on the popular areas at Sella. Not many climbers ever make the effort of actually walking up there which is a shame since it is one of the best crags in the area for people leading in the upper 6s and 7s. There are some superb, fully-bolted routes, with great lines, on perfect rock. Most of the pitches are at least 30m which makes lowering-off awkward. The best advice is to climb on two 50m ropes. Because it faces north, this wall is more attractive in warmer weather, although it does catch the evening sun in the Spring and Summer.

**APPROACH** - Park in the main area, below Techo del Rino. Go back down the road for about 100m until you find a path on the left. This leads steeply up through the trees to the bottom of the cliff. This path also seems to be a very popular toilet - please go somewhere else!

**DESCENT** - You can abseil straight back down most of the routes using double 50m ropes. Failing that, locate the anchor at the top of *Sonrisa Vertical*. One long abseil leads to the belay at the top of pitch 2. This is exactly 50m from the ground.

At the left-hand end is a large smooth wall. Surprisingly enough this wall is made of crappy rock and only has three poor lines on it - a chipped 8b, a project and an unknown.
The decent climbing starts on the left-hand side of the main wall, below a long diagonal slash high up.

**1. Luna** .................... 7a
1) 6b+, 2) 6b, 3) 6b+, 4) 7a. A good long route which starts up the left trending flake on a small clean slab. The last pitch is to the right of a large recess high on the face and provides a testing finale. The route is fully bolted.
*FA. Ruiz, Barber, Sánchez.*

**2. Esto escampa** ........ 7a+
1) 6b, 2) 7a+, 3) 7a, 4) 6c. Another majestic, fully-bolted route with two technical pitches in the middle on perfect rock.

**3. Lejos de la multitud** .... 7a
Direct up the wall with two hard pitches after an indifferent start.
1) 4. Scramble up the approach slopes to a belay.
2) 6c+, 3) 7a+. Direct up the wall left of the long curving corner.
*FA. J.M.García*

**4. Venus erycina** ...... 7b
A brilliant line up the long corner. Seldom climbed, probably because the top pitch is E6.
1) 4. As for *Lejos de la multitud*.
2) 6c, 3) 7b. Two desperate trad pitches up the corner.
*FA. J.M.García, N.Sanchez. FFA. M.Edwards.*

**5. El Ojo de Yavé** ........ 7a
33m. A scrappy start but fine climbing near the top.
*FA. N.Sánchez*

**6. Anillos de Saturno** .... 7b
30m. Another slow starter.
*FA. N.Sánchez*

**7. Molly Highins** ........ 6c
35m. A long single pitch. Excellent.

**8. El martillo de Thor** .... 6c
30m. A right-hand finish to *Molly*.
*FA. N.Sánchez*

**9. Tanit** ................ 6b+
A superb easier long route and the easiest way up the full wall.
1) 6b+, 2) 5+, 3) 6a+, 4) 6a+. The first three pitches are well bolted but there is little fixed gear on the last pitch so take a small rack.

**10. El endemoniado** ...... 7a
30m. A fine single pitch.
*FA. J.M.Ruescas, N.Sánchez*

# COSTA BLANCA - Sella

**Pared de Rosalia**

**11. La estación de la bruia** .... 6c
1) 6c, 2) 6b+, 3) 6b+. Another fully bolted mega route.
FA. N.Sánchez

**12. Armagedón** .......... 6c+
A left-hand start pitch to *Sonrisa*.
FA. J.M.Ruescas, N.Sánchez

**13. Sonrisa Vertical** ..... 7a
One of the best routes around with superb climbing on the first two pitches. Fully bolted and best done on 2 50m ropes.
1) 6c, 30m. Worth doing in its own right.
2) 7a, 20m. An immaculate sustained pitch.
3) 6a+, 40m. Straight to the top.
FA. Salva, Higinio, Jesús

**14. Calfamusculus** .......... 6a+
28m. The line above where the approach path arrives. Excellent grey limestone. Top-rope project below and right at 6b+.

**15. Caleidoscopio** .......... 6a
20m. A good route to the right of the corners of *Calfamusculus*.

**16. Barco pachero** ......... 6c
20m. More quality rock but a bit run-out.
FA. J.M.García, N.Sanchez.

**17. Línea caliente** .... 7b
Three great pitches plus one short connector.
1) 6c, 20m. 2) 7b, 30m. 3) 4, 15m. 4) 6b+, 35m.
FA. N.Sánchez

**18. Pretoriana** .......... 6b+
28m. The line of holes.
FA. Juan C. and Jesús Romero

**19. As de copas** .......... 7a
25m. Thin climbing with spaced bolts.
FA. N.Sánchez

**20. As de bastos** .......... 7a
28m. Another long line with an airy feel.
FA. N.Sánchez

**21. Sin comentarios** ... 7b
1) 7b, 35m. A desperately thin and fingery pitch.
2) 6b+, 30m. A long anti-climatic continuation.

**22. Arte del olvido** .......... 6c+
38m. An enormous single pitch.
FA. N.Sánchez

**23. Project** .............. (6c+)
38m.

**24. ?** ................ 7a+
A long and majestic trad route. Take a full rack.
1) 7a+. 2) 6b. 3) 6a. The odd bit of tat marks the way.
FA. M.Edwards, R.Edwards 1990

**25. Rosa de piedra** ........ 7a+
Two hard pitches but friable rock. 1) 7a. 2) 7a.
FA. N.Sánchez

**26. Project** .............. 7b

**27. La pistola** .......... 6b
18m. A crack and groove.
FA. Juan C. and Jesús Romero

**28. La Vergonya** .......... 4
20m. A scrappy pitch on the edge of the wall which is not worth walking up here for.

North facing wall
Long 30m pitches and 100m multi-pitch routes
Best grades - 6a to 7b

# COSTA BLANCA - Sella

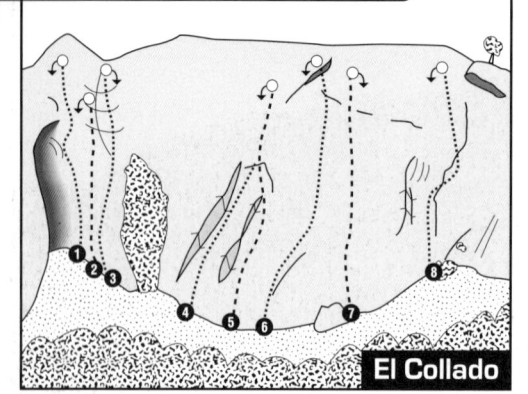

### El Collado

**EL COLLADO**
Up and right of the main face of Pared de Rosalía is a short wall in a bay.

**1. Manhatten Blues** ...... 7a
Start at the top of the slope, inside the cave. Climb the steep wall on pockets and tufas.
FA. An American

**2. Parado de larga duración** 6c+
30m.
FA. J.M.García

**3. La indecisa** ........ 7a/b
30m. A good route up the grey slab and into the open scoop right of the cave but with a perplexing move.

**4. ?** .................. 6c
25m. left-hand start to the next route.
FA. Javi Metal

**5. Quita la música, macarra** ... 7a+
25m. Superb steep climbing with too many holds on the crux.

**6. Final d'estiu** .......... 7b
25m. Good climbing up the steep wall.

**7. Felanicula** ................. (8a+)
25m. A former competition route so expect some chipped holds.
FA. M.Edwards 1989

**8. Los Avutardos** ....... 7c
25m. The overhanging crack and corner with hard moves to pull onto the headwall.

**GALERA DE TAFARMACH**
Right of El Collado is a massive wall which is in reality a continuation of Pared de Rosalía.
**APPROACH** - Walk up the clear area directly from the first bend in the track, after the refuge. This brings you out at the foot of *Mujer Lampréa*. There is also a path from below El Collado.

**9. ?** ....................... 6c
28m.

**10. Sporty Spice** ..... 7a+
A wild outing on a wall that has a big feel and remote atmosphere. It is partly bolted but take a small rack including some Friends. Start about 100m right of where the path arrives at the face. The first bolt can be seen about 20m up.
1) 6b+, 40m. Climb easily up a recess then move left to the bolt. Climb up to some good stuck-on holds to gain a line of undercuts leading left to a bolt before the belay ledge. 2 bolt belay.
2) 6b, 20m. Climb cracks past a bolt to the next belay on a bolt and peg.
3) 7a+, 40m. A long pitch needing 12 quickdraws and a Rock 5. Climb the beautiful pocketed shield up and right to belay in a deep cave. Nut belay.
4) 6b+, 30m. Leave the cave rightwards then move back left, past a peg, to the foot of a crack-line in an exposed position. Climb the crack to the top.
**DESCENT** - Walk down the ridge to the top of El Collado then off the back to a track which leads around to the main track.
FA. Andy Hyslop, Tim Lofthouse

### Galera de Tafarmach

El Collado

**El Collado**
North facing wall, 20m routes
Best grades - 6c+ to 7c

# COSTA BLANCA - Sella

## Badall de Tafarmaig

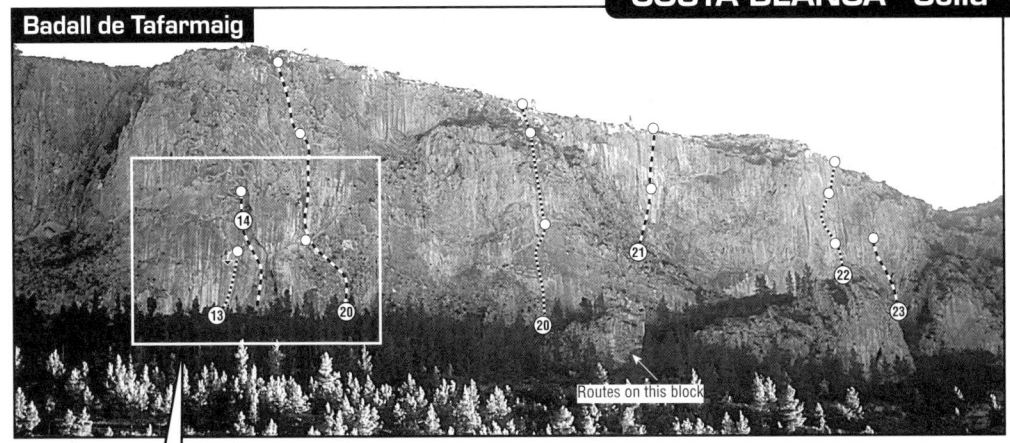

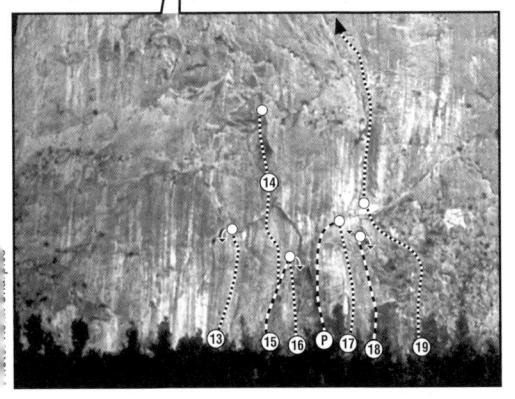

**15. ?** ................... 6b+
15m. The bolted right-hand finish to the previous route.
FA. J.M.García, S.Barber, J.C.Romero

**16. Vía de Bea** ........... 6c
15m. Direct to the lower-off on route 15.
FA. J.C.Romero

The next line is a project.

**17. La red del diablo** ..... 7b
22m.
FA. J.C.Romero, N.Sánchez

**18. Algol** ............... 7a
FA. J.C.Romero, N.Sánchez

**19. Zafiro** ............... 6b
The right-hand wall of the cave and the corner above.
1) 6a, 2) 6b, 3) 6a.
FA. R.Edwards, S.Perez

**11. Gato negro, gato blanco** ...... 7b
1) 6c, 2) 7b, 3) 7b.
Three very long pitches. Long ropes needed to abseil off.
FA. François Clair, Benjamin Stach

**12. Mujer Lampréa** .......... 6c
1) 6c, 2) 6b, 3) 6c, 4) 6c+.
The only details known are that it is fully bolted, brilliant and a little run-out.
FA. N.Sánchez

### BADALL DE TAFARMAIG
The continuation wall. The first routes are centred on a steep recess with well-featured rock.

**13. ?** ...................... (7c)
25m. The left-hand wall of the recess. Given 7c elsewhere but it is probably harder than that.

**14. Phoenix Zone** .......... 7a+
32m. A single pitch trad route.
FA. M.Edwards, R.Edwards

**20. Badall de Tafarmaig** ..... 6c
1) 6b, 2) 6c, 3) 6a.
FA. Albert Lloret, Sebastía Pérez

**21. Scenic Express** ......... 6c
A brilliant top pitch but it requires some effort to get there. It can be approached from above if you know where to abseil.
1) 6c, 2) 6b+.
FA. R.Edwards, M.Edwards

**22. Figures in the Mind** ..... 8a/7b
An impressive long route which is fully bolted.
1) 7a, 2) 7b
3a) 8a. The right-hand branch.
3b) 7b. The left-hand branch.

**23. Mighty Whitey** ......... 7c
The slab to the first belay of Figures in the Mind.
FA. A.Hocking 2001

**24. Gran diedro rojo** ......... 6c
The long red corner on the next section of the wall.
1) 6c, 2) 6a.
FA. R.Edwards

**Tafarmach and Tafarmaig** - North facing
20m pitches to 100m multi-pitch routes
Best grades - 6b to 8a

# COSTA BLANCA - Sella

**Líneas Naturales**

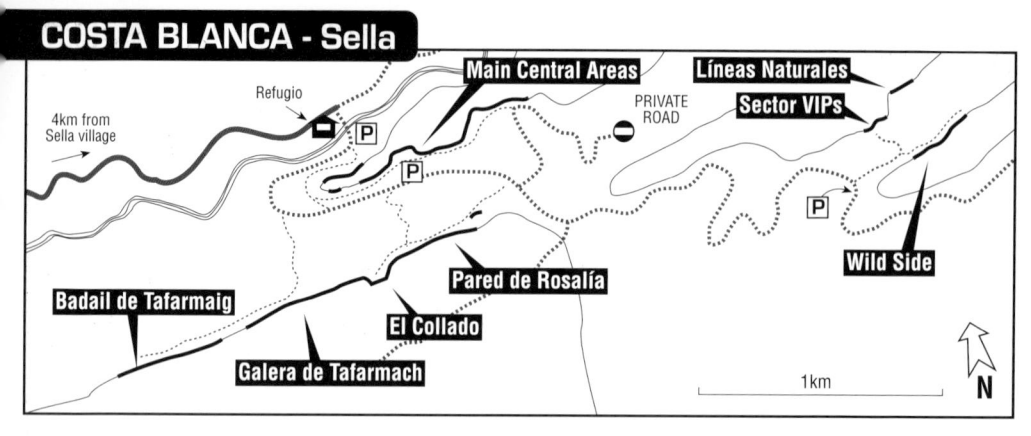

## HIDDEN VALLEY
This is an area of steep crags in a short deep valley to the east of the main areas. Most of the climbing is steep and overhanging with some superb routes in the grade 7 and 8 category. There is not much here for people who lead below 7a, to be precise, there is one route and a couple of poor variation pitches.
**APPROACH -** From the refuge, drive up the track past the main climbing areas and continue on the right fork of the road over the top of the ridge and down into another valley. Approximately 3km from the refuge you reach a sharp bend at the bottom of a valley. From here you can glimpse Sector Wild Side on the right-hand side of the valley ahead, through the trees. Park here and walk up the track. Wild Side is reached from the first bend and VIPs is further up the track.
**ACCESS -** Please do not park by the bend in the track, leave your car down on the main track.

## SECTOR LÍNEAS NATURALES
This is the large crag situated above Sector VIPs. The routes are long two and three pitch climbs which require some gear. They follow strong lines but the bolts are old and they are not frequently climbed. If they were re-geared then they would be high quality challenges.
**APPROACH -** From Sector VIPs, turn right and walk uphill under some big unstable looking cliffs to the base of the crag.

**1. Final Exam** ........ 7c
As its name suggests, this is the hardest route of the trio, up the smooth left-hand side of the wall.
1) 6a+, 20m. Scrappy climbing up and right to a ledge.
2) 7c, 35m. A big pitch but the bolts are not trustworthy.
3) 6c, 20m. Continue to the top.
Abseil off.
FA. R.Edwards, M.Edwards 1990

**2. Midterm Exam** ....... 7a+
The central crack line could also do with some new bolts.
1) 5+, 20m. easy climbing to the ledge.
2) 6c, 35m. The right-hand corner-line. Left-hand variation is 6a+.
3) 7a+, 20m. A hard final pitch.
FA. R.Edwards 1990

**3. Entrance Exam** .......... 6c
The first route of the degree course follows an elegant line up the right-hand side of the wall.
1) 6b+, 15m. Climb direct to the base of the slim groove.
2) 6c, 35m. Straight up the groove.
FA. R.Edwards, M.Edwards 1990

**4. Teorema Chino de los Restos** ... 7b+
The local topo lists a fully-bolted route somewhere near, probably up the hill to the right.
FA. Iván Hernández

South facing wall
50m to 70m multi-pitch
Best grades - 6c to 7c

# COSTA BLANCA - Sella

**Sector VIPs**

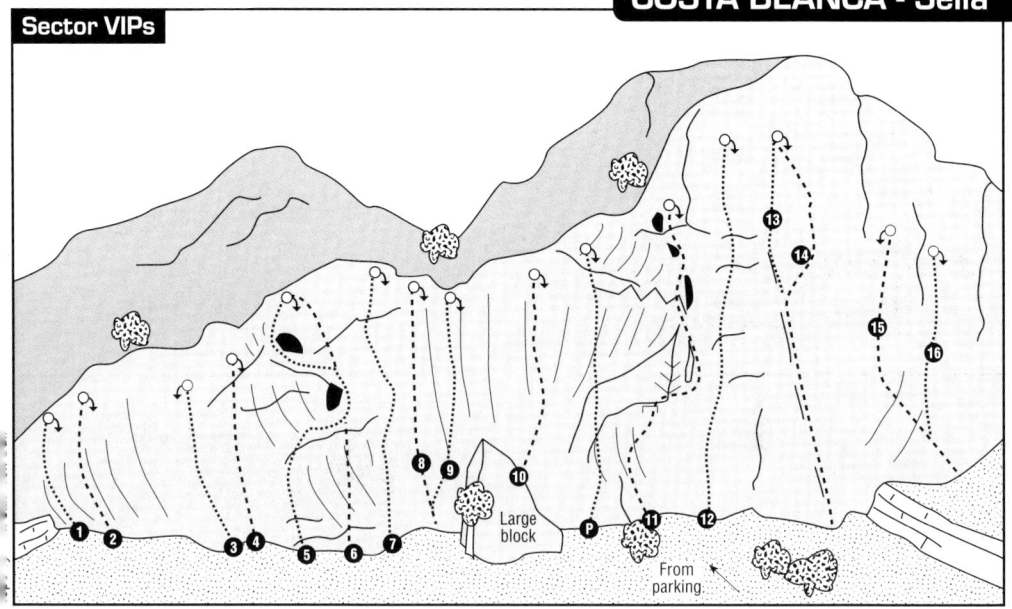

## SECTOR VIPs
This short overhanging buttress, of compact smooth limestone, is the home of some very difficult routes. The easiest route here is 7a, and even that one is a bit gnarly! There are some natural routes but most are heavily chipped and glued. This may create some good athletic exercises, it is up to you to make your mind up.

**1. ?** .................... 6c+
Above the wall.

**2. La invasión de las morcas** ......... 7b+
A short, sharp route!
FA. Carlos Porcell

**3. Hazlo ahora** ...... 8b
FA. Iván Hernández

**4. Jumping mecha flash** 8a
FA. Agustín Gómez, Mecha, I.Hernández

**5. Desert Storm** ....... 8a
A fingery boulder problem start followed by strenuous jugs and a powerful move to finish.
FA. M.Edwards 1989

**6. El valle de los locos** .... 8b
FA. Iván Hernández

**7. Ejecución radical** ... 8c+
Sella's hardest route.
FA. Iván Hernández

**8. Mark of the Beast** ...... 8a
More sustained but less cruxy than *Desert Storm*.
FA. M.Edwards 1990

**9. Torrente** ......... 8b+
Another outrageous looking line.
FA. Iván Hernández

**10. Bullarenque** ....... 8c
Starting from the top of the block.
FA. Iván Hernández

The next line is a project.

**11. La generación yogur** ... 7a+
Superb climbing with an E2 jamming crack to finish. The start is harder than it looks.
FA. J.García, I.Hernández

**12. La fuerza de la costumbre** ......... 7c
FA. J.García, I.Hernández

**13. Conecta cuarto** ...... 7c
The left-hand branch above the diagonal crack.
FA. Iván Hernández

**14. Estratego** ......... 7c
The diagonal pocket line has some reachy clips.
FA. Iván Hernández

The last two routes start above a wall.

**15. Copacabana** .......... 7b+
FA. Agustín Gómez

**16. El mejor matarife** ......... 7a

South facing wall
15m to 20m routes
Best grades - 7a to 8c+

# COSTA BLANCA - Sella

### SECTOR WILD SIDE
This large and impressive overhanging wall is one of the steepest crags in the area with some classic climbs up improbable tufas. If you climb 7b or above, this is the best crag at Sella, and one of the best in the Costa Blanca. If you don't climb that hard then the only reason to come here is for a look at some impressive rock formations.
The wall is very steep and sheltered and will stay dry in all but the heaviest of rain although it may seep if it has been very wet. It is north facing and gets very little sunshine so consequently can be cold.

**APPROACH (See map on previous page)** - From the parking area on the main road walk up the track to a bend. From here find a track through the woods which leads easily to a ledge below the wall.

**ACCESS** - Please do not park by the bend in the track, leave your car down on the main track.

**1. Si te dicen que caí** .......... 7a
The prominent corner gives intricate climbing. Finish up the right arete at the top.
FA. J.M.García

**2. Todos los caminos conducen al romo** .......... 7b
A good route up the vague tufa/crack system.
FA. J.M.García

**3. Llanuras bélicas** .......... 7b
Blue streak and tufas left of *Todos*.
FA. Goicoetxea, N.Sánchez

Past a 50m gap of blocky but climbable-looking rock is:

**4. Celia** .......... 7c+
7b up to the below the top tufa system (good rest). Then steep and powerful moves up the tufa to finish. Hard 7c+ but easy to read on sight and never 8a.
FA. Pep Ginestar

**5. La forqueta del diablo o Romocop** .......... 8a+
The line is marked by some double bolts with tats.
FA. Pep Ginestar

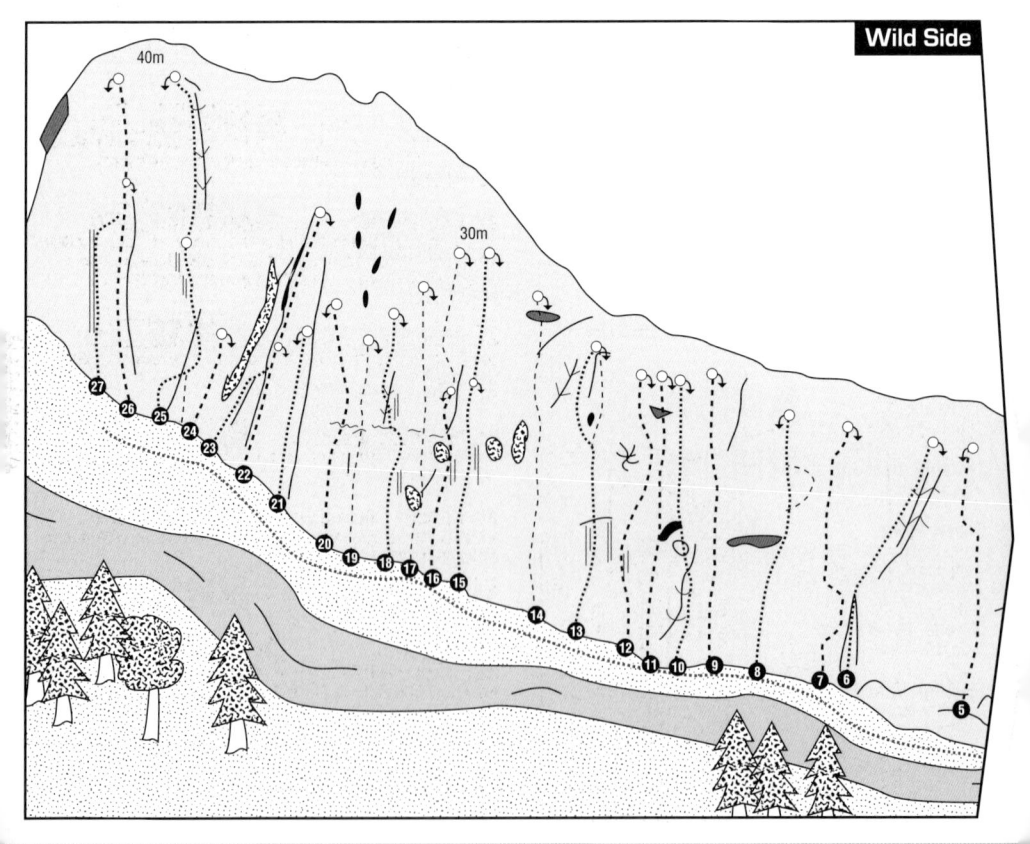

# COSTA BLANCA - Sella

**6. La hora de Millau** .. 7c
Start up the 'inverted-V' tufa. hardest at the start but sutained with a tricky upper section which is a bit run-out. Close to *El pito* in its middle section but still a brilliant route.
FA. Franceses

**7. El pito del sereno** ..... 7c+
A bouldery start leads to a virtual no-hands rest. Use it because the next 15m are steep and sustained on pumpy holds to a shake-out. The finish is hard, fingery and tricky to read.
FA. Iván Hernández

**8. El gremio** ........... 7c+
A superb climb up the blue streak. The start and finish are easy. The hard move is only short and can be by-passed on the right lowering the grade to 7b+.
FA. L.Birch, J.M.García

**9. Dimensión diamante** 8a+
Another excellent route. Climb past a long sling to a slot. Finish up a left-facing corner.
FA. A.Gómez

**10. Sweet Lady** ...... 8a
Start just right of a corner ramp and climb up to the blank headwall. A strange start and a boulder problem finish.
FA. A.Gómez

**11. Septiembre** ...... 8b+
Tufas up to the roof and then over roof. See photo page 13.
FA. A.Gómez

**12. La criatura** ...... 8b
Interesting despite 3 glued-on stones. The second bolt is very high.
FA. A.Gómez

**13. Nido amoroso** ....... 7b+/7c+
The right-hand finish provides the easier 7b+ option. Chipped.
FA. Iván Hernández

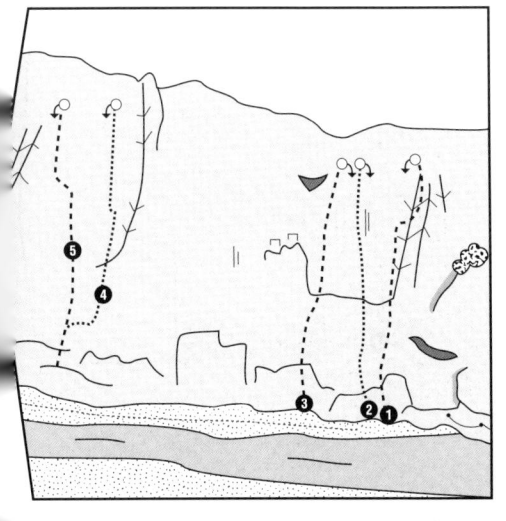

**14. Project** ....................
Pocketed wall. Bottom half looks okay.

**15. El último mono** ... 8b
35m. A stunning line up some vague tufas, all the way to the top. 8a+ to the first lower-off.
FA. Iván Hernández

**16. Océano** ........... 7b
Short 7b route to first belay chain. A project (8b+) to the top.
FA. A.Gómez

**17. Project** ....................
Another improbable-looking line.

**18. Ergometría** ......... 8a
A mini *Lourdes* (see El Chorro) with a hard start followed by pumpy moves up rounded tufas. There is one hands-off rest and several knee-bars if you can find them.
FA. J.M.García

**19. Project** ....................
Makes *Dosis* look like a path. Outrageous.

**20. Dosis** ......... 8b+
A very difficult line up the smooth overhanging wall. Chipped but still brilliant. See photo on page 146.
FA. Iván Hernández

**21. Cuestión de estilo** . 7c
The right-trending crackline has a distinct crux move. Finish on the belay of *Dosis* or continue to another lower-off (easy).
FA. J.M.García

**22. Keep the Faith** ....... 7c
Follow the overhanging ramp line to a crux on smooth rounded tufas and pockets. Can be split at a mid-height lower-off or continue in one long pitch to the top. Upper section is 7b.
FA. Unknown

**23. Nameless** ........... 7b
Left-hand start to *Keep the Faith*. Use the mini lower-off. Very worthwhile.
FA. Mechas, Sulcina

**24. Propiedad privada** .... 7b+
Short and hard up the tufa right of *Somos Olímpicos* to a bulge.
FA. S.M.Sánchez

**25. Ya Somos Olímpicos** .. 7b+
A brilliant route up overhanging tufas which can be lead in one mega 40m pitch from the ground.
1) 7b+. The direct start is harder.
2) 7a+. Continue up the corner in a spectacular situation.
FA. J.M.García

**26. Watermark** ....... 8a+
38m. A vague crack and tufa system up a big black wall which is led in one big pitch. To the first lower-off is an excellent 8a.
FA. M.Edwards 1991

**27. Black is Black** .......... 7b
25m. Tufa left of Watermark to the first lower-off.
FA. Iván Hernández

Steep, north facing wall
15m to 40m routes
Best grades - 7b to 8c

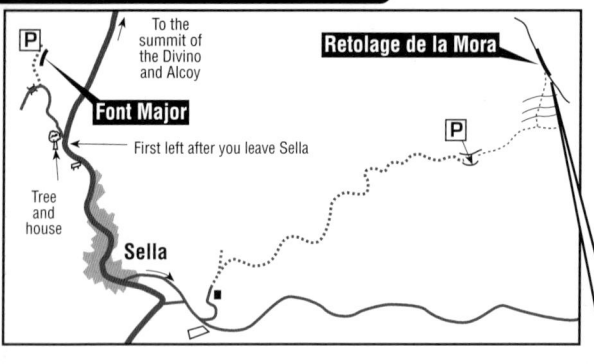

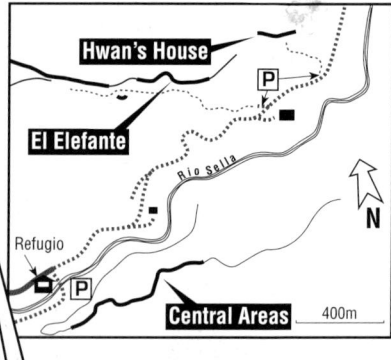

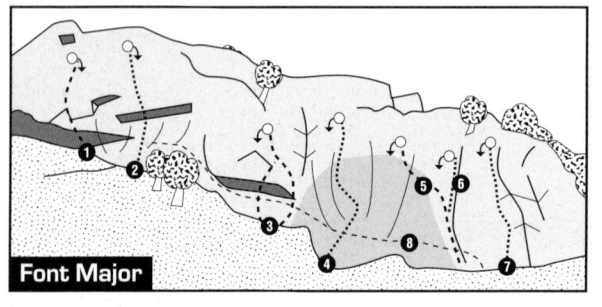

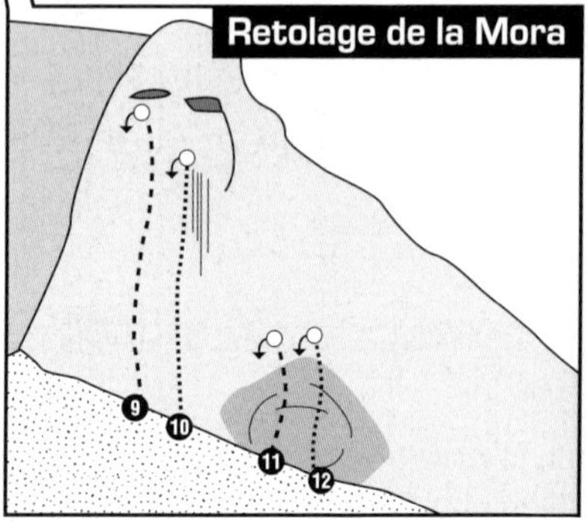

# COSTA BLANCA - Sella

## OUTLYING AREAS
There are three small crags in the Sella area with a handful of routes between them.

## FONT MAJOR
A small crag beyond the village of Sella which may be of interest to dedicated boulderers.
**APPROACH** - Drive uphill through the village of Sella. 300m after the 'village end' sign, turn left by a house with a large tree. Drop steeply downhill to a bridge on a bend. Continue straight and the crag will appear on your right.

1. Baldomero rey del mambo ....... 6c
   Out of the cave.

2. Hierbabuena ................. 7a

3. Calfadits .................. 7a
   A boulder problem with one bolt, and two starts.

4. ? ....................... Project
   Still an open project.

5. Malahierba ................. 6b
   Traverse the lip of the bulge.

6. Síndrome de la llampaça ........ 7a
   The crack.

7. Apología de destaino ......... 6b

8. La era ................... 8c+
   A boulder traverse - V10/11!

## RELOTAGE DE LA MORA
You get a good view of it on the approach drive to the main areas. It is the large scooped cave high up on the hillside to the left, just after you leave the village of Sella.
**APPROACH** - Before you enter the village of Sella, turn right and head towards the refuge and the main climbing areas. On the first bend on a small rise, turn sharp left up what looks like someone's driveway. Follow this track for about 2km, keeping right at the only fork. Eventually you arrive at a widening in the track. Park here and continue walking for about 400m, until you can break out leftwards up the hillside to the cave.

9. José Arcadio Buendía ... 7a+
   The left-hand line. Painful climbing on sharp holds.

10. Macondo ........ 7c+
    The right-hand line, finishing by a black streak.

11. Jugando en Kosovo ......... Project

12. ? ..................... Project

## HWAN'S HOUSE
A small wall further up the valley from the parking for the Elefante. Only two routes at present but lots of potential. It faces south and requires a 10 min uphill approach walk.

13. Everybody's Darling ... 7a+

14. ? ....................... (7c+)
    Probably still a project.

---

**Font Major**
NW facing, evening sun, roadside
Bouldering and short routes only

**Retolage de la Mora**
West facing, afternoon sun, 15min uphill walk
20m routes, 7a+ to 7c+

# COSTA BLANCA - Sella - Divino

**Divino Overview**

Labels on photo: Pared de la Cima; Line of terrace descent; Pared de la Taula; Sector Pertemba; Techo Placa; Sector CP10M; El Elephante; Approach scramble

## THE DIVINO
The most impressive bit of rock in Sella is also one of the least popular of the developed areas. The climbing is divided into two main categories. The lower walls which have some shorter (one or two pitch) sport routes; and the upper walls, which have some multi-pitch gear routes.

**APPROACH FROM ABOVE (Pared de la Cima and Pared de la Taula)** - The recommended approach for the upper sectors is by driving around the back to the summit of the mountain. A 4x4 or hire car is essential for this trip. Drive through Sella village. Check your kilometre meter as you leave the village. After 4.4km turn right onto a dirt track (signed ' Remonta Alemana'). Follow this track up the hill keeping right at 8.3km, left at 10.4km, left at 11.2km, over a tricky section at 11.5km, left at 11.6km then right at 12km, when you get the first view back down the valley. The top is reached at 13km, where there is a large chimney construction (apparently used for breeding pigeons - I didn't know they needed any help). Park here and walk to the actual summit. From here you can walk down the edge of the cliff to the grassy ramp between the 2 upper walls (see photo above). This ramp leads down, past one awkward section, to the terrace below both Pared de la Cima and Pared de la Taula.

**APPROACH FROM BELOW (El Elefante, CP10M, Techo Placa, Sector Pertemba) -** From the refuge, take the left-hand fork of the road up the valley. 100m past a house on the right, a track doubles back on the left, park here (space for 2 cars but don't block the road). Walk leftwards along a rough path up the hillside. The first buttress is El Elefante, to the left is Sector CP10M. Continue up the hillside to the cave of Techo Placa. Just beyond this is the rounded rib of *Espolón Pertemba*.
**For Pared de la Taula -** Continue walking up left to the foot of the long broken ramp dropping down from the upper walls. Scramble (3) up here and gain the diagonal ramp which runs up beneath the face. Walk up here to reach both upper sectors.

**DESCENTS -** These are listed with each section. The main terrace descent is indicated above. If you have approached the upper two sectors from below then the scramble down towards Sector Pertemba involves an awkward section which is equipped with a belay for abseil.

The route below is worth a brief mention because it provides a relatively easy way up the Divino, with continually interesting climbing. The line is marked on the photo above.

### 1. Amor de Odio ........ 6a
A great long expedition (12 pitches) which follows the lower ramp-line below Pared de la Taula, then continues up the slabs right of the diamond of Pared de la Cima. The hardest pitch is a 6a overlap half way up the lower ramp. Take a full rack of gear.

# COSTA BLANCA - Sella - Divino

**Pared de la Cima**

# COSTA BLANCA - Sella - Divino

## PARED DE LA CIMA

The splendid diamond-shaped buttress which rises to the summit of the mountain is home to some classic traditional challenges. The current routes follow the main lines of the wall and require a determined and competent approach. Inevitably there is some loose rock and route finding is intricate and complex but those up for a big-mountain adventure will find little better in this book.

**APPROACH** - The best approach for the wall is from above (see previous page).
**DESCENTS** - If you have parked at the top then you won't need to descend. If you approached from below then see the terrace descent from Pared de la Taula.

The first route follows the left-hand pillar high on the wall.

**1. Mamtastic** . . . . . . . . . . . . . . 6c+
A superbly positioned sport route on the upper left edge of the wall. Reach the start by locating some abseil bolts near the summit and abseiling down the line.
1) 6b, 25m.
2) 6b+, 15m.
3) 6c+, 25m.
FA. Andy Hyslop

**2. Diedro Edwards** . . . . . . . 6b
A striking line and the easiest way up the mountain. Start at the base of the ramp below the wall.
1) 5+, 25m. Climb a pillar to a slab then move up left to a ledge.
2) 6a+, 35m. Continue up the slab, over an overlap, to belay in a crack.
3) 6a, 20m. Move back onto the slab and follow it to a niche.
4) 6a+, 30m. The slab leads to a roof. Move left to a bolt belay.
5) 6b, 15m. Step left then go up right (bolt) to a bolt belay.
6) 5, 25m. Climb up and over a roof onto a slab. Move up left then climb a crack on the right to a ledge. (It is possible to continue leftwards in the same line an escape at grade 5).
7) 5, 25m. Climb the crack on the right, past some bolts (shared with *Mamtastic*) to a belay.
8) 6b, 25m. Follow the crack past 2 overhangs (2 bolts) to a edge.
9) 5+, 45m. Climb the groove and cracks above moving left to easy ground.
FA. R.Edwards, M.Edwards

**3. Notario** . . . . . . . . . . 7a
The original climb on this wall has become one of the great routes of the area. It follows the striking diagonal crack line, mostly on trad gear, with some bolted belays. The line described below shows many variations from the original aided line, and incorporates sections of the route *Angel's Highway*, but it is the most frequently climbed line, and arguably the best. Start on the slab below and left of the crack line.
1) 6a+, 25m. Climb a shattered pillar onto the slab on the right. Climb this and cross onto the wall then traverse the ledge to a thread (*Eye of the Wind* belay). Keep traversing to reach the right-hand side of a pillar and climb this to a belay on the top.
**Alternative starts** - The first free ascent reached the belay via the 4a option. The original aided start (**3b**) has yet to be freed.
2) 6b, 27m. Climb the broken cracks direct. At the top, move left to a sloping ledge and bolt belay.
3) 6a, 30m. Climb the slab on the left to a spike. Move right into a groove and climb up this until it is possible to move left and follow a fault to a bolt belay (same as *Eye of the Wind*).
3a) The original route followed a line to the left of this on aid.
4) 6b, Climb broken cracks on the left then follow the right-hand branch direct to a bolt belay. (The left-hand crack line is taken by *Eye of the Wind*).

**Notario continued...**
5) 6c, 32m. Climb left to a steep corner and pull around the arete leftwards into a diagonal hand traverse. Follow this to a corner (pegs and bolt). Move left and up to a spectacular hand traverse left across to a belays (bolts).
6) 6c, 50m. Follow the shallow depression to bolts above the roof. Pull over and traverse right into cracks. Follow these to the large ledge and traverse left to a bolt belay.
6a) 7b/c, 50m (original aided line). Once over the roof follow the bolts upwards to the fault running right across the face. Follow this and the crack above to reach a ledge and traverse left to a bolt belay.
7) 7a, 50m. Climb the short crack left to a shallow depression (bolt). Ascend leftwards (bolt) to the arete overlooking the crack (3 pegs) to ledges which lead to the top. The aided line was probably to the left of this.
FA. (Aid) P.Notario, Maldonado 14.1.83
FFA. R.Edwards, M.Edwards 3/4/5.1.93. Pitches 1) , 3) and 6) were climbed as Angel's Highway on 3.1.93

**4. Eye of the Wind** . . . . 7c
A superb route which takes an uncompromising line directly up the centre of this impressive wall. This route has now superceded *Angel's Highway* and incorporates the start that was originally climbed climbed with that route.
1) 6a+, 25m. Climb a shattered pillar onto the slab on the right. Climb this and cross onto the wall then traverse the ledge to a thread belay.
2) 6c+, 35m. Climb direct to a bolt then rightwards (2 bolts) to a groove. Climb this into another shallow groove and climb this (2 bolts) to its top. Move right to belay.
3) 6a, 30m. Climb the slab on the left to a spike. Move right into a groove and climb up this until it is possible to move left and follow a fault to a bolt belay.
4) 6b, 35m. Follow the shallow groove, passing below the broken cracks, until it is possible to climb along a faint crack which leads to a groove (bolt). Climb the groove (bolt) and cross right to a bolt belay.
5) 7c, 30m (E7 6c). Follow the fault to a good thread and flakes. Climb the groove (bolt) then move left onto a steep slab (bolt) and up to a roof. Pull over this (bolt) and climb the shallow groove (bolt). Continue up the cracks to a bolt belay.
6) 6b, 25m 6b. Follow the cracks, passing a small tree, and pull over a small overlap to a good ledge.
7) 4, 15m. Traverse the ledge left to a bolt belay.
8) 6c, 48m. Climb the slanting crack right for a short way, then move left onto the steep wall. Climb up then right to reach another crack. Follow this to a ledge on the right (possible belay). Move left to an undercling (bolt). Pull over this to a ledge and climb the slab (2 bolts) and move over the roof on the left.
9) 4, 15m. Climb up ledges to the top of the wall.
FA. R.Edwards, M.Edwards 19.3.93

**5. Angel's Highway** . . . 7a
The second major route to be climbed on this wall. All the pitches have now been incorporated into other routes but it is still an extremely good combination of pitches and worthy of a mention for its historical significance. Pitches 1) and 6) are the most popular version of *Notario* were originally climbed as part of this route.
1) to 4) As for *Eye of the Wind*.
4) to 7) As for *Notario*.
FA. R.Edwards, M.Edwards 3/4/5.1.93

The prominent crack to the right of the diamond is the line of *Ignasi Hernández*. This route is very loose and dangerous.
**DO NOT CLIMB IT.**

SW facing wall
90m to 230m multi-pitch routes
Best grades - 6b to 7c (trad)

# COSTA BLANCA - Sella - Divino

**Pared de la Taula**

# COSTA BLANCA - Sella - Divino

## PARED DE LA TAULA
This is the lower of the two diamond-shaped walls on the Divino. The routes on this wall are long, hard and of unquestionable quality but the easiest one has pitches of 6c and the rest are much harder. Most are traditionally protected, although there is some fixed gear, and there is also plenty of loose rock, as you would expect on a big mountain.
**APPROACH** - From above or below. See page 167.
**TERRACE DESCENT** - Climb up to the top point of the wall then scramble leftwards (looking in) down the back of the face. Follow the grassy ramp, past one awkward section, to the main terrace below. From your gear reverse back to the awkward section you scrambled up in the morning. You can abseil from here, or scramble if you feel up to it.

The first two routes are single pitches with bolt belays. The ledge beneath them is reached by a grade 4 scramble up a broken wall. Climb them with double ropes and abseil off.

**1. Class for Today** ....... 6a
40m. The route follows a cracks in the left-hand side of the wall, to a belay. Take a full rack.
FA. R.Edwards, S.Perez 1993

**2. Toda** ............. 7a
40m. The right-hand crack is harder. Take a full rack.
FA. F.Durá, J.F.Carbonell

The broken ledges beneath the centre of the wall are reached by scrambling up a pillar from the terrace below.

**3. La Taula**
**Regalo de díaz** ........ 7a+
A free version of the aid route *La Taula* with great climbing throughout. It has been fully bolted however there is some controversy involved. It is possible that the bolts may be removed at some stage - check at the Refuge before you climb it. Start on the left edge of the broken ledges, beneath a crack.
1) 6c, 45m. Climb the slab rightwards to the crack and follow it to a niche.
2) 7a, 40m. The crack leads to a stance below an overhang.
3) 7a+, 50m. Climb the roof on its left, then follow cracks to a peg. Traverse right into the wider crack/groove (possible belay) and follow this to the top.
FA. (Aid) Q.Soler, J.M.Orts. FFA. R.Edwards, M.Edwards 10.10.92

**4. Wish You**
**Were Here** ...... 8a
An extremely hard route with four exceptional main pitches. All the belays are bolted but there is no more fixed gear on the route. Take a full rack including lots of micro-wires. Start below a very faint crackline to the right of the wider crack of *La Taula*.
1) 3, 15m. Climb up easily to a ledge below the crack.
2) 6a+, 25m. Gain the crack and climb it to a bolt belay.
3) 7b, 25m. Continue in the same line.
4) 8a, 25m. The big pitch! Follow the very faint cracks above to another bolt belay. Small wires essential.
5) 7b, 25m. Continue up the cracks to a belay below a roof.
6) 7a, 25m. Climb the steep groove to the right of the roof, then the crack above, until it is possible to move right into another crack. Up this to belay and junction with *La Taula*.
7) 6a, 30m. Finish up the crack.
FA. M.Edwards, R.Edwards 1995

**5. Fisura de Edwards** .. 7a
A good route which takes the natural crack system in the middle of this impressive wall. Take a full rack of gear with a lot of quick-draws since the pitches are long. Start on the broken ledges in the centre of the wall.

### Fisura de Edwards continued....
1) 7a, 50m. Climb the cracks above until level with a bolt. Traverse right past this to a ledge, then move up over the bulge on the right. Move left out of the hollow above, past 2 bolts, to reach a flake. Climb this (bolt) to a crack which leads to a belay.
2) 7a, 25m. Descend right to a groove. Move up this past a bolt, then move left onto a wall. Cross this leftwards to a rest, then cracks lead back right to a hole. Climb the flakes and corner above to a ledge.
3) 7a, 40m. Traverse left, then move up into cracks. Follow these past threads, some difficult moves and 2 bolts, to a ledge.
4) 5+, 50m. Climb the groove above to an overhang. Step left to another groove and follow this to the top.
FA. R.Edwards, S.Perez 2.3.93

**6. Excitación/**
**Waiting for the Sun** ... 6c+
A fine route up the right-hand side of the wall based on the original route *Excitation*, with some new variations. Take a full rack. Start from the broken ledges in the centre of the face and descend rightwards to belay at the base of a long sloping crack.
1) 5, 25m. Climb cracks to a niche.
2) 6b, 25m. Climb the steep wall then move right and up another wall. Traverse left to a small cave and thread belays.
3) 6c+, 35m. Climb up then slightly right past a peg to cracks. Follow these to a ledge belay.
4) 6c, 25m. Climb cracks on the right past a peg and over a small roof to a stance in a niche.
5) 6b+, 25m. Follow the obvious traverse leftwards, past 2 bolts, to a crack. Climb up, then left and up to a ledge.
6) 6a+, 30m. Climb over the bulge on the left (bolt) and continue leftwards past a peg until you can climb direct to the top.
FA. (Excitación) J. , J.Garcés
(Waiting for the Sun) R.Edwards, S.Perez 11.2.94

**7. Edwards - Lloret - Pérez** 6c
The easiest line on this wall, with good protection, but still no picnic. Take a full rack with a lot of quick-draws. Start from the broken ledges by scrambling down rightwards to a rib.
1) 4, 40m. Climb the rib and wall to a ledge, then move up to another ledge with a small tree.
2) 5, 25m. Climb rightwards to a recess and bolt belay.
3) 6b, 50m. The crack on the right leads to a scoop.
4) 6c, 25m. Move left to a crack. Climb this then move left and back right past a bolt. Continue up the crack to a hanging stance.
5) 6a, 30m. Climb the crack then a shallow groove on the left, over an overhang to a ledge.
6) 5, 30m. Traverse left, then up to a small ledge and belay.
7) 5, 30m. Move left then climb up with a final leftwards move near the top.
FA. A.Lloret, S.Pérez, R.Edwards 1993

**8. Ópera Orni** ......... 7b
A lone sport route through the cave. The line continues with 2 aid pitches to join route 7.
FA. I.Sánchez

The right-hand side of this wall is bounded by a huge chimney/corner in its upper section - *La Canal*.

**9. La Canal** ........... 6a
The striking line has drawn many climbers to it but most come back with horrific tales of loose rock, thorns and gorse bushes. 8 pitches with a hardest grade of 6a.
FA. J.C.Chorro, M.Pomares

**10. La Chino** ........... 4
This line starts up *La Canal* but breaks rightwards acroos the wall from the base of the chimney. 7 pitches.
FA. Coves, Jiménez

South facing wall
40m to 120m single and multi pitch routes
Best grades - 6a, 6c to 8a (Trad)

# COSTA BLANCA - Sella - Divino

## Sector Pertemba

**SECTOR PERTEMBA**
The first two routes are classic long expeditions up the big wall left of the cave of Techo Placa. The most obvious feature is the rounded rib of *Espolón Pertemba*.
**APPROACH** - See page 167.
**DESCENT** - Walk UP the mountain side by scree slopes and short scrambles until you see Pared de la Cima (the upper wall). From here descend down the grassy ramp, past one awkward section, to the terrace below the upper walls. Drop down this until you are past a large cave on the left. Find the fixed belay and make 1 abseil to the ground (or reverse scramble at grade 3 or 4).

Up to terrace descent

**1. Blood on the Rocks** ... 7a+
A big route taking the impressive red-streaked wall left of *Espolón Pertemba*. A full rack is needed with a few thin threads. Start at the base of the easy ramp, right of the easy way up.
1) 3, 25m. Scramble up the ramp to the foot of a pillar.
2) 5, 40m. Climb the pillar to a ledge.
3) 4, 25m. Climb the groove on the right to a ledge.
4) 7a, 45m. Climb direct to a thread, then left up a pocketed slab, past some bolts, to a belay.
5) 7a+, 40m. Follow the fully bolted line above.
6) 6c, 40m. Climb a groove on the right then move left into a groove. Follow this past bolts to a ledge on the left.
7) 6b, 35m. Climb the wall above then swing left and follow grooves to a large ledge.
**DESCENT** - Make 5 abseils starting from threads and blocks down and left. Alternatively, walk across the ledge and follow cracks and slabs to the top (6a+). Then follow the descent as for *Pertemba*.
FA. M.Edwards, R.Edwards 1993

**2. Milongas sangrantes** 7a
Running parallel to *Blood on the Rocks* is a fully bolted route. No exact details are known but it is likely to be good.
1) 6b, 2) 7a/A0. This might be an aid point or just a short, hard section which is by-passable with a quick pull on a bolt.
3) 7b (6c+ with aid) 4) 6a+, 5) 6a+, 6) 6a
FA. Domenec Rus, E.Pereres

There are two long diagonal lines starting from the base of the crag. *Peligro de Extinción* and *Eclipse*. They both have pitch grades around 5 but *Eclipse* has a lot of aid including 1 pitch of A3+.

**3. Alcudia** ........... 5+
A diagonal line starting from just left of the pillar of *Espolón Pertemba*. 1) 4+, 2) 5+, 3) 4, 4) 4+, 5) 4+, 6) 4+, 7) 3
FA. R.Moltó, M.Pomares

**4. Espolón Pertemba** ..... 5
A fine line up the long rounded pillar which is the easiest long route on the Divino. However it is a serious undertaking on which route finding is awkward. Take a full rack. Start below the rounded rib left of the arching roof of Techo Placa.
1) 4+, 40m. The centre of the rib, past 2 ledges, to a 3rd ledge.
2) 5, 45m. Climb direct then trend left and back right to pegs. Move up and left again to a ledge. Pegs.
3) 4, 40m. Climb right then left over a bulge. Continue upwards, keeping right of the gully, to a ledge on the arete.
4) 4+, 30m. The vegetated groove, then press on up the slabs heading slightly left.
5) 4, 20m. Climb the slab then trend left to a belay.
6) 4, 40m. Move up rightwards to easier ground and the top.
**4a. Variation Finish**
6a) 5, 25m. Climb the slab on the left to blocks and a belay.
7a) 5+, 50m. Follow the slab above past a hard traverse right.
FA. J.García, M.Pomares, J.M.Ramírez. Variation - Edwards

South facing wall
150m to 200m multi-pitch
Best grades - 5 to 7b

Lots of sun | 30 min | Vertical | Slabby | Multi-pitch | Windy

# COSTA BLANCA - Sella - Divino

**Techo Placa**

## TECHO PLACA
To the right of the rounded rib of *Pertemba* is a long arching cave with a smooth wall under it. This is the home of a few good shorter routes.

**APPROACH** - See page 167.

The first two routes are near the steep cave down and left of the wall.

### 1. Enlaces ............... 6a
The left-hand line. It might have some fixed gear.

### 2. Tesores ......... 8a
The right-hand line covers some steep ground. Fully bolted.
*FA. N.Sánchez*

### 3. Voyages ......... 6c+
The left-hand side of the wall has a testing pitch on slightly suspect rock.
1) **6c+, 30m.** There is some fixed gear, but take a full rack of wires.
2) **4, 15m.** Traverse right to an abseil point.
*FA. R.Edwards, S.Perez*

### 4. Hidden Glory ....... 5+
Good climbing along the dog-leg cracks. Take a full rack.
1) **5, 20m.** Follow the crack up right to a stance in the middle of the wall.
2) **5+, 20m.** The leftwards crack leads to a belay on *Voyages*. Finish as for **Voyages**.
2a) **?, 20m.** There is a variation up the continuation line of the first pitch to another abseil point.
*FA. R.Edwards, S.Perez*

### 5. Techo Placa .... 7a
A good route on the right-hand side of the wall.
1) **6c, 30m.** Climb direct up the wall past some fixed gear (but not enough).
2) **7a, 25m.** Break right out from the stance up the bolt line. Abseil off.
*FA. R.Edwards, M.Edwards*

### 6. Duel in the Sun ....... 6a
Another amenable route following a line of weakness across the bolts of *Techo Placa*.
1) **6a, 30m.** Folow the line of weaknes to the belay.
2) **6a, 30m.** Head up leftwards to the main abseil point.
It has been extended upwards to the top of the crag in four more pitches (hardest grade 5).
*FA. R.Edwards, M.Edwards*

---

South facing wall
10m to 60m single and two pitch
Best grades - 6a to 7a & 8a

# COSTA BLANCA - Sella - Divino

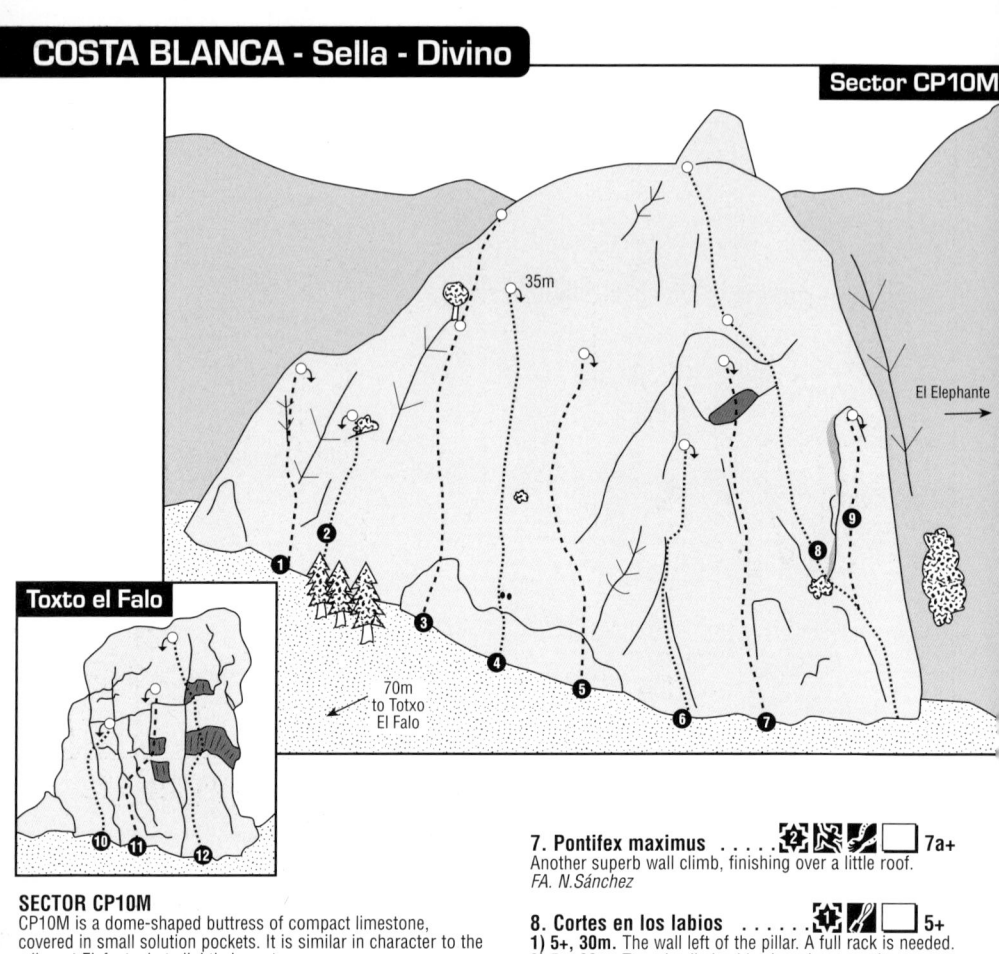

**Sector CP10M**

**Toxto el Falo**

## SECTOR CP10M
CP10M is a dome-shaped buttress of compact limestone, covered in small solution pockets. It is similar in character to the adjacent Elefante, but slightly less steep.
**APPORACH** - Sector CP10M lies immediately left of the Elefante.

**1. Jesusunu** .................... 6c
Old bolts up the nice looking hanging red groove. No lower-off.

**2. Rigoleto** .................... 6b
Old Bolts.

**3. CP10M** .................... 6b
30m. Abseil or continue to the top at 5+. Needs a small rack.

**4. Tramontana tremens** .... 7c
35m. A stunning long climb. Take care when descending.
*FA. N.Sánchez*

**5. Lyon's Den** ....... 8a
30m. Known locally as *Plasmagoratron*.
*FA. M.Edwards 1992*

**6. Hostia succidanea** ..... 7c
Technical climbing up some thin cracks.
*FA. N.Sánchez*

**7. Pontifex maximus** ..... 7a+
Another superb wall climb, finishing over a little roof.
*FA. N.Sánchez*

**8. Cortes en los labios** ..... 5+
1) 5+, 30m. The wall left of the pillar. A full rack is needed.
2) 5+, 20m. Two abseils lead back to the ground.

**9. Mediodía** .................... 4+
Bolts up the pillar.

## TOXTO EL FALO
Toxto El Falo is a small pinnacle of rock down and left of Sector CP10M. It provides some short hard routes with dubious bolts and lower-offs.

**10. Pene-tra-2** ............... 6c
Short and sharp.

**11. Morfigrey** ............... 6b+
Poor lower-off, so use the tree as well.

**12. Escalera De Color** .... 7c
A boulder problem start with difficult clips above. Keep left of the bolts over the roof.
*FA. I.Hernández*

South facing buttress
15m to 50m routes
Best grades - 5+ and 7a+ to 8a

# COSTA BLANCA - Sella - Divino

## El Elefante

### L ELEFANTE
his is the large smooth dome of rock situated at the base of the ivino which was long thought to be unclimbable. The few outes here are superb hard wall climbs which follow blank ooking lines, with only tiny pockets and edges for holds.
**APPROACH** - See page 167.

**. Candyman** ............... 6b
he left-hand edge of the wall has a sparsely bolted trad route.
1) **6b, 25m.** To a bolted stance.
2) **6a+, 25m.** To the top. Abseil off.
FA. R.Edwards, M.Edwards 1987

**. Scorpion** ............. 7a
big route which follows the line of grooves and tufas.
1) **6c, 20m.** If you haven't got any wires then, to reach the first olt, clip the thread on *Candyman*, traverse right, then back left o unclip it. Use the mini-lower-off to belay.
2) **7a, 40m.** A fine long pitch.
FA. R.Edwards, M.Edwards

**. Lupu** ................ 6c
short curving line past a hole.
FA. N.Sánchez

**. The Tongue of the Snake** ......... 7c
1) **7c, 20m.** A long sustained pitch.
2) **7c, 20m.** The left-hand variation middle pitch which is 7b+.
3) **7a, 20m.** The wall above.
FA. M.Edwards, R.Edwards 1987

**. Edward's Wall** ..... 8a
big 50m pitch. It is usually climbed to the mid-height lower-off a lesser 7b. Descend on a single 60m rope in 2 abseils.
FA. M.Edwards 1991

**6. Divine Inspiration** ..... 7c
1) **7b, 25.** Past some tufas to a ramp.
2) **7c, 30m.** Sustained wall climbing.
3) **7b, 20m.** To the top. Abseil back down.
FA. M.Edwards, R.Edwards 1986

**7. El Arúspice** .......... 7b+
A good single pitch to the lower-off on *Divine Inspiration*.
FA. N.Sánchez

**8. Wallmarks** .......... 8b
An old project with a good first pitch and a stunning second.
1) **6c+ 20m.** Sustained moves up the vertical, red wall.
2) **8b, 30m.** The continuation.
FA. M.Edwards 1997

**9. Gran fisura** .......... 6b+
The big corner gives a classic trad route.
1) **6b+, 30m.** Belay in the corner.
3) **6b+, 30m.**
**DESCENT** - Abseil via the fixed belay.
FA. R.Edwards, S.Perez, A.Lloret 1989

**10. The Naked Edge** ... 6c
A superb and sustained arete but with an awkward descent. See photo page 28.
1) **5+, 30m.** Climb the crack upwards to a single bolt belay on the pinnacle.
2) **6c, 30m.** Crank to the top - brilliant!
**DESCENT** - There is no fixed mid-route belay so you need 2 x 60m ropes to abseil off. Best done by leading on one and dragging up another when you are at the top.
FA. R.Edwards, M.Edwards 1987

South facing wall
25m to 85m routes
Best grades - 6b to 8b

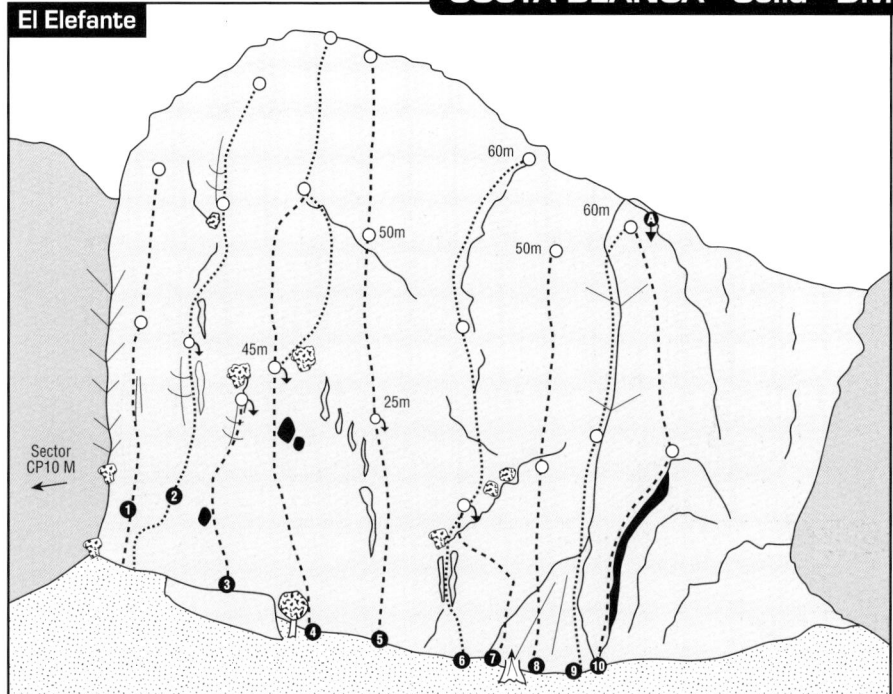

A climber making the hard move on *Acrobata porcino* (7a - page 152)
Sector Techo del Rino, Sella
Photo: Keith Sharples

# ALCOY

I have to admit that this crag nearly didn't make it into this book since nobody seems to like it much and we have never managed to get a decent approach map. However if you accept that it isn't the best crag in the area, and is poorly situated in a busy town, then you might have a good day's climbing since the actual routes are quite good, especially in the harder grades. It also has the added attraction that the bars and restaurants are only a short stumble down the hill, if you get bored or too hot. The crag consists of a small steep buttress of compact limestone just above the town. It is a highly-featured buttress covered in edges, tufas, pockets and big holes but despite this many of the routes have man-made holds. The routes are well equipped with new bolts and lower-offs. The grades tend to be a notch harder than elsewhere and it is probably only of interest to people who lead 7a and above. If this is your standard then prepare yourself for a battle and warm up first.

## ASPECT AND CLIMATE

The crag faces south and is quite sheltered making it a real sun trap. It may stay dry in light rain but will get wet pretty quickly in heavier stuff.

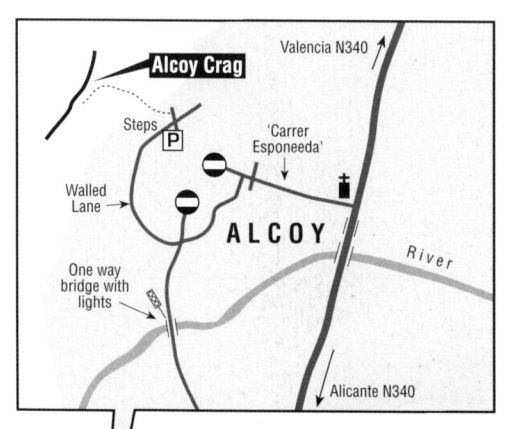

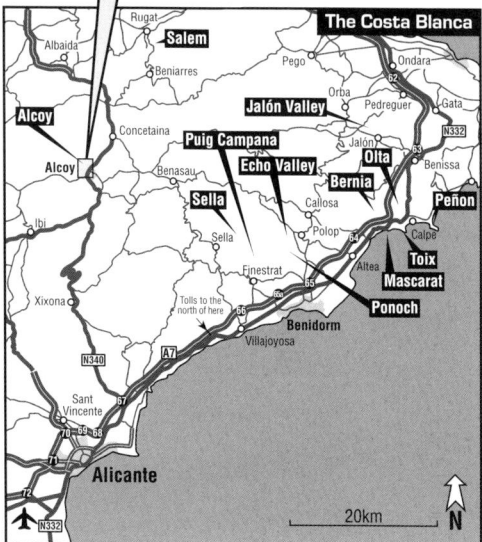

## APPROACH

Alcoy is approximately 50km north of Alicante, in the middle of the mountains.
**From the Coast** - Drive south on the A7 to junction 67. From here take the N340 north towards Alcoy. On entering the town you will cross a large bridge, continue on the same road into the centre, crossing another smaller bridge. Directly after this turn left (just before a church) onto the 'Carrer Esponeeda'. From here you should see the crag on the hillside directly in front. Try and fix this location in your mind because the best way to find the crag is to follow blindly your sense of direction through the maze of roads in the centre of the town. For what it is worth here is an attempt to write directions but I have yet to find anyone who has successfully followed this:

*Continue directly until you are forced to turn left. Keep going straight across every junction until you reach a high walled lane. Follow this until the road drops down and park under a tree. Locate some steps by a house (number 25). These lead to the base of the crag.*

**From Sella** - Drive over the hill from the village of Sella, past 'Alcolecha' and 'Benilloba'. After you enter the Alcoy, turn left onto the N340. Drive down here and turn right by the church and join the above description.

## THE ROUTES

I have no information on who has developed this crag but it is probably the local climbers of Alcoy.

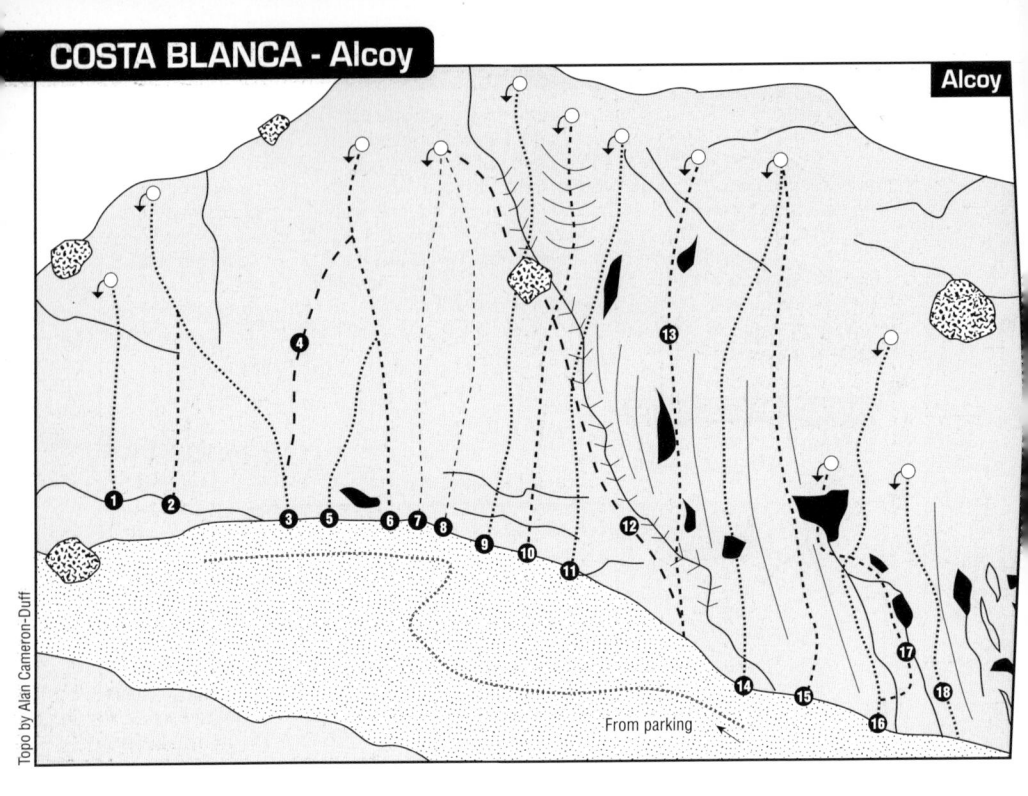

# COSTA BLANCA - Alcoy

Alcoy

*Topo by Alan Cameron-Duff*

From parking

## ALCOY
From the road follow the steps and a short path to the base of the cliff.
**GEAR -** Many routes have had their first bolts removed. A bit of trickery when lowering off should save you having to do the run-out more than once.

The first route is on a small grey wall at the left-hand side of the slab at the top left of the crag.

1. Gusano loco . . . . . . . . . . . . . . . . . . 5+
2. Nen butrut . . . . . . . . . . . . . . . . . . . 6a
3. Susi . . . . . . . . . . . . . . . . . . . 6a
4. Acido . . . . . . . . . . . . . . . . . . 6a+
5. Mireta . . . . . . . . . . . . . . . . . . 6a+
6. Mireta variation . . . . . . . . . . . . . . . 5+

The next two routes have been debolted.

7. Miguelín Schwarzeneger . . . . . . . . (5+)
8. Vampiro . . . . . . . . . . . . . . . . . (6a+)

9. Beso negro . . . . . . . . . . . . . . . . 6c
10. Flipo . . . . . . . . . . . . . . . . . . . 8a
Over the smooth bulge. Looks thin!

11. Orinal con pedales . . . . 6c+
The bulge to the right has considerably larger holds.

12. Mosca . . . . . . . . . . . . 6a+
Excellent climbing up the obvious corner. It has no bolts of its own but there are plenty of bolts on other routes.

13. Jetro . . . . . . . . . 7b
Up the bulging yellow wall, long reaches between big pockets.

14. Vómitos leprosos . . . . . 7b+

15. Pestañas postizas . . . . 7b
Pumpy!

16. Super flan . . . . . . . . 7c
Yow! A technical pumpy affair up the shallow corner, nasty!

17. Gapo del sapo . . . . 7b
Short, pumpy with a low crux but it is desperate!

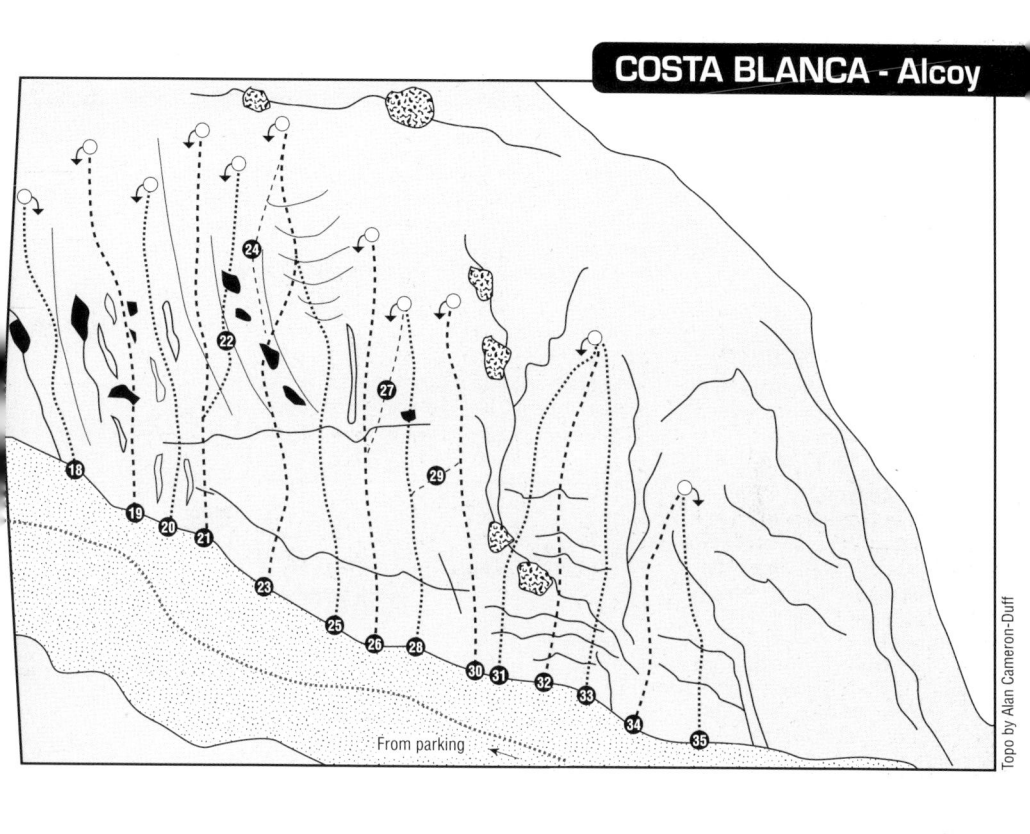

# COSTA BLANCA - Alcoy

**18. Mejillas tiernas** .............. 8a
Possibly chipped?

**19. Moldura** .................. 8a

**20. Mescalito** ................. 8a

**21. Dimitrius** ....... 7c+
A great route, powerful and with the crux near the top!

**22. Endavid** ....... 7b+
Another good route following the long reaches between pockets formula.

**23. Oleada pétrea** ....... 6c+
Brilliant climbing up the overhanging wall. Break right where the jugs run out.

**24. Espera de Joan Lerma** ....... 7a+
A more pumpy direct version of the last route

**25. Distrito** ......... 6c
Gain the scoop of *Oleada petrea* via the right-hand line finish as for that route.

**26. Vena Loca** ................ 7a+

**27. Que se mueran los feos** ......... 7a
An easier finish to *Vena Loca*.

**28. Veneno** .............. 6b

**29. Polos palos lolos** ......... 6a
A combination of the easier sections of the two adjacent routes.

**30. Araña** ................. 6b

The next five routes climb the broken block to the right of the corner. Most of the first bolts have been removed.

**31. Aniceto que te meto** .......... 6b

**32. Ventana electrónica** .......... 6b+

**33. Tentaculos** ............... 5+

**34. Griptorquidea** ............. 6a

**35. Los chinos** ............... 6a+

SE facing wall
10m to 25m routes
Best grades - 6a to 8a

# AGUJAS ROJAS

**by Karen Yeow**

Agujas Rojas is a small collection of pinnacles, in a picturesque woodland setting, on a hilltop near the town of Onil on the Costa Blanca. The orange and yellow coloured walls offer face-climbing enthusiasts well-bolted climbs on good quality rock. Most of the routes are in the high 6s and 7s with only 3 routes below 6a. The approach is very easy and the crag could be a good one to combine with a visit to Reconco or just to enjoy a bit of peace and quiet away from the crowds at Sella and Toix.

## ASPECT AND CLIMATE

Most of the crag faces west although the pinnacles can give shade if you find the right spots. The trees also offer some shelter from the sun and wind, however there is nothing to climb here in the rain.

## APPROACH

Recent road improvements have made getting to Agujas Rojas a bit easier although exactly where the new roads are going is not totally clear. Please inform of any new developments.

**From the Coast -** Leave the A7 at junction 70 which is initially signed to 'San Vicente' and then 'Alcoy'. Join a new road to Castalla. As you approach Castalla follow signs to Onil. Keep going into Onil until you arrive at a roundabout and turn right. This road turns into the Baneras Road - follow it for 2.5km past a traffic circle until you reach a fork in the road. Take a left fork along a rough surfaced road and continue for about 2km, past a pink house ('El Sucre') on the left. The crags are visible as a series of tawny-coloured faces uphill from the road. Park at a small gravelled shoulder off the road, within sight of the crag, just before a ruined stone hut. You've gone too far if you drive past some white stone blocks on your right. There are several paths leading from the road up through the woods to the crags.

**From Alicante -** Drive towards Madrid on the N330 (a free dual carriageway). Turn off this at the second junction signed to 'Sax'. Follow this road towards 'Castalla' but keep left towards 'Onil'. At a complex junction under a dual carriageway, continue straight past two small roundabouts. Reconco is up on the left. Keep going into Onil until you arrive at the roundabout mentioned above.

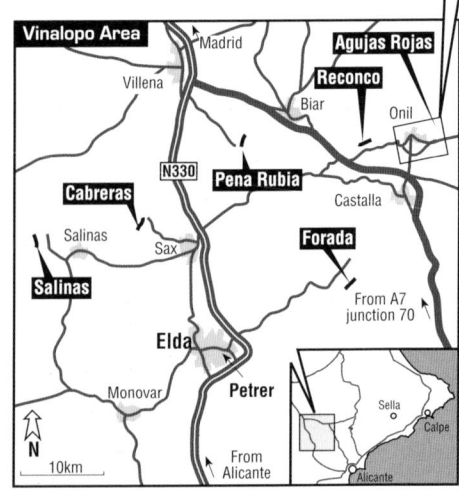

## THE ROUTES

Miguel Muñoz discovered, bolted and climbed every single route at this crag between 1991 and 1994.

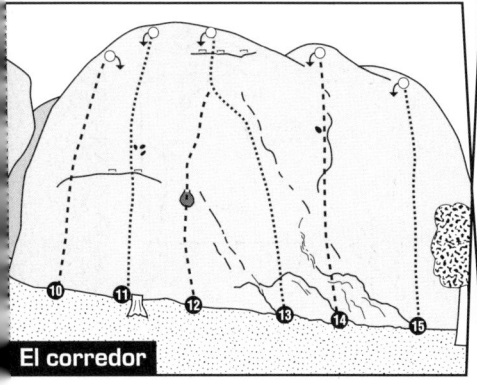

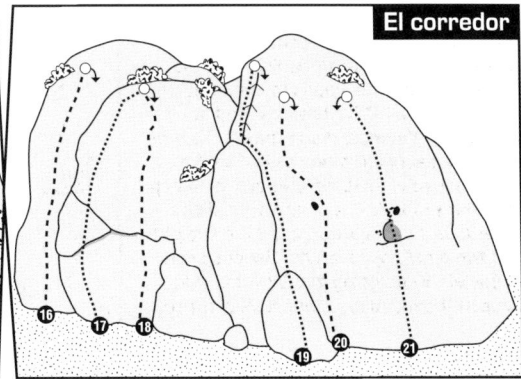

# COSTA BLANCA - Agujas Rojas

## Sector la Hiedra

### SECTOR MEDIA VUELTA
The pinnacle in front of Sector La Hiedra has three lines on it.

7. ? .................................... ?
The back of the pinnacle.

8. ? .................................... 6c
The central line.

9. ? .................................... ?
The right-hand line.

### SECTOR EL CORREDOR
This is the largest section of the crag.

10. Edu el travieso ............. 7b
11. Nit de bruixes ....... 7b+
12. My Gym .......... 7b+
The direct start to *L'Babao*. Start under a pocket.
13. L'Babao .......... 7a+
The thin, intermittent crack is superb.
14. Chip-chop ......... 7b+
The thin, winding crack.
15. Mama Chicho .... 7c
16. Mentireta .......... 6a+
A shallow groove up a slab.
17. Los taruges ........... 6b
A bulging start.
18. Un 6b i si no també ... 7a+
19. Turbo Diesel ......... 7a
A fine finish up the exposed arete.
20. Hay Bruneta ..... 7c+
Some large pockets but thin moves to connect them.
21. ? .................................... (7 ?)

### SECTOR LA HIEDRA
The crag is about 10m high and is situated about 10m above the track. It gives a small set of steep blobby routes with powerful moves and strange holds.
**Aspect** - The crag is in the shade until late in the afternoon.

The routes are described from left to right.

1. El Raco ................ 6b
Just right of the wall.
2. Stalak .................... (8a?)
3. Jumpin' Jack Flash ....... 7a
Up a slightly overhanging arete.
4. Niu de aranyes ............... 7c+
5. Jack el destrepador .... 7c+
An overhanging face climb with small shallow pockets.
6. Lagramusa ....... 8a

El corredor

El corredor

West facing pinnacles
15m to 20m routes
Best grades - 6a+ to 7c+

**181**

# COSTA BLANCA - Agujas Rojas

## SECTOR TOCHO PINCHOSO
A short, red tower has three lines on it.

**22. Marabu** .................. 7a+
The left-hand line.

**23. Cipriano toca el piano** ......... 6c
The middle line has a bulge at mid-height.

**24. Hay Madonna** ............... 6a+
The right-hand line.

## SECTOR A LA SOMBRE
This smaller pinnacle sits in the shade of the larger La Esfinge.

**25. Fumador no** ................ 6a

**26. Crus** .................... 6a+
The arete.

## SECTOR LA ESFINGE
This is the tower nearest the road. The first routes are around the back.

**27. ?** ..................... ?
An unknown new line.

**28. ?** ..................... ?
An unknown new line.

**29. A la sombre** ............... 6a

**30. Clip-clap** ................. 7b

**31. Rompe techos** .............. 7b
A very steep arete.

**32. Escupe cubatas** ............. 6b+
A hard slab finish.

**33. La tufona** ................. 7b
Just right of the large cross.

**34. Besuga** .................. 7c+
An impressive line but spoilt by bolt-on holds.

**35. ?** ..................... 6c+
A steep start.

**36. Gonso** ................... 4+
A hard start.

**37. Rufo** .................... 5+
An unbolted line. Top-rope it if you haven't got the gear to lead it.

**38. Pequeñecos** ................ 4+
A good beginners climb.

---

West facing pinnacles
15m to 20m routes
Best grades - 4+ to 7c+

# RECONCO

Reconco is a superb crag with a good range of middle grade routes on perfect, slabby rock. It is beautifully situated on a hillside above a pleasant rural valley and is easy to find. The only slight drawback is its distance from the main accommodation spots but stick to the motorway and you'll get there surprisingly quickly. As a venue it makes a superb alternative to the popular and polished areas at Toix and Sella with a similar grade range and and significantly less over-climbed routes.

Most of the routes are long single pitches, although there are some two pitch routes on the right-hand side which are particularly good. All the routes are clean and well-equipped but the rock is a bit sharp and taxing on the skin. Route finding shouldn't be a problem as the names and grades are stamped on tags on the first bolts.

## ASPECT AND CLIMATE

The crag faces southeast and is exposed so it also catches a lot of sun and wind. There is little shelter at the base of the wall apart from a single tree. Access isn't a problem at the moment but try to park with consideration to avoid antagonising the locals.

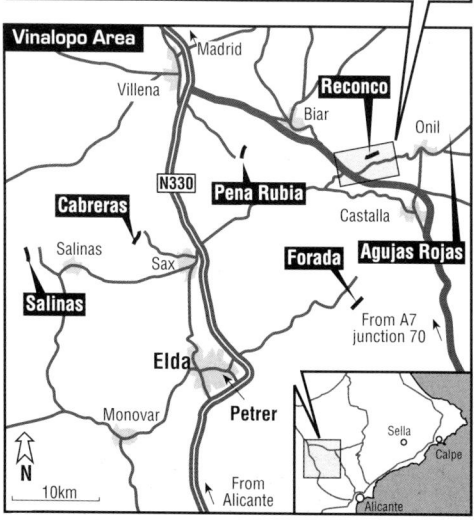

## APPROACH

Recent road improvements have made getting to Reconco a bit easier although exactly where the new roads are going is not totally clear. Please inform of any new developments.

**From the Coast -** Leave the A7 at junction 70 which is initially signed to 'San Vicente' and then 'Alcoy'. Join a new road to Castalla. After driving around Castalla exit on the next junction (signed to 'Sax') and turn towards Onil. 0.7km after the junction is a small white house on the right. Opposite this are two tracks, one with a fence. Continue for 100m to a third track and park a little way up this on the left. You should be able to see the cliff on the hillside directly above. Follow the sandy track up through the trees and the steep, open hillside above.

**From Alicante -** Drive towards Madrid on the N330 (a free dual carriageway). Turn off this at the second junction signed to 'Sax'. Follow this road towards 'Castalla' but keep left towards 'Onil'. At a complex junction under a dual carriageway, continue straight past two small roundabouts. 0.7km after the junction is a small white house on the right. Continue as above.

## THE ROUTES

All the routes have been equipped and climbed by Juan Mario Marcos and José Aurelio with a few additions by Miguel Muñoz.

# COSTA BLANCA - Reconco

## RECONCO
The left-hand side of the crag is a concave slab with some excellent routes on clean rock.

**1. Chino-Chano** .................... 6b
The right-hand variation start is 6c.

**2. Pata chula** ....................... 5+
Crack past a tree.

**3. El Rey del sis A** ................ 6a+
A short, rounded rib.

**4. Corbella** .......................... 6b
Climb up and out of the shallow scoop.

**5. Pa en cubitos** .................. 6a+

**6. Gorbachov** ....................... 6a

**7. Tacher** ............................ 6b+
Up a brown streak.

**8. Desconeguda** .................... 5
A good, long route on excellent rock.
1) 5, 25m. Worth doing on its own.
2) 5, 20m. A poor continuation. Much longer than it looks.

**9. Sexta** .............................. 6a+
1) 6a, 25m. Climb cracks to a slab.
2) 6a+, 20m. Traverse a long way up and right to the roof. Pull over to finish. Take care if you lower off.

**10. Paris-Texas** .................... 6a+

**11. Canal** ............................. 6a
Left-hand side of scoop.

**12. Servina** .......................... 6b+
Excellent climbing up the rounded scoop in the centre of the face. The crux is reaching the chain in the middle of nowhere.

**13. Directa** ........................... 6b
1) 6b, 28m. Up the rib to the right.
2) 6a+, 12m. A short pitch to the lower-off of *Sexta*.

**14. Dit-Laser** ....................... 6a+

**15. Llengua Free** ................... 6b+
A tricky route with a wandering line.

**16. La perla del Caribe** ........... 6c
An easier lower section leads to a sustained upper wall and a perplexing finish.

**17. Chunay-Free** ................... 6c+
Behind the tree.

# COSTA BLANCA - Reconco

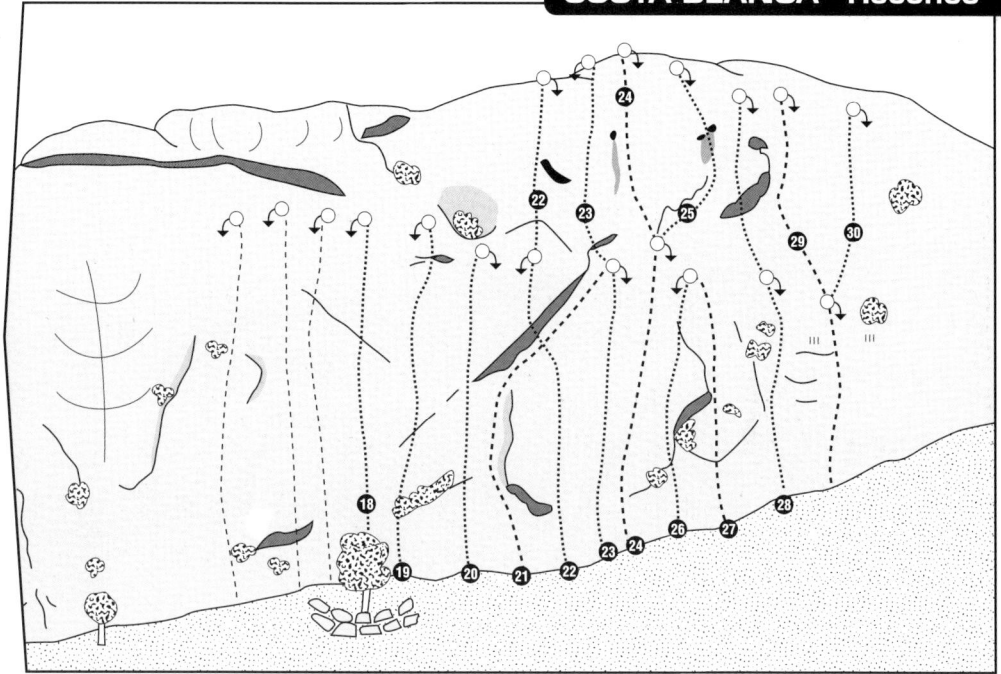

On the right-hand side of the crag, a large blank wall is split by a diagonal overlap. Most of the routes on this side have two pitches, with slabby and broken lower sections providing easy climbing, whilst the top is much steeper and more challenging.
**NOTE** - the top pitches of all these routes are a lot longer than they look although they do slab-off near the top.

**18. En buscat del Posets** 7b
Intricate climbing on solution pockets.

**19. No es tan guay** 7a+

**20. Gemma Boom** 7a
A broken start but a fine technical finish.

**21. Central** 5
This delightful route follows the big flake and leftward slanting overlap to a mid-height lower-off. The groove is mostly juggy but there is one tricky section.

**22. Chica de moda** 6b+
1) 6a+, 25m. A thin slab with a hard move to cross *Central*.
2) 6b+, 25m. A long and surprising pitch.

**23. Ruda** 6b
1) 6b, 25m. Another thin slab
2) 6b, 25m. Hard moves lead up a steep wall then it eases but the lower-off is miles away. Some loose holds.

**24. La llagrima** 6b
1) 6a, 30m. A good easier pitch worth doing on its own.
2) 6b, 25m. Steep moves lead to a hole. Leaving this is tricky.

**25. La llagrima Right** 7a
1) 6a, 30m. As for *La llagrima*.
2) 7a, 25m. A superb right-hand finish with some well-positioned moves into the scoop. An intense sequence.

**26. La Pilma** 5+

**27. Sense por** 5

**28. Fam de figa** 7a
1) 4, 20m. The easy slab
2) 7a, 25m. A sustained wall leads to the bulge before the pleasant finishing scoop.

**29. Super Ali** 6c
1) 4, 20m. The grassy slab.
2) 6c, 25m. A hard finish.

**30. Tedy Man** 7a
1) 4, 20m. As for *Super Ali*.
2) 7a, 25m. A reach-dependent alternative finish to *Super Ali*.

Right of here is a large roof with no climbs.

**RECONCO FAR RIGHT**
There is another small buttress down and right of the main wall which is worth seeking out if it is windy. The six routes are all good. From left to right:
1) 7a, 2) 6b+, 3) 6b+/6c, 4) 6b+, 5) 6a+, 6) 6b

South facing wall
15m to 45m routes
Best grades - 5 to 7a

# PEÑA RUBIA

This is not the most exciting crag in the guide but it has been quite popular in the past, and it does have some good climbing. Its main claim to fame is the proximity of the 'Boreal' factory and the thought that so many famous climbers have tested their sponsored boots on these humble walls. There is a full grade range from 4s to 8s. Most of the harder routes only have short technical sections on steep bulges and pockets. The easier routes are more interesting, especially some of the longer ones in the Centre Sector. The whole crag is fully equipped with good lower-offs. Some of the routes have two pitches but in most cases you can run them together with a 60m rope.

## APPROACH

Peña Rubia is very easy to get to. From Alicante, drive towards Madrid on the N330 (a free dual carriageway). 10km after passing the 'Sax' junction, is the 'Villena' junction. Turn off here and keep your eye open for a right turn signed 'Peña Rubia', which is virtually on the slip road. Take this turning and continue for 6km. The village of Peña Rubia never really materialises but you can see the crag on the hillside to the left for most of the 6km. See the map below for the few turnings. Eventually you reach a large gate, above a turning on the left, which is sometimes closed. If you can turn in here then turn left at the top junction and park by an old building. A short track leads up to the crag. Alternatively you can get around the gate by continuing and turning left onto the dirt track. Don't leave any valuables in your car.

## ASPECT AND CLIMATE

The crag faces northwest which means that it only gets the late afternoon sun. Despite this, the fact that it is relatively sheltered from any cooling breezes means that it will probably be too hot in the Summer months.

## THE ROUTES

The crag has been developed and equipped by many different people but principally Chimo, José Antonio and José Miguel. There is also one route by John Bachar climbed before most of the other in 1986.

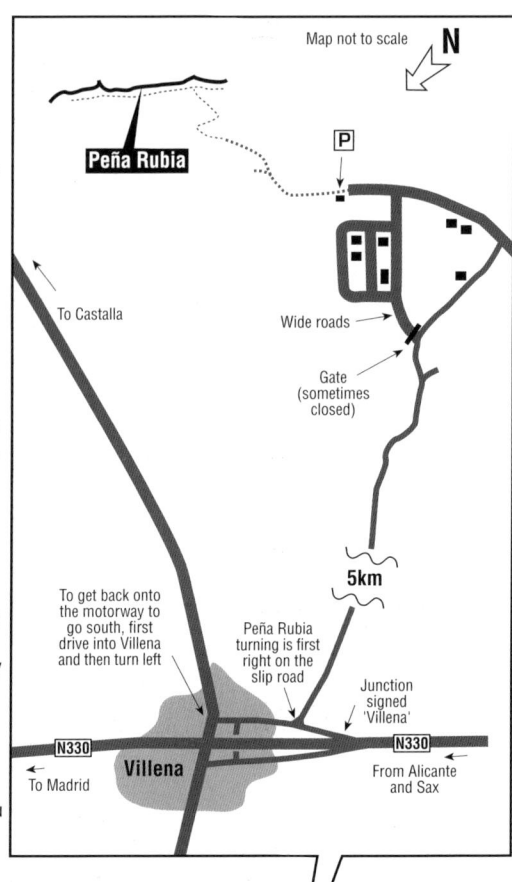

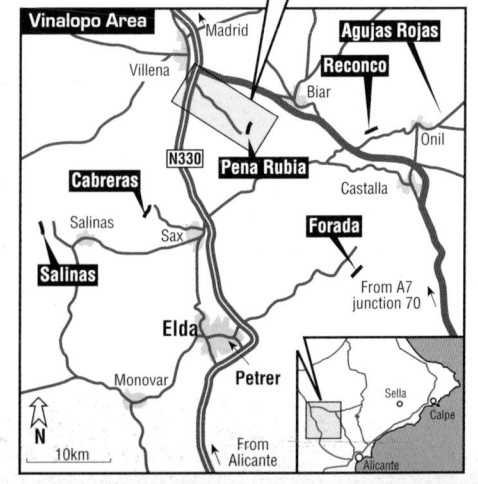

# COSTA BLANCA - Peña Rubia

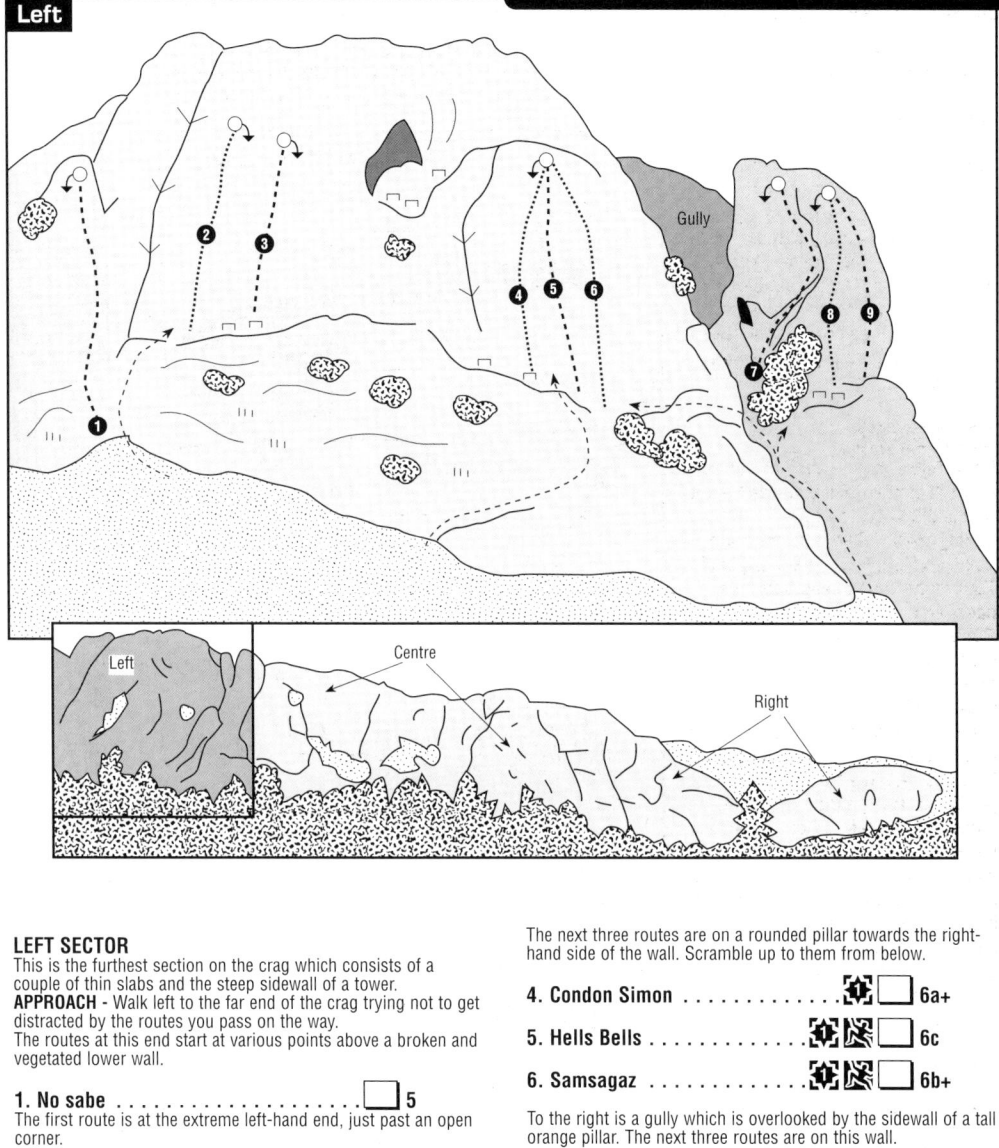

## LEFT SECTOR
This is the furthest section on the crag which consists of a couple of thin slabs and the steep sidewall of a tower.
**APPROACH -** Walk left to the far end of the crag trying not to get distracted by the routes you pass on the way.
The routes at this end start at various points above a broken and vegetated lower wall.

**1. No sabe** .................... 5
The first route is at the extreme left-hand end, just past an open corner.

**2. El espejo de Galadriel** ....... 7b+
Thin climbing up the slabby wall right of the corner.

**3. Sauron** .......... 7a+
More bald slab climbing.

The next three routes are on a rounded pillar towards the right-hand side of the wall. Scramble up to them from below.

**4. Condon Simon** ............ 6a+

**5. Hells Bells** ............ 6c

**6. Samsagaz** ............ 6b+

To the right is a gully which is overlooked by the sidewall of a tall orange pillar. The next three routes are on this wall.

**7. Me de la mismo** ........... 5
The twisting crack line. Good climbing.

**8. Smaug el dorado** .............. 6b+

**9. Gandalf el gris** ............... 6a+
Almost on the arete.

NW facing walls
10m to 20m routes
Best grades - 5 to 6b+

187

# COSTA BLANCA - Peña Rubia

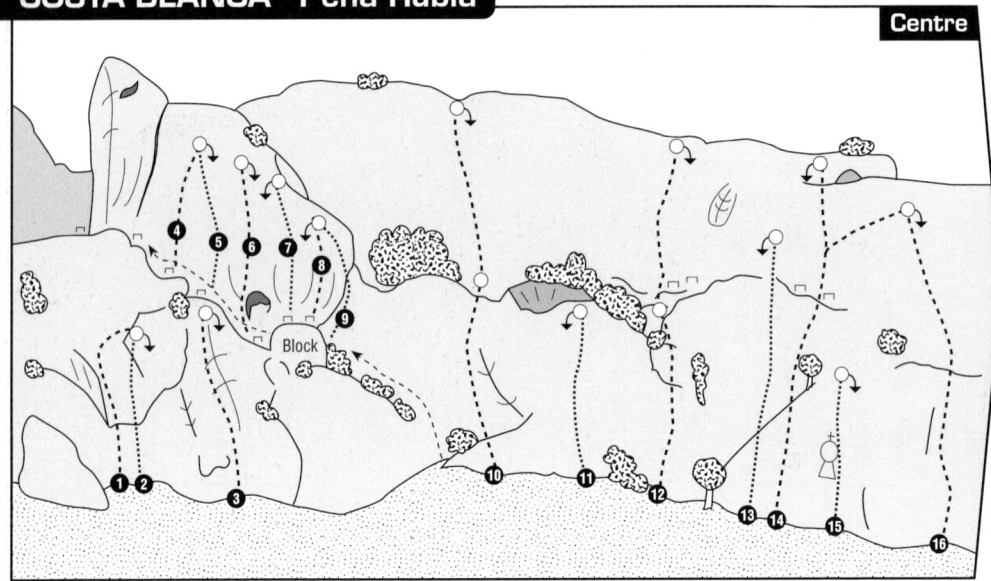

**Centre**

## CENTRE
The left-hand side of the main wall is a touch disappointing. It is broken up by ledges and most of the routes are very short.

The first routes start directly below the tall orange tower and, even by the standards set at this end of the crag, these are pretty crap.

**1. Piñerus** .................. 7a+
A contender for the most pointless route in this book.

**2. ¿Paraqué?** .................. 6b

**3. Pilarín** .................. 5+

The routes above this lower wall are a bit better. The starting ledges can be reached by an easy scramble from the right, or from the gully on the left.

**4. Voltage** .................. 6a+

**5. Semos peligrosos** .................. 6a+

**6. Por si el Sidra** .................. 6b+

**7. Póntelo Pónselo** .................. 6a
Start behind a block.

**8. Cinco contra el calvo** .................. 6a

**9. El chico del loro** .................. 5+

Before you reach the orange pillar is a tall slabby wall with a well vegetated mid-height ledge.

**10. El vuelo del Mono** .................. 5
A reasonable route which makes the best of the good rock. It can easily be done in one pitch if you have a 60m rope. If you do split it, both pitches are grade 5.

**11. Tampones lejanos** .................. 6a+
A short route which bales out before the ledge.

**12. Chimet** .................. 4+
Another 2 pitcher which can be done in one with a long rope.

**13. El ultimo Yeclano** .................. 5

**14. Caru** .................. 6b+ or 5
The right-hand finish is the easy option.

**15. Sharon Pistones** .................. 7a
Technical climbing past a bishop.

**16. Medio Metro** .................. 6a

# COSTA BLANCA - Peña Rubia

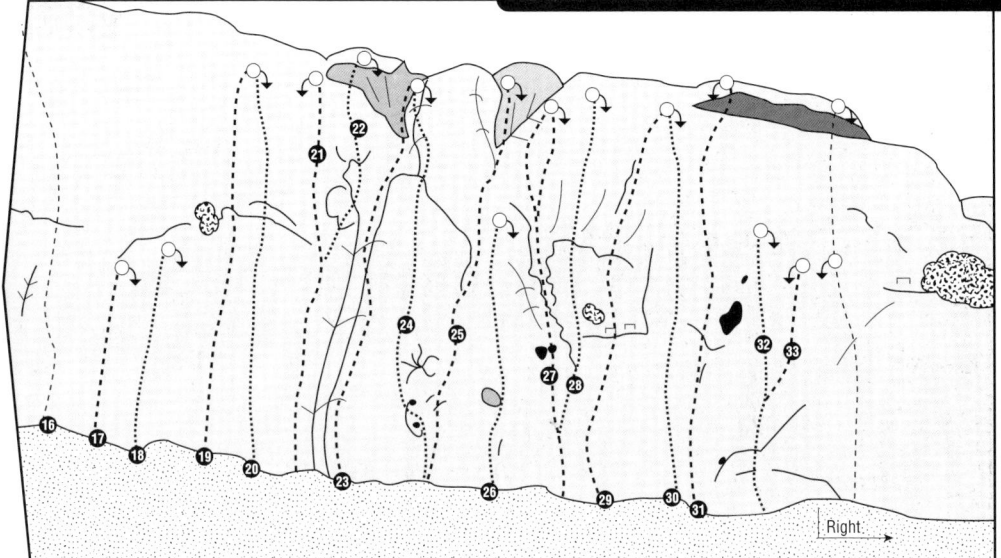

The best climbing at Peña Rubia is on the right-hand side of the main central area. The routes follow steep bulges and large pockets, with most of the hard climbing in the lower sections.

In the centre of the wall is a prominent corner. To the left of this is a steep bulge which the first two routes tackle.

**17. Pari-dakar** ....... 7b+

**18. Txavo tu vales mucho** .. 8a
5m of intense climbing!

**19. Kortatu** ........... 6c+

**20. Los 4 chinetes de la poca leche** ........ 6c+
A long bulging slab.

**21. Vacilando con lobos** ........ 6a+
An easier finish to the next route.

**22. Te cuelgan los Churumbeles** 6b+
The left-hand side of the red corner to a finish high up on the buttress, above a bulge.

**23. Verás que ferte te pones** ... 6a
Climb the blunt arete just right of the red corner.

**24. La muerte de la higuera** ... 6b
Finish to the left of the prow.

**25. Claveles** ............. 6b
A good route up the pocketed wall.

**26. Te tiemblan las piemblas** .. 7a+
Past a hole.

**27. Viviendo en una súplica** ...... 5+
The direct (right-hand) finish is 6b+.

**28. Anda tié huevos** ........ 7b

**29. Cocodrilo Din Don** .... 7b+
Finish up a steep diagonal crack. Spoilt by the mid-height ledge.

**30. La Ira del Tiempo** ....... 6c+
Up the rounded arete.

**31. El Amperio contra Paca** ... 7a+
A steep start and a slabby finish.

**32. Hambre de gamba** .... 8a
Short and hard.

**33. Txavito clavó un clavito** 7c

NW facing walls
5m to 20m routes
Best grades - 5+ to 7a+

# COSTA BLANCA - Peña Rubia

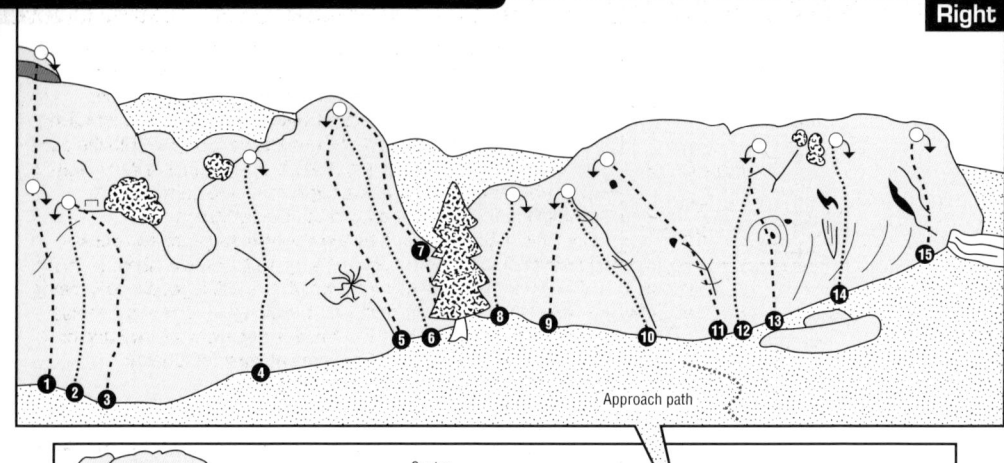

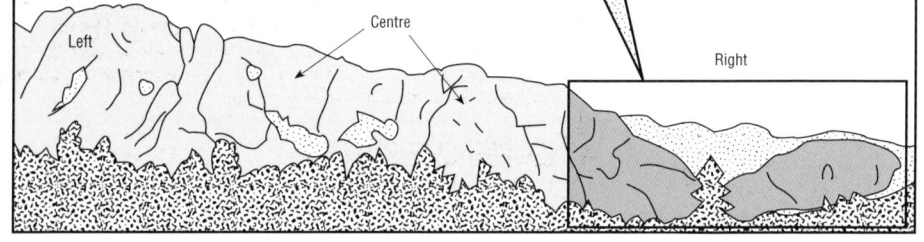

**Right**

Left — Centre — Right

Approach path

## RIGHT SECTOR
The first sector encountered when you arrive at the crag is an extremely steep and bulging wall, about 5m high. To the left of this wall is the main popular climbing area.

The next routes are on the right-hand side of the main wall.

**1. Rompe Pelotas** .......... 7a+
25m. Can be split at a mid-height belay but why would you want to do that.

**2. Wary Wary Yeah** ........ 7a+
Short and technical.

**3. En la espera te esquino mascando chicle** ............... 6a+
Yes, the name is longer than the route.

**4. María A** ................ 5+

Three routes are tightly packed in to the slab just left of the large tree.

**5. Vamos Joaquín** ................ 6c

**6. Placa Solar** ............... 5+
Entertaining for the grade.

**7. Huesitos Krac** ............... 6b

The bulging wall at the right-hand end of the crag is little more than a boulder but the routes pack a lot in. Unfortunately most of them are chipped.

**8. Aquaforce** ................ 7c
Terrible.

**9. A Bassi le faltó** .......... Project
Terrible and chipped.

**10. Lluvia de Arañas las Piembles** . Project
The diagonal crack-line.

**11. Pocker de Bassi** .......... 8a
Where is this route going?

**12. Hombres de Paja** ..... 7b

**13. Men of Still** ........ 6c
Pockets in a scoop.
FA. John Bachar 1986

**14. Estalactus Topus** ....... 7a
A steep tufa.

**15. Mantequila de Nápoles** ...... 6c+
Just left of the wall.

NW facing walls
5m to 25m routes
Best grades - 5+ to 7b

# CABRERAS

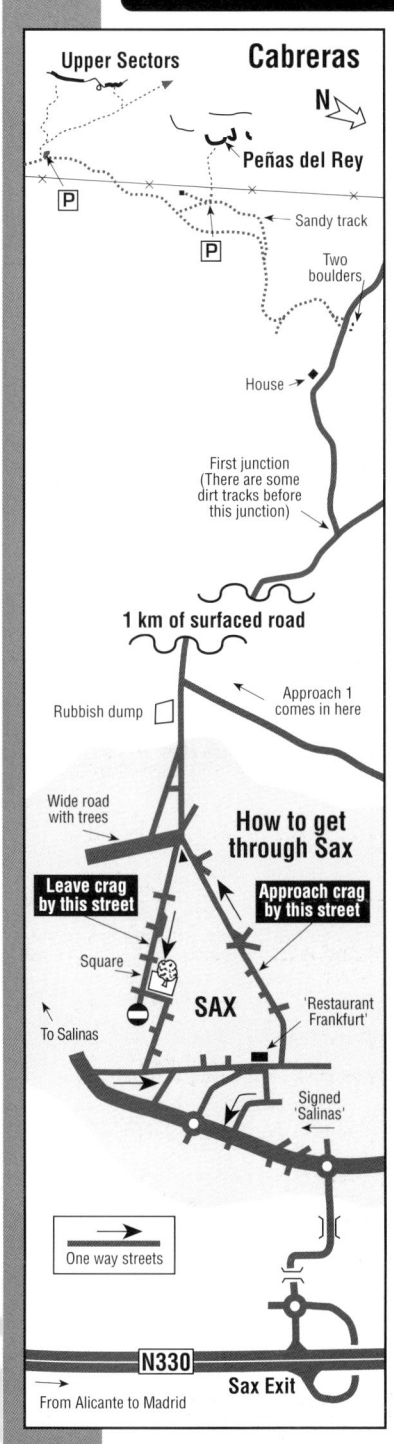

Cabreras comprises a series of pinnacles and walls perched high on the hillside above the historic maze of Sax. There are two main climbing areas; the Peñas del Rey, which is where the most popular climbing is, and Sector Cumbre which is a fine wall even higher up the hillside. Most of the climbing is slabby with the occasional bulging bit. The grade range is from delightful 4s to technical 6b's and climbers operating in the 5+ to 6a range will struggle to find a better crag in the Costa Blanca.

Cabreras has been used by the Spanish for years and consequently some of the routes feel very 'well climbed' although much of the gear has now being replaced. It is still a good idea to carry a selection of wires on some routes though. Many of the routes reach the top of the crag and there is not always a lowering or abseiling point, so take a few wires at least for a belay.

## ACCESS

**No climbing is allowed on the upper sectors of the crag from 1 February to 1 June be cause of nesting birds. Please respect this arrangement. It is sometimes starts earlier (December has been known) and stays on longer depending on the actual activities of the birds.**

## ASPECT AND CLIMATE

The main areas face east or northeast which makes it a good morning crag in Winter and a good afternoon crag in Summer. The exposed position on the hillside means that it will catch the wind although it is probably possible to still find some shelter on the Peñas del Rey.

## APPROACH

Drive from Alicante towards Madrid on the N330 (a free dual carriageway). Turn off at Sax and drive into the town.
**Approach 1** - This approach avoids the town centre but isn't on the map. At first roundabout in the town (second roundabout encountered after the motorway) turn right. Continue along passing below the Fort up on left. Take the next left (signed 'El Plano'). Follow this road for approximately 800m then turn right onto narrow lane (again signed 'El Plano'). From here, continue along a narrow road past the white house on the left. 400m further on turn left down a dirt track. Follow this towards the Peñas del Rey, which is now clearly visible on the hillside.
**For Peñas del Rey** - keep right at the first fork, and left at the second, then double back right and park under the crag.
**For the Upper Sectors** - keep right at the first fork, left at the second and continue up the hill to a level area some distance below the obvious Sector Cumbre.
**Approach 2** - A much more complex approach can be made through the town by following the map opposite. This approach isn't advisable, unless you get lost on Approach 1, or if you wish to stop at a cafe in the town.

## THE ROUTES

Climbing started at Cabreras back in the 70s and 80 with routes from Bravo, Pipona, Helios, Domingo and others. The crag was re-equipped in the 90s, and many routes added, by Chiri Ros, Manolo, Isabel Pagan and others.

# COSTA BLANCA - Cabreras

## Peñas del Rey - Left

2nd pitches about 30m

1st pitches about 35m

## PEÑAS DEL REY - LEFT

The lower section of the crags at Cabreras is centred on this superb tower of rock. Many of the routes converge at the top of the main pinnacle and following an independent line on these upper sections is often difficult. Usually this is above all difficulties.

**DESCENT** - For most of the routes walk off the back and down leftwards. It is possible to abseil off after some of the first pitches.

The main pinnacle has a clean slabby wall on its left-hand face, with a prominent cave high up.

**1. Espolón Mataix** . . . . . . . . . . . . . . . 4
1) 4, 20m. 2) 4, 30m. Full rack needed but there are fixed belays.

**2. ?** . . . . . . . . . . . . . . . . . . . . . . . . . . 5+
1) 5+, 25m. 2) (4), 35m.

**3. ?** . . . . . . . . . . . . . . . . . . . . . . . . . 6a+
1) 5, 25m. 2) 6a+, 35m.

**4. Blanes** . . . . . . . . . . . . . . . . . . . . . 4+
1) 4+, 25m. 2) 4+, 35m.

**5. Caballo Loco** . . . . . . . . . . . . . . . . 6a+
Small wires needed. Finish up *Blanes* or lower off.

**6. Anduriña** . . . . . . . . . . . . . . . . . . . 6a
1) 6a, 30m. Follow the slab to a belay left of the cave. Excellent.
2) 4+, 35m. The easy groove after a steep start.

**7. Liga Humana** . . . . . . . . . . . . . . . 6a+
An excellent route.
1) 6a+, 30m. Follow the slab to a belay in the cave.
2) 6a, 35m. Pull steeply up above, close to the line of *Tupungato*, to gain the upper wall.

**8. Tupungato** . . . . . . . . . . . . . . . . . . 5+
1) 5, 30m. The delightful slab leads to a comfortable belay in the cave.
2) 5+, 35m. Pull out leftwards into a smaller cave above (a wire may be needed by some).

**9. Muerte Sabrosa** . . . . . . . . . . . . . 6b
30m. Make a hard start to reach the orange patch beneath the cave. Abseil off or finish up one of the other routes.

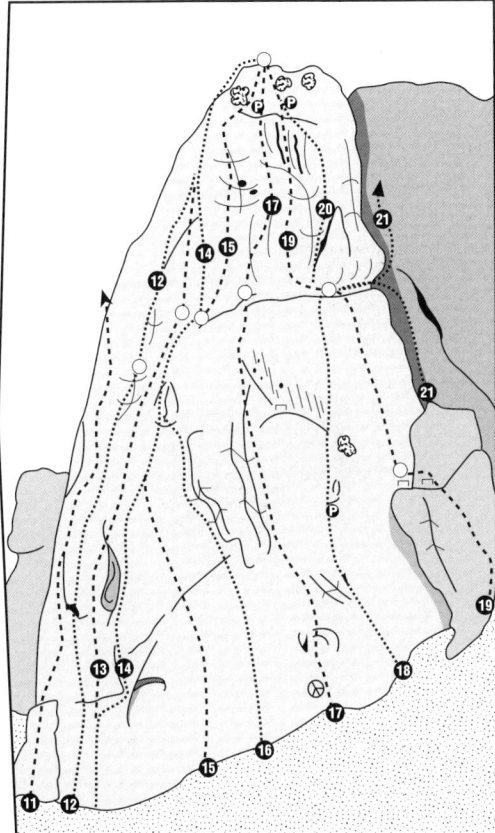

> # COSTA BLANCA - Cabreras

**13. La Mulxaranga** .......... 6b
1) **5+, 35m.** The direct line from the start of *Central*.
2) **6b, 35m.** The slab above leads to the top.

**14. Central** ................ 5+
1) **5+, 40m.** Climb to the right of a prominent oval cave and continue to a ramp.
2) **5+, 35m.** Straight up the rib and pull leftwards through the bulges above.

**15. Límites Realidad** ........ 6a+
Good bolts but a little run-out.
1) **6a, 40m.** Climb up leftwards to join *Central* and continue to its stance.
2) **6a, 35m.** Climb staright up the steep wall above to the top.

**16. Diedro Dinamita** ........ 6b
The left-facing corner needs wires. Finish up any of the other routes or abseil off.

**17. Polvos Mágicos** .......... 6a
The right-facing corner above the CND symbol.
1) **6a, 40m.** A bit run-out at the bottom.
2) **6a, 25m.** Climb up left of the rib to a corner.

**18. Hollywood** ............... 6a+
**35m.** A single pitch marked by a thread and a peg. Take some wires. Abseil off or continue up one of the upper pitches.

The next three routes are located in the back left-hand side of the gully, between the two pinnacles.

**19. Navarro 1** ............... 6a
An expedition up the front of the leaning block and wall above.
1) **5+, 10m.** Scramble up onto the top of the pinnacle (possible belay) then climb the steep wall above to the break.
2) **6a, 35m.** make a hard move up and left into a scoop and climb direct up the wall to eventually merge with the other routes.

**20. Navarro 1 Variante** ........ 6b
A variation to pitch three up the blunt rib on the right.

**21. Chimenea Groen 70** ...... 5
1) **5, 20m.** Squirm up the chimney at the back left-hand corner of the gully. Fun if you like that sort of thing.
2) **5, 35m.** Pull back right into the corner and contiue the fight to the top.

**10. ?** ..................... 6a+
1) **6a+, 30m.** The right-hand side of the orange patch to cave.
2) **?, 35m.** The narrowing slab to the top.

**11. Super Directa** ............ 6a
The front pillar of the main pinnacle.
1) **6a, 30m.** Start up a detached block and belay in the cave.
2) **5+, 35m.** Pull out right from the cave and climb the superb slab above.

The next routes are up the front pillar of the main pinnacle. They are illustrated on the topo opposite.

**12. Directísima** ............. 6a
The right-hand side of the front pillar.
1) **6a, 35m.** Climb the rib. The belay is marked by a red sling.
2) **6a, 35m.** The slab above leads to the top.

East facing slabby buttress
50m to 70m multi-pitch routes
Best grades - 4+ to 6a+

# COSTA BLANCA - Cabreras

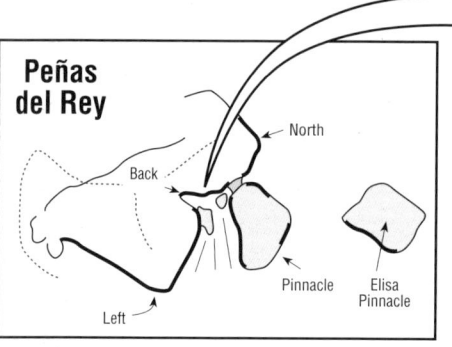

**Back Wall**

**Peñas del Rey**

North, Back, Left, Pinnacle, Elisa Pinnacle

Chimenea Groen 70

## PEÑAS DEL REY - BACK WALL
At the back of the gully between the two main pinnacles is an impressive steep wall which contains the best steep routes at Cabreras.
The big snake crack has an aid route up it. The next three routes have no belay at the top so take some wires and a sling. The 2nd pitches are much longer than they look.
**DESCENT** - Walk off the back left-hand side (looking at the wall) of the pinnacle.

**1. ?** .................... ? ?
A new route which looks quite hard. Two pitches.

**2. Elena de Pablo** ....... 7a
The magnificent route with 2 3-star pitches.
1) **6a+, 25m.** Steep and juggy climbing.
2) **7a, 35m.** More technical than the lower section although the real difficulties are only short.

**2a. Elena de Pablo (Pitch 1)** ... 6a+
For those who want a tick box for the first pitch only.

**3. Chinchey** .............. 6b
1) **5+, 25m.** Another superb first pitch.
2) **6b, 35m.** One hard move just above the stance then spaced gear to the top.

**3a. Chinchey (Pitch 1)** ........ 5+
Another tick box.

**4. Espolón Luis Rico** .......... 6a
1) **6a, 20m.** The chimney by the block on the right leads to a belay on the col.
2) **6a, 35m.** Finish up the arete above.

## PEÑAS DEL REY - PINNACLE
The right-hand side of the Peñas del Rey has a prominent pinnacle standing in front of the main crag.
**DESCENT** - For routes which reach the top of the Pinnacle, make one 30m abseil from the cable down into the central gully. For the other routes, and those on the Elisa Pinnacle, walk down.

The first routes are on the bulging wall on the right-hand side of the central gully.

**5. Retri** .................... (6a+)
A single pitch to the top of the tower. There are only two bolts visible.

**6. QE2** .................... 6a
Start as for *Retri* but break right and follow spaced gear to the top.

**7. Techo** ............... 7a+
The direct start to the next route is very technical. Finish up *Carrasco* or lower off from the mid-height belay.

---

**Back Wall**
North facing, 60m two pitch routes
Best grades - 5+ to 7a

# COSTA BLANCA - Cabreras

## Peñas del Rey
Back, North, Pinnacle, Left
Elisa Pinnacle Routes 15 to 17

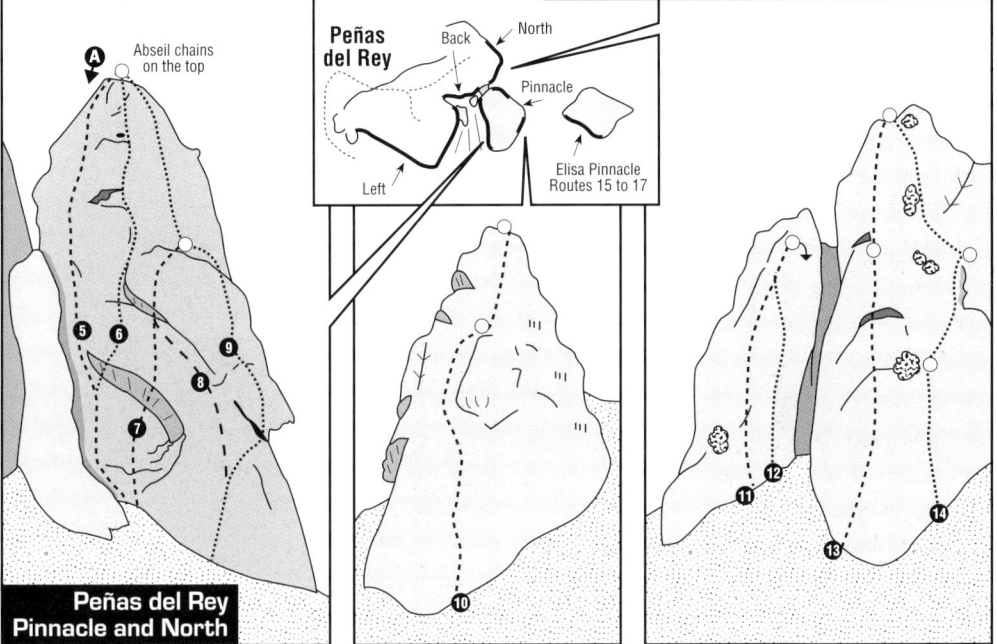

**Peñas del Rey Pinnacle and North**

---

**8. Con cutra basta** .............. 6a+
An eliminate which makes a rising traverse above the scoop. Join and finish up *Carrasco*.

**9. Carrasco** .............. 5
45m. A good route up the front left-hand side of the pillar. It can be split at the mid-height belay but there is no real need to do this.

The next route is around the other side of the pinnacle.

**10. Rafael Vercher** ............ 5
The line is marked by two pegs so take some wires. It can be split at a belay on a ledge.

At the back of the pinnacle is a narrow gully. The next two routes are on the left of this gully.

**11. Sombra del pájaro** ............ 6a+
Use the lower-off on *Carrozas Climb*.

**12. Carrozas Climb** ...... 7b
A wicked test-piece up the side wall.

## PEÑAS DEL REY - NORTH
Two more routes are on the wall beyond the pinnacle.

**13. Aspirante carroza** .......... 6a
A pleasant little route up the gentle rib.
1) 6a, 20m. Climb the rib past a small overlap.
2) 5+, 30m. Continue to the top.

**14. Marco Antonio** ............ 5
A long and wandering line which requires gear. It can be done in two pitches. All the pitches are grade 5.

## THE ELISA PINNACLE
To the right of the main sectors is another shorter pinnacle with a bulging side wall and a fine front arete.

**15. Moreno** .................... 6a+

**16. Super miembro** ........... 6c+

**17. Elisa-beltrán** ............. 4
45m. A good route up the front arete which can be split at a mid-height belay.

---

Sun and shade · 10 min · Slabby · Belay at top · Windy

**Pinnacle and North**
East and North facing, 20m to 45m routes
Best grades - 4 to 6a

# COSTA BLANCA - Cabreras

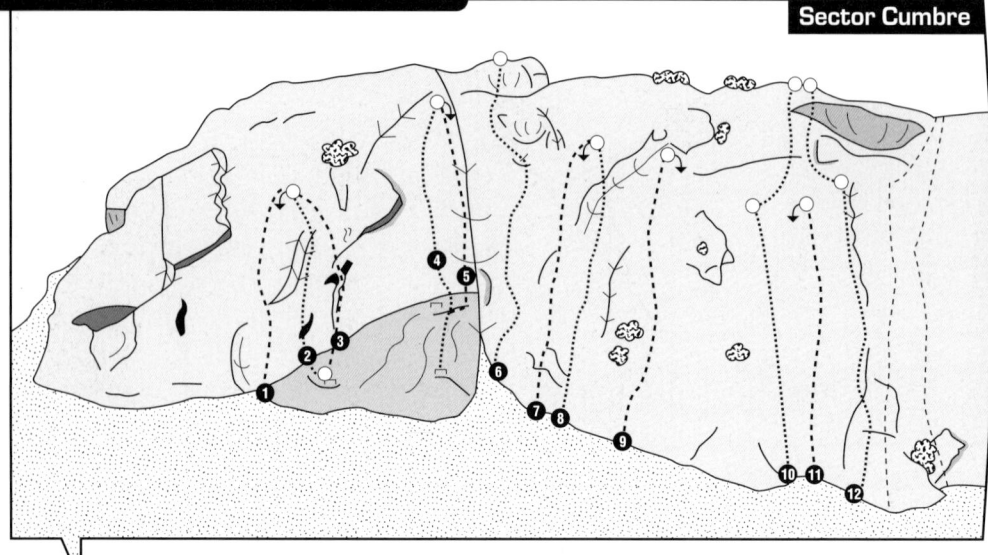

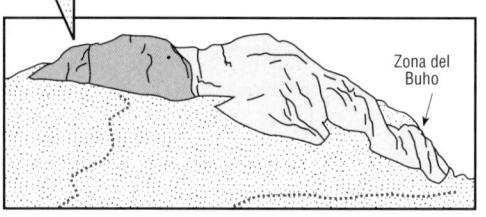

## Sector Cumbre

Zona del Buho

### UPPER SECTORS
The Upper Sectors of Cumbre and Zona del Buho are perched high on the hillside south (left looking in) of Peñas del Rey.
**GEAR** - The re-gearing of Cabreras is still not finished. At present a small rack of gear is needed for most of the older routes (marked with a nut symbol) and often for belays at the top.

⛔ **ACCESS** - NO CLIMBING FROM 1 FEBRUARY TO 1 JUNE BECAUSE OF NESTING BIRDS. This restriction is put in force when the birds nest and it has been known to have been in place as early as December.

### SECTOR CUMBRE
The main attraction of the upper walls is the long slabby Sector Cumbre. This gives a good selection of mid-grade routes with just the slight drawback of the steep ankle-scratching approach slog.
**APPROACH** - From the small parking area (see the general approach with the introduction) walk a little further up the track and find a faint path. The left-hand branch leads straight up the hill, along a sporadically-cairned path, to Sector Cumbre.
**DESCENT** - Some of the routes have lower-offs and some top-out. For the ones which top-out, a selection of gear is probably required for the belay, if not on the route itself. From the top, walk down the left-hand side (looking in) of the crag.

The first routes are on the short wall just left of the main buttress.

**1. Moreno machacón** .......... 7b+
Disproportionately hard for this crag.

**2. Rompe bragas** .............. 6a+
Up the right-facing corner.

**3. Polla asesina** ............. 6c
Past some holes and a bulge.

To the right is an attractive open groove/crackline.

**4. Homicidio frustrado** ....... 6c+
The wall left of the groove is thin.

**5. Asesinato premeditado** ..... 6b+
The crackline itself is not very helpful. The wall just left tends to be more helpful.

**6. Ingreso cadáver** ........... 6b+
A tricky wall climb. Wires needed for the belay.

**7. Pincha pansida** ............ 6a
A pleasant slab.

**8. Gorilero** .................. 6a
More delicate slab work.

**9. Tauro** ..................... 6a
The name is painted on the bottom. To get rid of the flutter symbol, carry some wires.

**10. Tubular Bells** ............ 6b+
The name is painted at the bottom.
1) **6b+, 20m**. A technical wall with spaced bolts.
2) **6b+, 20m**. Move back right and skirt a bulge on it left-hand side.

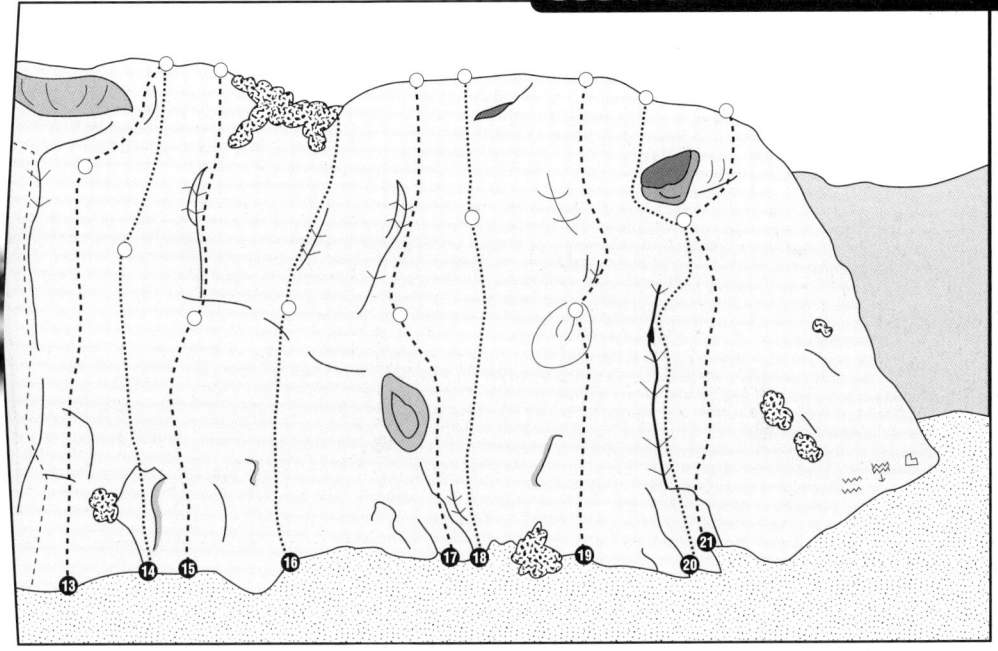

# COSTA BLANCA - Cabreras

**11. Zombis** .............. 6b
A shorter pitch with a lower-off.

**12. Fiesta salvaje** .......... 6b+
The central line of the face.
**1) 6a+, 20m.** Up a shallow corner to belay below the bulge.
**2) 6b+, 20m.** Move left of the bulge at the top.

**13. Busque y compare** .......... 6a+
Another route with spaced bolts and its name at the base.
**1) 6a+, 20m.** The wall just right of the central groove.
**2) 6a+, 20m.** Skirt right of the upper bulge.

**14. De película** .......... 6b+
**1) 6a+, 15m.** Start up a detached flake and head straight up the wall. New bolts.
**2) 6b+, 25m.** Continue directly to the top.

**15. Toreros muertos** ........ 6b+
**1) 6a+, 15m.** Name painted at base.
**2) 6b+, 25m.** Climb a small groove line high up.

**16. Demonio con faldas** ... 7a
**1) 6a+, 15m.** Spaced bolts but then again if you are up to pitch 2 then you won't mind.
**2) 7a, 25m.** A series of thin moves leads quickly to easier ground.

**17. Lucecitas de colores** ....... 6a+
**1) 6a+, 15m.** Start right of a shallow scoop, then traverse above it to gain a groove line.
**2) 6a+, 25m.** Climb the groove.

**18. Jabato con pie de gato** ..... 6a+
**1) 6a, 20m.** Name at its base.
**2) 6a+, 20m.** Direct to the top.

**19. Gringo** ............... 6a+
**1) 6a+, 15m.** Belay in a shallow scoop.
**2) 6a+, 25m.** Direct to the top.

**20. Civera** .............. 5+
**1) 5, 20m.** The prominent crackline is followed to the cave.
**2) 6a+, 20m.** Finish out left of the cave.

**21. Sensaciones azuladas** .... 6a+
**1) 5+, 20m.** The wall to the right of *Civerea*. Share its belay.
**2) 6a+, 20m.** Finish out right of the cave.

East facing wall
15m to 40m multi-pitch routes
Best grades - 6a to 6c+

# COSTA BLANCA - Cabreras

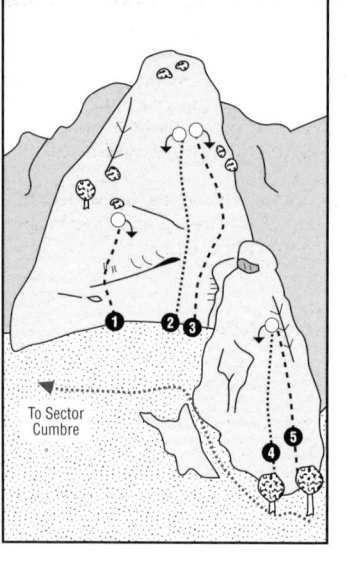

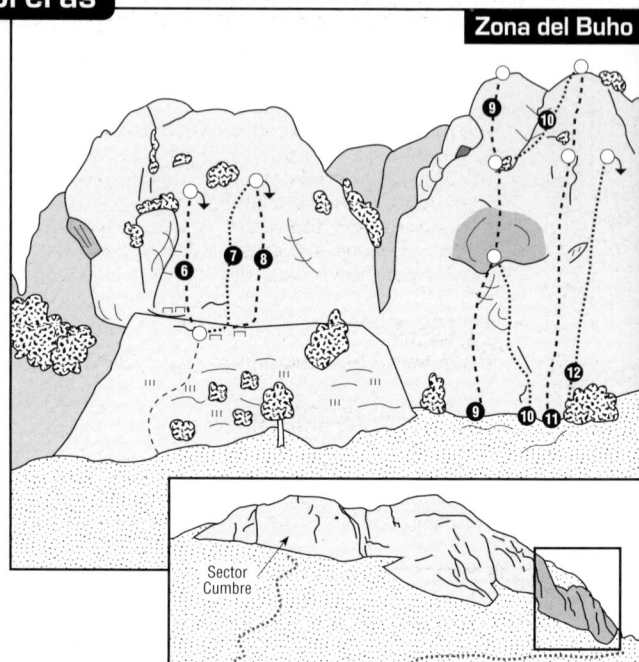

## Zona del Buho

### ZONA DEL BUHO
An obvious landmark on this sector is a small pinnacle with some trees at its base. This is the home of *Zipi* and *Zape*. The first routes are up and left of this pinnacle.

**APPROACH** - From the small parking area (see the general approach with the introduction) walk a little further up the track and find a faint path. The left-hand branch leads straight up the hill, along a sporadically-cairned path, to Sector Cumbre. The right-hand branch crosses under Zona del Buho and continues off into the wilderness.

**ACCESS** - NO CLIMBING FROM 1 FEBRUARY TO 1 JUNE BECAUSE OF NESTING BIRDS. This restriction is put in force when the birds nest and it has been known to have been in place as early as December.

**1. Sube si puedes** .............. 6c
Good while it lasts.

**2. Asignatura pendiente** ........ 7b
A technical horror straight up the blank wall.

**3. Prisionero** .................. 6c+
The best route on this sector up the right-hand side of the wall. New bolts.

Back down rightwards on the pinnacle are the two routes named after Spanish cartoon characters.

**4. Zipi** ........................ 5+

**5. Zape** ....................... 5+

Immediately right of the pinnacle is a clean wall above a vegetated lower section. Scramble up this to start them.

**6. Marionetas** ................. 6b+

**7. Titeres** .................... 6a+

**8. Bandolero** .................. 6b

The last routes are further right, on a wall with an obvious cave in its centre. Routes 9 and 10 are combinations of pitches which share their middle section using the only possible line to leave the cave.

**9. Rómulo/Perro Verde/Caligula** ... 7a
1) 5, 15m. Can be done on its own.
2) 7a, 10m. A hard middle pitch.
3) 6b+, 15m. Bumble on to the top.

**10. Remo/Perro Verde/Nerón** .... 7a
Much the same as Route 9, except that the top pitch is easier.

**11. Matojo de la bruja** ........ 6b+
There is a stance but it can be done in one pitch to the top.

**12. Fuego salvaje** ............. 6c
The furthest route right has a lower-off.

East facing buttresses
10m to 35m routes
Best grades - 5 to 6c+

# SALINAS

Salinas is a wonderful crag which is beautifully situated, superbly well-geared and has a good grade spread of high quality routes. What more could you ask for? Not much, but there is a down-side and in this case there are two small ones. Firstly, the lower-offs on many of the routes have been placed too low which often robs you of a worthy last move, and secondly, many of the harder routes are chipped. The chipping isn't as blatant as elsewhere but it sometimes leaves you with a bit of a hollow experience, as you reach off a chipped pocket to clip the lower-off chains, half way through a hard move.

Despite these reservations, the routes are mostly superb and sustained, following steep pockets and thin vertical walls. It shouldn't just be considered a hard crag since there are plenty of superb easier challenges on Sector Picara Viborita and on the edges of the higher sectors.

## ACCESS
**No climbing from 1 February to 1 June because of nesting birds.**

## ASPECT AND CLIMATE
The crag is basically a ridge with faces on either side. The upper section faces east and the lower section faces west. Most of the best routes are on the upper section so the crag is best considered a morning sun crag. It is not too exposed therefore it can be considered an all year round crag except perhaps on the coldest winter days, or when it is particularly windy. Most of the upper sectors are overhanging and may give some dry climbing in light rain, although only in the harder grades.

## APPROACH
The crag is situated near the town of Sax and is best approached from there. Drive from Alicante towards Madrid on the N330 (a free dual carriageway). Turn off at Sax and drive into the town. At the first roundabout turn left, signed 'Salinas'. Follow this for about 10km to the small village of Salinas and drive straight through it. (Note: water is available in the centre of the village). After you leave the town, continue for 1.5km and turn right (signed 'Finca Castillejos'). At this point the ridge of the crag can be seen ahead on the left. Ignore the first dirt track on the left and on the next bend continue straight onto a wide dirt track (signed 'Fontanos'). This track may soon be surfaced. Turn left off this onto another dirt track and follow it towards the crag past two sets of buildings. Keep left at the first branch and right at the second. The road after the second bend is particularly bad, but that's OK in a hire car, unless you puncture the fuel tank! Park at a clearing on the right. Continue walking up the track to find a path on a bend. This leads straight to Sector Picara Viborita. It is also possible to park just past the second building and be faced with a slightly longer walk.

## THE ROUTES
The crag was equipped by Juan Serrano, José Hernandez, Lola Justamante and others, between 1991 and 1993.

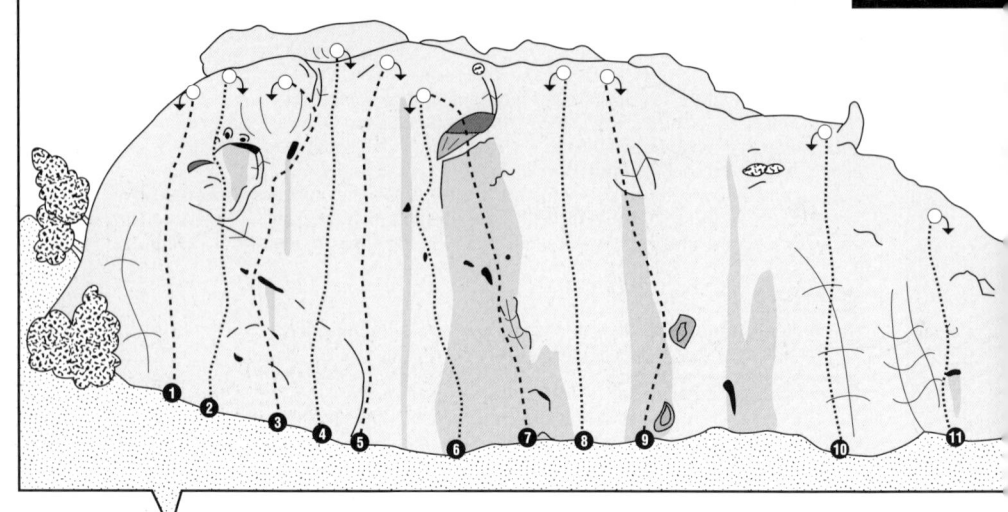

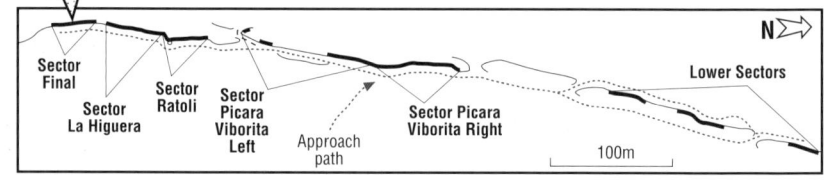

# COSTA BLANCA - Salinas

**Sector Final**

## SECTOR FINAL
The highest sector up the ridge is also one of the best. The routes are on superb rock, up some dramatic orange streaks, and are especially suited for those of you who like blank 7c's, with no holds and I know there are a lot of you out there! However there is also something for people who like swinging between juggy pockets at a slightly easier grade.

**APPROACH** - Walk left, under the main face, from where the approach path arrives at the crag. You will immediately pass over a lower wall of broken rock. A little further up is a gap in the ridge, keep left here. Continue uphill past Sector Ratoli and La Higuera.

**ACCESS** - NO CLIMBING FROM 1 FEBRUARY TO 1 JUNE BECAUSE OF NESTING BIRDS.

The first route is on the left-hand side, almost starting from a bush, and below a grey rib.

**1. Manzanita verde** .......... 6b+
The nice looking rib is a bit precarious and the finish has a hard move.

**2. Terranova** ............. 6c
A steep finish.

**3. ?** .................. 6b+
The bolts go over a steep bulge but you are forced rightwards onto a flake.

The next two routes are up an extremely blank wall.

**4. Crucifixión** ....... 7c
You'll just have to use your imagination since there aren't any actual holds.

**5. Ahí va la liebre** .... 7c
As blank as its neighbours.

**6. Danza interrumpida** . 7c
Between the two orange streaks. Chipped and sharp, but also brilliant.

**7. Mata-Hari** .......... 7a+
A stunning route up the pockets in the larger orange streak, finishing left or right via chipped pockets over the top roof.

**8. Metamorfosis** ..... 7c
Another hold-less horror!

**9. Línea maestra** ....... 7b+
The line of resin bolts has an outrageously hard start. Above that it gives a superb 7a+.

**10. Donde dices que vas** ........ 6a+
The curving rib.

**11. La silla de la reina** ...... 6b
Rounded holds on the crux bulge.

SE facing wall
10m to 20m routes
Best grades - 6a+ to 7c

# COSTA BLANCA - Salinas

**Sector la Higuera**

## SECTOR LA HIGUERA
The sectors at this end of the crag are all very similar; superb routes, orange streaks, interesting pockets, mainly harder grades, easy routes at the edges, all better than most of the bolted routes in Britain.

**APPROACH -** Walk left, under the main face, from where the approach path arrives at the crag. You will immediately pass over a lower wall of broken rock. A little further up is a gap in the ridge, keep left here. Continue uphill past Sector Ratoli and La Higuera.

**ACCESS** - NO CLIMBING FROM 1 FEBRUARY TO 1 JUNE BECAUSE OF NESTING BIRDS.

The first route is left of the steep middle section, just right of a curving groove.

1. ? .................... 6a
2. **Lloviendo sale corriendo** ........ 6a
The diagonal crack.
3. **Pequeña y juguetona** ...... 6c+
A short route with a delicate traverse and a drilled mono on the crux.
4. **Babieca** ............ 7b
A brilliant route which finishes just left of a thin roof.
5. **El gran cañon** ..... 7b+
Start in the same place as *Babieca* and finish over the thin roof. Hard!
6. **Reina de corazones** ...... 8a
Really hard.
7. **Africa** ............ 7c
8. **Puercoespín** ........ 7b+
A good route just right of a rightwards facing groove.
9. **Papa ven en tren** ...... 7a+
Looks unlikely!.
10. **Hay canto** ....... 7b+
11. **Directisima** ........ 6b+
The 'indirect' line to the right which swings under an old tree.
12. **Roca loca** ........... 6a
13. **Saltimbanqui** ........ 6a
14. **Pepito conejo** ......... 5

SE facing wall
10m to 20m routes
Best grades - 5 to 8a

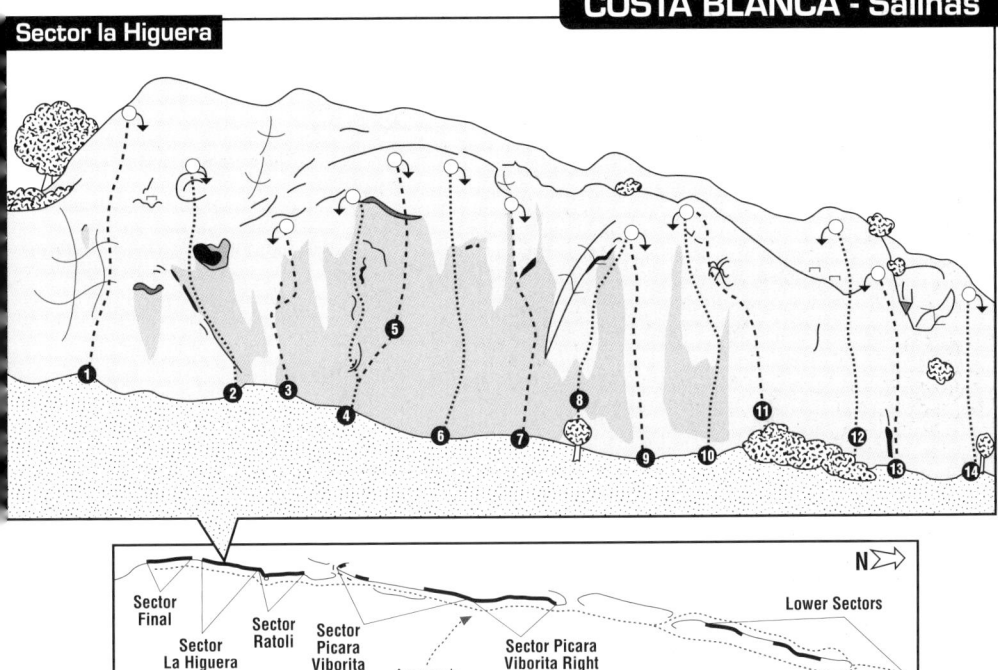

# COSTA BLANCA - Salinas

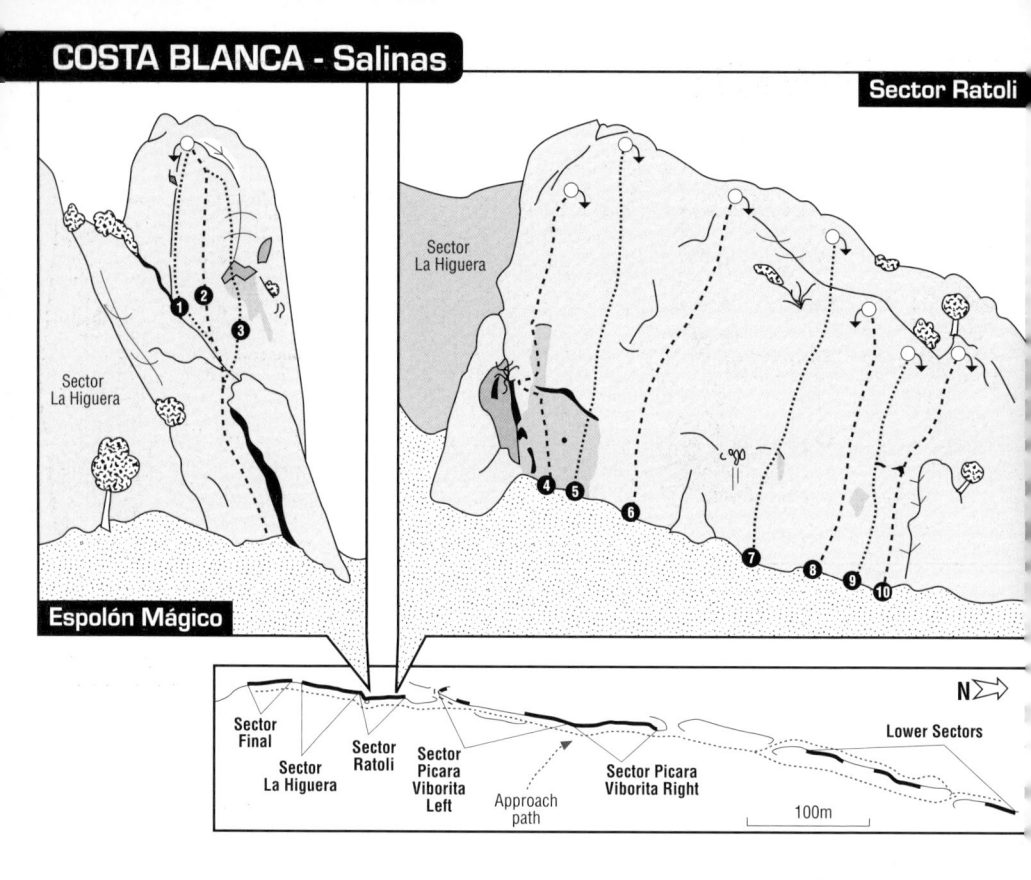

## Sector Ratoli

### Espolón Mágico

Sector Final — Sector Ratoli — Sector Picara Viborita Left — Sector Picara Viborita Right — Lower Sectors
Sector La Higuera
Approach path
100m
N

## SECTORS ESPOLON MAGICO AND RATOLI
The 'Magic Pillar' is slightly over sold by its name, but the wall to its right is good.

**APPROACH** - Sector Ratoli is the first decent wall you come to as you walk leftwards up the hill from the approach path. Take care to drop down leftwards at the col by the top routes on Sector Picara Viborita.

**ACCESS** - NO CLIMBING FROM 1 FEBRUARY TO 1 JUNE BECAUSE OF NESTING BIRDS.

## ESPOLON MAGICO
The pillar faces south and is next to the last routes on sector La Higuera.

1. **Fisura mágico** . . . . . . . . . . . . . . . . . . 6a+

2. **Placa mágico** . . . . . . . . . . . . . 6b+

3. **Espolón mágico** . . . . . . . . . 6b
   The rounded arete of the pillar.

## SECTOR RATOLI

4. **Los dedos del mono** . . . . . . 7a+
   Up the orange streak, right of the corner. At this grade, most people will accept the leftwards rest on the tree (7b without).

5. **Marca pasos** . . . . . . 7a+
   Brilliant climbing. The upper section is very blank.

6. **Agárrate donde puedas** . . 7b

7. **7b el plumero** . . . . . . . . . . 7a
   A good line just right of some blobs.

8. **Cangrena** . . . . . . . . . . . . . . . 6c+

9. **Paprika** . . . . . . . . . . . . . . . . . . . . 6b

10. **Avoriaz en pelotas me verás** . . . . . 5+
    There are better routes at this grade elsewhere.

SE facing wall
15m to 20m routes
Best grades - 6a to 7b

# COSTA BLANCA - Salinas

## Sector Picara Viborita - Left

Routes 1 to 4

Sector Ratoli

Sector Picara Viborita - Left

Approach path

Sector Picara Viborita - Right

## SECTOR PICARA VIBORITA

This is the main buttress at Salinas and has the best spread of grades. The routes vary from nice and slabby on the left-hand side to steep and orange on the right.

**ACCESS** - NO CLIMBING FROM 1 FEBRUARY TO 1 JUNE BECAUSE OF NESTING BIRDS.

The first routes are at the left-hand end.

**1. Dartacán** .................... 6c
The overhanging red wall almost on the back of the fin.

Back on the main face, just before the end of the buttress, is a small grey slab with three routes and one lower-off.

**2. Aramis** .................... 5

**3. Portos** .................... 5

**4. Atos** .................... (5)
No bolt hangars at the time of writing.

**5. No te lo pongas** .................... 4+
There is a hard move after the first bolt.

**6. Pónselo** .................... 6a
Good climbing up the blank scoop. Left of the scoop is easier (5+) but less worthwhile.

**7. Póntelo** .................... 5+
A hard finish.

**8. Jarpichuela** .................... 5+
Past an area of grassy, broken rock.

**9. Pero yeyo** .................... 5
Through the large diamond-shaped scoop.

**10. Amonite** .................... 5+

**11. Sancho Panza** .................... 6a
There is a scoop at the start.

**12. Ali Baba y los 40 mosquetones** .................... 6b
A very hard start.

**13. El canto de la abubilla** .................... 6b+

**14. Lolitus** .................... 7a
There is a 6c+ detour around the top hard section.

SE facing wall
15m to 20m routes
Best grades - 4+ to 7a

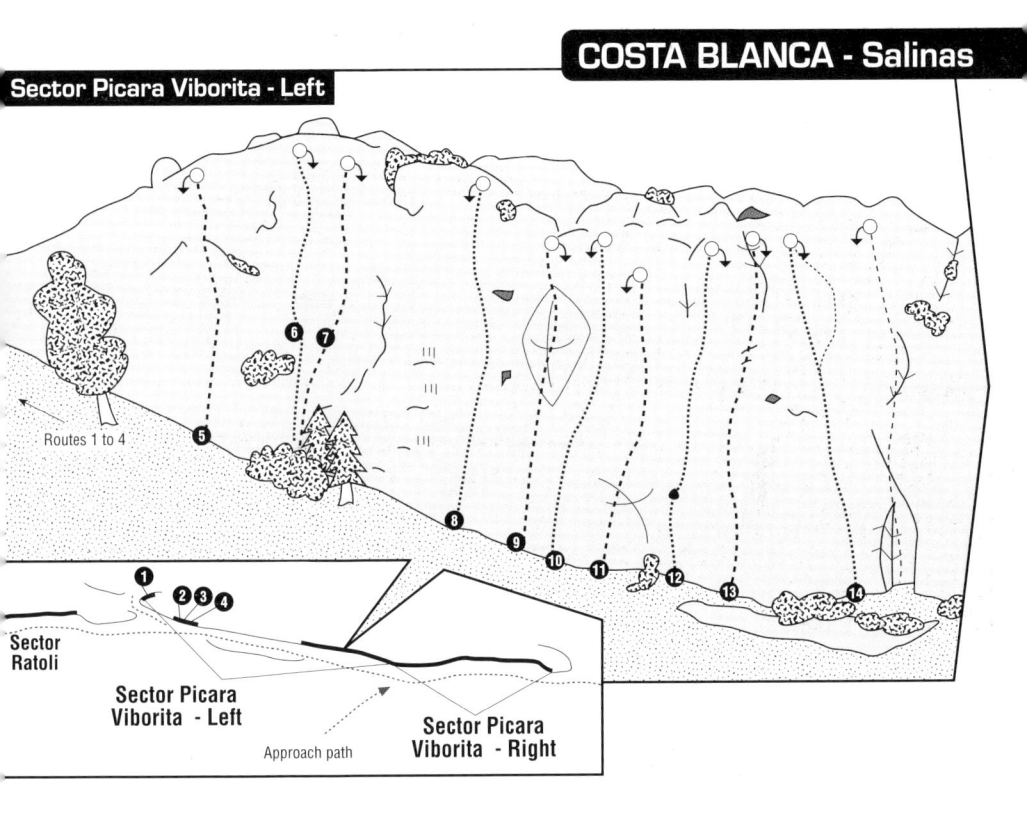

# COSTA BLANCA - Salinas

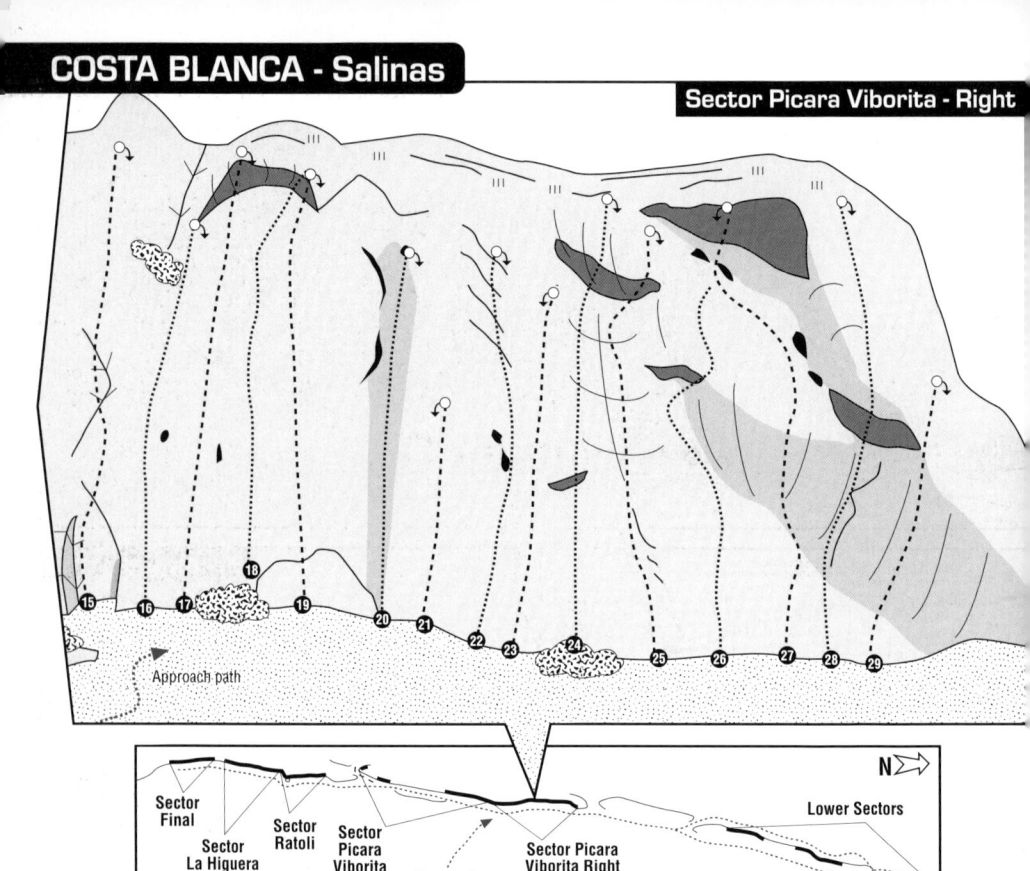

## Sector Picara Viborita - Right

### SECTOR PICARA VIBORITA - RIGHT
These routes are up the wall directly above where the approach path meets the crag.

**ACCESS** - NO CLIMBING FROM 1 FEBRUARY TO 1 JUNE BECAUSE OF NESTING BIRDS.

**15. Me estoy multiplicando** ......... 6b
A good route up the shallow, fingery corner.

**16. Así habelo Pepetrusta** ......... 6a

**17. Andrea** ......... 6b+

**18. Flash Bea** ......... 6b+
An eliminate.

**19. Bocadillos de microbios** ......... 6b

**20. Lenin** ......... 6c
Up the orange streak to a lower-off in the middle of nowhere.

**21. Cernicalus** ......... 7a
Finish in the middle of a blank wall.

**22. Cefalinpadus** ......... 6b
A brilliant route up the pocketed wall.

**23. El abominable** ......... 6b

**24. Machu que pichu** ......... 6b+

**25. Le puerta de Anubis** ......... 6a+
Climb up a shallow scoop and make a steep rightwards pull to finish.

**26. Sube golondrina** ......... 6c+
Probably 7a if you climb direct but it is very escapable on the left of the first bulge.

**27. Chirimoya** ......... 7c
A magnificent curving line of steep pockets with a desperate crux.

**28. Alicantorroca** ......... 8a

**29. Destroyer** ......... 6c+

204

SE facing wall
15m to 20m routes
Best grades - 6a to 7b+

# COSTA BLANCA - Salinas

**Sector Continuidad**

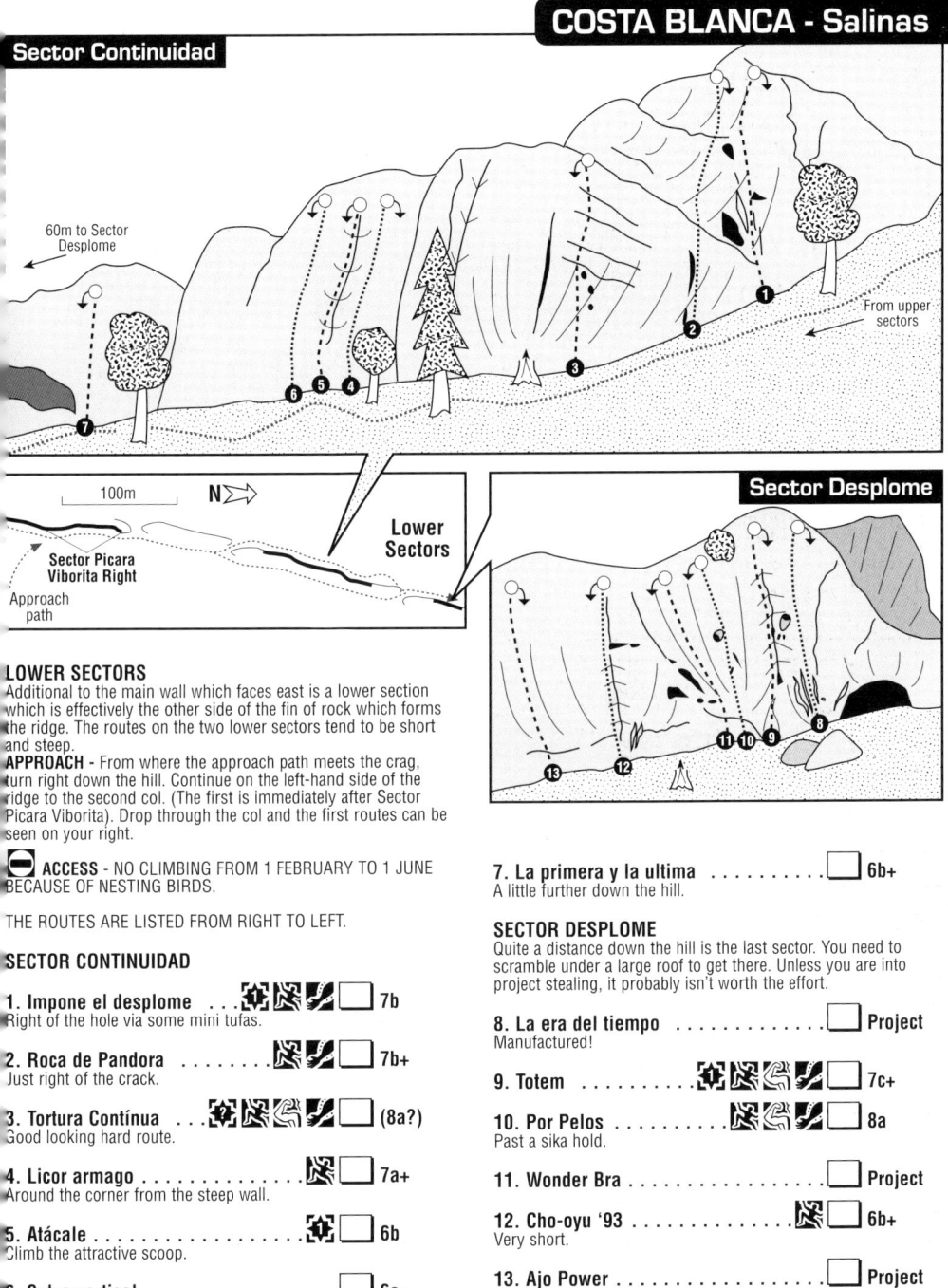

60m to Sector Desplome

**Sector Picara Viborita Right**

Approach path

Lower Sectors

From upper sectors

**Sector Desplome**

## LOWER SECTORS
Additional to the main wall which faces east is a lower section which is effectively the other side of the fin of rock which forms the ridge. The routes on the two lower sectors tend to be short and steep.

**APPROACH** - From where the approach path meets the crag, turn right down the hill. Continue on the left-hand side of the ridge to the second col. (The first is immediately after Sector Picara Viborita). Drop through the col and the first routes can be seen on your right.

**ACCESS** - NO CLIMBING FROM 1 FEBRUARY TO 1 JUNE BECAUSE OF NESTING BIRDS.

THE ROUTES ARE LISTED FROM RIGHT TO LEFT.

## SECTOR CONTINUIDAD

**1. Impone el desplome** .......... 7b
Right of the hole via some mini tufas.

**2. Roca de Pandora** ........ 7b+
Just right of the crack.

**3. Tortura Contínua** ..... (8a?)
Good looking hard route.

**4. Licor armago** ............ 7a+
Around the corner from the steep wall.

**5. Atácale** ................. 6b
Climb the attractive scoop.

**6. Selva vertical** ............... 6a+

**7. La primera y la ultima** ......... 6b+
A little further down the hill.

## SECTOR DESPLOME
Quite a distance down the hill is the last sector. You need to scramble under a large roof to get there. Unless you are into project stealing, it probably isn't worth the effort.

**8. La era del tiempo** ............ Project
Manufactured!

**9. Totem** .......... 7c+

**10. Por Pelos** .......... 8a
Past a sika hold.

**11. Wonder Bra** .................. Project

**12. Cho-oyu '93** ............... 6b+
Very short.

**13. Ajo Power** .................. Project

West facing wall
10m to 15m routes
Best grades - 6b to Project

Nick Wharton below the crux of *Elios* (7a+ - page 210)
Sector Super Heroes, Forada.
Photo: John Wilson

# FORADA

This is a truly brilliant crag which has a mega north facing wall which gives some of the best steep climbing around. The crag is a must for people into steep grade 7s, but it also has some attractive easier routes on the slabby southern side. Pride of place for the routes has to be Sector Super Heroes - a wonderful steep wall of soaring, overhanging pocket-lines. The other sectors on the north side are much the same as Super Heroes except on a smaller scale. The southern side is a totally different proposition with routes at a much friendlier angle and in a beautiful setting with magnificent views. Two sectors have the odd trad route, the rest routes are well bolted with good lower-offs. A 60m route is useful for Sectors Super Heroes and Elecciones.

## ASPECT AND CLIMATE

Apart from the 'soaring overhanging pocket-lines' the other major attraction of this crag is its usefulness in extreme weather. The Forada North Face is a great place to head for if it is hot and also has plenty to go at in wet weather, but it can be unusually cold compared to other crags in the area. In cold weather clever climbers will head straight for the South Face so that while the hard team are freezing themselves to death, in search of a 'big tick' on the North Face, the less ambitious members of the team can sun themselves on the much more pleasant South Face.

## APPROACH

Drive towards Madrid on the N330 from Alicante. After about 30km you will approach the towns of Elda and Petrer. There are three exits from the motorway to these two towns and you need the third one, signed 'Petrer, Elda, Centro Commercial'. Double back right off the exit road (see map below). The road you need to follow is signed 'Xorret de Cali' on red signs with white lettering. Drive along this road for 11km, always following the red signs, until you arrive at the Xorret de Cali. Turn right down a track (signed 'Coto Privado') and follow the dodgy main track over some bad sections to an open area by a small ruin. Double back and continue to another open section, on a rise and park here. Walk down the track with a cable across it, which soon turns into a path. Sector Villanos is on the right. See the close up map on the next page for approaches from here.

**Alternative approach for wet weather or fragile cars** - Follow the road to 'Xorret de Cali' as normal to a turning right, at 4.9km, to Rabosa. Take this and in about 0.5km where there is a track off to the left where the forest starts (there is a sign here for Rabosa (straight on) and a 'Peligro de Incendio' fire warning). Turn left onto the track, which is partially paved, to a junction at 2.1km. The right-hand branch is the main track and shortly passes between brick pillars. Ignore this and take the left-hand, minor track. Follow this for a further 3km to the ruin and eventually the highest car park. This approach is longer but kinder on the car.

## THE ROUTES

The crag was equipped by by Chiri Ros, Isabel Pagan, Pedro Luis, M.Amat, L.Montesinos, José Hernandez, Juan Serrano and others, mostly between 1989 and 1992. There were aid routes here in the 1970s.

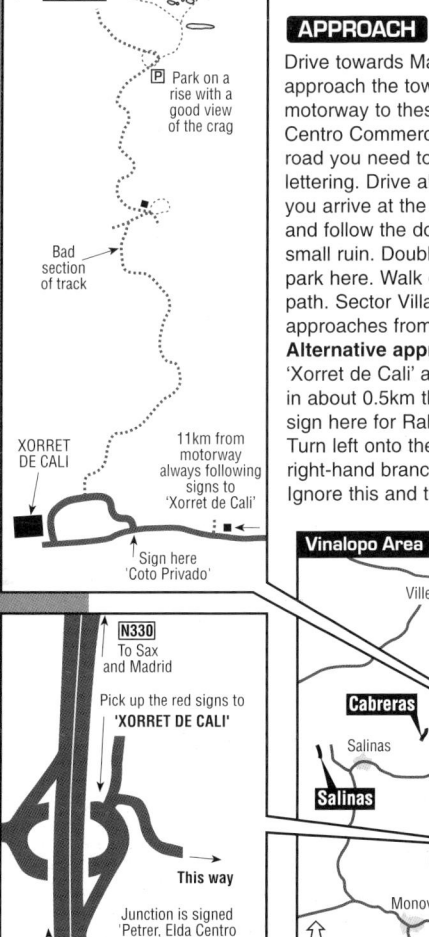

# COSTA BLANCA - Forada

## Sector Villanos

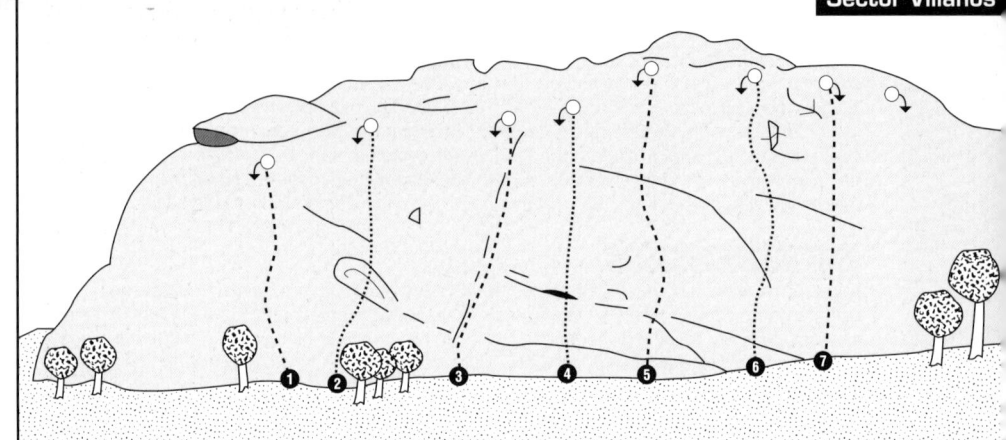

### SECTORS VILLANOS
This is the short wall on the right of the approach walk which has a few technical routes but is not in the same class as the offerings elsewhere.

**1. Joker** .................. 7a
A short, fingery wall.

**2. Pancho Villa** .......... 7a+
A small bulge provides the difficulties on this one.

**3. Doctor No** ............. 7a
The crack line is tricky.

**4. Lutor** ................... 6c+
Steep and crimpy.

**5. Esqueletor** ............. 6c+
More technical wall climbing.

**6. Phantomas** ............. 7a+
The hardest of the bunch.

**7. Barrabas** ............... 6c
The last route on the wall.

There is a random lower-off to the right which may have sprouted a route by the time you read this.

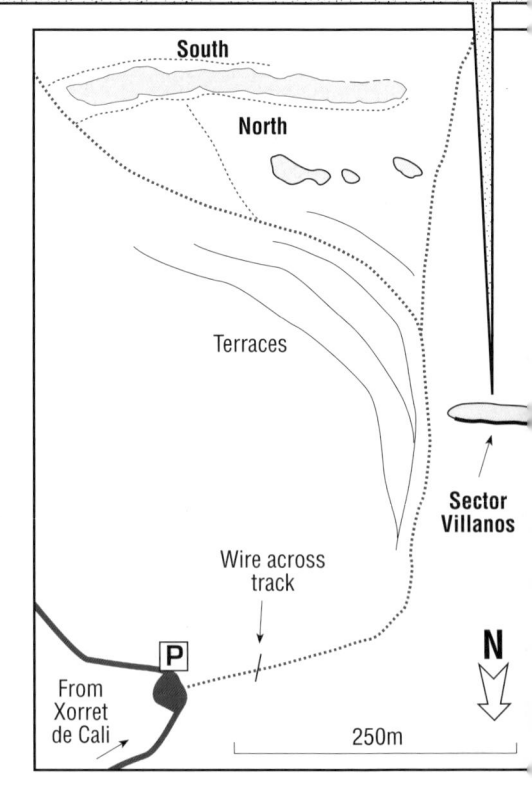

South facing wall
5m to 10m routes
Best grades - 6c to 7a+

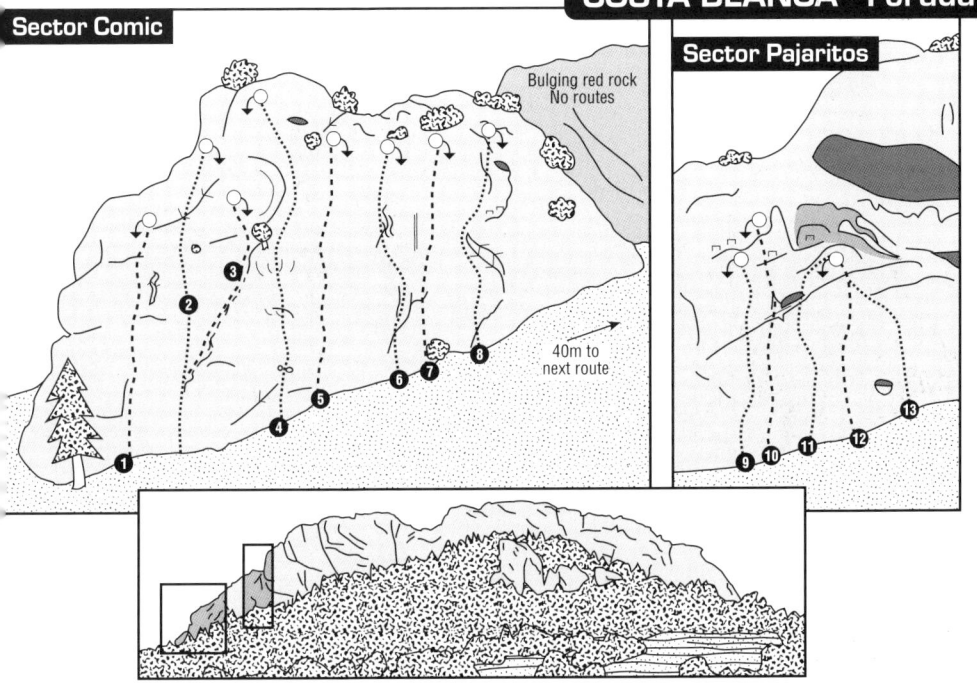

# COSTA BLANCA - Forada

## Sector Comic

Bulging red rock
No routes

40m to next route

## Sector Pajaritos

### SECTOR COMIC
The first section described on the magnificent North Face of Forada is at the extreme left-hand end. The left-hand branch on the approach track passes just under this sector.

**1. El pequeño Franenstein** .......... 6c
Starts just to the right of a huge fir tree.

**2. Mundo mutante** .......... 6c+
Direct above the rightwards-leaning crack.

**3. Pedrusco** .......... 6b+
The crack is very good.

**4. Sara** .......... 6c
A great little climb over two bulges.

**5. Torpedo** .......... 6b+
Less-steep climbing to the right.

**6. El mercenario** .......... 6c+
A bulging wall.

**7. Legionario** .......... 6c

**8. Comic** .......... 5+
Up the left-facing corner.

### SECTOR PAJARITOS
40m up the hill, past some bulging red rock with no routes, is a smaller wall below some large overhangs.

**9. Gorrión** .......... 6a
Quite good fun.

**10. ?** .......... 5+

The next three routes share the same lower-off.

**11. Golondrinas** .......... 6a

**12. Cucú** .......... 6a+
This route can be continued, on natural gear, to the top of the crag.

**13. Periquito** .......... 5

Sector Super Heroes is immediately to the right.

---

North facing wall
5m to 10m routes
Best grades - 5+ to 6c+

Not much sun · 10 min · Vertical · Lower-offs · Windy

# COSTA BLANCA - Forada

## Sector Super Heroes

### SECTOR SUPER HEROES
This is the best sector at Forada, in fact one of the best in the whole Costa Blanca. The climbing is unrelentingly steep but mostly on good pockets and cracks. It can be very cold in Winter but once you start wrestling with these routes you will soon warm up. Finding someone to belay can be tricky though, especially if you are in for a long session.

**1. ?** .......................... (8?)
**32m.** An immense and endless route of 8-something difficulty.

**2. Tundra** .......... 8a+
Pass the dead tree in the break and push on up the steep wall above. An unrelenting **30m** of effort!

**3. Batman** .......... 7b+
Direct over the bulge. Clipping the 4th bolt is challenging.

**4. ?** .......................... (8?)
The left-hand finish to *Batman*. Another hard 8 or a project.

**5. Muscleman** .......... 7b
The bulging pocket line is superb.

**6. Rock 'n Roll Express** .......... 8a
Less good than its neighbours with unpleasant moves.

**7. Radicales libres** .......... 8a+
**32m.** A long sustained route which leads onto the head-wall. Might be 8b.

**8. Thor** .......... 7b+
Intricate and sustained moves. Lower off or attempt *Plasticman*.

**9. Elios** .......... 7a+
The majestic diagonal pocket-line gives a superb pitch. Lots of hard moves broken up with reasonable rests and a distinct crux on the bulge. See photo on page 206.
FA. V.Freire, Santiago (aid) 1974. FFA. M.Amat, Tekila 1991
The only route climbed on the South Face until the late 80s

**10. Guerrero del antifaz** .......... 7b+
Hard climbing on rounded holds.

**11. Spiderman** .......... 7a
Powerful moves on slick buckets.

**12. Starman** .......... 7a
Smaller holds than Spiderman but not as steep and polished.

**13. Plasticman** .......... Project
Pitch 2 to *Thor* is a line of glued-on blobs at the moment.

The passage to the right of this can be used to access the South face but it is awkward with a sack on, but okay for between redpoint sun breaks. A better approach is around the bottom of the fin.

North facing wall
20m to 32m routes
Best grades - 7a to 8a+

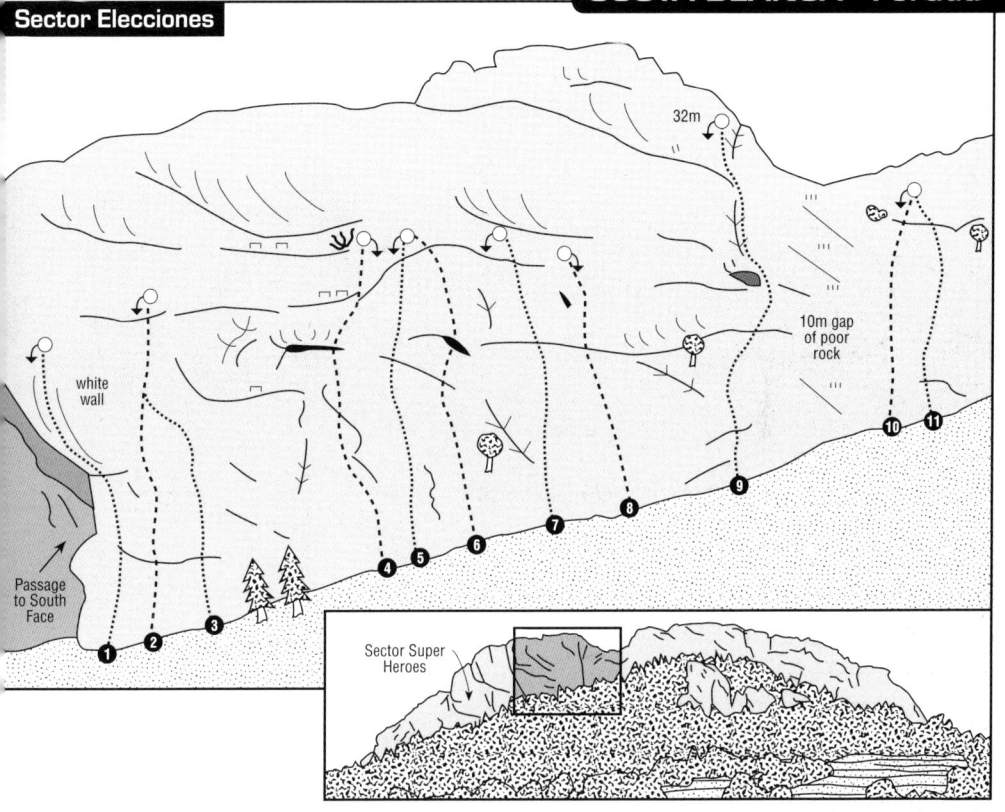

# COSTA BLANCA - Forada

## Sector Elecciones

*(topo diagram labels: 32m; 10m gap of poor rock; white wall; Passage to South Face; Sector Super Heroes)*

## SECTOR ELECCIONES

The section to the right of the diagonal slit is almost as impressive as Sector Super Heroes. It is made up of a series of bulges and open grooves leading to a breakline below a terminally bulging upper wall. Not surprisingly all the routes bale out at this point.

**1. ?** ............................ ?
A very hard project with glued-on holds.

**2. Los patos de la moncloa** ......... 7b+
The white wall direct is excellent.

**3. Cámara Alta** ............. 6c+
The indirect version is much easier.

**4. Disturbio vertical** ........ 6c
A wall and some bulges.

**5. El golfo de la guerra** ........ 6a+
Another bulge-laden line. Locally given 6b+ but it isn't anything like that hard.

**6. La guerra del golfo** ....... 6c
The line is just right of a groove.

**7. Abstención** ........... 6b+
A tricky lower wall.

**8. La fuerza del parabol** ...... 6a
Easy climbing leads to a hard finish past a hole.

**9. Galimatías** ............ 6c+
32m. A long route climbing in and out of the orifice. Highly entertaining.

The next section of rock has no routes. 10m further right is a much shorter wall.

**10. Pictolin** .................... 6a

**11. Sugus** .................... 6a+

North facing wall
15m to 32m routes
Best grades - 6a to 7b+

# COSTA BLANCA - Forada

## Sector Television

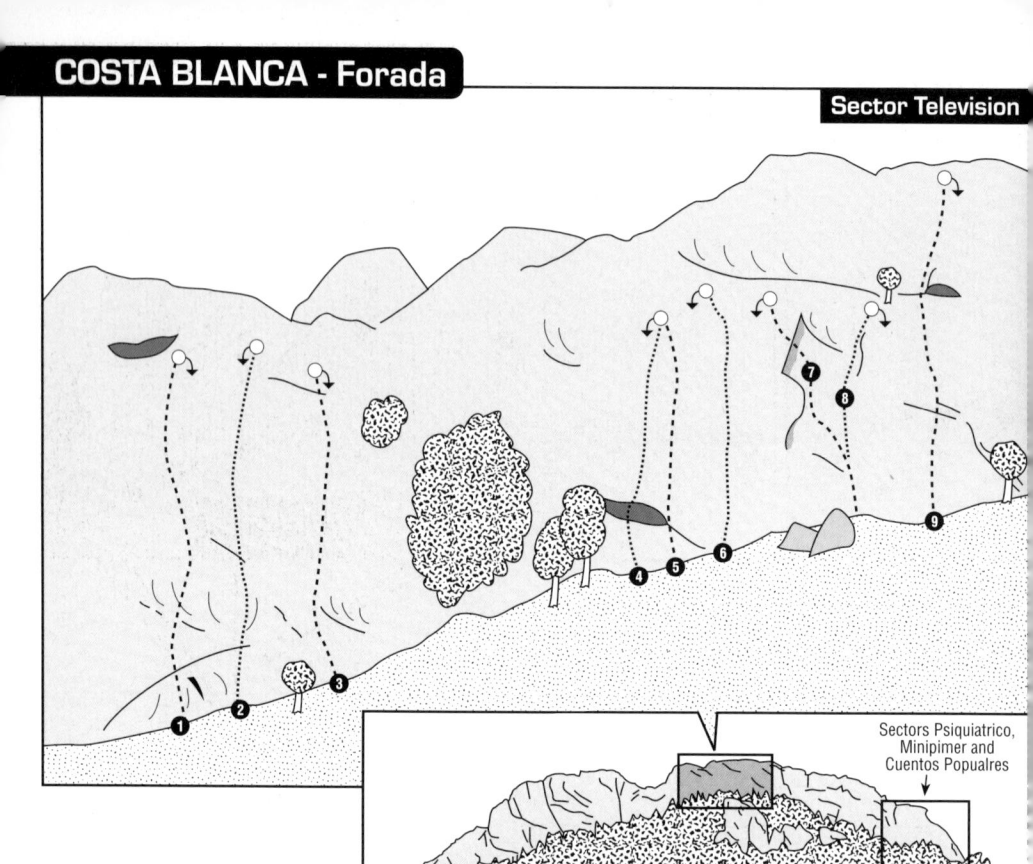

### SECTOR TELEVISION
At the highest point of the Forada ridge, the routes on the North Face become a bit more sporadic.

The first cluster of routes is about 30m right from the Sector Elecciones, just to the left of some BIG ivy.

**1. La calle de ritmo** . . . . . . 6c+
Two bulges. Lower off below a small roof.

**2. Waku-Waku** . . . . . . . . 6c
One larger bulge.

**3. Sesión de tarde** . . . . . . . . 6c
Just right of a small tree.

Further right, past the ivy, the routes begin again by a small roof.

**4. El último mohicano** . . . . . . . 7c
Over the roof on the left.

**5. Quieres que me coma el tigre** 7b+
The roof isn't much easier on its right-hand side.

**6. Bum-Bum** . . . . . . . . . . . . 7a+
A thin wall.

**7. ?** . . . . . . . . . . . . . . . . . . . . . (7a/b)
The large flake/corner.

**8. El precio justo** . . . . . . . . 7a
Start in the same place as the previous route but move right over a bulge, via a crack. The third clip is tricky.

**9. Carta de adjuste** . . . . . . . . 7a
The longest pitch on this wall at **25m**.

North facing wall
15m to 25m routes
Best grades - 6c to 7a

# COSTA BLANCA - Forada

## SECTOR PSIQUIATRICO
About 50m down the hill from the highest point on the ridge, is a short wall with two steep routes on it.

1. **Carne de psiquatrico** ......... 7a
Into a horizontal slot and over the bulge above.

2. **Bloqueo mental** ......... 7b
A harder version to the right.

## SECTOR MINIPIMER
At the very bottom of the ridge is a short wall that might even get some evening sun.

3. **Termomix** ......... 7b
The left-hand line is very technical.

4. **Picadora Mulinex** ......... 7a+
Same start as *Minipimer* but trend right across the wall.

5. **Minipimer** ......... 7a+
Steeper but less sustained than its neighbours.

## SECTOR CUENTOS POPULARES
In front of the main ridge of Forada are two sets of pinnacles. The left-hand (looking at the North Face) pinnacles have no routes but the right-hand set has a few routes on its northern side. It can be reached by hacking through the trees from Sector Psiquiatrico, or direct from the right-hand branch of the approach track (see map on page 208).

6. **Tres cerditos** ......... 6c
7. **Cuentos populares** ......... 7a
8. **Dumbo** ......... 7a+
9. **Pinocho** ......... 6b+
10. **Juan sin miedo** ......... 7a

On the south side of the pinnacle is a steep tufa line.

11. **Las botas de 7 leguas** ......... 6c+

The smaller pinnacle to the left (looking at the North Face) of the main pinnacle, has a solitary route.

12. **Chiquitín** ......... 6b+

North facing wall
10m to 20m routes
Best grades - 6b+ to 7b

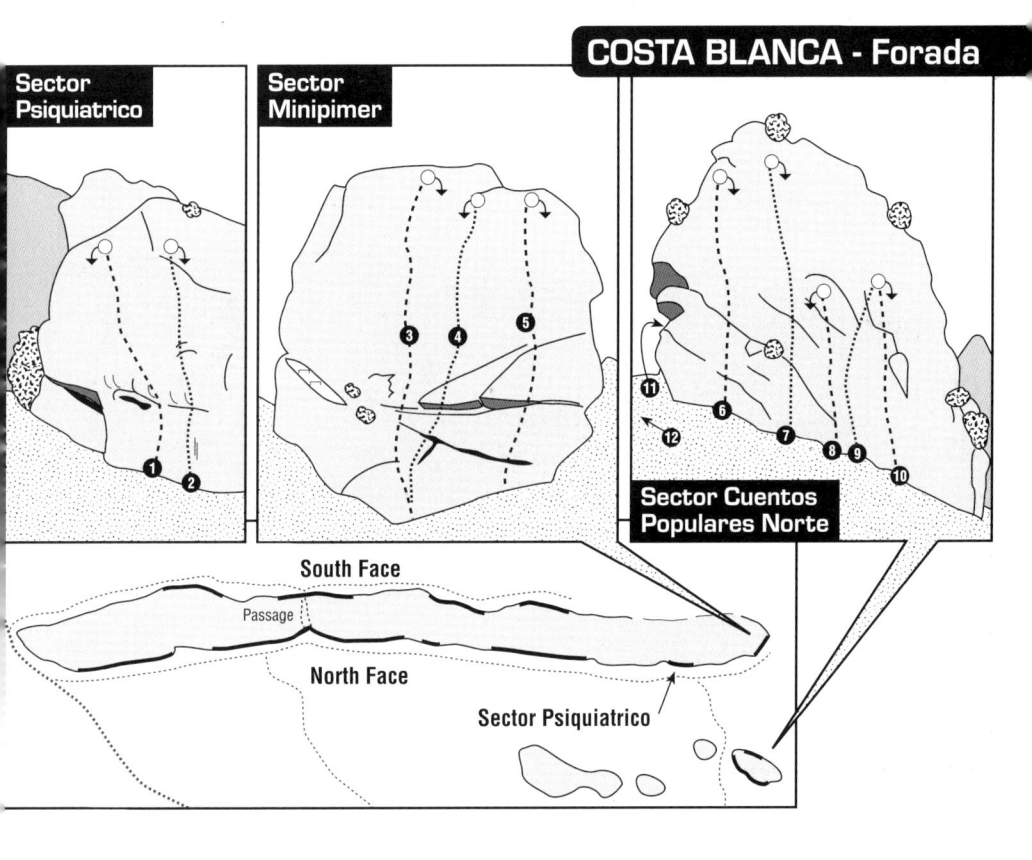

# COSTA BLANCA - Forada

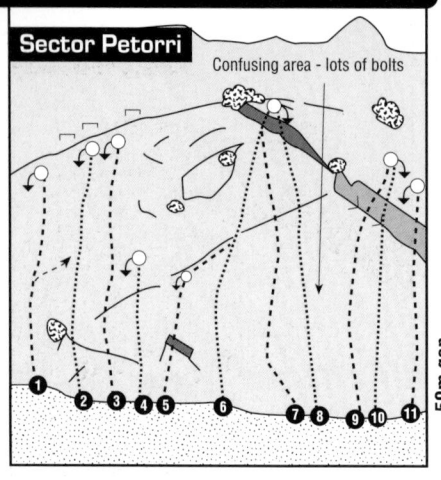

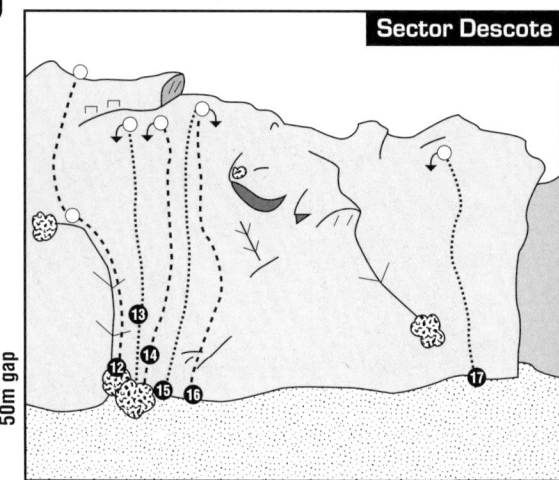

**Sector Petorri**

Confusing area - lots of bolts

50m gap

**Sector Descote**

## FORADA SOUTH FACE
The sunny south face has some very pleasant slab climbing and superb views. It is well worth considering as a venue in its own right even if the grades on the North face put you off. It is becoming a bit polished.

**APPROACH -** The easiest method is to approach via the track which passes under the lowest point of the ridge. Then turn the corner and head up the hill, arriving at Sector Goteta first. You can approach from the other end of the fin. It is even possible to scramble through the hole right of Sector Super Heroes but this is a bit awkward with a sack on.

## SECTOR PETORRI
This is virtually at the highest point of the ridge.

**1. ?** .................... 3+
An easy new route. There is a bolt to the right which connects this and the next route to give a better, and harder, variation.

**2. Bon día** ................ 5
A pleasant slab.

**3. Cursilania** ............. 4
The line of bolts curves rightwards.

**4. ?** ..................... 4+

**5. Fam de gos** ............. 5
There is a lower-off at the bend in the route but originally it continued to the shared lower-off.

**6. Pilar** .................. 5
The direct line is good.

The next section of the slab has a lot of bolts and it is very easy to get confused.

**7. Noche golfa** ............ 6a
Try to climb as direct as possible until you can no longer bare it, then reach left into *Pilar*.

**8. ?** ..................... 6a+
A narrow channel up the slab. If it gets easier then you have switched routes.

**9. Paula** .................. 5+
Climb through a slanting groove.

**10. Tiburón** ............... 5+
The large flake/corner.

**11. ?** .................... (4/5)
The right-hand end of the wall.

## SECTOR DESCOTE
The next climbs are 50m to the right.

**12. Caballari** ............. 4+
A two pitch route, on natural gear.
1) 4, 15m. The corner to a stance with pegs.
2) 4+, 15m. The wall above.
Walk down to the left (looking in).

**13. Marisol** ............... 6a
Just right of the corner.

**14. Freire sin aceite** ..... 6a
Thin moves at half-height give the crux.

**15. ?** .................... 6a+

**16. Mujer furtiva** ......... 6a+

**17. Cosme** ................. 5+
Further right, past a corner.

214 — Lots of sun · 10 min · Slabby · Lower-offs · Windy

South facing slab
15m to 20m routes
Best grades - 3+ to 6a+

ROCKFAX
rockfax.c

## COSTA BLANCA - Forada

### Sector del Forat

### Sector Goteta

**North Face**

**South Face** — Sector Petorri, Sector Descote — Passage — Best approach

## SECTOR DEL FORAT
The exit hole for the passage is in the middle of this wall. The first routes are on the bulging section to the left.

**1. La golondrina** .............. ☐ 6a+
Sustained.

The next three routes share a lower-off.

**2. Mama Ukri** ......... 🌞 ❄ ⚡ ☐ 6b
A tricky wall leading to a hard bulge to finish.

**3. Chorro sin agua** .......... 🌞 ☐ 6a

**4. Sube que es gratis** ...... 🌞 ⛓ ☐ 6a+

**5. Ana** .................... ☐ (A2,5+)?
Bits of gear show the line. It will be quite hard if/when it goes free.

**6. Del Forat** ............ 🌞 ⚡ ☐ 5+
A long, naturally-protected, diagonal line. The hole at half-height is the exit from the through cave next of Sector Super Heroes.

**7. Javier Muñoz** ............ ❄ ☐ 6a+
Short and steep with some awkward moves.

**8. Plutga** ................ 🌞 ⚡ ☐ 5+

## SECTOR GOTETA
Down the hill from the approach cave is an enormous curving roof. Below the right-hand end of this is a clean slab.

**9. Mayaya** ............... 🌞 ☐ 5

**10. Llei dels Maleans** ....... 🌞 ☐ 6a

**11. McFlay** ................ 🌞 ☐ 5
Do I detect some Scottish influence?

**12. Panchuflas** ............ 🌞 ☐ 5+
A shared first bolt with the previous route.

**13. Cristina** ............... 🌞 ☐ 5+
A thin slab with a scoop.

**14. Ligero de Equipaje** ........ ⚡ ☐ 6a
Not much fixed gear.

South facing wall
15m to 20m routes
Best grades - 5 to 6b

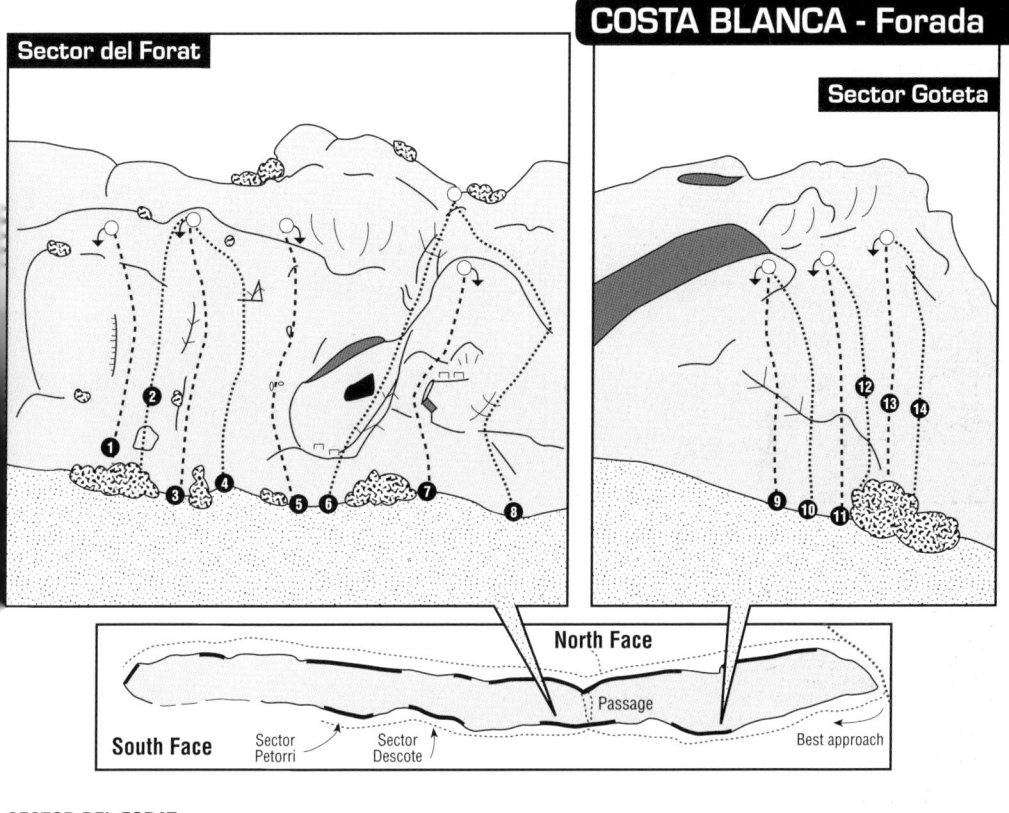

# MALLORCA

Climbing Information . . . . . . . . .218
Area Map . . . . . . . . . . . . . . . . .219
A Brief History . . . . . . . . . . . . . .220
Logistics . . . . . . . . . . . . . . . . . .223
Crag Selection Table . . . . . . . . .224

Andratx . . . . . . . . . . . . . . . . . .226
Santa Ponça . . . . . . . . . . . . . .229
S'estret . . . . . . . . . . . . . . . . . .231
Valldemossa . . . . . . . . . . . . . .236
Sa Gubia . . . . . . . . . . . . . . . . .240
Fraguel . . . . . . . . . . . . . . . . . .251
Port Sóller . . . . . . . . . . . . . . . .255
Ca'n Nyic (Torrella) . . . . . . . . . .258
Es Queixal . . . . . . . . . . . . . . . .260
Alaró . . . . . . . . . . . . . . . . . . . .262
Las Perxes (Caimari) . . . . . . . . .267
Creveta . . . . . . . . . . . . . . . . . .270
S'on Xanquete . . . . . . . . . . . . .274
Betlem . . . . . . . . . . . . . . . . . .277
Cala Magraner . . . . . . . . . . . . .280
Tijuana (Santanyi) . . . . . . . . . . .285

# Mallorca
## by Alan James

Dave Cross on
the magnificent *Buf!* (7a - page 266)
on Sector Chorreras at Alaró on Mallorca.
Photo: Lewis Grundy

# MALLORCA

The wonderful rock and mountains of Mallorca are now well known to most climbers and the Island has established itself as a favourite winter-sun destination. Several guidebooks have put an end to ground-up grade guessing, and scribbled approach descriptions, which used to be the norm back in the early 90s. Now it is possible to dedicate your entire trip to climbing and exploring this wonderful and beautiful island which is both compact and vast at the same time. You can drive to a crag on the other side of the island in under an hour and then lose yourself in a great sea of rock. However it is the potential of Mallorca which leaves the deepest impression. For every brilliant line there are another ten waiting to be done. There is still plenty to keep anyone busy, from the huge variety of Sa Gubia to the 30m pumping-tufas of Fraguel, from the barely-tapped splendour of Alaró to the intricate delights of Creveta. It is perhaps the atmosphere and the setting which provide the greatest attraction: beautiful cliffs of perfect rock, set amidst some majestic mountains with weather that you would expect in the Mediterranean. The potential of Mallorca has barely been touched, but it is already up there amongst the best.

In this edition of the book we have added a few new destinations and updated the information for all the other areas, including 26 new topos. Thanks to the hard work of Nick Verney we have established the correct names and spellings of several old areas which has resulted in a few crags changing names. This isn't to try and con you into thinking that there are more new crags, it is simply to make the book more accurate and in line with the local opinion. Nick has also written a short historical section in conjunction with Miquel Riera and Carlos Raimundo, two of the most prolific climbers on the island.

## CLIMBING INFORMATION

### Access
Access is a sensitive issue in Mallorca. The boulders at Boquer, the clean walls of Calvía and the steep tufas of Ca'n Torrat have all been lost to an uncooperative land owners and there are others which could go the same way if people aren't careful with car parking and following approach paths to crags. Please use all the described approaches and avoid antagonising locals. Also please avoid visiting any banned crag, especially Boquer and Calvía. Just because they are listed in previous editions of this guidebook, and in other guidebooks doesn't mean its okay to go there. Trespassing onto these crags will only make the likelihood of climbing ever being allowed again an even more remote possibility.

### Grades
Grades always used to be a bit of an oddity in Mallorca. It was not uncommon to find routes that were three or four notches undergraded. This was a consequence of the local climbers, for their own reasons, trying to establish a different scale than used elsewhere. The influence of visiting climbers has resulted in the grades being brought into line with those used elsewhere although overall the grades are probably still a touch on the hard side. See page 10 for a conversion table.

### Gear
For most of the routes all you will need is a long 60m rope and 15 or so quickdraws. A 50m rope will suffice for many routes but it is always better to be safe with a longer one. Some routes at Sa Gubia require abseil descent and using doubled 50m ropes will probably be more pleasant for most climbers. These same routes tend to offer the few traditional challenges on the Island. There are in fact only 4 trad routes listed but one of them is the classic *Gubia Normal,* or *Albahida* as it is more correctly known, and those with this on their tick list should bring a small rack of gear. For more information on gear see page 8. There is actually quite a lot of trad climbing on the island. The East Face of Alaró, Puig Major and Sa Calobra are the main areas.

### Missing Bolts
In Mallorca the bolts are sometimes removed from routes by the local climbers. This is done because one or all of the bolts on the route may be unsafe. The intention is to replace all the bolts on these routes but sometimes this takes a while.

## New Routes
Because there is so much potential climbing on the Island, the locals are more than happy for visiting climbers to put up their own routes, in fact they will go much further and positively help you in this. If you do wish to climb new routes then contact either of the two shops Foracorda or Es Refugi at the addresses shown in the small adverts.

## Other Books
*Guia de Escalada de Baleares* by Lluis Vallcaneras (1996) - English and German introductions topos and slightly dodgy crag approach maps.
*Rock Climbs in Mallorca* by Chris Craggs (2000) - English text descriptions for most destinations.

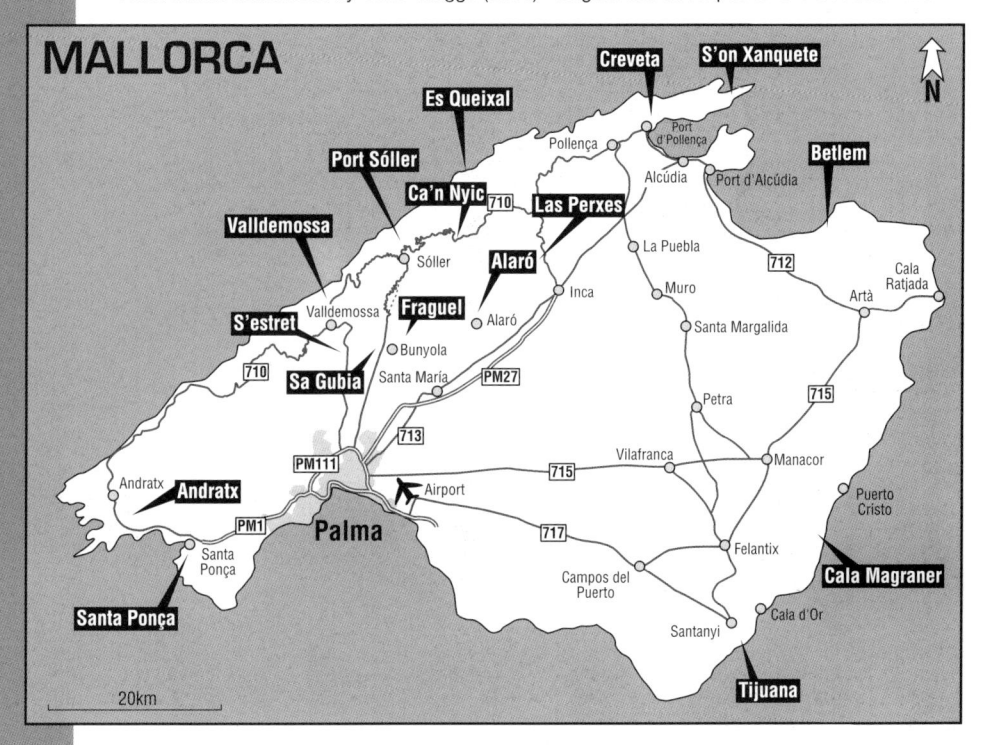

## Other Areas
On an island covered with climbable rock it comes as no surprise to discover that there are several other developed areas not documented in this book.

**Sa Forada** - A handful of mainly-hard routes down the coast from Valldemossa at the famous headland with a hole through it.

**Sa Coma** - A small crag with 4 routes only above the village of Sa Coma on the East Coast.

**Castell de Sanctueri (Felanitx)** - Eleven routes in the 7a and above grades near the castle above the town of Felanitx.

**Cala Figuera and Cala Llombarts** - Two small coves near Tijuana both with a handful of routes but old bolts.

There are also routes at Cap Formentor and Sa Calobra and I also have reports of a crags near Pollença and Almedra. Brief notes on approaches to these crags are on the ROCKFAX web site. If you do visit one of these crags then please write and let us know your improved description. Any maps or crag topos will also be gratefully received and such information will be put straight onto the web site so, if you are planning a trip, check rockfax.com/mallorca/ first.

# A BRIEF HISTORY

**By Nick Verney**

Climbing came late to Mallorca. Franco and then seaside package holidays ensured that it had never really been seen as a potential climbing destination. However, by the early 1970s a small group of climbers was working away, opening up the first routes on Mallorca. Almost always climbing artificially, climbers such as Guillem Martí, Bernat Torres, Tolo Quetglas, Joan Riera, Juan Valiente, and Adolfo Gregorio opened routes on nearly all the major walls of the island - Sa Gubia, the east face of Alaró, Puig Major, and in the Torrent de Pareis near Sa Calobra. Perhaps foremost amongst these names is Adolfo Gregorio, who after his return from university in Madrid began opening up the hardest routes on the island at that time.

In 1978 a new force arrived on the Mallorcan climbing scene. Repeating the hardest routes in record times, and freeing many of the most famous sections, Jaume Payeras started a revolution in Mallorcan climbing. Only 16 years old, climbing in rigid boots and on traditional protection, he, and an even younger Miquel Riera, amongst others, startled the climbing community with free ascents of routes. Climbing free "because free-climbing is more difficult," they began to open up new routes all over the island.

It was on a trip to the mainland whilst on military service that Jaume first saw a route equipped with bolts, and not long after his return the first bolted route - and his last new route - was completed. Although not of very great difficulty technically, *Seis Pelas* at Sa Gubia marked the beginning of a new generation of Mallorcan climbing. Traditional routes continued to be done by people such as Joan Riera and Tolo Quetglas, but it was with the new bolted routes that Mallorca's potential began to be realised.

Initially progress was slow. Everything had to be drilled by hand, and between the small band of climbers consisting - amongst others - of Miquel Riera, Alfonso Fitor, Eduardo Moreno and Carlos Raimundo, perhaps only 15 new routes would be equipped in a year. However, grades increased bit by bit, and soon the first 7as, and 7bs were completed - all on the large boulders below Alaró. By the end of the 1980s a new force was at work. 'Los Mexicanos' - otherwise known as Miquel Riera, Carlos Raimundo, Xisco Meca, Pepe Lopez, Juan Simonet and Micki Palmer - had given up everything to equip the huge amounts of virgin rock. The drill had arrived, and areas such as Tijuana, Port Sóller, Alaró, Sa Gubia and Valldemossa began to get developed. And then Fraguel was found...

Named after the children's TV series, as both feature large numbers of stupid people hanging around big rocks, Fraguel was stumbled upon by accident, and quickly became the epicentre for hard Mallorcan climbing - and one of Mallorca's worst-kept secrets. Under the influence of Laurent Jacob, one of the main protagonists at Buoux, and the author of such routes as *L'homme programmé* and most of the grade 8s at Fraguel, it was soon one of, if not the hardest sports crag in Spain. According to legend, a generator had to be lowered down the cliff to provide power for the spotlights and sound system at its inauguration party.

Miquel Riera on *Agent Orange* (8b - page 259), Ca'n Nyic (Torrella). Photo: Micki Palmer

Luís Alfonso climbing *Fes el que pugis* (7a+ - page 253) at Fraguel. Photo: Biel Santandreu

The early 1990s were a busy time in Mallorca. Los Mexicanos continued working away, developing more and more areas. The Pollença club was founded around 1990 and started developing the northern areas, such as Creveta, and later, Son Xanquete. Climbers from Artà, Manacor and Inca began equipping routes, giving us Cala Magraner, and adding routes to Las Perxes and Alaró. Years ahead of other areas in Spain in terms of hard, seriously overhanging routes, more and more foreign climbers began coming to Mallorca in search of warm, sunny climbing, many of them often leaving behind new additions.

And then, around 1995, it all slowed down. Many of Los Mexicanos gave up climbing and much of the impetus behind new routing was lost. New routes continued to be done, and new areas developed by people such as Jerry Castañeda, Llorenc Rosal, Biel Sureda - to name but a few - but not at the same rate as the years before. People such as Carlos Raimundo and Dani Andrada, on his frequent trips across from the mainland, began finishing off the hardest remaining projects. Essentially though, until around 1999 it was a case of plugging the gaps and polishing off the remaining projects. Often new crags were found, but lost due to landowners refusing to grant permission - a bigger, steeper version of Fraguel somewhere near Calvià - covered in tufas - was lost as it was on private land.

Even existing crags haven't escaped the problems with landowners. In Mallorca there is no such thing as a public right of way, and with increasing numbers of climbers in Mallorca, confrontations have become more and more common. Nonetheless, the last couple of years have been busy. A new wave of climbers have been hard at work equipping new crags all over the island, and adding new sectors to existing crags. Bouldering has taken off in a big way, with the ubiquitous Miquel Riera and others such as David Torres putting up some of the hardest problems in Spain. The scene is currently buzzing. It seems that every week new routes are being put up, and there is no shortage of available rock. Alaró, Andratx and the areas around Artà and Cap Formentor are the obvious areas, but the real gems waiting to be developed lie around the coastline, such as the legendary Cove De Ses Bruxes in the North of the island. As yet, many of the giant walls that exist on the island have barely any routes - traditional or bolted - on them, though people are beginning to gear themselves up for the challenges that they offer. It is only a matter of time before Mallorca needs a guidebook to itself.

Gràcies a tothom que m'ha ajudat amb aquesta historia - sobretot Carlos Raimundo i Miquel Riera - i també a tots els escaladors i escaladores de Mallorca amb qui m'ho he passat de puta mare.

# Alternative Mallorca
**Holidays Designed for You with Care**

**Villas & Apartments**
**Deià, Sóller and Pollença**
Tel : 0113 2786862
www.alternativemallorca.com
(See main advert on page 6)

## terracottages.co.uk

Holidays in Spain and Mallorca
Visit www.terracottages.co.uk
For a great selection of holiday accommodation
**Villas, Country Houses, Cottages, Apartments**

*Phone Stu 01695 624143*
SPANISH COSTAS, MALLORCA
EL CHORRO, COSTA DAURADA

**Car Hire**

## FORACORDA
muntanya i escalada

# you set the limit

The best equipment for every need and our advice according to your experience. In Foracorda you set the limits

If you need information about new sectors and routes, don't hesitate to contact us.

Carrer Miquel Marqués, 20.   07005 - Palma de Mallorca.   Tel/Fax (971) 46 30 04

## ES REFUGI

**ESPECIALISTES EN ARTICLES DE MUNTANYA, CAMPING, ESQUI I ESCALADA**

**¡T'EQUIPEM PER L'AVENTURA!**

Vía Sindicat, 21 - Pati
07002 Ciutat de Mallorca
Tel: 971 716 731
Fax: 971 718 597
refugi@detailsport.es

**Palma City Centre**

= 1 way streets

Foracorda
Miquel Marqués
Train Station
Park
Aragó
Cinema
Corte Ingles
From ring road
Avingudes
Pl. Espanya
Es Refugi
Syndicat
P
From sea front road
Cathedral
Pl. Major

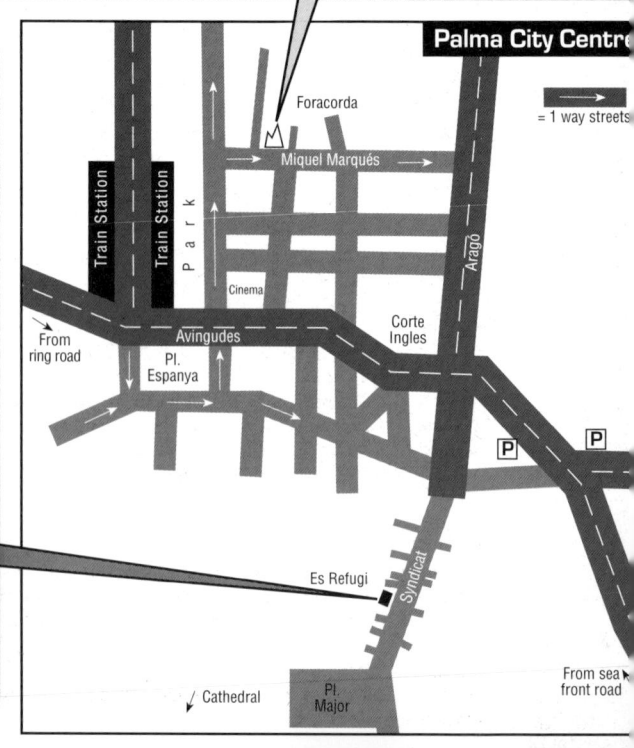

# MALLORCA LOGISTICS

More on the ROCKFAX web site at - rockfax.com/mallorca

## WHEN TO GO

The best time to visit Mallorca is in the Spring when the temperature will be pleasant and it is likely to be dry. Winter can be cold but you could get lucky and many people have had great holidays here over Christmas and New Year. If it rains then there are less options than the Costa Blanca but you can still often find dry rock on the east coast crags (Betlem, Cala Magraner and Tijuana). Autumn is the stormy season and, although the temperature will be fine, you could have problems with dripping tufas on certain crags although there is still likely to be plenty to do and full-week wash-outs are an extreme rarity. In the Summer it is too hot and expensive. It is worth remembering that Mallorca has the most north facing crags in this book which can be good options in hot spells although most only have routes in the higher grades.

## FLIGHTS

Palma is a popular package holiday destination and there are loads of charter flights leaving from most major European airports at every conceivable time of day, throughout the year. Prices vary from ultra-cheap £50 specials to £200+ in the most popular times. The best place to buy charters is from one of the many low-cost flight shops now in existence. Local ones (hence local phone calls) advertise in the yellow pages under 'Travel Agents and Tour Operators'. National ones advertise in the travel pages of the broadsheet newspapers. It is always worth at least two calls since prices, and availability, can vary dramatically. Palma is also on the destination list of EasyJet which means you can get bargain flights at off-peak times and reasonable value ones at popular times with the added advantage of being able to book your outward and return flight separately (www.easyjet.com). There are also plenty of other bargains to be had on the Internet these days.

## GETTING AROUND

A hire car is advisable for climbing in Mallorca. There is public transport from Palma but most people will need to speak good Spanish and avoid some of the more distant destinations to take advantage of it. Often you will be left with a long walk, or a difficult hitch, to get to the crag. The tourist information offices have good information about the buses, and they nearly all go from the area around the train stations. The most accessible crags are Port Sóller, Sa Gubia, Valldemossa and S'estret. Santanyi, Fraguel and Alaró are possible over the weekend.

For those who hire a car it is best to avoid the slow, hairpin-ridden roads in the mountains, unless you want a scenic trip. The longer, straighter roads to the south are a better option. A toll tunnel has been built from Bunyola to Sóller which is a bonus for those wishing to reach the crags north of the mountains.

## ACCOMMODATION

The most popular option for accommodation in Mallorca is to take advantage of the villas and apartments designed for the heavy Summer tourist trade. Package holidays can offer very good value but you have to be careful on Mallorca since you usually won't be able to choose your accommodation base and you are likely to end up a long away from the main climbing spots. Hiring a large villa is usually the most attractive option especially for those in a large group (6 to 10) since then it will offer remarkably good value. You may not get much use of the swimming pool but San Miguel's on the balcony, while the sun sets are close to an unbeatable experience after a good day's climbing. There are also plenty of apartments available outside package holidays and these represent good value for couples and small groups. Check some of the adverts to the left. There is an updated list, and more information, on the ROCKFAX web site at rockfax.com/mallorca/mlca_accom.html

## SHOPS

There are large supermarkets in most major towns. Opening times for most shops in Mallorca are 10am to 1:30 pm and 4pm to 8pm. Supermarkets stay open over the lunch break. Most shops will be shut on national holidays and many will be shut on Sundays.

### Climbing Shops

There are two climbing shops in Palma which are run by local climbers. They are both advertised opposite.

| MALLORCA | PAGE | No. of ROUTES | ↓VS ↓4 | VS 4 | HVS 5 | E1 6a | E2 6b | E3 6c | E4 7a | E5 7b | E6 7c | E7 8a↑ | Sport Routes | Other styles of climbing | Some Multi-Pitch |
|---|---|---|---|---|---|---|---|---|---|---|---|---|---|---|---|
| ANDRATX | 226 | 16 | | | 3 | 4 | 5 | | 1 | 1 | 1 | 1 | Sport | | |
| SANTA PONÇA | 229 | 7 | | | 1 | 1 | | 2 | 3 | | | | Sport | | |
| S'ESTRET | 231 | 26 | | 4 | 5 | 1 | 2 | | 5 | | 4 | 3 | Sport | Bouldering | |
| VALLDEMOSSA | 236 | 46 | | 3 | 8 | 6 | 12 | 4 | 6 | 5 | 2 | | Sport | | |
| SA GUBIA | 240 | 93 | 1 | 4 | 8 | 26 | 28 | 13 | 9 | 11 | 1 | 2 | Sport | Trad | ✓ |
| FRAGUEL | 251 | 51 | | 1 | 3 | 4 | 4 | 6 | 4 | 8 | 10 | 11 | Sport | | ✓ |
| PORT SÓLLER | 255 | 25 | | | | 2 | 6 | 6 | 3 | 3 | | | Sport | | |
| C'AN NYIC (Torrella) | 258 | 11 | | | 1 | 1 | 1 | 3 | 1 | 1 | 2 | 1 | Sport | | |
| ES QUEIXAL | 260 | 13 | | | 3 | 4 | 2 | 2 | 1 | | | | Sport | | |
| ALARÓ | 262 | 45 | | 1 | 4 | 8 | 4 | 4 | 9 | 10 | 5 | | Sport | | ✓ |
| LAS PERXES (Caimari) | 267 | 27 | | 2 | 2 | 2 | 3 | 2 | 3 | 2 | 4 | 7 | Sport | Bouldering | |
| CREVETA | 270 | 37 | | 5 | 4 | 8 | 11 | | 5 | 4 | | | Sport | | |
| S'ON XANQUETE | 274 | 14 | | | 2 | | 1 | 1 | 6 | | 1 | 2 | Sport | | |
| BETLEM | 277 | 20 | | | 2 | 3 | 6 | 3 | 5 | 1 | | | Sport | | |
| CALA MAGRANER | 280 | 58 | 1 | 3 | 10 | 13 | 7 | 9 | 10 | 2 | 2 | 1 | Sport | | |
| TIJUANA (Santanyi) | 285 | 35 | | 1 | 3 | 4 | 3 | | 7 | 6 | 9 | 2 | Sport | | |

| Approach walk | Sunshine or shade | Access restrictions | Dry in the rain | Windy and exposed | SUMMARY |
|---|---|---|---|---|---|
| 10 min to 15 min | Sun and Shade | | Dry in the rain | | Recently developed area with two distinct sections. One steep, sheltered and shady cave with good 6b to very hard routes, and one beautifully positioned, sunny and slabby area which only has a handful of climbs. Massive potential for the future. |
| 2 min | Morning | | | | Small isolated buttress situated over the town of Santa Ponça. Only worth a look in the 7a and above grades and most of the routes have a savage reputation. |
| 2 min to 10 min | Sun and Shade | | Dry in the rain | | An area with three separate sections. A wildly steep quarry wall with only hard routes but plenty to go at in the rain or when you need shade, a small sector with a few easy routes and sun in the afternoon, and one of the most extensive bouldering areas on the Island. Something for everyone. |
| Roadside to 2 min | Afternoon | | | | Accessible and popular roadside crag with a good spread of grades. Famous overhang above the road and attractive upper sector. Excellent crag for an airport day although the frequent passing cars can be an annoying distraction. |
| 20 min | Sun and Shade | | | Windy | Largest and best crag on Mallorca. Routes of all grades up to 7b including some superb fully-bolted, multi-pitch climbs and one great long traditional classic. Always possible to find sun or shade although the shady stuff won't be much good on very hot days. Slightly old gear on some routes. |
| 15 min | Morning | | Dry in the rain | Windy | The most important higher grade crags on the island with a stunning set of hard tufa climbs. Easier routes are also worthwhile. Can get very cold after the sun has gone but will give cool climbing in the hotter months. |
| 5 min | Afternoon | Restrictions | Dry in the rain | | A beautifully situated crag with a small selection of routes. Excellent cave with steep '6c to 7c routes. Dry and sheltered in bad weather. Access problems due to building work mean visits are best at weekends only however the work should be finished in the near future. |
| 10 min | Evening | | | Windy | Beautifully situated area in the mountains. Easy to tick in a day, unless you tackle the few harder climbs. Three excellent 6a to 6c routes. Can be a bit cold and exposed. Called 'Torrella' in the last books. |
| 25 min | Morning | | | Windy | Isolated tower in beautiful cove on the north coast. A long approach drive and exhausting, and tricky, approach walk make it a big effort. The few routes don't take full advantage of the potential of the face, however the setting will make it a rewarding experience for those wanting to get off the beaten track. |
| 15 min to 20 min | Afternoon | | | Windy | Major crag with an unbelievable potential. Currently three sectors with fantastic routes across the grade range. A 'must' for those who like tufa climbing in one of the most dramatic settings of any crag on Mallorca. The great restaurant can finish off a memorable day if you aren't too tired. |
| 5 min | Sun and Shade | | | Windy | Two small crags in a sheltered valley with easy access. An ultra-steep cave with brilliant and desperate routes which is sheltered and dry in bad weather. Also has some hard all-weather bouldering. A smaller buttress with easier routes is also worth a look. Called 'Caimari' in the last books. |
| 20 min | Afternoon | | | | Superb and well-positioned slab with a good spread of mid-grade routes up to 6c. Slightly exposed to the wind and very wearing on the finger tips. Recent additions include a set of superb vertical routes on the walls to the side of the main slab. |
| 10 min | Evening | | Dry in the rain | Windy | Two small blob-covered walls in a picturesque setting on Cap Formentor. Some great steep routes with weird stalactite moves but painful holds and sharp rock can make it hard work. Only for those operating at 7a and above. Sheltered from the rain but not from the wind. Shady for most of the day. |
| 2 min to 10 min | Evening | | Dry in the rain | | Delightful slabby buttress on the west coast with some excellent routes across the 6a to 6c range. Faces north but gets evening sun and probably doesn't offer much cool shade in the hotter months. Often has better weather when it is raining in the mountains. |
| 15 min | Lots of sun | | | | Interesting area by the sea. Good selection of short routes (grades 4 to 7a) and an impressive cave for the harder stuff. A bit of a suntrap but nice for swimming. Some bolts are old. Often has better weather when it is raining in the mountains. |
| 5 min | Lots of sun | | | | Superb sea cliff in a great position but usually a long drive from the accommodation centres. Most routes have steep undercut starts and technical upper sections. Very good sunbathing but also a suntrap. The best bet for good weather when it is raining elsewhere. Called 'Santanyi' in the last books. |

# ANDRATX

Andratx is another typical Mallorcan crag - a vast potential but as yet with only a handful of quality routes. The main face, which is of a similar size to the West Face of Alaró, will offer some major routes in the future, but at present the developed climbing is on the extreme left-hand end and on an excellent lower buttress. The main area of interest is a steep tufa-laden cave with several superb hard challenges and a couple of decent easier routes up the walls in between. There are some projects here and potential for a few even harder routes but there won't be a vast number of new routes on this section. Further left the cliff weaves its way down the hillside above Andratx but as yet only one tiny section has been developed. The higher walls have a beautiful aspect and provide some valuable easier routes. This is the area of major potential since 500m further up the hillside the cliff is nearly 100m tall with superb looking, solid rock.

## APPROACH

Leave Palma on the main A1 towards Andratx. Follow this to its end and at the roundabout follow keep following signs for 'Andratx'. (NOTE - the crag at Santa Ponça is straight on at this roundabout see page 229). After emerging from the second tunnel (a long one) you will see the huge face in front of you. Continue for 2.4 km to the brow of a hill which is half way between the 27km and 28km posts. Just after this turn right into a small road and park **before** the gate (which may be open but could also be closed and locked). Walk up the road towards some buildings and a locked gate on the left.

**For the Upper Wall -** Walk up a short ledge above the buildings and pick up a well-cairned path which wanders up the hillside. At the top walk rightwards to the climbs which are on the first bit of rock you encounter.

**For the Main Cave -** Crawl through a little gated-hole in the fence and follow the main track directly to the cave.

## ASPECT AND CLIMATE

The main cave is very well sheltered and should give some dry climbing in light rain. It faces north and gets no sun.

The upper wall is beautifully situated facing south, with views towards the coast. It is very sunny but is also exposed to the wind and rain.

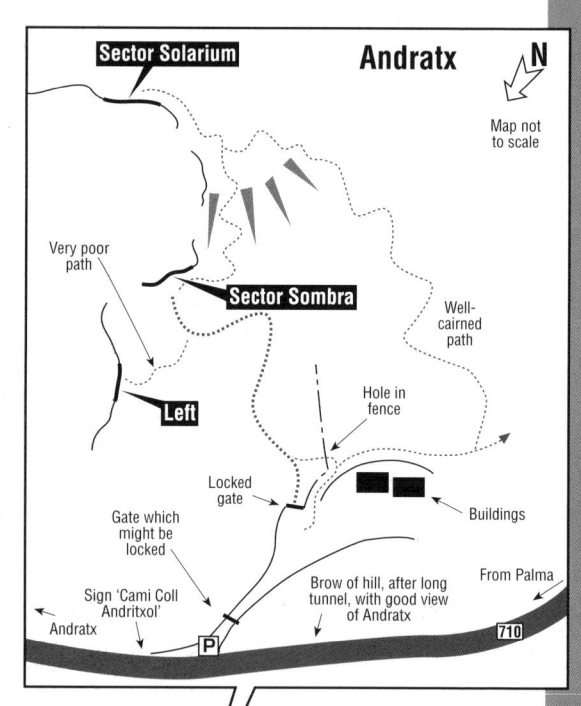

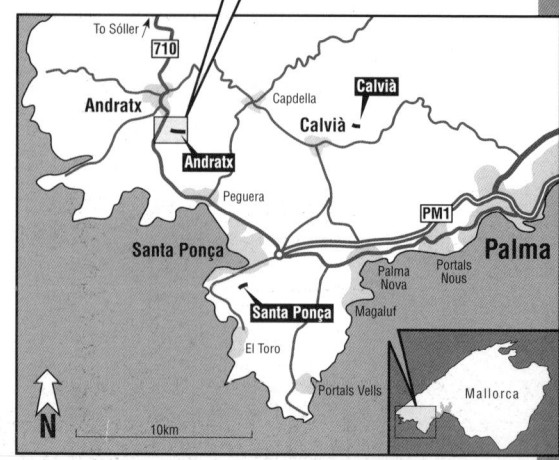

# MALLORCA - Andratx

**Sector Sombra**

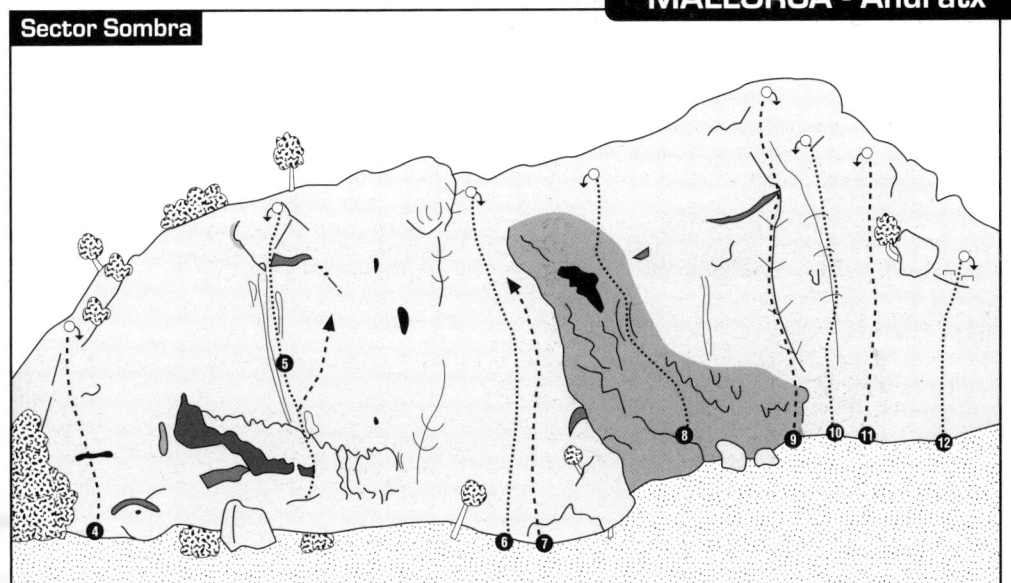

## LEFT
The first climbs described are on a short wall to the left of the main cave. It is reached by a very indistinct path which heads off from the main track about 30m before the cave.

**1. ?** .................... 6c
The left-hand line has some tricky moves in the middle section.

**2. ?** .................... 6a
The middle line past an undercut flake.

**3. ?** .................... 5
Just left of the corner. Only short.

## SECTOR SOMBRA
The main climbing is on the steep wall with caves, at the top of the track.

**4. Alacran** .................... 6a
Cracked wall just right of bushes.

**5. ?** .................... 7a
An impressive and unlikely line up the tufa. A right-hand finish has been bolted but is still a project.

**6. Chúpamela** .................... 6b
The left-hand line on the rib gives the best mid-grade route on the crag.

**7. Chúpamela por la derecha** .................... 6b
A little bit too close to its neighbour.

**8. ?** .................... Project
This one will be superb.

**9. ?** .................... 7c
The steep groove gives a magnificent pitch which looks a lot harder than 7c.

**10. ?** .................... (7a/b)
Great climbing up the long rib right of the groove.

**11. Soledad** .................... (6b/c)
Wall left of perched block.

**12. Diós no puedo** .................... (6a/b)
Poor short route on the right-hand end of the wall.

North facing cave
10m to 15m routes
Best grades - 6b to 7c

# MALLORCA - Andratx

## Sector Solarium

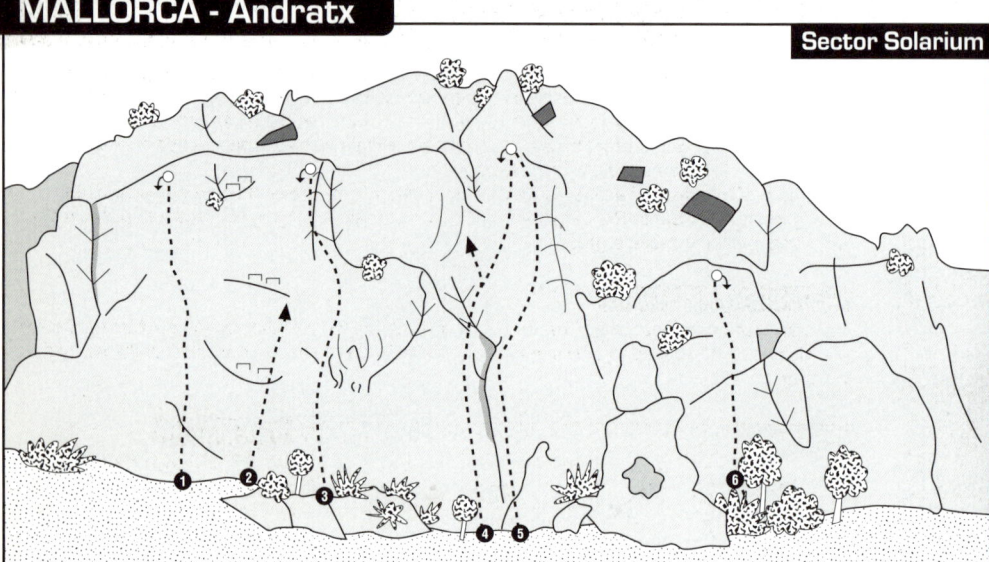

### SECTOR SOLARIUM
The sunny sector is higher up the hillside with magnificent views southwards over Santa Ponça. It is actually the extreme left-hand end of the huge face which you may well have spotted on the approach, if you came from Palma.

**1. Lúcifer** .................. 6a
Easy slabs leading to a steeper finish.

**2. ?** ...................... ?
2 bolts leading to nothing?

**3. Metállica** .................. (6a/b)
Climb over a bulge then move up the rib left of a short corner.

**4. Snoopy** .................. 5
Start left of the flake and climb the wall before moving right across a groove. there might be a left-hand finish as well.

**5. Mafalda** 19./12/04 .......... 5
Start up the chunky flake then step onto the delicate rib.

**6. Scooby doo** ............ 6a
A short route up the slabby wall right of a loose-looking pinnacle.

Further right is an impressive snaking crackline which is still an aid route but will probably go free soon to give a great pitch.

### NEW ROUTES
It is likely that there will be some new developments on this crag. Check rockfax.com/mallorca for more details.

Sector E..Z.. P..Z..
1                4 ?
2  19/12/04      4+/5 ?
3  19/12/04      4    ?
4  19/12/04      4+ ? 9 clips
gap
5

South facing slabs
15m to 20m routes
Best grades - 4 to 6b

Lots of sun • 15 min • Slabby • Lower-offs • Windy

# SANTA PONÇA

Santa Ponça is a small crag with a handful of high quality routes. In the past the grades here have been very ungenerous and several competent climbers have reported having a horrible day here after being repelled by most of the routes. I have upgraded things to try and bring the routes back in line with current thinking but, be aware that the routes pack a punch despite appearing relatively amenable from below.

The crag itself consists of a large 'sugarloaf' lump of rock perched high on the hillside overlooking the town of Santa Ponça. The climbing is mostly on overhanging walls with pockets or on blank and relatively delicate grooves.

## ASPECT AND CLIMATE

The crag faces northeast which means that it is shady for most of the day. Its position on the top of a hill makes it exposed to the wind although there is some shelter from trees at the base of the crag.

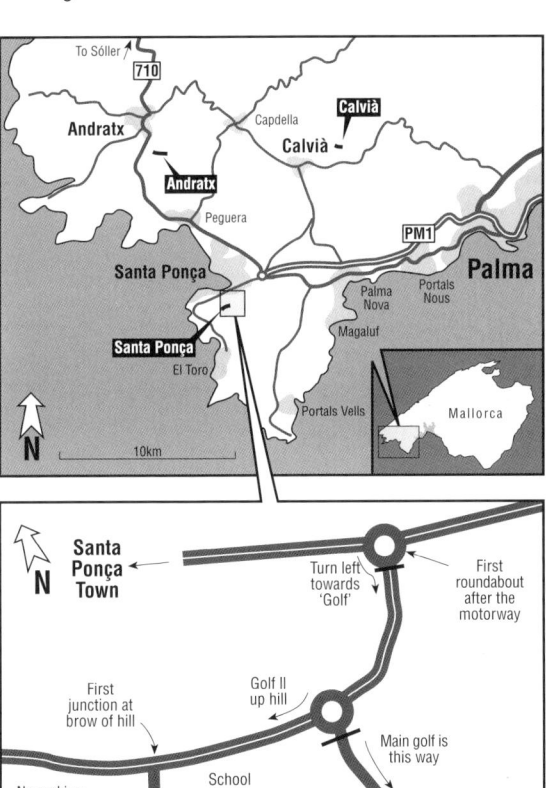

## APPROACH

The Santa Ponça lump is prominently positioned above the town of Santa Ponça. Leave Palma westwards on the PM1 motorway, towards Andratx. Continue to the end of the motorway to a roundabout. From the roundabout head roughly straight on towards 'Santa Ponça'. At the next roundabout turn left under a gate a pick up the signs for 'Golf' (an international word). Continue along a wide dual carriageway to another roundabout. Head up the hill (signed 'Golf I', not under the splendid entrance gate to 'Golf II'). At the brow of the hill turn left (unsigned) to a road with parking on the corner by a school entrance. The signs here suggest that parking isn't allowed however this probably only applies during school hours. If you can't park there then continue along the road for a short distance. Back at the parking spot, follow the track which leads uphill, past a few junctions, to the Santa Ponça lump.

**THERE ARE BREAK-INS TO CARS PARKED FOR THIS CRAG. LEAVE YOUR CAR EMPTY WITH THE GLOVE COMPARTMENT OPEN.**

229

# MALLORCA - Santa Ponça

## SANTA PONÇA
The two main features of the crag are the overhanging arete (route 3) and the gully between routes 5 and 6.

The routes are described from left to right and the first route is on the wall to the left of the arete.

**1. ?** ............................ 6a
Start up a flake and then step onto a steep, pocketed wall. Locally given 5 but that is a big sandbag.

**2. ?** ............................ 6b+
Start as for the previous route but move further right before tackling the wall with the red streak.

**3. ?** ............................ 7b
The prominent, white arete is hard from the word 'go'.

**4. ?** ............................ 7a+
The steep wall right of the arete has a hard lower section past a bulge, then a pumpy finish.

**5. ?** ............................ 7a+
This one tackles the cave with a roof and then finishes up the crack above. The first bolt is missing but this isn't a problem.

**6. ?** ............................ 7b
To the right of the gully is a deceptively awkward scoop that leads to a steep finish. High in the grade.

**7. ?** ............................ 7b+
The last route follows a technical, white groove with a dearth of holds.

NE facing pinnacles
10m to 20m routes
Best grades - 7a+ to 7b+

# S'ESTRET

S'estret is an old quarry which has been abandoned to leave a wildly overhanging wall. More recently routes have been added to the walls across the road from the quarry and also the boulders under the crag have been developed into a hard bouldering venue.

On the main crag most of the routes are in the upper grades, and many have been manufactured, but they mostly provide sensational climbing. Many of the 'Projects' have also been abandoned so feel free to have a go, however I have a feeling they might have been left for a reason. Sector Torrent now adds another dimension which should attract climbers operating in the lower grades. The routes on this wall aren't classic, and are well-spaced out, but they are in a pleasant setting. The bouldering covers the full grade range and there is plenty to go at if you are fed up with roped climbing elsewhere.

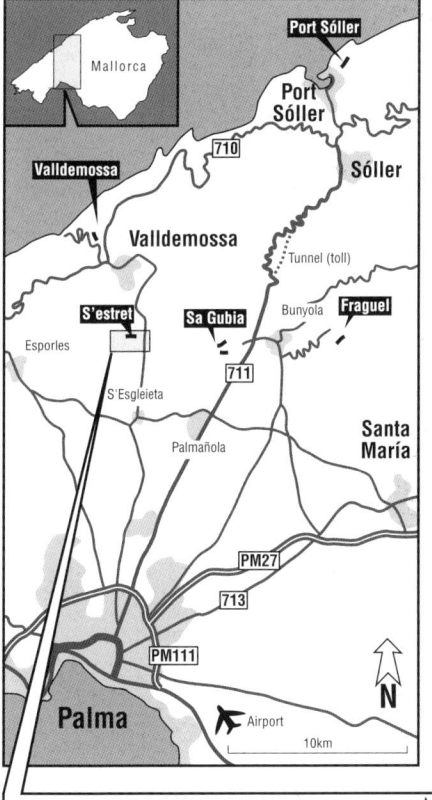

## APPROACH

Take the road from Palma towards Valldemossa. Start looking at the kilometre clock when you pass S'Egleieta. After another 4km, just past the 14km stone on the roadside, is a lay-by on the left by a bridge over a dry river bed. This lay-by is 3km before Valldemossa.

**THERE ARE BREAK-INS TO CARS PARKED FOR THIS CRAG. LEAVE YOUR CAR EMPTY WITH THE GLOVE COMPARTMENT OPEN.**

**Main Crag and Boulders -** From the parking, follow a track through the trees. The boulders are found after 250m. For the crag break off left up the hill.

**Sector Torrent -** From the parking, cross the road and find a path at the end of the crash barrier. Follow the path and after 50m, drop down some tiled steps. The path turns into a red-tiled path. Continue through a gap in the stone wall to the buttress above.

## ASPECT AND CLIMATE

The main crag faces due north and the base is shrouded by trees. This means sheltered and cool climbing. The hard routes are also likely to stay dry in heavy rain. Sector Torrent offers less shelter and will get the afternoon sun. The boulders are well-covered by the trees and should be cool enough except in very hot weather.

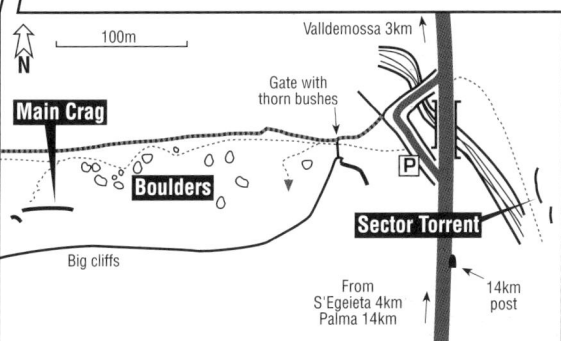

## ACCESS

There have been a few problems here in the past but as long as people park carefully, there should be no future problems. The road is used for accessing various properties so please don't double park or block access. The thorn bushes on the approach gate are to stop people leaving the gate open, hop over the wall instead.

# MALLORCA - S'estret

## Sector Torrent

*Handwritten annotation: 30/12/01 7a Next to tree. Climb round bulge 5+*

### SECTOR TORRENT
This area is on the opposite side of the road to the parking area and provides a good set of easier routes.

**APPROACH** - From the parking, cross the road and find a path at the end of the crash barrier. Follow the path and after 50m, drop down some tiled steps. The path turns into a red-tiled path. Continue through a gap in the stone wall to the buttress above. The routes here are numbers 4 and 5. The first routes are 25m to the left of this. *(handwritten: 8 6)*

**1. ?** .................... 5+  *30/12/01*
The slabs and bulge above.

**2. Movimiento sexy** .......... 5  *30/12/01*
Good climbing up the groove.

**3. Menage à trois** .......... 6a
Good fun until you arrive at the disappointing crux moves.

**4. Las cagao** ................ 4+  *30/12/01*
Great layback moves up the flake and cracks above. Coming in via the two bolts to the left of the rib is 5.

**5. Placa movio moreno** ......... 4+  *5/1/02*
Nice slab climbing.

**6. Placa movio moreno** ......... 5  *5/1/02*
The right-hand side of the slab.

*Handwritten: 3a grade 6a?*

**7. Zarza mora** *30/12/01* ............ 4+
Not certain of the exact location of this route.

There are a few more routes on the upper buttress including some two-pitchers.
**APPROACH** - Continue past the lower wall until you find a water pool. Take a path through a hole in the fence to the left and climb up to where the path splits. The next routes are along the left-hand branch of this path.

**8. ?** ...................... 5+
A better line than the next route.
1) 5, 30m.
2) 5, 30m. A great pitch of sustained slab climbing. Abseil off.

**9. Con el culo al aire** ........... 5+
An old route which has been tidied up.
1) 5+ 30m. Pull through the roof, past a peg and an old bolt, to join a line of new bolts.
2) 5, 30m. As for *Route 8* or lower off.

**10. Pasión oculta** ............. 4+
A lone route situated to the right of where the approach path hits the crag.

West facing wall
15m to 60m mostly single pitch
Best grades - 4+ to 6a

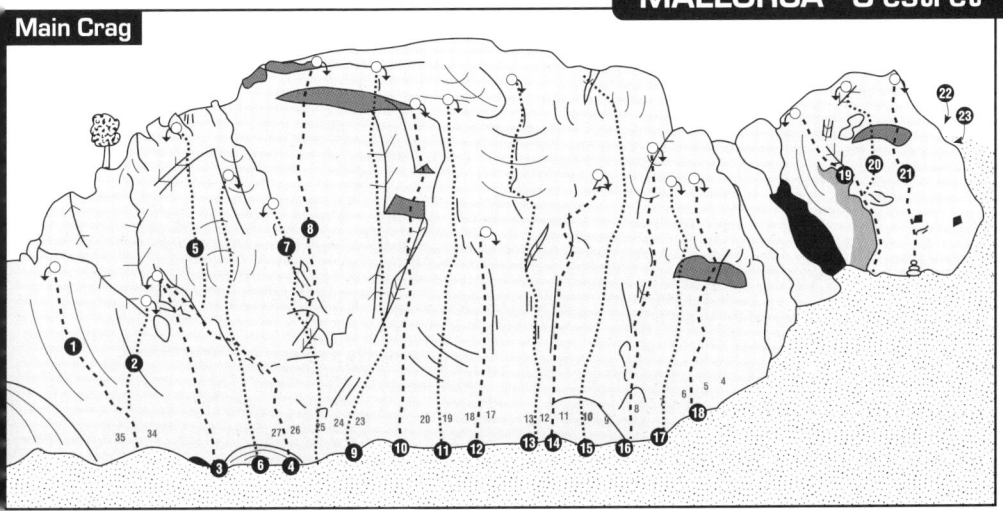

# MALLORCA - S'estret

## Main Crag

### MAIN CRAG
The first line of bolts is up a very steep bulging section on the left-hand side of the wall which looks to be completely unclimbable.

1. ? — 8b
2. La córte del faran — 8a
3. ? — 8a
   Very hard boulder problem near the bottom, then it eases above.
4. La travesia — 6c+
   The hanging, leftward-leaning groove, below the prow, gives a good pumpy route. Slightly too much for a 'warm up'.
5. Chappa y mata — 7c
   An extended finish to *La travesia*.
6. Fier hundert — 7c
   A stunning route.
7. ? — Project
8. ? — Project
9. ? — 8b
   A long pitch which finishes up a prominent left-facing groove, high on the face.
10. ? — ?
    This may be a route. Whatever it is, it is definitely hard.
11. ? — 8a
12. Si yo fuera presidente — 7a+
    Only short but it packs a lot in.
13. Odio a cobi — 7b
    The best route on the crag, which finishes up a steep, open groove at the top, via some sharp and positive pockets.
14. La sudaca — 7a+
    Originally a right-hand finish to *Odio a cobi* but now has its own set of bolts although the moves are much the same.
15. Tetris — 7c
    It is only 7b to the lower-off on *La sudaca*.
16. Buñocracia — 6b+
    This is the approved warm up, following the large groove and crack line. As is often the case with the one easy route on a hard crag, it is no push over.
17. ? — 7c
    Technical climbing with a hard crux to onsight.
18. ? — 7c

The last three routes are around the corner to the right on a smaller 'boulder-like' wall. They all look starightforward until you get on them and find that all the holds are rubbish.

19. La gigante verde — 7a
    The left-hand side of the overanging rib.
20. ? — 7a+
    The same start as the previous route, but pull right and hack on upwards to the top.
21. Bomber torrat — 7a+
    Use a pile of boulders to gain the first holds.

There are two more lines on the right of the block.

22. ? — 6b
    The left-hand line.
23. ? — 4

North facing wall
15m to 25m routes
Best grades - 6b+ to 8b

# MALLORCA - S'estret

## S'estret Boulders

To main crag

Charcoal circle

Gate

1 min from parking

Topo by Miquel Riera

234 | Not much sun | 2 min | Vertical | Steep

# MALLORCA - S'estret

## BOULDERING
The boulders past on the approach have been developed to give a good set of hard problems. Only the best of the problems are described here and there are a number of others.

1. Don Manolo .............. V4
2. D.J.Link .................. V3
3. D.J.Dan .................. V10
4. Dejota Dijei .............. V11
5. All Simpson .............. V4
6. Entre Dos ................ V3
7. Homer Simpson .......... V4
8. Alone in the Dark ........ V6
9. Respeta l'arbre .......... V3
10. El kamikaze ............. V3
11. El hueco ................ V4
12. Son rocas .............. V4
13. Mandel y skali .......... V4
14. Hip-hop de puta ........ V4
15. Jop .................... V8
16. Zubizarreta ............ V9
17. Pica paquito ........... V4
18. El crack ............... V3
19. Spanair ................ V7
20. D.J. Cervino ........... V8
21. Comando rasta ......... V5

22. Carta de plata .......... V2
23. Don Simón ............. V5
24. Golpesito Rodriguez .... V6
25. Skiatada ............... V1
26. Paco PP ............... V3
27. Aloete ................. V4
28. El rincón moro ......... V5
29. El cagatió ............. V4
30. 7 notas, 7 colores ..... V6
31. Siete, siete ........... V3
32. Nen's traverse ........ V7
33. Falsa identidad ....... V3
34. Chanelance ........... V8
35. El rimadero ........... V12
36. Señor Don Paco ...... V6
37. Sabio Joven Negro Estudiante .... V4
38. El comienzo .......... V3
39. Romano .............. V4
40. Los reyes del insomnio .. V6
41. Tetas valadores ...... V5
42. Chochos valdores .... V5

### UPPER BOULDERS
There are also loads more boulders above the main wall with some fantastic roof problems.
**APPROACH** - Walk to the right of the routes and climb up above them.

| Bouldering Grade | V0- | V0 | V0+ | V1 | V2 | V3 | V4 | V5 | V6 | V7 | V8 | V9 | V10 | V11 | V12 | V13 | V14 |
|---|---|---|---|---|---|---|---|---|---|---|---|---|---|---|---|---|---|
| UK Tech Grade | 4c or easier | 5a | 5c | | EASY | | 6b | | HARD | | EASY | | 7a | | HARD | | |
| | | 5b | | | 6a | HARD | | EASY | 6c | | HARD | | EASY | 7b | | | |
| Font Grade | | 4 | 4+ | 5 | 5+ | 6a | 6b | 6c | 6c+ | 7a | 7a+ | 7b | 7b+ | 7c | 7c+ | 8a | 8a+ | 8b | 8b+ |

Sheltered area under north facing wall
Boulder problems
Best grades - V1 to V12

# VALLDEMOSSA

Valldemossa is an accessible and popular crag which has a good selection of middle grade routes. It is situated in a delightful position high above the village of Port d'Valldemossa with splendid views over the village and the sea beyond. The only drawback to this idyllic setting is the proximity of the road, a situation made a bit worse by the fact that it is also a surprisingly busy road. However this does makes it a good airport day crag, when you can keep an eye on your gear.

The climbing is spread over three main buttresses which give good variation from steep slabs to vertical walls. There is the famous roof over the road and some interesting scooped runnels on the left-hand side of the main crag. Recent routes added further left have taken good lines on slightly dodgy rock. The Roadside Buttress is less interesting and also surprisingly dangerous owing to the sudden appearance of speeding cars. Up above the main crag are two considerably more isolated areas which contains some superb longer routes, some poor new ones and one stunning 7b.

## ASPECT AND CLIMATE

The crag faces west and gets the sun just after midday. It is reasonably sheltered and could well offer dry climbing if the more mountainous crags are wet. If it is raining there is one route to do, but that's about it. In the summer it will get as hot as everywhere else.

## APPROACH

Valldemossa is one of the larger towns situated on the north side of the mountains and is relatively easy to get to by following signs from the Palma ring road. Once in the town, head towards the coast. Ignore the first right turn (signed 'Sóller') and take the second right turn (signed 'Port de Valldemossa'). The crag is about 1km down this road. You will almost certainly drive past the first short wall. The main section of the crag is reached when a conspicuous beak of rock overhangs the road. Please park very carefully and keep in mind that some quite wide lorries come down this road. There is some extra parking further down the hill, or further up before the Roadside Buttress.

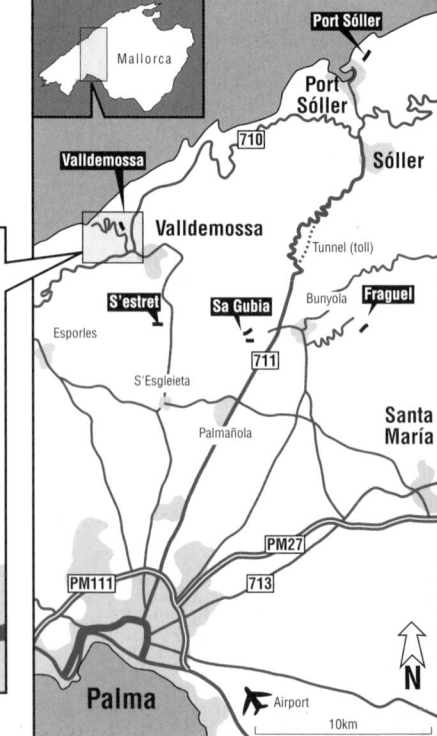

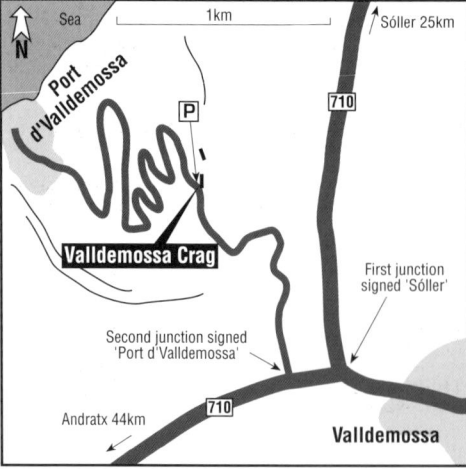

# MALLORCA - Valldemossa

*Top Buttress* — Topo by Nick Verney

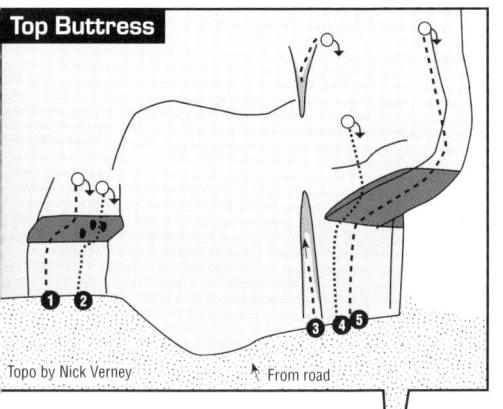

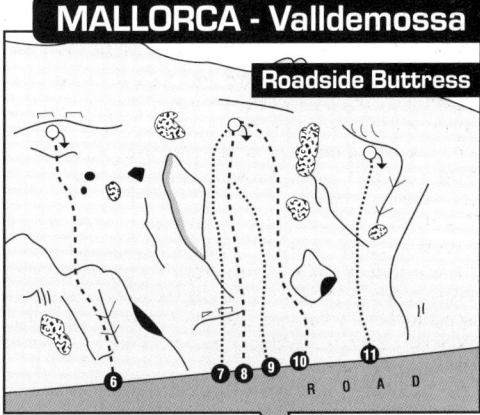

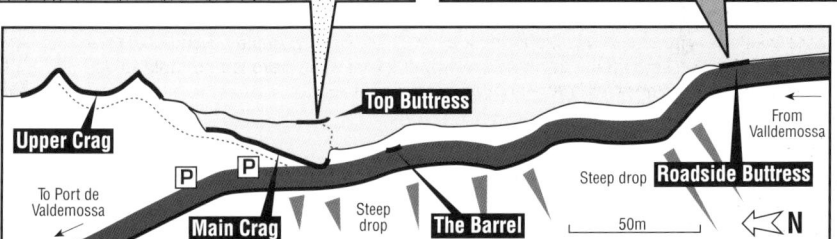

*Roadside Buttress*

## TOP BUTTRESS
At a late stage of the development of this book another buttress at Valldemossa came to light. It seems that this buttress isn't so much new as re-found since the routes have certainly been there for a while. The situation is spectacular and and the routes appear to be very high quality although not many more details are known, however route 5 is said to be "one of the best 7bs on the Island"!

**APPROACH** - To the right of the Valldemossa main crag is a rib and a path going steeply up by a big pine tree. This path leads steeply up to the huge roof of route 5.

**1. ?** .................................... (7a/b)
The left-hand side of the roof.

**2. ?** .................................... (7a/b)
The right-hand side of the roof.

**3. ?** .................................... 5
The crack and through cave are entertaining.

**4. ?** .................................... (7a/c)

**5. ?** .................................... 7b
The huge roof followed by the fly-away arete in a stupendous position.

Further right is a chimney which could be climbed on trad gear.

## ROADSIDE BUTTRESS
This is the short wall back up the road which you almost certainly drove past without noticing. Although the routes don't look too spectacular, they have some good climbing and are very popular. This wall is directly above the road. Please be very careful of cars coming speeding down the hill since there isn't really anywhere to hide.

The first route is a little way down the road from the main group. They are described from left to right.

**6. Zurdo** .................................... 6a
Up the short rib and wall above.

**7. Rompe dedos** ............................ 6a+
A touch scary at the top.

**8. Pérfido encanto** ......................... 6a+
The best of the routes on this buttress.

**9. Triplet derecho** ......................... 6b

**10. Recto cresta** ........................... 5+

**11. Derecho castilla** ....................... 6b
Fingery and technical near the top.

**THE BARREL** - Possibly the saddest buttress in this guidebook is 50m back up the road from the main crag overhang. Despite its size, it always seems to be very popular.

**12. Derecho** ................................ 4
The right-hand line.

**13. Centro** ................................. 4
The middle one.

**14. Izquierdo** .............................. 4+
The left-hand line.

**Roadside Buttress**
West facing wall, 5m to 12m routes
Best grades - 4 to 6b

237

# MALLORCA - Valldemossa

**Main Crag**

## THE MAIN CRAG
This area contains the best climbing at Valldemossa and consists of a fine buttress with a number of middle grade wall climbs and the spectacular roof. Most of the climbing can be viewed comfortably from the wall by the side of the road from where you can warn your mate lowering from the roof that he/she is about to be whisked away by a van.
The first route is to the right of the cave below the roof. They are described from right to left.

**1. Dali** .................... 5+
For some reason there is no lower-off so take a long sling to extend the bolt over the lip.

**2. Sostre den burot** ........ 6c+
The juggy roof is superb. Save a bit for the last heave up to the belay. See cover photo.

**3. Sostre den burot direct** .. 7a+
A hard boulder problem.

The wall to the left of the roof has some very fingery starts.

**4. Pepino** ................ 6b+

**5. Pepa** .................. 6a+

The next line of bolts can be used as an indirect start to *Another Roadside Attraction*, or a direct start to *El jubilado*. Whatever you do with it, it is a fingery 6b.

**6. Another Roadside Attraction** . 6b+
Take either of the two technical lines up the lower wall.

**7. Suphi** ................. 5+
A very good route through the crozzly holes. There is a 'hands and feet off' rest in the holes.

**8. El jubilado** ............. 5
An atypical sport route (ie. it follows a logical line) can be made by following the diagonal break rightwards to reach the easy upper groove and lower-off of routes 4 and 5.

**9. Vía des clau** ........... 6b
There is a peg after the 2nd bolt.

**10. ?** .................... 7a
The short crack is hard.

**11. Intrépido** ............. 6c
An excellent route interrupted by a grassy bit in the middle. The finish is exciting!

**12. Palmolive** ............ 7b
The left-hand finish to the above gives superb climbing with a short technical sequence.

**13. ?** .................... Project
A grade of 6b+ once appeared for this route.

**14. ?** .................... 6b
The scooped runnel climbed direct.

**15. Kiko** ................. 6b
The edge of the good rock.

**16. ?** .................... 6b
The middle of the not-so-good rock. Take care with your rope over the top roof edge.

238

West facing wall
10m to 25m routes
Best grades - 5 to 7b

# MALLORCA - Valldemossa

## Upper Crag

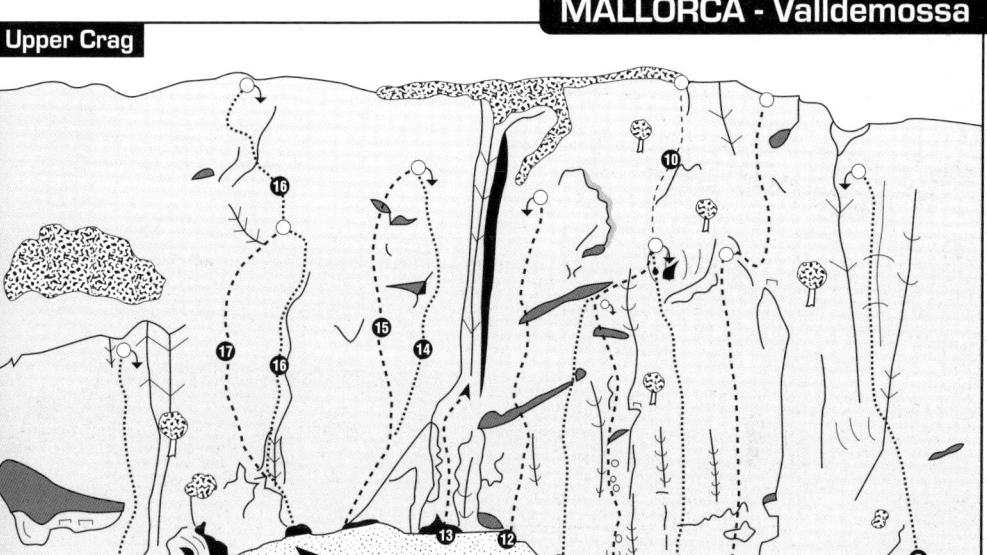

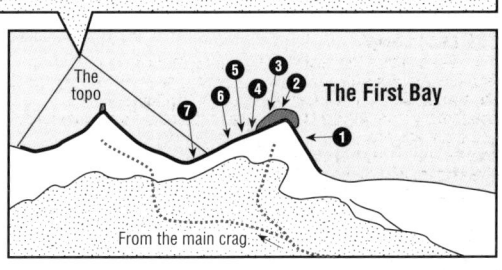

*opened out*

*From the first bay*

**The topo** — The First Bay

*From the main crag.*

### UPPER CRAG
By complete contrast the Upper Crag is strangely isolated compared to the hullabaloo below. The routes here vary from slightly pointless 'fillers in' to good long climbs on Verdon-esque rock. It is reached by walking up the hill leftwards from the Main Wall. The routes are described from right to left.

**1. ?** .................................... 5
The line right of the cave gives an awkward crack climb.

**2, 3 and 4** ........................... (7a/b)
The cave contains three vague crack lines all of which look to be steep and graunchy.

**5. ?** .................................... 6b+
A very poor and escapable route to the left of the cave.

**6. ?** .................................... 6c
Better than the last set of routes.

**7. ?** .................................... 7a+
A very poor route with a hard move low down.

**8. Shorty** ........................... 5+
A good long route up the right-hand edge of the wall. It can be split at a mid-height belay. The full route is 40m.

**9. ?** .................................... 6b
Straight up the wall to the new lower-off on *Lanky*. Good rock.

**10. Lanky** ........................... 6a
Another quality climb starting up an area of scoops and flutings. There is a new belay at 25m. Originally it continued more easily to the top (40m).

**11. ?** .................................... 6a

**12. ?** .................................... 6a+
Just right of the corner.

**13. ?** .................................... 5+
The central gully.

**14. ?** .................................... 7a+
Good climbing but escapeable where it matters.

**15. ?** .................................... 6c+
Fine climbing up the steep wall. Easier than it looks.

**16. ?** .................................... 6b+
The central flake line is good. It can be continued at 5+.

**17. ?** .................................... (7c)
A hard and unknown line to the left.

**18. ?** .................................... (7c)
Another unknown.

**19. ?** .................................... ?

West facing wall
15m to 40m, mostly single pitch
Best grades - 5 to 6c+

# SA GUBIA

Sa Gubia is a wonderful crag with a massive variety of climbing. It was one of the first areas on the island to be developed for climbing but still has plenty of potential left, however there have been relatively few recent additions. The climbing here is extremely varied and an most people will find a visit essential at some stage during their stay. There are plenty of single pitch routes across the grade range although it is a bit lacking in routes above 7b+. The upgrading of many of the easier pitches has lessened the crags savage reputation among visiting climbers when it used to be possible to start up a guidebook 5+ only to find you were on a route than elsewhere would be given 6b.

Probably one of the most appealing aspects of climbing out Sa Gubia as the wealth of classic longer climbs like *Excalibur*, *Estricina* and *La ley del deseo* at grade 5, and *Bomberos*, *Princesa* and *Sexo débil* in the higher grades. There is also a classic trad route which is correctly known as *Albahida* but in the past has been called *Gubia Normal*. This follows the majestic long ridge which dominates the crag and is visible from the plane if you know where to look. For routes harder than 7b+ Sa Gubia has now been surpassed by Fraguel, but in the grade range 6a to 7b+, it is the most varied and extensive area on the island.

## GEAR

Virtually all the routes are fully bolted with good belays. The one notable exception being *Albahida* which requires a small rack. Most of the single pitch routes can be climbed on a single 60m rope, although twin 50m ropes will also do, you just won't always be able to lower off. For the longer routes, twin 50m ropes are preferable to enable abseil descents.

## ASPECT AND CLIMATE

The different aspects of the various faces offer climbing in the sun and shade depending on your preference. The right-hand side (looking in) gets the sun for most of the day, except for the bit tucked around the back, in the bay (Sector Isla Bonita and the Sexo débil area). The Paret dels Coloms loses the sun in the early afternoon. It can be very windy in the gorge owing to the wind tunnel effect. In the unusual event that it is raining, there may be one or two hard routes which stay dry.

## APPROACH

From Palma take the C711 north towards Sóller. 4.5km after Palmañola, is a turning to Bunyola, park in the large car park next to the restaurant, just after this turning. If you are coming from the eastern side of the Island, there is a useful road connecting the motorway to Bunyola, from the junction after the Santa María junction. Walk up a track, almost opposite the turning to Bunyola, passing an old parking place on a track on the right. PLEASE DON'T PARK HERE.

Continue walking up the main track, passing a gate and another gate on the right which blocks off a track leading up to a large house.

Keep going until a dry river bed is reached and follow a good path next to the river bed. As you enter the trees near the crag you can branch right up the hill for the right-hand sectors or stay on the low path (river bed) for Paret dels Coloms.

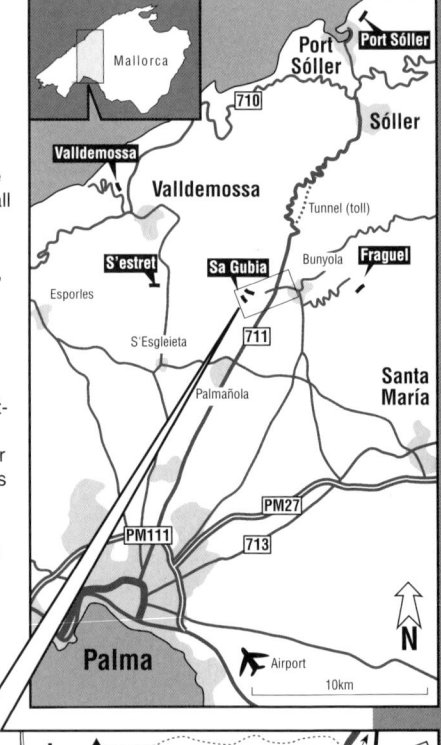

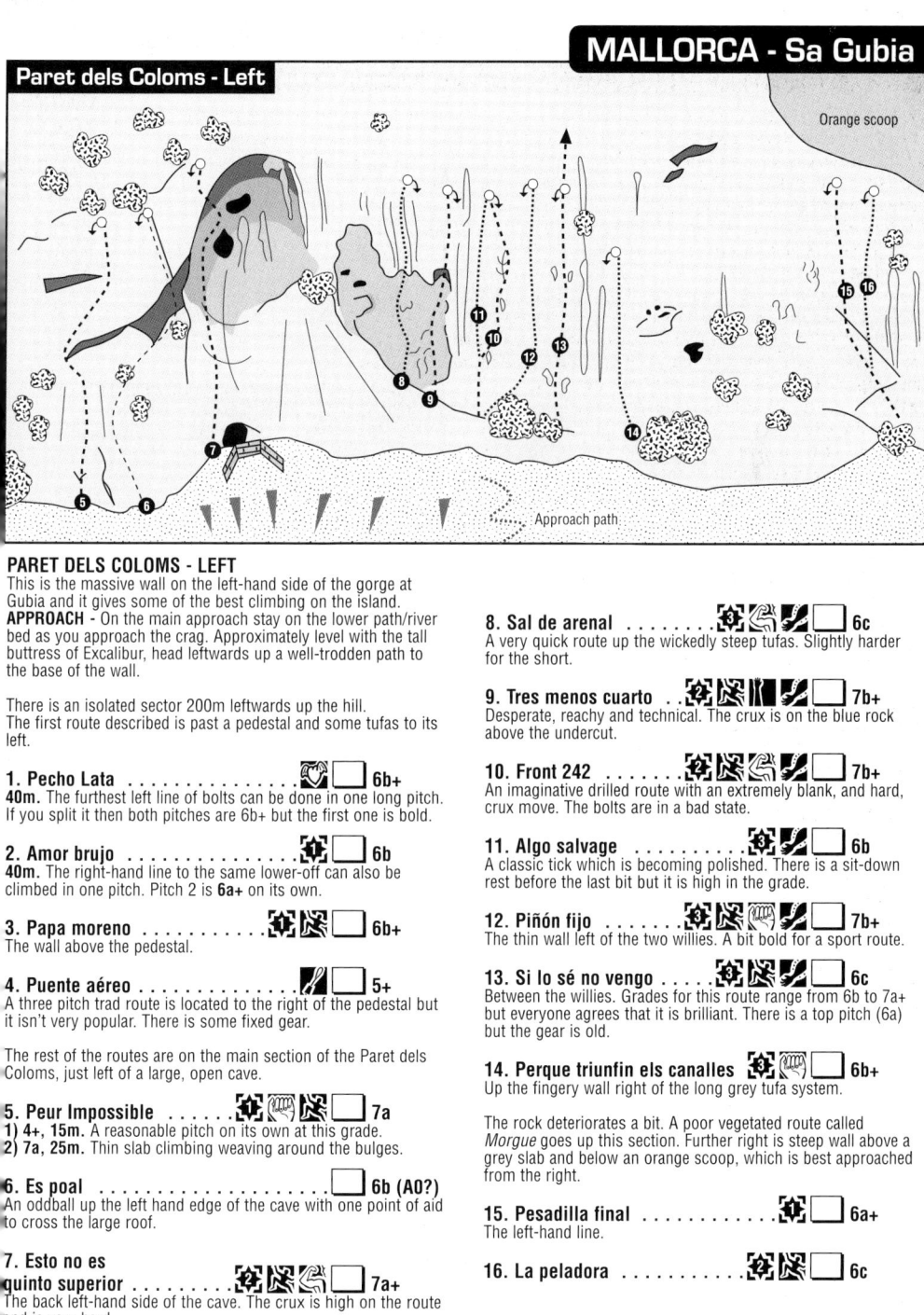

## Paret dels Coloms - Left

# MALLORCA - Sa Gubia

Orange scoop

Approach path

## PARET DELS COLOMS - LEFT
This is the massive wall on the left-hand side of the gorge at Gubia and it gives some of the best climbing on the island.
**APPROACH** - On the main approach stay on the lower path/river bed as you approach the crag. Approximately level with the tall buttress of Excalibur, head leftwards up a well-trodden path to the base of the wall.

There is an isolated sector 200m leftwards up the hill.
The first route described is past a pedestal and some tufas to its left.

**1. Pecho Lata** .............. 6b+
40m. The furthest left line of bolts can be done in one long pitch. If you split it then both pitches are 6b+ but the first one is bold.

**2. Amor brujo** .............. 6b
40m. The right-hand line to the same lower-off can also be climbed in one pitch. Pitch 2 is **6a+** on its own.

**3. Papa moreno** .............. 6b+
The wall above the pedestal.

**4. Puente aéreo** .............. 5+
A three pitch trad route is located to the right of the pedestal but it isn't very popular. There is some fixed gear.

The rest of the routes are on the main section of the Paret dels Coloms, just left of a large, open cave.

**5. Peur Impossible** .............. 7a
1) 4+, 15m. A reasonable pitch on its own at this grade.
2) 7a, 25m. Thin slab climbing weaving around the bulges.

**6. Es poal** .............. 6b (A0?)
An oddball up the left hand edge of the cave with one point of aid to cross the large roof.

**7. Esto no es quinto superior** .............. 7a+
The back left-hand side of the cave. The crux is high on the route and is very hard.

**8. Sal de arenal** .............. 6c
A very quick route up the wickedly steep tufas. Slightly harder for the short.

**9. Tres menos cuarto** .............. 7b+
Desperate, reachy and technical. The crux is on the blue rock above the undercut.

**10. Front 242** .............. 7b+
An imaginative drilled route with an extremely blank, and hard, crux move. The bolts are in a bad state.

**11. Algo salvage** .............. 6b
A classic tick which is becoming polished. There is a sit-down rest before the last bit but it is high in the grade.

**12. Piñón fijo** .............. 7b+
The thin wall left of the two willies. A bit bold for a sport route.

**13. Si lo sé no vengo** .............. 6c
Between the willies. Grades for this route range from 6b to 7a+ but everyone agrees that it is brilliant. There is a top pitch (6a) but the gear is old.

**14. Perque triunfin els canalles** .............. 6b+
Up the fingery wall right of the long grey tufa system.

The rock deteriorates a bit. A poor vegetated route called *Morgue* goes up this section. Further right is steep wall above a grey slab and below an orange scoop, which is best approached from the right.

**15. Pesadilla final** .............. 6a+
The left-hand line.

**16. La peladora** .............. 6c

East facing wall
20m to 40m routes
Best grades - 6a+ to 7b+

# MALLORCA - Sa Gubia

## Paret dels Coloms - Right

**PARET DELS COLOMS - RIGHT**
The right-hand side of the wall is dominated by a huge vertical cave. Right of the cave is a clean wall with a magnificent tufa - *Pasteles de Isabel*, and right again is a more slabby section with some longer, and slightly easier routes. Most of the routes here are two or more pitches long with well bolted, and worthwhile, upper sections.

**APPROACH** - One the main approach (previous page) stay on the lower path/river bed as you approach the crag. Approximately level with the tall buttress of Excalibur, head leftwards up a well-trodden path to the base of the wall.

The first routes are on the vertical grey wall, 20m up and left of the cave, below a huge orange section high on the cliff.

**1. Humi** .................. 6a+
Good climbing with a tricky crux bulge.

**2. Mes rapit suc el vent** ....... 6a
Similar quality climbing just to the right.

**3. Pellojo de tiburón** ..... 7a
Good technical climbing past a small hollow building to a fine finish on the upper wall.

**4. Seis pelas** ............ 6c
The original route of the face hasn't been re-geared yet.
1) **6a, 30m**. The diagonal cracks lead to a belay in the cave. A protectable pitch if you have a full rack of gear.
2) **6c, 30m**. Poor old gear leads rightwards to a high belay.

The next routes are in and around the huge cave. All the first pitches can be climbed and lowered in one, with a 60m rope, although care is needed since it can be a bit tight. The second pitches are well worth doing in which case a single 50m abseil on double ropes, or two shorter abseils, are required.

**5. Decadencia corporal** ... 7b+
A great route with a popular first pitch.
1) **6c, 30m**. The wall left of the cave is extremely sustained and on very small holds.
2) **7b+, 30m**. A stunning looking pitch but it has old bolts.

# MALLORCA - Sa Gubia

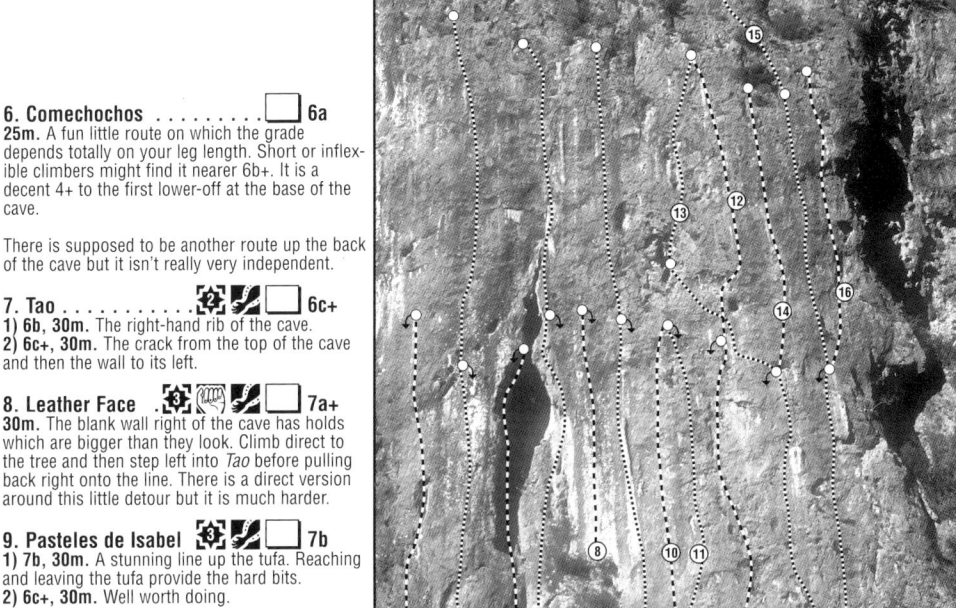

**6. Comechochos** ......... ☐ 6a
**25m.** A fun little route on which the grade depends totally on your leg length. Short or inflexible climbers might find it nearer 6b+. It is a decent 4+ to the first lower-off at the base of the cave.

There is supposed to be another route up the back of the cave but it isn't really very independent.

**7. Tao** .......... 🔲 6c+
1) **6b, 30m.** The right-hand rib of the cave.
2) **6c+, 30m.** The crack from the top of the cave and then the wall to its left.

**8. Leather Face** . 🔲 7a+
**30m.** The blank wall right of the cave has holds which are bigger than they look. Climb direct to the tree and then step left into *Tao* before pulling back right onto the line. There is a direct version around this little detour but it is much harder.

**9. Pasteles de Isabel** 🔲 7b
1) **7b, 30m.** A stunning line up the tufa. Reaching and leaving the tufa provide the hard bits.
2) **6c+, 30m.** Well worth doing.

**10. Gay Power** .. 🔲 7a+
**30m.** Technical face climbing on invisible holds.

**11. Vol de nuit** ...... 🔲 6b
**30m.** Good climbing up the easiest line right of the cave. A bit escapable where it counts. You can continue to the cave stance on *Estricina*.

**12. Tía Melis** ....... 🔲 6a
An excellent route which crosses *Estricina*.
1) **6a, 25m.** The scoop-cover wall.
2) **6a, 25m.** Swings rightwards and up from the belay. One 50m abseil descent.

The next routes start below an interesting pair of rock buttocks.

**13. Estricnina** ............ 🔲 5+
A popular and lengthy excursion which provides the easiest way up the wall.
1) **5, 20m.** Climb the wall past the buttocks.
2) **5+, 15m.** Traverse left below the belay of the previous route then make a hard move up and left to the belay.
3) **5, 20m.** Climb up and rigthwards across the wall to finish at the same belay as *Tia melis*. One 50m abseil descent or....
4) **5, 40m.** Continue to the top.
**DESCENT** - Make two abseils.

**14. Chungui chunguez** ....... 🔲 6c
A superb and direct second pitch above the buttocks. Pitch 1 is as for *Estricnina*.

**15. Danzomanía** ............ 🔲 6a+
A good long route which virtually reaches the top of the wall. Start at the bolt line right of the buttocks.
1) **5+, 15m.** Climb up rightwards to a prominent pillar. Pull up this and belay.
2) **6a+, 25m.** Follow a mixture of old gear up the wall above.
3) **6a+, 20m.** Climb the wall to the left of a groove. 2 abseils need for descent.

**16. Guatón** ............... 🔲 6a
Another good route which shares its first pitch with *Danzamonia*.
1) **5+, 15m.** as for *Danzamonia*.
2) **6a, 15m.** Step right and climb straight up the wall above. It is just possible to lower on a 60m rope but probably better to abseil.

There is another route marked to the right of this in the local topo but it has no fixed gear or obvious line.

**Paret dels Coloms - Right**

East facing wall
15m to 60m single and multi-pitch routes
Best grades - 5+ to 7b

# MALLORCA - Sa Gubia

Abseil descent down *La ley del deseo* possible from here

## 1. Albahida (Gubia Normal) .... 4+
The most poplar long route on the island is the long ridge of *Gubia Normal*. It is a full day's outing for most teams, including the long descent. There is some old fixed gear but take a full rack with you as well. The line of the route is a bit vague since it wanders around the rib however most of the stances have fixed gear, if in doubt, just follow the easiest line. Start at the base of the left-hand spur of the ridge by some red marks on the rock.
1) **3, 30m.** Climb the ridge by the easiest line, first right then left to a stance on a ledge. There is a bolt line exiting left from here.
2) **4+, 25m.** Move right then upwards with a hard move or two. Easier climbing leads back left to a recess.
3) **3+, 25m.** Climb the rib on the right to a big stance.
4) **3+, 35m.** Climb up right past some loose blocks and up a flake/corner to belay at a tree.
5) **4+, 35m.** The wall above leads awkwardly back left to the ridge. Follow this to a stance at some threads.
6) **3, 30m.** Follow the ridge to a bulge.
7) **3, 35m.** Move right to a corner, then climb up the corner to the top of the ridge.
**DESCENT 1** - Tricky but fast! Abseil down the last pitch. Then make one long (50m) diagonal abseil to the belay at the top of pitch 4, by a tree. From here abseil down the right-hand (looking in) side of the ridge, down the line of *La Ley del Deseo*. Don't commit yourself to the first two abseils until you know where you are going. After that it is straightforward.
**DESCENT 2** - Don't leave any gear at the base of the route. From the top of the climbing, walk along the ridge to the summit, then continue a short distance in the same direction to find a gravel road. This leads down past a farm to the main road. Turn right and head back downhill to the car (1 hour).
**DESCENT 3** - It is also possible to descend by continuing up the ridge and then heading leftwards and skirting back around and down the gully behind the main ridge and arriving back at the base. This is awkward and requires very careful route finding.
**Gubia Variante** - A right-hand start to the ridge can be made in three long pitches at about grade 5. No further details are known but the line looks fairly straightforward.

## 2. Quan es fa fosc ............ 5
This excellent variation follows the steeper rib to the left of *Albahida*. The main three pitches are well-bolted but you may require a few wires for the first pitch and you will require double ropes to descend.
1) **3, 30m.** As for *Albahida*.
2) **to 5) All 3 pitches grade 5 and about 30m long.** Follow the bolt line leading left from the stance.
**DESCENT** - Abseil off or continue right wards to join *Albahida*.

This is the short, compact wall at the toe of the main face. Some of the lower-offs on this wall are old. The left edge of this slab has a couple of bolts which may be part of a route but no details are known.

## 3. Chitas marchitas ......... 6b+
The left-most complete line of bolts leading to a crack.

## 4. Charly danone ....... 7a+
Very technical climbing past a short tufa.

## 5. Jódete y baila ........... 6b+
Roughly the centre of the slab.

## 6. Fill de ric ............ 6a
Follow the orange streaks.

## 7. Puta perro ............ 6a+
The right-hand edge of the slab.

### SECTOR ESPOLÓN
The largest and most complex area at Gubia is the huge bay which dominates the northern side of the gorge. It is an area with some magnificent multi-pitch routes, including the long and popular *Albahida* (formerly know as *Gubia Normal*) up the prominent ridge at the far side of the bay. From the ridge the crag sweeps around, past a superb vertical wall.
**APPROACH** - One the main approach (page 240) take the higher path, under Sector Silicona and Excalibur, and keep going across the bay to the far side.

# MALLORCA - Sa Gubia

To the right of the small slab is a much longer wall which has the best bolted, multi-pitch climbs at Sa Gubia.

## 8. La ley del deseo ......... 5+
This excellent route follows the right-hand side of the main ridge at a very amenable grade. It is fully bolted and very popular. The main drawback is people descending down it while you are on your way up. For this reason a helmet is advised.
1) **5, 25m.** Take the left-hand line of bolts, just right of a corner.
2) **5+, 25m.** Can be combined with pitch one.
3) **4+, 20m.** More straightforward bolt clipping.
4) **5, 30m.** Continue to a well-positioned stance.
**DESCENT** - Abseil off.

## 9. Sonrisa vertical ......... 6a
A variation pitch just right of pitch 2 of *La ley del deseo*.

The next three routes share a first pitch to a stance behind a large block with a cable belay.

## 10. The Master ............ 6a
Start up the right-hand first pitch.
1) **5, 20m.** The line of bolts just right of *La ley del deseo* starting from the same flat area.
2) **6a, 25m.** The left-hand line above. Good.

## 11. Polla Boba ............ 6a
2) **6a, 25m.** Direct from the stance to an awkward bulge.

## 12. Méjico Lindo .......... 6a+
2) **6a+, 25m.** The right-hand line to the same lower-off. Alternatively extend rightwards to the next lower-off up the wall.

Past a twisted tree are two short lines of bolts leading to a stance.

## 13. ? ................. 6a+
A superb route which can be done in one to the half lower-off but is better done in two pitches to the high lower-off.
1) **4+, 15m.** Either line of bolts to the scoop stance.
2) **6a+, 25m.** Great climbing between 2 tufas. Ignore the half lower-off unless you are belaying from the ground.
There are bolts above pitch 2 but not enough to make a pitch.

## 14. Oasis ............... 6b
**38m.** A huge single pitch between 2 tufas. Abseil off.

## 15. ? ................. 6c
**30m.** A direct version of pitch 1 of *Bomberos*. Aim for the chunky, white tufa. Tricky in its middle section.

## 16. Vía de los bomberos .... 6b
A great route which takes the best line of unvegetated rock up the huge wall of the bay. The climbing is sustained but never desperate and the views from the stances are excellent. Start at a clear area below a big white tufa in a hollow.
1) **6a, 30m.** Take the right-hand line of bolts to the white tufa.
2) **6a+, 25m.** Pull up right and climb the blunt rib.
3) **6a, 40m.** A long pitch, take lots of quick-draws.
4) **6b, 40m.** Steady climbing leads to the route's crux, about 10m from the last belay.
**DESCENT** - Abseil off on double ropes.

## 17. Hambre eterna ........ 6a+
**28m.** The last line on this section of wall.

South facing ridge and wall
15m to 200m single and multi-pitch routes
Best grades - 4+ to 6c

# MALLORCA - Sa Gubia

**Sector Princesa**

**Sexo Débil**

## SECTOR PRINCESA
The huge rear wall of the bay is an immense and well-featured section or rock. At present it is home to just a handful of climbs but two of them are mega-classics.

**APPROACH** - One the main approach (page 240) take the higher path, under Sector Silicona and Excalibur. Then head steeply upwards through the tress to the lower slabs of the *Sexo débil* Area. *Princesa* is further around to the left.

### 1. Princesa Original ............ 6b+
This superb, fully-bolted route tackles the full length of the back wall of the bay. There are two starts to the route and the number of pitches can vary depending on how you combine them. Start on the grey slabs below and left of the vast orange scoop in the back wall. You can either belay at the tree line or scramble up to where the wall steepens. The original version follows the left-hand line of bolts and the first bolt is old (the rest are new).
1) 6a, 20m from first bolt, 30m from trees. Climb the wall to a hanging stance below a steep section.
2) 6c (6a/A0) 20m. Make a hard pull past the steep section (slightly easier on the left) and continue to a stance.
3) 5, 48m. Climb to a stance on a ledge with trees.
4) 6a, 48m. Climb straight past a bulge to a ledge (optional stance). Traverse right to a small stance.
5) 5, 48m. Climb straight up past another possible belay at 20m. Continue to the top more easily.

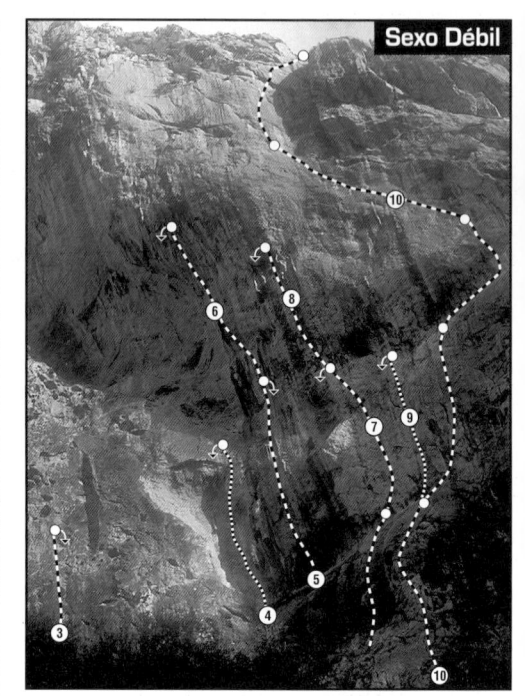

### 2. Princesa Left-hand ........ 6b+
There is a marginally easier left-hand start which leap-frogs one pitch on the original. Start below the right-hand line of bolts.
1) 6b+, 48m from first bolt, 58m from trees. Climb the new bolts up the steep wall.
2) 6a, 45m. Climb up left then back right to a ledge with a tree and junction with the top of pitch 3 of the *Princesa Original*. From here finish up *Princesa Original* pitches 4 and 5.
**DESCENTS** - Abseil down the route. This requires 4x50 abseils or 6x30m abseils.

### 3. Placa aspera .............. 6a+
A lone pitch up the dark grey wall, beneath the big orange gash. It is difficult to spot until you get close and is about 20m right of the *Princesa* starts.

### 4. Tierra al reves ........... 6a+
An impressive route up the steep scoops left of the huge willy.

### 5. Moca de pavo ........... 7c
The steep wall right of the big willy. Scramble up easy rock to start.

### 6. Foracorda ........... 8b
The continuation pitch to *Moca de pavo* is an awesome route

### 7. Idem ............ 7b+
Scramble up easy rock to get to the steep wall.

### 8. De gorrones hasta los cojones ......... 8a
The continuation to *Idem*.

### 9. ? ................. (7a/b)
Direct up the steep groove above the pillar of *Sexo débil*.

**246**

**Sector Princesa**
West facing wall, 200m route
Best grades - 6b+ to 6c

# MALLORCA - Sa Gubia

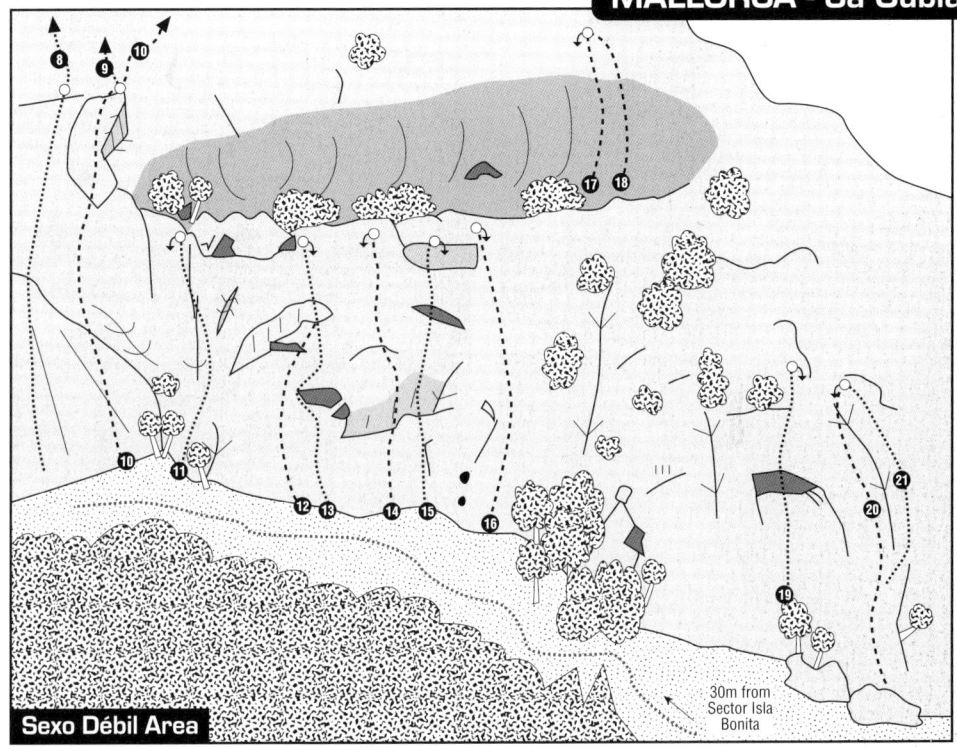

## SEXO DÉBIL AREA

**10. Sexo débil** . . . . . . . . . . . . 6b+
This amazing route weaves its way up the shady right-hand side of the bay through some dramatic rock territory. If you can come to terms with the ethical dilemma of the bolt-on holds on pitch 3, then you will be able to reach the last two pitches which ARE utterly sensational. Start below the pillar of rock below the right-hand side of the cave.
1) 4, 20m. Climb to the base of the corner.
2) 6a+, 20m. Pull up and right onto and climb to the monkey (sadly he may now be missing or damaged).
3) 6b+, 15m. Traverse right then heave up the tufas and 'bolt-on's. One of them spins for the real climbing wall feel.
4) 6b, 25m. Make a superb rising traverse leftwards, on immaculate rock and just enough holds, to a hanging belay.
5) 6b, 15m. Traverse back right and up.
**DESCENT** - Abseil down the route. With a single 60m make three abseils via stances at end of pitches 3 and 1.

Down the slope are several more routes on the slabby wall.

**11. ?** . . . . . . . . . . . . . . . . . . . . . . . . . (3/4)
An easy slab leading to a crack. the first bolt is high but this shouldn't be a problem.

**12. ?** . . . . . . . . . . . . . . . . . . . . . . . . . 3+
An easy left-hand start to the next route.

**13. Cannabis in vitro** . . . . . . . . . 4
Negotiate the protruding roof on its left-hand side.

**14. Pataje español** . . . . . . . . . . . 5
The next line has a red bolt and a leaning wall at mid-height.

**15. El jardín de la abuela** . . . . . . 4+
The flake and wall.

**16. Tantum ergo** . . . . . . . . . . . 5
The furthest right line has a tricky move past the 4th bolt.

The next two routes start from the ledge above the easy slabs. Do one of the previous 5 routes to get to the ledge.

**17. Mi pichica** . . . . . . . . 7b
The left-hand bolt line up a very steep, bulging wall.

**18. Miju** . . . . . . . . . . . . 7b+
The right-hand line.

The last three routes on this sector are down the slope, past some bushes.

**19. Caperucita...** . . . . . . . . . . . . 6b
A short wall behind some trees past a square-cut roof. poor.

**20. ?** . . . . . . . . . . . . . . . . . . . . . . 6a
The curving groove.

**21. ?** . . . . . . . . . . . . . . . . . . . . . . 6b
Same start as the previous route but step right onto the rib.

**Sexo Debil Area** - NW facing wall
15m to 110m single and multi-pitch
Best grades - 3+ to 8a

# MALLORCA - Sa Gubia

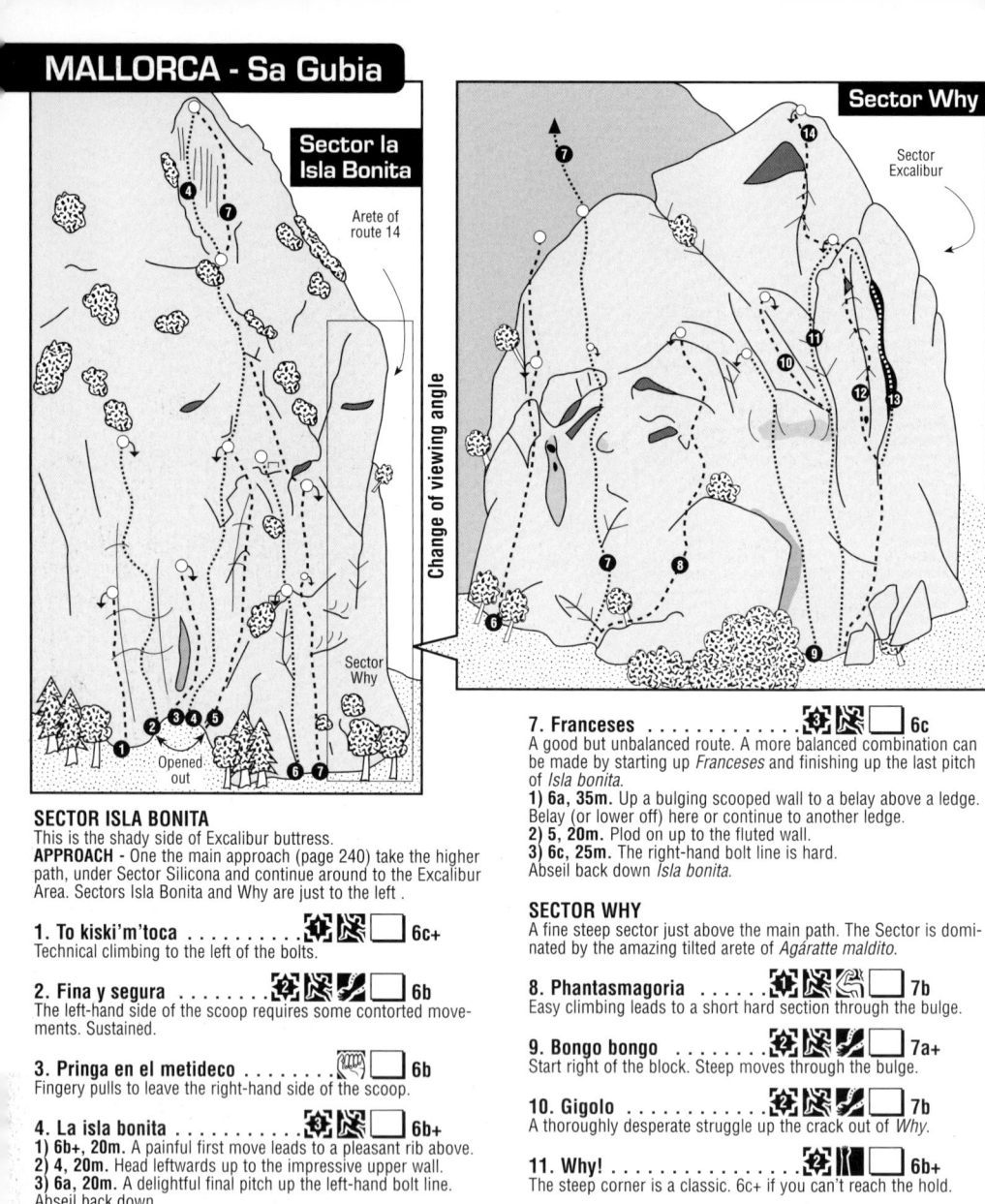

## Sector la Isla Bonita

Arete of route 14

Change of viewing angle

Opened out

Sector Why

## Sector Why

Sector Excalibur

### SECTOR ISLA BONITA
This is the shady side of Excalibur buttress.
**APPROACH** - One the main approach (page 240) take the higher path, under Sector Silicona and continue around to the Excalibur Area. Sectors Isla Bonita and Why are just to the left.

**1. To kiski'm'toca** .......... 6c+
Technical climbing to the left of the bolts.

**2. Fina y segura** ......... 6b
The left-hand side of the scoop requires some contorted movements. Sustained.

**3. Pringa en el metideco** ......... 6b
Fingery pulls to leave the right-hand side of the scoop.

**4. La isla bonita** .......... 6b+
1) 6b+, 20m. A painful first move leads to a pleasant rib above.
2) 4, 20m. Head leftwards up to the impressive upper wall.
3) 6a, 20m. A delightful final pitch up the left-hand bolt line. Abseil back down.

**5. ?** ..................... 5+
An easier alternative to the desperate first move of *Isla bonita*.

**6. Climber gay** .......... 6b
Starting at a lower level.
1) 5+, 20m. Cracks and corner lead to a lead. A good pitch.
2) 6b, 20m. A fingery extension.
Abseil down leftwards from the belay of *Isla bonita*.

**7. Franceses** .......... 6c
A good but unbalanced route. A more balanced combination can be made by starting up *Franceses* and finishing up the last pitch of *Isla bonita*.
1) 6a, 35m. Up a bulging scooped wall to a belay above a ledge. Belay (or lower off) here or continue to another ledge.
2) 5, 20m. Plod on up to the fluted wall.
3) 6c, 25m. The right-hand bolt line is hard.
Abseil back down *Isla bonita*.

### SECTOR WHY
A fine steep sector just above the main path. The Sector is dominated by the amazing tilted arete of *Agáratte maldito*.

**8. Phantasmagoria** ...... 7b
Easy climbing leads to a short hard section through the bulge.

**9. Bongo bongo** ........ 7a+
Start right of the block. Steep moves through the bulge.

**10. Gigolo** ........... 7b
A thoroughly desperate struggle up the crack out of *Why*.

**11. Why!** ............... 6b+
The steep corner is a classic. 6c+ if you can't reach the hold.

**12. Cortocircuito** ........ 6b
Superb climbing up the blunt arete with a hole.

**13. Zaragüay** .......... 6a
Graunchy climbing up the wide crack.

**14. Agárrate Maldito** ..... 7b+
A stunning and obvious extension to any of the last three routes up the arete.

---

248 | Afternoon | 20 min | Vertical | Steep | Lower-offs

West and NW facing walls
20m to 60m single and multi-pitch
Best grades - 5+ to 7b+

rockfax.c

# MALLORCA - Sa Gubia

## SECTOR EXCALIBUR
This is the buttress perched above and behind Sector Silicona. The route lines here are a bit complex but the classic *Excalibur* is well worth the effort, following a superb natural line up the wall.

**APPROACH** - Take the higher approach path past Sector Silicona and scramble up rightwards to the base of the tall wall.

**1. K.G.B.** ....... 6c+
At a lower level to the rest of the routes, climb a corner to reach a pocketed crack. This leads up right then back left to easier ground. There is an alternative line of bolts just right which is probably a right-hand start.

**2. Na guarra** ........ 6a
A good route up the wall left of the Excalibur groove, behind a small tilted block. Higher up step right and broidge up the corner and crack.

**3. Excalibur** ........ 5+
A superb climb following the logical line up the ramp and corner above.
1) 5+, 20m. Follow the curving ramp/groove. At its end pull over the bulge and belay on a tree.
2) 5+, 25m. The corner leads past a couple of overlaps to the top.
**DESCENT** - Abseil off (45m).

**4. Ópera prima** .... 6a+
A direct on *Excalibur*. Continue up above a ramp to an optional lower-off (5+). The steep wall above leads to the tree stance.

**5. Horrible belleza** .... 7a
A wicked technical extension to any of the last few routes.

**6. Trampera matinera** 6b
Start up *Excalibur* but at the top of the ramp pull through the leaning wall by the middle line of bolts.

**7. IL panzerotto** .............. 6a+
The right-hand line goes through the steep section just left of the bulge on *Excalibur*.

**8. No haces más grado..** 6c
Start right of *Excalibur* and pull over some bulges onto a slab. Cross *Excalibur* and tackle the left-hand line on the leaning wall above.

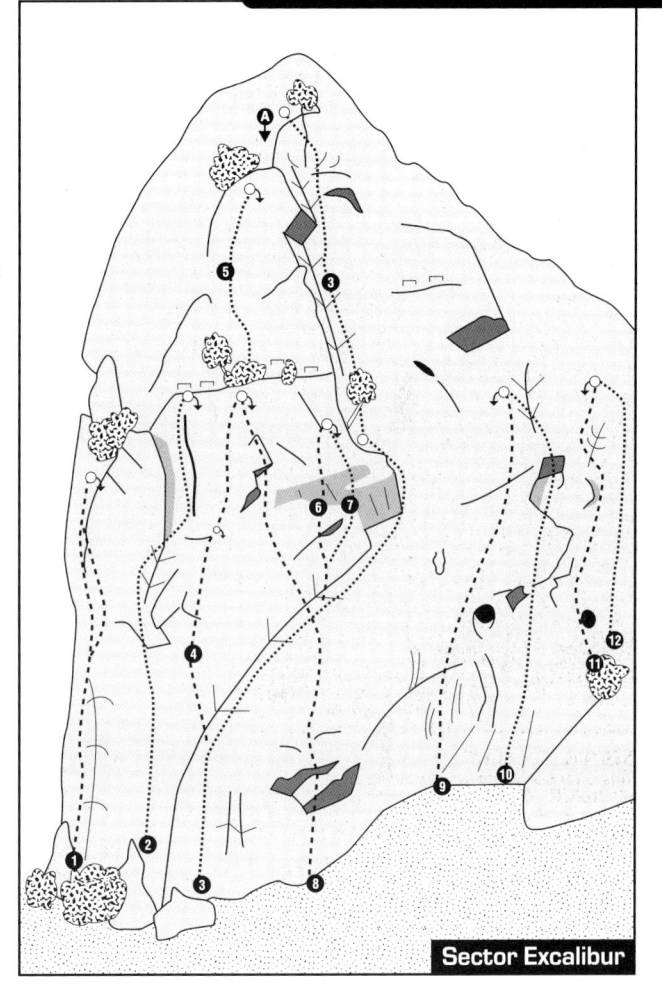

The last 4 routes are up the side slope.

**9. Bofetadas de placer** .... 7b+
Very steep climbing up the tufas.

**10. Charismatic** .......... 6c
Steep climbing through the holes and past a glued-on flake.

**11. Hot consuela** ......... 6c+
Start up the side slab then climb the short technical wall to reach good holds above.

**12. Ingleses** ............. 6b+
Starting in the same place as *Hot consuela*, climb the technical wall to the same poor lower-off.

Sector Excalibur

SW facing wall
15m to 45m routes
Best grades - 5+ to 7b & 7b+

249

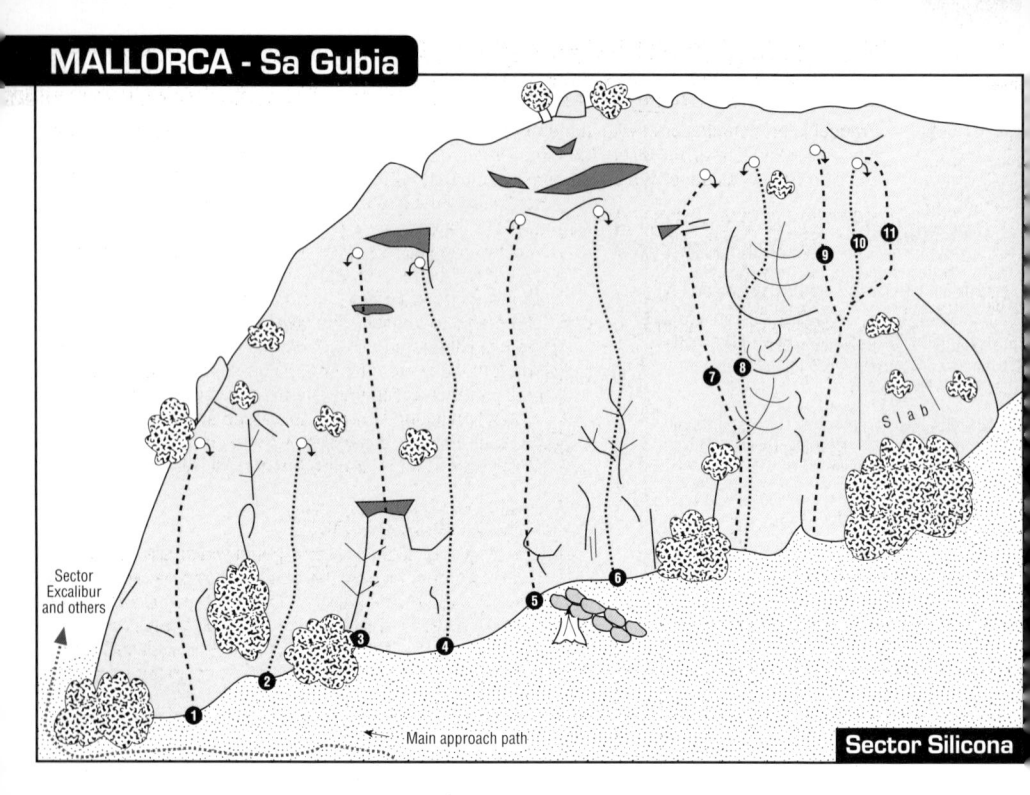

# MALLORCA - Sa Gubia

**Sector Silicona**

## SECTOR SILICONA
This popular sector is often the first section of Sa Gubia sampled by visiting climbers. The climbs are mostly slabby or gentle walls with some hard, technical moves and they have all become a bit polished.
**APPROACH** - It is situated above the higher approach path.

**1. Hawaii 5-0** .............. 4+
Scratched slab up the left-hand edge of the wall.

**2. Silicona** .............. 6b+
A thin slab starting between 2 bushes.

**3. Lulu** .............. 6b
The groove right of some bushes. The move above the low roof is hard and there is a second curx on the upper wall. A popular sandbag at 6a!

**4. Proteina vegetal** .............. 6a
Good holds up a rib. The hard section can be passed on the left. Sadly it is very polished.

**5. Totom fa el que vol** .............. 6a+
Start by the wall. A steep finish.

**6. Resaca** .............. 6a+
Above a wall is an open groove. Climb the groove easily to a hard finish over a small overhang.

The next lines start at a higher level between two bushes.

**7. Gran pis** .............. 6b
The left-hand line leads to a steep bulging finish which needs to be crossed rightwards to the belay.

**8. Rustic pogo** .............. 6b+
The next line has an extremely hard crux to leave the scoop in the middle of the wall. Another old sandbag at 6a+!

The last three routes share a start up the slabby rib right of the groove.

**9. ?** .............. 6a+
The left-hand line is a bit closde to its neighbours.

**10. Familia Iscariote** .............. 6a
A fine finish on the wall above.

**11. Familia variante** .............. 6b
The last line on the wall.

South facing wall
15m to 25m routes
Best grades - 6a to 6b+

Lots of sun | 20 min | Slabby | Lower-offs

# FRAGUEL

Fraguel is an amazing crag with some of the most important hard sport climbing in Europe. The central section is a massive overhanging wave of rock, laced with tufas. In fact most of the climbing here is all about tufas - big ones, little ones, fat ones, thin ones and erotic ones. If you don't like 'em, keep away; if you do like 'em then you may spend most of your holiday here. It is situated in a beautiful wooded valley, hidden from almost every direction, including the one you use to approach the crag. It is almost as if nature didn't want people to find this crag. The crag's reputation may give you the impression that there is little here of interest to people who lead less than 7b+, but there are a few excellent easier routes on the two ends of the crag, some of them almost fitting into the 'slabby' category! However it is steep and hard routes that are what Fraguel is really about and you will have to travel a long way to find a better collection of this type of climb.

### ASPECT AND CLIMATE

The crag only gets the morning sun which is a benefit in warm weather since by the time most people arrive, it will have slipped into the shade. However if you are in search of warm conditions then be warned that it can also be extremely cold here, even in April. This is especially true when there is any wind since it howls down the gorge below the crag.
If you intend a long spell of belay duty, while your mate 'dogs' his or her 8a, take a big duvet jacket. Most of the harder routes will stay dry in all conditions. The easier routes at either end won't.

### APPROACH

From Bunyola drive towards Santa María. Turn left as you leave the village, 200m before the bar on the left. Follow the track, gradually gaining height, through lots of hairpin bends. (There is a gate on this bit of the road which is sometimes locked). When you pass the 5km post, park the car carefully by a path on the right-hand side of the track. leave enough room for a large lorry to get past. Follow the path by the parking area for about 60m, to a small clearing. Keep to the left-hand fork. 15m after the fork, dive left into the bushes, emerging immediately into an old charcoal pit (a grassy circle). Leave this on its opposite side and wander through the trees. Take care not to miss a right-hand turn in the path and continue until a tree blocks the path. At this point break out rightwards to the cliff edge and scramble down a short, awkward groove. The path leads back easily rightwards under the cliff.

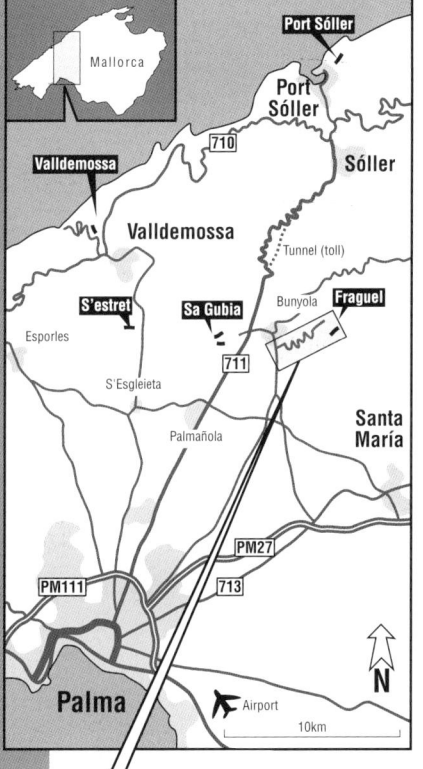

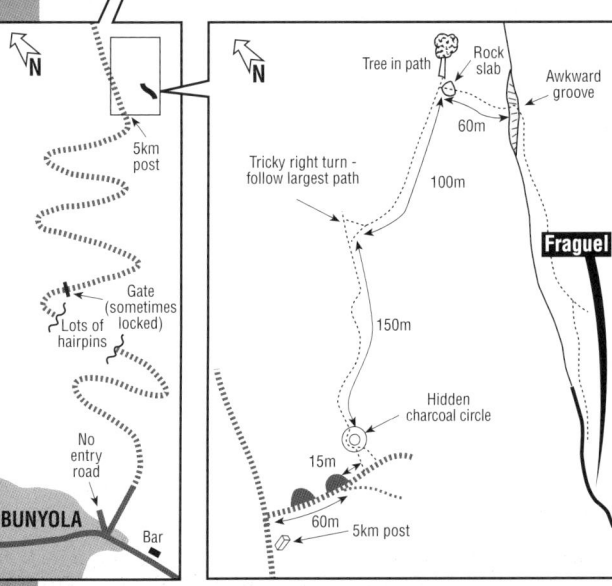

# MALLORCA - Fraguel

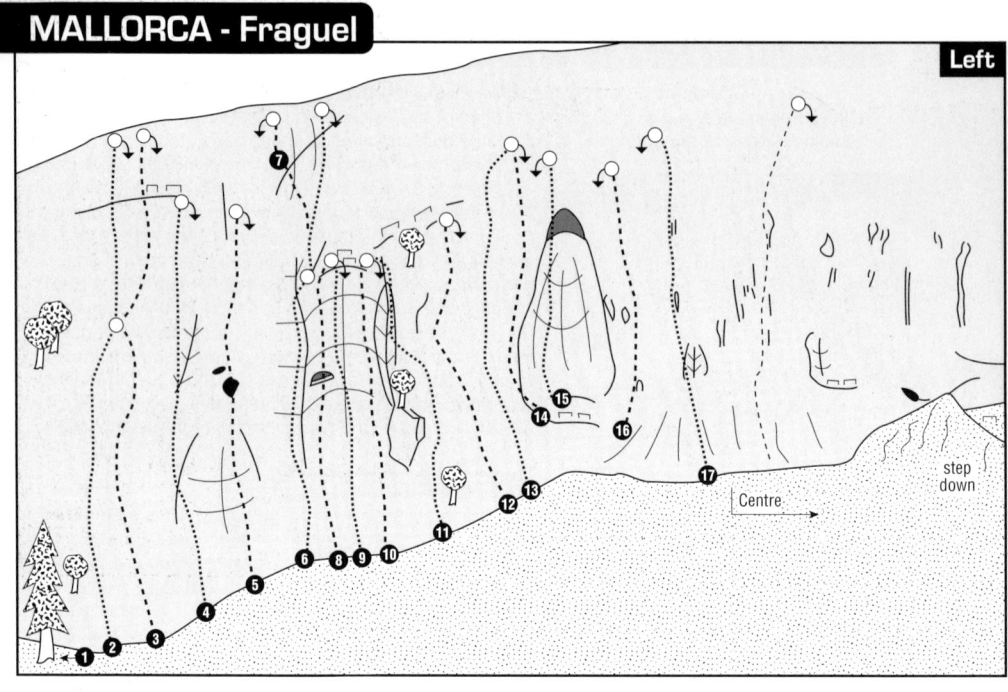

**Left**

## LEFT
At the far end of the crag, beyond a step down in the terrace, is a tall pillar. The first routes start just beyond this pillar.

**1. La casa de la pradera** ....... 6a
A poor route with spaced bolts and little decent climbing.

**2. Ojo climbico** ............. 6c+
1) 6c. A thin middle section. It has blue bolts at the bottom.
2) 6c+. The second pitch has some tricky moves.

**3. 666** ................. 6c
1) 6b+. Technical and fiddly but very worthwhile.
2) 6c.

**4. Tabasco** ............. 7a+
The left-hand side of the scoop.

**5. Harissa** ............. 7b
The right-hand side of the scoop has a desperate move near the bottom. A bit run-out above.

**6. Pink panther** .......... 6a+
1) 5. The corner gives one of the best easy routes on the crag.
2) 6a+. Excellent climbing and a lot easier than it looks.

**7. El terrat** ............. 6b
A short left-hand finish to *Pink Panther*.

**8. Caca de colores** ........ 7a+
The left-hand line up the pillar.

**9. Rosa de sanatorio** ..... 7b+
The blank-looking central line.

**10. Fakir** ............... 6c
The right-hand line.

**11. ?** ................. 5+
An easy route up the flake and groove above.

**12. Psycho Killer** .......... 6c+
Good climbing but a touch escapable higher up.

**13. Jungle hop** ........... 7a
Superb, sustained and twice as pumpy as it looks considering that it looks like a slab!

Further right is a tall oval cave with two lines of bolts.

**14. Salpicón de menisco** .. 8a
The first of the mega hard, mega classic stamina tests.

**15. Solo sex** ........ 8a+?
This route may have been climbed.

**16. ?** ................. (8b/c)
Right of the cave. Probably climbed by now.

**17. Goo goo mack** ....... 8a
The line of blue bolts up the wall right of the oval cave.

# MALLORCA - Fraguel

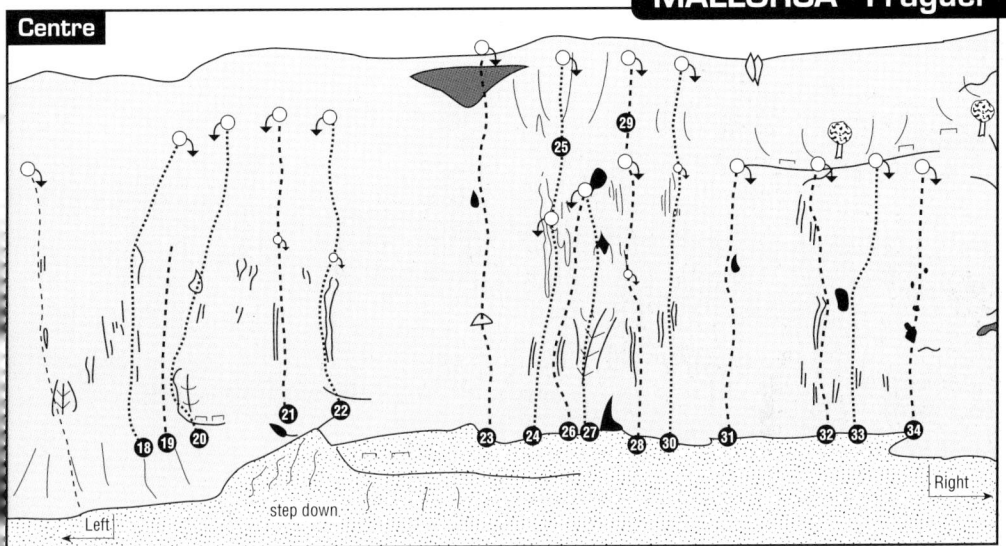

## Centre

## CENTRE
In the centre of the main section of the crag is an distinct step down to a lower level. The routes to the left of this step are long, hard and impressive.

**18. Le gorille a une bonne mine** .... 7c
A long curving line up sustained tufas. People have been known to spend most of their holiday on this route.

**19. Amnesia** ............... (8b+)
An old project which may now have been climbed.

**20. Football fan** ....... 8a
One of the best hard routes on the Island - 'Baby 8a'.

**21. Shabada** ....... 8a+
Above the step in the crag base. Only 7a+ to the first lower-off.

**22. Ramadán** ....... 8b+
To the top of the tufa is 6a+ and very worthwhile. The wall above gives a magnificent continuation.

The next routes are situated around a big open cave above the ledge below the crag.

**23. French kiss** ... 8b
A huge pitch which just goes on and on.

**24. Terre d'adventure** ....... 7b+
The tufas left of the central cave give a short pitch.

**25. Terre d'adventure (Pitch 2)** .......... 8a+
If pitch 1 wasn't enough then just keep going. You are allowed a break at the belay though.

**26. Fes lo que puguis** ....... 7a+
A good route up the big tufas on the left-hand side of the cave. It is the crag 'warm-up' which means it is very polished but still worthwhile. See photo on page 221.

**27. Miss Palma** ....... 7b+
The groove at the back of the cave requires some contorted manoeuvres.

**28. Bobo dodo** ....... 7c
Just to the right of the cave is a tufa system (surprise, surprise). This route is 6c+ to the 'nowhere' lower-off and 7c to the proper one.

**29. ?** ....... ?
The extension to *Bodo Dodo* may be a project.

**30. Humanoide** ....... 8a+
As far as the first lower-off is a very popular 7c+.

**31. No Name** ....... 8b+
One of the hardest routes at the crag.

**32. Pantano boas** ....... 7c+
Up a large tufa and then the wall above.

**33. Muguelín y los probetas** ....... 7c+
Past a deep hole.

**34. Aloha from Hell** ....... 7c
Follow the line of big pockets then when you are totally pumped make the crux pull onto the wall above. Less enjoyable than it looks.

East facing wall
15m to 20m, mostly single pitch
Best grades - 5 to 8b+

# MALLORCA - Fraguel

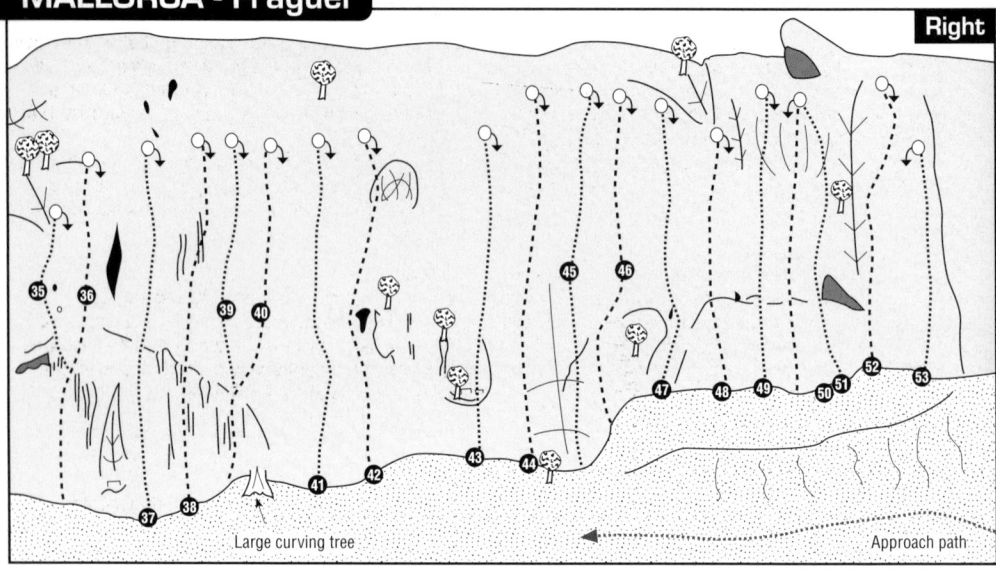

**Right**

Large curving tree — Approach path

## RIGHT
The routes on the right-hand end of the crag start from a ledge at its base. There are a number of quality easier routes here for people who find the central challenges a bit hard, or who are just tired at the end of the day.

**35. Glasnost** ........ 7b
The infamous 'mono' is well chalked up.

**36. Tête de pene** ..... 7c+
Start up the same line of bolts as *Glasnost* but branch right.

**37. El último vals** ........... (7c+)
Up the wall to the right of a cave, past a curving break.

**38. Rock punk** ........ 7c+
More tufa pulling.

**39. Cuencamelo** ........ 7c
Start behind the large, curving tree.

**40. On es l'avi** ..... 7b+
One of the more popular routes which regularly spits people off from high up. Harder for the short and the bolts are awkwardly placed.

**41. Pastanaga punyetera** ........ 8a
There are not so many tufas on this one.

**42. 7b el plumero** .... 7b+
Sustained and technical despite being broken by two rests in holes.

**43. Cotorrot** ........ 7c+
Above a ledge with two trees.

**44. Cous-cous** ........ 6c
One of the best of the (relatively) easy routes on the crag. Start just to the left of a rounded rib.

**45. Esto no es Calvià** ........ 6b+
The wall just to the right of the rib.

**46. Sementir** ............. 6a+
Start in the same place as the above but branch right on gold bolts.

**47. Comando rasta** ............ 6a
The slabby wall to the right gets gradually harder.

**48. D** ................ 6b+
Another one that packs it in at the top.

**49. Peep show's garriga** ... 7b+
A created line up the bulge.

**50. Marmade** ........ 7b
Slightly bigger chipped holds on this one.

**51. Tofol** ............. 6b+
A superb little route just left of the tree.

**52. Churropino** ............. 6a
At last something a bit easier. Don't be fooled - the bulge at the bottom is still hard.

**53. Chris line** ................ 4
This one really is easier, but it's not very good.

East facing wall
20m to 30m routes
Best grades - 5+ to 8a

# PORT SÓLLER

Mallorca specialises in small crags, with about 20 routes in total, all of which are better than most of the sport routes in Britain. Port Sóller is one of these places, in a beautiful location, perched high above the sea, surrounded by pine trees and with perfect solid rock. There used to be a blemish which was the small selection of easier routes which were really not up to standard but fortunately they have all been demolished.

The best routes are steep and sustained pitches on weird droopy blobs of rock. Many of them are extremely unlikely jug-hauling extravaganzas which make a visit to the crag essential for any strong team. *Blobland* and *Ja Som Five* are both superb and well worth the trip on their own.

## ACCESS

The area above the crag is being developed with new houses which has caused access problems in the past. AT the time of writing (Feb 2001) the work is coming to an end and once it is finished there should be no problems getting to the crag. Until then you may find that you are turned away during the week, when workmen are present. It is probably a good idea to follow their advice since they do have a habit of chucking large items off the cliff top.
Check rockfax.com/mallorca for more information.

## ASPECT AND CLIMATE

The crag faces northwest over the sea, getting all the mid to late afternoon sun that's going, as well as any decent sunset. Although it is quite close to the town of Port Sóller, it can feel isolated because of the trees at its base. These also give it shelter from any wind. The cave routes will give dry climbing in the rain, but some of the tufas may seep after long spells of bad weather.

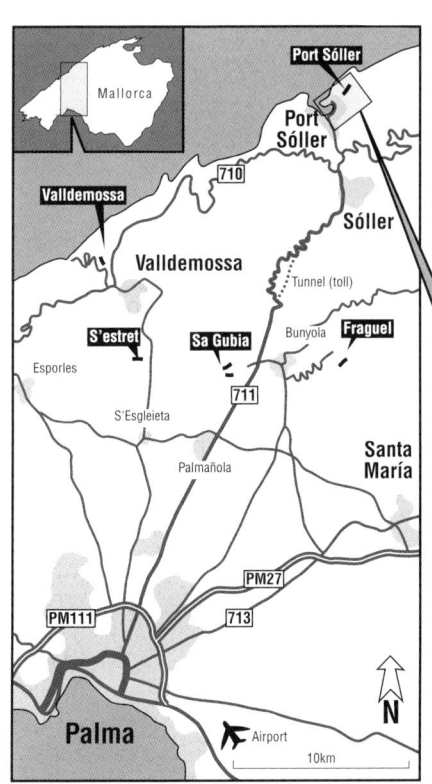

## APPROACH

Drive to Port Sóller through the tunnel. When you reach the bay in the town, follow the road around to the right along the sea-front. Continue all the way around until you reach two 'no entry' roads directly in front of you. Turn sharply right up the hill and continue through two hairpins. Park on a bend by an abandoned old bar or further down the road. Walk down the track next to the bar and you will see the crag ahead of you. There is some fencing on this track a present but there is a path maintained down the side.

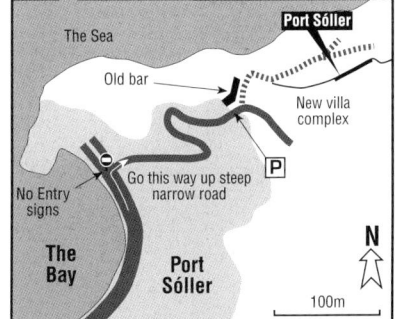

# MALLORCA - Port Sóller

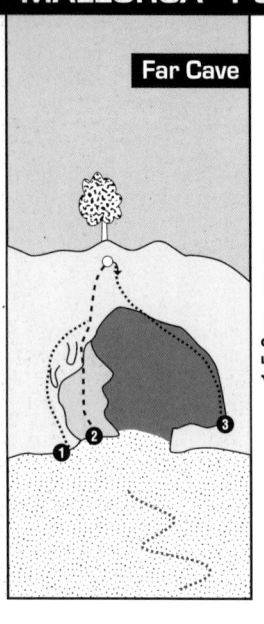

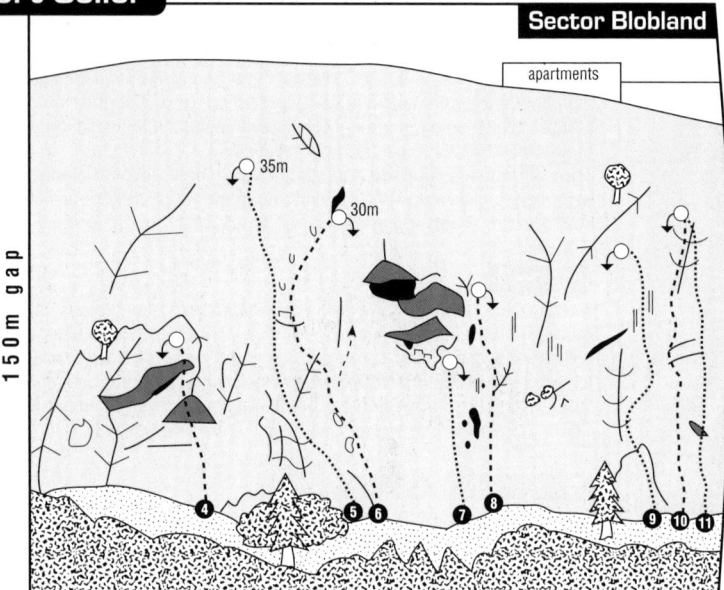

**Far Cave**

**Sector Blobland**

apartments

150m gap

35m
30m

## FAR CAVE
The first routes detailed are in a cave 150m left of the main crag. This is a mini-version of the main cave.

**1. ?** ............................... 6c
A strange route with a huge gap between the middle bolts. Clip a bolt on the next route or, better, join and finish up it.

**2. ?** ............................... 7a
Start in the cave and swing out leftwards.

**3. ?** ............................... 8a
The hard line on the right-hand side of the cave.

## SECTOR BLOBLAND
This is the left-hand side of the main area. It is a bit overgrown at the far end, and sadly, this is also a popular toilet. If you are desperate, try walking a bit further.

The first route starts just left of a very big tree.

**4. Doris** ............................... 7b
A relatively short route over a couple of roofs.

The next to routes start to the right of the big tree.

**5. Directland** ............................... 7c
**35m.** It is possible (and easier) to join *Blobland* higher up.

**6. Blobland** ............................... 6c
**30m.** A stunning and unlikely route up the line of golden bolts. The crux is at the top of the lower wall and the headwall is outrageous.

**7. Bon vi** ............................... 6a
Good climbing with one awkward move.

**8. Els salvatges** ............................... 6b+
A steep finish.

Further right is an area of well-featured, easier-angled rock with three good pitches.

**9. ?** ............................... 6c
The bolts are to the right at the bottom.

**10. ?** ............................... 6a

**11. ?** ............................... 6b

# MALLORCA - Port Sóller

**Sector Sa Cova**

**Far Right**

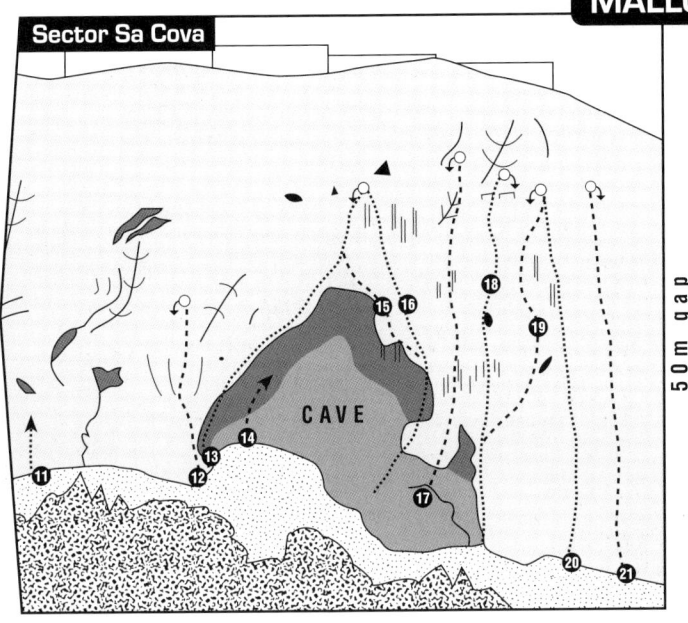

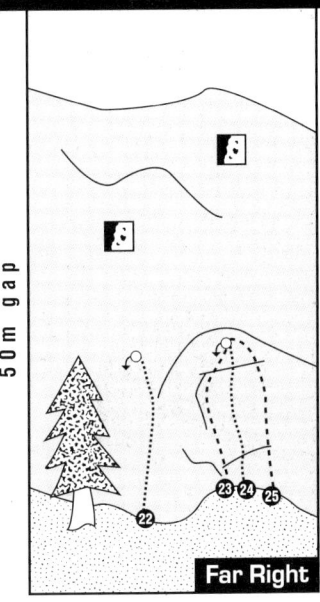

## SECTOR SA COVA
The most important area is centred on the large cave which dominates the right-hand side of the crag.

**12. Dit I fet** .......... 7a
The left-hand edge of the cave is short but demanding.

**13. Virgin** ......... 8a+
Extremely strenuous and sustained. There is a cop-out mid-route lower-off which downgrades the route to 8a.

**14. ?** ........................ Project
A really hard version of the previous route.

On the right-hand side of the cave the routes get even better but the first two have old bolts (as of 12/2000) and shouldn't be climbed in their present state.

**15. Phantomas** ......... 7b
Superb jug-pulling up the steep right edge of the cave. I have been given grades of 7a+ and 7b+ for this one. Take your pick but it helps if you are a gorilla.

**16. Ficalito** ......... 7c
Old bolts. From the 'rest' on the last route, power straight up the wall.

**17. Club super tres** ...... 7b
Great climbing on tufa-covered rock with a disappointingly hard crux move.

**18. Ja som five** ......... 6c+
A superb sustained route which is desperate if you are short (7a) and a path if you are tall (6c) therefore hardly anyone will agree with the 6c+ grade.

**19. Picnic** .............. 6b+
Start as for the previous route but break rightwards up the wall. An early exit from the fixed krab gives a good 5+.

**20. ?** ................. 6b+
30m. Steady climbing to the last bolt then the tricky crux of the previous route.

**21. ?** .................. 6b
30m. The last of the longer lines.

## FAR RIGHT
Further right, down the hill is an unspectacular wall just past a large tree. Three of the routes share one lower-off.

**22. ?** .................... 6c
**23. ?** .................... 6b+
**24. ?** .................... 6c
**25. ?** .................... 7a

There used to be a set of easy routes on the walls further right, above the approach track. These are now completely unclimbable and covered in fencing. It is not clear whether the fencing will be removed when the building work is finished and even if it is the routes will take some time before the clean up.

NW facing wall and cave
10m to 30m routes
Best grades - 6a to 8a+

# CA'N NYIC (Torrella)

Ca'n Nyic is a beautiful crag situated in the mountains to the east of Sóller. There isn't much to do here so it is an easy place to tick in a day, or even half a day, however the routes are all high quality challenges. A good idea is to combine a visit with a trip to the gorge of 'Torrent de Pareis' or, if you have less time, a drive to the base of the gorge at 'Sa Calobra'. The crag was called Torrella in earlier editions of this book.
The climbing is mainly vertical on the customary immaculate rock. Routes 5, 6 and 7 are the three classic and popular ticks of the place but the rest are also worthwhile. Some of the harder routes appear to be of the same high quality as the three easier climbs however they do suffer from lack of attention and are often a bit dirty.

## ASPECT AND CLIMATE
Torrella is virtually a mountain crag hence it can be windy and cold. It makes a pleasant venue in hot weather since it only receives the late afternoon sun.

## APPROACH
Cross over the mountains on the hairpin-ridden C711. Once in Sóller, turn towards Pollença, on the twisting coast road, C710. (This road is also signed to 'Lluc'). Keep driving until you are just before the first proper tunnel. This is about 10km from Sóller and is just after the 38km post. Park in a lay-by, opposite a belvedere view point. A faint path leads leftwards (looking in) up the steep slope towards the crag.
If you are staying near Pollença, it is probably quicker to drive down the road south of the mountains, and cross the C711 as described above. The long north coast road is a very picturesque road, but it is popular with large coaches and groups of cyclists and therefore it is extremely slow. If you do approach on te north coats road then watch out for the tunnel after the 39km post and park at the belvedere just after this.

**THERE ARE BREAK-INS TO CARS PARKED FOR THIS CRAG. LEAVE YOUR CAR EMPTY WITH THE GLOVE COMPARTMENT OPEN.**

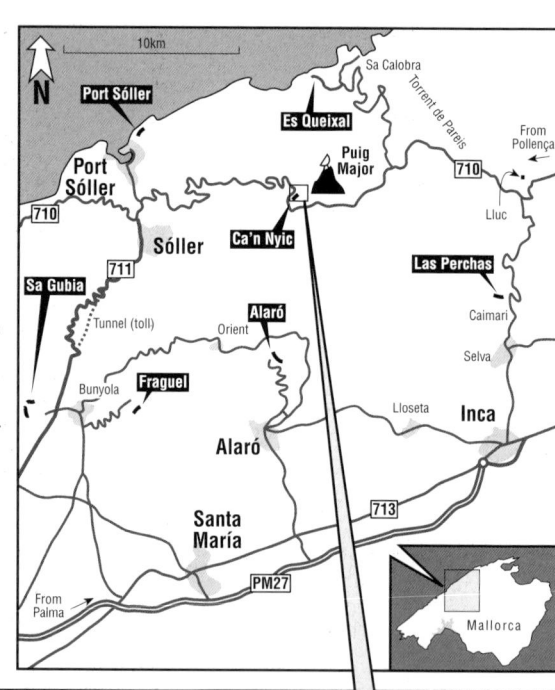

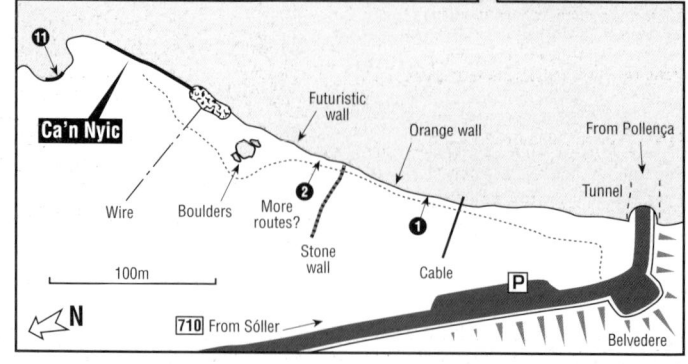

# MALLORCA - Ca'n Nyic (Torrella)

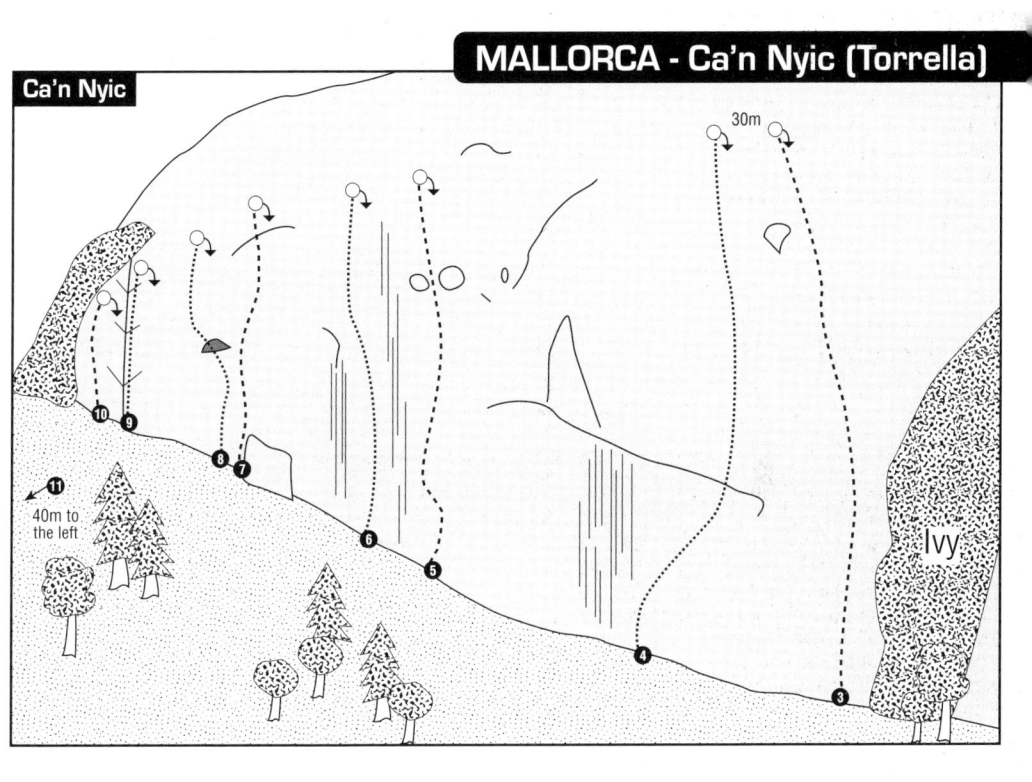

## CA'N NYIC

The path leading up the slope to the main crag passes under a lot of just climbable rock. At present hardly any of this has been developed but there are two routes.
The routes are listed from right to left.

**1. Max Cady** . . . . . . . . 7c
Climb the orange streak just past a cable lying on the ground.

**2. Agent Orange** . . . . . 8a+
Past a stone wall is a faint, left-facing groove. This gives a hard and sustained pitch. See photo on page 220.

There may also be two other bolt lines in this area but no details are known.

Once you have passed some boulders, and a wire, the routes become more concentrated. The first two pitches follow awesome lines up the wall just left of a large patch of ivy.

**3. S'Horabaixa** . . . . . . 7c
High in the grade.

**4. Na faresta** . . . . . . . . 7b+
A superb looking route which is low in the grade. However the start is sometimes wet and the holds are often dirty.

**5. Tutup** . . . . . . . . . . . 6c
A magnificent wall climb with a hard start. The leftwards move at the bottom requires lateral thinking otherwise you may find it worth 6c+.

**6. Molins de paper** . . . . . . . 6b
Equally as good as its neighbour. Pumpy, not too technical and high in the grade.

A little further up the slope is a detached flake.

**7. Bona nyic** . . . . . . . . . . 6a+
Superb climbing up the wall and bulges left of the flake. It keeps going all the way to the lower-off.

**8. Ho passam pillo** . . . . . 7a
Hard climbing up the bulging wall to the left.

There are supposed to be two projects to the left, although there was only one when I was there. Neither looks very good.

**9. Borinot** . . . . . . . . . . . . 6c
The blank groove is awkward.

**10. Nycinyatos** . . . . . . . . . 4+
An unspectacular route up the rib.

There are reports of two more routes up the gully to the left of the main wall. The final route, which is well worth seeking out, is across the gully on a prow down and left.

**11. Bernadí Company** . . . . 6c+
Excellent moves and is a touch easier than first appearance suggests.

NW facing wall
10m to 30m routes
Best grades - 6a+ to 8a+

# ES QUEIXAL

This is a curious crag which puts to rest the rumour that modern climbers are only interested in developing bits of rock that they can walk to within 10 minutes from the car. The approach drive passes through some spectacular scenery but involves tackling the endless hairpins on the road which descends to Sa Calobra. The spectacular pinnacle of Es Queixal is actually situated in in the next cove along from Sa Calobra which is called Cala Tuent.

As is often the case in Mallorca the potential of the crag exceeds the reality which may come as a bit of a disappointment if you have struggled to get the crag, especially if you lose your way on the approach path. However, don't be put off, the situation and atmosphere at Es Queixal are magnificent and, for those who wish to explore the island further than the usual haunts, you could not wish for a more beautiful location.

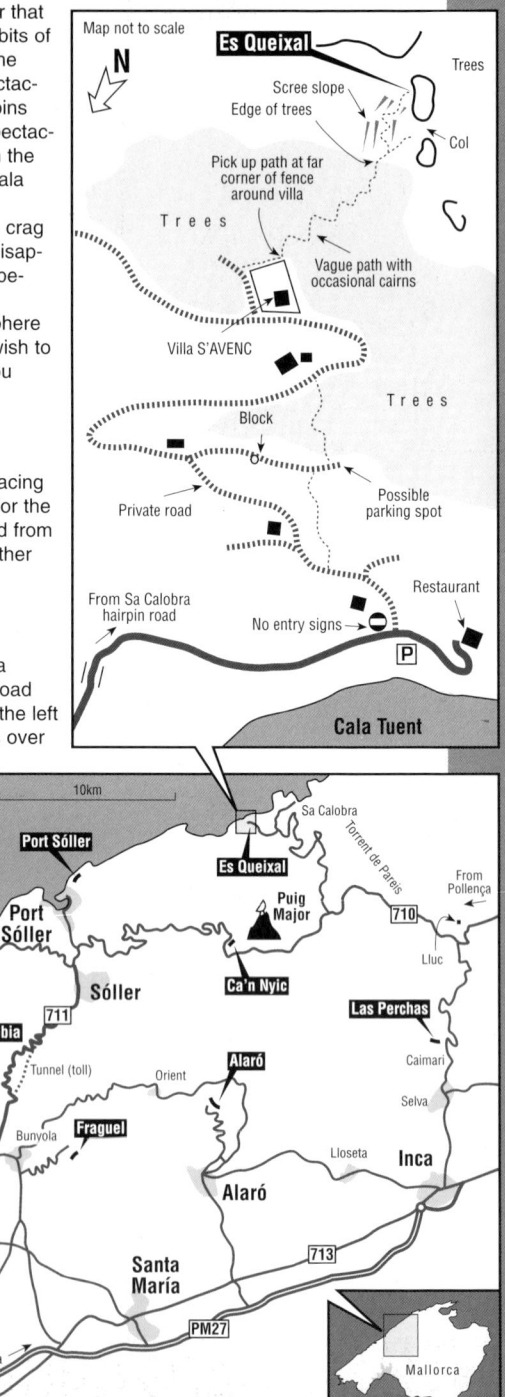

## ASPECT AND CLIMATE

The climbing is a northeast facing wall, in a north facing cove. It were receive some early-morning sun but for the most part will be shady. It is unlikely to be sheltered from the wind and there will be nothing here in bad weather but if hot, it could provide a pleasant retreat.

## APPROACH

Of from the north coast road descend towards a Sa Calobra. After 15 minutes of tortuous hairpins the road opens out at the bottom and there is a junction on the left signed to 'Cala Tuent' and a restaurant. Follow this over the brow and wind down into the cove with the the characteristic tooth of Es Queixal prominent on the hillside opposite (and depressingly far up the hillside). As you round the cove there is a road on the left signed as 'no entry'. Either park somewhere near here and start walking up the road, or chance your luck and drive up it (see map opposite). From wherever you park get yourself to the top bend by Villa S'AVENC. Now comes the hard bit. Walk down the short track beside the Villa and follow the fence around to the far corner. From here very carefully pick up the vague path which winds slowly up the hillside past the occasional cairn. As you exit the trees the col between the two pinnacles is visible above you. At this point branch left up a scree slope and head as directly as possible for the base of the crag. If you lose this path then the going gets very tough so try and back track. If you successfully followed the path on the way up then help subsequent visitors by building more cairns on your way back down.

# MALLORCA - Es Queixal

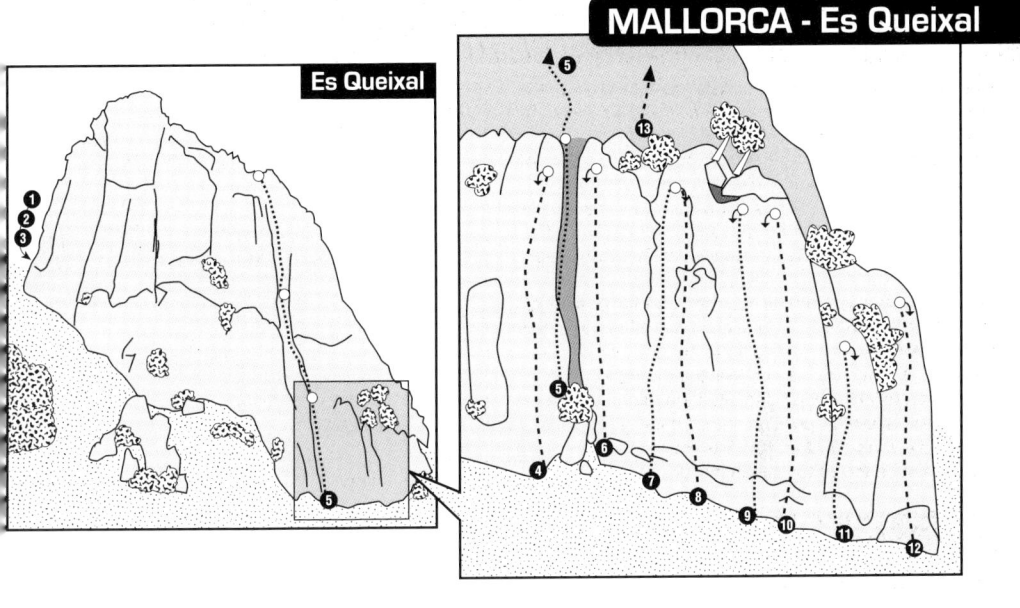

## ES QUEIXAL
There are three isolated short routes situated on the very top left-hand side of the wall. The extra effort to reach these will prove beyond even the most dedicated of explorers.

**1. Los tuberculosos van al campo** .. 5+
Around the corner from the next two routes.

**2. Es mirador** .............. 5+
The left-hand line.

**3. Idò a què esperes** .......... 6a+
The right-hand line.

The main attraction is on the bottom right-hand corner of the pinnacle where there is a short compact wall of grey rock with the obligatory vast expanse of similar rock above it.

**4. No és es dragó el que em fa por** ........ 6c+
The scooped wall left of the chimney.

**5. Es queixal corcat** ........ 6a+
The chimney is the beginning of a three pitch route which reaches the top of the crag.
1) 6a+, 20m. The first pitch is fully bolted.
2) 6a+, 25m. The corner above is followed on trad gear.
3) 6a+, 30m. Continue to the top.
**DESCENT** - Abseil back down the route.

**6. Sa travessa des queixal** .... 6b
The right-hand edge of the chimney.

**7. Gelat i desrinyonat** ....... 6a+
Crozzly wall leading to a crack.

**8. Jose's show** ........... 7a+
Another crozzly wall.

**9. Pepa Pattisier** ........ 6c
Technical climbing on sharp edges.

**10. Rintintín** ............ (6b/c)
More painful holds.

**11. Santas pascuas** ............. 5+
The short slab.

**12. Canta y no llores** ........ 6a
Right of a chimney is a short slab route.

There is one extension pitch from the ledge at which the rest of the routes finish. This may be excellent but no details are known.

**13. La paz de Andy Sheridan** ..... ?

East facing pinnacle
15m to 20m routes
Best grades - 5+ to 7a+

# ALARÓ

This is one of the most impressive crags in Europe which has only just begun to be developed. It is so big that, if you know where to look, it is easy to spot from the plane as you fly into Palma. The size of the place will also strike you as you look up to the west wall from the restaurant. It therefore comes as a bit of a disappointment to find out that many of the routes are on the teeny wee section on the left-hand end, below the castle. Don't worry though because when you go and stand underneath it you will discover that it is neither teeny nor wee.

The other two developed areas are essential for those of you who like tufa climbing and if you don't what are you doing in Mallorca?

The massive southern wall which is passed on the approach, and which can be clearly seen from most of the Island, is home to a few traditional routes. The sister lump to the east of Castillo Alaró is known as Soncadena. It also has a few traditional routes and slightly more potential than even Alaró. The restaurant is excellent; there tends to be only one meal on the menu but you can be sure it is a good one. You can also stay the night there very cheaply.

The Paret de sa Porta area (formerly Castillo Wall) sits directly over the path leading to the castle. This path is very popular, which is no problem if you are a poseur, but if you are a bit shy, or if you like your peace and quiet, then keep away from the crag at weekends. The routes on this sector vary from good easier slab climbs to steep, hard and technical grade '7s. The routes on the tufa walls are amongst the best of their type found anywhere, and an ascent of *Buf!!* will be a memorable experience, even if you do fall off while staring at the chain!

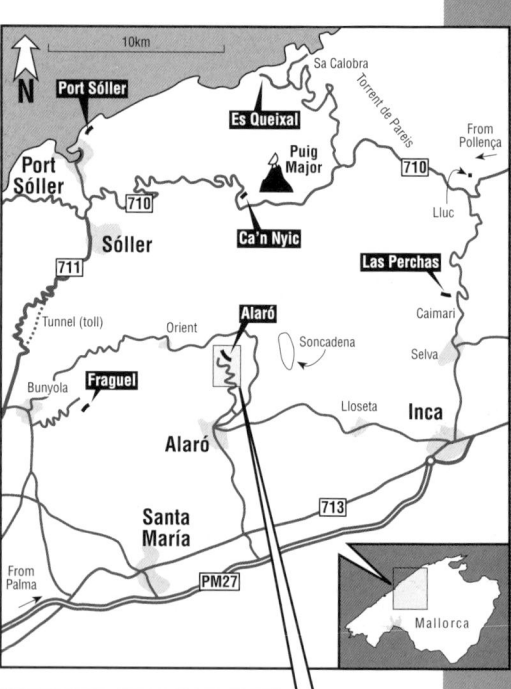

## ASPECT AND CLIMATE

The Castillo d'Alaró is high and exposed hence it can be windy and cold. It receives the sun at around midday so make sure that you aren't half way up one of the tufas when the sweat starts pouring off your hands. Sector del medio faces more northwest than the others and as such stays in the shade for longer. It is worth remembering that tufas are formed by drainage streaks, which means that the face is usually wet after rain. This is often the case in Sept -Oct time.

## APPROACH

The town of Alaró can be easily reached from the main C713 road, to the south of the mountains. From the town follow the road which is signed for 'Castillo de Alaró'. This soon turns into a twisting dirt track. (There are several boulders beside the road here which have routes on them). Eventually the track arrives at the restaurant where you can grab some refreshment before joining the crowds walking up to the castle. It is also possible to continue up the road to a higher car park from where a slightly shorter walk reaches the Castillo Wall but the road is very rough, the car park not as secure and no use if you intend to climb on Sector Chorreras.

For the detailed approaches to the two sectors see the individual descriptions with the routes.

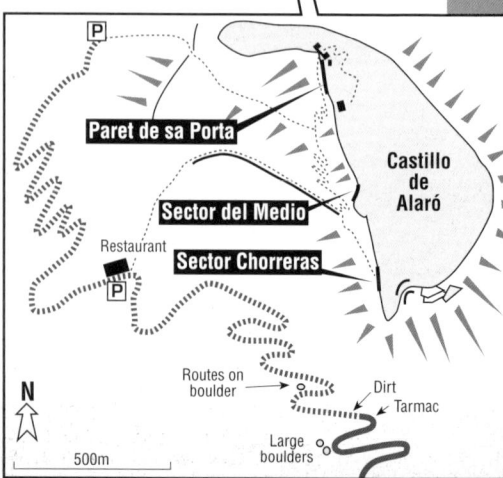

# MALLORCA - Alaró

**Paret de Sa Porta - Left**

**Paret de sa Porta - Right**

To Castle

Paret de Sa Porta

Sector del Medio

Sector Chorreras

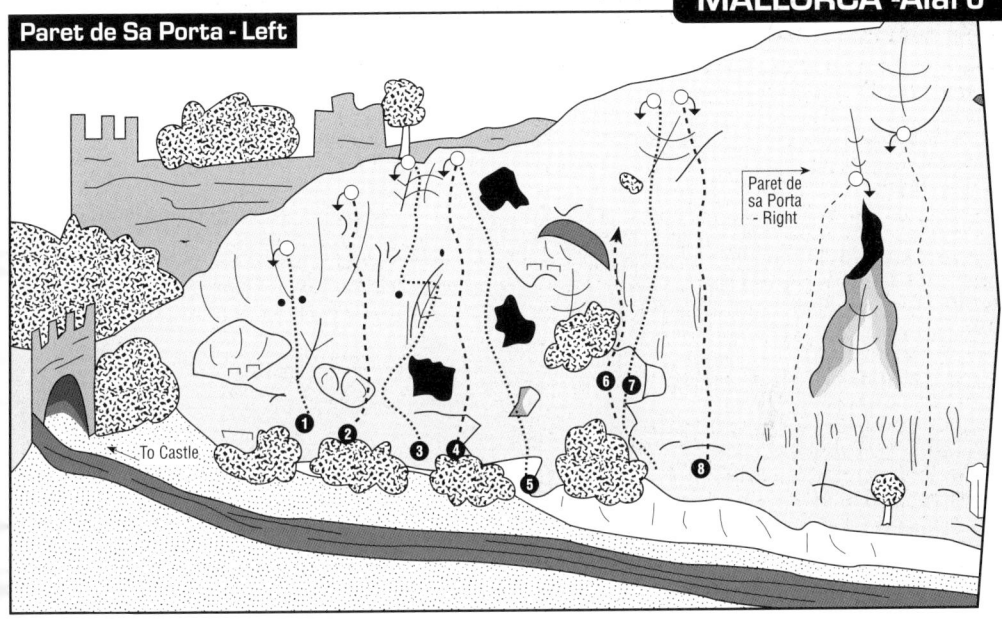

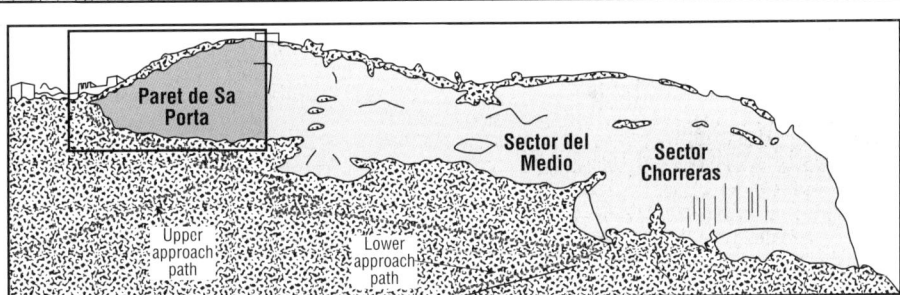

Upper approach path

Lower approach path

## PARET DE SA PORTA (formerly CASTILLO WALL)
The wall under the extreme left-hand end of the massive main face is relatively small compared to the stuff to the right but it still manages to give some superb long pitches.

**APPROACH** - Follow the obvious popular path from the restaurant, which leads diagonally up below the cliff. It then zig-zags back leftwards towards the castle. Alternatively use the upper car park and follow the less steep and slightly shorter path to the same point.

The first routes start on the bulging wall at the far left-hand end, behind some bushes.

**1. ?** .................... (7b+)
Short and steep past 2 pockets. Glue-in bolts.

**2. A** .................... 7b
The steep pocketed wall behind the bushes. Hard to on-sight but the difficulties are only short.

**3. B** .................... 7a
Superb climbing up the tufa with a long reach left for the crux.

**4. C** .................... 6c
There is a drilled mono on the crux but it is possible to do it without. A bit artificial.

**5. D** .................... 6a
Steep juggy climbing but the hard bits are escapable. If you stick to the direct line it is 6b.

**6. ?** .................... Project
The left-hand of two bolt lines is a project which may now have been climbed at 7b.

**7. Esteban** .................... 7b+
The wall on the right is superb and has a strange crux sequence.

**8. ¿Amigos para siempre?** .................... 7c+
Wonderful technical and sustained! Sadly also outrageously hard.

West facing wall
15m to 25m routes
Best grades - 6a to 7c+

# MALLORCA - Alaró

## Paret de Sa Porta - Right

### PARET DE SA PORTA - RIGHT
The next routes are around the tall cave, left of the plinth.

**9. Foam Party** ........................ 7c
Another hard and brilliant line to the left of the tall orange cave.

**10. ¡Muérete ya!** ..................... 7c
The right-hand side of the cave is equally hard.

**11. Zatropeck** ........................ 7c
The long tufa line behind a curious plinth.

**12. ?** ................................ (7b/?)
The old bolt line to the right is probably about 7b to the lower-off on *Aferra el tul*. It may now continue higher up the wall.

**13. Aferra el tul** .................... 6c
At last something a bit easier; at least as far as the last bulge, then it has a bit of a sting but it is only one move.

**14. Mata guiris** ...................... 7a+
A superb and testing route which has a hard crux followed by a long arete on cheese-grater rock. It is a pleasent 5+ to the twin ring lower-off.

**15. No res** ........................... 7a+
Similar climbing but slightly easier than *Mata guiris* and also 5+ to the half-height lower-off.

**16. Frit** ............................. 6a
A pleasant little route up the short wall to a lower-off on a ledge.

**17. Sobrassada** ....................... 5
First bolt is missing, clip the bolt on *Frit*.

The next route starts 10m further right, just above the path.

**18. ?** ................................ 6a+
A long pitch with a hard finish past a bulge which can be by-passed on the right at 6a.

**19. Snowboard** ........................ 5+
Climb the slab directly above the path. There is a loose flake on this route.

**20. Fido-dido** ........................ 6a
Just to the right, climb over a bulge.

The last three routes are further right, above a bend in the path. The bolts are missing from some of these. Try climbing the right-hand one and then top-roping the other two.

**21. Vagon roll** ....................... 4+
The left-hand side of the slab. Only one bolt.

**22. Las mallas de cristo** ............. 5
Old rusty bolts and a peg.

**23. Hola qué tal** ..................... 6a
The right-hand side of the slab is still fully bolted.

West facing wall
15m to 25m routes
Best grades - 5 to 7c

# MALLORCA - Alaró

**Sector del Medio**

Huge 'mouth' which is clearly visible from the restaurant

Slabs

Approach from hairpin

## SECTOR DEL MEDIO

This excellent area is situated to the right of the huge mouth in the middle of the west face. It gets the sun later in the afternoon than the other two main areas.

**APPROACH** - From the restaurant follow the path up towards the face to the first hairpin. Instead of jumping over the wall (as for Sector Chorreras) pick up a vague path that leads up and slightly leftwards under the wall. The routes are about 75m up through the trees.

**1. ?** ............................. 5+
The left-hand line.

**2. ?** ............................. 6b
The right-hand line is high in the grade. Photo page 25.

**3. ?** ............................. 6c
A brilliant three-pitch route which reaches the top of the wall.
1) **6c.** Pull steeply out of the cave. belay in an orange recess.
2) **6c.** Exit right from the recess onto a crozzly wall.
3) **6b.** A wide groove leads to the top.
Abseil off on double ropes.

**4. Lute** ............................. 7a
Gain the droopy tufa blob then head right and up the thin wall.

**5. Superchorrera access** ....... 6a
The access pitch for the next routes has a hollow feel and is bolted for 7b climbers!

**6. Superchorrera** .............. 7b
Struggle up the inner thighs of this elegant route.

**7. XTR** ............................. 7b+
Start from the right-hand cave and head for the crack.

**8. Therapy** ....................... 7b
Start from the right-hand cave, pull left from the tufas onto the thin wall.

**9. Sánchez** ....................... Project
There is a rumour that this is an open project.

**10. Magnum** ...................... 7a+
A stunning, long route.
1) **7a+.** Up tufas and the white wall above to a hanging belay in the cave. Technical in its middle section.
2) **6c.** The magnificent diagonal crack to the ledge.
3) **6b.** Step back left and head for the short hanging corner high on the wall.

West facing wall
20m to 30m, mostly multi-pitch
Best grades - 6b to 7b+

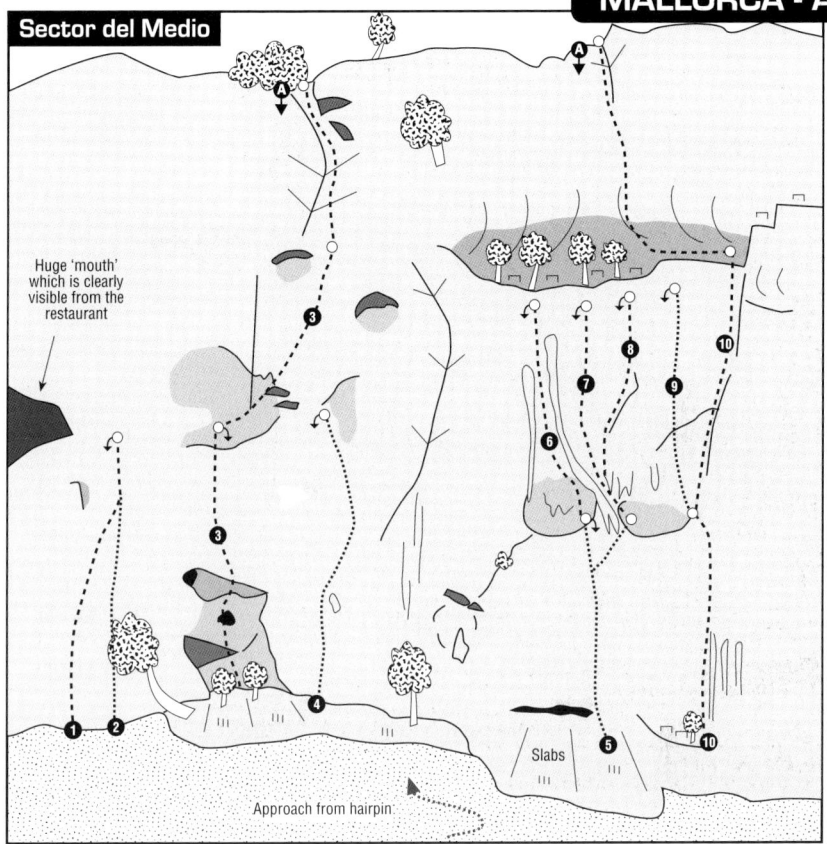

# MALLORCA - Alaró

**Sector Chorreras**

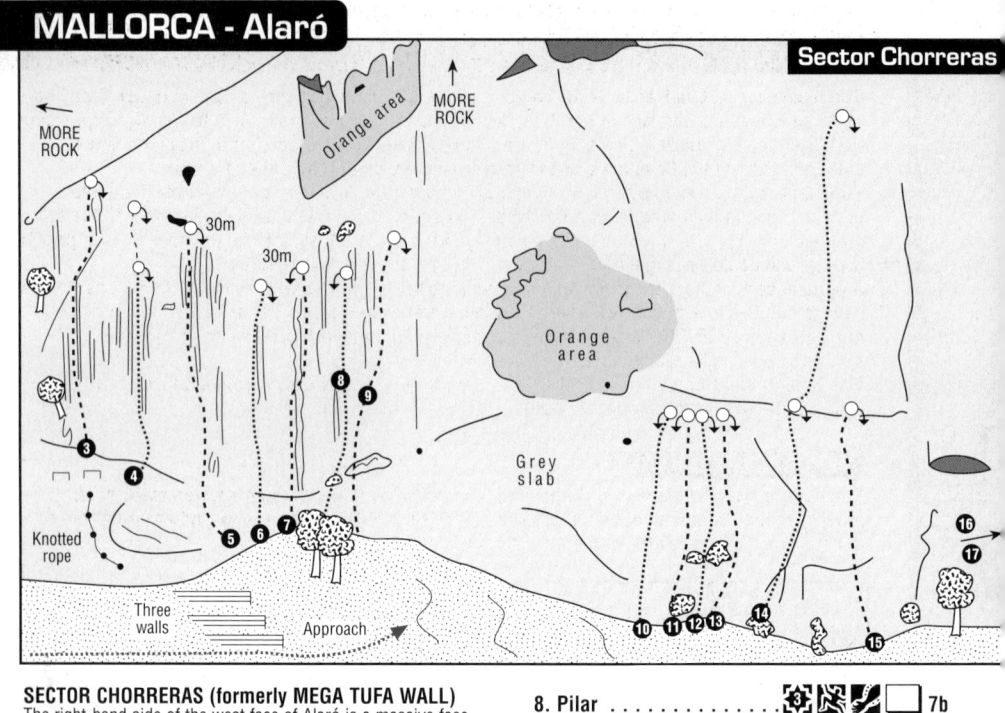

## SECTOR CHORRERAS (formerly MEGA TUFA WALL)
The right-hand side of the west face of Alaró is a massive face laced with tufas, home to some of the best climbs on the Island.

**APPROACH** - From the restaurant, walk up a long diagonal path by a wall, to the point where the path turns away from the wall. On the corner, jump down over the wall and continue rightwards under the face. Pass a small grey slab and continue along some walls to a larger grey slab underneath the massive wall.

The first two routes are on an orange wall which is directly up and left after jumping over the wall on the approach.

**1. ?** .................... (6b/c)
Orange wall, over a bulge, into a groove.

**2. ?** .................... (6c/6c+)
The rest of the routes are on the topo.

**3. ?** .................... (8a)
The left most line reached by the rope. May still be a project.

**4. Hob nops** .................... 6c+
There is some evidence of activity above the belay.

**5. Buf!!** .................... 7a
One of the best tufa climbs in the world! It's got everything; hands-off rests, back and footing, knee bars, egyptians and a terrible name. 30m long and many fail at 29.5m. Photo page 217.

**6. To pa ti** .................... 7a+
A superb climb which feels more than a '+' harder than *Buf*.

**7. Cloncion** .................... 7b
Much the same as the others only with a glued-on blob to pass a blank bit.

**8. Pilar** .................... 7b
The last long tufa on the wall.

**9. ?** .................... Project
With a hanging rope.

The next 6 routes are on the lower slab.

**10. ?** .................... 6c
The fingery slab left of the bulge.

**11. ?** .................... 6b+
Climb the bulge directly.

**12. ?** .................... 6c
The right-hand side of the bulge past a small loose flake. Escapable rightwards at 6a+.

**13. ?** .................... 6a+
The slab to the right past the same loose flake.

**14. Pincha uvas** .................... 5
The crack is a delightful. The extension is a whole different ball game and may never have been climbed although the local topo quotes an extremely unlikely grade of 7b+, therefore it is either brilliant or chipped.

**15. Kiko** .................... 6a
An enjoyable slab climb just to the right.

**16. Xavier** .................... 7a+
Of the topo to the right.

**17. ?** .................... 7c
Worth seeking out.

West facing wall
15m to 30m, mostly single pitch
Best grades - 5 to 7b

# LAS PERXES (Caimari)

The main cave at Las Perxes is for bored muscle-monsters who fancy a little work out. A day at here will leave you with little strength to pick up your bottle of San Miguel and also the impression that "Fraguel is actually a bit slabby"! The main climbing is in a steep, north facing cave with three soft ticks at 6b, 6c and 7a, but the quality routes start at 7b and end at 8b+.
The other crag is known as Hairpin Wall and is much more friendly and amenable. It should provide a good day's entertainment for those operating around 5 to 6b. Despite the fact that the approach walk is only 1 minute, this is not a good crack for an airport day because the car park is busy and could be targeted by thieves.
A general comment for those wishing to have a good day on the steeper routes in the Las Perxes cave is that it is a very good idea to wear long trousers so that you can take advantage of the numerous knee-bars and leg-locks without the need for hospitalisation when you lower off bleeding from the incredibly rough tufas.
The cave at Las Perxes has become a popular all-weather bouldering venue and we have included the best of the problems here.

## ASPECT AND CLIMATE

The cave is a useful place in extreme weather conditions (ie. too hot or too wet) since it will provide shelter from both of these extremes. The Hairpin Wall is more exposed and won't stay dry in the rain but is relatively sheltered from strong wind.

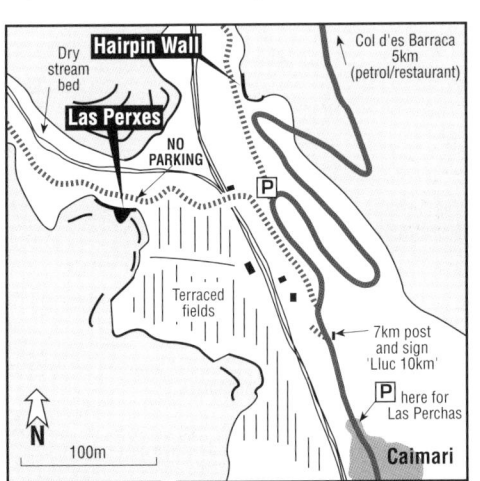

## APPROACH

The village of Caimari is situated to the north of Inca, on the road which crosses the mountains to the C710 north coast road. From Inca follow signs for 'Selva' and then 'Caimari'.

**For Las Perxes** - Park your car near the far side of Caimari and continue up the road on foot. After 200m you will pass a sign 'Lluc 10km' and a 7km post. Take the second track on the left after this, which is marked by a small red arrow on the wall. The crag is on the left after 200m.
It is also possible to use the parking for Hairpin Wall, and walk back down the road, if the first spot is full.
**It used to be customary to park under the crag at Las Perxes. Please don't do this since the road is someone's driveway and the crag is on private property. Access could easily be banned.**

**For the Hairpin Wall** - Continue driving up the road past the turning to Las Perxes and park on the first hairpin bend. Walk along a track to the crag.

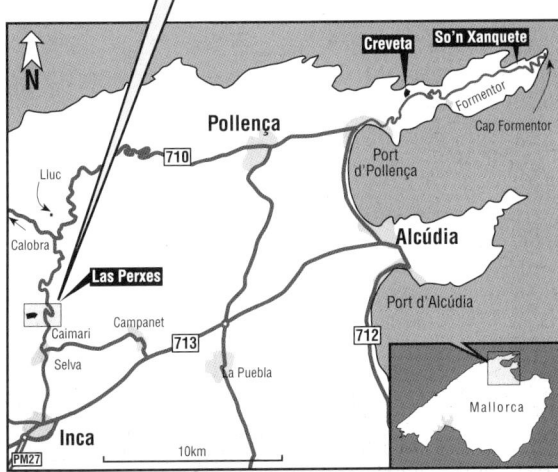

# MALLORCA - Las Perxes

Las Perxas

## LAS PERXES CAVE
The first routes are on the pillar to the left of the main crag.

**1. ?** .......................... 6b
Slabby line of the far left-hand side of the crag.

**2. Petit poi** .............. 6c
Up a hanging groove. A bit too technical for a warm up.

**3. Ball de bot** ............ 7a+
Hard at the bottom with an awkward crux.

**4. Empire State** ...... 8b
As you delve further into the cave things start getting a bit harder. The start is close to *Ball de bot*.

**5. Peu deret** ........ 8b+
The left-hand finish to *Commando Madrid*.

**6. Commando Madrid** .. 8b+
An unbelievable route.

**7. American Express** .. (8a+?)
The steepest section of the cave. I have a grade of 8a+ for this route but it looks a bit harder than that.

**8. Master hit** ........ 8b+
The right-hand side of the cave has another ultra-steep pitch. A 'path' 7c+ to the lip lower-off.

**9. ?** ..................... ?
Looks to be in the 8a/b range but may still be a project.

**10. Colago** ........... 7b
A superb route split by a rest ledge on the right. The upper section involves swinging around on the blobs getting pumped while you tie yourself in a knot.

**11. Es Penjat** .......... 7a+
The right-hand line from the rest.

**12. A vista de pajaro** .. 8a+

**13. Motorhead** ........ 7c+
Just to the right of a small cave. A bouldery start but the route is low in the grade.

**14. Terrorvisión** ........ 8a
Another bouldery start. 1st bolt missing (2/2001) and others look a tad old.

**15. Toten hosen** ....... 7c
Past some pockets with a move right at the top. Easier for the tall. A seepage line so it is sometimes wet.

**16. Nota petit** ........ 7c
Twin bolts at the start. High in the grade and usually requires a dyno.

**17. Penhouse** .......... 8a
An independant line squezzed in to the right of *Nota petit*.

**18. Hoodoo gurus** ...... 7b+
The second last line on the wall.

**19. Picados** ........... 7c+
The last line has old bolts. There is a project right-hand start.

## LAS PERXES BOULDERING
The right-hand side of the crag gives some excellent all-weather bouldering which mostly consists of the starts of the routes. There are two traverses possible and there are plenty of variations on the problems mentioned below.

**20.** Left-hand start to *Motorhead* ........ (V8)

**21.** Right-hand start to *Motorhead* ....... (V9/10)

**22.** Between *Motorhead* and *Terrorvision* ... (V9)

North facing cave
10m to 25m routes
Best grades - 7b to 8b+

268

# MALLORCA - Las Perxes

## Hairpin Wall

23. Start to *Terrorvision* . . . . . . . . . . . . . . . (V9)
24. Start of *Toten Hosen* . . . . . . . . . . . . . V5
25. Start to *Nota petit* . . . . . . . . . . . . . . . V5
26. Sitting start from left into *Penhouse* . . . . V6
27. Sitting start to black cave between . . . . . V6
*Penhouse* and *Hoodoo gurus*

## HAIRPIN WALL

This interesting little crag provides a complete contrast to the mega-steep routes of the Las Perxes cave. The small set of routes should prove entertaining to mid-grade climbers.
**APPROACH (see previous page)** - Drive up the road from the town of Caimari and park at a good parking area on the first hairpin. The crag is 100m up the track which leads off from this parking area.

The routes are listed from left to right starting on a slabby wall on the left.

1. ? 21/12/04 . . . . . . . . . . . . . . . 5   *1st hanger missing*
Slab left of curving groove. Curious gear placements but well-bolted where you need it. *Spaced bolts*

2. ? 21/12/04 . . . . . . . . . . . . . . . 5+   *10 quick draws, 1st hanger missing*
The well-bolted central line.

3. ? 21/12/04 . . . . . . . . . . . . . . . 4/5   *3 hangers missing*

The next lines are right of a curving tree.

4. ? . . . . . . . . . . . . . . . . . . . . . . . . 7a
Steep and technical. The first bolt is high but the climbing is easy.

5. ? . . . . . . . . . . . . . . . . . . . . . . . . 6c
The easy slab to a steepening. Use the blob to get onto the upper wall.

6. ? . . . . . . . . . . . . . . . . . . . . . . . . 6b
Start as for route 4 then climb direct to the rope lower-off.

7. ? 21/12/04 . . . . . . . . . . . . . . . . . . 5+
Climb direct to the lower-off of the last route.

Further right past a bush is a long slab.

8. ? . . . . . . . . . . . . . . . . . . . . . . . . 6a+
Start up blocky rock then continue via a pocket.

9. ? . . . . . . . . . . . . . . . . . . . . . . . . 6a
Start in the same place but move right after the second bolt to the centre of the slab.

Up the slope to the right of the buttress is one last route.

10. ? . . . . . . . . . . . . . . . . . . . . . . . 6b+
A poor route with a high first bolt.

West facing wall
10m to 20m routes
Best grades - 4 to 6b

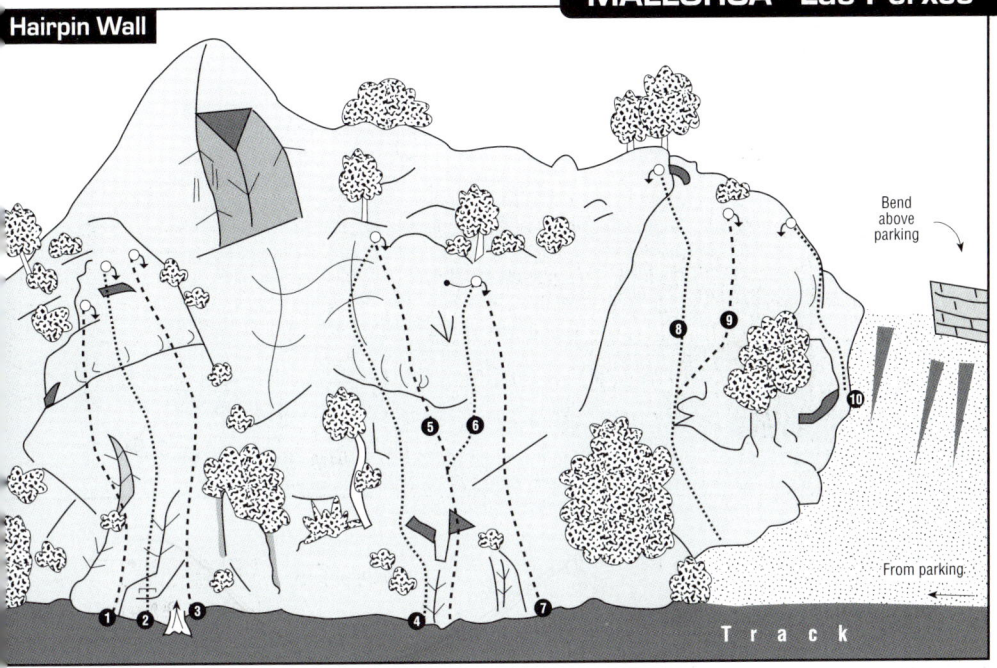

# CREVETA

Creveta is a superb little crag situated amid some impressive rock scenery on the northeastern tip of the island. The cliffs beyond Creveta stretch into the Mediterranean but few have been developed with any climbing apart from S'on Xanquete (see page 274). The two main buttresses here offer contrasting climbing but there should be plenty to appeal to all climbers leading from grade 4 to 7a. At first appearance the routes on the main slab look like friendly mid-grade slab climbs on perfect rock. The 'friendly' and 'mid-grade' attributes are in somewhat short supply so they are welcome. The only drawback is the sharpness of the holds. A days climbing here is guaranteed to leave those little pink spots all over your finger tips. However the sacrifice is worth it since many of the routes here, especially on the right-hand side of the crag, are amongst the best of their grade on the island. The other area described is the walls above the approach walk which have been viewed by many over the past 10 years but have only recently been developed (by Rab Anderson, author of the El Chorro section of previous ROCKFAX guidebooks). The routes here have contributed an extra aspect to the climbing at Creveta by offering some superb vertical challenges, once again on immaculate rock.

## ASPECT AND CLIMATE

The buttresses are situated high above a valley to the north of Port d'Pollença. This exposed position means that it can suffer from high winds and offer little shelter from any bad weather. However it faces west and will receive all the afternoon sun that's going.

## APPROACH

Leave Port d'Pollença towards Cap Formentor. The road winds uphill for 5km, eventually arriving at a viewing area ('Mirador d'es Columet') with plentiful parking. Walk back from the parking area, down a vague track, next to an old pipeline. Just before you reach an old sign post, break out rightwards up the hillside along a cairned path towards the second of two cols in the ridge. Cross the col and head down leftwards under the cliff face. Keep walking around leftwards under the Approach Wall. The Main Wall is a little further on.

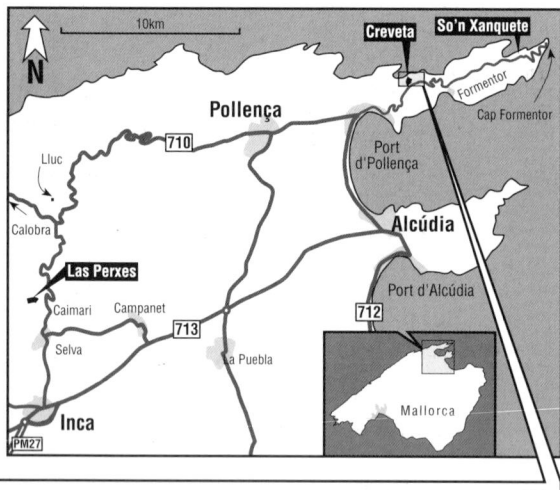

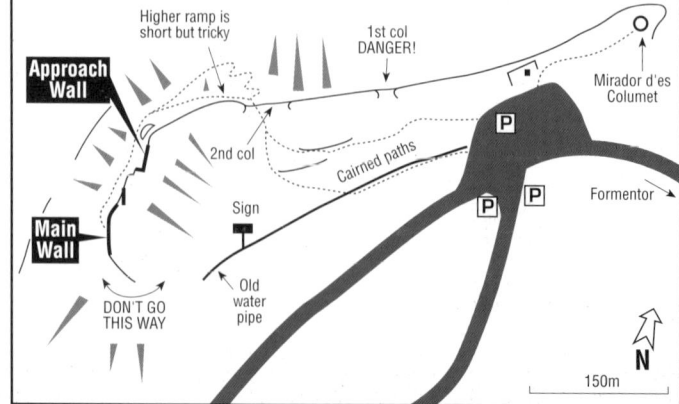

# MALLORCA - Creveta

## Approach Wall - Left

*Two old bolt lines*

*Approach*

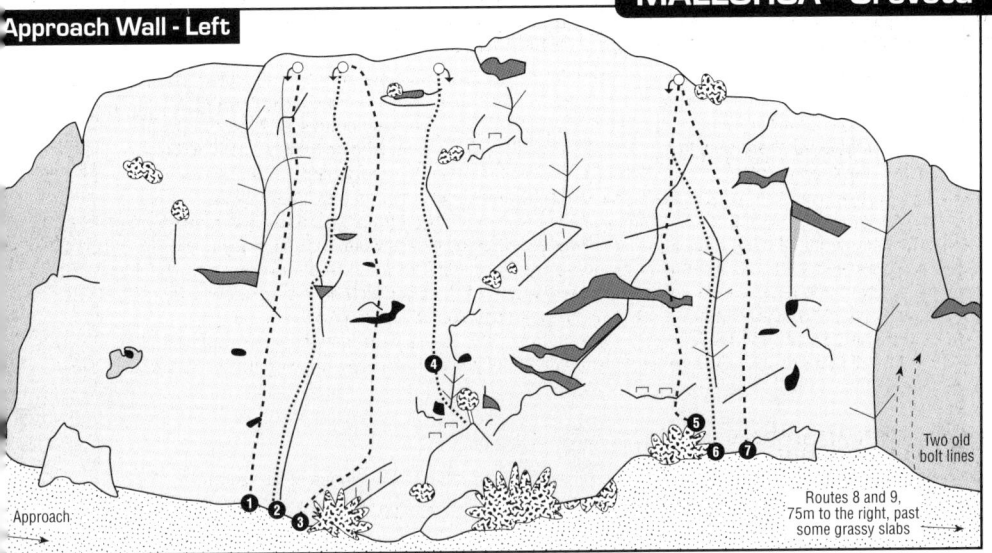

*Routes 8 and 9, 75m to the right, past some grassy slabs*

### APPROACH WALL
The steep walls passed on the approach to the main slab have been developed with a fine set of long routes on superb rock.
**APPROACH** - After you scramble down from the col, keep walking past a pinnacle. The routes start on the wall above.

**1. Gringo Star** ........... 6b+
30m. The black streak and blunt arete is much more climbabale than it looks with plenty of good positive holds when you need them.

**2. Pammi-A** ........... 6b+
30m. The long crack-line to the right gives great sustained climbing which increases in difficulty as you get higher.

**3. Cool Max** ........... 7a
30m. The middle of the pillar has a hard move to get established on the wall. Above is easier but still demanding.

**4. Frank Tapas** ........... 6c+
30m. The right edge of the pillar and crack gives another fine route. Start by scrambling up to a ledge.

**5. Much Azure About Nothing** .. 7a+
30m. Hard moves over the overlap.

**6. Azure Like It** ........... 6b+
30m. pleasant climbing with a tricky section. A bit reachy.

**7. Northern Exposure** ........ 6c+
30m. A short hard section.

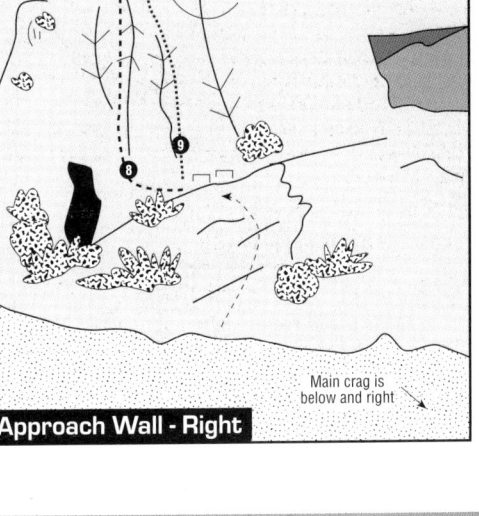

*75m further on, past a corner with old bolts, are 2 more routes.*

**8. Braveheart** ........... 7a
25m. The left-hand grovve to start. Superb moves over the top roof.

**9. Lion Rampant** ........... 7a
25m. Slim groove in blunt arete.

## Approach Wall - Right

*Main crag is below and right*

West facing wall
**Long 25m to 30m routes**
Best grades - 6b+ to 7a

Afternoon | 20 min | Vertical | Lower-offs | Windy

# MALLORCA - Creveta

**Main Wall**

From Approach Wall

Creveta Right

## MAIN WALL
The left-hand side of the wall is terminated at a large semi-detached flake. The first route is on the front of this flake.

**1. ?** .................... 5+
A technical start which may require a pile of stones for some people.

The next routes are on the main face starting almost in the gully behind the semi-detached flake. The first two are full 25m routes so take care when lowering off if you have a 50m rope.

**2. Nordcad** ............ 6b+
25m. Start up the next route and step left for a pleasant alternative at a much more friendly grade of 6a.

**3. ?** .................... 4+
25m. A thin start easing gradually above.

**4. Coordina coordinator** ....... 4+
A delightful route with a hard lower section and a fine finish.

**5. Curset** ............... 4
A slightly easier line just to the right.

**6. Baba** ................ 4+
The prominent flakeline/groove has some loose stuff at the top.

Right of the groove is a short, triangular slab.

**7. Camisasque** ........... 5
The left-hand side of the slab is hard at the bottom.

**8. Krilin** ................ 6a+
A rather pointless little route with a hard last move to the low lower-off.

**9. Hyperion** .............. 5+
The right-hand side of the slab and the wall above (not the bolts on the right). A reachy move to the second bolt.

**10. Hyperion derecho** ....... 6a+
Climb the line to the right of the upper section of *Hyperion*. The traverse right is the awkward bit.

The next two routes start from a ledge behind the prickly bushes. This is best reached from the right. The gap in the middle is only used when you lower off.

**11. Els corderos atacan de nuevo** ......... 6b
Good climbing up the wall past the triangular niche.

**12. Jerita** ............... 6b+
The steep and blank wall gives an excellent technical pitch.

272

Afternoon | 20 min | Slabby | Lower-offs | Windy

ROCKFAX
rockfax.c

# MALLORCA - Creveta

The next route starts just right of some large bushes.

**13. Hussein** .......... 6c
Fingery wall climbing with a distinct crux move.

**14. Terapia de grupo** ........ 6b+
Direct up the wall on razor-sharp holds.

**15. Ca magre, puçes** ........ 6a+
Up the open black scoop roughly in the centre of the wall.

**16. Ja me pagaràs** ...... 6c
Sustained and fingery climbing up the right-hand side of the scoop.

**17. Lastrolophithicus** ..... 6c
Probably the hardest route here up the slightly bulging wall.

At the right-hand end of the wall is a tall grey slab with a cave in its centre.

**18. 150 Sipis** ............ 6a+
Sustained climbing up the wall just right of the large flake, reaching the flake near the top.

**19. Récords de Bunyola** ...... 6a+
One of the classics of the crag. It follows the blank-looking wall in between the large flake and the cave. Sustained but never desperate.

**20. El Sant Crist** ............... 6a+
Another good route. From just left of the cave, pull out rightwards across the lip.

**21. Som-hi** .................... 6a
A devious climb which avoids the bulge near the top by a sly traverse left at the cave.

**22. Ball o'en banyeta verda** ...... 6b
More thin wall climbing. Move left at the top to tackle the bulge. Ignore the rusty lower-off to the right.

**23. Somni Bucolic** ........ 6b
The last route on the wall is particularly tricky for the short, leaving the ledge is the crux.

The far right-hand end of Creveta has some routes above a jumble of blocky ledges. Scramble across to the starts.

**24. Glückspitz** ................ 4+
Easy line on the left.

**25. ?** .................. 6a+
Good climbing up the crozzly black streak.

**26. Leucht Turm** .......... 6b+
A fingery route left of the ragged crack.

**27. Just Married** ........ 6b+
Reachy climbing up and right of the crack.

**28. Angsthase** ............ 5+
Crozzly wall up and left of the big flake.

West facing slab
15m to 20m routes
Best grades - 4 to 6c

# S'ON XANQUETE

S'on Xanquete is a marvellous steep crag situated towards the end of Cap Formentor. This peninsula is covered in impressive rock walls but, as yet, few have been developed. In comparison S'on Xanquete appears to be somewhat small and insignificant, consisting of an overhanging wall of tufa-laced bulges reaching about 20m in height. However, don't be fooled, the routes here pack a punch and a day wrestling with the rough tufas is sure to leave its impression on your biceps and skin.

The the crag offers little to those climbing below 7a, and even those operating 7a will want to have a bit of fuel in their tanks otherwise they could find a trip to the bar becomes necessary after only one route. At the time of writing the crag is having new routes added and some seemed to still be in the planning stage since the local topo indicated route lines where there were no bolts. Most of the new additions will be in the hard, and very hard, grades.

## ASPECT AND CLIMATE

The crag faces northwest and only receives the Sun late in the day. Most of this headland is exposed to the wind although you may be able to get some shelter by tucking yourself in underneath the crag. In the rain S'on Xanquete is one of the best venues on the island with many of the routes staying dry at all times, although it is likely that after very heavy rain that tufas will begin to seep.

## APPROACH

The crag is easy to get to and the drive along the headland is very pleasant, unless you get stuck behind a coach.
Drive from Port de Pollença towards Cap Formentor, turning left at the only major junction. The crag is situated just beyond the exit of the only tunnel on this road which is after the 13km post. There is one parking place on the left as you exit the tunnel and some more lay-bys further on near the Mirador. From the parking place by the tunnel, walk up the road and jump over the crash barrier on the bend of the road, above the crag. Drop down towards the crag-top and skirt rightwards until you can walk down to the base (don't try and scramble down too early). The crag can also be reached from the other end.

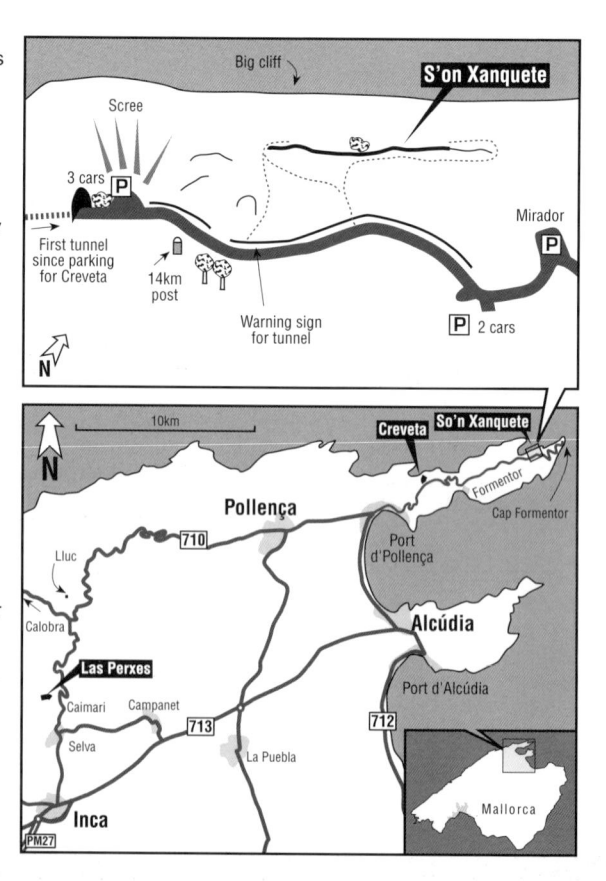

274

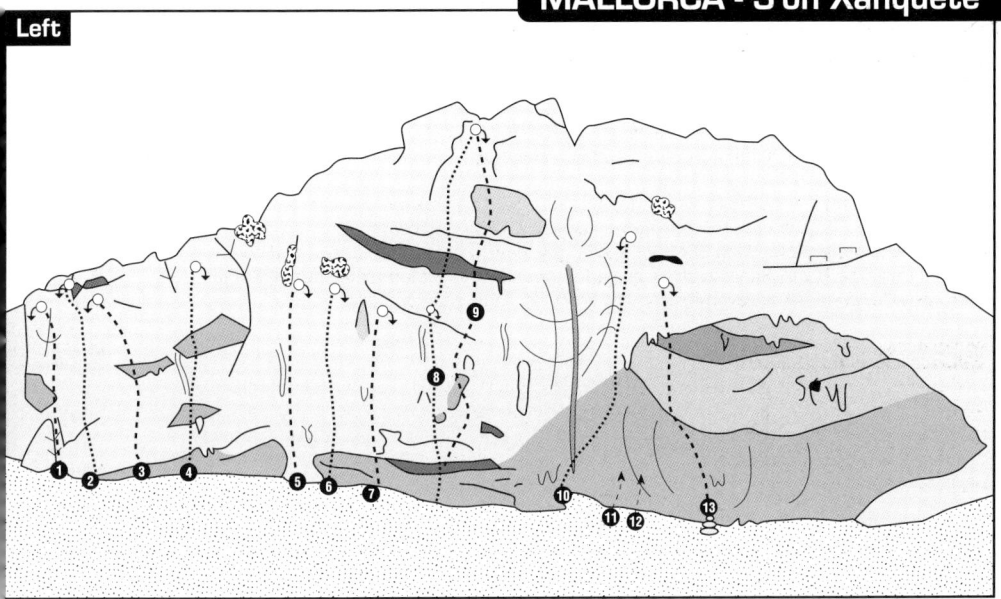

# MALLORCA - S'on Xanquete

Left

## S'ON XANQUETE - LEFT
The first routes are on the short left-hand side of the crag.

**1. Cachi kai** .................... 5+
Two bolts up a rib at the left-hand end of the wall.

**2. Chi craku** .......... 6b+
A hard top bulge.

**3. Planqui xanqui** .... 7c
Very thin moves past the first bolts and continuing hard above.

**4. Fledi ulkel** ...... 8a
Two hard bulges.

**5. Fam un fumfi** ................ Project

**6. ?** ...................... Project

The middle section of this crag has a steep lower wall with a conspicuous chalked-up handrail below the route *Cuki*.

**7. Xao xoxin** .......... 7a+
An entertaining blob move.

**8. Cuki** .............. 7a+
Staples past two first slots to half lower-off. Rest then continue on older bolts to the top.

**9. Teta blik** .................... Project
An unclear line with a gap between the 3rd and 4th bolts.

**10. Tlasmeditelanea** ............. Project

**11. Tila pa tlas** ................ Project
No bolts in place at the time of writing.

**12. Glillo aglidulce** ............. Project
No bolts in place at the time of writing.

**13. Xin Xubi** .......... 7a+
A hard start leading to the tufa roof.

Steep NW facing wall
15m to 25m routes
Best grades - 7a to 8a

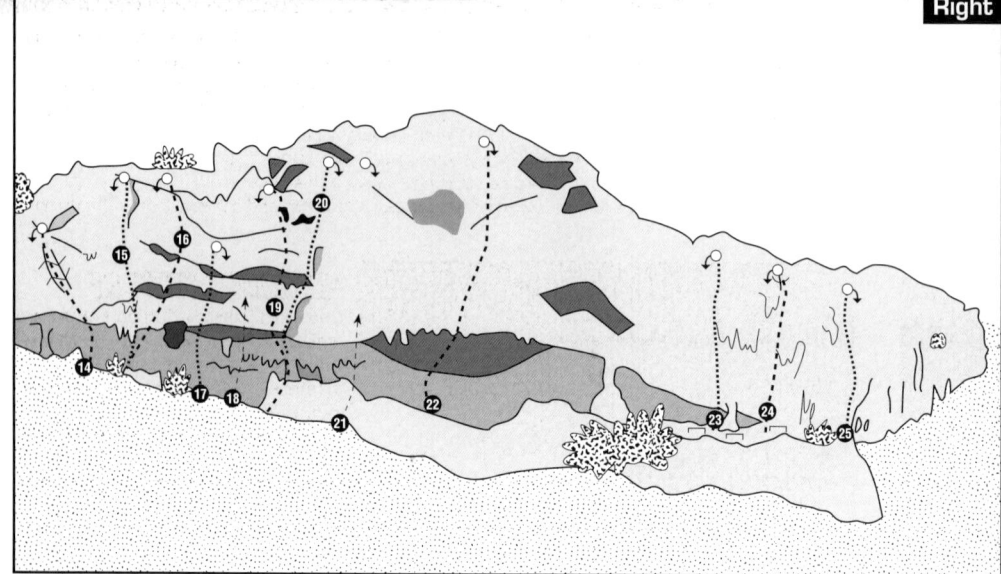

# MALLORCA - S'on Xanquete

**Right**

## S'ON XANQUETE - RIGHT
The right-hand sector is reached by walking towards the impenetrable vegetation and passing by it under the roof.

**14. ?** .......................... ☐ Project
Up a diagonal ramp.

**15. Xin xampu** ............. 🔲🔲 ☐ 7c+
Climb to first and then a move left of roof to flake high up. One of the few routes which is easier for the short!

**16. Brut Lee** .............. 🔲🔲 ☐ 7a+
The crux is holding a tiny hold to connect some larger blobs.

**17. Xop suey
de vaca loça** ...... 🔲🔲🔲 ☐ 7b
Steep and hard.

**18. Tai xixa** .................. ☐ Project
Rusty studs on a hard-looking line.

**19. Xin peldon** ......... 🔲🔲🔲 ☐ 7a
The longest route here which seems to need a large bolt-on hold to cross the incredibly steep final section.

**20. Patxi aloz cena** .............. ☐ Project
Steep start to hands off ledge on right. Then things get a bit harder.

**21. ?** .......................... ☐ Project
No bolts in place at the time of writing.

**22. Xoriguer amb ximonada** ....... ☐ Project
Very, very, big project out over the huge roof.

**23. Quin Fum Fa** ......... 🔲🔲 ☐ 7b
Where the angle eases the holds get thinner.

**24. El cacho del
chichi más chachi** ......... 🔲🔲 ☐ 6c+
Easy to the third bolt then comes the stopper-crux.

**25. Mao se la tu** ............. 🔲 ☐ 5+
The three-bolt warm-up. Bridge off the droopy tufa.

There is another route (grade 5+) marked on the local topo but there are no bolts in place.

---

276

Evening | 10 min | Steep | Lower-offs | Dry in the rain | Windy

Steep NW facing wall
15m to 25m routes
Best grades - 7a to 7c+

ROCKFAX
rockfax.c

# BETLEM

Lying on the northeastern tip of the island of Mallorca, on the Badia d'Alcudia on the way to Cap de Ferrutx, are the fine little crags at Betlem. The two buttresses offer contrasting climbing, on fine rock, in a beautiful setting. Betlem Two, in particular, has a fine set of middle-grade routes and is a great place to appreciate sunsets as you squeeze every last bit of light out of the day. The central slab dome has two magnificent technical climbs and the walls on either side are home to contrasting steeper numbers. Betlem One is only of interest to those who really enjoyed S'on Xanquete and need to get a bit more steep tufa-action under their belts.
The routes are well-bolted with good lower-offs and can all be climbed comfortably on a standard rope.

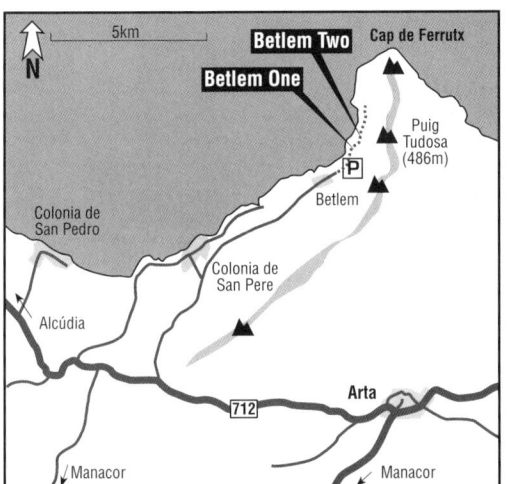

## ASPECT AND CLIMATE

The mountains on Cap de Ferrutx are isolated from the rest of Mallorca and often experience very different weather conditions. It can be rainy or cloudy in the mountains and yet the sun will still be shining on Betlem. As mentioned, both crags face northwest and get the evening sun although the left-hand side of Betlem Two faces northeast and gets some sun in the early morning. Despite the general northerly aspect Betlem Two will not be a very cool crag when the sun is blazing down.

## APPROACH

Although a little off the beaten track the crags are relatively easy to get to and make a good stop-off on the way back from Cala Magraner.
Head towards Arta on the eastern side of the island. 6km to the west of Arta, on the main C712, take a minor turning towards 'Colonia de Sant Pere'. The stark Arta mountains are up on your right. Follow the road for 5km to a sharp left turning to Sant Pere. Continue straight on for another 5km, on a rough road, to the villa settlement of Betlem. Drive straight through Betlem to where the surfaced road stops. This point is about 45 minutes drive from Pollenca. You can park here and walk for 10 minutes along the track to Betlem One, and a further 10 minutes to Betlem Two. Alternatively drive along the rough track and park, off the road, at a layby between Betlem One and Two. Passing vehicles coming in the other direction could be awkward so don't drive too fast.

# MALLORCA - Betlem

Hard

Topo by Rab Anderson

## Betlem One

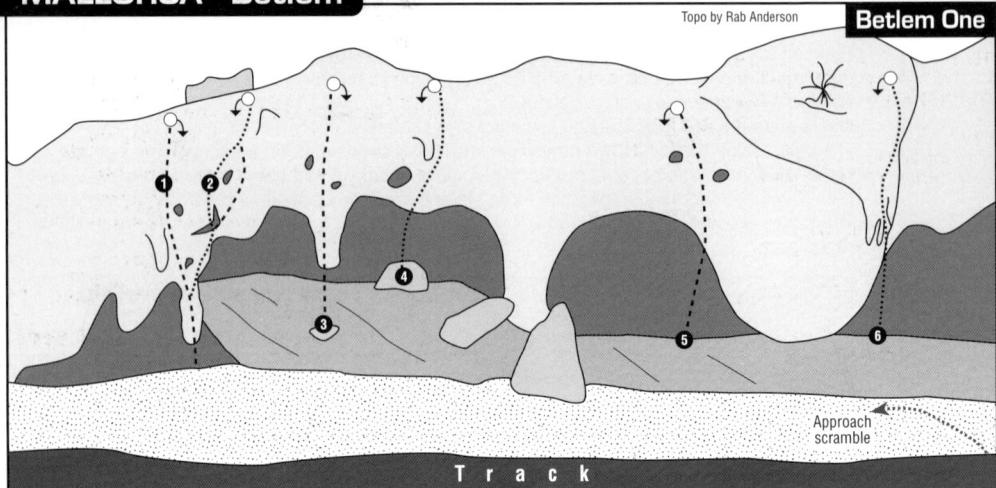

### BETLEM ONE
The crag is about 10m high and is situated about 10m above the track. It gives a small set of steep blobby routes with powerful moves and strange holds.

The routes are described from left to right.

**1. ?** .................... 6b
Possibly harder for short (6b+). Make a long reach from a side-pull to a concealed slot.

**2. ?** .................... 7b+
More long reaches. The chalked-up line goes right and is hard. There is an easier left-hand version (7a+).

**3. ?** .................... Project
Up hanging tufa. Use block to start.

**4. ?** .................... ?
Either a project or a very hard route.

**5. ?** .................... (6c/7a)
Out of right-hand side of the cave.

**6. ?** .................... ?
Up the steep nose.

### BETLEM TWO
This is a very pleasant location with pine trees at the base and the Med down below. The routes are a complete contrast to Betlem One offering fingery climbing up walls and slabs some 20m high. The crag is easily visible along the track from Betlem One and it takes about 10 minutes to walk there.
**ASPECT** - The buttress faces east for morning sun on one side (routes 7 to 13) and west for evening sun (routes 8 to 25).

The routes are described from left to right.

**7. ?** .................... (6c/7a)
On a buttress further left on the main one. Steep in its upper section.

The next routes are on a clean grey slab above and left of the main buttress.

**8. ?** .................... 6a+
The left-hand side of the slab and groove above. Bolts removed.

**9. ?** .................... 6b
Excellent sustained climbing with a high crux.

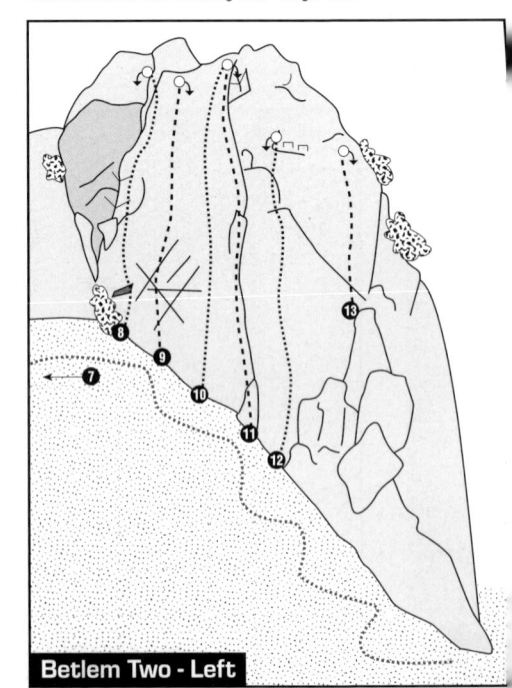

## Betlem Two - Left

**Betlem One**
NW facing, short 15m routes
Best grades - 6b to ?

278

# MALLORCA - Betlem

**10. ?** 6b+
Good climbing but slightly spoilt by being too close to the crack. Harder than its left-hand neighbour.

**11. ?** 13/2/04 5+
Good climbing up the crack but a bit loose near the top. The bolts are on the right at the start.

**12. ?** 6a
Good little route right of the crack.

**13. ?** Project
An impressive project up the high face. Very thin!

The main climbing is on the clean grey dome of rock, with a man and dog, just above the track.

**14. ?** 7a
Thin moves on drilled pockets gain the runnel.

**15. ?** 7a
Sharp, crozzly wall with a thin 'stopper' move.

**16. The Dog Walker** 6b+
The best route on the crag up the central slab, just left of the man walking his dog.

**17. ?** 7a+
A superb, technical slab route.

**18. ?** 6b
A crack and the overlap. Use a long extender on the bolt on the lip.

**19. ?** 18/12/04 a bit 6b
The crozzly wall left of the groove. Slightly escapable.

**20. ?** 18/12/04 5+
Pleasant climbing up the groove.

**21. ?** 18/12/04 sort of 6a
The awkward, short, blocky rib. Harder of you climb direct.

**22. ?** Project
Drilled pockets at the start and a thin flake above.

**23. ?** 6c
Up left-slanting crack. A short-lived crux.

**24. ?** (7a/b)
Direct from the start fo the slanting groove.

**25. ?** 6c+
Good reachy climbing up the slab on the right-slanting groove. Sting in the tail for sore fingers.

slab up hill or right 18/12/04

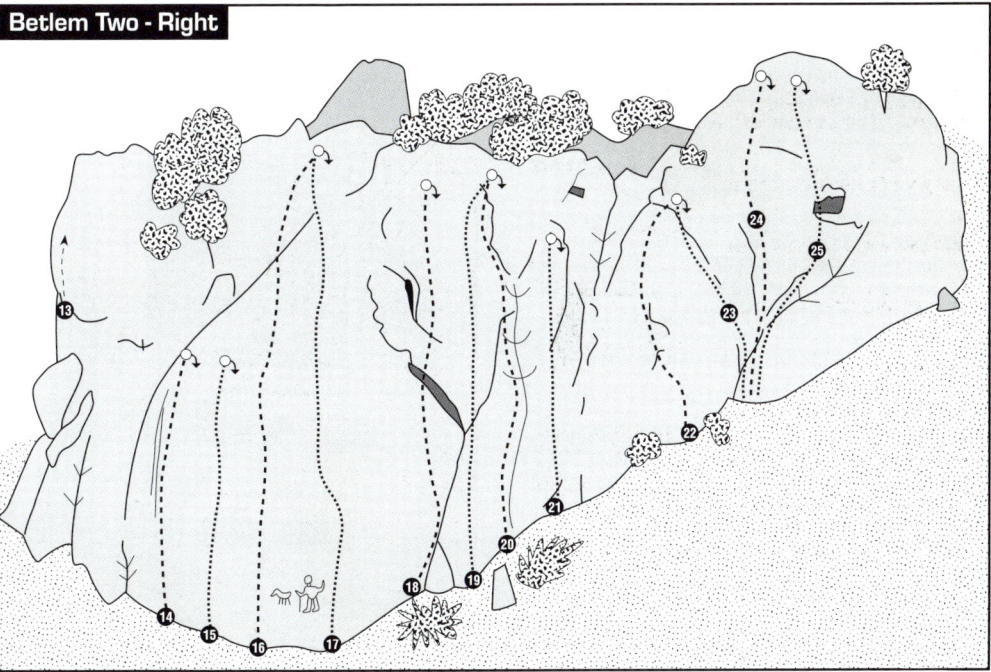

## Betlem Two - Right

**Betlem Two**
NW facing, 5m to 20m routes
Best grades - 5+ to 7a+

# CALA MAGRANER

Cala Magraner is a great little crag especially for those in groups of climbers of mixed abilities. There are some pleasant, easy slabs for beginners, and loads in the middle grades. The routes tend to be technical wall climbs, with tricky, fingery cruxes, although there are a couple of steeper areas for variety. It is pleasantly situated and climbing here can have a real holiday atmosphere, especially if you combine it with a quick dip in the Med. The main cliff is similar in character to Santanyi, although it is barely a sea cliff since the crags line the side of a small dry river estuary. As a final bonus, groups with the one of those annoying hotshots who always says "Fraguel" when asked which crag they want to go to in the morning, Cala Magraner has a thoughtfully-positioned cave with plenty that should keep them busy.

## ASPECT AND CLIMATE

The main area is a south facing, sheltered, sun-trap which is great if you are here in January and everywhere else is freezing, but it is serious pink-skin time in the warmer months. The hardman's cave offers one of the few hard climbing venues on the island that gets a lot of sun - not always what you want but great in cold weather. It should also be remembered that the East Coast of Mallorca is often dry when it is raining in the mountains.

## APPROACH

The crag is situated on the east coast of the Island, near many of the popular tourist areas. Drive to Manacor and locate the main street with all the tourist shops on it. Pick up signs for 'Calas de Mallorca' and follow them southwards out of the town. After about 8km you arrive a 'T' junction where you should turn right. Continue to a sharp bend in the road and turn into a track on the inside of the bend signed 'Agroturismo'. Drive down here and park by the first gate taking great care not to block the track. Continue walking down the track past a farm and another gate. Keep going to a sharp right turn then continue on a small path first straight and then rightwards across a wide open field. head down towards the dry river and follow this until the first cave appears on your left. the rest of the crags are further down the dry river estuary.

**THERE ARE FREQUENTLY BREAK-INS TO CARS PARKED FOR THIS CRAG. LEAVE YOUR CAR EMPTY WITH THE GLOVE COMPARTMENT OPEN.**

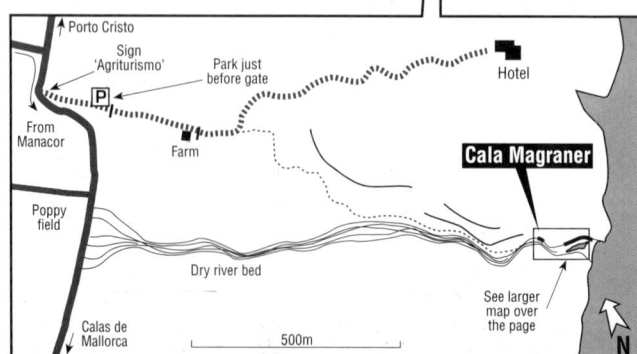

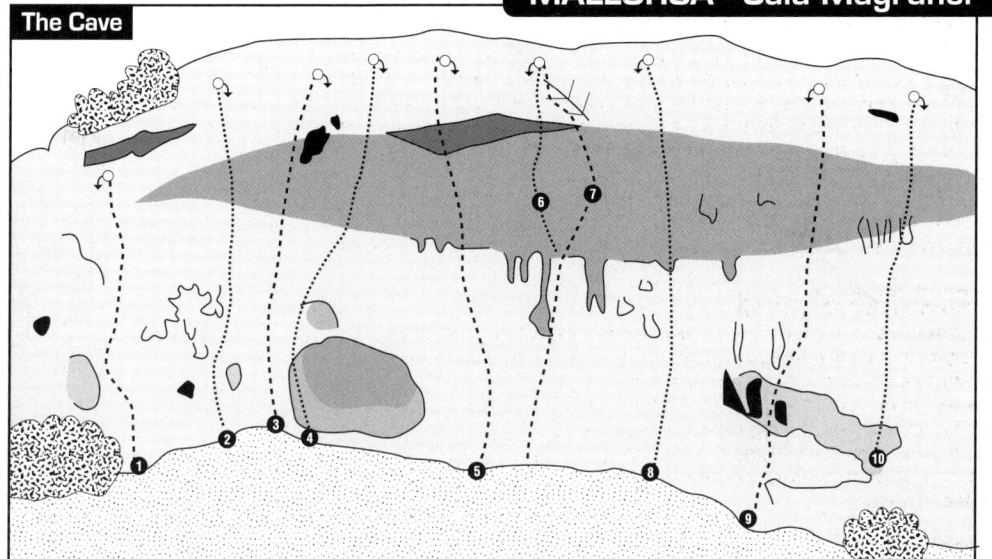

# MALLORCA - Cala Magraner

## The Cave

**CAVE**
The first sign of climbing encountered on approaching the crag, is a large cave. This now has some superb hard routes although no specific star ratings are known.

**1. ?** .................................. 7a
The short left-hand side of the cave.

**2. ?** .................................. 7c+
One extremely hard move but otherwise relatively straightforward.

**3. ?** .................................. 7c
A powerful single move.

**4. ?** .................................. 8a
Much more sustained than its neighbours but no move harder than routes 2 or 3.

The local topo has another line in here but there are no bolts.

**5. ?** .................................. 7a+
The unlikely looking central line (might be 7c+).

**6. ?** .................................. 7b+
The direct line above the big tufa.

**7. ?** .................................. 7b+
The right-hand finish has a surprise on the lip. Once graded 7a+ but either this was wrong, or it has lost holds.

**8. ?** .................................. Project
Given 7a+ in the local topo but, if it has been climbed, then it is a lot harder than that.

**9. ?** .................................. 7a+

**10. ?** .................................. 7a

**FAR LEFT**
This small cave has three short routes. It is visible from the path and can be reached direct from the river bed. Do not try to reach it from the main Left sector.

**11. ?** .................................. 7a+
Short. Tape a finger.

**12. ?** .................................. 7b
Hardest and steepest of the three.

**13. ?** .................................. 7a
A bit of unnecessary chipping.

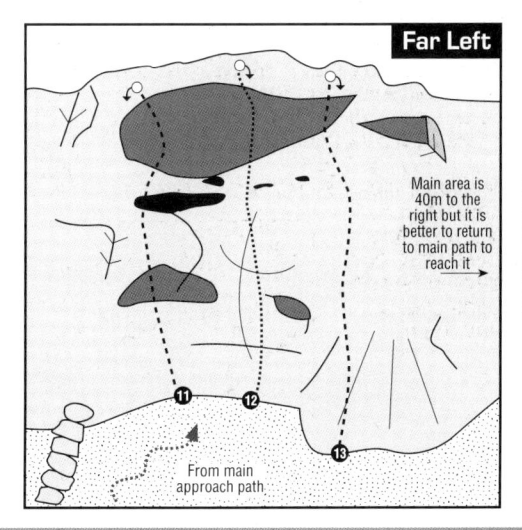

## Far Left

Main area is 40m to the right but it is better to return to main path to reach it →

From main approach path

South facing caves
10m to 20m routes
Best grades - 7a to 8a+

Lots of sun | 15 min | Steep | Lower-offs

# MALLORCA - Cala Magraner

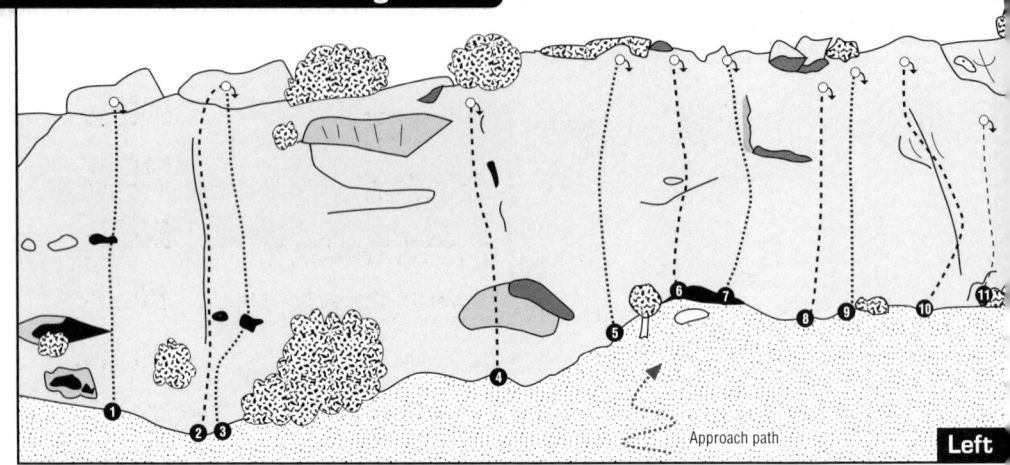

## LEFT
The left-hand sector is above the most usual arrival point at the crag (somtimes people walk onto the ruin before approaching the crag in which case this area is 100m to the left). It consists of a fairly continuous, short, vertical wall. The first routes are just to the left of where the path arrives.

**1. ?** .............................. 5
Stiff pull past the first bolt.

**2. ?** .............................. 6a
The crack.

**3. ?** .............................. 6a+
An eliminate. Harder if you keep away from the crack.

**4. ?** .............................. ?
Very thin, old bolts.

The next route is above where the path arrives.

**5. Al loro Manolo** .............. 6c
Just left of a tree, past some red rock.

**6. Meta Fatigue** ................ 7a+
The wall above a tiny cave.

**7. Lladre de somnis** ........... 6c
Finish by a flake.

**8. ?** .............................. 6a+
Pocketed wall to a threaded lower-off.

**9. Sense voler** .................. 6a

**10. ?** ............................. 6a+
Start up diagonal pockets, move left to higher lower-off.

**11. ?** ............................. 6a+
Very short.

**12. ?** ............................. 6c
Tricky moves left of a very big red stain.

**13. Tootsie** ..................... 6b+
The tufa.

**14. Mou els peus** .............. 6b+
The fiddly wall to the right of the tufa.

**15. Miguelín el travieso** ..... 6c
The wall using some very small and sharp holds.

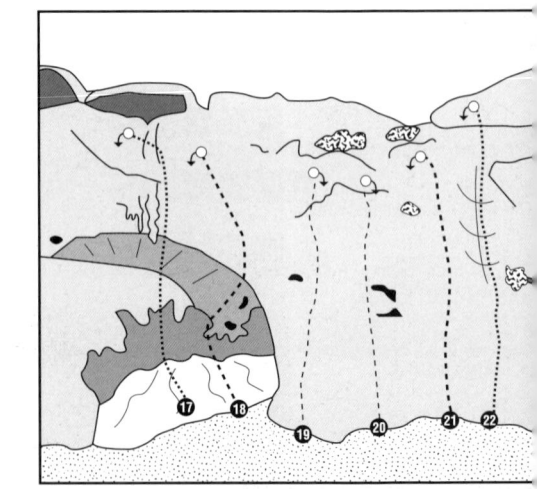

**16. ?** ............................. 5+
The crack.

South facing wall
10m to 15m routes
Best grades - 5 to 7a

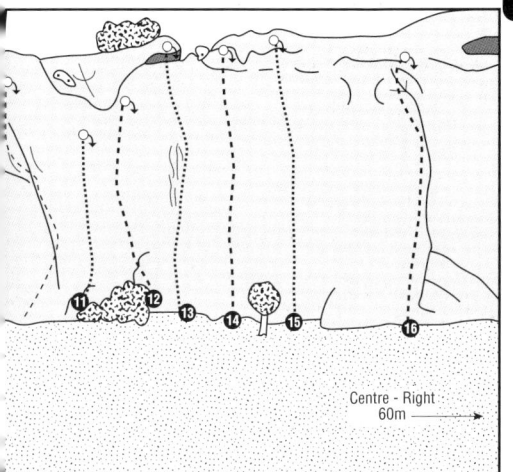

# MALLORCA - Cala Magraner

**19. Sa nyoscla** .............. 5+
No bolts in place.

**20. Paramuero** .............. 5
No bolts in place.

**21. Herbofilia** .............. 4
One staple bolt at the start.

**22. Jardiners sense fronteres** ..... 3
A line of staples up the scoop.

**23. Perelló** .............. 4+

**24. Pixotades per ses galtes** ... 6c
Hard moves on monos with a tricky clip.

**25. Penta** .............. 6c+
A zig-zag line left of the cave.

**26. Galiana m'engana** ....... 6c
A hard start and not much easier above.

**27. Sa sesta** .............. 6b+
Another hard start but good higher up.

**28. Pipiricot** .............. 6b+
Pull out right from the cave to a scoop.

**29. ?** .............. 5+
Pocketed wall and groove.  31/12/01

**30. Florinotto** .............. 5
The hard section is escapeable on the its left-hand side.

## CENTRE
60m right of the last routes, and 60m left of the ruin, is a large, blobby cave. The next route two routes are in this cave.

**17. ?** .............. 7a+
Direct through the cave past the tufa on the lip.

**18. ?** .............. 6c+
Pull out rightwards through the cave and continue up the hard wall above.

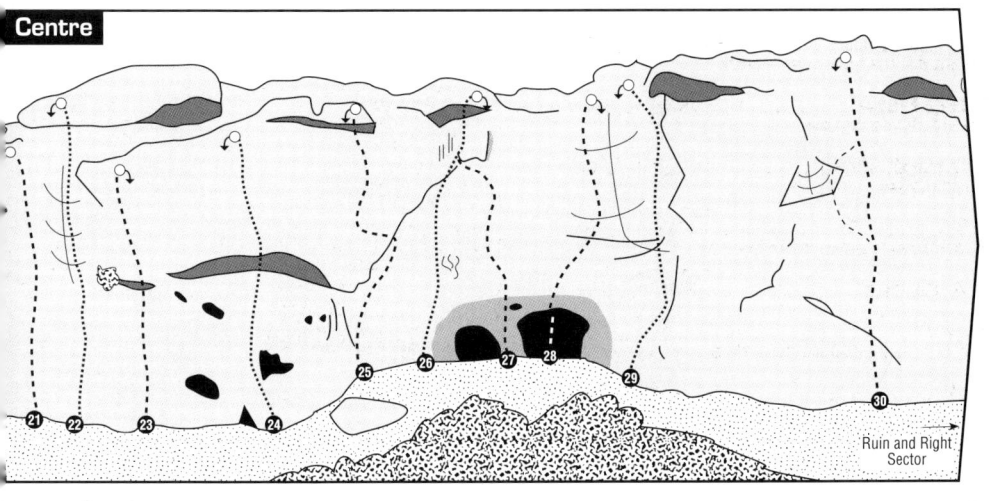

South facing wall
10m to 15m routes
Best grades - 3 to 7a+

Lots of sun — 10 min — Vertical — Lower-offs

# MALLORCA - Cala Magraner

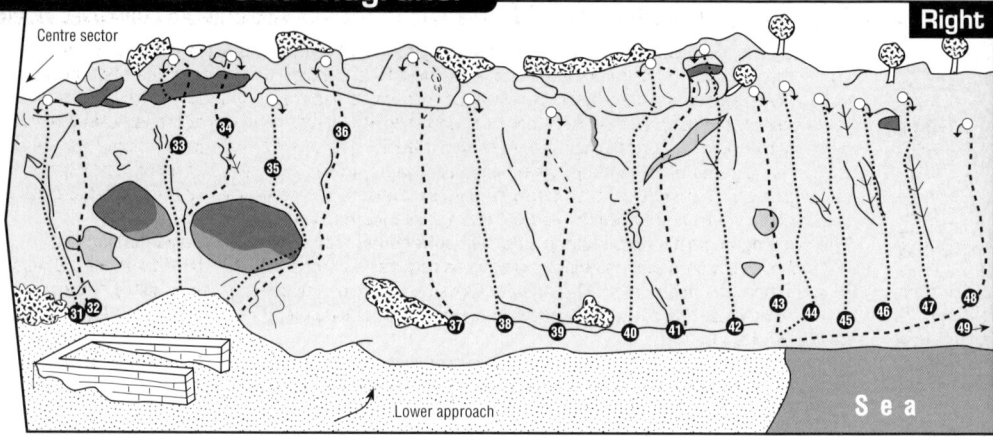

**Right**

Centre sector

Lower approach

Sea

## RIGHT
The largest sector is at the right-hand end of the cliff and is the first place you arrive on the approach. There is a ruined building under some large caves on its left-hand side.

**31. ?** .................... 5+
The crack left of the caves leads to a steep finish.

**32. ?** .................... 6c+
The reachy crux is about 6a for those of 1.80m or more. It can also be by-passed on the left at about 6a+ by all climbers.

**33. Only you** ............ 6c+
Through the middle of the two caves. At the top finish either left (slopy) or right (reachy).

**34. ?** .................... 5+
Steep, juggy and excellent.

**35. Joc de mans** ........ 7a
Very technical.

**36. ?** .................... 6b
Start from right edge of cave. Dangerous bolt on the crux.

**37. Els xorigs** .......... 6b
The right-hand finish makes the route an excellent **6a**.

**38. Es rupaça** .......... 6a
Left of a diagonal crack.

**39. ?** .................... 6a
A delightful little route which can be tricky if you try to go too direct.

**40. Ses tres Maries** .... 6a
The crux is standing on the large blob.

**41. ?** .................... 6a
The slanting groove to the right.

**42. ?** .................... 6b+
Only **4+** to the first lower-off.

**43. L'amo de Baltix m'envia** .... 6a
Above the water's edge, climb past 2 scoops.

The rest of the routes are currently above the sea, although this does change from time to time. Reaching the starts is awkward but possible if you take a hanging belay on the first bolts.

**44. ?** .................... 5+
Poor gear.

**45. Elvigilant de la platja** ...... 4
A long groove gives a great easy route.

**46. Sa clàssica** .......... 5
A rib right of the groove.

**47. Ses panxetes** ........ 6a
A fingery start into a scoop.

**48. ?** .................... 5+
Past some small bushes.

**49. ?** .................... 6b+
Even further right is another old line. Climb out of the cave.

284

South facing wall
10m to 15m routes
Best grades - 4 to 7a

ROCKFAX
rockfax.c

# TIJUANA (Santanyi)

The sea cliffs near Santanyi, known as Tijuana by the local climbers, provide yet another variation in the wide variety of climbing available on the island of Mallorca. Although the rock quality is not always as good as elsewhere, the situation and the routes make up for this. Climbers who enjoy powerful undercut starts with technical upper walls will find plenty to go at here, however it is not all biceps and bulges since there are some easier slabby routes at the left-hand end of the crag. It is also one of the most pleasant locations on the Island for a lazy day's sun bathing, although swimming should be treated with caution owing to the sharp rock and potential strong undercurrents which could whisk you out into the Mediterranean.

The climbing is mostly on the steep side with outrageous roof starts and barely-relenting thin walls above. In some places chipped holds are required to cross the initial roof but there are less of them than you might think. The easier climbs here are less appealing being mostly short and on unspectacular bits of rock, but they do provide a bit of sideline entertainment from the serious business of sunbathing.

The crag is still in the process of being re-geared with stainless steel U-bolts. Be very wary of anything that isn't a U-bolt.

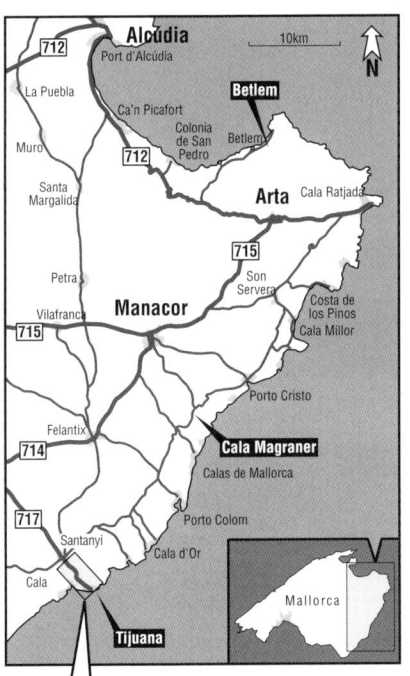

## APPROACH

The cliffs of Santanyi are situated on the south-eastern tip of the Island. The drive to this corner is relatively easy though it can take a while to negotiate your way through all the small villages and towns encountered on the way. From Santanyi, follow signs for 'Cala Santanyi' out of the village. Take the second turning signed to 'Cala Santanyi' off this road (ignore the first turning). Then take the first left turn and then the first right turn (signed 'HR Palmaria'). Continue along this road, past a roundabout with a tree, to a parking area on the cliff top by a ruined tower. LEAVE NOTHING VALUABLE IN THE CAR. From here walk rightwards (looking out) and descend to the platform below the crag.

## ASPECT AND CLIMATE

It is such a good sun-trap that it is often too hot, even in winter. If you have already overdone your sunburn then keep away since there is nowhere to hide on the platform beneath the crag. There is sometimes a sea breeze but this tends to effect the routes around the arete of *Arista* and the stuff further right is relatively sheltered.

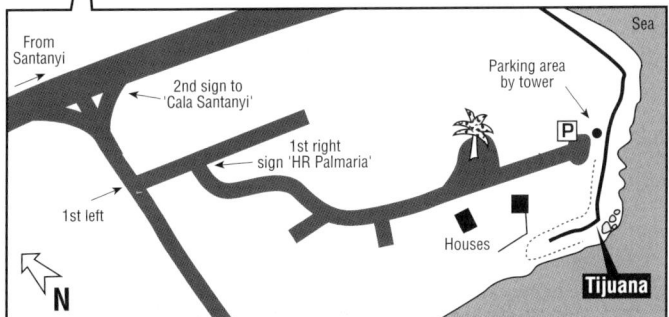

# MALLORCA - Tijuana

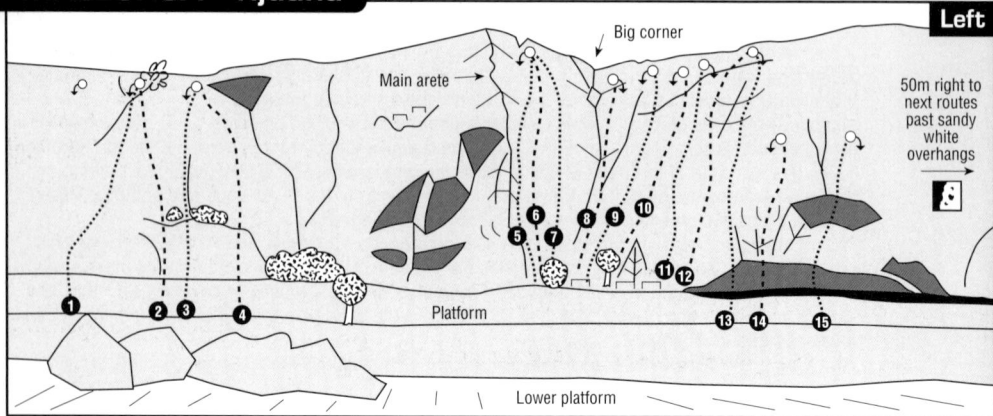

*Big corner*
*Main arete*
**Left**
50m right to next routes past sandy white overhangs
Platform
Lower platform

**Centre**
Platform
50m from last routes
Lower platform

## SANTANYI
The first feature you encounter as you walk around the wave cut platform at Santanyi is the prominent arete of *Arista*. The first routes are on the slabby wall to the left of this arete, starting from a ledge reached by a short scramble.

**1. Left Wing** .................... 6a
A hard start.

**2. Tom and Jerry** ............. 5
The lower-off is by a cactus.

**3. Ebam** ........................ 4+
Finish either left or right.

**4. Ebamsa** ..................... 5
Another tricky start.

The open corner to the right of the arete contains 8 routes.

**5. Arista** ....................... 6b
The right-hand side of the impressive arete.

**6. Finger Killer** ............. 6c
Direct is 6c, left then up is only 6b+.

**7. Foot-hook** ................. 6c
A thin wall climb with a hard crux.

**8. Corner** ..................... 5+
Start in the corner, then the right wall.

**9. Vino Tinto** ................ 6a

**10. Tapas** ..................... 6a+
Requires a bit of a reach.

**11. Blame it on the Rain** ..... 6c+
Start at the right-hand end of the ledge.

**12. Honeymoon** .............. 7a
Traverse right from the ledge, then up.

**13. Never Mind the Bollocks** ..... 7a
The left-hand edge of the lower roof.

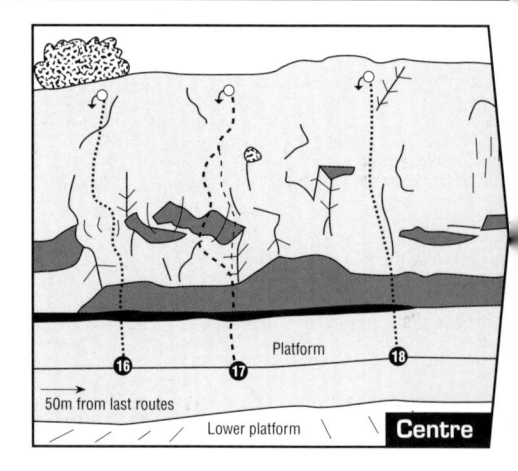

**14. Xiscu que reiliscu** ....... 6b
Thuggy! A high first clip - spotter advised.

**15. Tupé de Rocké** ......... 6c
The double roof to the right is harder and even more spectacular.

There is then a gap of about 50m past a section of white, crumbly overhangs. The next route is below a large tree on the cliff top.

**16. ?** .............................. 6b
Superb juggy climbing through the roofs.

**17. Un dimange à la campange** ......... 7a
The direct version, *Tocino for Pepino* - 7a, now has old bolts.

**18. Flesh for Dani** .......... 7b
The drilled roof at the start is reached from some else's shoulders. The wall above is steep and sustained.

# MALLORCA - Tijuana

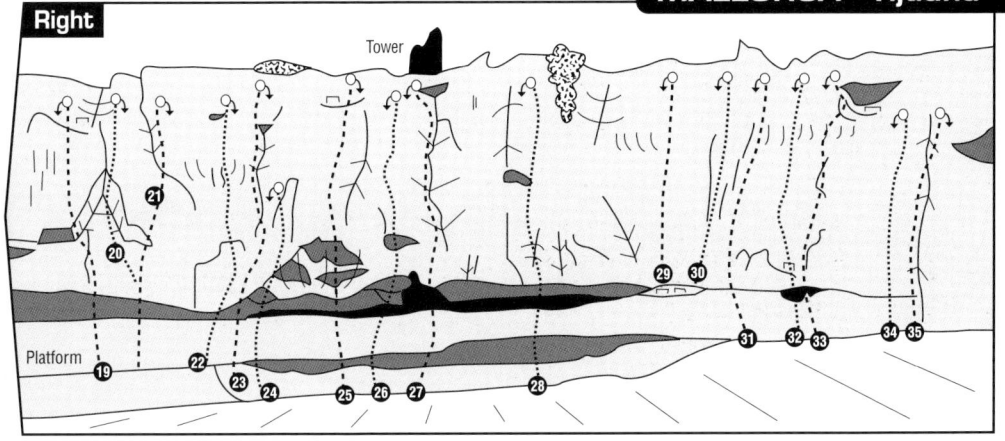

As the cliff continues rightwards the huge roof which dominates it relents a bit to let a few more climbs through. The first one starts below and left of an inverted V-niche on the wall above.

**19. Comepiedras** . . . . . . 7b+
The roof is desperate and above that it doesn't get much easier.

**20. Darsa prisa** . . . . . . . . 7b
The centre of the inverted V is tackled by this technical-despo! The final moves can be avoided by a slightly bold left-hand variant.

**21. Miquel's** . . . . . . . . . . . 7b
One of the best routes on the crag. Start as for the last route and continue up the sustained wall to a depressingly awkward finish.

**22. La calle de ritmo** . . . . . . . . 7b
At last a route without a desperate start, however it makes up for it higher up. I have been given grades of 7a to 7b+ for this route.

**23. Psicomambo** . . . . . . . . . 6c
The substance of this superb route is the slim groove high on the face.

The upper platform, from which all the previous routes have started, drops away at this point adding an extra move or two onto the bottom of the routes.

**24. ?** . . . . . . . . . . . . . . . . . 7b
Glued, chipped, short and sad.

**25. Cocina ligera** . . . . . . 7b
Brilliant climbing through the steep starting roofs and up the arete above.

**26. Na c'al les Seychelles** . . . . 7a+
A good route just to the left of the big corner of *Colesterol Party*.

**27. Colesterol party** . . . . . . . . 6a
The most popular route on the crag. A powerful start allows access to the delightful, easier upper section.

Some of the next climbs haven't been re-bolted yet (12/2000). Be very wary of trusting the old bolts.

**28. Batchcamp** . . . . . . . . . . . 7a+
Technical climbing up the blunt arete right of the corner, finishing just left of the cactus. Old bolts.

**29. Tenacidad** . . . . . . 8a
A very hard pitch starting from a little ledge level with the end of the main lower roof. Old bolts.

**30. Poseidon** . . . . . . . . . 7b
An excellent pitch starting from the little ledge. A rapid finish.

**31. Chuteur fou** . . . . . . . 7b+
The steep tufa/fluting system is brilliant with a slightly reachy crux. Low in the grade.

**32. Go Johnny** . . . . . . 8a
It doesn't look as hard as it actually is. Old bolts.

**33. Rompepierna** . . . . . . . . 6c
The wall just right is a touch easier than its left-hand neighbour. Finish via the scoop/cave on the right.

**34. Naranje** . . . . . . . . . . . 7a
The wall just left of the arete is hyper-technical. Old bolts.

**35. Espolón** . . . . . . . . . . . . 6c
The arete itself is good. Old bolts.

To the right of the arete the cliff swings around and presents a similar, very climbable, wall which stretches rightwards for some distance. One route has been 'built' here at about 7b/c. This is a bit sad since the the cliff has a lot of good natural lines. This potential may be exploited some time in the future.

South facing sea cliff
15m to 20m routes
Best grades - 6a to 8a

287

# EL CHORRO

| | |
|---|---|
| Climbing Information | 290 |
| Area Map | 291 |
| Logistics | 293 |
| Crag Selection Table | 294 |
| | |
| Las Frontales | 296 |
| Lower Gorge | 308 |
| Central Gorge | 319 |
| Upper Gorge | 330 |
| Desplomlandia | 335 |
| Campillos Gorge | 340 |
| Túron | 344 |
| El Torcal | 348 |
| Archidona | 353 |
| Loja | 356 |

Look very closely
and you may see James McHaffie
on *Danza agresiva* (7a+ - page 355)
in the cave at Archidona.
Photo: Mark Glaister

# El Chorro

## by Mark Glaister

Additional topos and text
by Rab Anderson

# EL CHORRO

El Chorro is an extraordinary place. Where else can you find climbing with the weird atmosphere that is associated with the Gorge? Towering walls, outrageously exposed routes and a belay ledge that is slowly falling apart! These features on their own would be enough to attract the attention of many climbers, but the area also has superb slab climbs, fully bolted multi-pitch epics and some stunning steep walls. You can have hard days, easy days, long days and short days and all within a short walk of the lively post-crag attractions of the refugio and station bars. The compact nature of the climbing here is what a lot of people come for, since it is possible to get to almost every crag on foot. For those with a desire to travel beyond the confines of El Chorro the multitude of other venues in the region also provide some exquisite climbing ranging from the nearby slabs and walls of Desplomlandia and Turón to the simply awesome Archidona and route-packed Loja.

A climber on *Arabesque* (8a - page 302) on Escalera Arabe, on the Frontales Area. Photo: Mark Glaister

In this edition of the book we have added many of these outlying areas as well as refining and updating most of the information about the Gorge and Frontales areas. Sadly we have not had the time, or resources, to seek out any significant historical details for El Chorro, however we would like to acknowledge the contribution of the local climbers in equipping and maintaining the routes. Without their work we would have nothing to climb. Two people who do need a mention are Jon Hofor, who runs Finca la Campana, and is responsible for much of the more recent bolting work, and Bernabé Fernández who is one of the most understated climbers around but is responsible for most of the routes in this section of the book of 8c and above including *Orujo* - 9a+ at Archidona.

## CLIMBING INFORMATION

### Access
In 1995 a climbing restriction was placed on certain areas in El Chorro which meant that you could only climb on these cliffs with a permit. The reason for the restriction was never very clear but environmental concerns were mentioned. In practice getting a permit proved to be difficult and the policing of the restriction was sporadic. The system adopted in the end was to hand out the permits on a day-to-day basis to climbers at the crags, as long as they were carrying a passport. The ban appears to be more rigorously enforced in the Upper Gorge where all climbers are moved on, permit or none. It is not clear how this situation will develop but at present it shouldn't be seen as serious enough to hamper your trip.

### Grades
The grades at El Chorro have been a little on the soft side over the years. Hopefully (or sadly!) most have now been brought in line with those found elsewhere in the Costa Blanca and Mallorca. See page 10 for a table.

## Gear
Most of climbs in the El Chorro area are fully bolted sport routes requiring quickdraws only. The bolts are also well placed and in good condition. However a number of routes require a small rack to be carried. These routes are found in the Lower Gorge and on Los Cotos and are denoted with the 'nut' symbol. A 60m rope is essential on many of the climbs. An abseil device will also be found necessary on many of the multi-pitch routes either to access or descend. An abseil will often be required to access the numerous single pitch climbs in the Gorge. A long sling will be a comfort to most for clipping into the fixed wires that are fixed on the really scary sections of the walkway. A good windproof and a warm jacket will come in very useful in the confines of the Gorge. Sun screen and water should also be carried.

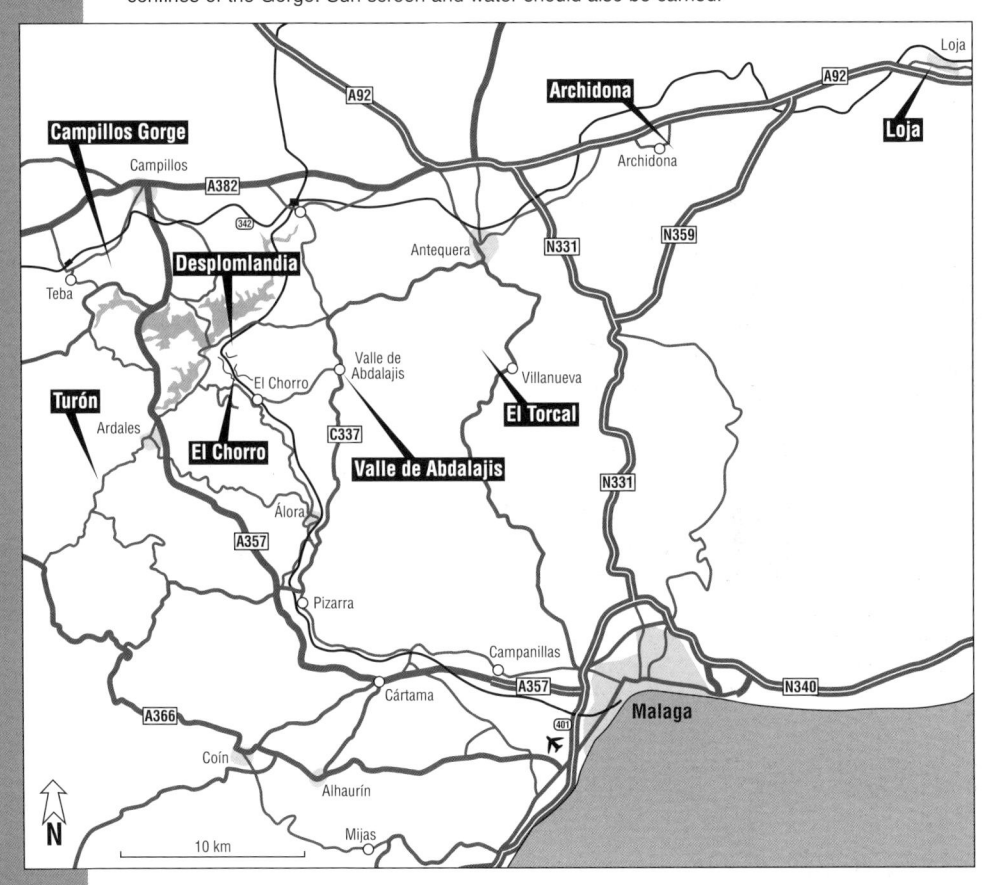

## Other Books
There is a local guidebook called *El Chorro* by Pedro Garcia and Juan Carlos Perez (1995). This is now difficult to get hold of but photocopies can be bought at the Refugio shop. The area is also covered in *Andalusian Rock Climbs* by Chris Craggs (1992) and semi-covered in *Sun Rock - Band 1* (1992).

## Other Areas
There are many other excellent climbing areas within striking distance of El Chorro and worth checking out. On the coast Mijas and Cala de Moral are good and may have better weather than the inland crags as well as being closer to the sea. Further afield Los Vados and Cahorros are major crags. A useful source of information on many climbing areas within Spain is the Desnivel website which has a searchable index www.desnivel.es .

# Finca la Campana

**El Chorro Accommodation**
Tel (0034) 626 963 942
Fax (0034) 952 112 019

## terracottages.co.uk

**Holidays in Spain and Mallorca**
Visit www.terracottages.co.uk
For a great selection of holiday accommodation
**Villas, Country Houses, Cottages, Apartments**

*Phone Stu 01695 624143*
SPANISH COSTAS, MALLORCA
EL CHORRO, COSTA DAURADA

**Car Hire**

## La Alimona Chica — EL CHORRO

Spend your holiday in 130 year old cottages set amongst olive and almond groves, between two National Parks with a backdrop of mountains. Situated between the station and Las Encantadas and just a five minute walk from both.
4 cottages to sleep 2/3/4/5 from 150 + 7% VAT a week. Besides climbing, also ideal as a base for discovering Andalucia and relaxing round the pool.
Call Susan or Dell on (0034) 952119872
or e-mail us at sumitch@teleline.es

The entrance to the Lower Gorge at El Chorro. Photo: Mark Glaister

# EL CHORRO LOGISTICS

More on the ROCKFAX web site at - rockfax.com/el_chorro

### WHEN TO GO
The best times to come are Spring and Autumn when the temperature will be comfortable and you will have the full choice of all area s. In Winter there are often long periods of good weather it can be very cold in the shade, and in the Gorge, and some rain is likely at times. Summer is way too hot.

### FLIGHTS
El Chorro is located 50km inland from Málaga, Andalucia, in Southern Spain. There are many low costs charter, or scheduled, flights to Málaga leaving from all major airports throughout the year. The best place to buy charters is from one of the many low-cost flight shops now in existence. Local ones (hence local phone calls) advertise in the yellow pages under 'Travel Agents and Tour Operators'. National ones advertise in the travel pages of the broadsheet newspapers. It is always worth at least two calls since prices, and availability, can vary dramatically. Málaga is also on the destination list of EasyJet which means you can get bargain flights at off-peak times and reasonable value ones at popular times with the added advantage of being able to book your outward and return flight separately (www.easyjet.com). There are also plenty of other bargains to be had on the Internet these days.

### GETTING TO AND AROUND EL CHORRO
It is easy to walk to most of the climbing in and around the Gorge from the village of El Chorro, but, to access the outlying areas, a car is essential. Car hire is easily arranged prior to departure or on arrival at Málaga.
**Getting to El Chorro by Car (See map on previous page)** - Leave the airport and turn left on the N340 following signs for 'Ronda de Málaga'. Once on the main ring road look for exit signs for CARTAMA and the UNIVERSITY. Follow these (junction 231A/B which becomes 233B) and continue past Cartama (14km) on the C341/A357. Continue for another 32km to the El Chorro exit. Take this and after 6km turn right at another sign for El Chorro. A further 5km down a very steep and winding road leads to the dam. Turn left and cross the dam into El Chorro itself (1 hour 15 min from the airport).
**Getting to El Chorro by Train** - To get to the village of El Chorro from the airport, first take the underground train to the main station - Málaga Renfe. From here there are many trains to Álora and a few trains straight to El Chorro. The times have been changed recently, and may also have changed by the time you read this. As of February 2001:
Málaga to El Chorro - leaves at 18.55 arrives El Chorro at 19.40.
El Chorro to Málaga - leaves El Chorro at 09.00 an arrives at Málaga Renfe at 09.46
El Chorro to Málaga - leaves El Chorro at 15.00 an arrives at Málaga Renfe at 15.41
There are trains from Málaga to Álora every hour roughly and one bus from Álora to El Chorro at 12.30 leaving from *Avda. de Cervantes* by the Health centre (Sunday service is different). From Álora a Taxi is about 2000psts as far as the station.

### ACCOMMODATION
Unlike Mallorca and the Costa Blanca, cheap coastal package accommodation isn't such a good option is El Chorro. The drive from the coast is too long each day. It is better to stay locally and there is a small amount of excellent accommodation available (see adverts opposite and on page 14). There is also a climber's refuge in the village. A good campsite is located a few minutes walk from El Chorro and is central for the climbing and village. It is not particularly cheap but is quiet and located in a lovely bit of woodland. For the location of the refuge and the camp site see the map on page 296.

### SHOPS
A small climbing shop is located above the Refugio bar in El Chorro and supplies all essential items including rock boots. Food is available from a number of very small shops in El Chorro. Larger and cheaper shops, and large supermarkets, are located in Álora and on the outskirts of Málaga.

# EL CHORRO

| Area | Page | No. of Routes | ↓VS ↓4 | VS 4 | HVS 5 | E1 6a | E2 6b | E3 6c | E4 7a | E5 7b | E6 7c | E7 8a↑ | Sport Routes | Some Trad Routes | Some Multi-Pitch |
|---|---|---|---|---|---|---|---|---|---|---|---|---|---|---|---|
| ALBERCONES | 297 | 31 | | | 2 | 1 | 9 | 5 | 4 | 6 | 2 | 1 | 1 | Sport | | |
| AMPTRAX AREA | 298 | 21 | | | 1 | 3 | 4 | 2 | 3 | 5 | 3 | | | Sport | Trad | ✓ |
| POEMA DE ROCA | 300 | 30 | | | | 1 | 2 | 4 | 10 | 7 | 4 | | | Sport | | ✓ |
| ESCALERA ARABE | 302 | 37 | 1 | 2 | 6 | 7 | 3 | 10 | 5 | 2 | 1 | | | Sport | | ✓ |
| LAS ENCANTADAS | 304 | 32 | | 1 | 1 | 6 | 1 | 5 | 7 | 7 | | 4 | | Sport | | |
| CALIZA | 306 | 12 | | | 2 | 5 | 4 | | | | 1 | | | Sport | | |
| VALLE DE ABDALAJIS | 307 | *30* | *10* | *10* | *10* | | | | | | | | | Sport | Trad | |
| LOWER GORGE | 308 | 98 | | | 4 | 8 | 17 | 23 | 14 | 13 | 9 | 10 | | Sport | Trad | ✓ |
| LOS COTOS | 320 | 62 | 1 | 5 | 18 | 11 | 10 | 9 | 8 | | | | | Sport | Trad | ✓ |
| EL POLVORIN | 324 | 23 | | | | 2 | 5 | 5 | 8 | 2 | 1 | | | Sport | | |
| INVENTO/BLOQUES | 326 | 24 | | | | | 2 | 8 | 7 | 2 | 3 | 1 | 1 | Sport | | |
| EL MAKINODROMO | 328 | 27 | | | | | | 1 | 3 | 7 | 8 | 3 | 5 | Sport | | |
| UPPER GORGE | 330 | 64 | | | | 5 | 6 | 8 | 11 | 10 | 7 | 3 | 4 | Sport | | |
| DESPLOMLANDIA | 335 | 56 | | | | 4 | 2 | 5 | 9 | 12 | 12 | 8 | 4 | Sport | | |
| CAMPILLOS GORGE | 340 | 34 | | | 2 | 2 | 2 | 10 | 3 | 6 | 5 | 2 | 2 | Sport | | |
| TÚRON | 344 | 65 | | 1 | 11 | 13 | 9 | 12 | 8 | 8 | | 2 | 1 | Sport | Trad | ✓ |
| EL TORCAL | 348 | 47 | | | 5 | 8 | 5 | 7 | 11 | 6 | 1 | 4 | | Sport | | |
| ARCHIDONA | 353 | 22 | | | 2 | 1 | | | 2 | 4 | 4 | 3 | 5 | Sport | | |
| LOJA | 356 | 50 | | | 2 | 7 | 6 | 10 | 7 | 11 | 3 | 4 | | Sport | | |

| Approach walk | Sunshine or shade | Access restrictions | Dry in the rain | Windy and exposed | SUMMARY |
|---|---|---|---|---|---|
| Roadside | Lots of sun | | | | A very popular area due to its ease of access. The climbing is pretty good but a bit over-climbed. The location close to the railway line is not great. Better to head up the hill a little way. |
| 15 min | Lots of sun | | | Windy | Huge wall on the lower end of Las Frontales. A select bunch of long and popular easier routes. Also some really good single pitches at the base of the wall. |
| 10 min | Lots of sun | | Dry in the rain | | Impressive cave and wall above with a lot of potential. Some of the most blobby tufa routes around plus two 6-pitch fully-bolted epics. Not many pitches of interest in the lower grades. |
| 10 min | Lots of sun | | | Windy | A nice crag high up the long ridge of Las Frontales. Looks tiny until you get up to it. Good selection of routes in the low to mid grades. |
| 5 min | Lots of sun | Restrictions | Dry in the rain | | **CURRENTLY ACCESS PROBLEMS.** Brilliant buttress of particular appeal to harder climbers. Not much in the lower grades. |
| Roadside | Morning | | | | Little roadside buttress which has been developed by the local shop. Nothing very special but worth a look if you are passing. |
| 5 min | From mid morning | | | | A very good lower grade venue within easy reach of El Chorro. A pleasant outlook and plenty of routes only spoilt by a lack of detailed information at present. |
| 15 min to 25 min | Sun and Shade | | | Windy | One of the main reasons for coming to El Chorro - experience the walkway and some amazingly atmospheric climbing. Plenty of single pitch wall climbs plus some good long routes. Lots to do in hot weather. |
| 30 min | Lots of sun | | | | Immaculate grey slabs covered in superb routes. The best place in El Chorro for low to mid-grade leaders. A bit of a sun-trap and some of the gear is getting old. |
| 35 min | Afternoon | | | | The place to climb if you like 6c wall climbs on amazing rock. Superbly positioned and very different from the other wall climbing in the area. |
| 40 min | Lots of sun | | | | Mini versions of Makinodromo but not in the same class. Tend to get climbed on by people who can't be bothered to walk to the top of the hill. One or two good (harder) routes. |
| 1 hour | Lots of sun | | Dry in the rain | | Magnificent cave like sector and featured wall to its right. Home of El Chorro's most famous route, *Lourdes*, and also its most famous walk-in. A 1 hour slog but worth every step. Nothing much below 6c. |
| 40 min | Shade | Restrictions | | Windy | **CURRENTLY CLIMBING IS BANNED HERE.** Double the atmosphere of the Lower Gorge; even narrower and even taller. Amazing setting but can be cold, dark and windy. |
| 10 min | Shade | Restrictions | Dry in the rain | | A good selection of crags with something for everyone. None of them get much sun so only go in reasonable or hot weather. Plenty of quality routes across the grade range. |
| 5 min | Sun and Shade | | Dry in the rain | Windy | Gorge 30km north of El Chorro with a good selection of routes across the grade range. Spooky cave for hard (and dry) stuff. A lot of new development here in recent times. |
| 10 min | Sun and Shade | | | | A lovely area with a lot of easier climbing on sheets of slabby and vertical limestone. Very quiet spot. The eastern crag is a good place in hot weather. |
| 10 min | Lots of sun | | | Windy | A wonderful and weird place consisting of millions of pinnacles. Finding your route can take most of the day but this doesn't matter since it is such a beautiful place. Previously published climbing now banned. New areas are more open with great views down to the Med. Don't go in anything but good weather. |
| 5 min | Shade | | Dry in the rain | | Awesome arena with state-of-the-art pitches. Can be cold and may seep after rain. |
| 5 min | Shade | | | Windy | Lots of routes all easily accessed and with many good pitches lined up for the taking. High, exposed and north-facing make this an ideal warm-weather venue. Tufas can seep. |

# LAS FRONTALES

The huge frontal line of cliffs which tower above El Chorro, and visible from miles away, are known as Las Frontales. This is in fact one huge fin of rock that starts down by the lake and stretches diagonally up the hillside, above the village. Although the majority of the routes here are single pitch climbs on steep rock at the bottom, many are being extended upwards to take advantage of the vast potential of these huge walls. The main Frontales cliffs are split into three areas - Bajas (lower), Medias (middle) and Atlas (upper).

In front of these cliffs, and to some extent dwarfed by them, is a fine line of easily-accessed low cliffs, a short distance above the village of El Chorro. These lower cliffs comprise of the superb Las Encantadas, and the smaller Bedees.

An adventurous outing can be had by climbing the crest of the Frontales fin from just above the lake to the col which forms the first break in the chain at Escalera Arabe.

The climbing on Las Frontales varies from well-travelled, slippery horrors on Albercones, to the long, multi-pitch, stamina routes around the Poema de Roca area. In amongst it all are some super-classics on tufas and flowstone across the grade range. One slight drawback is the lack of concentration of routes in any one area and you may need to move around a bit to find routes at your grade. A little adventurous spirit will be rewarded though since there are some particularly fine routes to be found which are rarely busy.

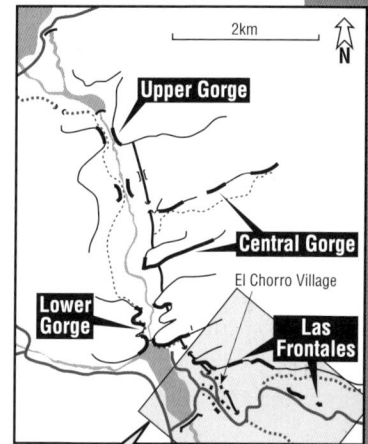

## ASPECT AND CLIMATE

The main Frontales cliffs face southeast, with most of them receiving sun until mid to late afternoon. Escalera Arabe catches the sun until much later which makes it a superb evening venue. It is worth remembering that the sun is particularly unforgiving on exposed flesh which has been hung out to dry on the belay of a multi-pitch route, so slap on some factor 20 and climb in a long sleeved shirt. Nowhere in this area is particularly sheltered, although it is not as windy as in the Upper and Lower Gorges. When it rains, some dry climbing can be found in the Poema Roca cave and at Las Encantandas.

## APPROACH

All of the cliffs detailed in the Frontales area are accessible on foot from the village, however, since it can be hot and the approaches are uphill, it is a lot easier to drive to them. Although the road surface runs out at El Chorro, the main route to Valle de Abdalajis continues up the hill as a dirt track which soon becomes paved. Various minor tracks lead off this which can be followed to the different sectors.

Full approach details are included with the route pages but you may need to refer back to this map.

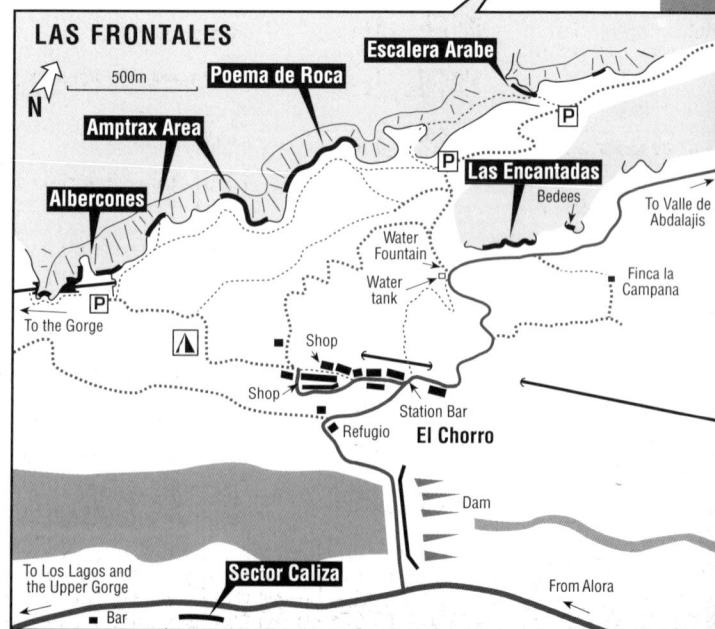

# EL CHORRO - Frontales Bajas

**Albercones**

**Sector Luna**

Amptrax Area

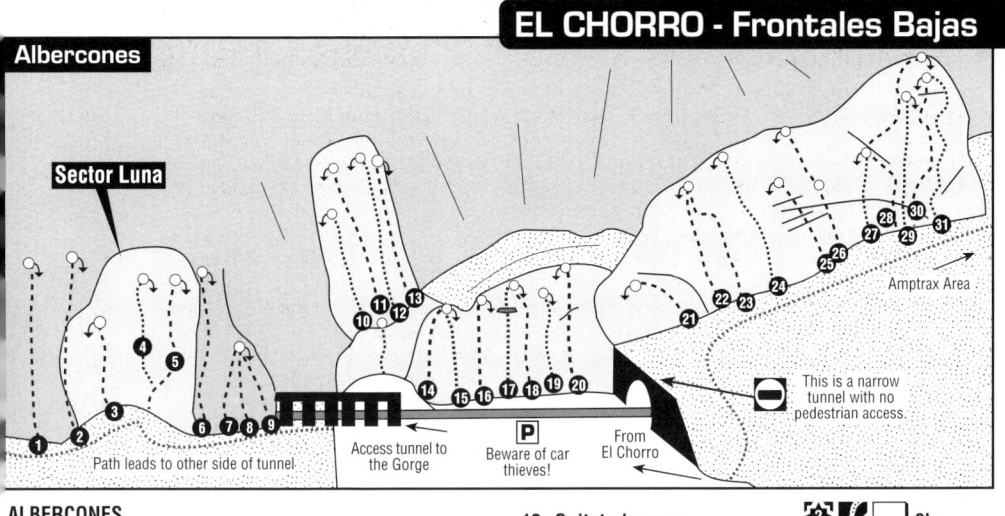

This is a narrow tunnel with no pedestrian access.

Path leads to other side of tunnel. — Access tunnel to the Gorge — Beware of car thieves! — From El Chorro

## ALBERCONES
This crag is probably the most popular bit of El Chorro but it certainly isn't the best the area has to offer, however there are a number of good pitches.
**APPROACH** - It is situated at the end of the track which heads towards the Gorge from the station bar in the village.

## SECTOR LUNA
The first routes are on the outside wall of the tunnel leading to the gorge. There are some poor routes to the left of route 1.

**1. Little Brown Baby** . . . . . . . . 7a+
Steep climbing up the pocketed brown wall.

**2. Simon ha perdido el panadero** . . . 6c+
A steep juggy groove with a low crux.

**3. Luna** . . . . . . . . . . 6c+
Polished and fingery.

**4. Instinto** . . . . . . . . . . . 6a
The crux is reaching the lower-off.

**5. Big fun** . . . . . . . . . . . . 6a+
Nice layback moves.

**6. Montou de chattara** . . . . . . . . 6a
Up via left edge of scoop.

**7. Vas pisando huevas** . . . . . . . . . . . 4
Easy route with a tricky finish.

**8. La corona** . . . . . . . . . . . . . . . 4+

**9. Punto de salida** . . . . . . . . . . . 5

The next four routes are reached by a short access pitch of 4+ via the telegraph pole.

**10. Sapillo momificado** . . . 7b+

**11. Saca la lengua** . . . . . . . . 6b+
Nice groove climbing.

**12. Cosas de dos** . . . . . . . . . 6c+
Jp the blank wall. Very good.

**13. Quitate la ropa** . . . . . . . . 6b+

**14. Troncómovil** . . . . . . . . . . . 6a

**15. Ganímedes** . . . . . . . . 6b+

**16. Engrase la bisgara** . . . . . . . . . 6c+

**17. Estas porido chaval** . . . . . . . 7c+

**18. ?** . . . . . . . . . . . . . . . 8a

**19. Chicüelito querido** . . . . . . . 6b+

**20. Arzapua** . . . . . . . . . 7b

The next routes are on the right above the tunnel.

**21. Océano gris** . . . . . . . . . . . 7a

**22. Me deseos los nuevos** . . . . . . 7a

**23. Zulú exprés** . . . . . . . . 6a+
A tricky traverse.

**24. La chica pelirroja** . . . . 6a
30m. Good wall climbing.

**25. Babi** . . . . . . . . . . . . . . 6a

**26. Puitferio** . . . . . . . . 6a

**27. Er vuelo de los peluos** . . . . . . . 6a+

**28. El virgo de vencenteta** . 6b+

**29. Cita en Sevilla** . . . . . . . . 7a+

**30. El truco del almendruco** . . 7a

**31. Sufre mamón** . . . . . . . . . . . . . 7a+
Same lower-off as the previous route.

South facing walls
15m to 30m routes
Best grades - 5 to 7a

Lots of sun | Roadside | Vertical | Lower-offs

# EL CHORRO - Frontales Bajas

## Amptrax Area

### AMPTRAX AREA
This is the large area of cliff overlooking El Chorro and to the left of Poema Roca. Several long climbs have been put up here and there is much scope for more long new routes at relatively amenable grades.
**APPROACH** - From the station bar in El Chorro, go down the track which heads towards the Gorge. Park at the road end by Albercones and walk up the path, over the tunnel, and up the hillside.

The first two routes are on the wall to the left of the famous Amptrax and are fully bolted.

**1. Pa lante amigos** ......... 6c
1) 6a, 20m, 2) 6c, 30m.

**2. Son quatros** ............ 6b+
1) 4, 15m, 2) 6b+, 35m.

**3. Amptrax** .............. 5+
This is the most popular route on this section of cliff which gives excellent, steep climbing for the grade. It is fully bolted from pitch 2 to pitch 4. Some gear will be required for the first pitch (which is very easy) and, if you intend to go to the top, the last three. Reach the start by scrambling up to the grassy bay above the path beneath an obvious ramp.
1) 3, 35m. Follow the ramp until you need to put a rope on.
2) 5+, 15m. Climb steeply up and left, then make an exposed move right to stand on top of a flake. Continue to 2 bolt belay.
3) 5, 15m. Another steep pitch on good holds.
4) 5, 20m. Straight up to a belay below a roof.
5) 5, 20m. Continue straight up for about 10m and then traverse out horizontally right to another belay.
6) 4+, 25m and 7) 4+, 30m. Two more pitches to the top.
**DESCENT** - From the top of pitch 4 abseil back down the route. From the top walk down heading leftwards down the mountain.

**4. Las cabras** .......... 5
A long wide groove located at a prominent wide groove in the face. The pitches are all long (30m +).
1) 5, 2) 4, 3) 4+ 4) 4
**DESCENT** - Either abseil carefully back down the rotue, or try walking over the back into the next valley.

The next three routes are on a small wall, in the trees, and slightly proud of the main wall. The routes need some traffic.

**5. Superpotencia** .......... 6a

**6. Maspotencia** .......... 6a+

**7. Prepotencia** .......... 6a+

The next routes are on the red overhanging wall accessed via a gully on the right. This is a particularly good section of cliff with some brilliant stamina pitches.

**8. Coño paco** .......... 7a
A technical route on the far left.

**9. Sesso, drogas y flamenco** .. 7a+
Steep climbing up the yellow wall.

**10. Alicia** ............. 7b+
Superb moves on a gently leaning wall. Harder than it appears from the bottom.

**11. Bienvenidos al circo** ..... 7b
Another quality pitch at the lower end of the grade.

# EL CHORRO - Frontales Bajas

**Amptrax Area**

**12. Que leche que tengo** 7a+
1) **6b.** A good warm-up in its own right.
2) **7a+.** Can be combined on a 60m rope.

**13. Judea del frenta popular** 7a+
The steep groove right of the red wall is a tremendous line and it used to be one of the most over-graded routes in the world at 7b+. A double rope would be useful for getting down, otherwise an intermediate lower-off from a single bolt will have to be made.

**14. Frente judea de popular** 6c
1) **6b, 40m.** The wall to the right of the groove gives a superb pitch. Abseil off or continue up....
2) **6c,** 3) **6a,** 4) **6a.** Three more good pitches above.
DESCENT - Abseil back down on double 50m rope.

**15. No esta acabda** 6b+
40m. The wall left of a long groove is another very long pitch. There is a mid-height lower-off but take great care descending. This route can be dirty at times.

**16. Soñador de grado** 4
This pitch is used to access the following three climbs. Only one bolt to the belay.

**17. La niña de mis ojos** 6c+
The left-hand line.

**18. La urriki** 7a+
This central line.

**19. Ajon joli** 7b+
This right-hand line.

**20. Quatro elephants** 5

Below route 20 is a tiny insignificant set of 7 routes. From the left they are - **5, 6c+, 5+, 6c+, 6a, 6b+, 5+** These are not all be bolted.

One more route is encountered before Poema de Roca.

**21. 'Route number 13'** 6a+
A fine open face climb.
1) **6a+,** 2) **6a,** 3) **6a.**

South facing wall
10m to 100m routes
Best grades - 5 to 7b+

# EL CHORRO - Frontales Medias

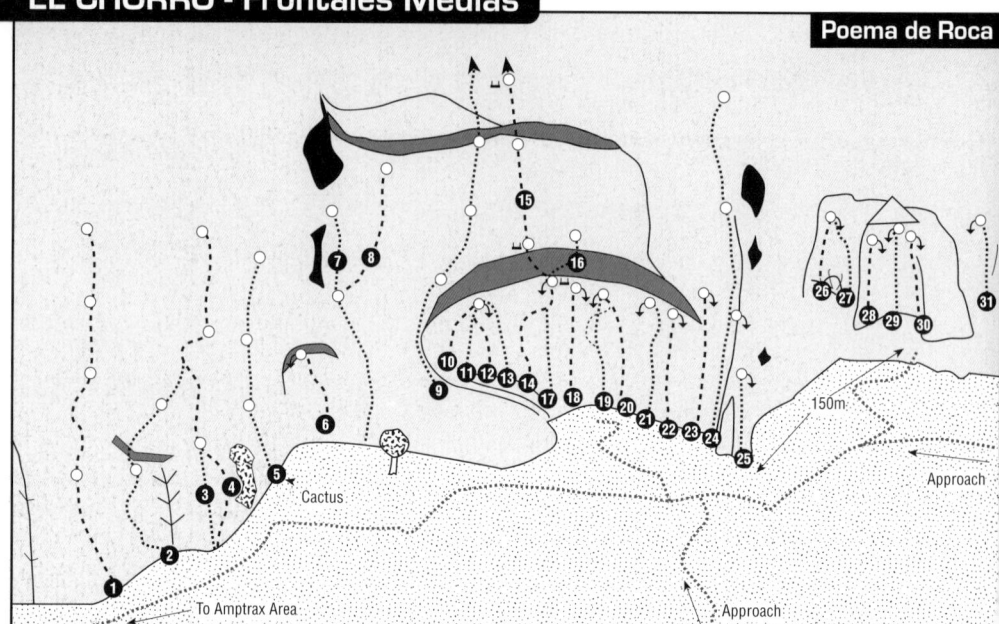

## Poema de Roca

### POEMA DE ROCA
Poema de Roca is the huge oval cave below the tallest section of Las Frontales. It has some superb routes on immaculate rock and many of the routes are now being extended upwards to create companions to the amazing route called *Poema de Roca* which must rank as one of the best of its type in Europe. It is a very popular area and the routes are starting to get polished. This area gets very warm so it is better to climb in the cave when it is cool to get the best conditions and avoid slipping around on the polish.

**APPROACH** - Follow the dirt track up the hill out of El Chorro, towards Valle de Abdalajis, to a square water tank. Take the upper of two tracks which branch off left at the side of Encantadas. Drive along this past a farm turning on the right after 100m, keeping right at the first branch on the main track. Park by the next track on the left and walk down it to a collection of boulders. Then walk up and rightwards to the large oval-shaped cave above you. Alternatively, carry on along the main track to a parking place on a sharp bend just before a quarry. Now traverse the hillside to the cave (parking 1.1km from the water tank).

The first routes are down the hill beyond the cave.

**1. Café burbuscon** ......... 7a
A superb third pitch and a wild fourth.
1) 5+, 2) 6c, 3) 7a, 4) 6b+.

**2. Gaia** ......... 7a+
The roof on pitch 2 is desperate. If you haven't had enough continue up pitch 3 of route 4. 1) 6c, 2) 7a+, 3) 6b+.

**3. Insominio de equipmiento** ... 6c+
Direct to the lower-off on the next route.

**4. Seco y Pedro** ......... 7a+
A good top pitch. 1) 6b, 2) 6c, 3) 7a+.

The next route is up and right, just left of an arched recess.

**5. ?** ......... 7a+
1) 6a, 2) 6c+, 3) 7a+.

**6. Black cave** ......... 7b
Steep climbing in the arched recess. Can be wet.

**7. Verdes venenas** ......... 7a+
1) 6b, 2) 7a+.

**8. Hierbes letales** ......... 7a+
An alternative right-hand pitch 2 to the previous route.

**9. Maquina cualquiera** ......... 7b+
Another mega-route which is of a similar stature to *Poema de Roca*. Start up the left edge of the cave and continue for 6 sustained pitches.
1) 7a+, 2) 6c+, 3) 7a+, 4) 7b+, 5) 7a+, 6) 6b+.

The main attraction of this area is the huge oval cave. The next 11 routes are in, or around, it.

**10. Lavia stragniato** ......... 7b+

**11. Eye of the storm** ......... 7c
Shares the last 2 bolts with *Thunder Struck*.

**12. Thunder struck** ......... 7c+

**13. Swimming through a shark attack** ......... 8a+

# EL CHORRO - Frontales Medias

**Poema de Roca**

The wacky blobby rock in the cave is tackled by one of El Chorro's most famous routes.

**14. Poema de roca (pitch 1)** — 7a
Brilliant! No grabbing the seat at the lower-off.

**15. Poema de roca** — 8a/8a+
1) 7a, 2) 8a/8a+, 3) 7b, 4) 7a, 5) 6c.
Five mighty pitches with little respite. It is fully bolted. The lose of a hold on the second pitch has pushed the grade up.

**16. ?** — 7c
A variation second pitch to *Poema de Roca* full version.

**17. Rima libra** — 7c+
A hard direct on *Poema de Roca*.

The next three routes all have second pitches which are at the present time projects.

**18. Viejo traidor** — 7b+

**19. Morritos Jeagger** — 7b
There is an often-climbed variation which wanders around up an easier line at 7a+.

**20. Viejo amigo** — 7a
A flowstone start leads to a bad crux.

**21. García aguas** — 6b
Good climbing up the flowstone at the right-hand edge of the cave.

**22. Suizo** — 5+

Right of the cave is a prominent corner.

**23. Vivac porus** — 7a+
A long pitch left of the corner.

**24. El señor de las tinieblas** — 7a
1) 6b+, 2) 7a, 3) 6a. The final pitch is poor.

**25. Block** — 6c

150m further right again is a recess with a cave. The next route follows the left-hand side of the cave.

**26. Solarium** — 7b
A touch loose

**27. Lobo López** — 7b
The right-hand side. Some poor rock.

**28. Deprisa y con bulla** — 6c
Short and thuggy.

**29. Agip** — 6a
Wall of 'Verdon-esque' rock.

**30. Nanuz** — 6a+
More of the same, just left of the corner.

A short distance up the hill is one final route.

**31. A pique de un repique** — 6c
Some loose rock on the finish spoils this one a bit.

South facing wall
15m to 180m routes
Best grades - 6a to 8a

# EL CHORRO - Frontales Atlas

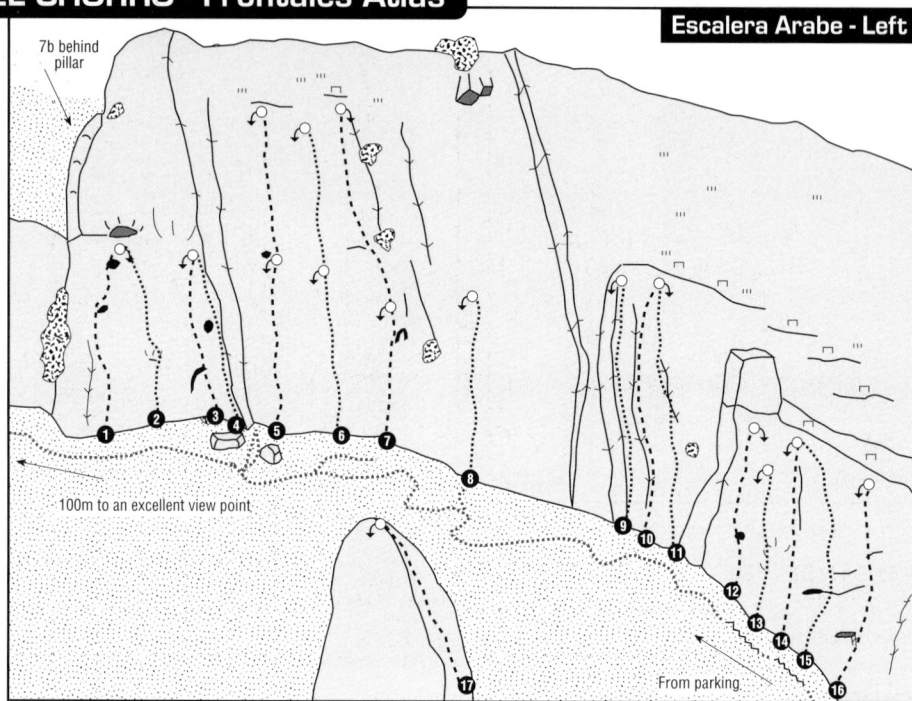

## Escalera Arabe - Left

7b behind pillar

100m to an excellent view point

From parking

### ESCALERA ARABE - LEFT
The upper right-hand end of the Frontales ridge is known as Frontales Atlas. Much of it this broken and slabby but in amongst it are several good quality buttresses which have become known as 'Escalera Arabe', or 'Arab Steps', after a series of steps underneath the first section.

**APPROACH** - Follow the track from the station up a steep hill. At the water tank, bear left and follow the road around the back of Las Encantadas. Pass a small farm turning after 100m and then keep right at the next two junctions until a quarry appears on the left at 1.1 km from the water tank. Continue up the track beyond the quarry around a bend for a further 1km and park by a cairn. This point is 20m after the power lines cross the road and where a ramp cuts up left below the main face and above a lower series of cliffs. Walk up through the trees and find the old steps by a large tree.

1. El beso de la flaca .......... 5+
2. Lucky no come pan ......... 6a
3. Filou ...................... 6a
4. Blanca .................... 6a
   Hangers missing.
5. Engendro caneki ......... 6c
   1) 6b+, 2) 6c.
6. El amor sandunguero ... 6c
   1) 6c, 2) 6c.
7. Escalopendra guajani ...... 6a+
   1) 6a, 2) 6a+. The second pitch isn't very good.
8. El árabe perdido ........ 6c+
9. Lococolo ................. 7a+
10. Diedre torpedol ........ 6c
    A great line and excellent moves. Best to move right to finish at the lower-off of the next route.
11. Arabesque ............. 7a
    The pillar has a blind pocket on the crux. Photo page 290.

The next routes are on a short steep wall above the steps.

12. Sheik tu dinero ........ 6c+
13. Birdy .................. 7b+
14. Calvo potrun ........... 7c
    Polished on the crux bulge.
15. Coming on strong ....... 7a
16. Rock the Kasbah ........ 7b
    Start by a bend in the steps.
17. El pilarito ............. 3
    Up the little pinnacle in front of the crag.

The next 4 routes are not on the topo. 30m right of *Rock the Kasbah* is a little pitch.

18. Sólo afeitar ............ 6a
    Climb over a bulge

## Escalera Arabe - Right

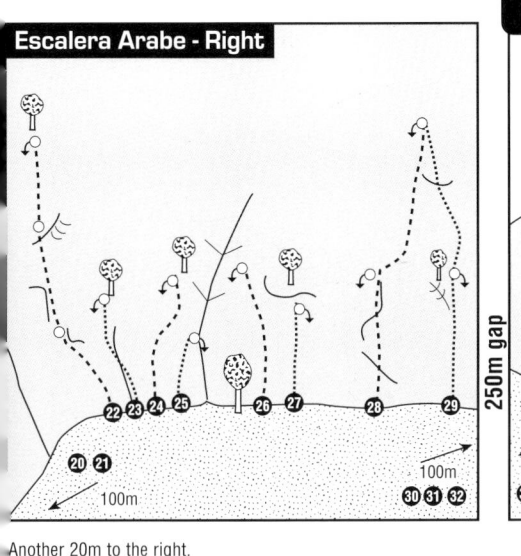

## EL CHORRO - Frontales Atlas

### El Pilar

Another 20m to the right.

**19. La Raya a la Izquierda** ......... 5
Follow the small slab.

200m to the right is an excellent buttress.

**20. For fite** ............ 6b
35m. If you attempt to lower off then please take great care.

**21. Double edged** ......... 6b
Harder if you climb to the left.

### ESCALERA ARABE - RIGHT
Another 100m up the hill rightwards.

**22. La chillona** ........... 6a
1) 4. An easy start.
2) 6a. A tricky, and poorly bolted, slab
3) 6a. A steep finish.

**23. O sole mio** ........... 4
Up over the edge.

**24. Los timbales** ......... 4
Long and pleasant.

**25. El artista** ............ 4
Up a ramp.

**26. Dos tetas tiran** ....... 6b
Great climbing up the yellow arete.

**27. Mas que un carreta** ........... 6a

**28. Highway to Africa** ....... 6b
1) 5+. A good pitch worth doing on its own.
2) 6b, 35m. A very long pitch with a belay well back.

**29. Marlen suzuky** .......... 6c
1) 6a+, 2) 6c. A good second pitch.

100m further uphill, and about 150m left of the prominent pillar, are three little climbs which aren't on the topo.

**30. ?** ........................ 4+
Only two well-spaced bolts to the belay.

**31. Kiwi** .................. 5

**32. La gaita** ............... 4+

### EL PILAR
On the far right-hand end of Las Frontales is a tall pillar.
**APPROACH -** It is most usually reached from further up the approach track.

**33. El Navigator** .......... 7a+
A long, fully-bolted route, which goes to the top of the pillar. Start just right of a small cave. You can abseil back down on one 60m rope doubled. Some of the bolts are not well positioned especially one on the crux of pitch 6.
1) 6c, 2) 6a, 3) 6c, 4) 4, 5) 6b+, 6) 7a+

The next routes are all at least 30m so take care when lowering.

**34. Los genelos** ............ 6c
30m. To the left of the hole.

**35. Los genelos right** ....... 7a
30m. To the right of the hole.

**36. La sonrisa vertical** ....... 6c
30m. Start in the small cave. It can be finished at the mid-height lower-off on the next route (6b+).

**37. Longarone** ............ 6c
35m. An excellent long climb. Use the mid-height lower-off to descend.

Southwest facing wall
15m to 150m routes
Best grades - 5 to 7b

# EL CHORRO - Frontales Area

## Las Encantadas

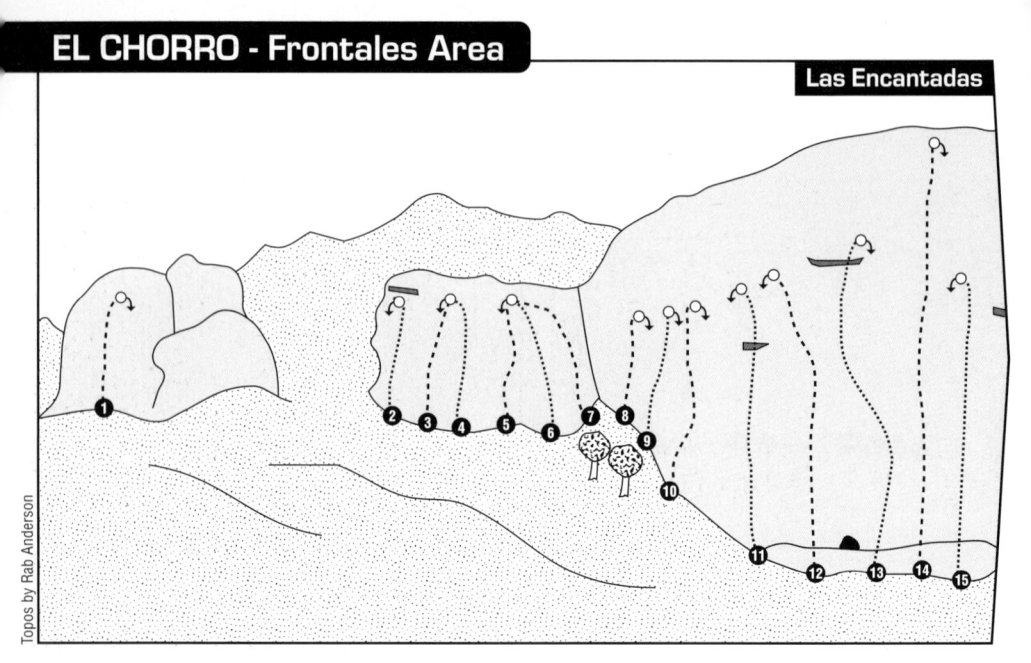

### LAS ENCANTADAS
This superb crag is one of the best at El Chorro. It is situated away from the gorge, high above the road which leads up the hill from the village. The rock is superb, compact and solid limestone which varies from the steep red stuff at the bottom to the slabby grey and sharp stuff at the top.

**APPROACH** - From the station follow the track towards Valle de Abdalajis, up a steep hill. The cliff lies above the road after about 500m and is impossible to miss.

🚫 **ACCESS** - Unfortunately at present there is an access dispute. The situation is that the owner, who also owns the building beneath the crag, is actively moving people off the crag. The building used to be a cafe but this has now closed. Also the first couple of bolts on all the routes have been removed. However if a friendly approach is made **BEFORE** climbing, by going to the house and asking if it is okay to climb, permission **MAY** be given. Absolutely no dogs are allowed at the crag.

To get around the problem of missing first bolts you can either use a clip-stick, or pre-arrange your first clips from the lower-off of the adjacent route which you have just climbed.

**1. Bolondro** .................. 6a+
An isolated route on a short wall to the left of the main buttress. Take a small rack.

**2. Nombro propio** ........ 6a

**3. Bohem destrell** ........ 6a+

**4. Poum poum ram ram** ...... 6a

**5. Para que disfrute la canalla** . 6b

**6. Crisis de identidad** ....... 6a+

**7. Tipo poloki** .............. 6a+
There is an unbolted line just to the right finishing at the same anchors as *Crisis de identidad*, grade 6a+.

**8. Atenea** ................ 4
An easy route for this crag, with one bolt.

**9. Geisha** ................ 6a

**10. Program genocida** .... 6c
Thin climbing up a slabby rib with some 'awkward to clip' bolts.

**11. Mañon tropo** ........ 7b
A chipped pocket above the roof.

**12. Las mulas comen muchas cuerdas** ........ 8a+

**13. Un lait fraiche pour monsieur** ........... 7b+
Start up a technical groove. Sustained above.

**14. Generación límite** ....... 7b+
A small rack is required.

**15. Mam endika** ....... 8a+

Topos by Rab Anderson

# EL CHORRO - Frontales Area

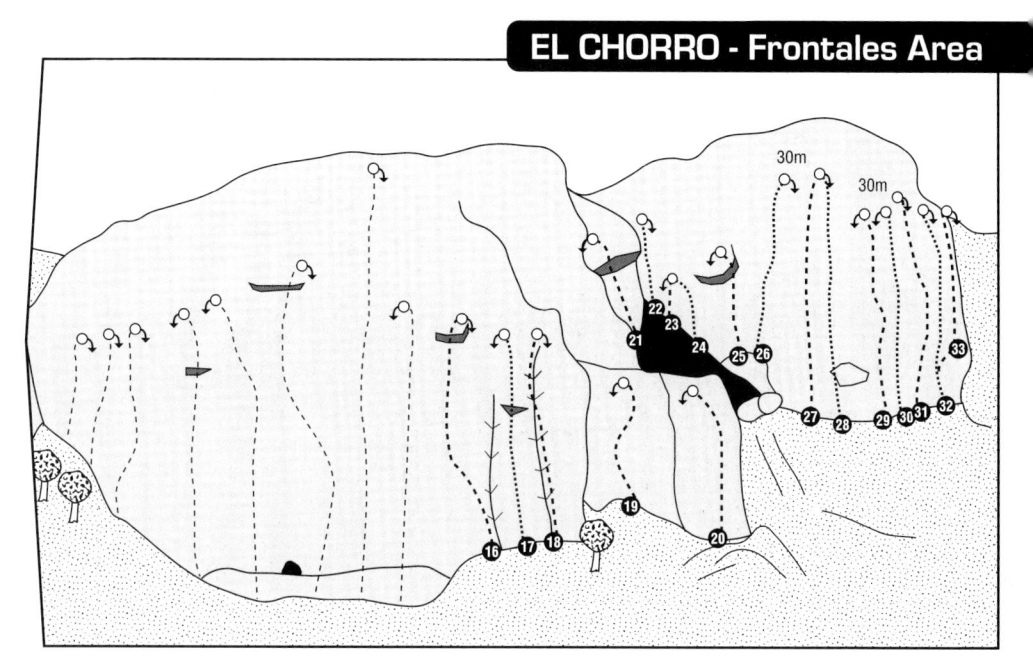

**16. Bueno, bonito y barato** — 6c+
Rib to the left of a corner.

There is a traditional route up the corner system to the right, at about 6b.

**17. Chorro mundo** — 7a+

**18. La ley del cateto** — 7a
The open groove.

**19. Mataillos lugareños** — 6c

**20. Artemisa** — 5+
Up a narrow rib.

The next routes lie higher up, on the side walls of a gully. There may be two routes on the left wall of the gully.

**22. Tipo indio** — 7b+

**22. No me miras mal** — 8a
The right-hand wall of the gully.

**23. No puedo controlarme** — 6c+

**24. Espoloa nombrada** — 7a+
A puzzling, fingery little number.

**25. Un poco vicioso** — 7a+
The obvious bulge high up.

All the next 8 routes require a 60m rope to lower off safely.

**26. Mezcia explosiva** — 8a
30m. Past a bolt-on hold.

**27. Kit grimpe** — 7b+
30m. Another bolt-on hold.

**28. Gros rouge** — 7b
30m. A long pitch.

**29. ?** — 7a
30m. A long pitch with the crux right at the top.

**30. Sara** — 7a+
30m.

**31. ?** — 7b
30m. Weaves its way up the front of a pillar.

**32. Dura vida la de un frekee** — 6c+
30m. A nasty start is followed by superb climbing above leading to a fluttery finish.

**33. Fiebra de Sur** — 7a
30m. Start up the previous route to the first bolt then break out right.

South facing wall
15m to 30m routes
Best grades - 6b to 8a+

**305**

# EL CHORRO - Frontales Area

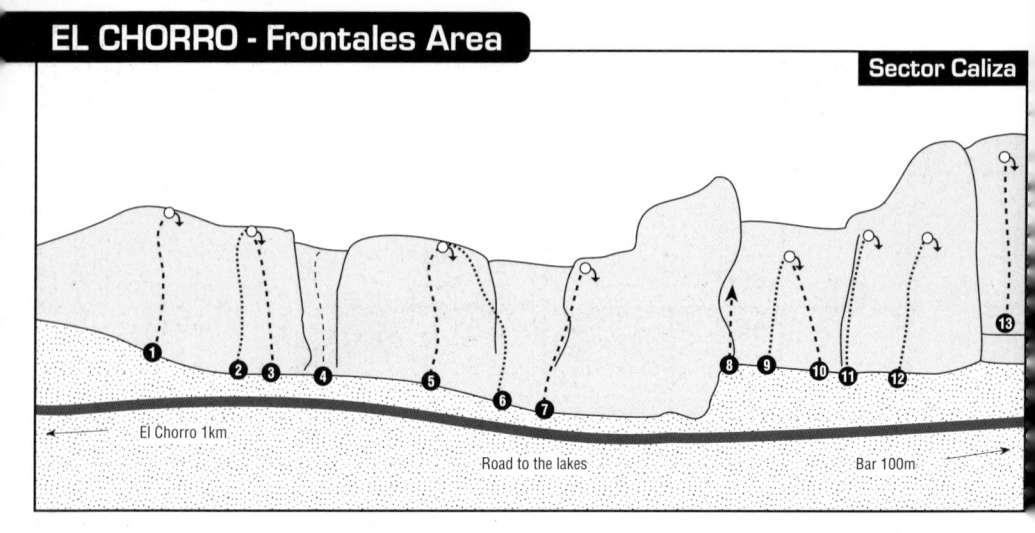

**Sector Caliza**

El Chorro 1km • Road to the lakes • Bar 100m

## SECTOR CALIZA
This is a relatively small sector, which has been bolted and developed by the shop owners in the village, hence it carries its name. Although the climbs aren't very long, or spectacular, they are very accessible.

**APPROACH -** It is situated 2 minutes drive along the road which goes from El Chorro to the lakes at the top of the Gorge, overlooking the dammed lake. Drive from the dam towards the lakes until the crag appears on the left of the road.

1. Caliza .................... 6b+

2. Parecia .................... 6b

3. Aranpicare con Adan .......... 6b+

4. La abujeritos ............... 6a
A line of bolts with no lower-off.

5. No más té ................... 6a
Bolts missing.

6. Harte un té ................. 5+
Bolts missing.

7. Santiana .................... 5

8. ? ........................... 6b+
The next line is a project next to it which may well have been climbed by now.

9. Medio dia ................... 6a

10. Nocturna ................... 6a+

11. Diurana .................... 6a+
A crack line which needs wires.

12. ? .......................... 6a+

13. ? .......................... 7b+
Excellent wall climbing. Starting from a ledge. But at present overgrown

East facing wall
10m to 15m routes
Best grades - 5+ to 7b+

# EL CHORRO - Frontales Area

**Valle de Abdalajis**

Location of routes

## VALLE DE ABDALAJIS

The friendly, tiered walls and slabs situated above the village of Valle de Abdalajis is an ideal spot for those seeking good quality easy climbs, or for those just starting and wishing to find their feet. Fine views, easy access and a sunny aspect add to the appeal of this venue. There is no shelter from the elements here which would make it a poor choice in bad weather.

**APPROACH -** From El Chorro take the road to Valle de Abdalajis which climbs the hill and passes under Las Encantadas. The road winds its way over the range and then slowly drops until the outskirts of Valle de Abdalajis come into view. The crags are easily seen up on the left. Take the road into the village (which narrows) and follow it as it contours above the main centre down on the right. After a few hundred metres a small sign for El Chorro will be seen on the left. Turn sharp left here (the first turning on the left that actually leads anywhere). The narrow road soon turns into a rough track and leads out of the houses and towards the crags. After 0.9km an open parking area is reached which is opposite a building. From the parking walk up the road and take a steep rough track uphill on the right. This leads up to beneath the obvious slabby corner which is not developed and then on to the main crag.

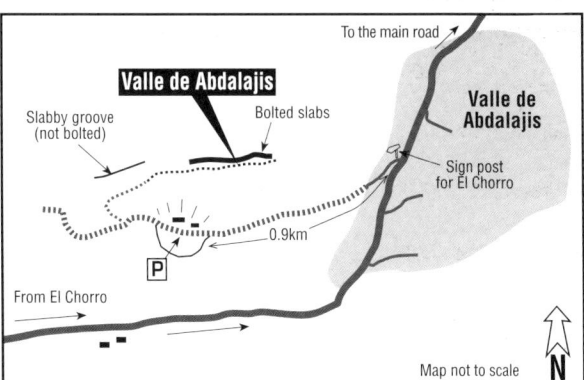

Valle de Abdalajis
Slabby groove (not bolted)
Bolted slabs
To the main road
Valle de Abdalajis
Sign post for El Chorro
0.9km
From El Chorro
P
Map not to scale
N

**THE CLIMBING -** Unfortunately there is no topo available to this crag at the present time. Originally the route names, grades and general line of the routes were painted at the base but this information has now weathered away. Nevertheless the climbing is excellent and the lack of details should not discourage a visit as the majority of the routes are on excellent compact rock which is off vertical. The grades are mainly in the 3 to 5 range. All the pitches have good lower-offs. Some of the routes follow crack lines, these pitches are less well bolted and a rack will be required by most.

South facing slabs
10m to 30m routes
Best grades - 3 to 5

# LOWER GORGE

The Lower Gorge is the impressive defile which cleaves its way through the towering crags of Cerro Cristo and Los Venenos. At some point in the distant past the rock structure has been eroded through by the river to form the magnificent spectacle we see today. At some point in the not so distant past 'Man' has had a hand in the matter and seen fit to construct a pipe system and a walkway, complete with bridge, that runs the full length of the Gorge. Not content with nature's route, Man has also driven tunnels straight through the bands of rock to make a route for the railway. This is a bonus for climbers since both man-made routes provide convenient and rather interesting access to the base of the climbs and the Central Gorge beyond. It is mainly because of the unique method of reaching the routes that the Gorge provides some of the most atmospheric climbing to be found anywhere.

Apart from the routes to the right of the entrance, there is little in the way of easy climbing and a general air of seriousness prevails. This can be particularly unsettling for first-time visitors unused to the instant exposure just after you make the first move. Thankfully the climbing is mainly vertical which allows you to lower off back to the walkway without too many scary antics.

The best climbing is dotted about a bit although there is a good concentration of technical wall climbs in Sector Recodo. For the longer routes you need look no further than the classic *Zeppelin* which is the best long route of its grade in the area.

## THE WALKWAY

The walkway, or *Camino del Rey*, is an amazing narrow, concrete path that runs the full length of both the Lower Gorge and the Upper Gorge. It was originally constructed in the 1920s to allow the King to view the engineering work carried out by his subjects. Sadly the walkway is is now slowly dropping into the gorge, however it is still possible to walk along its full length, but those of a nervous disposition may require a harness and a sling.

## ASPECT AND CLIMATE

The Gorge runs from west to east, and due to its extreme narrowness, receives very little in the way of sunshine, apart from at the entrances. Once in the depths though, not only does the sun rarely shine, but the wind can howl through it. This can be welcome in really hot weather but can make it freezing (and worrying as you teeter along the walkway) in cold weather.

## APPROACH

From the Albercones car park walk through two tunnels and over two bridges, to reach a large vertical wall through which there is another tunnel. The walkway cuts across the face to the left, the large broken wall on the right is Los Venenos. The walkway gives access to Pasarela de los Venenos, Santimonia, Juaja, Africa and El Recodo and continues all the way to the Upper Gorge. The tunnel is followed for Zeppelin and the central area including Los Cotos. TAKE CARE WHEN WALKING DOWN THE TUNNELS, THE TRAINS ARE VERY FAST!

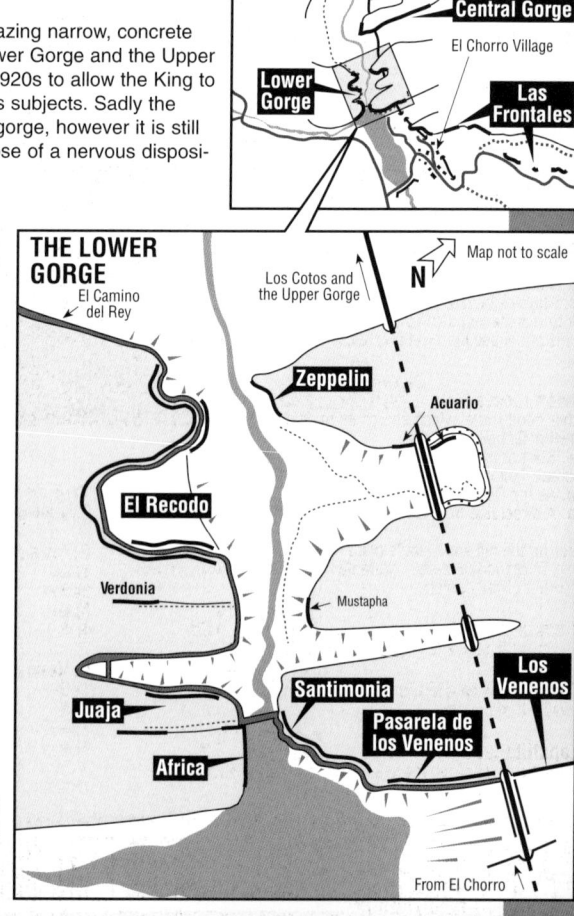

# EL CHORRO - Lower Gorge

**Los Venenos**

## LOS VENENOS
The huge wall which marks the front of the Lower Gorge stretches far up the hillside above the railway bridge. Although on first impression the crag looks a bit rambling and broken, it does contain some good pitches. On most of the routes it is worth carrying a small rack to supplement the fixed stuff.
**DESCENT -** Abseil back down the route lines on double 50m ropes.

The first four routes start from a ledge above and right of the bridge. It is possible to scramble up to this ledge from the right, but a little more entertaining is the steep groove just right of the tunnel - this is the first pitch of -

### 1. El techito del pirata  6a
A good long route. A rack is needed for the first and last pitches.
**1) 6a.** Start up the groove, to the ledge.
**2) 5.** Continue up to a tree.
**3) 5+ (6b+).** Follow some corners to another ledge, or climb over the bulge onto the slab on the right and continue direct at 6b+.
**4) 5+, 5) 5+.** Continue for two more long pitches, marked by occasional fixed gear.

### 2. La ampola  6a
**1) 5.** From the ledge, traverse across leftwards over the tunnel.
**2) 6a, 3) 6a, 4) 6a, 5) 5+.** Climb the wall above in four more pitches.
There is a left-hand finish at 5+, 5+.

### 3. Octopus dey  6c
An excellent long wall climb. Start on a ledge.
**1) 6c.** Move right across a wall.
**2) 6a.** Climb this and a crack to a good stance. The wall above is followed, past a ledge to another stance.
**3) 6c.** Move right and climb the hard thin crack to reach a ledge and an iron bar. There is a report of a loose block on this pitch. Abseil off.

### 4. Avión rockero  6a
Another good route, which shares its middle pitch with *Octopus dey*.
**1) 5+.** Start at the right-hand end of the ledge and climb a flake to a crack. Follow this to a ledge then traverse left to belay.
**2) 6a.** As for *Octopus dey*.
**3) 6a.** A direct line from the ledge in one 30m pitch.

Further up the hill are 3 single pitch routes left of a prominent corner. To get to the starts, scramble first left then back right to a ledge left of the corner.

### 5. Victima de la evidence  6a
A short pitch from the left-hand end of the ledge.

### 6. Empotrador at atómico  5+
The wall left of the corner.

### 7. Zapatilla jebe  7a
Start up the corner then move left onto a technical slab.

There are two more routes even further up the hillside. Only the grades are known.

### 8. Excedente de cupo  6b
**1)** 6a
**2)** 6a+
**3)** 6b
**4)** 5.

### 9. Venecia celeste  5+
**1)** 5+
**2)** 5+
**3)** 5+
**4)** 4.

East facing wall
20m to 120m routes
Best grades - 6a to 6c

Photo: Mark Glaister

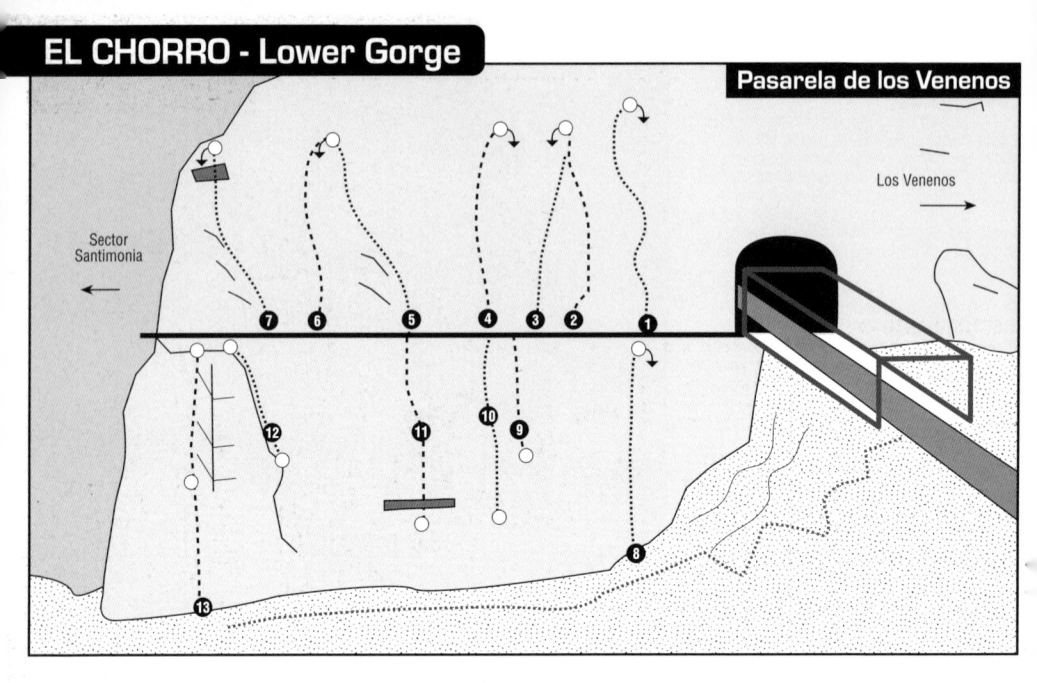

# EL CHORRO - Lower Gorge

## Pasarela de los Venenos

Los Venenos →

← Sector Santimonia

## PASARELA DE LOS VENENOS

The mouth of the gorge is flanked on its northern side by a large vertical wall split by the famous walkway. This is the location of a few single pitch routes which are all very fingery and technical.

The first route starts about 10m along the walkway and the routes are listed from right to left.

1. **Camino shuffle** ........ 7b

2. **No seas pesada nena** ... 6c+
A hard start leads to a good groove.

3. **Demócratas y cristianos** . 7a+
The right-facing corner.

4. **Pedorro y macaco** ..... 7c+
A technical horror up the blank wall.

5. **Les cutres** ............ 6b+
The leftwards rising line.

6. **Jaque el rey** .......... 7c+
Another vertical 7c+ - horrific!

7. **Aixamatinae** .......... 7c+
.. and another! Less technical then the others since the last move requires a dynamic approach.

The routes below the walkway require an abseil to reach their starts. There is not always a bolt in place to do this so you may have to climb one of the routes above, or use the walkway in some way. Routes 8 and 13 can be accessed by scrambling down to their bases from the railway line. The walkway itself provides a spectacular finishing roof to the routes, however you also get a good view of what its made of, which makes your subsequent trips onto it even more exciting!

8. **Ace ventura** ............ 8a

9. **?** ...................... 6c+

10. **Fruto prohibido** ........ 8b
This one must be awesomely technical!

11. **La cupla la tiene el bar de isabel** 7a
Start below a thin roof.

12. **Luz verde** ............. 7b
A wall and arete.

13. **Diedro de hercules** ..... 6b+
Start by scrambling down the slope or by abseiling down the line. 1) 6b+, 2) 6b.

East facing wall
15m to 40m routes
Best grades - 6b+ to 7c+

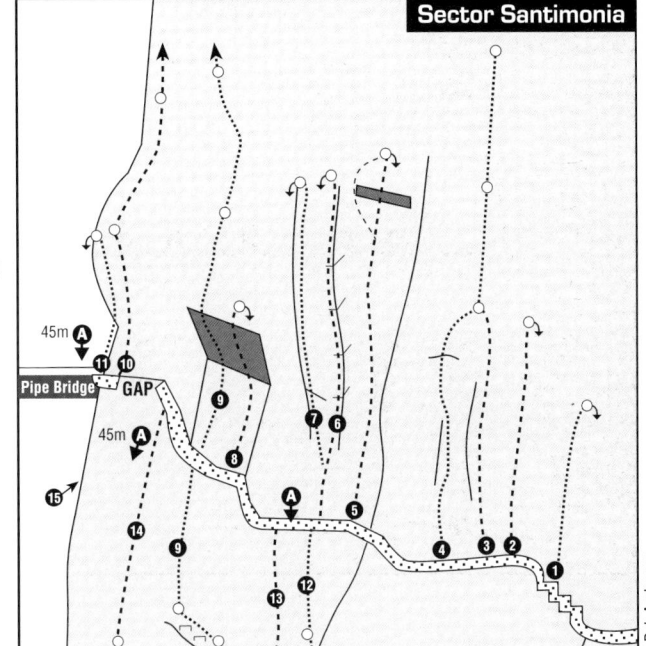

# EL CHORRO - Lower Gorge

## Sector Santimonia

**SECTOR SANTIMONIA**
This sector has the dubious distinction of having the most dodgy sections of walkway underneath it, including the infamous gap, just before the pipe bridge. This gap is pretty frightening first time you cross it, but it is easy to get used to it after a few trips.
The routes tend to be steep wall climbs with fingery little holds and phenomenal exposure after you have done a couple of moves.
**APPROACH** - Continue along the walkway, around the corner from Pasarela de Los Venenos. The first routes are above some steps.

**1. Moco de hierro** — 6c
A short route with a tricky start.

**2. Jabega** — 7b+
This was once given 8b. Someone hacked it about with a chisel and now it's a bit easier.

**3. Desos de domino** — 7a+
The right-hand of two cracks.

**4. Santimonia** — 6c+
1) 6c+. The left-hand crack is excellent.
2) 6a. The middle pitch leads to a belay below(!) a ledge. This pitch is harder if taken direct.
3) 6b+. The last pitch gives more finger crack climbing.
**DESCENT** - Abseil off.

**5. La tregua del pedal** — 7c+
A scrappy start. The last move can be by-passed on the left, but it ain't much easier (7c)!

**6. Sangre latina** — 6c

**7. Hartelo** — 7b
The superbly-positioned arete.

**8. Polva de angel** — (8b?)
The line of pockets.

**9. Sendero luminoso** — 6c+
A huge expedition which starts at the base of the gorge with a hard aid pitch.
1) 5+/A2, 2) 6a, 3) 3. The starting pitches.
4) 6b. The pitch above the walkway is worthwhile.
5) 6a+. This one is also worth the effort if you are up to it.
**DESCENT** - Lower off pitch 4 or abseil from higher up

**10. Camino sin ander** — 6a+
Past the gap is another long route starting from the walkway.
1) 4, 2) 6a, 3) 6a+, 4) 4.

**11. Ventana en el tropico** — 7a+
A short problem above the pipe.

The last three routes require abseils, on two 50m ropes, to get to their starts.

**12. Chupa la gamba** — 6c
Recently re-bolted.
1) 6c. Excitingly bolted. make sure you are confident at 6c before attempting this pitch.
2) 6b.

**13. Er-Mouriadine** — 6c
Recently re-bolted.

**14. Lobo de mar** — 7a+

**15. Libertad de movimiento** — 7a+
Reached from the far side of the bridge. The seemingly pointless 1st pitch is used to access the 7a+ pitch.
1) 3, 2) 7a+.

East facing wall
15m to 60m+ routes
Best grades - 6c to 7b

Topo by Rab Anderson

# EL CHORRO - Lower Gorge

## Sector Juaja

### SECTOR JUAJA
The routes here are spread over the walls at different levels. The lower section gives some steep wall climbs. The upper section is rarely explored, possibly because the easiest route is 7b+!
**APPROACH** - Continue across the pipe bridge from Sector Santimonia and you are under the lower section.

The first route is on the front of the buttress.

**1. Enimigo público** . . . . . . . . . . . . 7b+
A desperate finishing roof.

**2. Juaja** . . . . . . . . . . . . . . . . . . . . . 7a+
Gets harder higher up.

**3. E por doquier** . . . . . . . . . . . . . 8a+
The wall left of the crack.

**4. Granainos '85** . . . . . . . . . . . . . 6b
Starts as for the previous route but moves right to the steep crack. Large gear is needed for the crack.

**5. Atlética y Ilorica** . . . . . . . . . . . 7b

If you continue along the walkway, around a corner, there is another clean wall.

**6. Una española nunca mea sola** . . 7b+
Good, sustained wall climbing.

Up the gully to the right of the first wall are more routes. Approach by an awkward and precarious scramble up banking where cable end is attached.

**7. ?** . . . . . . . . . . . . . . . . . . . . . . . 7c

**8. ?** . . . . . . . . . . . . . . . . . . . . . . . 7b+

Right again is a stunning wall containing two of the hardest routes in El Chorro. They share the same start.

**9. Cangreo** . . . . . . . . . . . . . . . . . 8c
The left-hand line.

**10. Monsters forever** . . . . . . . . . 8b+
The right-hand line.

In front of, and to the right of, *Monsters Forever*, is -

**11. Verbene de lapiz** . . . . . . . . . 7c+

NE facing wall
10m to 25m routes
Best grades - 7b+ to 8c

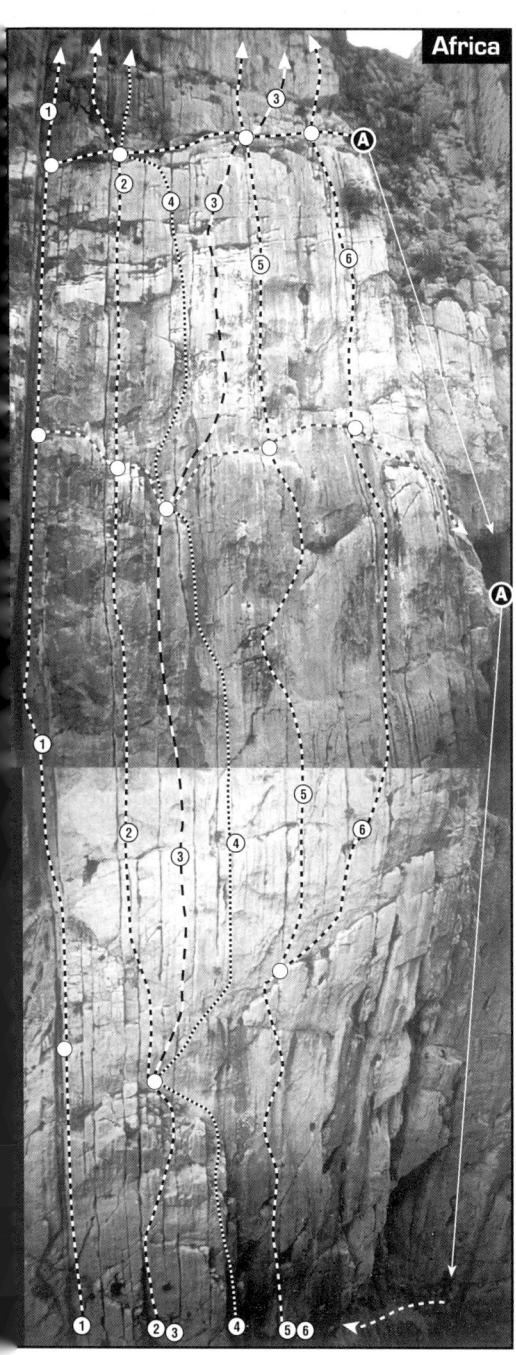

# EL CHORRO - Lower Gorge

**Africa**

### SECTOR AFRICA
Opposite Sector Santimonia is a massive wall lined with vertical crack systems, this is the well named sector Africa - a huge wilderness where it is easy to get lost! The routes on the wall have a big feel about them and it is advisable to take a full rack with you although some are reasonably well bolted.

**APPROACH -** All the routes start from the lowest ledge, which can be reached by crawling along a tunnel marked on the topo for Sector Juaja (opposite). From its end, make a 52m abseil (exciting!) to the ledge, which is 30m above the water. From here traverse leftwards across the wall.

**DESCENT -** Traverse rightwards along one of the ledge systems and abseil, or scramble, back to the cave entrance. If you are unfortunate enough to have failed before you have got above the cave, then you will have to abseil into the river and swim for it. This is not recommended as anything other than a good story to tell your friends.

The first three routes start at the left-hand end of the ledge. Traverse left past the bolt belay of routes 4 and 5, around a rib to a peg belay in a crack.

### 1. Material belico ..... 6a
This route follows the crack and corner system to the left of the belay. The climbing is relatively straight forward but there is not much fixed gear to point the way. Take a full rack including some large stuff. There is a curious lower pitch at A2, which presumably starts from a boat.
1) 4, 2) 5, 3) 5, 4) 6a.

### 2. Africa ............. 6b+
The classic route of the wall follows grooves and cracks.
1) 6a+, 2) 6b+, Two well-bolted pitches lead to the mid-height ledge. Escape rightwards is possible. Don't get confused with pitch two of the next route.
3) 5, 4) 6b. There is a hard direct finish to the right of the last pitch at 7a+.

### 3. La bella y la bestia .... 7a+
A hard and sustained route which starts as for *Africa*, then continues straight up the blank wall above. It is said to be fully bolted but take a small rack just in case.
1) 6a+, 2) 7a+, 3) 7a, 4) 7a.

The next three routes start from the bolt belay at the base of the approach abseil.

### 4. Chiripitiglauticos ....... 6b+
A variation on *Africa*. The line goes up leftwards to the first belay on *Africa*. From here it wanders up the wall on the right, eventually finishing up the last pitch of *Africa*. Take a full rack of gear.
1) 5+, 2) 6a, 3) 5+, 4) 6b+.

### 5. La dame del viento ..... 6c+
A magnificent route up the right-hand side of the wall. Mostly bolted but take a large wire for the start of pitch 1.
1) 6c, 2) 6c. Climb direct from the bolt belay to the mid-height ledge.
3) 6b+, 4) 7a. Two long, crack systems above to a final pitch up the head wall.

### 6. Cuando se lo diga a mis amigos 6c+
This route takes a direct line up the wall, starting up *La dame del viento*. Take a full rack.
1) 6c. As for *La dame del viento*.
2) 6b, 3) 6c+, 4) 6b+. Three pitches up the crack system on the right-hand side of the wall.

North facing wall
100m to 150m routes
Best grades - 6a to 7a+

# EL CHORRO - Lower Gorge

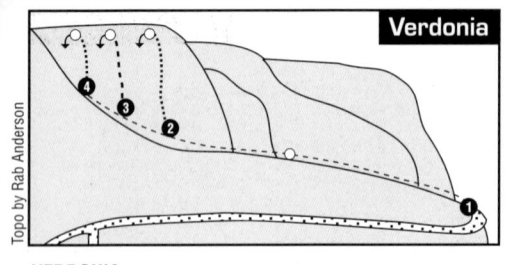

### Verdonia

### EL RECODO - LEFT
The left-hand side of the bowl has some left-facing grooves running up it.

1. Pixci . . . . . . . . . . . . . . . . . . . . . . ☐ 6b+

2. Dixci . . . . . . . . . . . . . . . . . . . . . . ☐ 6c+

3. La canastera . . . . . . . . . ▣▣▣ ☐ 7b+
A brilliant wall climb which would be worth three stars if it were not escapable after the crux.

4. Tipo sueca . . . . . . . . . . ▣▣▣ ☐ 6c+
Another stunning wall climb with a hard move low down and a tricky finish. High in the grade. Photo page 318.

5. Calígula . . . . . . . . . . . . ▣▣▣ ☐ 7b+
A superb second pitch.
1) 6c, 14m. Climb the shallow corner groove to a hanging belay at the prominent hole.
2) 7b+, 14m. Excellent moves up the arete and right wall.

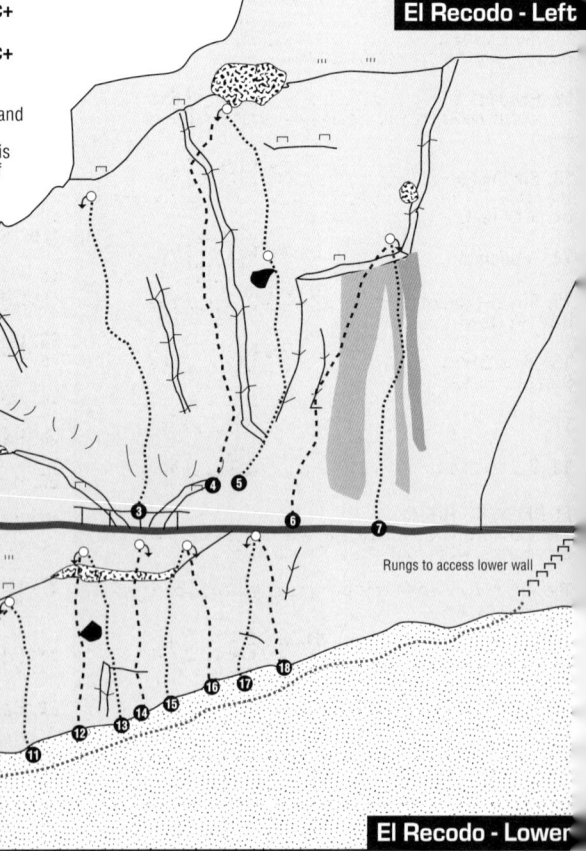

## VERDONIA
A short wall mainly of interest to 6c+ climbers.
It is located above and behind the bowl of El Recodo.
**APPROACH** - Start from the walkway and use route 1 to access the upper three routes.

1. Verdonia . . . . . . . . . . . . . . . . . . ☐ 5
1) 5, 2) 5. Access route to the next 3 routes.

2. Moloko plus . . . . . . . . . . . . ▣ ☐ 6c+

3. Verdonia . . . . . . . . . . . . . . . ▣ ☐ 6c+

4. Enano pagano . . . . . . . . . . . ▣ ☐ 6c+

## EL RECODO
This superb and varied sector gives the most accessible and developed climbing in the Lower Gorge. It is usually very popular and busy, especially during the local holidays. It is also a total 'shade-trap', receiving only a small amount of morning sun.
**APPROACH** - Continue walking down the walkway from the pipe bridge and you can't miss it. The first two routes are at the left-hand end of a ledge above the walkway.

El Recodo - Left

Rungs to access lower wall

El Recodo - Lower

Topo by Rab Anderson

**Verdonia**
East facing wall
Grades - 6c+

# EL CHORRO - Lower Gorge

### El Recodo - Right

**6. El campista** .......... 7b+
Thin and insecure moves via the slim groove.

**7. Musas inquientantes** 8a
Magnificent moves on surprisingly un-worn rock leads to a tense throw for the finishing hold.

## EL RECODO - LOWER WALL
The wall beneath the walkway has a few good routes.
**APPROACH** - Descend iron rungs beneath the walkway at the back of the bowl.

**8. Todos pretenden saber** .. 6c+
Abseil off bolts behind the walkway, below *Pixci* and *Dixci*.

**9. Los gozas y las sombras** . 7a
Abseil in from anchors on the far left. It is probably easier to reach this from below *Zeppelin*, water depth permitting.
1) 6c+, 2) 7a

**10. King Kong** .......... 6b+
Start at a bolt belay and finish at a hard crack.

**11. Indio jumeli** .......... 6c
The start is hard and below the first bolt!

**12. Recodo** .............. 6a+
The relatively unspectacular route which gives the sector its name.

**13. Six Vicious** .......... 6b+
The rightward facing corner. Possibly called *Sid Vicious* but this is a better name.

**14. Tumisimo** ............ 7a+

**15. Sietebe del plumero** ... 7b+
Hard and cruxy!

**16. Miss Dedos** .......... 6c+
Start below a hole.

**17. ?** .................... 6c

**18. ?** .................... 6c

## EL RECODO - RIGHT
The final routes on this side of the Lower Gorge are on the right-hand buttress which forms the El Recodo bowl.

The next three routes are reached by scrambling up iron rungs into the large cave.

**19. Iriquieza** ............ 7c+
1) 7b+. The incredibly well-chalked flake is very popular.
2) 7c+. The extension is less popular.

**20. Hari-Kiri** ............ 8c+
45m. John Dunne's stunning realisation of one of the most impressive lines in the world, which is only slightly spoilt by the bolt-on holds it uses. A mere 8c, 8a+ if you split it at a hanging stance.

**21. Bon voyage** .......... 6c
An excellent route up the right-hand side of the cave.
1) 6c, 2) 6b+

**22. ?** .................... 7a+
1) 6b, 2) 7a+

**23. Lluvias otoñales** ........ 5+
Below the walkway. Abseil from two bolts.

The rest of the routes are around the corner, just off the topo.

**24. Rasta de posta** ........ 6b+

**25. Come unas** ............ 6a+

**26. Bob Marley** .......... 7c
Superb and technical all the way. Lost holds hence now 7c.

**27. Los capitalistas** ........ 7c+
A desperate route up the blank wall. maybe harder.

**28. Rovicunda** ............ 6b
Fun climbing up and around the cave.

**29. Haale Bop** ............ 6b

Three routes have been recorded on the lower wall to the right of this but no deatilas are known.

**30. Maestro golpeador** ...... 6b
Abseil from below *Rovicunda*.

---

**El Recodo**
North facing bowl, 20m to 50m routes
Best grades - 6b to 8c+

# EL CHORRO - Lower Gorge

## Sector Zeppelin

**SECTOR ZEPPELIN**
The vast north side of the Gorge is characterised by three huge buttresses which the railway tunnels cut through. Between the second and third buttresses the gorge opens out and the wall behind contains three massive caves (Los tres techos). The main area of climbing interest is the last buttress which contains the superb long route *Zeppelin*.

**APPROACH** - Walk down the railway towards the gorge and continue through two tunnels after passing the walkway.
**For Routes 1 to 5 and 10 and 11** - Descend down the unstable slope behind the bridge to beneath the arches. From here you can either abseil or descend a fixed cable to the (even more) unstable slope below. Alternatively you can abseil directly off the railings on the bridge to the lower slope but **BEWARE OF GREASE AT BASE OF ABSEIL.**

**For Routes 7 to 9** - Walk to the starts behind the bridge.
**For Routes 12 and 13** - Continue through the tunnel and they are on your left.

# EL CHORRO - Lower Gorge

## Zeppelin

**1. Zeppelin** ........... 6c+
This superb long route is fully equipped but take a small rack to supplement the fixed gear on the easier pitches. Pitches 4 and 5, which are much harder than the others, can be climbed using some aid. Start at the base of the long slab which leads up to the prominent roof on pitch 4.
1) to 3) 70m. Climb the slab following the fixed gear. Can be done in two long pitches.
4) 6c, 20m. The roof is strenuous to a stance on the lip.
5) 6c+, 25m. Hard moves above the stance lead to easier climbing above. Don't go too far left after the hard moves. Worth 7a if you join it with the last pitch since the belay becomes a significant point of aid.
6) 5, 30m. The slab is a bit thin on bolts.
7) 6b+, 25m. Follow the crack in the groove above then move right and up onto the ridge.
8) 3, 40m. Scramble easily rightwards to belay behind a tree.
9) 6b, 35m. Climb the corner to the top of a pinnacle then continue up the wall above.
10) 70m. Scramble up the left-hand side of the ridge to the top.
**DESCENT** - Continue right up a rocky rib until it is possible to scramble down left through scrub, eventually arriving at the railway between the Gorge and Los Cotos.

**2. Espolón Masay** ............ 6b+
A long, and seldom climbed traditional route which bumbles easily up the wall until 2 hard pitches near the top, where it joins *Zeppelin*. Take a full rack.
1) 3, 2) 5+, 3) 5+, 4) 5, 5) 5+, 6) 6b+, 7) 3, 8) 6b, 9) 4.

The next routes are situated on the very steep wall right of the start of *Zeppelin*.

**3. ?** .................. 8c
The left-hand line starts up the slope.

**4. Shaka Zulu** .......... 8b
The well-chalked line.

**5. Perspectiva Neiwski** .... 8b+
Follow the vague arete.

The line to the right was once given 7c+ but it is so hard that it is still a project.

The next route is reached by precarious abseil from a bolt on the left-hand side of the railway to a belay behind a tree.

**6. Lactarius Deliciosus** ......... 6b+

There are three routes underneath the walkway which follows the back of the bay behind the bridge.

**7. La Peña se Despeña** ........ 6c+

**8. Acuario** .............. 6a+

**9. Papalillo Pafuena** ........ 6a

There are two more routes on this side of the gorge. To get there scramble down the slope as for *Zeppelin*, but turn left (downstream) and scramble up to the wall which forms the central pillar between the two tunnels.

**10. Mustafa** ........ 7c+
1) 6c+, 2)7c+, 3) 5+.

**11. Estrella de Sur** ........... 7a
1) 6c+, 2)7a,
Right of the arete.

The last two routes are on the left-hand wall as you exit the gorge, facing Los Cotos. Scramble down to the starts.

**12. Bahia Cochino** ............ 7a+
The left-hand line

**13. ?** .................... 6b+
The right-hand line.

Photo: Mark Glaister

**Zeppelin** - West facing wall
15m to 200m routes
Best grades - 6c+ to 8b

James McHaffie
on *Tipo sueca* (6c+ - page 314)
on El Recodo, the Lower Gorge.
Photo: Mark Glaister

# CENTRAL GORGE

This is the area where the valley opens out after the narrow ravine of the Lower Gorge. When exiting the tunnels on the approach walk, a long ridge of perfect grey slabs, slanting down towards the river, comes into view. This is Los Cotos - one of the best areas for limestone slab climbing in Europe. At the base of this ridge is the vertical wall of El Polvorin and below it a pleasant level area of trees and grass. This used to be an idyllic camping spot but now it has been spoilt by unthoughtful campers, hence the total ban on camping in the whole area. Beyond Los Cotos, and parallel to it, is a much larger wall. This is where El Invento and Makinodromo are located. The routes span a broad range of grades and styles, from the technical slabs on Los Cotos, to the steep overhangs and tufas on El Makinodromo. Most of the routes are fully bolted but, for some routes on Los Cotos and El Polvorin, it is worth carrying a small rack to take the sting out of some of the run-outs.

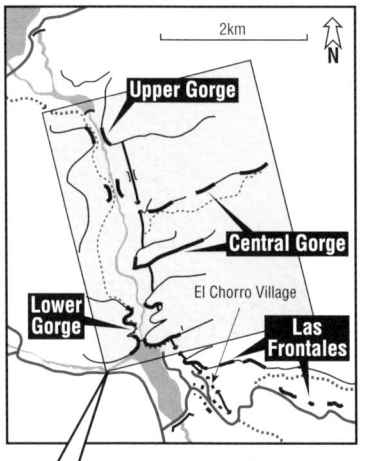

## ASPECT AND CLIMATE

Los Cotos, El Invento and El Makinodromo are south-east facing and usually extremely hot, with little shade to be found anywhere except for the odd small bush. El Polvorin faces west and is in the shade until the afternoon. The sun does slide off El Makinodromo late in the day and if you are waiting for the right time, and temperature, to make an ascent then take a head torch for the return walk through the tunnels.
Overall the Central Gorge is less windy than the two narrower ends, however there can still be a breeze but usually this is welcome in the heat.
If it is raining then El Makinodromo should provide some dry rock but you will get very wet getting there. Also, in heavy rain, the tufas will start running with water and this could be awkward since, frequently, they are the only holds.

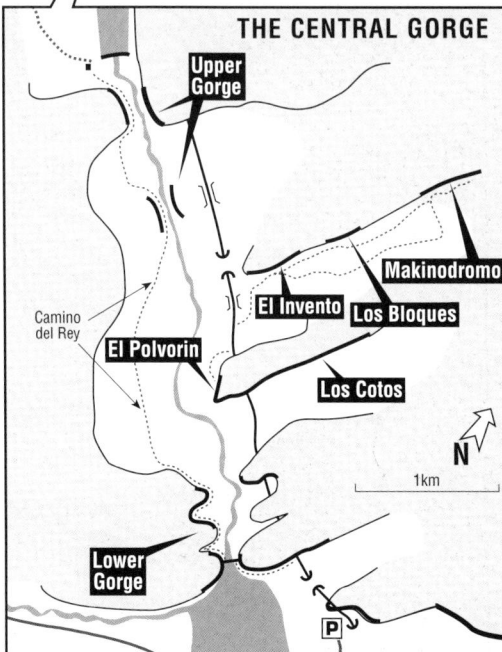

## APPROACH

From El Chorro village drive down the road towards the Gorge, and park underneath Sector Albercones, between two railway tunnels. Walk through the tunnel on the left and continue towards the gorge, over a bridge and through another tunnel. Where the walkway departs on the left, keep on the railway through three more tunnels. This leads to the open Central Gorge. The long ridge of Los Cotos is the first obvious feature which you come to. The tunnel through this ridge leads around the back to El Polvorin and beyond to the Makinodromo area. Approaches to the sectors are listed with the route pages but you may need to refer back to this map.

# EL CHORRO - Central Gorge

**Cotos Bajas**

EL POLVORIN

30m

From Cotos Medios

From the railway

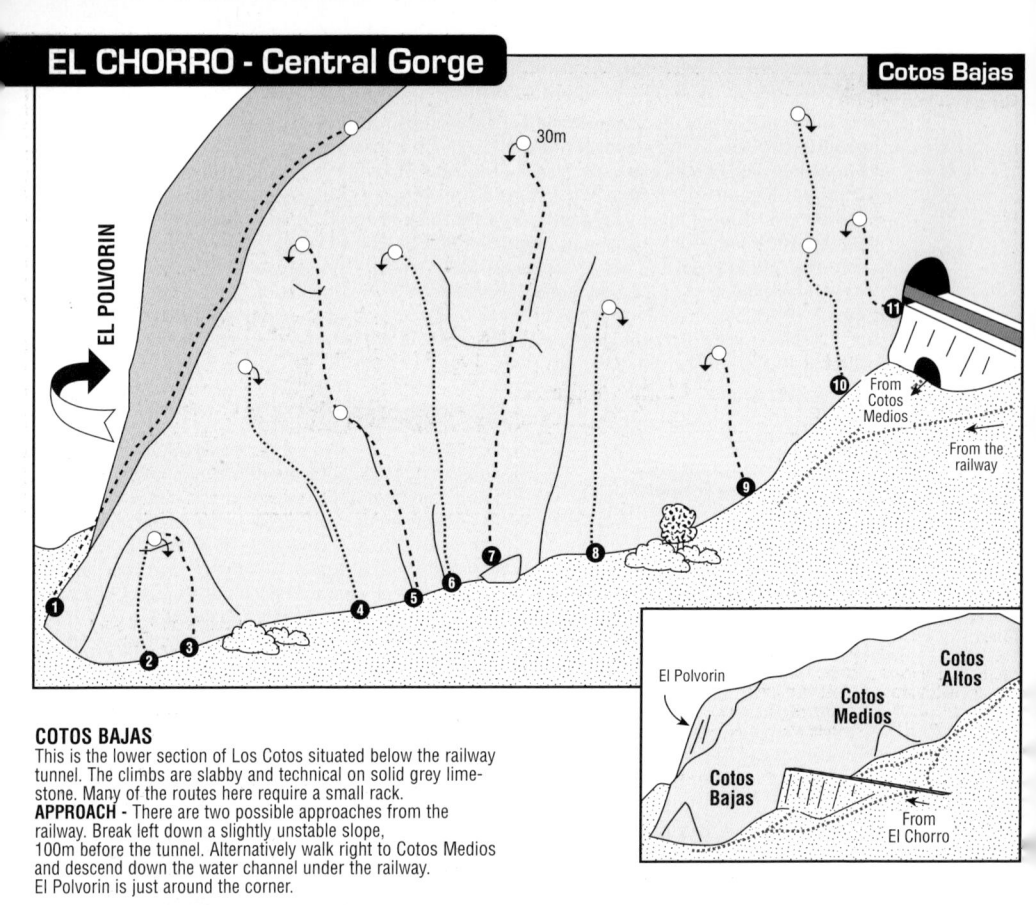

El Polvorin — Cotos Altos — Cotos Medios — Cotos Bajas — From El Chorro

## COTOS BAJAS
This is the lower section of Los Cotos situated below the railway tunnel. The climbs are slabby and technical on solid grey limestone. Many of the routes here require a small rack.
**APPROACH -** There are two possible approaches from the railway. Break left down a slightly unstable slope, 100m before the tunnel. Alternatively walk right to Cotos Medios and descend down the water channel under the railway. El Polvorin is just around the corner.

The first route follows a long line starting below the arete between Cotos Bajas and El Polvorin.

**1. Diedro y quique** . . . . . . . . . . . 3+
Follow the corner in one or two pitches. Take a full rack. Abseil off on double ropes.

At the toe of the buttress is a short triangular slab with two routes.

**2. Ordinada salvaje** . . . . . . . . 6a+
Hard past the first bolt.

**3. Mama quiero ser torero** . . . . . . . 6b
The right-hand line is even more fiddly.

Past some bushes, the routes get a bit longer.

**4. San satanas** . . . . . . 6a+
A diagonal line above the bushes. Wires needed at the start.

**5. San Gabriel** . . . . . . . . . . . . 5+
The flake-line. The name is painted on the rock.
1) 4+. No fixed gear on this pitch.
2) 5+.

**6. La hora del maquis** . . . . 5+
The crack needs a few medium sized wires. At the top, either lower off the last bolt or continue to the belay on the next route.

**7. La placa morrocotuda** . . 6a
30m. A good long pitch to the right with a high crux. Take some large wires or a Friend 2.5.

**8. Berrinche de chinche** . . . . . . 6b
Before some bushes is a short, and well protected pitch.

Further up the hill are a couple more routes.

**9. El yerno de Abraham** . . . . . . . . 6a
No fixed gear.

**10. Les muelles de guite** . . . . . 7a
1) 6a+. A poor easy approach pitch which needs wires.
2) 7a. An excellent upper pitch which is fully bolted.

**11. 4 mejilliones 20 duros** . . . . . . . 6c+
Starting from the railway, climb past 2 bolts and lower off the third.

320

Lots of sun — 30 min — Vertical — Slabby — Lower-offs

SE facing wall
10m to 30m routes
Best grades - 5+ to 6b

rockfax.c

# EL CHORRO - Central Gorge

**Cotos Medios**

## COTOS MEDIOS
The most popular climbing area in the whole of El Chorro is the section of Los Cotos just to the right of the railway. This is not surprising since it contains the best selection of easy to mid-grade routes around. Most of them are well bolted with good lower-offs but they are also very polished.

**APPROACH** - The first route starts from the railway.

**1. Rafael anyaya** ............ 5
A small rack is needed.

The next few routes start from the water channel.

**2. Camella cojo** ........ 5
Climb the crack past one bolt.

**3. Fisuroterapia** ........ 5
A good sustained pitch. Take some large wires.

**4. Fisura de los santos** .... 5
Start and finish as for the previous route.

**5. Fisura de hombre** ........ 5+
A superb climb left of a break in the slabs. The start is bold.

Past the break is another shorter slab.

**6. Bitchitos on the wailers** ........ 4+
The bulge at the bottom is the crux.

**7. El Monstruo de las galletas** ....... 5+
The first of the 'biscuit' routes has an overgrown start.

**8. Mordiscos de amor** ........... 5
To the same poor belay as the previous route.

**9. ?** ................. 6a+
A poor route.

The main attraction of this area is the large triangular slab.

**10. Alucinosis** ............ 4+
The first bolt is blue.

**11. ?** ................. 5
Superb climbing.

**12. Mitad hombre' mitad galleta** .. E4 5c
A trad route which is probably still awaiting a second ascent.

**13. Number one** ..... 4
The crack with a crux move back left at the top.

**14. Bruja intrepida** ........ 5
A direct variation on the last route, which starts between two bushes.

**15. Numero dos** ............. 5
Start between the next set of bushes.

**16. Galleta** ............ 4
The original 'biscuit' route follows the diagonal break.

**17. Super galleta** ...... 5+
Superb climbing direct from the start of the last route. Its name is painted on the rock.

**18. Gaby** ............ 6b+
A hard left-hand finish to the next route.

**19. Los mandriles no comen galletas** 6a+
The leftwards slanting groove gives a brilliant pitch.

**20. Madriles** ............... 7a
Steeper than most of the other routes around here.

SE facing wall
15m to 35m routes
Best grades - 4 to 6a+

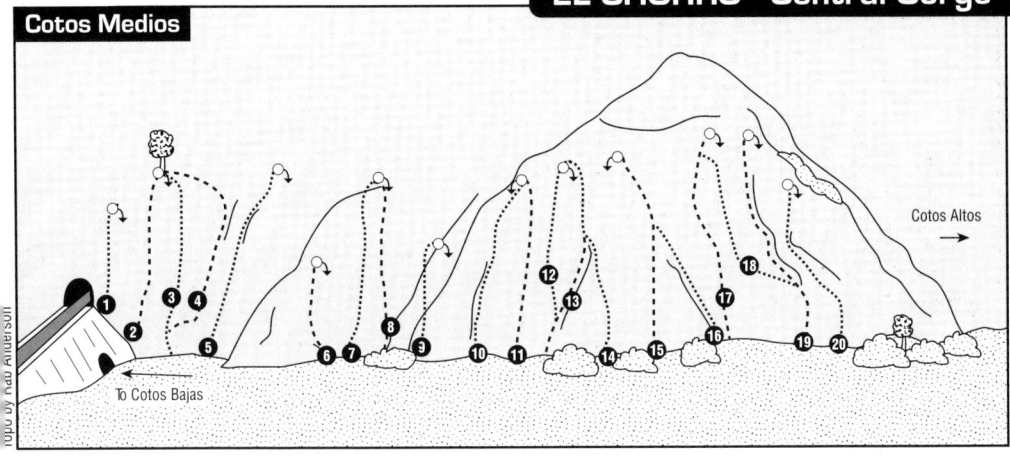

**321**

# EL CHORRO - Central Gorge

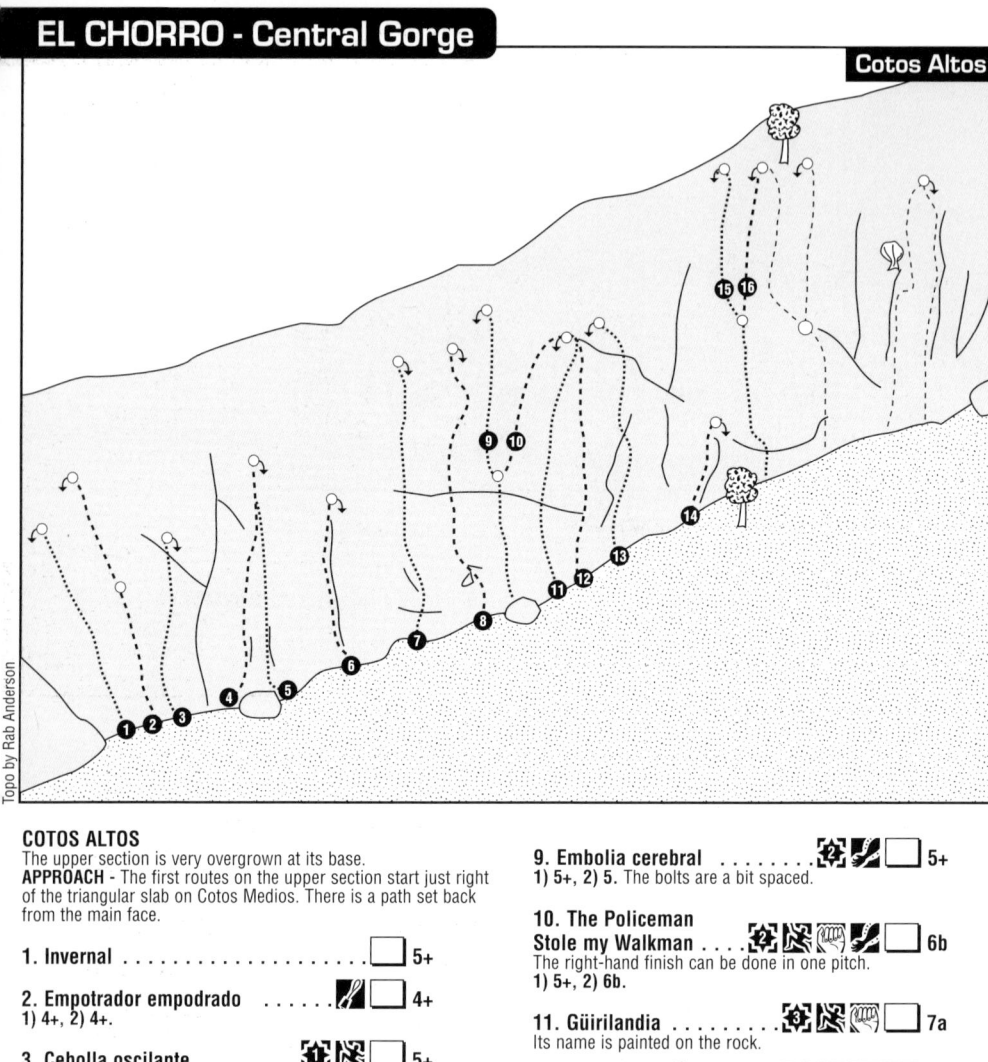

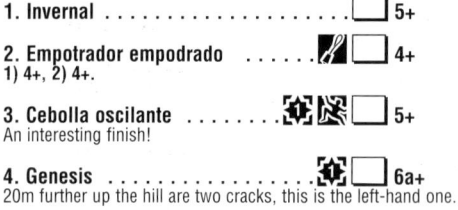

**Cotos Altos**

## COTOS ALTOS
The upper section is very overgrown at its base.
**APPROACH -** The first routes on the upper section start just right of the triangular slab on Cotos Medios. There is a path set back from the main face.

**1. Invernal** .................... 5+

**2. Empotrador empodrado** ...... 4+
1) 4+, 2) 4+.

**3. Cebolla oscilante** ....... 5+
An interesting finish!

**4. Genesis** .................. 6a+
20m further up the hill are two cracks, this is the left-hand one.

**5. Mongroni free** ......... 6a+
The right-hand crack.

**6. Arbola** ............. 6a+
The next crack up the hill.

**7. Bruner and the bruna** ... 6a+
Good climbing direct or otherwise, past a prominent hole.

**8. Ley de la selva** ....... 6b+
Its name is painted on the rock.

**9. Embolia cerebral** ........ 5+
1) 5+, 2) 5. The bolts are a bit spaced.

**10. The Policeman Stole my Walkman** .... 6b
The right-hand finish can be done in one pitch.
1) 5+, 2) 6b.

**11. Güirilandia** ........ 7a
Its name is painted on the rock.

**12. Cafe bonk** .......... 7a+
Another technical test-piece.

**13. Penetración analgésica** . 6c
Hard for the short.

**14. Si te caes pega una voz** ...... 6c
Short and desperate.

**15. Amarilla** .......... 5+
Wires needed for the second pitch.
1) 5, 2) 5+.

**16. Fanáticos del atico** . 6c
The fully-bolted right-hand variation pitch 2 to *Amarilla*.

# EL CHORRO - Central Gorge

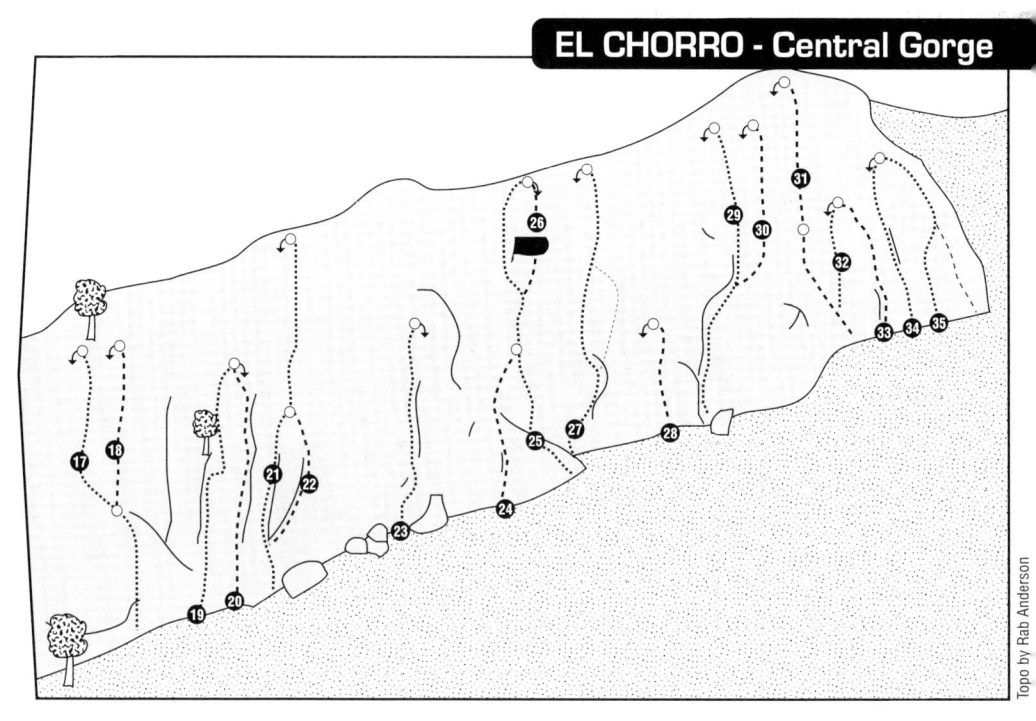

The upper section of the crag is to the right of a prominent right to left slanting break. The first route starts below and left of this break.

**17. El ventorro** . . . . . . . . . . . 6a+
Climb direct through the break.
1) 5, 2) 6a+.

**18. La blanca** . . . . . . . . . . . 6b
A hard right-hand finish to *Ventorro*.

**19. Guerrero del abismo** 7a
Superb slab climbing.

**20. Exceso de equipaje** . . . 6c
The next crack to the right may require a wire or two.

**21. Chungo superior** . . . . . . . 6a
Start just left of a boulder.
1) 5+, 2) 6a.

**22. Quasimodo** . . . . . . . . 7a+
The right-hand branch of the crack provides a testing alternative. Bolt missing on the crux.

**23. Profanes y blasfemos** . . 6b+
Further up the hill, between some more boulders.

**24. Pisto gilguero** . . . . . . . . . . . 6c+
A short and technical crack.

**25. Que te den por culo** . . . . . . 6b
1) 6b.
2) 5. The roof on its left needs wires.

**26. El dinamitate te espera** . . . 6c
1) 6b.
2) 6c. The roof itself is something different!

**27. Yu yu** . . . . . . . . . . . . . . . 6c
The right-hand variation is easier - 6a.

**28. Chulo de madriza** . . . . . . . 7a

**29. El piqui** . . . . . . . . . . . . . 6c
A desperate start, use some blocks.

**30. Petamorfosis** . . . . . . . 7b
A wicked right-hand finish to *El Pique*.

**31. Mister proper** . . . . . . . . . 5+
Well-spaced bolts.
1) 5+, 2) 4+.

**32. El viajero amable** . . . . 6b+

**33. Adeli** . . . . . . . . . . . . . . 6b+
Same lower-off as *El viajero amable*.

**34. Electro volt** . . . . . . . . . 6b+
The last groove on the wall.

**35. Exodo** . . . . . . . . . . . . . 6a+
Can be started direct at **7b+**.

West facing wall
15m to 45m single and two pitch routes
Best grades - 5+ to 7b

323

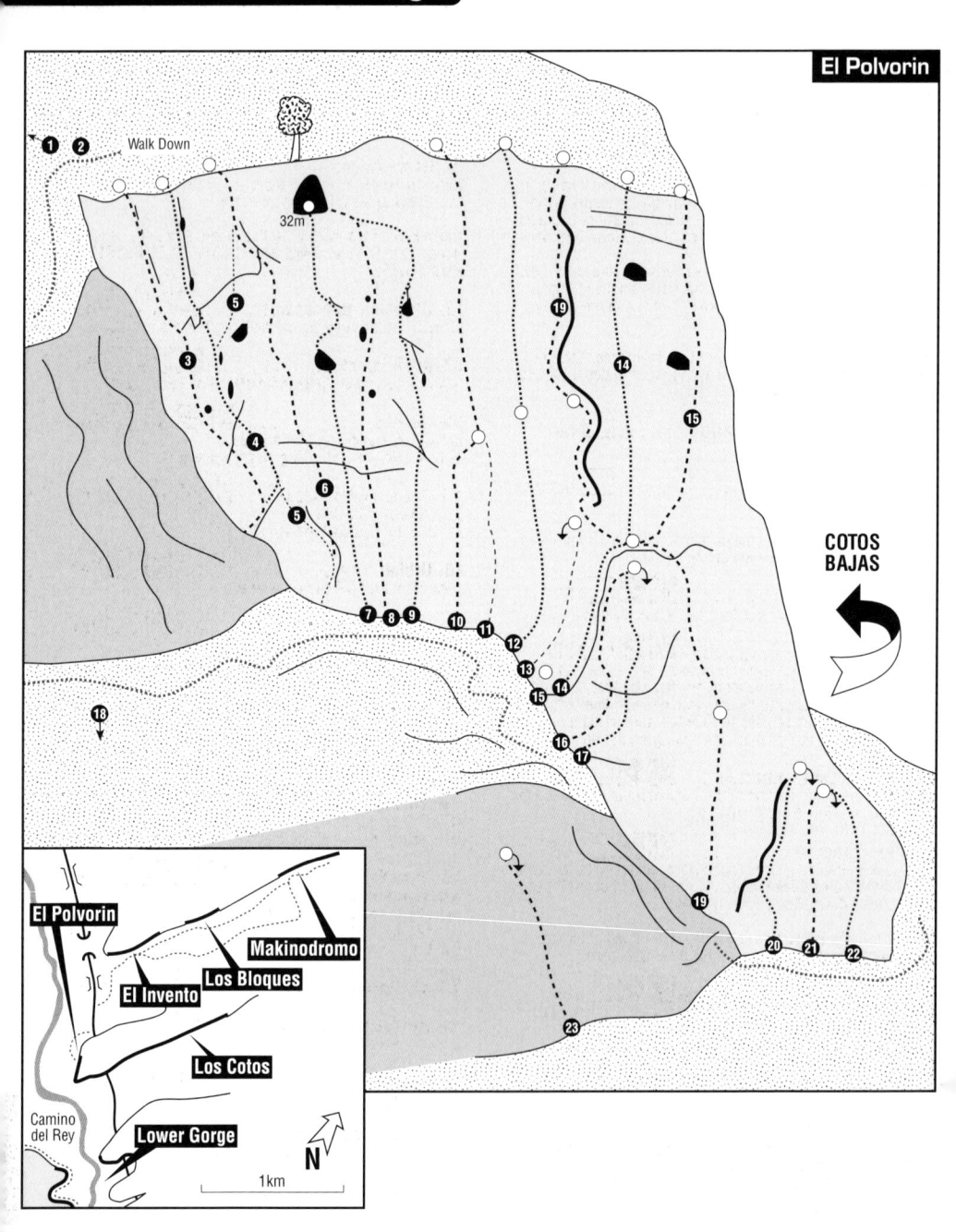

# EL CHORRO - Central Gorge

El Polvorin

COTOS BAJAS

Walk Down

32m

El Polvorin
Makinodromo
El Invento
Los Bloques
Los Cotos
Camino del Rey
Lower Gorge

N
1km

324
Afternoon | 35 min | Vertical | Multi-pitch

rockfax.com

# EL CHORRO - Central Gorge

### EL POLVORIN
If 6c wall climbing is your 'bag' then don't look any further. At the end of the Los Cotos ridge is a magnificent west facing wall of vertical rock, giving sustained, but seldom desperate routes on superb featured rock. Some people may find the bolts a bit far apart but they are usually in the right place when it matters.
**APPROACH (Routes 1 to 18)** - Walk through the tunnel in the Los Cotos ridge and double back left when you exit on the other side. A small path leads to a pleasant picnic platform overlooking the crag.
**DESCENT** - You can abseil off most of the main routes with two 50m ropes. It is also very easy to walk down on the left-hand side of the crag. Do not try and lower from any of the routes unless you have a 60+m rope!

The first two routes are up and left of the main face. They are best left for those who have done all the other routes to attempt while walking back down.

**1. El gordo ya no come guarro** ....... 5+
30m left of the descent path.

**2. Pedro el grande** ............. 6a+
Above the descent path.

The main routes are on the magnificent main face. Routes 3 to 17 start from the sloping ledge below the face.

**3. Alerta roja** ............ 6b+
30m. A good pitch which is a bit close to the gully at the bottom.

**4. Sueño de venus** ........ 6a+
The original and easiest route on this part of the wall has been slightly superseded by some more direct variations. Start in the gully and climb up to gain the leftwards trending line. A long sling for a thread can be used to ease the run-out higher up. Originally climbed in 2 pitches with a belay on the right at 10m.

**5. Sueño de venus varacion** ... 6b
32m. Gain the upper section of the original route from the right, then break out right from it higher up.

**6. Pilier dorada** .......... 6c
35m. Climb direct to a ledge (optional stance) then trend left to finish at the top of *Sueño Variacion*. Abseil off or scramble to the top and walk down. See photo on page 15.

Routes 7, 8 and 9 finish in a cave high on the wall. You can just lower from here with a 60m rope but take great care.

**7. Generación spontanea** .. 6c
32m. Climb straight up past the optional stance to belay in a large cave.

**8. Revuelta en el frenopático** 6c+
32m. The thin wall to the right leads to the cave.

**9. Habitos de un perturbado irrderiable** .... 6c
35m. The best route on the wall. You can crawl into the mid-height cave for a rest. Finish leftwards to the other cave.

**10. La pregiera tonta** .. 6c
35m. Another long 6c which is an indirect start to the next route. The stance is small and optional. A long runout near the top!

**11. Games moya** ............ 6a+
35m. An inferior start to the previous route, but it is the original one. Either lower off or continue at 6c.

The next 6 routes start at various points down the disintegrating slope below the wall. **TAKE GREAT CARE WHEN DESCENDING THIS SLOPE.**

**12. Obsesion permanente** .... 6c
38m. A superb route which can be split at a small stance.

**13. Araña mecánica** ....... 6b+
15m. A short route to the third stance of *Paca Eugene*.

**14. Nirvana** .......... 6b+
1) 5, 15m. Up the crack to a ledge.
2) 6b+, 30m. Fine climbing on the upper wall.

**15. Romo y extraploma** ... 6c
1) 5, 15m. As for *Nirvana*.
2) 6c, 30m. The wall to the right.

**16. Urbi et orbe** ............. 7a
15m. Very artificial and escapable.

**17. Los crocodrilos no lloran** .. 7a+
15m. Slightly better than its sister.

Below the gearing up area is a lone pitch reached by abseil from above.

**18. La triaición de willobi** ....... 6a+

**APPROACH (Routes 19 to 23)** - The rest of the routes could be reached from above but this involves a dodgy scramble, or abseil, down the gully below the crag. It is better to reach them by walking underneath Cotos Bajas.

**19. Paco Eugene** ....... 6a
A long and classic expedition.
1) 5, 2) 4. Wires are required for these two pitches.
3) 5, 4) 6a. If you wish to do the upper section of the route, you can reach it via pitch 1 of *Nirvana*.

**20. El engendo** .......... 5+

**21. Rebuzonos de amor** ... 7b+
Steep and technical.

**22. Jaquima** .......... 6c
Steep and juggy.

The last route is situated on the slabby wall to the left of the possible descent gully from the upper routes.

**23. Al Chorro con un porro** ........ 6b

West facing wall
20m to 60m single and two pitch routes
Best grades - 6a+ to 6c+

# EL CHORRO - Central Gorge

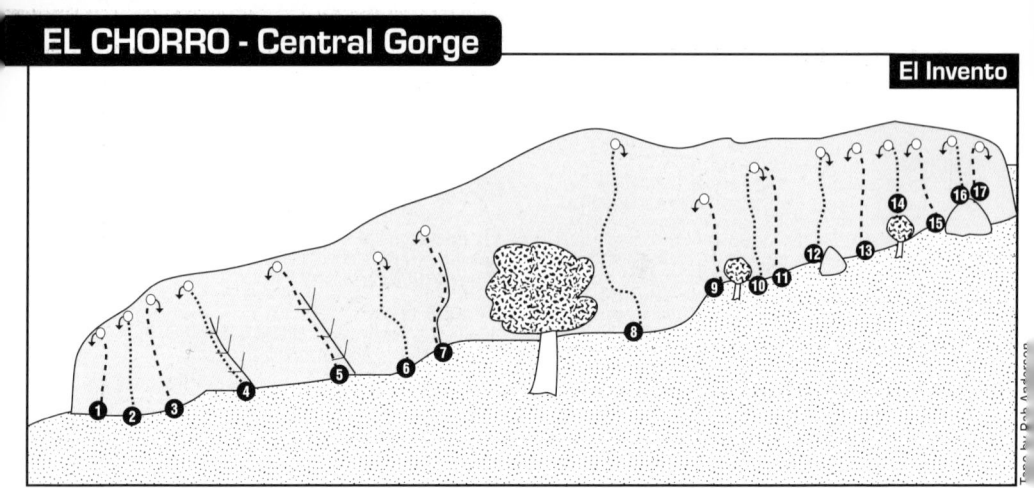

## El Invento

### EL INVENTO
This is the lowest section of the long cliff running up the hillside above and beyond Los Cotos. The cliff starts small at this end and reaches a crescendo at the Makindromo end. However, although the routes on El Invento are are only short, they pack a lot in.

**APPROACH -** Walk along the railway and continue through the tunnel under Los Cotos. A short distance after the tunnel is a bridge just before another tunnel. Break out rightwards up the hillside and head for the large tree below the crag.

The first routes are all short and unimpressive.

**1. Fresquito fresquito** .......... 6c

**2. Me empino con un chumino** .... 6b

**3. Discordia** ............ 6b
A steep and thin slab.

**4. Alucina por la esquina** ........ 7b+
An impressive steep groove and continuation arete.

**5. Diedro veneno** ....... 6a
The slanting groove doesn't contain much fixed gear.

**6. La leche que mamaste** ..... 7b
Steep climbing, but there is a rest!

**7. Ahora que te pilo sola** ..... 7a+
The best route on this sector follows the sustained and technical crack which eases towards the top.

The next major feature is the splendid tree, which makes an idyllic picnic spot.

**8. Sabrino royal** ......... 6c
A wicked start!

A gap of 40m.

**9. Pantomines** ............. 6b+

**10. Esclavo del grado** ......... 6c+
The left-hand of two close lines.

**11. Lo tomas o lo dejos** ........ 7b
The right-hand line.

**12. Champamania** ........... 6c+
Start just left of a large flake.

**13. La via shin** ............ 6b

**14. Peripecias de invalido** ....... 6c

**15. Nacida para la critica** ....... 6c+
Start left of a really big flake.

**16. Hemoglobina** ............. 6b
Start from the flake.

**17. Juego Duro** ............ 6c

---

326 | Lots of sun | 40 min | Vertical | Steep | Lower-offs | SE facing wall — 5m to 20m routes — Best grades - 6b to 7b+ | ROCKFAX — rockfax.c

# EL CHORRO - Central Gorge

## Los Bloques

## LOS BLOQUES
Further up the hill from El Invento is an area where some huge blocks have fallen away from the main face. This is Los Bloques, a complex area with only a few routes at present.
**APPROACH -** Continue past El Invento to where the path moves away from the cliff to get around the boulder field. Cut back left towards the cliff at this point.

The first routes are on the main wall behind a huge tilted block.

**1. Comicos y modistas** ........ 6b+
Interesting flowstone holds. Lower-off missing (11/2000).

**2. Em** ................ 7a+
A juggy start leads to a crimpy and balancy finish.

**3. Straw donkey** ........ 7b
A famous soft touch when it was graded 7c.

The overhanging front face of the huge tilted block contains a tiddly little pitch.......

**4. La tete de Mari** .... 8b
..however the grade isn't tiddly!

In front of, and right (looking in) from these routes, is a block with at least two more routes and possibly three.

**5. Hay un Guarillo en la tapia** ....... 6a
The right-hand line.

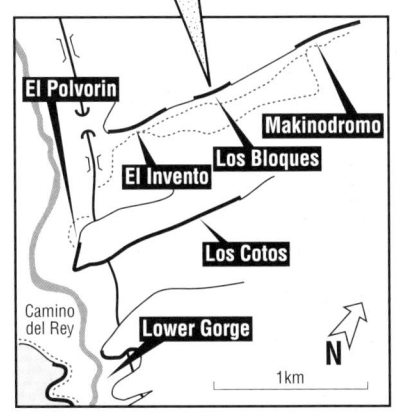

**6. Salto del Grato I** ........... 6b
The left-hand line.

**7. Salto del Grato II** .......... 6b
If there is a third bolt line then it is 6b+, otherwise it is just a right-hand variation of this using the same bolts.

**8. Per peroi** ............... 7c

**9. Project** .................. ?

Further right are three more projects.

Southeast facing wall
10m to 25m routes
Best grades - 6a to 7b

# EL CHORRO - Central Gorge

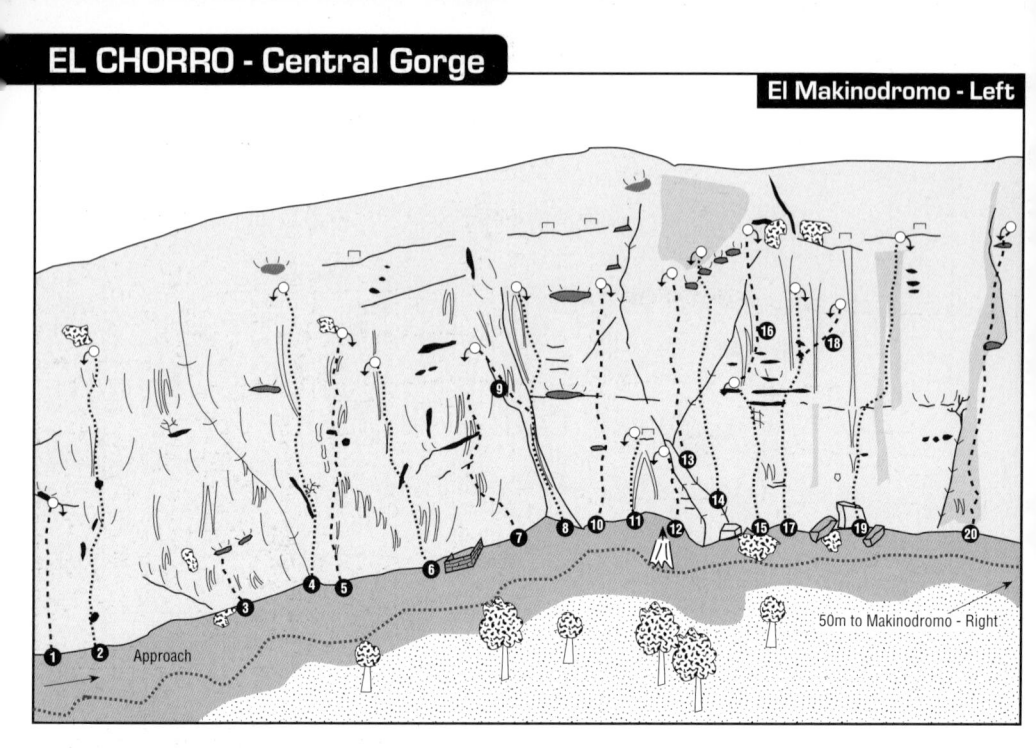

## El Makinodromo - Left

Approach

50m to Makinodromo - Right

## EL MAKINODROMO
The Makinodromo is the most impressive cliff in El Chorro, with *Lourdes* being one of Europe's best hard routes. Many climbers travel to El Chorro just to climb this route. However Makinodromo is also wrongly thought to be just *Lourdes* and a few 8c's. The wall right of the main cave contains some brilliant routes in the 6c to 7b range.

**APPROACH** - Walk along the railway past Los Cotos and through the tunnel. On emerging from the tunnel a bridge will be seen ahead. Walk towards the bridge and look for a small building 100m up the hillside on the right. Head for this and pick up a vague path which winds its way up to the Makinodromo. 20 minutes from the railway line.

**LOWERING OFF** - Note that many of the routes are at least 30m in length and very steep. It is possible to reach the ground on *Lourdes* with a 60m rope, but it is a close thing and there's nowhere to go if you find you are a few metres too short. On the less steep routes, keep in touch with the other rope as you lower.

**1. Trainspotting** .......... 7b+
A good route which, unfortunately, is not as long as it promises. Fairly tough.

**2. Samarkanda** ...... 8b+
A mind-blowing pitch. Very sustained and with the crux in the final 8m.

**3. Randi** .................. (8?)
Project.

**4. Al-Hakan** .......... 8b+
The blank and leaning wall to the left of *Lourdes*.

**5. Lourdes** .......... 8a
30m. The central line of weakness provides the line for this justifiably famous pitch. The really hard bit is right at the top. The rest is brilliant climbing on generally good holds. There are at least two hands-off rests! See photo page 4.

**6. Cous cous** ........ 8c
An awesome pitch linking some large tufas and blobs on the lower wall to finish up the obvious protruding tufa in its second half.

**7. Project** .................. (8?)
Between *Cous Cous* and the corner.

**8. Atlas shrieked** .......... 7c+
Start right of the corner and traverse back above the corner.

**9. Smashing pumpkins** ...... 7c+
30m. The direct version.

**10. ?** .................. 7c+
30m. A popular outing.

**11. Mutemroy** .......... 8a
A short and technical pitch. Watch out for the bees' nest!

**12. Vette al infierno** ........ 7b
Another short and tricky route.

There is a three pitch gear route up the corner which does not see a lot of traffic.

**Makinodromo Left**
SE facing wall, 15m to 35m routes
Best grades - 6c to 8c

328

# EL CHORRO - Central Gorge

**El Makinodromo - Right**

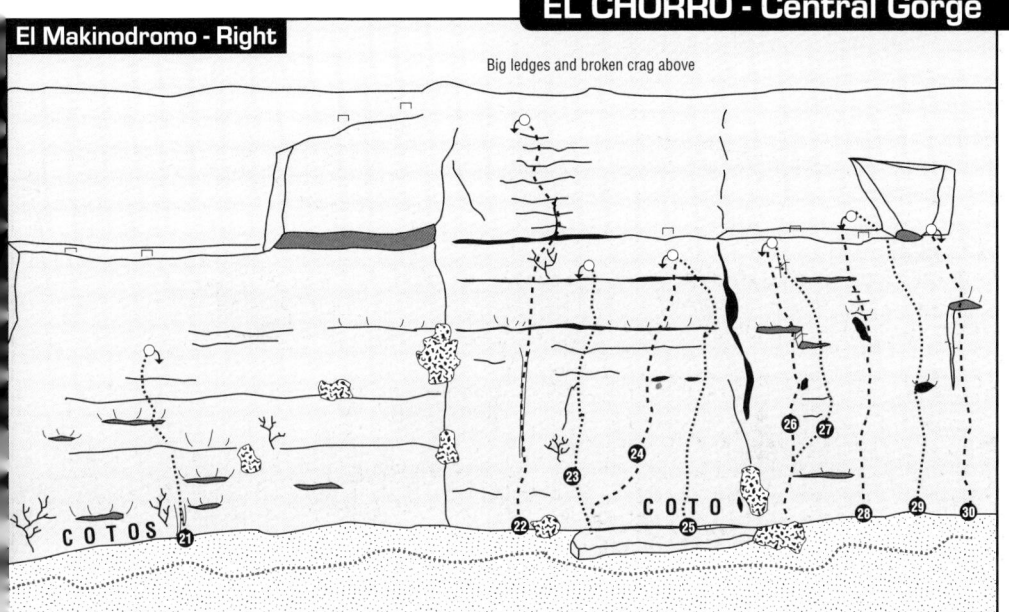

Although not as impressive as the left-hand side of the crag the right-hand side has some very good pitches in a slighty more reasonable grade range.

**APPROACH** - 50m uphill from the last route on sector Makinodromo is a steep wall with 'COTOS' painted on the rock.

**13. Hakuna mata** .......... 7a+
Fine climbing starting up the ramp.

**14. Las loi laufen** ....... 7b
Another quality pitch finishing through the upper bulges.

**15. Salida de emergencia** .... 6c

**16. ?** ................. ?
An extention to *Salida de emergencia*.

**17. Mystic rhythem** ........ 6b+

**18. Rhythem method** ..... 7b
35m. A right-hand extension to the previous route is also worthwhile.

**19. Life is sweet** ......... 6c
32m. A brilliant long pitch, just grab the small 'ice cream cone' tufa and keep going up the long upper wall. A 60m rope just reaches the ground.

**20. ?** ................. 7a+
A long pitch up the grey streak.

**21. Anatema** ............. 7b
Very steep.

**22. Heat exchange** ......... 6c
Start right of a corner with a bush.

**23. Canto pecato** .......... 7a+

**24. One bastiamba** ......... 7b
Sustained steep climbing up the bulging wall.

**25. Post festum** ......... 7b

**26. Mega flash** ............ 7a+
Its name is painted on the rock. Chipped.

**27. Grimal el curtido** ......... 7a
A right-hand variation on *Mega flash*.

**28. Punk street** ........... 7a
The wall into a prominent niche below the roof then out and over.

**29. Holé** ............. 7b+
Interesting climbing through a hole.

**30. Howling Madness** ....... 7a+
Steep and juggy but slippery at the final bulge.

**Makinodromo Right**
SE facing wall, 15m to 30m routes
Best grades - 7a to 7b

**329**

# UPPER GORGE

The Upper Gorge has some wild and varied climbing in a similar style to the Lower Gorge. It is possibly more atmospheric since it is even narrower. As with the Lower Gorge the method of reaching the routes provides one of the great attractions of the area. The climbs on the walkway side tend to be short and fingery; a good place to clock up the mileage as long as your skin lasts. Many of the other routes require more committing approaches, often by abseiling blindly into the abyss.

## ACCESS

The recent access arrangements for the whole area of El Chorro have been a little curious. The one area where the climbing ban seems to remain, and be enforced, is the Upper Gorge from Las Baneras (on both sides) to Sector Brasil (ie. not including the Petit Desfiladero). The reason for the special ban is because of a rare plant called 'Ruphicapnus Africana', which grows all over the place here, but doesn't grow anywhere else in the world. As with the other areas the access situation may change. Whatever happens, please take care with all the plants on these walls. The climbing information is included here for completeness only.

## ASPECT AND CLIMATE

It can be very cool owing to the wind tunnel effect but can also be pleasant in the summer when everywhere else is too hot.

## APPROACH

**From the Lower Gorge -** The Upper Gorge can be reached by walking the full length of the walkway, or the railway, past all the other crags, eventually arriving at Petit Desfiladero. This is the best way to reach Petit Desfiladero.

**From the Top -** If you have a car, it is better to follow the road from El Chorro across the dam and then turn right. Continue up this road keeping right to a T-junction after about 5km. Turn right alongside the lakes until just before a Bar, above the road, where there is a track on the right. Park at this point and walk down a track, through a tunnel, to the old car park beside a lake. From here take a path around a building to the very narrow Upper Gorge, where the walkway starts (about 25 minutes).

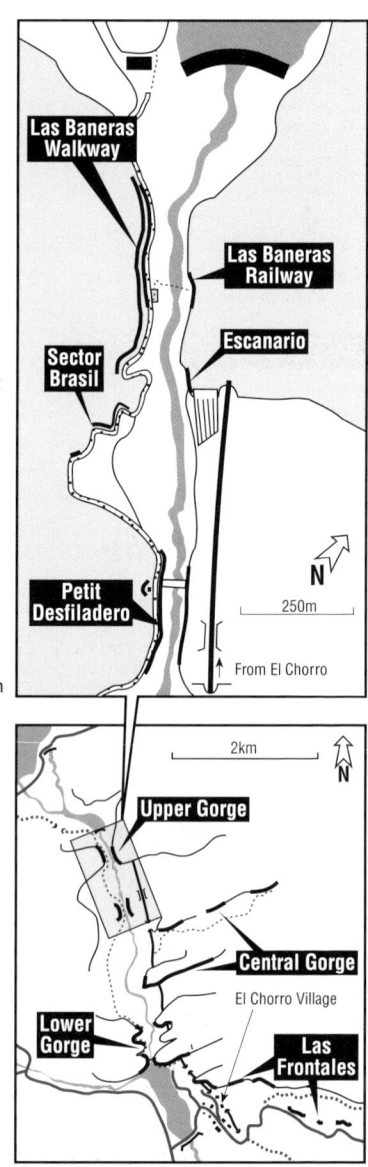

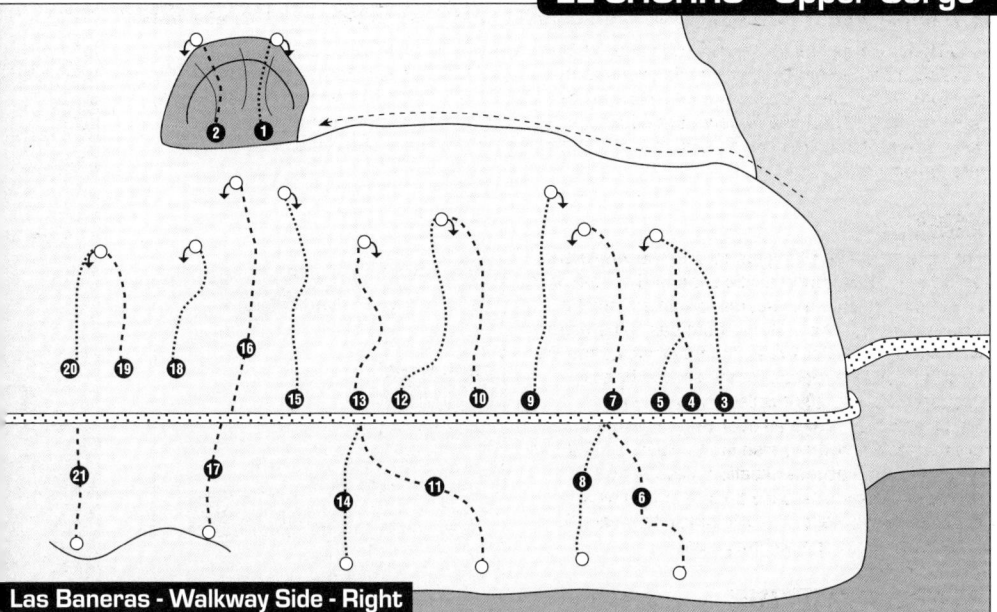

# EL CHORRO - Upper Gorge

## Las Baneras - Walkway Side - Right

**LAS BANERAS - WALKWAY SIDE - RIGHT**
The first routes are in a cave above the walkway, which is approached on foot from the entrance to the Upper Gorge.

**ACCESS** - Climbing is not allowed in the Upper Gorge. The routes are only inlcuded here for completeness.

1. Hercules poirot . . . . . . . 8b
2. Ojos saltones . . . . . . . . 7b
   I suppose this is the warm up! Steep!

The main event is the very narrow and deep section of the gorge with the walkway providing the only conceivable access method.
**APPROACH** - The routes start 70m beyond the gateway and are described from right to left.

3. Menbrillo . . . . . . . . . . 5
   A steep slab, moving left to the belay.
4. Hijo puta el que quite la chapa . . . . . . . . 6a
   A more direct line to the same lower-off.
5. Bordillo de los chicillos . . . . 7a
   A technical left-hand start.
6. Tubular bells . . . . . . . 6c+
   Stunning climbing up the water scoop. Abseil to the start.
7. Walkway waltz . . . . . . . 6b+
   The blunt tufa with some metalwork moves at the start.
8. Mola más que America . . 6a+
   Abseil to the start, from below route 9.
9. Replicando y co el mazo dando . . . . . . . . 7c+
   An incredible sustained route.
10. A golpe de mazo . . . . . 7b+
11. Saga corniz . . . . . . . . . . 6c+
    Abseil to the start below the walkway. A long diagonal line.
12. Algo sobre la virgen . . . . 6b+
    Start by a small walled cave.
13. Perro violador . . . . . . . 6b+
    Past a small hole.
14. El ultimo blues . . . . . . . 6c
    Abseil to the start.
15. Sin columpiarse . . . . . . 7a+
    A long pitch with a short crux to reach a large flake.
16. Vulture culture . . . . . . . 6b
    A long and pleasant pitch.
17. Moco . . . . . . . . . . . . 6b
    Abseil to the start.
18. Al verdón con un melón . . . . . 6a+
19. El perito caliente . . . . . . . 6a+
    Black bolts.
20. El robo del siglo . . . . . . 6b
21. ? . . . . . . . . . . . . . . 6a+
    Abseil to the start, from below route 20.

Deep gorge wall
15m to 30m routes
Best grades - 6a+ to 8b

# EL CHORRO - Upper Gorge

## LAS BANERAS - WALKWAY SIDE - LEFT
The routes are described from right to left.

■ **ACCESS** - Climbing is not allowed in the Upper Gorge.

**1. Pinchito moruno** ........ 6c
A steep wall climb starting from the back of a small bay.

**2. Imperio de sentidos** ..... 6c

**3. Morocioputa** ........... 6c+
Climb up and through a scoop.

**4. Color dominante** ........ 7a+
A wall and roof and then some bold moves above.

**5. Aspromanix** ............ 5+
Start 10m before some steps. An excellent route.

Just above the steps is the start of -

**6. Vendaval de antigüedades** .. 8a
A mega route which soars upwards in 5 pitches. It is fully bolted and can be done with a single 60m rope. The longest pitch is 30m so abseil descent is also possible. Sounds great, shame pitch 3 is so bloody hard!
1) 3, 2) 6b+, 3) 8a, 4) 7a, 5) 7a+.

**7. ?** ..................... 7a
A variation to the right for which few details are known.
1) 3, 2) 6b+, 3) -, 4) 7a.

## SECTOR BRASIL
Further down the walkway is an isolated slab which is crossed by some prominent cracks. This is the home of three pleasant easy routes.

**8. El pudor de un sola dios** .... 5

**9. Joyous medio** ........... 5

**10. Izquierdo camino** ....... 5+

There are two more routes around the corner, on a wall above a water channel.

**11. Instinto asesino** ......... 7a+

**12. Instinto cabrero** ......... 7b+

There are apparently three more routes below the walkway, before you get to the first slab. They may be quite good.

**13. ?** ..................... 6c+

**14. Maverick** .............. 7a

**15. Pachanga** ............. 7b

## LAS BANERAS - RAILWAY SIDE
The railway side of the gorge had a series of wild pitches which are mostly inaccessible now. Four routes which start from the bottom of the gorge are described briefly here.
**APPROACH (Routes 16 to 19)** - Descend the steps on the walkway side and scrambling over the boulders across the river.

**16. ?** .................... 7a+
The left-hand line.

**17. Giganta verde** ......... 8a
A monstrous, huge extravaganza up the full height of the wall. It is fully equipped but sadly uses bolt-on holds for the blank bits.
1) 7b+, 2) 8a, 3) 7b, 4) 7c+, 5) 8a, 6) 7a+, 7) 6c.

**18. Onda vital** ............ 8c

**19. No acabada** ........... (8c+)
May have been climbed.

## SECTOR ESCENARIO
Further down on the railway side are two more routes which are supposed to be fully bolted, but there is no obvious way of getting to the starts. They are situated around the corner from the railway tunnel exit.

**20. Escenario de bufones** .... 7a
1) 6a+, 2) 7a.

**21. Avecrem a Mano** ....... 6a+
1) 5, 2) 5, 3) 6a+.

Deep gorge wall
Mostly 15m to 30m routes
Best grades - 6c to 8c

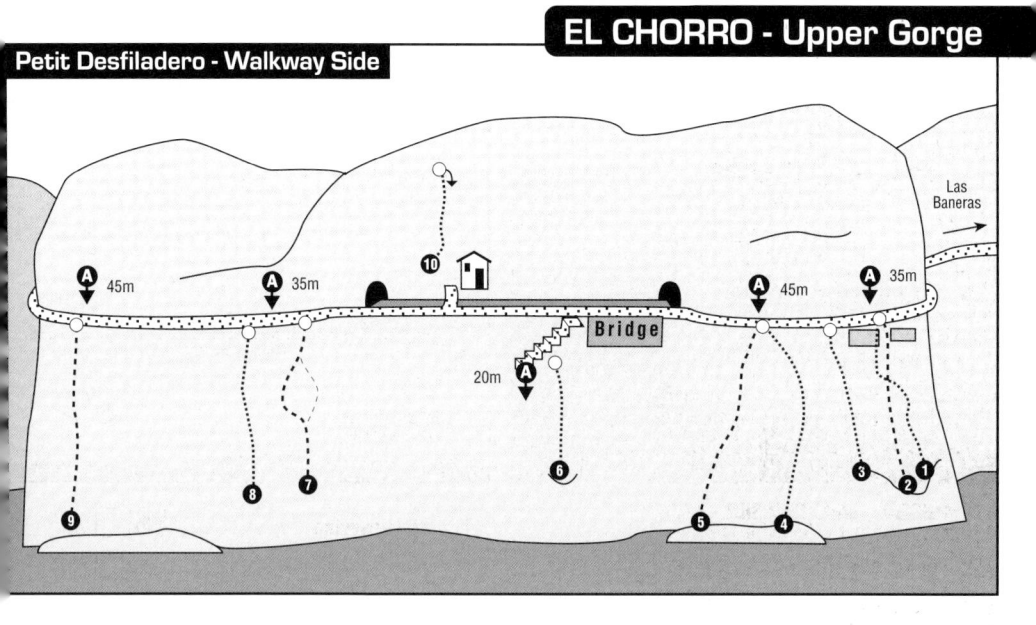

# EL CHORRO - Upper Gorge

## Petit Desfiladero - Walkway Side

## PETIT DESFILADERO - WALKWAY SIDE
This relatively small gorge gives yet more amazingly atmospheric climbing. The climbs are mostly situated below the walkway on weird water-worn scoops and bulges and they have an added degree of commitment required because they are the only way out (unless you wimp out and top-rope them).
**APPROACH** - It can be approached from either end but since the road at the top of the gorge has been closed off, it is probably better to approach them from the Lower Gorge.
Since the routes mostly require long abseils to reach the starts, you will need double 50m ropes. Sometimes there are abseil bolts in place but often these are stolen. Use either the walkway itself or carry some hangars with you since there are often studs in place.

The routes on the Walkway side are described from right to left. The first route is before the bridge, just after the water channel has disappeared into a tunnel. The route names are painted at the top.

**1. Torturas ninjas** . . . . . . . . . . . 5
Abseil 35m to a ledge above the water. Be certain you can climb back out before pulling your ab-rope!

**2. ?** . . . . . . . . . . . . . . . . . . . . . 5
A counter diagonal of the same grade.

**3. La puta del gurda** . . . . . . . . . . 6b

The next twin bolts above the walkway are used to gain the starts of two routes, which are way below at the base of the gorge.

**4. Les papanates** . . . . . . . 7b
Stunning, steep and superb! A belay may be required before the top.

**5. Les batatiste** . . . . . . . . . . 6c
Equally as good as its neighbour.

Just past the bridge, some steps drop down. An abseil from the bottom of these gains...

**6. Tito Camarón** . . . . . . . . . . 6b
Good varied climbing and surprisingly steep. Didn't he play for Liverpool?

A little further along, after the water channel has again disappeared into a tunnel, are two more bolts. Abseil from these to;

**7. Tú veras** . . . . . . . . . . . . . 7c
A big pitch.

**8. Empacho de gobacho** . . . . . . 7a+

A good distance further along the walkway is one last bolt. A long abseil from here reaches the base of the gorge, and the start of;

**9. El Último mangante** . . . . . . 6b

There is an isolated pitch above the walkway which is nowhere near as good as the stuff below. It is behind a small hut behind the water channel.

**10. Robert Curtio** . . . . . . . . . . . . . . . . 7a

Deep gorge walls
10m to 45m routes
Best grades - 5 to 7c

333

# EL CHORRO - Upper Gorge

## Petit Desfiladero - Railway Side

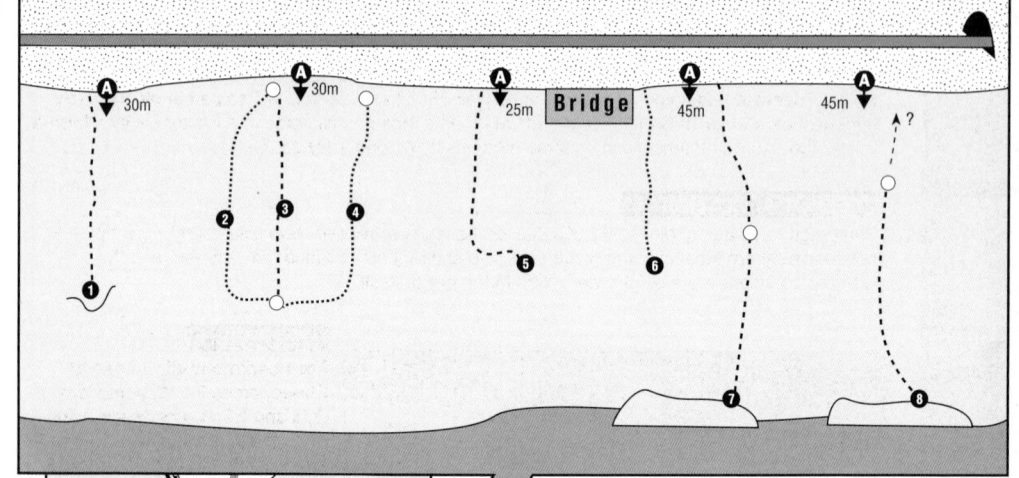

### PETIT DESFILADERO - RAILWAY SIDE

**APPROACH** - The starts of the routes on this side can prove awkward to find. Take care when searching since the bolts are near the edge. In fact the best idea is to take a look at your chosen line from the other side first.
The first route is 50m upstream from the bridge.

**1. Ruta de la Lycra** ......... 7a
Scoops and bulges with two very hard moves.

30m upstream from the bridge is a pair of bolts which give access to a belay below the next three routes.

**2. La Higuerola** ......... 7b
The left-hand line.

**3. Escuela sin Grado** ..... 7c+
The middle one.

**4. Paseo por el Limbo** ....... 7a
The right-hand line.

The approach to this one is just upstream from the bridge.

**5. Latex Lubricated** ......... 6c+

There is supposed to be another route just south of the bridge now.

**6. ?** ......................... ?
Details unknown.

The last two require long abseils to the base of the gorge.

**7. Charro del Charro** .......... 6c+
1) 6c, 2) 6c+

**8. Cantos Nibelungos** ....... 7b
The top of this route is below the top of the gorge. Haul yourself out on your ab rope.

Deep gorge walls
10m to 45m routes
Best grades - 6c to 7c+

# DESPLOMLANDIA

To the north of El Chorro are two venues with some excellent routes which provide good alternatives in hot weather, or for those seeking a change of scenery. Desplomlandia has a lot of quality single pitch routes all easily accessed and El Pozo de la Mona has a slightly lower grade spread. The majority of the routes are in the 6b to 7c grade range and most of these are very good. Sector Triangulo has some very hard, steep wall climbs and Sector La Boda a handful of lovely 30m pitches. Sector El Cable is more suited to the stamina afficionado and Sector La Vida Misma will be the haunt of teams wanting some high quality 6s and easy 7s.

## ASPECT AND CLIMATE

The crags have a very pleasant outlook over the lake but receive very little, if any, sunshine and consequently are ideal in warm weather. Some shelter can be found from the rain and the weather can clear more quickly here than in the gorge itself.

## APPROACH

**For Desplomlandia** - From El Chorro, cross the dam and turn right and follow a narrow winding hill to the lakes at the top of the gorge. At the T-junction turn right and follow the road past a bar and the turn off to the Upper Gorge. Continue past a good restaurant, across a dam and through a village. A few kilometres further after crossing another dam follow signs for Antequera. The first crags appear on your right. The first climbing is in a bowl, just off the road, above a hairpin bend - Sector Buena Sombra. 100m further on are two dirt tracks which join and lead up the hillside to a col. Park at the bottom of the first.

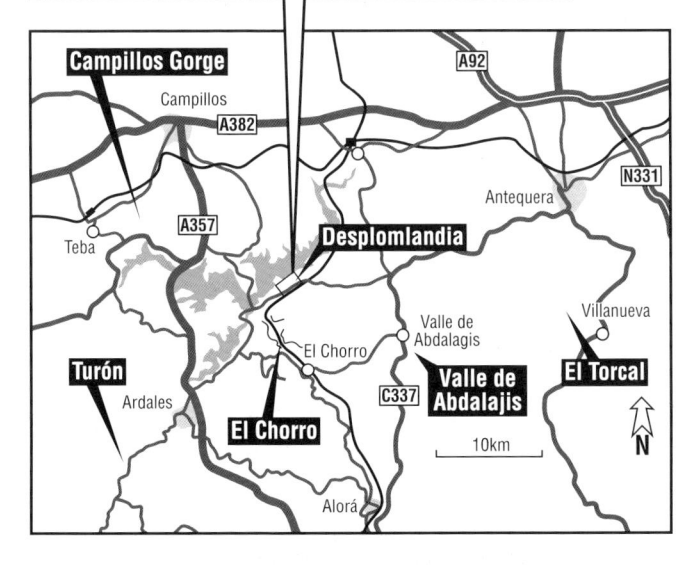

335

# EL CHORRO - Desplomlandia

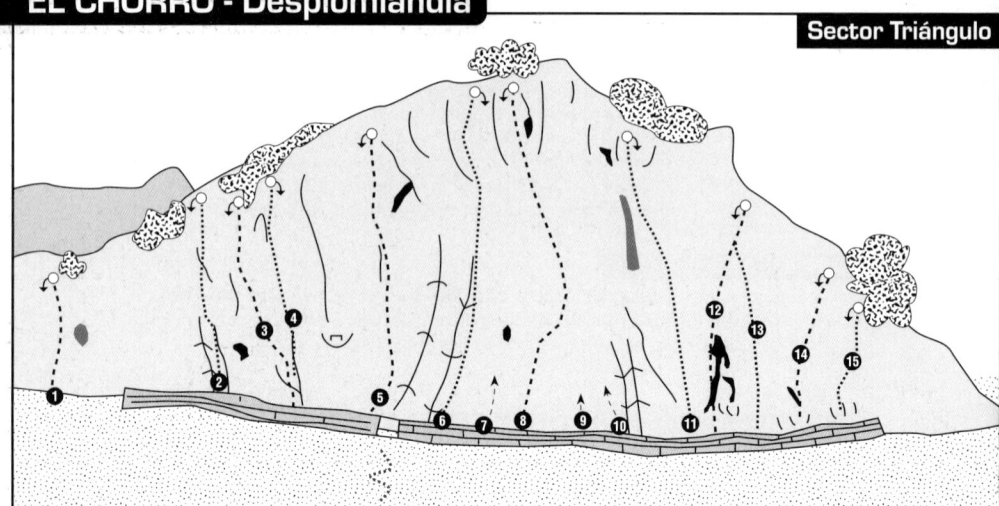

**Sector Triángulo**

## SECTOR TRIÁNGULO
This appealing crag is the continuously steep wall just to the east (left) of the col. The routes are very good sustained stamina affairs. The only off-putting aspect is that the base is used as a corral and shelter for goats so it can be a little dirty at times (bring a rope bag!). Some of the lines described have been debolted, but this may change. These lines can be easily top-roped from other route's lower-offs.
**APPROACH** - Walk up the hill from the parking spot and head to the left of the col.

1. **Triángulo** .................... 7a+
The far left-hand line.

2. **Maligno catarro** ........ 6c
The ramp and wall

3. **Aljamar** ............. 7b

4. **?** .................... 7b+

5. **Reina mora** ........... 7c
A brilliant and very impressive wall climb.

6. **Zeus kapotas** ................ ?

7. **Mar de Ortigas** ............. 8a
Not bolted at the present time

8. **No toques a tu madre** 8a+

9. **Madre Salvaje** .......... 7c
Not bolted at the present time

10. **Oasis de cristal** ...... 7c
Not bolted at the present time

11. **La Conexión pelirroja** ....... 8a

12. **¿Que tal mea tu padre?** ... 7b
Hard last move.

13. **Mas que Money** ........ 7b+
Sustained climbing. Same finish as route 12.

14. **De copas** .............. 7b

15. **La copa** .................... 7b

## SECTOR EL CABLE
A fine area with a few excellent long pitches. This sector does not receive any sunshine and is fairly exposed.
**APPROACH** - The sector is just west (right) of the col and is easily identified by the pylon above and slightly behind it. A path leads from the track to the crag just before the col.

16. **Puto cable** .............. 5+
The first line on the far left is not worth seeking out

17. **La flaca** ............. 6c+

18. **La decepción** ......... 7a+
A good route starting by a small corner

19. **Uretrofilo** ........... 7a
A very good pitch with some tricky moves.

20. **Akira** ............. 7b
The shallow groove provides the line for this excellent and difficult climb.

21. **Oleanna** ....... 7b+
The very blank and crimpy wall.

22. **Mamabi** ............. 7b
1) 6b, 2) 7b.

23. **El angel flamenco** ......... 7a
Starts just right of the blunt arete.

**336**

**Triangulo and El Cable**
NW facing walls, 10m to 30m routes
Best grades - 6c to 8a+

# EL CHORRO - Desplomlandia

**Sector El Cable**

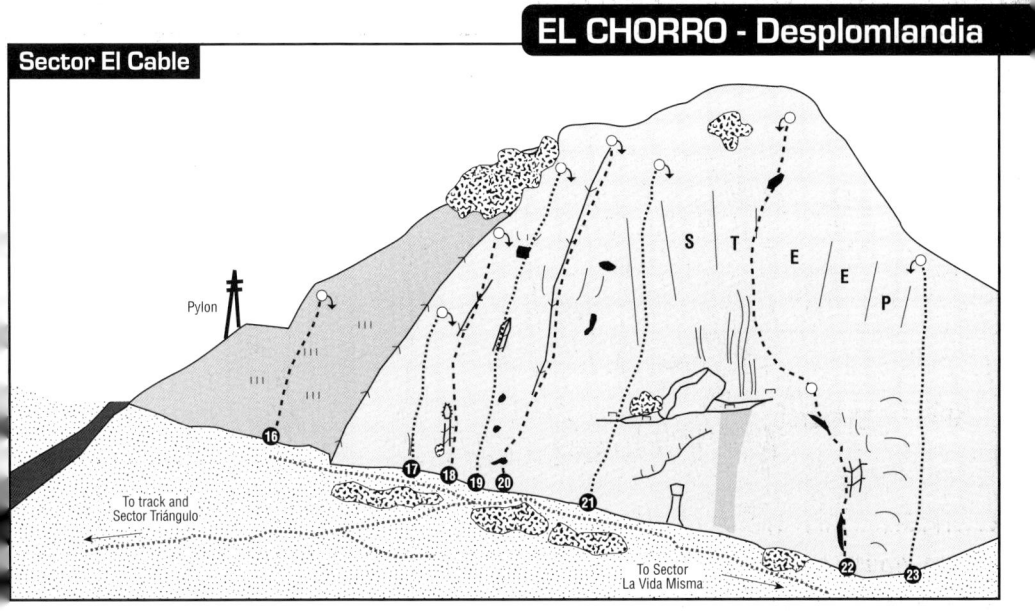

## SECTOR LA VIDA MISMA - LEFT
Good rock and a pleasing grade spread make this a popular spot. As with many other sectors at Desplomlandia it can be chilly here in cold weather and it gets no sun. Obviously this makes it a great hot weather venue.
**APPROACH** - A path leads to the sector from just before the col passing beneath sector El Cable.

**24. ?** .................... 5
An easy route that serve as a good warm up.

**25. Mamabi** .......... 6c+
Fine technical wall work.

**26. Manzanilla Madness** ..... 7a
Tricky climbing over the bottom bulge, which is best tackled from the right. Above things are a little reachy.

**27. Cheyenne** ......... 7a+
Nice wall climbing, with a pressing finish to gain the still awkward slab.

**28. Maquina Pestosa** ..... 7b+
More good sustained climbing which starts up the steep tufa before a bouldery move gains easier ground.

**29. Ankana wanamio** ..... 8a
The left-hand line of bolts leading out from Al andalú has a surprisingly decent amount of independent climbing.

**30. Al andalú** ............ 6c
A really good line that is a touch on the worn side, but still one of the best here.

**31. Sandokan** .......... 7c
Impressive climbing up the lefthand side of the arete

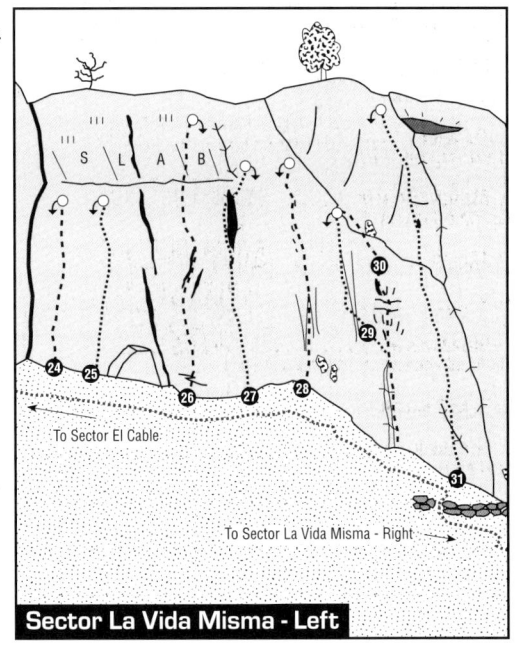

**Sector La Vida Misma - Left**

**La Vida Misma**
NW facing wall, 20m to 30m routes
Best grades - 6c to 8a

337

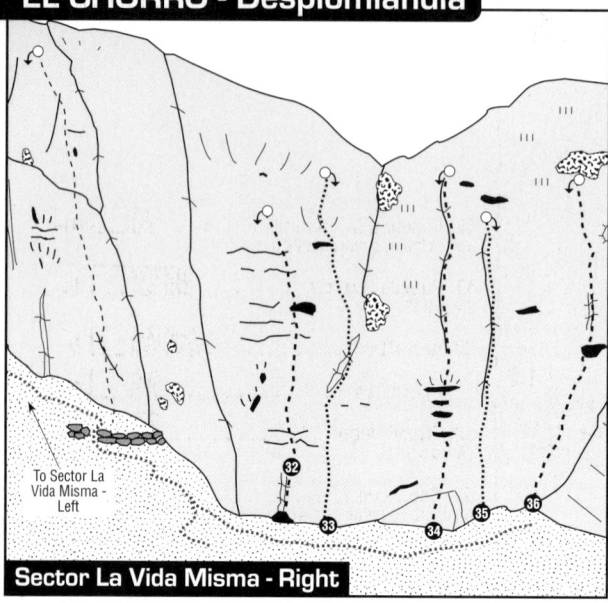

# EL CHORRO - Desplomlandia

**Sector Buena Sombra**

**Sector La Vida Misma - Right**

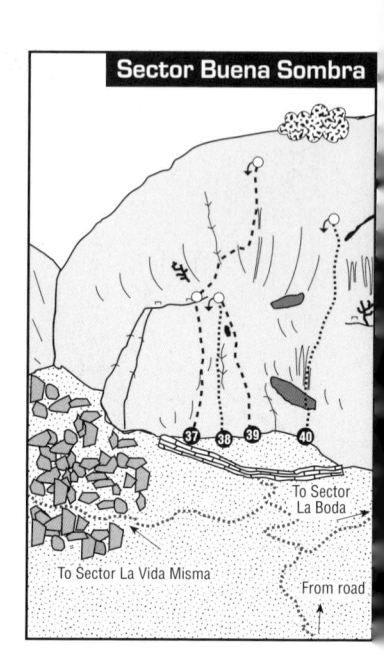

## SECTOR LA VIDA MISMA
Good rock and a pleasing grade spread make this a popular spot. As with many other sectors at Desplomlandia it can be chilly here in cold weather and it gets no sun, However conditions can be good here in hot weather.
**APPROACH** - A path leads to the sector from just before the col passing beneath sector El cable.

**32. Si te gusta el pique, pique** .......... 6b+
The first of three excellent, long, easier routes.

**33. Captain sardina** ....... 6c

**34. Calidad alemana** ....... 6b

**35. El emigrante** ............ 7a+

**36. El chupacabras** ....... 7a+
A dramatic pitch which makes up for its lack of length with some fine moves. Go easy with the large fragile flake, in fact give it a miss altogether!

## SECTOR BUENA SOMBRA
A convenient, although uninspiring sector, but useful in very hot weather.
**APPROACH** - The crag is very easily reached from the hairpin bend just before the parking.

**37. Lirón Careto** .......... 7c
1) 7a, 2) 7c.

**38. Escombros** ............ 5+

**39. Autan** ................ 5+

**40. Los Zauden** .......... 7a
A fair pitch.

## SECTOR LA BODA
A recently developed sector wih some excellent 30m pitches that are worth the steep walk up.
**APPROACH** - The sector is roughly 300m up the hill to the right of Sector Buena Sombra.

**41. El testigo** ............ 7b
The steepest and hardest on this section of crag following the line of tufas in the steep bay set back from the main wall.

**42. La fea** ............... 6a
A good warm up following the small corner and arete. The bolts take a little bit of spotting.

**43. El novio** ............. 6c
The best route on the sector with a sharp crux close to the top.

**44. El novia** ............. 7a
A tricky climb with a bit of a nasty clip. Watch out!

**45. La svegra** ............ 6b
Steady away until the final bulge.

**46. El anillo perdido** ....... 6b
A fine pitch.

**47. la marcha atras** ....... 6c
Cruxy on the final moves.

**Buena Sombra and La Boda**
North facing wall, 20m to 30m routes
Best grades - 5+ to 7b

# EL CHORRO - Desplomlandia

## Sector La Boda

From road (300m) and Sector Buena Sombra.

**48. Subete a la Higuera** .......... 6a+
Good climbing between ledges.

**49. Pogeda Higuera** .......... 6b+
Sustained.

**50. Abrasibra** .......... 6c

**51. Malva Loca** .......... 6c+

**52. Fleton Negro** .......... 7a+
Sharp holds.

**53. Bee...bee...** .......... 6c
A superb route up the groove and tufa.

**54. Silicon Beach** .......... 7b+

**55. ?** .......... 7c

**56. Escremento** .......... 7a
The impressive corner.

**57. Iracundias** .......... 7c+

**58. Silicon Beach** .......... 7c

**59. Prosynesky** .......... 7c+
32m. Take care when lowering!

### SECTOR El POZA DE LA MONA
This sector is just along the road from Desplomlandia. The climbing is similar to Desplomlandia, with short steep routes mainly in the harder grades. It faces north and is well sheltered.

**APPROACH** - From the parking spot for Desplomlandia continue down the main road for 3km until the crag comes into view on the right by a building. Park here and walk up to the base of the crag. The route names are painted on the bottom.

**ACCESS** - Climbing is only allowed at this crag during the Summer as the base is used by the farmer as a corral for his stock during the winter.

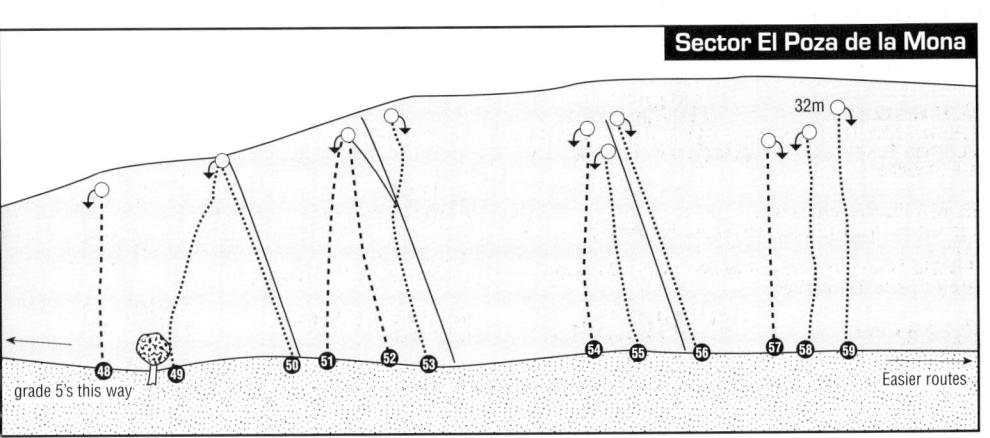

## Sector El Poza de la Mona

grade 5's this way                    Easier routes

**Poza de la Mona**
North facing wall, 15m to 32m routes
Best grades - 6a+ to 7c+

339

# CAMPILLOS GORGE

A pleasant and easily accessible gorge, which should probably be known as the Rio de la Venta Gorge, but tends to be called the Campillos Gorge by climbers. The routes detailed here lie close to the road on the less high section of the cliff. There is already a report of new routes on the higher section of the East Wall. The nearby pig farm used to give the place a distinctive country fragrance but they have been made to clean up their act recently and the atmosphere is now more pleasant. There is a bar and a petrol station at the junction to Teba mentioned below. The climbing in the gorge is varied with a good spread of grades, ranging from steep 7s to slabby 4s. The cave is an atmospheric and unusual place containing about 11 steep routes which are ideal for muscular thugs with night vision! All the climbs are well-equipped with good lower-offs.

The information included on the next four pages is the same that was produced in the last two editions of the guidebook. We know that new routes have been climbed on both sections, and further into the gorge, but no exact details are known. Please inform us of any developments (alan@rockfax.co.uk) which we will put up on the ROCKFAX web site - rockfax.com/el_chorro

### ACCESS
**No climbing from 1 January to 1 April because of nesting birds.**

### ASPECT AND CLIMATE
Since the walls face east and west, the climbing can be in or out of the sun as one desires. The gorge itself can get very windy and cold but the routes in the cave are sheltered and dry in the rain, though they will seep after rain.

### APPROACH
It is situated some 25 minutes drive (30kms) to the north of El Chorro, on the northern side of the Lakes. From El Chorro, cross the dam, turn right and follow the narrow road up to a junction at the Lakes. Turn right and follow the road over a dam. Continue over another, larger, dam then turn left along a new road signed to 'Campillos'. Follow this road to a junction where 'Campillos 12km' is signed to the right. Turn left towards 'Ronda' and continue past an impressive crag towards the fort on a hill at Teba. Just before the turn off to Teba, is a bridge over the Rio de la Venta. Park in a lay-by over the bridge. The gorge is clearly visible some 2 minutes walk from the car.

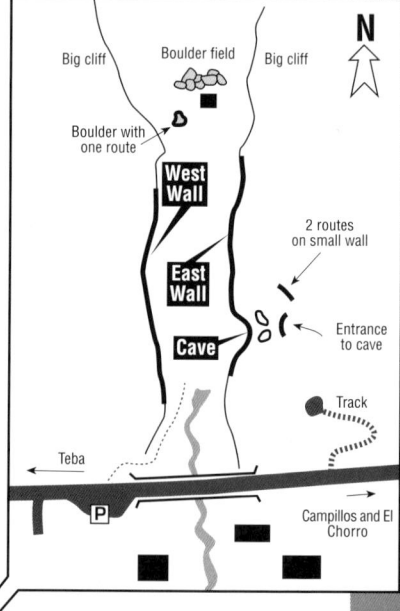

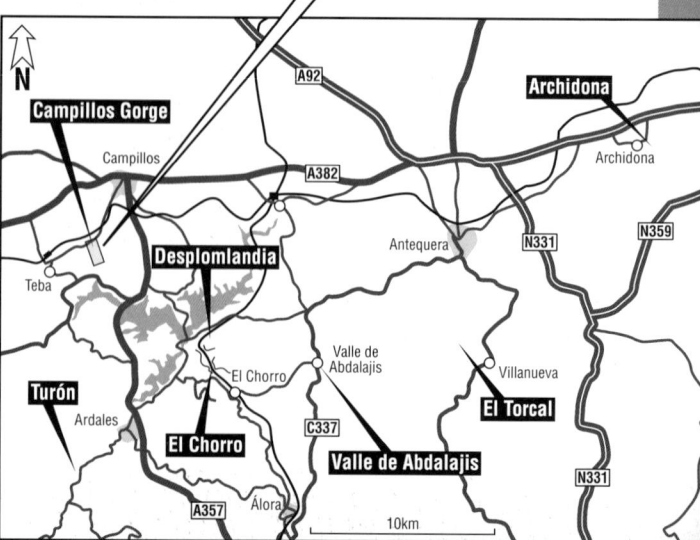

340

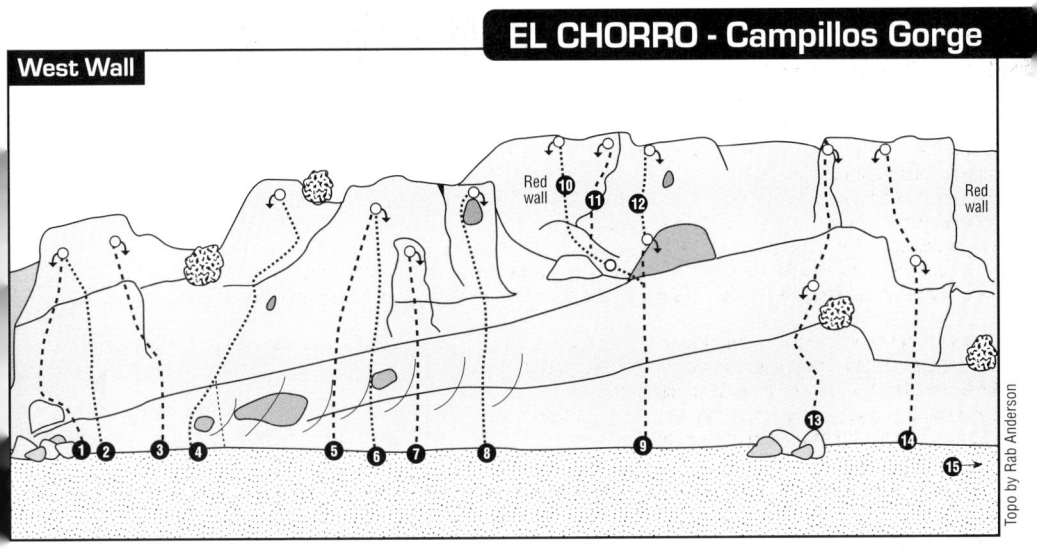

# EL CHORRO - Campillos Gorge

## West Wall

## THE WEST WALL
This is on the left-hand side as you walk into the gorge from the road. There may well be more development further to the right now.

**ACCESS** - NO CLIMBING FROM 1 JANUARY TO 1 APRIL BECAUSE OF NESTING BIRDS.

No character symbols have been added to these routes.

**1. Yo quierosa papa** .............. 6b+
Awkward and reachy.

**2. Below tijo lands** .............. 7b

**3. Pegaso** .................... 6c+
Only one hard move.

**4. El mono sin nombre** ......... 6b+
It can be started more directly on the right, at an unknown grade. The first bolt is high.

**5. Ya son muchas pechas** ....... 6c

**6. Mujer sin nombre** .......... 6b+

**7. ?** ...................... 6c

**8. Nostalgia de antono** ........ 6b+

**9. El grado viene despue** ....... 5
An easy access route to gain the higher section of the wall.

The next three routes start at the top of route 9.

**10. Elo** .................... 7b

**11. ?** ..................... 7a

**12. ?** ..................... 6c
Good climbing up a tufa.

Further right are a couple of two pitch routes.

**13. ?** ..................... ?
No details are known.

**14. Rodolfa y su cochine** ...... 6a+
1) 6a.
2) 6a+, 30m.

**15. ?** ..................... 6b+
Just off the topo to the right.
1) **15m.** Scramble past two bolts.
2) **6b+, 30m.** Up a long groove and arete.

East facing gorge wall
20m to 40m routes
Best grades - 6b+ to 7b

341

# EL CHORRO - Campillos Gorge

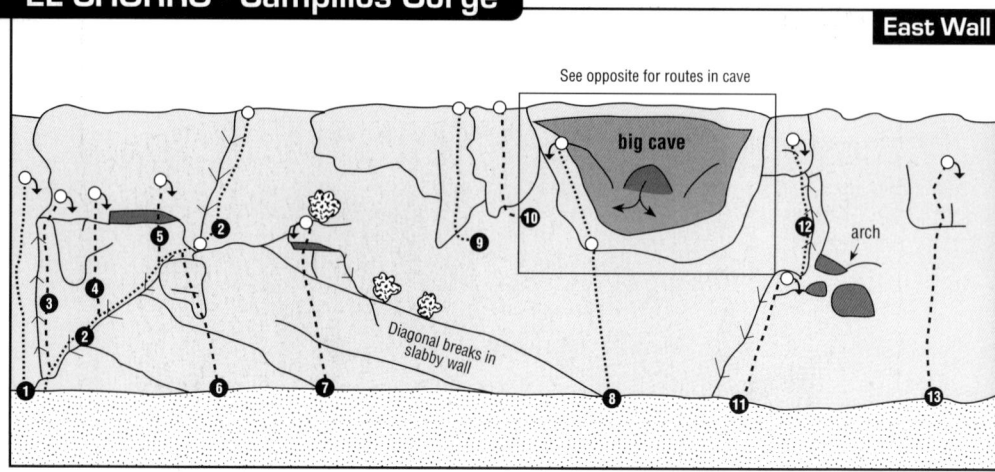

**East Wall**

See opposite for routes in cave

big cave

Diagonal breaks in slabby wall

arch

## THE EAST WALL
This is on the right-hand side as you walk into the gorge from the road. The section to the left of the topo may well have some more routes now. The star ratings of the first 10 routes are not known.

**ACCESS** - NO CLIMBING FROM 1 JANUARY TO 1 APRIL BECAUSE OF NESTING BIRDS.

No character symbols have been added to these routes.

The first listed route starts at an arete next to a diagonal groove.

1. ? ........................ 8a
2. ? ........................ 6a
   1) **4+** The long diagonal groove line.
   2) **6a.** The continuation groove to the top.

The next three routes start at various points above the diagonal line of route 4.

3. ? ........................ 7b
4. Amarreto de canto ............ 7a
5. ? ........................ ?
6. Cudadin .................... 6b+
7. Gasofa ..................... 6a+

8. **Pasta de basta** ............. 5
   A long route up to the left-hand side of the big cave.
   1) **5.**
   2) **5.**

For the next two routes either start from the cave (see opposite) or do *Pasta de Basta*.

9. ? ........................ 6b+
10. ? ....................... 6b

Below and right of the cave is a groove.

11. **Introduction al tema** ....... 4
    The groove.
12. **La costurera** ............. 6b+
    The arete above the groove is much harder than its approach pitch.
13. **Gorilla** ................. 7a

---

342 | Afternoon | 10 min | Vertical | Lower-offs | Windy | Restrictions | West facing wall 15m to 20m routes Best grades - 6a to 7b | ROCKFAX rockfax.c

# EL CHORRO - Campillos Gorge

## The Cave

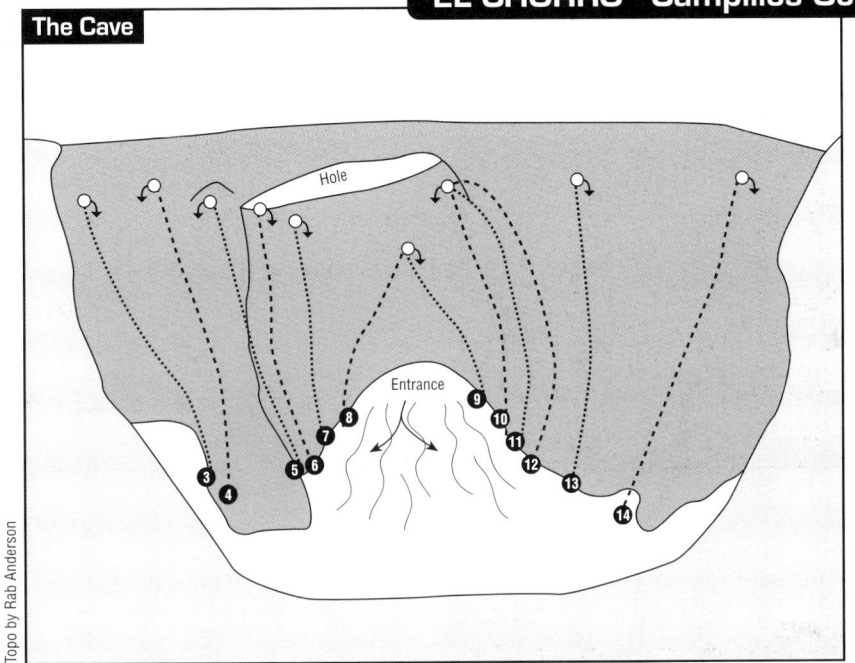

*Topo by Rab Anderson*

## THE CAVE
The huge cave high in the east wall, gives some eerie and atmospheric climbing.

**APPROACH** - It can be reached from the base of the gorge, via *Pasta la basta* opposite. Alternatively reached it from above by walking down the road from the parking and up a track to the cliff top. Locate the entrance to the cave and descend into it from above.

⊖ **ACCESS** - NO CLIMBING FROM 1 JANUARY TO 1 APRIL BECAUSE OF NESTING BIRDS.

No character symbols have been added to these routes.

There are two short routes on the wall to the right of the cave entrance. No details are known except that one of them is called *Hey Bubu*.

Routes 1 and 2 are in the cave entrance.

**1. Asi kaska la baska** . . . . . . . . . ?
**2. Note extranes...** . . . . . . . . . . . . ?

The rest of the routes are in the cave.

**3. Ritual habitual** . . . . . . . . . . . . 7a
Steep and juggy with a technical move to finish.

**4. House of Pain** . . . . . . . . . . . . ?

**5. Lavialatua de mach** . . . . . . . . ?
Powerful climbing across the roof.

**6. Nequaquam vacuum** . . . . . . . . ?

**7. El guru** . . . . . . . . . . . . . . . . . 7a

**8. Putas fever** . . . . . . . . . . . . . . 6b+
A poor route.

**9. Violento express** . . . . . . . . . . 7c
Short and powerful.

**10. Karo shi** . . . . . . . . . . . . . . . . 7c
Climb past a hole.

**11. Arande notivo rea** . . . . . . . . . 7b+

**12. Posey-don** . . . . . . . . . . . . . . 7b+

**13. Historia de una chica mala** . . . . 8a

**14. Kami-kaze** . . . . . . . . . . . . . . ?

Dark cave
15m to 20m routes
Best grades - 7a to 8a

343

# TÚRON

Túron is a beautifully located area, set in a quite and isolated valley and it is is easily reached from El Chorro via the white-washed Andalucían village of Ardales. The crags of Túron will appeal to teams looking for good pitches in the lower grades on excellent sheets of off-vertical limestone. It is also worth noting that you could well find the place deserted during the week.
Undoubtably the best climbing found here is in the 6th grade although a number of the 7s are also worthwhile. On the west side the climbs are on water-worn slabs, or sparsely featured vertical walls, of up to 30m in height. The east side is steeper and less well travelled but worth a look at the end of a day, or to escape the heat.

### ASPECT AND CLIMATE
The western sectors are lower-lying and receive sun from early morning until late afternoon. The east sector is slightly higher and very exposed to the elements. Also, it is in the shade until mid afternoon making this a good crag in warm weather. Túron is not the place to be in rain or wind as there is little in the way of shelter, or overhanging rock.

### APPROACH
From El Chorro take the road Ardales. Drive into the village on the main road and up the hill into a small, open square in the centre. Turn right and immediately pick up a sign for 'El Burgo'. This takes you left into a small street and out of the village and into the hills on a dirt road. Follow the track (which becomes paved) for 6.5km until the crags come into view.
**Túron West -** Park at the point where the old road has been crossed by the the new road and follow a vegetated gully down to the river. About 50m upstream from the base of the gully, the river can be crossed (this will be difficult if there is a lot of water). The crag can then easily be reached by a variety of goat tracks. Alternatively, continue on the old road and turn right towards a farm. Cross a bridge and park. Now pick up a path that leads towards the crag.
**Túron East -** Turn right onto a dirt track on the left as you approach the crag (this turn off is 1.6 km back towards Ardales from the parking for Túron West). Follow this for 1km to parking on top of the crag. Take a path that drops steeply down the northern flank of the cliff to its base.

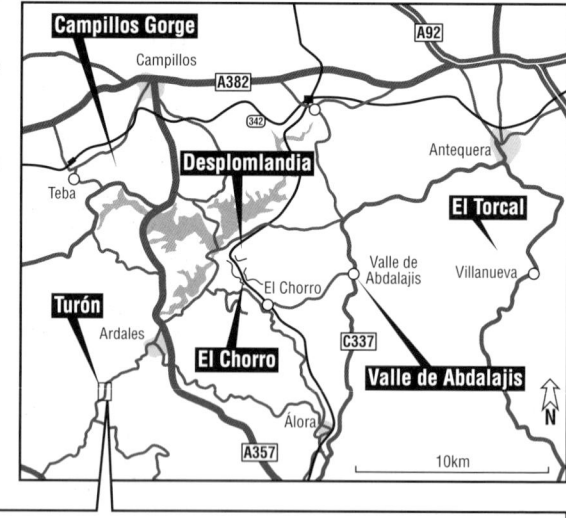

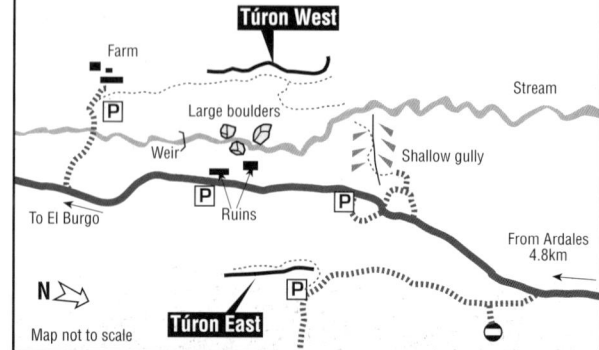

344

# EL CHORRO - Túron

**East**

## EAST
This impressive crag is easily identfied from the road that runs beneath it but on close inspection is not quite as good as it would first appear. Nevertheless it is well worth a quick visit to pick off the best on offer. The views are fantastic.
**APPROACH -** From the parking take a path that drops steeply down the northern flank of the cliff to its base.

1. **Cabrero Blanco** ............ 6a+
Start is just left of the arete.

2. **Placa la cascabulla** .... 6a+
Pull over the bulge just right of the arete to start.

3. **La condena** ........ 7a

4. **Ascenso al reino de los ciegos** 6b+
The crack.

5. **Banana melosa** ............ 6c

6. **Estrella del sur** ....... 7b

7. **Si te quieres comer un higo** ....... 5+

8. **Ensancha el alma** ........ 6b+

9. **Al filo del escualo** ............ 6a+
The arete of the large detached block.

10. **Mamon no comas aleta de tiburón** . 5+

11. **El dia de la bestia** .... 7b+
The impressive arete.

12. **Pato palo** ........ 6a+

13. **Vía del topo** ........ 6a

14. **Última del año** ............ 5+

15. **Todo tiene su fin** .... 8a
A very thin looking pitch.

16. **Vía del maki** ........ 6c+
Another impressive line.

17. **Cuerpo jodio** ............ 7a+
1) 7a+, 2) 6b+

18. **Que cojones el del palo** ... 7b+

19. **Mustang** ............ 7b
1) 5+, 2) 7b 3) 6b.

20. **Al roja vivo** ............ 6c+
1) 6a+, 2) 6c+, 3) 6a+.

21. **El indeciso** ............ 6c/A0
1) 6c/A0, 2) 6b+.

22. **El esparragueo** ........... 7b

23. **No eres naide tú** ....... 7b+
Bolt-ons show the way.

24. **La ley del deseo** .......... ?

25. **El guaichichi de wankatanka** 7c
Climb the fine tufa system.

26. **Con tus huesos en el suelo** .... 7c
Start up the ramp.

27. **Jack el destrepador** ......... 6c+

28. **Tierra de nadie** ....... 7b+

29. **Alma gitana** ............ 6a+

30. **Diedrin II** ............ 5+

East facing wall
15m to 50m routes
Best grades - 5+ to 8a

**345**

# EL CHORRO - Túron

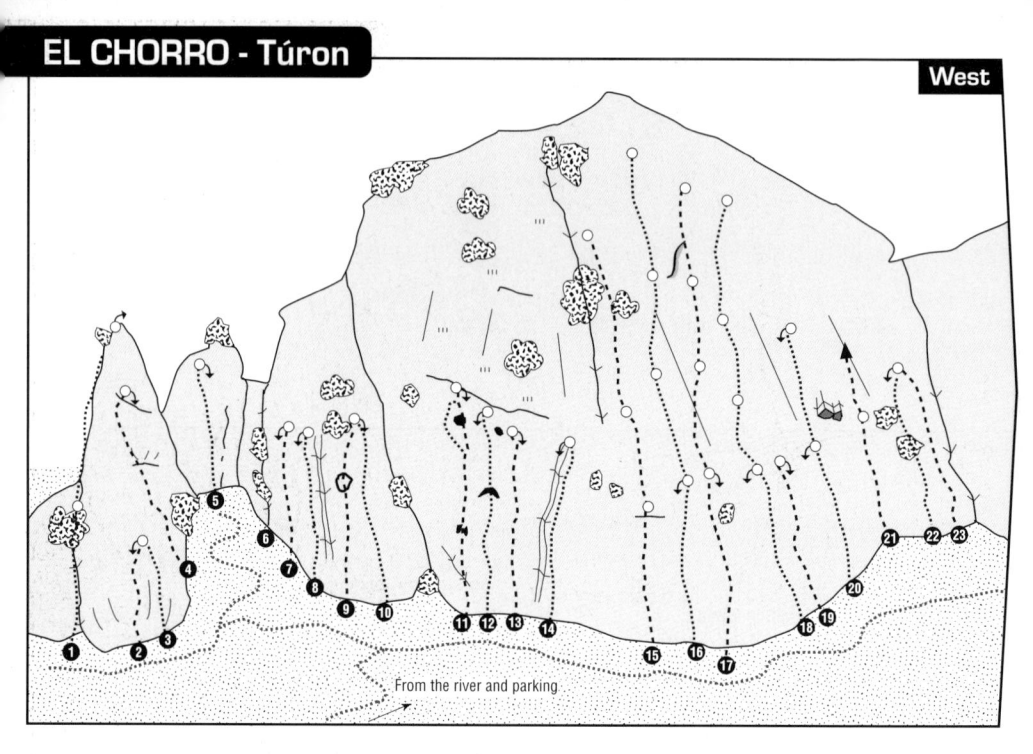

**West**

## WEST
The pinnacles are best left out of the sports plan as the better climbing is to be found on the slabs and steep walls of the main buttress.
**APPROACH** - All routes are accessed from a network of small paths beneath the crag.

**1. Sin bragas y a lo loco** .......... 4,5+
1) 4, 2) 5+.

**2. Dónde están mis amigos** ... 6c

**3. Potage de lentejas** ....... 6c+

**4. Kavernicola** ............... 6c
Tough at the top.

**5. Gualtrapidos sin fronteras** 7a+
Good moves combined with an exciting finish.

**6. Diedrin 1** .................. 5

**7. Bolleré** ................. 6b+
An enjoyable steep slab.

**8. Chupaté ésa teresa** ........ 6a+
Cracks up the pillar.

**9. la grieta de tu nieta** ........ 6b

**10. El payaso decotador** ..... 7a

**11. Apolonio** ............ 7b+
Great climbing. Steep pocketed rock.

**12. Los malos también lloran** .. 7a+
Varied and airy climbing on immaculate rock.

**13. Cuasimodo** ............ 6c
Coral like rock.

**14. Suspiros nostálgicos** ........ 6a+
The leaning corner/groove.

**15. La libertad de expansión** ..... 6b
1) 4+, 2) 6b, 3) 4+,

**16. Julay Lama** ............ 6a
1) 4+, 2) 6a, 3) 4+, 4) 5.

**17. Floja y pendulona** .......... 5
1) 4+, 2) 5, 3) 4+, 4) 4+.

**18. Guevos con bechamel** ....... 5+
1) 4, 2) 5, 3) 5+, 4) 4.

**19. Vestigios** ............. 5

**20. Acosa y derribo** ......... 6a
1) 6a, 2) 5+.

**21. La prima** ............. 5
1) 5, 2) 4+.

# EL CHORRO - Túron

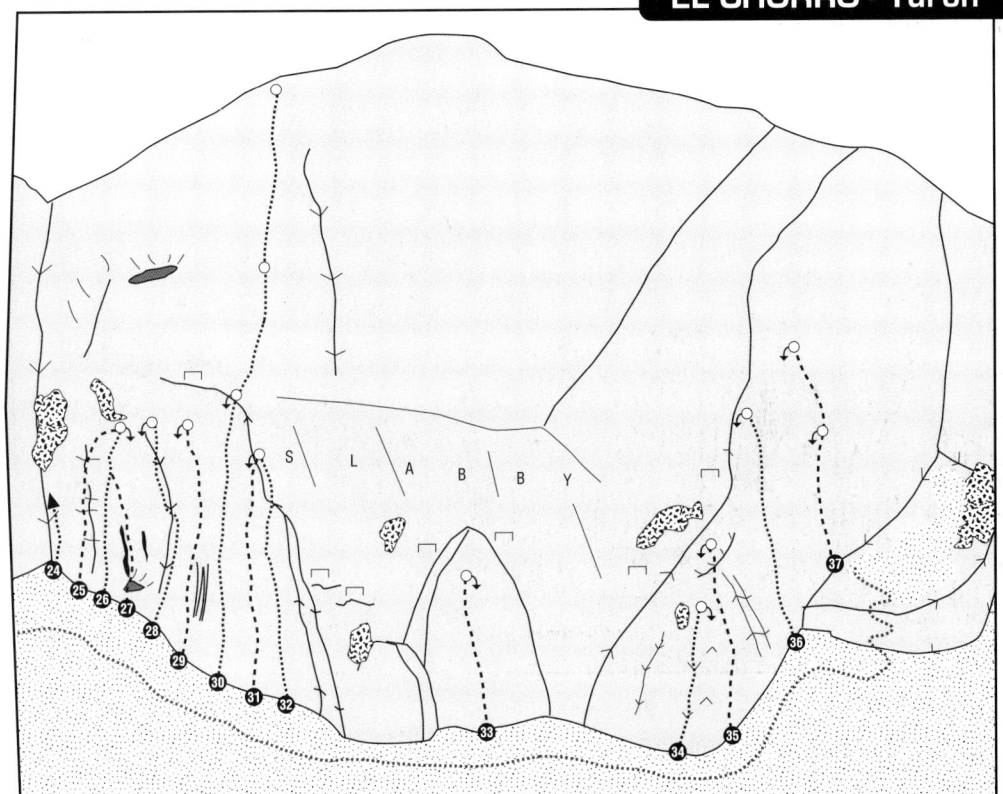

**22. Sombra gris** .......... 6b

**23. Diedro polvarea** ....... 6a

The right-hand side provides some more worthwhile pitches. There is a number of easy multi-pitch traditional routes up the broken and line-less headwall above the slabby central area (not described).

**24. Kanal del jabalix** ....... 4+
The line that divides the west and east sectors.

**25. Sector Olletas** .......... 5+
Climbs the cracked wall.

**26. Pitiflan exprés** .......... 6a+

**27. La raja del siesso** ........ 7a
Very sharp rock.

**28. Manteca colorá** ......... 6b+
Very enjoyable climbing on large holds.

**29. Como un burro amarao** .... 6c
A bit of lateral thinking will be required on this one.

**30. Paco Micro y su Niva** ..... 6b
1) 6a+, 2) 4+, 3) 6b

**31. Lo que no puede sar** 7a+

**32. Condón Goretex** ... 7b+

**33. Me cago en la benemérita** ....... 6c+

**34. Almoraju** ............. 6a+

**35. Agustitu** .............. 6c

**36. Calostro** .............. 7a
Dirty.

**37. Sabor salado** ........... 6b+
1) 6a+, 2) 6b+

SW facing wall
15m to 50m single and multi-pitch routes
Best grades - 5 to 7b+

**347**

# EL TORCAL

Some 10km to the south of the town of Antequera is a small national park which sits on top of a limestone peak at an elevation of about 1300m. The plateau top of this peak has been heavily eroded to form some typical 'karst' scenery, a geological curiosity. It is therefore, an amazing climbers playground, set amidst a myriad of spectacular pinnacles and spires. The shallow grassy valleys and hollows between the pinnacles make lovely picnic and sunbathing spots. It is as relaxing as you want it to be; a very pleasant place to climb and well worth a visit. Since the last edition of the guidebook a ban has been imposed on the climbing described in the main area adjacent to the visitor centre. However the areas described in this edition are all without restrictions and are well worth seeking out.

There isn't very much climbing at El Torcal, and much of it isn't as good as many of the other areas described in this chapter, but what is on offer is worth a day of anyone's time. Much of the climbing is very technical and, although often less than 15m in height, the pitches are sustained and in magnificent surroundings.

## ASPECT AND CLIMATE

The altitude can make it a bit chilly at times and during the winter it is probably worth avoiding if it is at all windy or cloudy. However, on a still winter's day, once the sun has warmed the place up, it can take on a magical atmosphere. Much of the climbing faces south but there are a few north facing routes for those here in the hotter months.

## APPROACH

From El Chorro, take the winding paved road up the hill past Las Encantadas, to the town of Valle de Abdalajis. Go through the town (driving straight ahead above the town is best). Turn left and continue for 20km towards Antequera. (This main road can also be reached by driving around to the lakes above the gorge and picking up the road to the north of the El Chorro massif). Just before you reach Antequera, turn right (signed 'El Torcal de Antequera') and follow the road up and around the side of the mountain, for about 10km, to the park entrance. Drive into the Park to reach the visitor centre. This drive takes about 1 hour from El Chorro. For those who are approaching from the coast, it is possible to take a more direct route. Simply follow signs for Antequera and keep an eye open for the park, which you will pass on your left, as you approach the town.

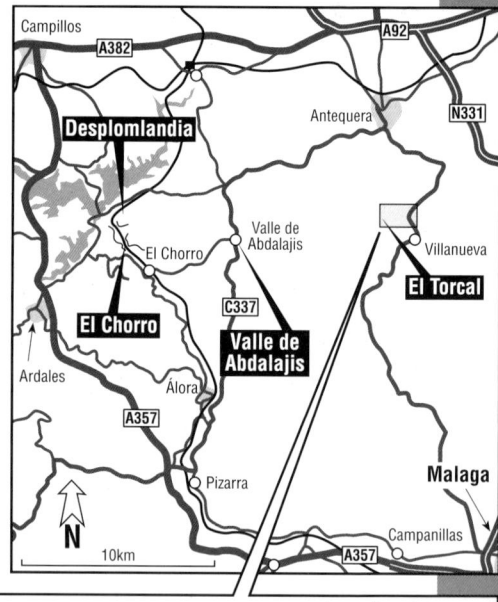

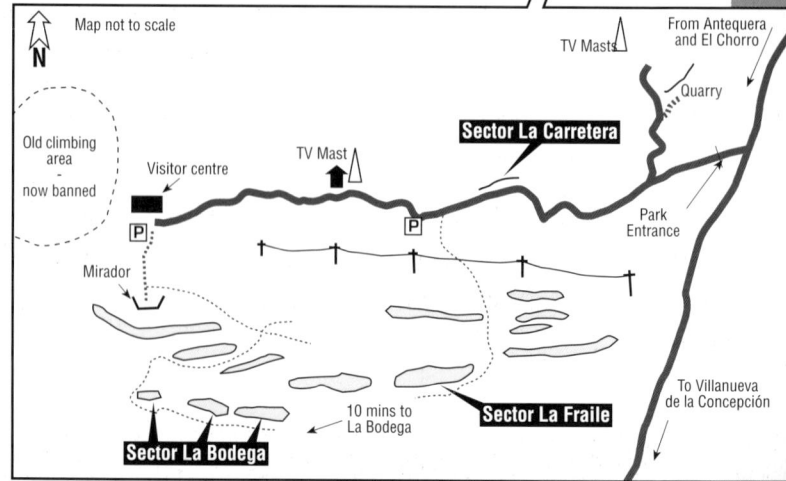

# EL CHORRO - El Torcal

## Sector El Fraile

**SECTOR EL FRAILE**
A beautifully located crag with a spread of grades.

**APPROACH** - This sector is not far from the road but is tricky to locate on first aquaintance. From the parking area 150 metres beyond sector La Carretera walk back down the road and after 70m pick up a faint path on the right that leads through some thorny bushes and under a power-line. Now head for the col on the near horizon (see diagram right). The crag is just over the col on the right.

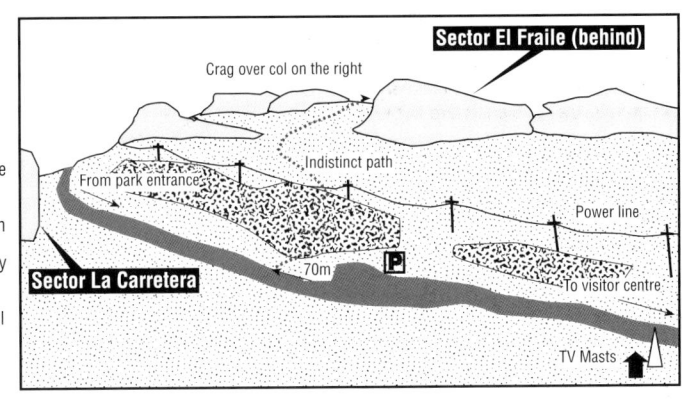

1. Sacrifice . . . . . . . . . . . . . . . . 7b
2. Los golfos del golfo . . . . . . . . . . 6b
   Joins up with route number 2 at mid-height.
3. A vista de pájaro . . . . . . . 7a
   Via the short crack in the wall.
4. Hotel California . . . . 7a+
5. Turboniajas . . . . . . . 7a
6. Villanueva city . . . . . . . . 6b
7. El trepaollas . . . . . . . . 6a+
8. La grieta de Julieta . . . . . . . 5
   Good climbing up the right-hand corner.
9. Paraiso de los cazos romos . . . 7a
10. Choralasmirlas Froe . . . . . . . 6a
11. Té en el Sahara . . . . . . 8a+
    The first of four extremely hard routes on this beautifully located sector. Start up the crack before heading up the arete.
12. Hierba Luisa . . . . . 8b+
13. Menta Poleo . . . . . 8c
14. ? . . . . . . . . . . . . . 8a+
15. Cowboy . . . . . . . . . . . . 7b
    The excellent and exposed rampline in the headwall.

South facing wall
10m to 20m routes
Best grades - 5 to 8c

# EL CHORRO - El Torcal

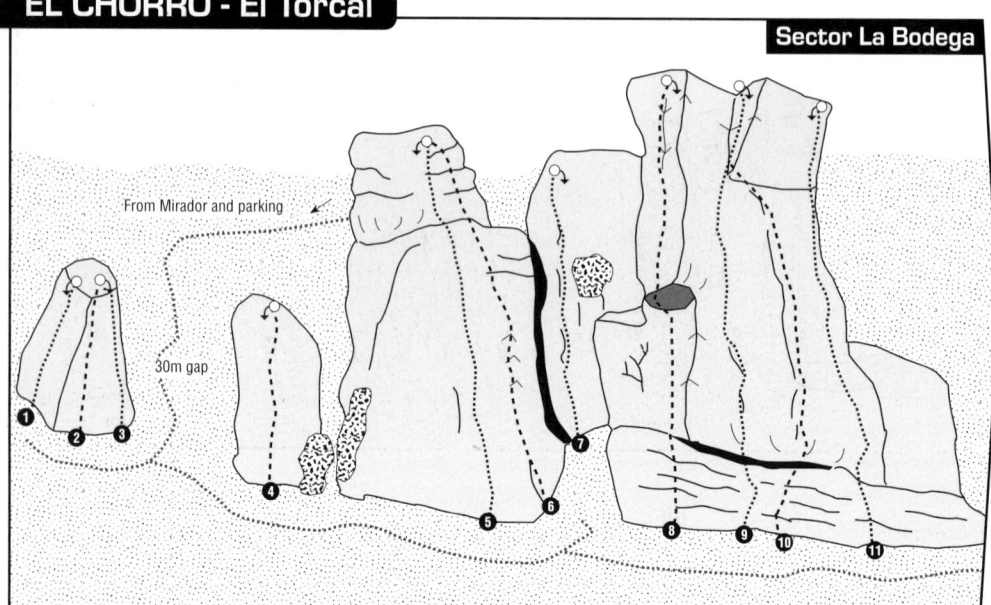

## Sector La Bodega

### SECTOR LA BODEGA
A good little area with lots of shortish routes on great rock and with a stunning view down to the coast.

**APPROACH** - Although only a stones throw from the Mirador this sector is pretty tricky to access, go slowly and try not to lose the way. (Map on previous page) Park at the visitor centre and take the path to the Mirador. Looking straight ahead a short pinnacle can be seen about 100m away on the edge of the escarpment. This is where routes 1,2 and 3 are located. Now back track to a bin and take a path behind it which is vague for the first 5 metres. Follow the rocky boot-worn path for 130m until it drops down into a shallow gully. At this point loop back hard right under the large face and continue to an open area (Bolted lines here - not described). Now head out to the escarpment and the aforementioned routes.

No character symbols have been added to these routes.

The first three routes are on an isolated pinnacle

1. Sol y sombra . . . . . . . . . . . . . . . 5
2. Martini Bianco . . . . . . . . . . . . . 6b
   The central arete.
3. ? . . . . . . . . . . . . . . . . . . . . . . . . 5

Route 4 is on a small detached butress.

4. Dahikiri . . . . . . . . . . . . . . . . 7c

The remaining routes are all on the main edge.

5. Tequila . . . . . . . . . . . . . . . . . . 7b
6. ? . . . . . . . . . . . . . . . . . . . . . . 7a
7. ? . . . . . . . . . . . . . . . . . . . . . . 6c
8. ? . . . . . . . . . . . . . . . . . . . . . . 6c+
9. Tinto con Limón . . . . . . . . . . 7a+
10. Tinto con Casera . . . . . . . . . 6c+
11. Pacharán con endrinas . . . . . 6c
12. Calimocho . . . . . . . . . . . . . . 6b
13. Licor . . . . . . . . . . . . . . . . . . 6a
14. Faustino . . . . . . . . . . . . . . . 7b+
15. Moscatel . . . . . . . . . . . . . . . 6c+
16. Pacharán con mier . . . . . . . . 7a+
17. Frexinet . . . . . . . . . . . . . . . . 7a+
18. Cruzcampo . . . . . . . . . . . . . 6a+
19. Don Perignon del 69 . . . . . . . 5+
20. ? . . . . . . . . . . . . . . . . . . . . . 5+
21. ? . . . . . . . . . . . . . . . . . . . . . 6b+

**Sector La Bodega**
West facing wall, 15m to 20m routes
Best grades - 5 to 7b+

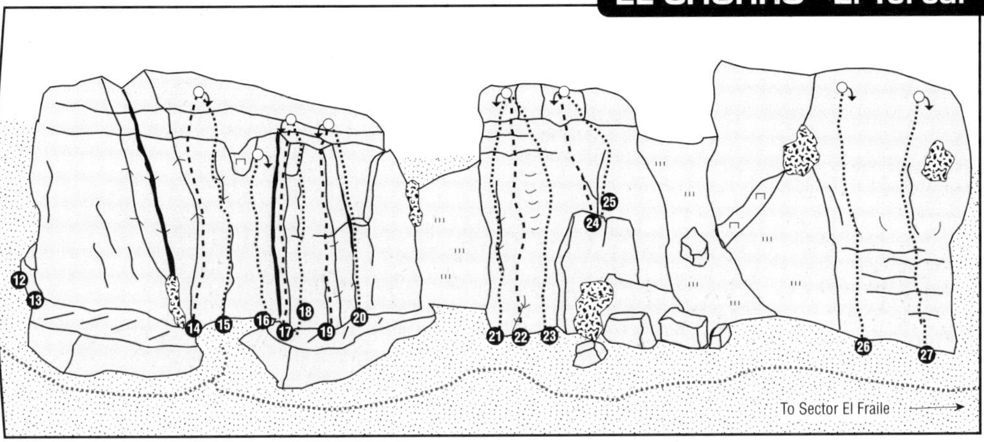

# EL CHORRO - El Torcal

To Sector El Fraile →

| | | |
|---|---|---|
| 22. Cervezas . . . . . . . . . . . . . . . . | | 7a+ |
| 23. Ante la rasca coñac pal cuerpa . | | 6c+ |
| 24. Coctel tropical . . . . . . . . . . . . . | | 6a |
| 25. Tómato algo . . . . . . . . . . . . . . | | 6a |
| 26. Sugumu . . . . . . . . . . . . . . . | | 6c+ |
| 27. Los niños del Rioja . . . . . . . . | | 6c |

## SECTOR LA CARRETERA

A compact wall of excellent rock provides some intense pitches which are easily found but not as easily ticked!

**APPROACH** - This is the first roadside wall on the right as the road levels out after climbing up to the plateau from the El Torcal Park entrance. See map on page 348.

**28. Domingacios crack** . . . . . . . . . . 7a
The crack on the far left to the tree.

**29. Ero ergo sur** . . . . . . . 7a
The wall to the left of the wide crack, Which is unclimbed at present.

**30. Mercedes 26 años** . . . . . . . 7b
Hard climbing up the central wall.

**31. Asfalto** . . . . . . . . 6a
Fine moves up the open corner/groove.

**32. La fuerza del destino** . . . . 7b+
Tough stuff starting just to the left of the butress.

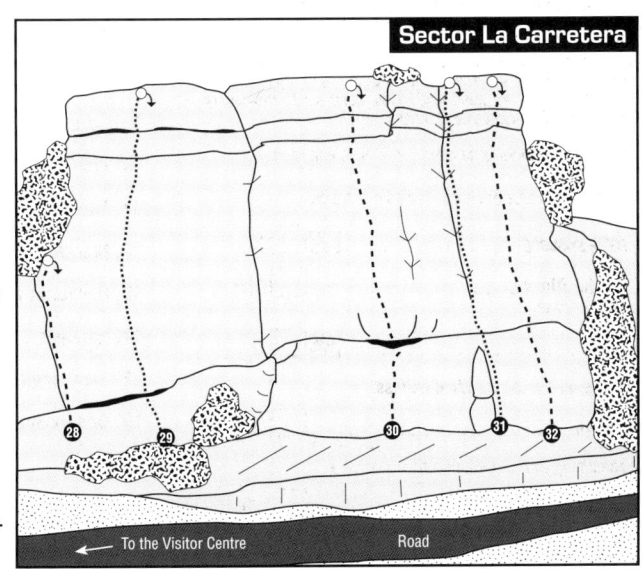

### Sector La Carretera

← To the Visitor Centre    Road

**Sector La Carretera**
West facing wall, 15m to 20m routes
Best grades - 6a to 7b+

Lots of sun | Roadside | Vertical | Lower-offs

351

One of the Bindhammer brothers high on *Kallisté* (8c)
in the cave at Archidona.
Photo: Mark Glaister

# ARCHIDONA

The massive cave of Archidona is a daunting site. Its weird angles and beautiful white and grey, tufa-streaked, concave walls give the place a very strange ambience - at times impenetrable-looking and at others surprisingly amenable. Archidona is a crag for the very accomplished climber only, but is worth a look by anybody with an interest in seeing what is the 'State of the Art'.

All the worthwhile routes are very hard and extremely sustained. Much of the climbing is steep and based on pockets and tufas. A few less steep pitches can be found on the left-hand side of the cave but these are still no push-over. *Orujo*, by Bernabé Fernandez, is one of the most difficult climbs in the world, and it looks it!

## ASPECT AND CLIMATE

The crag is north facing and receives no sun apart from on its margins late in the day. During the winter it is generally cool but climbable and is a good venue in spring and autumn. Most of the hard routes will be climbable in heavy rain although some of the tufas will begin to seep if it is prolonged.

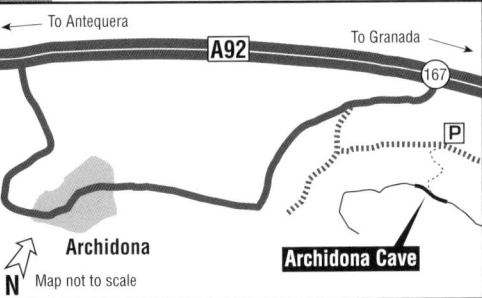

## APPROACH

From El Chorro head for Antequera via Valle de Abdalajis. Go through Antequera following signs for Granada and pick up the main dual carriageway (A92) heading west towards Granada. Follow this to the second Archidona exit (Junction 167). Head towards Archidona and after 0.9km turn left onto a dirt road and then after 0.4km turn left again. 0.6km along this dirt road is the parking (do not block the road). The crag is obvious. Follow a path through the olive grove up into the cave. (1 hour and 10 minutes from El Chorro depending on traffic)

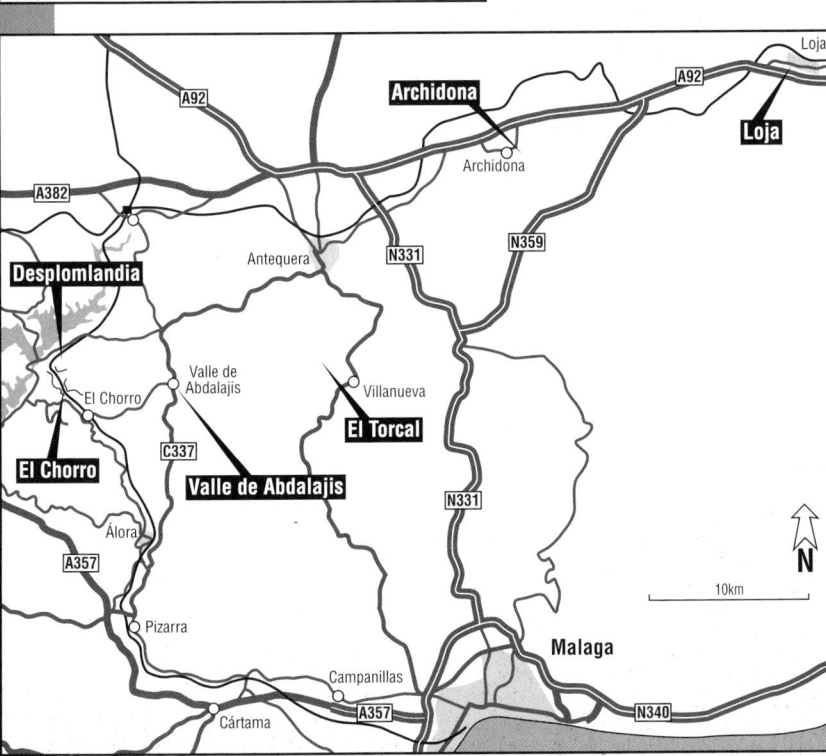

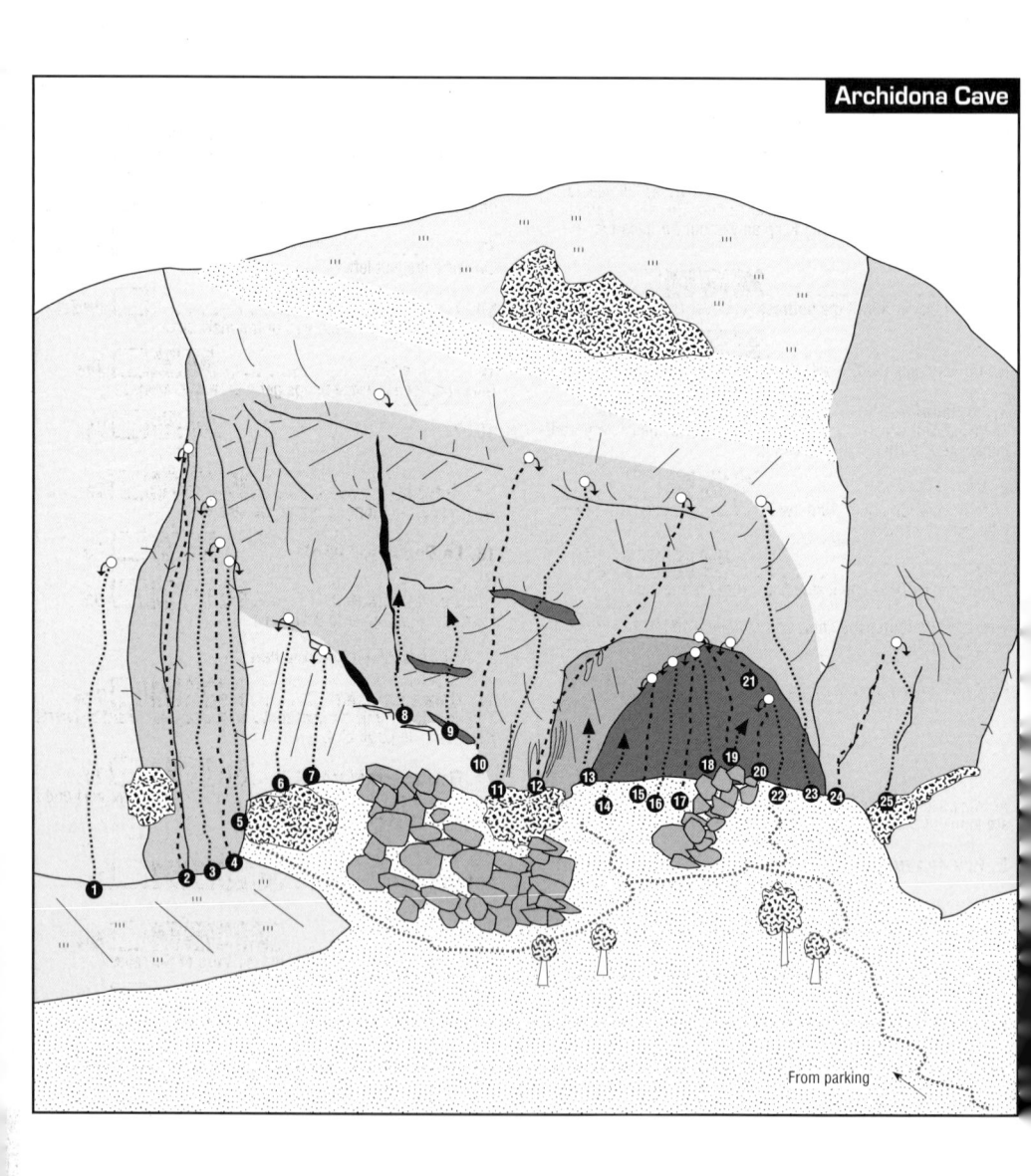

# EL CHORRO - Archidona

**Archidona Cave**

# EL CHORRO - Archidona

## ARCHIDONA CAVE
The approach to the crag via the olive grove eventually leads through a gate in a large fence and into the gaping mouth of this awesome arena. The first routes encountered are those in the large cave itself, whilst the left side of the cave provides the longest and hardest of the pitches on offer. Further left several less steep but only marginally easier routes. There is a number of projects on the go here so keep an eye out for lines that are only partially bolted.

1. ? .................... 7a
Starts on the far left of the buttress just over the small fence.

2. ? .................... 7a
A very good pitch which will stretch even a 60m rope.

3. La canal .................... 5+
The wide cleft which narrows at mid-height provides a very traditional line in a very modern setting.

4. ? .................... 7b
Another very long pitch, with its fair share of precarious and a little fluttery climbing.

5. ? .................... 7a+
Climbs the obvious line just to the left of the main corner.

The next two routes are short and provide a couple of very gentle warm ups.

6. ? .................... 4+

7. ? .................... 4+

At this point the climbing becomes very impressive. Indeed these are some of the most intimidating lines anywhere.

8. Rey de azucor .................... Project

9. Happy hardcore .................... Project

10. Kallisté .................... 8c
The first of a trio of stunning routes which gives unrelenting climbing via the lefthand side of the mid-height roof.

11. Alpechin .................... 8c
Climbs via tufas up to and through the mid-height roof before cranking out the daunting headwall.

12. Orujo .................... 9a+
Starts just to the left of the cave. A truly astounding mission that traverses the cave via the obvious hanging blobs before pulling onto the impossible-looking headwall. A route the fits the grade.

13. ? .................... Project
Line of bolts just left.

14. ? .................... Project
The first line on the back wall of the main cave.

15. Lindo gatito .................... 7b+
After a bit of a bumble things get a bit more radical!

16. ? .................... 7b

17. Antonia .................... 7c
This one is a bit longer, but no less steep.

18. La Penita del perito .................... 7b

19. Campo amango .................... 8a
A great trip into upside-down land.

A project heads up right from here.

20. Danza agresiva .................... 7a+
The first half of this brilliant route ends at a mid-height lower-off. See photo on page 288.

21. Danza... (full pitch) .................... 7c
From the cave moves out left bring some big tufas to hand and a race for the chains.

22. Precario del calvario .................... 7c+

23. ? .................... 8b+
A superb pitch up the right-hand buttress of the cave.

24. Gurú .................... 6c

25. Demolition Man .................... 6c+

North facing cave
15m to 40m routes
Best grades - 7a to 9a+

# LOJA

Loja is an excellent collection of accessible crags located high above a barren landscape which is home to the large town of Loja itself. The vast majority of the climbing is single pitch, steep and sustained wall climbing often on tufas and pockets. If you are looking for mileage then this is a great place to head for with lots of quality climbs. The 70 or so climbs described here are only a small sample of the climbing available around Loja and a number of other sectors are easily accessed from the parking area. Being high up (altitude 1000m), and mostly shady, this area should only be considered in warm and dry weather. Although Loja is the most distant crag from El Chorro, described in this guide, it is a pleasant drive and the climbing is well worth the effort involved. There are many fine pitches on the sectors described some of which are deceptively long. Those without a 60m rope should take great care when lowering off. There is plenty here for those climbing in the 6a to 7c range.

## ACCESS
**No climbing from 1 January to 1 May because of nesting birds.**

## ASPECT AND CLIMATE
The crags of Loja face north and northwest and receive very little sunshine and this, combined with their altitude at 1000m, exposed aspect and prolific tufas, means that the climbing hereabouts is ideally suited to warmer and drier periods. Nevertheless conditions will rarely be bad enough for plans to be abandoned. This would be a great place in spring or autumn.

## APPROACH
The drive to the crag from El Chorro takes approximately one and a half hours. From El Chorro head for Antequera via Valle de Abdalajis. Go through Antequera following signs for Granada and pick up the main dual carriageway (A92) heading west towards Granada. Follow this to the first exit signed for the town of Loja (junction 187). Exit here and continue for 3.8km straight ahead on a road that overlooks the main town of Loja on the left. After passing a hotel on the left carry on a little way and turn right on a tarmac road (signed Sierra de Loja - this is a VERY tiny sign!). Immediately turn right again onto a steep dirt track and follow this uphill and under the dual carriageway. turn right and follow the track uphill for 3.3km to the parking spot.

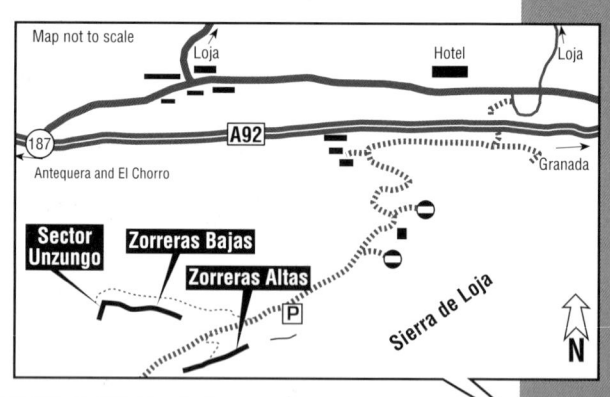

# EL CHORRO - Loja

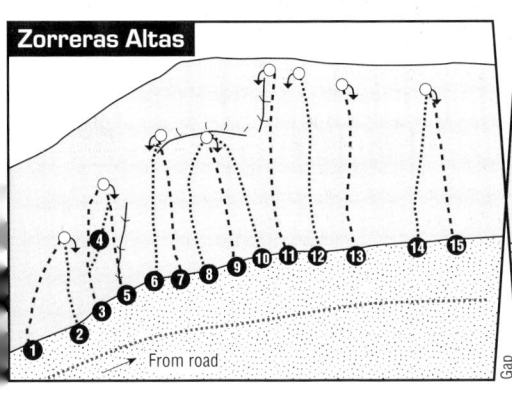

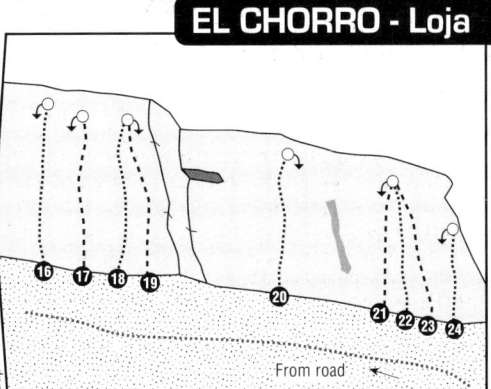

## ZORRERAS ALTAS

A good wall with a pleasing collection of routes. No star ratings or character symbols are known for these routes. We have left space for you to write your own comments. Please feel free to e-mail these to ROCKFAX (alan@rockfax.co.uk) for inclusion in future guides.

**APPROACH -** This sector is located just above and to the right of the parking and easily accessed in a couple of minutes.

**ACCESS -** NO CLIMBING FROM 1 JANUARY TO 1 MAY BECAUSE OF NESTING BIRDS.

No character symbols have been added to these routes.

1. Trepazarzas . . . . . . . . . . . . . . . 5+
2. Danza prima . . . . . . . . . . . . . . 6a
3. Buraka . . . . . . . . . . . . . . . . . . 6a+
4. Cepillos free . . . . . . . . . . . . . . 6a+
5. Exculibertu . . . . . . . . . . . . . . . 5+
6. Bonguiboy . . . . . . . . . . . . . . . 6c
7. Hoito con el hito . . . . . . . . . . . 6c
8. Nirvana . . . . . . . . . . . . . . . . . 6b+
9. Dominio paria . . . . . . . . . . . . . 6c
10. Aprendiz de fakir . . . . . . . . . . 6c+
11. Albergue de emplumados . . . . 7b+
12. Ukachaka . . . . . . . . . . . . . . . 7c
13. Perros de presa . . . . . . . . . . . 8a
14. Hasta los güevos . . . . . . . . . . 7b+
15. Perchomanía . . . . . . . . . . . . . 7a+
16. D'lulu . . . . . . . . . . . . . . . . . 6b+
17. Patrañus . . . . . . . . . . . . . . . 6a+
18. Sidroterapia . . . . . . . . . . . . . 6b+
19. D'ayo . . . . . . . . . . . . . . . . . 6b
20. Mostacho . . . . . . . . . . . . . . 7a
21. Rosky . . . . . . . . . . . . . . . . . 6b
22. Sir Lancelot . . . . . . . . . . . . . 6c
23. Arcadia . . . . . . . . . . . . . . . . 6b
24. D'Brokers . . . . . . . . . . . . . . 6a

NW facing wall
15m to 20m routes
Best grades - 6a to 7a

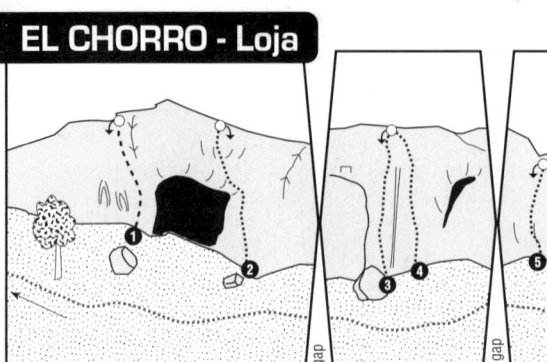

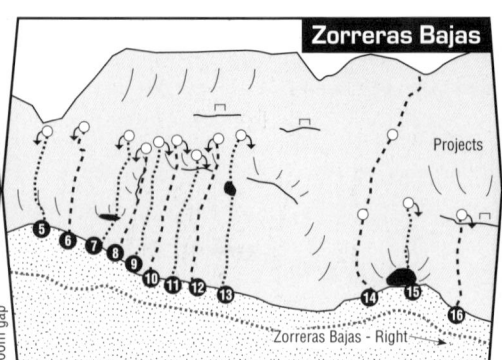

# EL CHORRO - Loja

## Zorreras Bajas

### ZORRERAS BAJAS
Thi is a fine sector with many excellent pitches, particularly towards the right-hand side where there are some superb overhanging walls streaked with tufas. Unfortunately, some of these tufas can seep.
We have added visual star ratings but no character symbols. Please feel free to email these to ROCKFAX (alan@rockfax.co.uk) for inclusion in future guides.
**APPROACH** - From the parking pick up a good path which leads down and left to the start of the cliff-line.

**ACCESS** - NO CLIMBING FROM 1 JANUARY TO 1 MAY BECAUSE OF NESTING BIRDS.

No character symbols have been added to these routes.

1. Colorin colorado . . . . . . . . . . 7c+
2. Idioma galveciano . . . . . . . . . 7b
3. Atila matutino . . . . . . . . . . . 7b
4. Zingaros . . . . . . . . . . . . . . 7a
5. La cima del mirdo . . . . . . . . . ?
6. Desperado . . . . . . . . . . . . . ?
7. Ososcan . . . . . . . . . . . . . . ?
8. Como gato panzamba . . . . . . . ?
9. Tarari que te vi . . . . . . . . . . ?
10. Espaldus el mundo . . . . . . . . ?
11. Al abordaje . . . . . . . . . . . . ?
12. A la derva . . . . . . . . . . . . ?
13. A la mierda . . . . . . . . . . . . ?
14. La zorra y las chapas . . . . . . . 7a+
A three-pitcher which starts just left of a small cave.
1) 7a+, 2) 6a+, 3) 7b+
15. Violaciones de un monaguillo . . 7c+
Desperate sequence out of the cave.

16. El tratante . . . . . . . . . . . . . 6a
Above this pitch is a number of projects.
17. La sombra de Cain . . . . . . . . ?
18. Vibraciones positivas . . . . . . . 8a
19. Morada de vampiros . . . . . . . 7a+
20. La rambla del mago . . . . . . . . 7b
21. La pálide . . . . . . . . . . . . . 8a+
22. Dos itanos . . . . . . . . . . . . . 7b+
23. Hasta luego Luca . . . . . . . . . 7b
24. La perversa . . . . . . . . . . . . 8a
25. Tela marinera . . . . . . . . . . . 6b
26. Enrezabiá . . . . . . . . . . . . . 6b
27. Panceta . . . . . . . . . . . . . . 6a+
28. A sombrao . . . . . . . . . . . . . 7b+
29. Piperra . . . . . . . . . . . . . . . 6c+
30. Puta Navidad . . . . . . . . . . . 6c
31. Helao recalentao . . . . . . . . . 6c+

### SECTOR UNZUNGO
This sector picks up a bit of sun in the late afternoon. Although worthwhile it is not as good as Zorreras Bajas.
**APPROACH** - From the right-hand end of Zorreras Bajas, continue along the base of the crag for 100m to the first route at an arete.

**ACCESS** - NO CLIMBING FROM 1 JANUARY TO 1 MAY BECAUSE OF NESTING BIRDS.

No character symbols have been added to these routes.

32 . Unzungo . . . . . . . . . . . . . 8a
The arete.

**Zorreras Bajas**
North facing wall, 15m to 30m routes
Best grades - 6b to 8a+

# EL CHORRO - Loja

## Zorreras Bajas

|  |  |  |
|---|-------|-------|
| 33. | Cortes | 7b+ |
| 34. | Tauncro | 7b+ |
| 35. | La demonia | 7a+ |
| 36. | Kalahary | 7b |
| 37. | Aborigen | 7a+ |
| 38. | Gentuza | ? |
| 39. | Locos de atar | 6c |
| 40. | Tremalleta | 6b+ |
| 41. | Trogloditas sibaritas | 6b+ |
| 42. | Dragones y mazmorras | 6c+ |

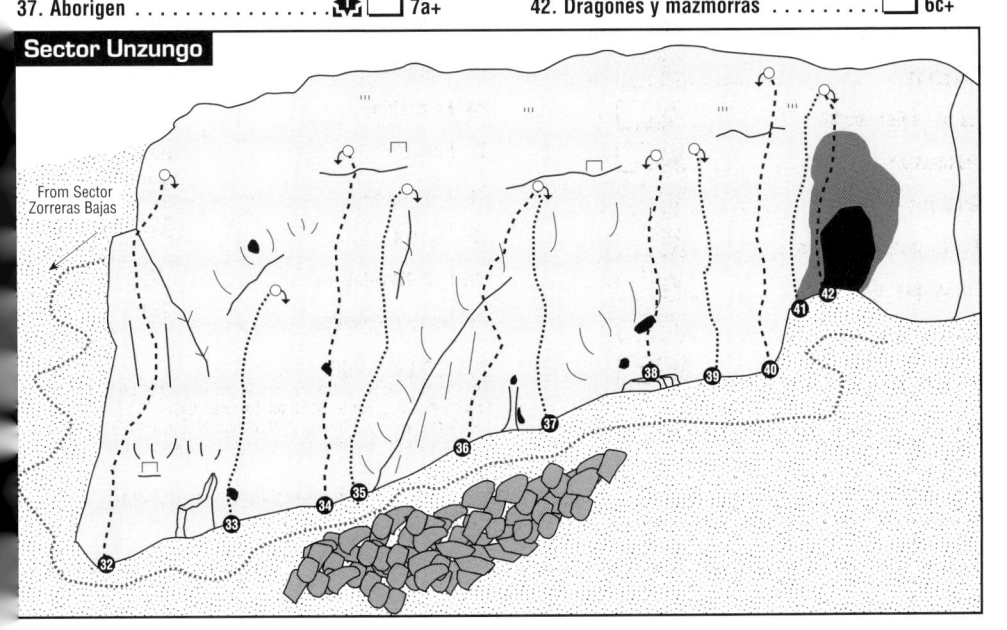

## Sector Unzungo

From Sector Zorreras Bajas

100m to Sector Unzunga

Broken ground

**Sector Unzungo**
NW facing wall, 15m to 20m routes
Best grades - 6b+ to 8a

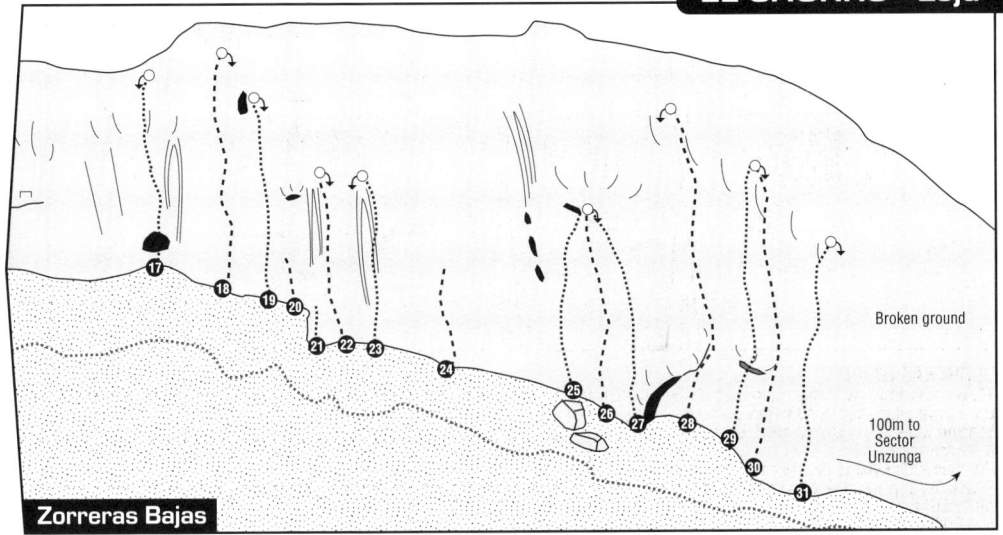

359

# INDEX

| | |
|---|---|
| *Acknowledgments* | 27 |
| *Advertiser Directory* | 24 |
| **Agujas Rojas** | **180** |
| **Alaró** | **262** |
| **Alcoy** | **177** |
| **Andratx** | **226** |
| **Archidona** | **353** |
| **Aventador** | **59** |
| **Bellús** | **64** |
| **Bernia Ridge Area** | **110** |
| Altea Col | 111 |
| Dalle d'Olla | 110 |
| **Betlem** | **277** |
| Boquer | 218 |
| *Bouldering Grade Table* | 235 |
| Ca'n Torrat | 218 |
| **Ca'n Nyic** | **258** |
| **Cabreras** | **191** |
| Peñas del Rey | 192 |
| Upper Sectors | 196 |
| **Caimari** | **267** |
| **Cala Magraner** | **280** |
| Calvià | 218 |
| **Campillos Gorge** | **340** |
| **Central Gorge** | **319** |
| El Invento | 326 |
| El Makinodromo | 328 |
| El Polvorin | 324 |
| Los Bloques | 327 |
| Los Cotos | 320 |
| **Costa Blanca** | **29** |
| Access | 31 |
| Accommodation | 33 |
| Classified Adverts | 30, 32 |
| Climbing Information | 31 |
| Crag Table | 34 |
| Flights | 33 |
| Gear | 31 |
| Getting Around | 36 |
| Grades | 31 |
| Introduction | 31 |
| Map | 36 |
| Other Areas | 31 |
| Other Books | 31 |
| Shops | 33 |
| When to Go | 33 |
| **Creveta** | **270** |
| **Desplomlandia** | **335** |
| *Deutsch* | 22 |
| **Echo Valley** | **113** |
| Castillo | 115 |
| Col Llama | 131 |
| Echo One | 119 |
| Echo Placa | 130 |
| Echo Two | 122 |
| Haunted Walls | 133 |
| La Capella | 135 |
| Senyera | 134 |
| *Einfuhrung (Deutsch)* | 22 |
| **El Chorro** | **289** |
| Access | 290 |
| Accommodation | 293 |
| Classified Adverts | 292 |
| Climbing Information | 290 |
| Crag Table | 294 |
| Flights | 293 |
| Gear | 291 |

| | |
|---|---|
| **El Chorro continued...** | |
| Getting Around | 293 |
| Getting To El Chorro | 293 |
| Grades | 290 |
| Map | 291 |
| Other Areas | 291 |
| Other Books | 291 |
| Shops | 293 |
| When to Go | 293 |
| **El Torcal** | **348** |
| **Es Queixal** | **260** |
| *Español* | 18 |
| **Forada** | **207** |
| North Face | 208 |
| South Face | 214 |
| **Fraguel** | **251** |
| *Français* | 20 |
| **Gandía** | **37** |
| El Bovedón | 46 |
| *Gear* | 8 |
| *Grades* | 10 |
| *Introducción (Español)* | 18 |
| *Introduction* | 5 |
| *Introduction (Français)* | 20 |
| **Jalón Valley** | **71** |
| Alcalalí | 71 |
| Covatelles | 77 |
| Coves Rojas | 77 |
| Font d'Axia | 76 |
| L'Ocaive | 74 |
| Lliber | 72 |
| **Las Frontales** | **296** |
| Albercones | 297 |
| Amptrax Area | 298 |
| Escalera Arabe | 302 |
| Las Encantadas | 304 |
| Poema de Roca | 300 |
| Sector Caliza | 306 |
| **Las Perxes** | **267** |
| Bouldering | 268 |
| **Loja** | **356** |
| **Lower Gorge** | **308** |
| El Recodo | 314 |
| Los Venenos | 309 |
| Pasarela de los Venenos | 310 |
| Sector Africa | 313 |
| Sector Juaja | 312 |
| Sector Santimonia | 311 |
| Sector Zeppelin | 316 |
| **Mallorca** | **217** |
| A Brief History | 220 |
| Access | 218 |
| Accommodation | 223 |
| Classified Adverts | 222 |
| Climbing Information | 218 |
| Crag Table | 224 |
| Flights | 223 |
| Gear | 218 |
| Getting Around | 223 |
| Grades | 218 |
| Map | 219 |
| New Routes | 219 |
| Other Areas | 219 |
| Other Books | 219 |
| Shops | 223 |
| When to Go | 223 |

| | |
|---|---|
| **Mascarat Gorge** | **104** |
| **Montesa** | **56** |
| **Olta** | **78** |
| **Peña Rubia** | **186** |
| **Peñon d'Ifach** | **80** |
| North Face | 81 |
| South Face | 83 |
| **Ponoch** | **136** |
| **Port Sóller** | **255** |
| **Puig Campana** | **138** |
| Aguja Encantada | 143 |
| Sector Central | 140 |
| **Reconco** | **183** |
| *ROCKFAX* | 12 |
| **S'estret** | **231** |
| Bouldering | 234 |
| **S'on Xanquete** | **274** |
| **Sa Gubia** | **240** |
| Paret dels Coloms | 241 |
| Sector Espolón (Gubia Normal) | 244 |
| Sector Excalibur | 249 |
| Sector Isla la Bonita | 248 |
| Sector Princessa | 246 |
| Sector Silicona | 250 |
| Sector Why | 248 |
| **Salem** | **47** |
| **Salinas** | **199** |
| **Santa Ponça** | **229** |
| **Santanyí** | **285** |
| **Sella** | **146** |
| Badall de Tafarmaig | 161 |
| Cabeza de Rino | 149 |
| Culo de Rino | 150 |
| Divino | 167 |
| El cajon de los Cuartos | 152 |
| El Collado | 160 |
| El Elefante | 175 |
| Galera de Tafarmach | 160 |
| Hidden Valley | 162 |
| Líneas Naturales | 162 |
| Ojo de Odra | 156 |
| Outlying Areas | 166 |
| Pared de la Cima | 169 |
| Pared de la Cima | 169 |
| Pared de la Taula | 171 |
| Pared de Rosalía | 158 |
| Sector Competcion | 155 |
| Sector CP10M | 174 |
| Sector Final | 157 |
| Sector Marión | 154 |
| Sector Pertemba | 172 |
| Sector VIPs | 163 |
| Techo del Rino | 153 |
| Techo Placa | 173 |
| Wild Side | 164 |
| **Sierra de Toix** | **88** |
| Sea Cliffs | 99 |
| Toix Este | 90 |
| Toix Norte | 89 |
| Toix Oeste | 92 |
| Toix Placa | 95 |
| Toix TV | 97 |
| **Tijuana** | **285** |
| *Topo and Symbol Key* | 17 |
| **Torrella** | **258** |
| **Túron** | **344** |
| **Upper Gorge** | **330** |
| Petit Desfiladero | 333 |
| **Valldemossa** | **236** |
| **Valle de Abdalajis** | **307** |